国家领土主权与海洋权益协同创新中心

武汉大学边界与海洋问题研究丛书
海洋文库·研究丛书

武汉大学边界与海洋问题研究丛书编委会

主　编　胡德坤
副主编　易显河　余敏友

委　员（按姓氏笔画排序）
丁　煌　孔令杰　匡增军　关培凤　杨泽伟　李仁真
李　斐　余敏友　张　彬　易显河　周茂荣　胡德坤
秦天宝　谈广鸣　彭敦文　韩永利

海上共同开发
协定汇编（汉英对照）

International Agreements on the Joint Development of Marine Resources
(Chinese – English Bilingual Version)

（上）

杨泽伟　主编
邓妮雅　黄文博　副主编

社会科学文献出版社
SOCIAL SCIENCES ACADEMIC PRESS (CHINA)

本书得到了教育部哲学社会科学研究重大课题攻关项目"海上共同开发国际案例与实践研究"(项目批准号：13JZD039)、中国海洋石油总公司国际合作部以及"国家领土主权与海洋权益协同创新中心"(武汉大学总部)的资助，特致谢忱。

前　言

　　一般认为，海上共同开发是指两个或两个以上的政府在协议的基础上，共同勘探开发跨界或争议海域的自然资源。例如，德国教授雷纳·拉戈尼（Rainer Lagoni）认为，海上共同开发是建立在协议的基础上，以对一块有争议海域的非生物资源进行开发为目的的国家间经济合作方式。[①]日本学者三好正弘（Masahiro Miyoshi）强调，"共同开发是一种临时性质的政府间安排，以功能性为目的，旨在共同勘探和（或）开发领海之外海床的碳氢化合物资源"[②]。中国学者高之国博士也指出，"共同开发是指两个或两个以上国家达成的政府间协议，其目的是开发和分配尚未划界的领土争议重叠区的潜在自然资源，而共同行使在此区域内的主权和管辖权。"[③]

　　从国际法角度来看，海上共同开发是和平解决国际争端原则的具体化。按照《联合国海洋法公约》第 74 条和第 83 条的规定，在达成划界协议前，"有关各国应基于谅解和合作的精神，尽一切努力作出实际性的临时安排，并在此过渡期间内，不危害或阻碍最后协议的达成。这种安排应不妨碍最后界限的划定"。此外，国际法院在 1969 年"北海大陆架案"（the North Sea Continental Shelf Cases）的判决中也确认，大陆架划界可通过协议解决，达不成协议时可通过公平划分重叠区域，或通过共同开发的

[①] See Rainer Lagoni, "Oil and Gas Deposits Across National Frontiers", *American Journal of International Law*, Vol. 73, 1979, p. 215.

[②] Masahiro Miyoshi, "The Joint Development of Offshore Oil and Gas in Relation to Maritime Boundary Delimitation", *Maritime Briefing* (International Boundaries Research Unit), Vol. 2, No. 5, 1999, p. 3.

[③] Zhiguo Gao, "The Legal Concept and Aspects of Joint Development in International Law", *Ocean Yearbook*, Vol. 13, 1998, p. 112.

协议解决。① 可见，无论是国际条约还是国际司法实践，都把海上共同开发看作是相关海域划界前的一种临时性安排。

自 1958 年巴林与沙特阿拉伯签订《巴林—沙特阿拉伯边界协定》、实施海上共同开发以来，共同开发跨界或争议海域资源的国家实践已成为一种较为普遍的现象，迄今海上共同开发的国际案例也有近 30 例。海上共同开发 50 多年的发展历程，可以分为以下四个阶段。第一，海上共同开发的产生阶段（1958~1969 年），在波斯湾和西欧一共出现了 5 例海上共同开发案。第二，海上共同开发的发展阶段（1970~1993 年），一共出现了 14 例海上共同开发案，涉及 26 个国家，包括亚洲国家 11 个，欧洲国家 5 个，非洲国家 7 个，美洲国家 2 个及大洋洲的澳大利亚。第三，海上共同开发的回落阶段（1994~2000 年），只有一例海上共同开发案，即 1995 年 9 月英国与阿根廷签订的《关于在西南大西洋近海活动进行合作的联合声明》。第四，海上共同开发的平稳阶段（2001 年至今）。进入 21 世纪以来，海上共同开发活动又渐趋增多，产生了近 10 例海上共同开发实践。

就中国而言，中国拥有约 1.8 万千米的大陆海岸线，海上与 8 个国家相邻或相向。中国与一些周边海上邻国存在岛屿主权争议和海域划界争端。虽然早在 20 世纪 70 年代末，中国国家领导人就提出了"主权属我、搁置争议、共同开发"原则，试图解决中国与周边海上邻国间的岛屿主权和海洋权益争端；然而，30 多年过去了，从作为整体的中国周边海域来看，海上共同开发举步维艰，迄今尚未得到真正实现。值得注意的是，2013 年 10 月中国、文莱两国一致同意支持两国相关企业开展海上共同开发活动，勘探和开采海上油气资源；紧接着，中国、越南两国也同意积极研究和商谈共同开发问题，在政府边界谈判代表团框架下成立中越海上共同开发磋商工作组，本着先易后难、循序渐进的原则，稳步推进湾口外海域划界谈判并积极推进该海域的共同开发。2014 年 11 月，中国国家主席习近平分别会见前来参加亚太经合组织第 22 次领导人非正式会议的文莱苏

---

① 杰塞普（Jessup）法官在该案的个别意见中也强调，在有争议但尚未划界而又有部分领土重叠的大陆架区域，共同开发的方法更合适。See the North Sea Continental Shelf Cases (Federal Republic of Germany/Denmark, Federal Republic of Germany/Netherlands), Judgments, I. C. J. Reports 1969, available at http://www.icj-cij.org/docket/files/52/5561.pdf，最后访问日期：2015 年 11 月 5 日。

前　言

丹哈桑纳尔、马来西亚总理纳吉布时也指出，中方愿意同文方加强海上合作，推动南海共同开发尽早取得实质进展；中、马双方要推进海上合作和共同开发，促进地区和平、稳定、繁荣。可以预见，海上共同开发问题将成为未来中国对外关系的重要内容之一。因此，全面深入研究"海上共同开发国际案例与实践"，无疑具有重要的理论价值与现实意义。

为了进一步推动海上共同开发的国际法理论与实践研究，2013年10月，在武汉大学中国边界与海洋研究院和国际法研究所的鼎力支持下，特别是在胡德坤老师的鼓励和帮助下，我以首席专家的身份，联合国内外20多家教研机构和实务部门的专家，成功申报了教育部哲学社会科学研究重大课题攻关项目——"海上共同开发国际案例与实践研究"，并被批准立项。经过几年的悉心研究，我们逐步推出了一些研究成果。

本书系由我主持的教育部哲学社会科学研究重大课题攻关项目——"海上共同开发国际案例与实践研究"的阶段性研究成果，也是"海上共同开发国际案例与实践研究"系列丛书之一。

本书主要收录并翻译了1958年巴林与沙特阿拉伯共同开发波斯湾大陆架案等17个海上共同开发案例中较为重要的法律文本，以及1990年英国国际法与比较法研究所推出的"海上共同开发协定示范文本"，旨在为进行海上共同开发问题研究的广大同仁提供某些便利和参考。在翻译的过程中，我们参考了蔡鸿鹏的《争议海域共同开发的管理模式：比较研究》（上海社会科学院出版社1998年版）、萧建国的《国际海洋边界石油的共同开发》（海洋出版社2006年版）等论著。

本书由我主编，邓妮雅和黄文博为副主编，董世杰、申钟秀、宗吕谦、张慧芬和王晓梅参与了相关文本的翻译、校对工作，具体分工如下：

（一）1958年巴林与沙特阿拉伯共同开发波斯湾大陆架案：宗吕谦译，黄文博、杨泽伟校；

（二）1962年荷兰与联邦德国埃姆斯河口资源共同开发案：申钟秀译，邓妮雅校；

（三）1965年沙特阿拉伯与科威特共同开发案：董世杰译，黄文博、杨泽伟校；

（四）1974年日本与韩国共同开发东海大陆架案：邓妮雅译，黄文博、杨泽伟校；

（五）1974年法国与西班牙划界与共同开发案：黄文博译，邓妮雅、杨泽伟校；

（六）1976年英国与挪威共同开发弗里格天然气案：邓妮雅译，黄文博校；

（七）1979年泰国与马来西亚有关泰国湾的共同开发案：王晓梅译，邓妮雅校；

（八）1981年冰岛与挪威扬马延岛共同开发案：宗吕谦译，黄文博校；

（九）1989年澳大利亚与印度尼西亚共同开发案：董世杰译，黄文博校；

（十）1992年马来西亚与越南共同开发案：邓妮雅译，黄文博校；

（十一）1993年哥伦比亚与牙买加共同开发案：宗吕谦译，黄文博校；

（十二）1993年几内亚比绍与塞内加尔共同开发案：黄文博译，邓妮雅校；

（十三）2001年尼日利亚与圣多美和普林西比共同开发案：张慧芬、黄文博译，邓妮雅校；

（十四）2001年东帝汶与澳大利亚共同开发案：董世杰译，邓妮雅校；

（十五）2003年圭亚那共和国和巴巴多斯国共同开发案：董世杰译，邓妮雅校；

（十六）2012年美国和墨西哥共同开发案：宗吕谦译，邓妮雅校；

（十七）2012塞舌尔和毛里求斯共同开发案：申钟秀译，黄文博、杨泽伟校；

海上共同开发协定示范文本：邓妮雅译，黄文博校。

个别协议附带的地图等附件，因过于专业等原因未收入本书中。

由于对法律文本的理解仁智各见，加上水平的限制，本书难免会有诸多纰漏甚至错误，恳请读者批评指正。

我们仅从学术研究角度出发，对有关协议进行整理、翻译等工作，并不代表我们同意协定有关安排，也与中国政府立场无关。特此声明。

杨泽伟

2015年3月27日

于"国家领土主权与海洋权益协同创新中心"（武汉大学总部）

目 录
CONTENTS

一 海上共同开发的产生阶段

（一）1958 年巴林与沙特阿拉伯共同开发波斯湾大陆架案 ………… 3
  1.《巴林—沙特阿拉伯边界协定》………………………………… 3
  2. Bahrain – Saudi Arabia Boundary Agreement, 22 February 1958 ……… 6

（二）1962 年荷兰与联邦德国埃姆斯河口资源共同开发案 ………… 10
  1.《荷兰王国与德意志联邦共和国签署的〈关于在埃姆斯河口合作安排的条约〉（〈埃姆斯—多拉德条约〉）之补充协定》………… 10
  2. Supplementary Agreement to the Treaty Concerning Arrangements for Cooperation in the Ems Estuary (Ems – Dollard Treaty), Signed between the Kingdom of the Netherlands and the Federal Republic of Germany ………………………………………………………… 18

（三）1965 年沙特阿拉伯与科威特共同开发案 …………………… 28
  1.《沙特阿拉伯王国—科威特国划分中立区的协定》…………… 28
  2. Agreement between the Kingdom of Saudi Arabia and the State of Kuwait on the Partition of the Neutral Zone …………………… 32
  3.《沙特阿拉伯王国和科威特国有关毗邻分隔区的水下区域的协定》……………………………………………………………… 39

4. Agreement between the Kingdom of Saudi Arabia and the State of Kuwait Concerning the Submerged Area Adjacent to the Divided Zone, 2 July 2000 …………………………………………………… 42

二　海上共同开发的发展阶段

（四）1974 年日本与韩国共同开发东海大陆架案 ……………… 49
　1.《日本和大韩民国关于共同开发邻接两国的大陆架南部的协定》…… 49
　2. Agreement between Japan and the Republic of Korea Concerning Joint Development of the Southern Part of the Continental Shelf Adjacent to the Two Countries ……………………………………… 64
　3.《日本和大韩民国关于共同开发邻接两国的大陆架南部的协定的会议纪要》……………………………………………………… 84
　4. Agreed Minutes to the Agreement between Japan and the Republic of Korea Concerning Joint Development of the Southern Part of the Continental Shelf Adjacent to the Two Countries ………………… 87

（五）1974 年法国与西班牙划界与共同开发案 ………………… 91
　1.《法兰西共和国政府与西班牙王国政府划分两国在比斯开湾大陆架的公约》………………………………………………………… 91
　2. Convention Between the Government of the French Republic and the Government of the Spanish State on the Delimitation of the Continental Shelves of the Two States in the Bay of Biscay ……………… 96

（六）1976 年英国与挪威共同开发弗里格天然气案 …………… 103
　1.《关于开发弗里格气田并向联合王国输送天然气的协定》……… 103
　2. Agreement Relating to the Exploitation of the Frigg Field Reservoir and the Transmission of Gas therefrom to the United Kingdom ………… 117

目 录

3. 《大不列颠及北爱尔兰联合王国政府与挪威王国政府关于修改 1976 年 5 月 10 日有关开发弗里格气田并向联合王国输送天然气的协定的协定》 …………………………………………… 137

4. Agreement between the Government of the United Kingdom of Great Britain and Northern Ireland and the Government of the Kingdom of Norway Relating to the Amendment of the Agreement of 10 May 1976 Relating to the Exploitation of the Frigg Field Reservoir and the Transmission of Gas therefrom to the United Kingdom ……………… 153

(七) 1979 年泰国与马来西亚有关泰国湾的共同开发案 ……………… 177

1. 《马来西亚和泰王国为开发泰国湾两国大陆架划定区域内海床资源而设立联合管理局的谅解备忘录》 …………………………… 177

2. Memorandum of Understanding between Malaysia and the Kingdom of Thailand on the Establishment of the Joint Authority for the Exploitation of the Resources of the Sea Bed in a Defined Area of the Continental Shelf of the Two Countries in the Gulf of Thailand ……… 181

3. 《马来西亚政府和泰王国政府关于设立马来西亚—泰国联合管理局及其他事项的 1990 年协定》 ……………………………………… 186

4. 1990 Agreement between the Government of Malaysia and the Government of the Kingdom of Thailand on the Constitution and Other Matters Relating to the Establishment of the Malaysia–Thailand Joint Authority …………………………………………………………… 195

5. 《泰国—马来西亚联合管理局第 2533 号法令 (1990)》 ………… 209

6. Thailand–Malaysia Joint Authority Act, B. E. 2553 (1990) ……… 218

7. 《马来西亚和泰国联合管理局第 440 号法令 (1991)》 …………… 230

8. Malaysia–Thailand Joint Authority Act 440 ……………………… 239

9. 《马来西亚—泰国联合管理局石油作业准则》 ……………………… 252

10. Malaysia–Thailand Joint Authority Standards of Petroleum Operations ………………………………………………………… 257

（八）1981年冰岛与挪威扬马延岛共同开发案 …………………… 263
　1.《关于冰岛和扬马延岛之间的大陆架协定》 ……………… 263
　2. Agreement on the Continental Shelf Between Iceland and Jan Mayen …………………………………………………………… 267

（九）1989年澳大利亚与印度尼西亚共同开发案 ………………… 272
　1.《澳大利亚与印度尼西亚共和国在印度尼西亚东帝汶省与澳大利亚北部之间的区域设立合作区的条约》 ………………… 272
　2. Treaty between Australia and the Republic of Indonesia on the Zone of Cooperation in an Area between the Indonesian Province of East Timor and Northern Australia ………………………… 289

（十）1992年马来西亚与越南共同开发案 ………………………… 313
　1.《马来西亚与越南社会主义共和国关于两国大陆架划定区域内石油勘探和开采的谅解备忘录》 ………………………… 313
　2. 1992 Memorandum of Understanding between Malaysia and the Socialist Republic of Vietnam for the Exploration and Exploitation of Petroleum in A Defined Area of the Continental Shelf Involving the Two Countries …………………………………………………… 316

（十一）1993年哥伦比亚与牙买加共同开发案 …………………… 320
　1.《牙买加与哥伦比亚共和国海域划界条约》 ……………… 320
　2. Maritime Delimitation Treaty between Jamaica and the Republic of Colombia ………………………………………………………… 324

（十二）1993年几内亚比绍与塞内加尔共同开发案 ……………… 329
　1.《几内亚比绍共和国与塞内加尔共和国管理和合作协定》 … 329
　2. Agreement on Management and Cooperation between the Republic of Guinea – Bissau and the Republic of Senegal ………………… 331

3.《几内亚比绍共和国与塞内加尔共和国关于通过 1993 年 10 月 14 日协定设立的管理和合作局的组织和运作的协定的议定书》……… 334

4. Protocol to the Agreement between the Republic of Guinea – Bissau and the Republic of Senegal Concerning the Organization and Operation of the Management and Cooperation Agency Established By the Agreement of 14 October 1993 ……………………………… 347

三　海上共同开发的平稳阶段

（十三）2001 年尼日利亚与圣多美和普林西比共同开发案 ………… 367

1.《尼日利亚联邦共和国与圣多美和普林西比民主共和国共同开发两国专属经济区的石油及其他资源的条约》……………… 367

2. Treaty between The Federal Republic of Nigeria and The Democratic Republic of São Tomé e Príncipe on the Joint Development of Petroleum and other Resources, in Respect of Areas of the Exclusive Economic Zone of the Two States ……………………………… 391

3. 2003 年《尼日利亚与圣多美和普林西比共同开发管理局石油法规》………………………………………………………… 427

4. Nigeria – Sao Tome and Principe Joint Development Authority Petroleum Regulations 2003 ………………………………………………… 457

（十四）2001 年东帝汶与澳大利亚共同开发案 ……………………… 499

1.《东帝汶政府与澳大利亚政府间帝汶海条约》………………… 499

2. Timor Sea Treaty between the Government of East Timor and the Government of Australia ……………………………………… 515

3.《澳大利亚政府和东帝汶民主共和国政府关于 Sunrise 和 Troubadour 油田统一开发的协定》……………………………………… 536

4. Agreement between the Government of Australia and the Government of the Democratic Republic of Timor – Leste relating to the Unitisation of the Sunrise Troubador Fields ·· 551

5. 《澳大利亚与东帝汶民主共和国关于帝汶海的特定海上安排的条约》 ·· 571

6. Treaty between Australia and the Democratic Republic of Timor – Leste on Certain Maritime Arrangements in the Timor Sea ················ 581

（十五）2003 年圭亚那共和国和巴巴多斯国共同开发案 ············ 594

1. 《圭亚那共和国—巴巴多斯关于在其他国家专属经济区外部界线以外两国专属经济区外部界线以内的双边重叠区中的专属经济区行使管辖权的专属经济区合作条约》 ·· 594

2. Exclusive Economic Zone Cooperation Treaty between the Republic of Guyana and the State of Barbados Concerning the Exercise of Jurisdiction in Their Exclusive Economic Zones in the Area of Bilateral Overlap Within Each of Their Outer Limits and Beyond the Outer Limits of the Exclusive Economic Zones of Outer States ············ 599

（十六）2012 年美国和墨西哥共同开发案 ·························· 607

1. 《美利坚合众国政府与墨西哥合众国政府关于墨西哥西部海湾 200 海里以外大陆架划界条约》 ·· 607

2. Treaty between the Government of the United States of America and the Government of the United Mexican States on the Delimitation of the Continental Shelf in the Western Gulf of Mexico beyond 200 Nautical Miles, 9 June 2000 ·· 611

3. 《美利坚合众国与墨西哥合众国之间关于墨西哥湾跨界油气储藏的协定》 ·· 616

4. Agreement between the United States of America and the United Mexican States Concerning Transboundary Hydrocarbon Reservoirs in the Gulf of Mexico ………………………………………………… 630

（十七）2012年塞舌尔和毛里求斯共同开发案 ………………… 650

1. 《塞舌尔共和国政府与毛里求斯共和国政府关于共同管理马斯克林高原地区大陆架的条约》……………………………………… 650
2. Treaty Concerning the Joint Management of the Continental Shelf in the Mascarene Plateau Region ………………………………… 665
3. 《塞舌尔共和国政府与毛里求斯共和国政府关于共同行使马斯克林高原地区大陆架主权权利的条约》……………………………… 686
4. Treaty Concerning the Joint Exercise of Sovereign Rights over the Continental Shelf in the Mascarene Plateau Region …………… 689

四 海上共同开发协定示范文本

1990年英国国际法与比较法研究所的修订示范文本 ………… 695

1. 《X国和Y国共同开发两国大陆架和/或专属经济区区域内石油的修订示范协定》………………………………………………… 695
2. The Revised Model Agreement between State X and State Y on the Joint Development of Petroleum in Areas of the Continent Shelf and /or the Exclusive Economic Zone of the Two Countries …………… 712

一

海上共同开发的产生阶段

（一）1958年巴林与沙特阿拉伯共同开发波斯湾大陆架案

1.《巴林—沙特阿拉伯边界协定》

（1958年2月22日订于利雅得）

宗吕谦译，黄文博、杨泽伟校

注意到沙特阿拉伯王国与巴林政府之间的海域多有交集，却因其各自的海岸线而被忽略，意识到沙特阿拉伯王国于1368年的第一个舍尔邦月（即1949年5月28日）颁布王室公告、巴林政府于1949年6月5日颁布法令，宣布开发海床，认识到两国达成划定下覆水域协定的必要性，考虑到两国之间的感情与彼此友谊，以及沙特阿拉伯国王陛下愿尽一切可能协助巴林政府，遂达成以下协定。

第一条

1. 沙特阿拉伯王国和巴林政府之间边界依中间线原则从坐标点一开始，坐标点一位于巴林最南端巴尔角（Ras al Bar）（A）与位于沙特阿拉伯王国海岸线的穆哈拉角（Ras Muharra）（B）连线的中点。

2. 上述中间线再由坐标点一延伸至坐标点二，坐标点二位于A点与扎那尼亚（Zakhnuniya）岛最北端（C）之间连线的中点。

3. 此线再由坐标点二延伸至坐标点三，坐标点三位于A点与赛亚角（Ras Saiya）（D）连线的中点。

4. 此线再由坐标点三延伸至坐标点四，坐标点四位于E点与F点连线的中点，坐标点四、E点、F点位置见所附地图。

5. 此线再由坐标点四延伸至坐标点五，坐标点五位于 G 点与 H 点连线的中点，坐标点五、G 点、H 点位置见所附地图。

6. 此线再由坐标点五延伸至坐标点六，坐标点六位于 I 点与 J 点连线的中点，坐标点六、I 点、J 点位置见所附地图。

7. 此线再由坐标点六延伸至坐标点七，坐标点七位于乌姆纳桑（Umm Nasan）岛西南角（K）与库赖雅角（Ras Al Kureya）（L）连线的中点。

8. 此线再由坐标点七延伸至坐标点八，坐标点八位于拜勒阿斯塞赫（Al Baina As Saghir）岛的最西端，从该岛向巴林政府方向延伸。

9. 此线再由坐标点八延伸至坐标点九，坐标点九位于拜勒凯比尔（Al Baina Al Kabir）岛最东端，从该岛向沙特阿拉伯王国方向延伸。

10. 此线再由坐标点九延伸至坐标点十，坐标点十位于法西湾（Khor Fasht）西北角（M）与恰什修斯（Chaschus）岛最南端（N）连线的中点。

11. 此线再由坐标点十延伸至位于 O 点与上述第十款中 N 点连线中点的坐标点十一，O 点位于法西雅里姆（Fasht Al Jarim）最西端。

12. 此线再由坐标点十一延伸至坐标点十二，坐标点十二约位于北纬 26°31′48″、东经 50°23′15″。

13. 此线再由坐标点十二延伸至坐标点十三，坐标点十三约位于北纬 26°37′15″、东经 50°33′24″。

14. 此线再由坐标点十三延伸至坐标点十四，坐标点十四约位于北纬 26°59′30″、东经 50°46′24″，从伦尼（Rennie）浅滩（奈季沃特里杰和法西安洛伊雅，Najwat Al Riqai and Fasht Al Anawiyah）转向沙特阿拉伯王国方向。

15. 此线再由坐标点十四向东北方向延伸至沙特阿拉伯王国于 1368 年的第一个舍尔邦月（也就是 1949 年 5 月 28 日）颁布的王室公告以及巴林政府于 1949 年 6 月 5 日颁布的法令中宣告的长度。

16. 上述边界左侧属于沙特阿拉伯王国，右侧属于巴林政府。两国政府有义务接受下述第二条的内容。

第二条

划界区域为下文所描述的六边形闭合区域：

1. 第一条边的起点约位于北纬 27°、东经 50°23′。

2. 第一条边的终点约位于北纬 26°31′48″、东经 50°23′15″。

4

3. 再连接至约北纬 26°37′、东经 50°33′。

4. 再连接至约北纬 26°59′30″、东经 50°46′24″。

5. 再连接至约北纬 26°59′30″、东经 50°40′。

6. 再连接至约北纬 27°、东经 50°40′。

7. 再由该点连接至起点。

依照巴林国王殿下的意愿，以及经沙特阿拉伯国王陛下同意，上述区域主权归属于沙特阿拉伯。该区的石油开采以沙特阿拉伯王国国王选择的方式进行，沙特阿拉伯将上述石油开采中所获的一半净收入归于巴林政府，资源的共享不影响沙特阿拉伯政府对该区域的主权和管辖权。

第三条

该协定附两张地图副本，尽可能清晰地说明上述条款中的位置与坐标，地图由下文第四条规定的委员会最终确定。该地图在经两国政府代表签字后成为该协定确定的、不可分割的一部分。

第四条

两国应选择一个技术机构来采取必要的措施，以确定边界符合本协定条款的规定，该技术机构应在合同履行后两个月内完成工作。

第五条

在第四条规定的委员会完成其工作、两国确定地图的最终选本后，双方将安排大量技术代表着手按照地图最终选本中的细节部分，放置标记、划定边界。

第六条

本协定在两国政府签署后生效。

2. Bahrain – Saudi Arabia Boundary Agreement, 22 February 1958

Whereas the regional waters between the Kingdom of Saudi Arabia and the Government of Bahrain meet together in many places overlooked by their respective coasts,

And in view of the royal proclamation issued by the Kingdom of Saudi Arabia on the 1st Sha'aban in the year 1368 (corresponding to 28 May 1949) and the ordinance issued by the Government of Bahrain on 5 June 1949 about the exploitation of the sea – bed,

And in view of the necessity for an agreement to define the underwater areas belonging to both countries,

And in view of the spirit of affection and mutual friendship and the desire of H. M. the King of Saudi Arabia to extend every possible assistance to the Government of Bahrain,

The following agreement has been made:

Article 1

1. The boundary line between the Kingdom of Saudi Arabia and the Bahrain Government will begin, on the basis of the middle line from point 1, which is situated at the mid – point of the line running between the tip of the Ras al Bar (A) at the southern extremity of Bahrain and Ras Muharra (B) on the coast of the Kingdom of Saudi Arabia.

2. Then the above – mentioned middle line will extend from point 1 to point 2 situated at the mid – point of the line running between point A and the northern tip of the island of Zakhnuniya (C).

（一） 1958 年巴林与沙特阿拉伯共同开发波斯湾大陆架案

3. Then the line will extend from point 2 to point 3 situated at the mid-point of the line running between point A and the tip of Ras Saiya (D).

4. Then the line will extend from point 3 to point 4, which is defined on the attached map and which is situated at the mid-point of the line running between the two points E and F which are both defined on the map.

5. Then the line will extend from point 4 to point 5, which is defined on the map and which is situated at the point [sic] of the line running between the two points G and H which are defined on the map.

6. Then the line will extend from point 5 to point 6, which is defined on the map and which is situated at the mid-point of the line running between the two points I and J which are defined on the map.

7. Then the line will extend from point 6 to point 7 situated at the mid-point of the line running between the south-western tip of the island of Umm Nasan (K) and Ras Al Kureya (L).

8. Then the line will extend from point 7 to point 8 situated at the western extremity of the island Al Baina As Saghir, leaving the island to the Government of Bahrain.

9. Then the line will extend from point 8 to point 9 situated at the eastern extremity of the island Al Baina Al Kabir, leaving the island to the Kingdom of Saudi Arabia.

10. Then the line will extend from point 9 to point 10 situated at the mid-point of the line running between the north-western tip of Khor Fasht (M) and the southern end of the island of Chaschus (N).

11. Then the line will extend from point 10 to point 11 situated at the mid-point of the line running between point O situated at the western edge of Fasht Al Jarim and point N referred to in subsection 10 above.

12. Then the line will extend from point 11 to point 12 situated at latitude 26 degrees 31 minutes 48 seconds north and longitude 50 degrees 23 minutes 15 seconds east approximately.

13. Then the line will extend from point 12 to point 13 situated at latitude 26 degrees 37 minutes 15 seconds north and longitude 50 degrees 33 minutes 24 sec-

onds east approximately.

14. Then the line will extend from point 13 to point 14 situated at latitude 26 degrees 59 minutes 30 seconds north and longitude 50 degrees 46 minutes 24 seconds east approximately, leaving the Rennie Shoals (known as Najwat Al Riqai and Fasht Al Anawiyah) to the Kingdom of Saudi Arabia.

15. Then the line will extend from point 14 in a north – easterly direction to the extent agreed upon in the royal proclamation issued on the 1st Sha'aban in the year 1368 (corresponding to 28 May 1949) and in the ordinance issued by the Government of Bahrain on 5 June 1949.

16. Everything that is situated to the left of the above – mentioned line in the above subsections belongs to the Kingdom of Saudi Arabia and everything to the right of that line to the Government of Bahrain, with the obligation of the two Governments to accept what will subsequently appear in the second clause below.

Article 2

The area situated within the six defined sides is as follows:

1. A line beginning from a point situated at latitude 27 degrees north and longitude 50 degrees 23 minutes east approximately.

2. From there to a point situated at latitude 26 degrees 31 minutes 48 seconds north and longitude 50 degrees 23 minutes 15 seconds east approximately.

3. From there to a point situated at latitude 26 degrees 37 minutes north and longitude 50 degrees 33 minutes east approximately.

4. From there to a point situated at latitude 26 degrees 59 minutes 30 seconds north and longitude 50 degrees 46 minutes 24 seconds east approximately.

5. From there to a point situated at latitude 26 degrees 59 minutes 30 seconds north and longitude 50 degrees 40 minutes east.

6. From there to a point situated at latitude 27 degrees north and longitude 50 degrees 40 minutes east approximately.

7. From there to the starting point.

This area cited and defined above shall be in the part falling to the Kingdom of Saudi Arabia in accordance with the wish of H. H. the Ruler of Bahrain and the agreement of H. M. the King of Saudi Arabia. The exploitation of the oil resources in this area will be carried out in the way chosen by His Majesty on the condition that he grants to the Government of Bahrain one half of the net revenue accruing to the Government of Saudi Arabia and arising from this exploitation, and on the understanding that this does not infringe the right of sovereignty of the Government of Saudi Arabia nor the right of administration over this above-mentioned area.

Article 3

Two copies of a map shall be attached to this agreement, making as clear as possible the positions and points referred to in the foregoing subsections, subject to the map being made final by the expert knowledge of the committee defined in the fourth clause below. This map shall become final and an integral part of this agreement after approval and signature by the accredited representatives of the two Governments on behalf of the two parties.

Article 4

The two parties shall choose a technical body to undertake the necessary measures to confirm the boundaries in accordance with the provisions of this agreement on the condition that this body shall complete its work two months at the most after the date of execution of this agreement.

Article 5

After the committee referred to in the fourth clause has completed its work and the two parties agree on the final map which it will have prepared a body of technical delegates from both sides shall undertake the placing of signs and the establishing of the boundaries in accordance with the detailed announcements made clear in the final map.

Article 6

This agreement shall come into effect from the date on which it is signed by the two parties.

（二）1962 年荷兰与联邦德国埃姆斯河口资源共同开发案

1.《荷兰王国与德意志联邦共和国签署的〈关于在埃姆斯河口合作安排的条约〉（〈埃姆斯—多拉德条约〉*）之补充协定》**

（1962 年 5 月 14 日订于宾尼哥姆）

申钟秀译，邓妮雅校

荷兰王国与德意志联邦共和国，为促进埃姆斯河口水下自然资源的勘探，在此本着《埃姆斯—多拉德条约》第 48 条的精神进行合作，达成如下协定。

第一条

本协定中：

"边界地区"是指本协定附图①的阴影部分的区域及其之下的范围；

"分界线"是指在附图中用绿色标注的纵向平分边界地区的线段；

"自然资源"是指根据任一缔约方的采矿立法，获得特许权，而从地下开采的所有固态、液态和气态的物质；

"特许经营者"是指被授权勘探或开采自然资源的人（下文中称"特许"）。

---

* 参见《联合国条约集》第 508 卷。
** 1963 年 8 月 1 日生效；参见《联合国条约集》第 508 卷第 20 页脚注 1。
① 参见《联合国条约集》第 508 卷第 138 页与第 139 页内容。

（二） 1962年荷兰与联邦德国埃姆斯河口资源共同开发案

第二条

缔约方应本着睦邻的精神，在勘探与开采埃姆斯河口水下自然资源时产生的，可能影响其利益的所有问题上进行合作。

第三条

本协定第四条至第十条的规定，应适用于开采开始前在边界地区发现的石油和天然气矿藏，以及开采过程中发现的其他物质。对边界地区的其他资源，若任一缔约方认为有必要，缔约方应比照适用上述条款内容，做出个别安排。

第四条

（1）在边界地区，在不影响《埃姆斯—多拉德条约》的前提下，对以下事项荷兰法律适用于分界线荷兰一侧，德国法律适用于分界线德国一侧：

（a）勘探与开发；

（b）与勘探及开发相关的作为与不作为；

（c）为勘探与开发而建造的设施；

该款同样适用于有关当局与法院的事项；《埃姆斯—多拉德条约》第33条第2款至第6款应比照适用于为勘探或开采而使用的固定设施。

（2）缔约方应依据其国内法授予在整个边界地区有效的特许。但是，这种特许与本协定生效时已经存在的特许，应只能依据本协定的条款加以使用。

（3）任一缔约方应毫无迟延地通知另一缔约方已存在的特许，当授予新的特许时或者特许废除或修改时同样适用。

第五条

（1）德国的特许经营者与荷兰的特许经营者，对开采出的石油和天然气，及在开采过程中发现的其他物质，享有同等的份额。

（2）经其政府同意，特许经营者可放弃其全部或部分份额的权利，或同意现金结算。

（3）勘探和开发双方共享的或者现金结算的产品所产生的合理费用，应与所得产品相同的比例承担，除非特许经营者按照第七条达成了其他一致。

第六条

（1）在分界线荷兰一侧的勘探及开采，应由荷兰的特许经营者实施；在分界线德国一侧的勘探及开采，应由德国的特许经营者实施。

(2) 若分界线一侧的特许经营者提出分界线另一侧的特许经营者采取合适的勘探与开采工作要求后一年内，后者仍未满足其要求，那么前者可依据该特许中施加于他方经营者的所有条件，进行勘探与开采。如果后者已建立了开采设施且不适合建立新的设施，经特许经营者要求，其必须同意其他特许经营者支付合适的报酬后使用这些设施。

(3) 在适用第2款第1句时，如果特许经营者发现了位于分界线另一侧的油田或天然气矿藏，且另一特许经营者依据第五条主张其对从矿藏中开采的物质全部或部分份额，或协定采用现金支付，那么前者不仅对依据第五条第3款产生的费用，而且对适当的风险津贴均享有份额，除非特许经营者间依据第七条第2款达成其他一致。

第七条

(1) 在勘探与开采中，边界线一边的特许经营者应与另一边的特许经营者密切合作。为了此目标，他们应交换在边界地区的经营计划以及经营结果的报告。

(2) 为了此种合作，特许经营者应在以下事项上尽早达成协议：

(a) 石油与天然气的储量和产量的计量方法；

(b) 依据第五条，产品分享与费用相关的细节，及记账与审查的程序；

(c) 第六条第3款提到的风险津贴是不是可支付的，若可支付，应支付多少；

(d) 争端的解决。

(3) 特许经营者在与合作相关的问题上自由达成协议；这些协议应提供第六条第3款规定之外的其他风险津贴。

(4) 应通知缔约方政府第2款与第3款中的协议。第2款所指的协议，及规定风险补贴或分担第五条第3款所规定费用之外的其他费用的其他规定，须经双方政府的同意。

(5) 若特许权经营人由新的特许经营者继任，后者应受第2款所涉协议的约束，直至达成新的协议。

第八条

依据第七条第2款的规定，若一项协议未能在合理的时间期限内达成，缔约方政府应进行谈判以为特许经营者做出一项联合提议。如果政府的努力仍未能使特许经营者之间达成协议，任一政府可依据《埃姆斯—多拉德条约》第 12 章诉诸仲裁法庭。

第九条

若在 4 个月期限内，任一或两个政府都没有授予第七条第 4 款要求的批准，政府间应进行磋商。若磋商未达成协议，任一政府可诉诸仲裁法庭。磋商亦可达成联合提案，应比照适用第八条规定。

第十条

（1）在依据第八条或第九条诉诸仲裁法庭的案件中，《埃姆斯—多拉德条约》第 12 章的规定应比照适用，除非本条下述款项中做出其他规定。

（2）德意志联邦共和国应依据第 51 条①的规定，从联邦法院院长任命的四个联邦法院法官中任命特别顾问。荷兰王国应依据第 51 条②的规定，从最高法院院长任命的四个最高法院法官中任命特别顾问。

（3）第 52 条③第 1 款与第 4 款提及的主张声明中，应包括解决争议问题的提案。

（4）提交申请书的政府应向任一受到影响的特许经营者送交一个副本。第 52 条④第 2 款不应当适用。

（5）任一受影响的特许经营者都应作为一个当事方参与仲裁程序。受影响的特许经营者也应参与第 52 条⑤第 3 款和第 5 款规定的讨论程序。

（6）仲裁法院应对所有的法律问题或自由裁量的问题，做出约束缔约方与受影响的特许经营者的裁决。仲裁法庭在其决议里应考虑公平问题。

（7）仲裁法庭应制定其程序规则，使得本条的适用有必要偏离第 12 章规定的程序性安排。

（8）在第八条所指案件中，仲裁法庭可判定某一或所有参加仲裁程序的特许经营者承担部分或全部仲裁费用。

第十一条

依据《埃姆斯—多拉德条约》第 46 条第 2 款达成的任何协定都不影响本协定。

---

① 指《埃姆斯—多拉德条约》第 51 条。——译者注
② 指《埃姆斯—多拉德条约》第 51 条。——译者注
③ 指《埃姆斯—多拉德条约》第 52 条。——译者注
④ 指《埃姆斯—多拉德条约》第 52 条。——译者注
⑤ 指《埃姆斯—多拉德条约》第 52 条。——译者注

第十二条

该协定的最后议定书与附后的今日换文都构成条约的一部分。

第十三条

该协定亦适用于柏林地区，除非在《埃姆斯—多拉德条约》生效后的三个月内德意志联邦共和国政府做出与荷兰王国政府相反的声明。

第十四条

该协定应被批准。批准文书应尽快在波恩进行交换。

第十五条

该协定应在批准书换文一个月后生效，成为《埃姆斯—多拉德条约》的一部分。

下列签署人，经其各自政府正式授权，在本协定上签字，以昭信守。

1962 年 5 月 14 日签署于宾尼哥姆，原本为两个，一为荷兰语文本，一为德语文本，两个文本具有同等效力。

荷兰王国

H. R. 万·豪滕

德意志联邦共和国

拉尔

最后议定书

关于签署 1960 年 4 月 8 日荷兰王国与德意志联邦共和国于宾尼哥姆签署的《关于在埃姆斯河口合作安排的条约》[①]（《埃姆斯—多拉德条约》）之补充协定[②]，缔约方全权代表协定如下。

第一条

（1）为了适用该补充协定，"德国法"意指在邻接边界地区德国一侧的领土内现行有效的法律，尤其指矿产法，劳动与社会法，税收与海关法。

（2）"荷兰法"尤其指矿产法，劳动与社会法，税收与海关法。

第二条

为了实现该补充协定第六条第 2 款之目的，"条件"仅指授予有关管理

[①] 参见《联合国条约集》第 508 卷第 64 页。

[②] 参见《联合国条约集》第 508 卷第 140 页。

(二) 1962年荷兰与联邦德国埃姆斯河口资源共同开发案

与组织采矿工作、自然资源的勘探开采、地理数据的披露的荷兰的特许权时，施加于或应施加于特许经营者的条件。

第三条

若荷兰未授予部分边界地区的特许权，在德意志联邦共和国政府的请求下，为了实现该补充协定的目的，荷兰王国政府应指派人员，该人员被视为勘探特许经营者。

第四条

如果某一缔约方没有对某部分边界地区授予开采特许，当于此处发现石油或天然气矿藏时应授予此种许可。尽管有补充协定第五条第1款的规定，如果没有在合理的时间期限内授予开采许可，在该边界区域持有另一缔约方开采许可者，在开采操作开始前有权处置位于该边界区域的全部石油或天然气矿藏。

第五条

（1）为了适用《埃姆斯—多拉德条约》第32条与第36条，位于分界线荷兰一侧的用以勘探或开采的固定设施应被视为荷兰的一部分，位于分界线德国一侧的用以勘探或开采的固定设施应被视为德国的一部分。为了适用《埃姆斯—多拉德条约》第40条，该规定同样适用。

（2）双方同意，《埃姆斯—多拉德条约》第34条第3款第1句不涉及矿业管理机构对在船舶上实施的勘探作业的监督，在该情况下，该适用何国法律与哪个矿业机构拥有管辖权的问题应由分界线来决定。

（3）双方同意，若钻井活动从移动设施或船舶上实施，则该移动设施或船舶应被视为固定设施。

第六条

双方同意，在不影响该补充协定（第八条至第十条）规定的特殊仲裁管辖的情况下，《埃姆斯—多拉德条约》第50条至第54条亦适用于缔约国之间与补充协定解释或适用有关的争端。

1962年5月14日签署于宾尼哥姆，原本为两个，一为荷兰语文本，一为德语文本，两个文本具有同等效力。

荷兰王国
H. R. 万·豪滕
德意志联邦共和国
拉尔

换　文

I

外交部长

宾尼哥姆，1962年5月14日

尊敬的阁下：

在促成今天于宾尼哥姆签署的《1960年4月8日荷兰王国与德意志联邦共和国签署的〈关于在埃姆斯河口合作安排的条约〉（《埃姆斯—多拉德条约》①）之补充协定》②的谈判中，本人声明，在不损害《埃姆斯—多拉德条约》第33条与第36条的情况下，为了适用德国税收和海关法，位于分界线荷兰一侧的地区视为荷兰的领土。

在不损害《埃姆斯—多拉德条约》第33条与第36条的情况下，联邦政府在这一前提下开展工作，即为了适用荷兰税收和海关法，位于分界线德国一侧的地区视为德国的领土。

若您确认您的政府同意前述内容，我将不胜感激。

尊敬的阁下，请接受我崇高的敬意。

拉尔

H. R. 万·豪滕阁下
荷兰王国外交部长

II

外交部长

宾尼哥姆，1962年5月14日

尊敬的阁下：

很荣幸地告知您，我已收到您今天的来信，文本以荷兰语表述如下：

[参见照会 I]

我很荣幸地确认荷兰政府同意您照会的内容。

---

① 参见《联合国条约集》第508卷第64页。
② 参见《联合国条约集》第508卷第140页。

（二）1962年荷兰与联邦德国埃姆斯河口资源共同开发案

尊敬的阁下，请接受我崇高的敬意。

H. R. 万·豪滕

R. 拉尔阁下
德意志联邦共和国外交部长

2. Supplementary Agreement[*] to the Treaty Concerning Arrangements for Cooperation in the Ems Estuary (Ems – Dollard Treaty), Signed between the Kingdom of the Netherlands and the Federal Republic of Germany[**]

Signed at Bennekom, on 14 May 1962

The Kingdom of the Netherlands and the Federal Republic of Germany,

Desiring to promote the exploitation of natural resources underlying the Ems Estuary and proposing, in so doing, to co – operate in the spirit of article 48 of the Ems – Dollard Treaty,[①]

Have agreed as follows:

Article 1

In this Agreement:

The term "frontier area" means the area hatched on the map annexed[②] to this Agreement, together with the ground beneath it;

The term "line" means the line, marked in green on the attached map, bisecting the frontier area lengthwise;

The term "natural resources" means all solid, liquid or gaseous underground substances for the extraction of which, under the mining legislation of one of the

---

[*] Came into force on 1 August 1963; see footnote 1, p. 20 of volume 508 of the United Nations. Treaty Series.

[**] See p. 64 of this volume.

[①] See p. 64 of this volume.

[②] See insert between pp. 138 and 139 of this volume. No. 7404.

two Contracting Parties, a concession is required;

The term "concessionnaire" means a person who has authorization to prospect for or to extract natural resources (hereinafter referred to as "a concession").

Article 2

The Contracting Parties shall co-operate in a spirit of good-neighbourliness with respect to all questions arising in connexion with prospecting for and the extraction of natural resources underlying the Ems Estuary which may affect their interests.

Article 3

The provisions of articles 4 to 10 of this Agreement shall apply to deposits of petroleum and natural gas present in the frontier area before the commencement of extraction and to other substances recovered in the course of extraction. The Contracting Parties shall make arrangements in a separate agreement for the application of these provisions mutatis mutandis to other natural resources in the frontier area, if one of the Contracting Parties declares this to be necessary.

Article 4

(1) In the frontier area, without prejudice to the terms of the Ems-Dollard Treaty, Netherlands law shall apply on the Netherlands side of the line and German law shall apply on the German side of the line to:

(a) Prospecting and extraction;

(b) Acts and omissions connected with prospecting and extraction;

(c) Installations erected for prospecting and extraction purposes.

The same shall apply with respect to the competence of the authorities and the courts; article 33, paragraphs 2 to 6, of the Ems-Dollard Treaty shall apply mutatis mutandis to fixed installations used for prospecting or extraction operations.

(2) The Contracting Parties may in accordance with their domestic law grant concessions valid for the whole of the frontier area. However, such concessions, and concessions already existing at the time of the entry into force of this Agreement, may be utilized only in accordance with the terms of this Agreement.

(3) Each of the Contracting Parties shall without delay notify the other Party of the concessions already in existence. The same shall apply when new conces-

sions are granted or when concessions are amended or revoked.

Article 5

(1) German concessionnaires and Netherlands concessionnaires respectively shall be entitled to an equal share of the petroleum and natural gas extracted and of other substances recovered in the course of their extraction.

(2) A concessionnaire may with the consent of his Government waive the right to the whole or a part of his share, or agree to a cash settlement.

(3) Expenses reasonably attributable to prospecting for and the extraction of products which are shared or for which a cash settlement is made shall be shared in the same proportion as the products, unless the concessionnaires agree otherwise in accordance with the terms of article 7.

Article 6

(1) Prospecting and extraction shall be carried out on the Netherlands side of the line by Netherlands concessionnaires and on the German side of the line by German concessionnaires.

(2) If a concessionnaire does not within one year accede to a request by the concessionnaire on the other side of the line to carry out appropriate prospecting or extraction operations on his side of the line, the last-mentioned concessionnaire may himself, subject to any conditions imposed on the other concessionnaire by the terms of his concession, proceed with the prospecting or extraction operations. If the first-mentioned concessionnaire has set up any extraction installations, he must allow the other concessionnaire, upon request, to use such installations against suitable remuneration, provided that it is inexpedient to set up new installations.

(3) If a concessionnaire, in the application of the first sentence of paragraph 2, discovers deposits of petroleum or natural gas on the other side of the line, and if the other concessionnaire claims the whole or a part of his share of the products extracted from such deposits in accordance with the terms of article 5, or a cash settlement is agreed upon, the first-mentioned concessionnaire shall be entitled not only to the share of the expenses already incurred provided for in article 5, paragraph 3, but also to an appropriate risk bonus, save as other-

wise agreed between the concessionnaires in accordance with the terms of article 7, paragraph 2.

Article 7

(1) The concessionnaires of one side shall co-operate closely with those of the other side in prospecting and extraction. To this end, they shall exchange all plans for operations in the frontier area and reports on the results of such operations.

(2) With a view to such co-operation, concessionnaires shall conclude agreements as soon as possible on the following matters:

(a) Methods of calculating petroleum and natural gas reserves and output;

(b) Details relating to the sharing of products and costs in accordance with the terms of article 5, and book-keeping and auditing procedures;

(c) Whether the risk bonuses referred to in article 6, paragraph 3, are to be payable and, if so, in what amount;

(d) The settlement of disputes.

(3) Concessionnaires shall be at liberty to conclude agreements on other matters connected with co-operation between them; such agreements may provide for risk bonuses in cases other than those referred to in article 6, paragraph 3.

(4) The Governments of the Contracting Parties shall be notified of the agreements referred to in paragraphs 2 and 3. The agreements referred to in paragraph 2, and clauses in other agreements providing for the payment of a risk bonus or the sharing of costs otherwise than as prescribed in article 5, paragraph 3, shall require the approval of each of the two Governments.

(5) If a concessionnaire is succeeded by a new concessionnaire, the latter shall be bound by one of the agreements referred to in paragraph 2 until such time as a new agreement is concluded.

Article 8

If an agreement under the terms of article 7, paragraph 2, is not arrived at within a reasonable period of time, the Governments of the Contracting Parties shall enter into negotiations with a view to presenting a joint proposal to the concessionnaires. If the endeavours of the Gouvernments do not result in an agreement between the concessionnaires, either Government may appeal to the arbitral tribunal provided for in chapter 12 of the Ems – Dollard Treaty.

Article 9

If the approval required under the terms of article 7, paragraph 4, is not granted by one or both Governments within a period of four months, the Governments shall enter into consultations. If the consultations do not result in agreement, either Government may appeal to the arbitral tribunal. The consultations may also result in a joint proposal, to which article 8 shall apply mutatis mutandis.

Article 10

(1) In cases where an appeal is made to the arbitral tribunal under the terms of article 8 or article 9, the provisions of chapter 12 of the Ems – Dollard Treaty shall apply mutatis mutandis, save as otherwise provided in the succeeding paragraphs of this article.

(2) The Government of the Federal Republic of Germany shall appoint the assessor whom it is entitled to appoint under the terms of article 51 from among four judges of the Federal Court of Justice nominated by the President of that Court. The Government of the Kingdom of the Netherlands shall appoint the assessor whom it is entitled to appoint under the terms of article 51 from among four judges of the Supreme Court of the Netherlands nominated by the President of that Court.

(3) The statements of claim referred to in article 52, paragraphs 1 and 4, must include a proposal for a settlement of the questions at issue.

(4) The Government submitting the statement of claim shall forward a duplicate thereof to each of the affected concessionnaires. Article 52, paragraph 2, shall not apply.

(5) Each of the affected concessionnaires may participate in the proceedings as a party. The affected concessionnaires shall also participate in the discussions provided for in article 52, paragraphs 3 and 5.

(6) The arbitral tribunal shall lay down a settlement binding upon the Contracting Parties and the affected concessionnaires with respect to all questions of

law or discretion which are at issue. In its decision, the arbitral tribunal may also take into account considerations of equity.

(7) The arbitral tribunal shall establish its own rules of procedure, wherever the application of this article makes it necessary to deviate from the procedural arrangements provided for in chapter 12.

(8) In the cases referred to in article 8, the arbitral tribunal may award the whole or a part of the costs of the proceedings against the concessionnaire or concessionnaires participating in the proceedings.

Article 11

Any settlement under the terms of article 46, paragraph 2, of the EmsDollard Treaty shall not affect this Agreement.

Article 12

The Final Protocol to this Agreement, and the exchange of notes of today's date annexed hereto, form part of this Agreement.

Article 13

This Agreement shall also apply to Land Berlin unless the Government of the Federal Republic of Germany makes a declaration to the contrary to the Government of the Kingdom of the Netherlands within three months after the entry into force of the Ems – Dollard Treaty.

Article 14

This Agreement shall be ratified. The instruments of ratification shall be exchanged as soon as possible, at Bonn.

Article 15

This Agreement shall enter into force one month after the exchange of the instruments of ratification. It forms part of the Ems – Dollard Treaty.

IN WITNESS WHEREOF the plenipotentiaries of the Contracting Parties have signed this Supplementary Agreement.

DONE at Bennekom, on 14 May 1962, in two original copies, each in the Dutch and German languages, both texts being equally authentic.

For the Kingdom of the Netherlands:

(Signed) H. R. VAN HOUTEN

For the Federal Republic of Germany:

(Signed) LAHR

FINAL PROTOCOL

On signing the Supplementary Agreement[①] to the Treaty concerning Arrangements for Co-operation in the Ems Estuary (Ems-Dollard Treaty), signed between the Kingdom of the Netherlands and the Federal Republic of Germany on 8 April 1960,[②] the plenipotentiaries of the two Contracting Parties have agreed as follows:

Article 1

(1) For the purposes of the application of the Supplementary Agreement, the term "German law" means the law in force in the territory adjoining the frontier area on the German side. It means, in particular, mining law, labour and social law, and tax and customs law.

(2) The term "Netherlands law" means, in particular, mining law, labour and social law, and tax and customs law.

Article 2

For the purposes of article 6, paragraph 2, of the Supplementary Agreement, the term "conditions" means only such conditions as have been or shall be imposed on the concessionnaire on the occasion of the granting of a Netherlands concession with respect to the management and organization of mining operations, prospecting for and the protection of natural resources, and the disclosure of geological data.

Article 3

If no concession has been granted by the Netherlands for a part of the frontier area, the Government of the Kingdom of the Netherlands shall upon the request of the Government of the Federal Republic of Germany designate the person deemed to be the prospecting concessionnaire for the purposes of this Supplemen-

---

① See p. 140 of this volume.

② See p. 64 of this volume.

tary Agreement.

Article 4

If one of the Contracting Parties has issued no extraction concession for a part of the frontier area, it shall do so in the event that a deposit of petroleum or natural gas is discovered there. If the extraction concession is not granted within a reasonable period of time, the holder of an extraction concession granted by the other Contracting Party for that part of the frontier area shall have the right, notwithstanding the provisions of article 5, paragraph 1, of the Supplementary Agreement, to dispose of the entire deposit of petroleum or natural gas present in that part of the frontier area before the commencement of extraction operations.

Article 5

(1) For the purposes of the application of articles 32 and 36 of the EmsDollard Treaty, any fixed installation for prospecting or extraction purposes on the Netherlands side of the line shall be deemed to be a Netherlands port, and any such installation on the German side of the line shall be deemed to be a German port. The same shall apply for the purposes of the application of article 40 of the Ems – Dollard Treaty.

(2) It is agreed that supervision by the mining authorities of prospecting operations carried out from aboard a vessel is not covered by article 34, paragraph 3, first sentence, of the Ems – Dollard Treaty; in such cases, the question which law is applicable and which mining authorities have jurisdiction shall be determined by the line.

(3) It is agreed that mobile installations or vessels shall be deemed to be fixed installations if drillings are carried out from them.

Article 6

It is agreed that, without prejudice to the special arbitral jurisdiction provided for in this Supplementary Agreement (articles 8 to 10), articles 50 to 54 ofthe Ems – Dollard Treaty shall also apply to disputes between the Contracting Parties relating to the interpretation or application of this Supplementary Agreement.

DONE at Bennekom, on 14 May 1962, in two original copies, each in the Dutch and German languages, both texts being equally authentic.

For the Kingdom of the Netherlands:

(Signed) H. R. VAN HOUTEN

For the Federal Republic of Germany:

(Signed) LAHR

EXCHANGE OF NOTES

I

THE MINISTER OF STATE FOR FOREIGN AFFAIRS

Bennekom, 14 May 1962

Sir,

During the negotiations which resulted in the signing today of the Supplementary Agreement① to the Treaty concerning Arrangements for Co-operation in the Ems Estuary (Ems-Dollard Treaty),② signed between the Kingdom of the Netherlands and the Federal Republic of Germany on 8 April 1960, I stated that, without prejudice to articles 33 and 36 of the Ems-Dollard Treaty, the area on the Netherlands side of the line is to be regarded as Netherlands territory for the purposes of the application of German tax and customs law.

In this connexion, the Federal Government proceeds on the assumption that, without prejudice to articles 33 and 36 of the Ems-Dollard Treaty, the area on the German side of the line is to be regarded as German territory for the purposes of the application of Netherlands tax and customs law.

I should be most grateful if you would confirm that your Government agrees with the foregoing.

Accept, Sir, the assurances of my highest consideration.

(Signed) LAHR

His Excellency Dr. H. R. van Houten

Minister of State for Foreign Affairs of the Kingdom of the Netherlands

---

① See p. 140 of this volume.

② See p. 140 of this volume.

(二) 1962 年荷兰与联邦德国埃姆斯河口资源共同开发案

II
THE MINISTER OF STATE FOR FOREIGN AFFAIRS

Sir, Bennekom, 14 May 1962

Sir,

I have the honour to acknowledge receipt of your letter of today's date, the text of which reads in Dutch as follows :

[See note I]

I have honour to confirm that the Netherlands Government agrees with the contents of your note.

Accept, Sir, the assurances of my highest consideration.

(Signed) H. R. VAN HOUTEN

His Excellency Mr. R. Lahr

Minister of State for Foreign Affairs of the Federal Republic of Germany

（三）1965 年沙特阿拉伯与科威特共同开发案

1.《沙特阿拉伯王国—科威特国划分中立区的协定》

（1965 年 7 月 7 日订于哈达）

董世杰译，黄文博、杨泽伟校

以慈悲宽容的真主之名义，

鉴于缔约国双方在共享区域内享有平等权利，此共享区边界依据 1922 年 12 月 2 日（回历 1341 年 4 月 13 日）《欧奎尔公约》和 1961 年 3 月 29 日（回历 1380 年 10 月 12 日）于科威特签订的《协议记录》的规定而划定（以下称为"分隔区"）。

然而前述公约并不规制权利的行使，且事务仅具有临时性，进而产生了严重的现实困难。

缔约国双方于 1963 年 8 月 5 日（回历 1383 年 3 月 15 日）就划分中立区互换照会，同意将中立区分割为两部分来结束临时状态，其中一部分归属科威特，另一部分归属沙特阿拉伯。原本《欧奎尔公约》中规定缔约国双方平等享有的权利，将在整个分隔区被全部保留，且受国际责任条款的保障。据此，缔约国双方达成以下一致。

第一条 中立区两部分的边界线应当是一条将中立区划分为均等两部分的界线，该界线的起点位于中部东海岸低潮线上，终点位于中立区西部边界线上。此边界线由调查和划分中立区边界线的委员会划定。该委员会

（三）1965年沙特阿拉伯与科威特共同开发案

是依1963年8月5日（回历1383年3月15日）两国于吉达签订的外交换文附件中的规定而建立的。边界线将由缔约国双方在补充协定中予以确认。

第二条 在不损害本协定条款的前提下，分界线以北的区域作为科威特的领土不可分割的部分归属科威特；分界线以南的区域作为沙特阿拉伯的领土不可分割的部分归属沙特阿拉伯。

第三条 在遵守协定其他条款，以及不损害缔约国双方对于整个分隔区自然资源的权利的情况下，缔约国在划归自己的分隔区内，行使和自己原有领土一样的行政、立法和防卫权利。

第四条 缔约国在归属自己领土的分隔区内，应当尊重其他缔约国对共享自然资源的既有权利以及将来可能出现的权利。

第五条 若任一缔约国放弃或向其他国家让与，本协定条款所保护的并在分隔区内任一区域行使的全部或部分权利，对方缔约国应免除本协定所规定的义务。

第六条 每一缔约国不得采取任何国内或国际措施或行为，若该措施或行为可能有损另一缔约国行使本协定所保护的权利；该缔约国有责任同另一缔约国全面合作以保护另一缔约国的权利。

第七条 在毗邻分隔区且属于缔约双方各自领土的领水内，缔约各方行使与其所属分隔区相同的权利。缔约国双方同意划定毗邻分隔区的领水的分界线。

基于开发分隔区自然资源的目的，毗邻分隔区的6海里以内的海床和底土，为附属分隔区的主要领土。

第八条 划定毗邻分隔区的水下区域的北部边界线时，应将该区作为整体进行划定，不考虑本协定的内容。

缔约国双方以共同开发的方式，在前述条款6海里界线之外的水下区域内行使平等权利，除非双方另有约定。

第九条 对于一缔约国在另一缔约国所属分隔区内的装置，从事行政管理和司法工作的政府人员应将其撤离，并移交对方。但是该条款不适用于雇员用于石油计量、核查与账目审计、技术监督、采购以及其他类似监督工作的装置。

第十条 如果缔约一方委托双方当事国共同特许的公司，根据特许条款，在归属自己的分隔区内，建设司法和行政设施。建设这些设施的合理必要支出，可以从特许公司的资本支出中扣减。

第十一条 现有的石油特许协议继续有效，缔约国双方在其各自的分隔区内，应当尊重现有石油特许协议的条款及其修订文本。缔约国双方也要通过必要的立法和法律措施，确保特许公司持续行使权利和履行义务。

第十二条 根据现有特许协议规定的义务，每一缔约国在其所属的分隔区内负有保护和保卫的责任。

第十三条 为了避免双重征税，每一缔约国应采取立法保障措施，对在分隔区内从另一缔约国获得特许权的公司，不征收税收、关税或者特许权使用费。

第十四条 任一缔约国的公民，作为公职人员、雇员、劳工以及承包商根据特许协议或附属协议而进入分隔区，从事自然资源的开发，应有对方缔约国签发的有效护照，或者有一方缔约国制作的特殊形式的通行证，但有进入签证者是不需要的。

第十五条 每一缔约国在其所属的分隔区内，不得损害已生效的石油特许协议，应当确保无论是现有石油特许协议还是将来任何石油特许协议，另一缔约国的公民与本国公民一样，在从事与石油有关的工作时，享有工作自由以及平等参与的权利。

缔约国双方还同意，对于任何将来可能发现的资源，双方公民都有从事相关工作的权利。

第十六条 每一缔约国在其所属的分隔区内，应当尊重另一缔约国公民对现有设施和建筑物的权利。

第十七条 为了确保缔约国双方为分隔区内自然资源的最有效开发而持续努力，应当设立一个常设联合委员会，命名为"委员会"。

第十八条 委员会由缔约国双方相同人数代表组成。由两国的自然资源部长协商委员会成员的人数、运行规则以及财政保障。

第十九条 委员会拥有以下职权：

（1）方便政府人员以及特许石油公司、附属公司和机构的雇员（除缔约国公民以外）在分隔区内出入；

（2）研究共享自然资源的开发项目；

（3）审查与共享自然资源相关的许可、合同以及特许权，并向缔约国双方的自然资源部长提出适当建议。

（4）讨论缔约国双方的自然资源部长提出的任何问题。

为了履行职责，委员会有权缔结合同。委员会直接向缔约国双方的自然资源部长提出报告和建议。

第二十条　两缔约国的自然资源部长，应就有关共享自然资源特许权的授予或修订相互协商。一缔约国不同意另一缔约国观点时，在特许权授予或修订前，应当书面告知另一方不同意的理由。

若任何其他实体或公司允许替代现有实体或公司在分隔区内开发自然资源，此种替代不应被认为是一项新的特许，因为对方当事国未受影响。

第二十一条　委员会为履行职责而要求的数据、信息和文件，缔约国双方应当提供。

第二十二条　一旦因本协定的解释或适用，或者权利义务而产生争端，缔约国双方应当寻求友好方式解决争端，其中包括寻求阿拉伯联盟的帮助。

如果证明上述方式无法解决争端，应将争端提交国际法院。

缔约国双方应当就此接受国际法院强制管辖。

如果一缔约国反对另一缔约国采取的某一行动，反对的一方可请求国际法院采取临时措施以中止对方当事国采取的行动，或者允许对方当事国的行动继续直到国际法院做出最终决定。

如果任一缔约国不遵守对其不利的判决，另一缔约国将免除本协定所规定的义务。

第二十三条　本协定需要缔约国双方根据各自的宪法程序予以批准，自交换批准文书之日生效。

本协定缔结于回历1385年3月9日，即公元1965年7月7日，双方的条约正本均以阿拉伯语作准。

沙特阿拉伯王国代表　　　科威特国代表
艾哈迈·扎基·亚迈尼　　吉巴·阿尔－艾哈迈德·阿尔－沙巴

2. Agreement between the Kingdom of Saudi Arabia and the State of Kuwait on the Partition of the Neutral Zone

In the Name of God the Compassionate, the Merciful.

Whereas both Contracting Parties have equal rights in the shared zone whose territory is defined in the Convention of Al – Uqair dated 13 Rabi, II A. D. 1341, corresponding to 2 December A. D. 1922, and the Agreed Minutes signed at Kuwait on 12 Shawwal A. H. 1380, corresponding to 29 March A. D. 1961 (hereinafter referred to as "the Partitioned Zone"),

Whereas the aforementioned Convention did not regulate the exercise of those rights and that state of affairs was of a provisional nature and gave rise to serious practical difficulties,

Whereas both Contracting Parties have agreed, by an exchange of notes (on partition of the Neutral Zone) dated 15 Rabi, I A. H. 1383, corresponding to 5 August A. D. 1963, to put an end to that provisional state of affairs by partitioning that Zone into two sections, whereby one section shall be annexed to the territory of the State of Kuwait and the other shall be annexed to tiie territory of the Kingdom of Saudi Arabia, provided that the equal rights of both Parties as originally established by the Convention of Al – Uqair and shared by both Parties shall be preserved in the entire partitioned Zone and shall be safeguarded by the provisions of international responsibility,

They have agreed as follows:

Article 1

The boundary between the two sections of the Zone shall be the line which divides the Zone into two equal parts and which begins from a point at the middle of the shore to the east at the low – tide line, and ends at the western boundary of the Zone. That boundary line shall be demarcated by the Commission for the survey and delimitation of the Neutral Zone whose establishment was agreed on in the annex to the notes exchanged between the two Parties at Jeddah on 15 Rabi, I A. H. 1383, corresponding to 5 August A. D. 1963. 3 The boundary line shall be confirmed by both Parties in a Supplementary Agreement.

Article 2

Without prejudice to the provisions of this Agreement, the area lying to the north of the line dividing the Partitioned Zone shall be annexed to Kuwait as part of its territory, and the area lying to the south of the line dividing the Partitioned Zone shall be annexed to the Kingdom of Saudi Arabia as part of its territory.

Article 3

Each of the Contracting Parties shall exercise over that part of the Partitioned Zone annexed to its territory the same rights of administration, legislation and defence as those exercised in the rest of its territory, while observing the other provisions of this Agreement, and without prejudice to the rights of both Contracting Parties to the natural resources of the entire Partitioned Zone.

Article 4

Each of the Contracting Parties shall respect the rights of the other Party to the shared natural resources either existing at present or which may in the future exist in that part of the Partitioned Zone which is annexed to its territory.

Article 5

If one of the Parties cedes or otherwise alienates all or part of the aforementioned equal rights which are safeguarded by the provisions of this Agreement and which are exercised over any part of the Partitioned Zone to some other State, the other Party shall be relieved of its obligations under this Agreement.

Article 6

Each Contracting Party undertakes not to take any domestic or international measure or action which may in any way cause the other Party to be impeded in the exercise of the rights safeguarded by this Agreement, and each Party undertakes to cooperate fully with the other Party in protecting those rights.

Article 7

Each of the Contracting Parties shall exercise over the territorial waters adjoining that part of the Partitioned Zone which is to be annexed to its territory the same rights as those exercised over the part annexed to its territory; and both Contracting Parties agree to determine the boundary line dividing the territorial waters adjoining the Partitioned Zone.

For the purpose of the exploitation of the natural resources in the Partitioned Zone, no more than 6 nautical miles of the seabed and subsoil adjoining the Partitioned Zone shall be annexed to the mainland of the Partitioned Zone.

Article 8

The northern boundary of the offshore field adjoining the Partitioned Zone shall be delimited as if the Zone had not been partitioned and without regard to the provisions of this Agreement.

The two Contracting Parties shall continue to exercise their equal rights in the offshore field beyond the 6 – mile limit referred to in the preceding article by means of joint exploitation, unless both Parties agree otherwise.

Article 9

Each of the Contracting Parties shall, in the part of the Partitioned Zone annexed to the other Party, evacuate the facilities occupied by its government officials who perform administrative and judicial work and hand tiiem over to the other Party; however, this provision shall not apply to facilities occupied by government officials engaged in oil gauging, the checking and auditing of accounts, technical supervision, procurement and other similar supervision work.

Article 10

If either of the Contracting Parties entrusts the companies that have been granted a joint concession by both Parties with the construction of judicial and administrative facilities in that part of the Partitioned Zone annexed to its territory, in accordance with the terms of the concession, the cost of constructing such facilities shall be deducted from the capital expenses of the concessionary companies, provided that such costs shall be limited to necessary and reasonable expenses.

Article 11

The present oil concession agreements shall remain in force, and both Parties undertake to respect, each in the half of the Partitioned Zone to be annexed to its territory, the provisions thereof and any amendments thereto. They also undertake to adopt the necessary laws and regulations to ensure the continued exercise by the concessionary companies of their rights and the discharge of their obligations.

Article 12

Each Contracting Party shall, in the part of the Partitioned Zone to be annexed to its territory, assume the responsibility for protection and security devolving on the other Party under the obligations laid down in the concession agreements currently in force.

Article 13

For the avoidance of double taxation, each Contracting Party undertakes to enact legislative safeguards to ensure the non – imposition of taxes, customs duties or royalties on the companies that have been granted a concession in the Partitioned Zone by the other Party.

Article 14

Entry into and movement in the Partitioned Zone of citizens of either Contracting Party who are working as officials, employees, labourers and contractors in establishments and firms engaged in the exploitation of natural resources under concessions or affiliated firms shall be by a valid passport issued by that Party or by a card of agreed design to be issued by one of the Contracting Parties, but a visa shall be required upon entry.

Article 15

Without prejudice to the concessionary oil agreements in force, each Party shall, in the part of the Partitioned Zone to be annexed to its territory, guarantee the citizens of the other Party the freedom to work and the right to engage on an equal footing with its own citizens in any profession or occupation connected with the oil resources granted under current concessions or any concessions that may supersede them in the future.

With regard to such natural resources as may be discovered in the future, both Parties shall agree on the rights of each other's citizens to work and to engage in any profession or occupation relating thereto.

Article 16

Each of the Contracting Parties shall, in the part of the Partitioned Zone to be annexed to its territory, respect the rights of the citizens of the other Party in the installations and buildings currently existing in that Zone.

Article 17

In order to ensure the continuation of the efforts of both Contracting Parties for optimal exploitation of the natural resources in the Partitioned Zone, a standing joint commission shall be established, hereafter referred to as 'the Commission'

Article 18

The Commission shall be composed of an equal number of representatives of both Contracting Parties. The competent Ministers for Natural Resources in both Contracting Governments shall agree on the number of members of the Commission, its rules of procedure and the manner of securing the necessary appropriations for it. Both Contracting Parties shall endeavour to ensure that the Commission is ready to start work within six months at most from the date of entry into force of this Agreement.

Article 19

The committee shall have the following powers:

(a) To facilitate passage of officials and employees (other than the nationals of either Party) of concessionary companies and of ancillary companies and establishments in the Partitioned Zone;

(b) To undertake studies on projects for the exploitation of the shared natural resources;

(c) To examine new permits, contracts and concessions relating to the shared natural resources, and to make appropriate recommendations thereon to the two competent Ministers;

(d) To consider whatever matters the two competent Ministers see fit to refer to it.

For the purpose of performing its mandate, the Commission shall have the right to make contracts.

The Commission shall submit its reports and recommendations directly to the two competent Ministers.

Article 20

The two competent Ministers shall consult each other on the granting or amendment of any new concession relating to the shared natural resources. The Party that cannot agree to the view of the other Party must inform that Party of its reasons in writing before the granting or amendment of such new instrument.

The replacement of an establishment or company currently exploiting the natural resources in the Partitioned Zone by another establishment or company shall not be considered a new concession, provided that the rights of the other Party are not prejudiced.

Article 21

The two Contracting Parties undertake to supply the Commission with such data, information and documents as it may require to facilitate its task.

Article 22

In the event of a dispute over the interpretation or application of this Agreement or the rights and obligations arising therefrom for either Contracting Party, the Contracting Parties shall seek to settle such dispute by amicable means for the settlement of disputes, including recourse to tiie League of Arab States.

Should it prove impossible to settle the dispute by such methods, the dispute shall be brought before the International Court of Justice.

The two Contracting Parties shall accept the compulsory jurisdiction of the International Court of Justice in this regard, should either Contracting Party take some action to which the other Contracting Party objects, the objecting Party may request the International Court of Justice, as a matter of urgency, to issue a judgement of principle either for the halting of the action to which there is an objection or for its continuation pending a final settlement of the dispute.

Should either Contracting Party fail to abide by the judgement pronounced against it, the other Party shall be released from its obligations under this Agreement.

Article 23

This Agreement shall be subject to ratification by both Contracting Parties, each in accordance with its constitutional procedure, and shall enter into force on the date of exchange of the instruments of ratification.

Done on 9 Rabi, I A. H. 1385, corresponding to 7 July A. D. 1965, in two original copies in the Arabic language.

For the Kingdom of Saudi Arabia: For the State of Kuwait:
AHMAD ZAKI YAMANI   JABIR AL – AHMED AL – SABAH

3. 《沙特阿拉伯王国和科威特国有关毗邻分隔区的水下区域的协定》

（2000 年 7 月 2 日订于科威特城）

董世杰译，杨泽伟、黄文博校

以仁慈的神的名义，沙特阿拉伯王国与科威特就毗邻分隔区的水下区域达成协议。加强和巩固两国人民之间的相互信任以及兄弟般的纽带；确认两个兄弟国家间根深蒂固且不可动摇的友爱之情；鉴于两国领导人，沙特阿拉伯国王——法赫德·本·阿卡杜勒—阿齐兹·阿萨德，以及科威特埃米尔——贾比尔·艾哈迈德·贾比尔·萨巴赫，渴望以一种服务于两个兄弟国家利益并尊重它们区域权利，以及遵循1965 年 7 月 7 日（回历1385 年 3 月 9 日）《划分中立区协定》和 1969 年 12 月 18 日（回历 1389 年 10 月 9 日）《有关确立两国间中立区中间线的协议》之规定，确定毗邻分隔区的水下区域的界线。两兄弟国家协议如下：

第一条

1. 毗邻分隔区的水下区域的分界线，代表着两国的边界。该分界线始于海岸上的地理坐标 G 点（北纬 28°32′02.488″，东经 48°25′59.019″），经过下列四个坐标：

坐标点	北纬	东经
1	28°38′20″	48°35′22″
2	28°39′56″	48°39′50″
3	28°41′49″	48°41′18″
4	28°56′06″	49°26′42″

从第 4 个点起，毗邻分隔区的水下区域的分界线向东延伸。

2. 本条第 1 款的规定不得损害本协定附件 1 的规定。

第二条

毗邻分隔区的水下区域最北部界线，始于基点 1（地理坐标为北纬 28°49′58.7″，东经 48°17′0.188″），基点 1 根据距离低潮线等距离原则确定，适当考虑《中立区划分协定》第 8 条之规定，岛屿、沙洲、暗礁对划界无影响。

第三条

根据本协定第二条确定的最北边界线，进行调整时应当充分考虑 Faylakah 群岛，但是不得影响本协定附件 1 之规定。

第四条

毗邻分隔区的水下区域的最南部界线，应当是两国目前使用的界线，始于海岸基点 5（地理坐标为北纬 28°14′05.556″，东经 48°36′06.916″）。

第五条

缔约国之间有关毗邻分隔区的水下区域的自然资源所有权问题的协议，包含在本协定附件 1 中，是本协定的一部分。

第六条

缔约国双方任命的负责毗邻分隔区的水下区域勘查和绘图的公司，应当根据本协定第 2、3 条之规定确立最北边界线的坐标，并绘制最终地图。地图由缔约国双方的代表签署并被视为本协定的组成部分。

第七条

有关毗邻分隔区的水下区域的东部界线的划定问题，沙特阿拉伯王国和科威特国应当作为单一谈判主体。

第八条

缔约国当局之间，应就有关毗邻分隔区的水下区域的休闲垂钓的措施和安排达成一致。

第九条

本协定的条款不损害 1965 年 7 月 7 日《中立区划分协定》以及 1969 年 12 月 18 日《确定中立区中点协定》中的条款。

第十条

本协定需要缔约国双方予以批准，自交换批准文书之日生效。

两原始文本签署于科威特城，2000 年 7 月 2 日（回历 1421 年 3 月 31 日）。

沙特阿拉伯王国代表　科威特国代表

沙特·阿尔—费萨尔　萨巴赫·艾哈迈德·阿尔—贾贝尔·阿尔—萨巴

外交大臣　　　　　第一副首相兼外交大臣

以仁慈的神的名义。

附件 1
《沙特阿拉伯王国和科威特国有关毗邻分隔区的水下区域的协定》

两国同意毗邻分隔区的水下区域的自然资源共享。两国共享的自然资源应当包括，加龙（Qaruh）和乌姆—马拉迪姆（Ummal‑Maradim）岛上的自然资源，以及根据第二条划定的北部界线与根据第三条修订后的北部界线之间区域内的自然资源。

沙特阿拉伯王国代表　科威特国代表

沙特·阿尔‑费萨尔　萨巴赫·艾哈迈德·阿尔‑贾贝尔·阿尔‑萨巴

外交大臣　　　　　第一副首相兼外交大臣

4. Agreement between the Kingdom of Saudi Arabia and the State of Kuwait Concerning the Submerged Area Adjacent to the Divided Zone, 2 July 2000

In the Name of God, the Merciful, the Compassionate

Agreement between the Kingdom of Saudi Arabia and the State of Kuwait concerning the submerged area adjacent to the divided zone.

Strengthening and reinforcing the ties of faith and brotherhood between the fraternal peoples of the State of Kuwait and the Kingdom of Saudi Arabia;

Affirming the unshakeable and deeply rooted relationship and bonds of love and affection between the two fraternal countries;

In view of the desire of the Custodian of the Two Holy Mosques, King Fahd Bin Abdul – Aziz Al Saud, King of Saudi Arabia, and his brother His Highness Sheikh Jaber Al – Ahmad Al – Jaber Al – Sabah, Amir of the State of Kuwait, to determine the line dividing the submerged area adjacent to the divided zone in a manner that will serve the interests of the two fraternal countries and respect their regional rights, and pursuant to the Agreement on the partition of the neutral zone between the two countries signed on 9 Rabi' I A. H. 1385 (7 July A. D. 1965) (hereinafter referred to as the divided zone) and the Agreement concerning the designation of the median line of that neutral zone between the two countries signed on 9 Shawwal A. H. 1389 (18 December A. D. 1969),

The two fraternal countries have agreed as follows:

Article 1

1. The line dividing the submerged area adjacent to the divided zone, which

represents the border between the two countries, begins on the coast at point G at geographical coordinates 28° 32′ 02.488″ north and 48° 25′ 59.019″ east and passes through four points with the following geographical coordinates:

Point	Latitude north	Longitude east
1	28° 38′ 20″	48° 35′ 22″
2	28°39′56″	48°39′50″
3	28°41′49″	48°41′18″
4	28°56′06″	49°26′42″

From Point 4, the line dividing the submerged area adjacent to the divided zone continues in an easterly direction.

2. The provisions of paragraph 1 of this article do not prejudice the provisions of Annex 1 to this Agreement.

Article 2

The northernmost limit of the submerged area adjacent to the divided zone, beginning on the coast at point No. 1, at geographical coordinates 28° 49′ 58.7″ north and 48° 17′ 00.188″ east, shall be determined on the basis of the principle of equal distance from the low-water mark. With due regard for the provisions of article 8 of the Agreement on the partition of the neutral zone, the islands, shoals and reefs shall have no effect on this limit.

Article 3

The northernmost limit fixed in accordance with article 2 of this Agreement shall be amended by taking fully into account the Faylakah group of islands, while not prejudicing the provisions of Annex 1 to this Agreement.

Article 4

The southernmost limit of the submerged area adjacent to the divided zone shall be the line between the two countries currently in use, which starts at point No. 5 on the coast, at geographical coordinates 28° 14′ 05.556″ north and 48° 36′ 06.916″ east.

Article 5

The agreement between the two Contracting States concerning ownership of the natural resources in the submerged area adjacent to the divided zone is contained in Annex 1 of this Agreement, of which it is an integral part.

Article 6

The company commissioned by the two countries to survey and prepare maps of the submerged area adjacent to the divided zone shall determine the coordinates of the northernmost limit in accordance with articles 2 and 3 of this Agreement and prepare the maps in their final form. Those maps shall be signed by the representatives of both countries and considered an integral part of this Agreement.

Article 7

The Kingdom of Saudi Arabia and the State of Kuwait shall be considered as a single negotiating party with regard to the designation of the eastern limit of the submerged area adjacent to the divided zone.

Article 8

The competent authorities in each country shall agree upon the measures and arrangements concerning recreational fishing in the submerged area adjacent to the divided zone.

Article 9

The provisions of this Agreement do not prejudice the provisions of the Agreement on the partition of the neutral zone between the two countries signed on 9 Rabi' I A. H. 1385 (7 July A. D. 1965) or of the Agreement concerning the designation of the mid - point of that neutral zone between the two countries signed on 9 Shawwal A. H. 1389 (18 December A. D. 1969).

Article 10

This Agreement shall be subject to ratification by both countries and shall enter into force from the date on which the instruments of ratification are exchanged.

DONE in the city of Kuwait in two original copies on the thirty - first day of the month of Rabi'I in year A. H. 1421 (2 July A. D 2000).

On behalf of the Kingdom of Saudi Arabia

Saud Al - Faisal

Minister for Foreign Affairs

On behalf of the State of Kuwait

Sabah Al – Ahmad Al – Jaber Al – Sabah

First Deputy Prime Minister and Minister for Foreign Affairs

In the Name of God, the Merciful, the Compassionate

Annex 1
Agreement between the Kingdom of Saudi Arabia and the State of Kuwait Concerning the Submerged Area Adjacent to the Divided Zone

The two countries have agreed that the natural resources in the submerged area adjacent to the divided zone shall be owned in common. Those resources shall include the islands of Qaruh and Umm al – Maradim and the area lying between the northernmost limit referred to in article 2 of the Agreement and the northernmost limit as amended in accordance with article 3 of the Agreement.

On behalf of the Kingdom of Saudi

Arabia Saud Al – Faisal

Minister for Foreign Affairs

On behalf of the State of Kuwait

Sabah Al – Ahmad Al – Jaber Al – Sabah

First Deputy Prime Minister and Minister for Foreign Affairs

二

海上共同开发的发展阶段

（四）1974年日本与韩国共同开发东海大陆架案

1.《日本和大韩民国关于共同开发邻接两国的大陆架南部的协定》[*]

（1974年1月30日订于汉城）

邓妮雅译，黄文博、杨泽伟校

日本和大韩民国愿意为促进两国间现有的友好关系，考虑到对邻接两国的大陆架南部的石油资源进行勘探和开发符合两国的共同利益，双方决定达成开发这种资源最终可行的解决方案，遂达成如下条款。

第一条

依本协定：

（1）"自然资源"是指石油（包括天然气）资源以及与这种资源相结合而产生的其他地下矿物；

（2）"特许权持有人"是指任何一方依据该方法律和法规授权的，在共同开发区内勘探和/或开发自然资源的人；

（3）"双方的特许权持有人"是指在共同开发区内同一分区内，双方分别授权的特许权持有人；

（4）"经营协议"是指为了在共同开发区内勘探和开发自然资源，双方的特许权持有人签订的合同；

---

[*] 此协定严重侵犯了中国的主权，中国政府对此表示了强烈反对和抗议。——译者注

(5)"经营者"是指根据共同开发区内某一区块的经营协议,被指定担任经营活动的特许权人。

第二条

1. 共同开发区是一块由连接下列相关点的直线所构成的大陆架区域:

第 1 点	北纬 32°57′00″	东经 127°41′06″
第 2 点	北纬 32°53′24″	东经 127°36′18″
第 3 点	北纬 32°46′12″	东经 127°27′48″
第 4 点	北纬 32°33′36″	东经 127°13′06″
第 5 点	北纬 32°10′30″	东经 126°51′30″
第 6 点	北纬 30°46′12″	东经 125°55′30″
第 7 点	北纬 30°33′18″	东经 126°00′48″
第 8 点	北纬 30°18′12″	东经 126°05′30″
第 9 点	北纬 28°36′00″	东经 127°38′00″
第 10 点	北纬 29°19′00″	东经 128°00′00″
第 11 点	北纬 29°43′00″	东经 128°38′00″
第 12 点	北纬 30°19′00″	东经 129°09′00″
第 13 点	北纬 30°54′00″	东经 129°04′00″
第 14 点	北纬 31°13′00″	东经 128°50′00″
第 15 点	北纬 31°47′00″	东经 128°50′00″
第 16 点	北纬 31°47′00″	东经 128°14′00″
第 17 点	北纬 32°12′00″	东经 127°50′00″
第 18 点	北纬 32°27′00″	东经 127°56′00″
第 19 点	北纬 32°27′00″	东经 128°18′00″
第 20 点	北纬 32°57′00″	东经 128°18′00″
第 1 点	北纬 32°57′00″	东经 127°41′06″

2. 连接共同开发区的直线由本协定附图标示。

第三条

1. 共同开发区应划分为若干区块,每个区块由双方的特许权持有人进行勘探和开发。

2. 每个分区都应当按照本协定附图的地理坐标加以编号并识别。附图可以在不修改本协定的情况下经双方同意予以修改。

第四条

1. 本协定生效三个月内,各方应当在每个分区内将特许权授予一人或多人。如果一方就某一分区授予了多个特许权持有人,所有的特许权持有人的利益应当不可分割,并且,依本协定,应当由一个特许权持有人作为代表。如果特许权持有人或者分区有任何变化,该方应当尽快授予一个或者多个新的特许权持有人。

2. 各方应当毫不延迟地将授予的一个或者多个特许权持有人通知对方。

第五条

1. 双方的特许权持有人应当签订一项经营协议,以实施共同开发区内自然资源的共同勘探和开发活动。经营协议尤其应当包括:

(a) 按照第九条分享自然资源和分担费用的细节;

(b) 经营者的指定;

(c) 单一风险条款的处理;

(d) 渔业利益的调整;

(e) 争端的解决。

2. 经营协议及其修改应经双方政府批准后生效。经营协议或者其修改提交政府批准2个月内,除任何一方明确不同意经营协议及其修改外,应当被视为已被批准。

3. 双方应当尽力保证经营协议在依据第四条第1款确定特许权持有人后6个月内生效。

第六条

1. 经营者应当由双方的特许权持有人一致指定。如果双方的特许权持有人在获得特许权3个月内,无法就经营者的指定达成一致,双方应该就经营者指定问题进行协商。如果在开始协商后2个月内仍无法指定,双方的特许权持有人应当通过抽签的方式确定。

2. 经营者应对依照经营协议的一切活动享有专属控制权,雇用此种经营活动所需的一切人员,支付和免除与经营活动有关的所有费用,并且获取经营活动所必需的所有资产,包括设备、材料和供给。

第七条

一方特许权持有人可以在另一方领土上，按照另一方的法律和法规取得、建造、维护、使用和处置共同开发区内勘探或开采自然资源所必需的建筑、平台、油槽、管道、码头以及其他设施。

第八条

一方的特许权持有人不能干涉对方特许权持有人依对方法律和法规履行义务，但此义务须在本协定规定的范围内。

第九条

1. 双方的特许权持有人均应当有权平等分享从共同开发区内开采出的自然资源。

2. 双方的特许权持有人应当平等分担为勘探和开发这种自然资源产生的合理费用。

第十条

1. 依据本协定，特许权持有人享有勘探权和开采权。

2. 勘探权的期限为 8 年，从经营协议生效之日起算，但本条第 4 款第（3）项规定的情形除外。

3. 开发权的期限为 30 年，从权利确定之日起算。双方的特许权持有人可以向相应各方申请延展 5 年。这项申请可以于必要时多次提出。在收到此项申请时，一方需要立即与另一方协商决定是否批准此项申请。

4.（1）如果在勘探权期限内发现了有商业价值的自然资源，双方的特许权持有人可以分别向各方申请确定开采权。收到这种申请后，双方应当立即协商并毫不迟延地批准申请。

（2）当双方承认有商业价值的发现，各方应当要求相关的特许权持有人提交确定开发权的申请。特许权持有人应当在收到这种要求后的 3 个月内提交申请。

（3）如果在勘探权存续期间确定了开采权，勘探权在开采权确定之日届满。

5. 如果一方的特许权持有人发生变化，新的特许权持有人的勘探权或开采权的期限应于原特许权持有人的勘探权或开采权届满之日终止。

6. 特许权持有人可以在获得授权方批准，且同一区块其他特许权持有人同意的情况下，将勘探权或开采权全部转让，但应以特许权持有人在本协定和经营协议中享有的权利和义务的整体转让为限。

第十一条

1. 在勘探权有效期间,双方的特许权持有人应当按照双方的另行安排钻一定数量的井。从经营协议生效之日起,在最初 3 年、随后 3 年以及剩下 2 年期间内,每个分区最低钻井数量分别不应当超过两口。双方在确定每个分区最低钻井数量时,需要考虑到上覆水域的深度以及分区的大小。

2. 如果双方的特许权持有人钻井数量超过了本条第 1 款所指的任一期间的要求,这些超过的钻井应当被视为后期所钻的井。

第十二条

双方的特许权持有人应当于勘探权或开采权确定之后 6 个月内开始经营活动,且不应当停止经营活动连续 6 个月以上。

第十三条

1. 依据本条第 2 款的规定,双方的特许权持有人应当自经营协议生效之日起,三年内放弃原分区 25% 的权利,6 年内放弃该分区 50% 的权利,8 年内放弃该分区 75% 的权利。

2. 拟放弃的区域的大小、形状和位置,以及放弃的时间,由双方的特许权持有人协议决定。但是,除根据本条第 3 款外,任何放弃的区域不能小于 75 平方千米。

3. (1) 如果双方的特许权持有人无法就本条第 1 款规定的放弃区域达成一致,双方特许权持有人应于放弃届满之日,放弃共同提议的区域和各自提议区域的 50%,但应尽可能使所有拟放弃区域成为一个单一区块。

(2) 如果不存在拟共同放弃的区域,双方的特许权持有人应该分别放弃 50% 拟放弃的区域。

4. 除本条第 2 款规定之外,双方的特许权持有人可自愿放弃任何区域。

5. 虽然有本条第 2 款的规定,但在经营协议生效 2 年后,特许权持有人可以单边放弃整个区块。

第十四条

1. 如果特许权持有人不履行本协定或者经营协议的任何义务,任何一方可以根据该方保护特许权持有人相关法律和法规的程序性规定,在与另一方协商之后撤销己方特许权持有人的勘探权或开发权。

2. 当任意一方意图按照其法律和法规撤销其特许权持有人的勘探权或开发权时，除本条第 1 款之外，该方应当至少于撤销前 15 日通知另一方撤销意图。

3. 一方撤销勘探权或开发权，应当毫不延迟地通知另一方。

第十五条

1. 当一方的特许权持有人依据协定第十三条第 5 款的规定单边放弃整个区块，或一方特许权持有人的勘探权或开发权依据第十四条被撤销，或者一方特许权持有人停止存在（以下将这些情形称为"前特许权持有人"），相关分区现存的特许权持有人，在前特许权持有人授权一方授予新的特许权持有人之前，经该授权一方批准，可以依据单一风险经营条款，以及其与前特许权持有人之间签订的经营协议相关条款，进行自然资源的勘探或开发。

2. 依本条第 1 款，现存的特许权持有人，在特许权持有人的权利和义务方面，应被授予前特许权持有人一方视为特许权持有人，同时保留自己一方特许权持有人资格。但该规定不适用于特许权持有人依据本条第 1 款勘探或开发自然资源所得收入的征税。

3. 当一方授予新的特许权持有人，新的特许权持有人和现有的特许权持有人应受经营协议的约束，此经营协议由现有的特许权持有人和前特许权持有人签订，直到新的经营协议生效。如果现存的特许权持有人，依据本条第 1 款的规定已经开始勘探或开发自然资源，在上述新的经营协议生效之前，可以根据其与前特许权持有人签订的经营协议的单一风险经营条款的规定，继续勘探或开发工作。

第十六条

在适用与共同开发区内开采出来的自然资源有关的法律和法规时，各方特许权持有人依据第九条规定享有的那部分自然资源，应当被视为从各方享有主权权利的大陆架上开采出来的自然资源。

第十七条

1. 任何一方（包括地方当局）不应向特许权持有人就下列事项征收税收或其他费用：

（a）共同开发区内的勘探或开采活动；

（b）此类活动所产生的收益；

（c）共同开发区内进行此类活动所必需的固定资产；或

（d）特许权持有人被授权的分区。

2. 各方（包括地方当局）可以向己方特许权持有人就下列事项征收税收和其他费用：

（a）共同开发区内的勘探或开采活动；

（b）共同开发区内进行此类活动所必需的固定资产；以及

（c）特许权持有人被授权的分区。

第十八条

在适用各方关于关税、进口和出口有关的法律和法规时：

（1）共同开发区内，自然资源的勘探和开采必须引进的设备、材料以及其他货物（以下称为"设备"），嗣后在该地区使用或运出该地区，均不应视为进口或出口；

（2）设备从一方管辖地区运至共同开发区内，不应当被视为该方的进口或出口；

（3）使用人将设备从任何一方管辖地区引入共同开发区内，可能被要求向该方就设备的使用情况提交报告；

（4）虽然有本条（1）的规定，但是本条（3）所指的设备从共同开发区内运至该方管辖权以外的地区，应被视为该方的进口或出口。

第十九条

除非本协定另有规定，一方的法律和法规适用于该方特许权持有人被指定且作为经营者行事的分区内，与自然资源勘探或开采有关的事项。

第二十条

双方应该就采取措施达成一致，以防止共同开发区内与自然资源的勘探或开采有关的活动可能产生的海上碰撞，并防止和消除海洋污染。

第二十一条

1. 如果任何一方的国民或居民，遭受共同开发区内因自然资源勘探或开采所引起的损害时，该国国民或者其他人可以在以下法院提起损害赔偿：（a）损害发生地的法院，（b）该国国民或其他人居住地的法院，或（c）发生损害事故的区块内，作为经营者的特许权持有人授予国的法院。

2. 本条第 1 款情形下，接受损害赔偿诉讼一方的法院，应当适用该方的法律和法规。

3. (1) 当本条第一款所指的损害是由海床和底土的挖掘作业，或者矿水和废水的排放所引起时：

（a）此种损害发生时，相关区块内享有勘探或开发权的双方的特许权持有人，

（b）此种损害发生时，如果相关区块内没有享有勘探或开发权的双方的特许权持有人，则该区块内最近曾享有勘探权或开发权的特许权持有人，或者

（c）此种损害发生时，如果相关区块内只有一个享有勘探或开发权的特许权持有人，此特许权持有人和第十五条第1款所指的前特许权持有人，

应根据本条第2款，适用相应的法律和法规，对损害共同地、分别地承担赔偿责任。

（2）依本款（1），本款（1）所指的损害发生后，在勘探权或开发权已经转让的情形下，转移勘探权或开发权的特许权持有人以及获得此种权利的特许权持有人应当共同地、分别地承担赔偿责任。

第二十二条

1. 各方为了勘探或开发共同开发区内的自然资源，在固定装置上的无线电站设置频率时，应当在设置这种频率之前尽早通知对方频率、发射级别、无线功率、站台位置以及其他必要的细节。各方也应将上述事项的后续变化通知对方。

2. 双方应当在任何一方的要求下，就上述细节的必要调整进行协商。

第二十三条

1. 如果任何一种自然资源的单一地质结构或者油田，跨越了第二条第1款所规定的任何一条线，且位于该线一边的结构或油田从另一边全部或部分是可开采的，特许权持有人以及任何一方授权开采此种地质结构或油田的个人（以下称"特许权持有人和其他人"），应经协商之后对最有效开发的方式达成一致。

2. （1）如果特许权持有人和其他人在开始协商后6个月内，没有就本条第1款所指的开发方式达成一致，双方应当进行协商，并在合理期限内尽全力就特许权持有人和其他人的开发方式提出联合建议。

（2）如果所有人或部分特许权持有人和其他人就开发的方式达成协议，该协议（包括修改）应当于双方批准时生效。该协定应该按本条第3

款就自然资源的分享和费用分担做出详细规定。

3. 依据本条第 2 款（2）进行开发时，从该地质结构或油田开发出来的自然资源以及为此目的而产生的合理支出，应当在特许权持有人和其他人之间，按照位于该方授权的区域内，该结构或油田的相应部分产油储量的比例，进行分配。

4. 本条上述各款的规定应准用于跨越共同开发区各分区界线的单一地质结构或油田内自然资源的开发。

5. （1）为了实现第二十六条之目的，一方按照本条第 3 款授权和本条第 2 款（2）授权的人（除特许权持有人外），有权和一方授权的特许权持有人一样，分享共同开发区内开采出来的自然资源。

（2）为了实现第二十七条之目的，一方所授权的人（除特许权持有人外），作为本条第 2 款（2）协议的当事人，应当被视为该方的特许权持有人。

（3）任何一方（包括地方当局）都不应对任何一方的特许权持有人就下列事项征收税收或其他费用：

（a）根据本条第二款（2）所指的协议，在共同开发区外进行的勘探活动；

（b）该活动的收益；或

（c）进行该活动所必须占有的固定资产。

第二十四条

1. 双方应当建立并维持日本—大韩民国联合委员会（以下称为"委员会"），并作为对执行本协定有关事项进行协商的机构。

2. 委员会由两国国民小组组成，每一小组分别由各方任命两个成员组成。

3. 委员会的所有决意、建议和其他决定都只能由这两个国民小组协商一致达成。

4. 委员会可以通过并于必要时修订其会议程序规则。

5. 委员会应当每年至少召开一次会议，并经任一国民小组要求随时召开会议。

6. 在第一次会议时，委员会应当从两个国民小组中分别选出主席和副主席。主席和副主席的任期为一年。国民小组对主席和副主席的选择应以各方均可轮流担任此职位的方式进行。

7. 应当建立一个永久秘书处，其从属于委员会，处理委员会的事务性工作。

8. 委员会的工作语言为日语、韩语和英语。提案和数据可以其中任意一种语言提交。

9. 如果委员会决定有共同开支的必要，这项费用应当由委员会从双方的缴费中支付，该费用由委员会建议并经双方批准。

第二十五条

1. 委员会应当履行以下职责：

（a）审查本协定的执行情况，必要时仔细讨论并向双方建议改进协定执行的措施；

（b）接受特许权持有人的技术和财务年度报告，双方应每年提交该报告；

（c）向双方建议特许权持有人无法解决的争端的解决方案；

（d）监管经营者的经营活动，以及共同开发区内自然资源勘探和开发设施和其他设备的作业情况；

（e）研究本协定生效时未能预料到的问题，包括关于双方法律法规的适用问题，并于必要时向双方建议解决这些问题的合理措施；

（f）接受双方提交的关于颁布与共同开发区内自然资源勘探和开采相关的法律和法规的通知；

（g）讨论与本协定执行相关的其他措施。

2. 双方应当尽可能尊重委员会在本条第1款下提出的建议。

第二十六条

1. 双方有关本条约解释和执行的争端，首先应当通过外交途径解决。

2. 任何未能通过本条第1款解决的争端，应该提交仲裁委员会解决。仲裁委员会由3位仲裁员组成，在一方收到另一方请求将争端提交仲裁照会的30天内，双方各任命一位仲裁员；第三位仲裁员由已任命的两名仲裁员在30天内协商确定，或者由已任命的两名仲裁员在30天内协商同意的第三国指定，但是第三名仲裁员不得为任意一方国民。

3. 如果双方任命的两名仲裁员，没有在本条第2款规定的期限内，就第三名仲裁员或者第三国达成一致，双方应当请求国际法院主席指定第三名仲裁员,该仲裁员不得为任意一方国民。

4. 在任意一方的请求下,仲裁委员会可在紧急情况下,在裁决做出前发布一项临时命令,该命令应当得到双方的尊重。

5. 仲裁委员会按照本款所做出的任何裁决,双方应当遵守。

第二十七条

共同开发区内自然资源的勘探和开采,应当确保共同开发区及上覆水域内其他合法活动,如航行和渔业,不受过度影响。

第二十八条

本协定的任何条款都不应视为,对共同开发区任何部分或全部区域上主权权利的确定,也不应影响任何一方在大陆架划界的相关立场。

第二十九条

在任意一方的请求下,双方应当就本协定的执行进行协商。

第三十条

双方应当采取一切必要的国内措施以执行本协定。

第三十一条

1. 双方应当批准本协定。批准文书应尽早于东京进行交换。本协定从互换批准文书之日开始生效。

2. 本协定有效期限为50年,且在依据本条第3款规定终止以前继续有效。

3. 任意一方可在给予对方3年的书面通知方式,在最初50年期限到期之后或其后任一时间终止本协定。

4. 虽然有本条第2款的规定,但是当任意一方认识到共同开发区内自然资源不再具有商业可开采性时,双方应就是否修改或终止本协定进行协商。如果就本协定的修改或终止无法达成一致,协定应在本条第2款规定的期限内继续有效。

下列签署人经双方政府正式授权签署本协定,以昭信守。

本协定在汉城以英语作成,一式两份,并于1974年1月30日签订。

日本代表	大韩民国代表
后宫虎郎	金东祚

附 录

共同开发区内的分区是连接下列点的直线所构成的区域：

分区 I

第1点	北纬 32°57′00″	东经 127°43′00″
第2点	北纬 32°39′30″	东经 127°32′36″
第3点	北纬 32°39′36″	东经 127°39′12″
第4点	北纬 32°38′36″	东经 127°39′12″
第5点	北纬 32°39′06″	东经 128°18′00″
第6点	北纬 32°57′00″	东经 128°18′00″
第1点	北纬 32°57′00″	东经 127°43′00″

分区 II

第1点	北纬 32°57′00″	东经 127°41′06″
第2点	北纬 32°53′24″	东经 127°36′18″
第3点	北纬 32°48′06″	东经 127°30′00″
第4点	北纬 32°39′30″	东经 127°30′00″
第5点	北纬 32°39′30″	东经 127°32′36″
第6点	北纬 32°57′00″	东经 127°43′00″
第1点	北纬 32°57′00″	东经 127°41′06″

分区 III

第1点	北纬 32°48′06″	东经 127°30′00″
第2点	北纬 32°46′12″	东经 127°27′48″
第3点	北纬 32°40′12″	东经 127°20′16″
第4点	北纬 32°40′18″	东经 127°25′42″
第5点	北纬 32°39′24″	东经 127°25′42″
第6点	北纬 32°39′30″	东经 127°30′00″
第1点	北纬 32°48′06″	东经 127°30′00″

分区 IV

第1点	北纬 32°39′30″	东经 127°30′00″
第2点	北纬 32°35′00″	东经 127°30′00″
第3点	北纬 32°39′30″	东经 127°32′36″

(四) 1974年日本与韩国共同开发东海大陆架案

  第1点   北纬32°39′30″   东经127°30′00″
分区Ⅴ
  第1点   北纬32°40′12″   东经127°20′48″
  第2点   北纬32°33′36″   东经127°13′06″
  第3点   北纬32°10′30″   东经126°51′30″
  第4点   北纬30°53′06″   东经126°00′00″
  第5点   北纬30°35′12″   东经126°00′00″
  第6点   北纬30°33′18″   东经126°00′48″
  第7点   北纬30°31′00″   东经126°01′30″
  第8点   北纬30°31′00″   东经126°43′00″
  第9点   北纬31°56′00″   东经127°07′00″
  第10点   北纬32°35′00″   东经127°30′00″
  第11点   北纬32°39′30″   东经127°30′00″
  第12点   北纬32°39′24″   东经127°25′42″
  第13点   北纬32°40′18″   东经127°25′42″
  第1点   北纬32°40′12″   东经127°20′48″
分区Ⅵ
  第1点   北纬30°53′06″   东经126°00′00″
  第2点   北纬30°46′12″   东经125°55′30″
  第3点   北纬30°35′12″   东经126°00′00″
  第1点   北纬30°53′06″   东经126°00′00″
分区Ⅶ
  第1点   北纬32°39′30″   东经127°32′36″
  第2点   北纬32°35′00″   东经127°30′00″
  第3点   北纬31°56′00″   东经127°07′00″
  第4点   北纬30°31′00″   东经126°43′00″
  第5点   北纬30°31′00″   东经126°01′30″
  第6点   北纬30°18′12″   东经126°05′30″
  第7点   北纬29°38′36″   东经126°41′48″
  第8点   北纬29°39′42″   东经127°45′24″
  第9点   北纬31°47′00″   东经128°32′36″

第 10 点	北纬 31°47′00″	东经 128°14′00″
第 11 点	北纬 32°12′00″	东经 127°50′00″
第 12 点	北纬 32°27′00″	东经 127°56′00″
第 13 点	北纬 32°27′00″	东经 128°18′00″
第 14 点	北纬 32°39′06″	东经 128°18′00″
第 15 点	北纬 32°38′36″	东经 127°39′12″
第 16 点	北纬 32°39′36″	东经 127°39′12″
第 1 点	北纬 32°39′30″	东经 127°32′36″

分区 Ⅷ

第 1 点	北纬 31°47′00″	东经 128°32′36″
第 2 点	北纬 29°39′42″	东经 127°45′24″
第 3 点	北纬 29°38′36″	东经 126°41′48″
第 4 点	北纬 28°56′36″	东经 127°19′36″
第 5 点	北纬 29°08′54″	东经 127°32′36″
第 6 点	北纬 29°09′00″	东经 127°40′06″
第 7 点	北纬 29°21′24″	东经 127°58′18″
第 8 点	北纬 29°47′12″	东经 127°57′54″
第 9 点	北纬 30°16′48″	东经 128°16′12″
第 10 点	北纬 30°16′54″	东经 128°32′00″
第 11 点	北纬 30°57′24″	东经 129°01′30″
第 12 点	北纬 31°13′00″	东经 128°50′00″
第 13 点	北纬 31°47′00″	东经 128°50′00″
第 1 点	北纬 31°47′00″	东经 128°32′36″

分区 Ⅸ

第 1 点	北纬 30°57′24″	东经 129°01′30″
第 2 点	北纬 30°16′54″	东经 128°32′00″
第 3 点	北纬 30°16′48″	东经 128°16′12″
第 4 点	北纬 29°47′12″	东经 127°57′54″
第 5 点	北纬 29°21′24″	东经 127°58′18″
第 6 点	北纬 29°09′00″	东经 127°40′06″
第 7 点	北纬 29°09′54″	东经 127°32′36″

(四) 1974 年日本与韩国共同开发东海大陆架案

第 8 点　　　　　北纬 28°56′36″　　　　东经 127°19′36″
第 9 点　　　　　北纬 28°36′00″　　　　东经 127°38′00″
第 10 点　　　　 北纬 29°19′00″　　　　东经 128°30′00″
第 11 点　　　　 北纬 29°43′00″　　　　东经 128°38′00″
第 12 点　　　　 北纬 30°19′00″　　　　东经 129°09′00″
第 13 点　　　　 北纬 30°54′00″　　　　东经 129°04′00″
第 1 点　　　　　北纬 30°57′24″　　　　东经 129°01′30″

2. Agreement between Japan and the Republic of Korea Concerning Joint Development of the Southern Part of the Continental Shelf Adjacent to the Two Countries

Signed at Seoul on 30 January 1974

JAPAN AND THE REPUBLIC OF KOREA,

DESIRING to promote the friendly relations existing between the two countries,

CONSIDERING their mutual interest in carrying out jointly exploration and exploitation of petroleum resources in the southern part of the continental shelf adjacent to the two countries,

RESOLVING to reach a final practical solution to the question of the development of such resources,

HAVE AGREED as follows:

Article I

For the purposes of this Agreement

(1) The term "natural resources" means petroleum (including natural gas) resources and other underground minerals which are produced in association with such resources;

(2) The term "concessionaire" means a person authorized by either Party under the laws and regulations of that Party to explore and/or exploit natural resources in the Joint Development Zone;

(3) The term "concessionaires of both Parties" means a concessionaire of one Party and a concessionaire of the other Party respectively authorized with re-

spect to the same subzone of the Joint Development Zone;

(4) The term "operating agreement" means a contract concluded between concessionaires of both Parties for the purpose of exploring and exploiting natural resources in the Joint Development Zone;

(5) The term "operator" means a concessionaire designated and acting as such under the operating agreement with respect to a subzone of the Joint Development Zone.

Article Ⅱ

1. The Joint Development Zone shall be the area of the continental shelf bounded by straight lines connecting the following points in the sequence given below:

Point 1	32°57.0′N	127°41.1′E
Point 2	32°53.4′N	127°36.3′E
Point 3	32°46.2′N	127°27.8′E
Point 4	32°33.6′N	127°13.1′E
Point 5	32°10.5′N	126°51.5′E
Point 6	30°46.2′N	125°55.5′E
Point 7	30°33.3′N	126°00.8′E
Point 8	30°18.2′N	126°05.5′E
Point 9	28°36.0′N	127°38.0′E
Point 10	29°19.0′N	128°00.0′E
Point 11	29°43.0′N	128°38.0′E
Point 12	30°19.0′N	129°09.0′E
Point 13	30°54.0′N	129°04.0′E
Point 14	31°13.0′N	128°50.0′E
Point 15	31°47.0′N	128°50.0′E
Point 16	31°47.0′N	128°14.0′E
Point 17	32°12.0′N	127°50.0′E
Point 18	32°27.0′N	127°56.0′E
Point 19	32°27.0′N	128°18.0′E

| Point 20 | 32°57.0′N | 128°18.0′E |
| Point 21 | 32°57.0′N | 127°41.1′E |

2. The straight lines bounding the Joint Development Zone are shown on the map annexed to this Agreement.

Article Ⅲ

1. The Joint Development Zone may be divided into subzones, each of which shall be explored and exploited by concessionaires of both Parties.

2. Each subzone shall be numbered and defined by reference to geographical coordinates in the appendix to this Agreement. The appendix may be amended by mutual consent of the Parties without modification of this Agreement.

Article Ⅳ

1. Each Party shall authorize one or more concessionaires with respect to each subzone within three months after the date of entry into force of this Agreement. When one Party authorizes more than one concessionaire with respect to one subzone, all such concessionaires shall have an undivided interest and shall be represented, for the purposes of this Agreement, by one concessionaire. In case of any change in concessionaire or in subzone, the Party concerned shall authorize one or more new concessionaires as soon as possible.

2. Each Party shall notify the other Party of its concessionaire or concessionaires without delay.

Article Ⅴ

1. Concessionaires of both Parties shall enter into an operating agreement to carry out jointly exploration and exploitation of natural resources in the Joint Development Zone. Such operating agreement shall provide, inter alia, for the following:

(a) Details relating to the sharing of natural resources and expenses in accordance with article Ⅸ;

(b) Designation of operator;

(c) Treatment of sole risk operations;

(d) Adjustment of fisheries interests;

(e) Settlement of disputes.

2. The operating agreement and modifications thereof shall enter into force upon approval by the Parties. Approval of the Parties shall be deemed to have been given unless either Party explicitly disapproves the operating agreement or modifications thereof within two months after such operating agreement or modifications thereof have been submitted to the Parties for approval.

3. The Parties shall endeavour to ensure that the operating agreement enter into force within six months after concessionaires of both Parties have been authorized under paragraph 1 of article IV.

Article VI

1. The operator shall be designated by agreement between concessionaires of both Parties. If concessionaires of both Parties fail to reach agreement between themselves as to the designation of the operator within three months after such concessionaires have been authorized, the Parties shall hold consultations concerning the designation of the operator. If the operator is not designated within two months after such consultations have started, concessionaires of both Parties shall determine the operator by lot – drawing.

2. The operator shall have exclusive control of all operations under the operating agreement and employ all personnel required for such operations, pay and discharge all expenses incurred in connection with such operations, and obtain all assets, including equipment, materials and supplies, necessary for carrying out such operations.

Article VII

A concessionaire of one Party may acquire, construct, maintain, use and dispose of, in the territory of the other Party, buildings, platforms, tanks, pipelines, terminals and other facilities necessary for exploration or exploitation of natural resources in the Joint Development Zone in accordance with the laws and regulations of that other Party.

Article VIII

A concessionaire of one Party shall not interfere with the discharging by a concessionaire of the other Party of its obligations under the laws and regulations of that other Party, insofar as such obligations are consistent with the provisions of this Agreement.

Article IX

1. Concessionaires of both Parties shall be respectively entitled to an equal share of natural resources extracted in the Joint Development Zone.

2. Expenses reasonably attributable to exploration and exploitation of such natural resources shall be shared in equal proportions between concessionaires of both Parties.

Article X

1. The right of concessionaires under this Agreement shall be exploration right and exploitation right.

2. The duration of exploration right shall be eight years from the date of entry into force of the operating agreement, subject to the provisions of paragraph 4 (3) of this article.

3. The duration of exploitation right shall be thirty years from the date of the establishment of such right. Concessionaires of both Parties may apply to the respective Parties for an extension of an additional period of five years. Such application may be made as many times as necessary. The Parties shall, upon receipt of such application, consult with each other to decide whether to approve such application.

4. (1) When commercial discovery of natural resources is made during the period of exploration right, concessionaires of both Parties may apply to the respective Parties for the establishment of exploitation right. When the Parties receive such application, they shall promptly hold consultations and shall without delay approve such application.

(2) When the Parties recognize that commercial discovery is made, each Party may request its concessionaire concerned to present an application for the establishment of exploitation right. Such concessionaire shall present such application within three months after receiving the request.

(3) If exploitation right is established during the period of exploration right, the period of exploration right shall expire on the date of the establishment

of exploitation right.

5. In case of any change in concessionaire of one Party, the period of exploration right or exploitation right of a new concessionaire shall expire on the date of expiration of the period of exploration right or exploitation right of the original concessionaire.

6. Exploration right or exploitation right of a concessionaire may be transferred in its entirety subject to the approval of the Party that has authorized it and to the consent of the other concessionaire authorized with respect to the same subzone, provided that the rights and obligations of that concessionaire under this Agreement and the operating agreement are transferred in whole.

Article XI

1. Concessionaires of both Parties shall be required to drill a certain number of wells during the period of exploration right in accordance with a separate arrangement to be made between the Parties. However, the minimum number of wells to be drilled in each subzone shall not exceed two respectively for the first three-year period, the following three-year period and the remaining two-year period, from the date of entry into force of the operating agreement. The Parties shall, when agreeing upon the minimum number of wells to be drilled in each subzone, take into account the depths of the superjacent waters and the size of each subzone.

2. If concessionaires of both Parties have drilled wells in excess of the requirements during any of the periods referred to in paragraph 1 of this article, such excess wells shall be regarded as having been drilled in the succeeding period or periods.

Article XII

Concessionaires of both Parties shall start operations within six months from the date of the establishment of exploration right or exploitation right and shall not suspend operations for more than six consecutive months.

Article XIII

1. Subject to the provisions of paragraph 2 of this article, concessionaires of both Parties shall release twenty-five per cent of the original subzone concerned

within three years, fifty per cent of such subzone within six years, and seventy – five per cent of such subzone within eight years, from the date of entry into force of the operating agreement.

2. The size, shape and location of the area to be released and the time of release shall be determined by agreement between concessionaires of both Parties. However, no single area smaller than seventy – five square kilometres shall be released except under paragraph 3 of this article.

3. (1) If concessionaires of both Parties are unable to agree on the area to be released under paragraph 1 of this article, concessionaires of both Parties shall release, on the date of the expiration of the release period concerned, the area mutually proposed for release and fifty per cent of the areas respectively proposed for release in such a way that the total area to be released will be a single area whenever possible.

(2) If there is no area mutually proposed for release, concessionaires of both Parties shall release fifty per cent of the areas respectively proposed for release.

4. Concessionaires of both Parties may release voluntarily any area subject to the provisions of paragraph 2 of this article.

5. Notwithstanding the provisions of paragraph 2 of this article, a concessionaire may unilaterally release the total subzone concerned after two years have elapsed from the date of entry into force of the operating agreement.

Article XIV

1. Either Party may, by pertinent procedures laid down in its laws and regulations concerning the protection of concessionaires, cancel exploration right or exploitation right of its concessionaire after consultations with the other Party if such concessionaire fails to discharge any of its obligations under this Agreement or the operating agreement.

2. When either Party intends to cancel in accordance with its laws and regulations exploration right or exploitation right of its concessionaire, that Party shall notify the other Party of its intention at least fifteen days prior to such cancellation, except under paragraph 1 of this article.

3. The cancellation of exploration right or exploitation right by one Party shall be notified to the other Party without delay.

Article XV

1. When a concessionaire of one Party has unilaterally released a subzone under paragraph 5 of article XIII, when exploration right or exploitation right of a concessionaire of one Party has been cancelled under article XIV or when a concessionaire of one Party has ceased to exist (any such concessionaire hereinafter referred to as "the former concessionaire"), the remaining concessionaire in the subzone concerned may, until such time as the Party that has authorized the former concessionaire authorizes a new concessionaire, carry out exploration or exploitation of natural resources under the terms of the sole risk operation clauses and under other relevant provisions of the operating agreement to which such remaining concessionaire and the former concessionaire were parties, subject to the approval of the Party that has authorized the former concessionaire.

2. For the purposes of paragraph 1 of this article, the remaining concessionaire shall be regarded as a concessionaire of the Party that has authorized the former concessionaire in respect of rights and obligations of a concessionaire, while retaining its own concessionaireship. The provisions of the above sentence shall not apply to taxation upon the remaining concessionaire with respect to its income derived from exploration or exploitation of natural resources under paragraph 1 of this article.

3. When a new concessionaire is authorized by one Party, the new concessionaire and the remaining concessionaire shall be bound by the operating agreement to which the remaining concessionaire and the former concessionaire were parties until such time as a new operating agreement enters into force. The remaining concessionaire who has started exploration or exploitation of natural resources under paragraph 1 of this article may continue such exploration or exploitation under the terms of the sole risk operation clauses of the operating agreement to which such remaining concessionaire and the former concessionaire were parties until such time as the new operating agreement referred to above enters into force.

Article XVI

In the application of the laws and regulations of each Party to natural resources extracted in the Joint Development Zone, the share of such natural resources to which concessionaires of one Party are entitled under article IX shall be regarded as natural resources extracted in the continental shelf over which that Party has sovereign rights.

Article XVII

1. Neither Party (including local authorities) shall impose taxes or other charges upon concessionaires of the other Party with respect to:

(a) Exploration or exploitation activities in the Joint Development Zone;

(b) Income derived from such activities;

(c) The possession of fixed assets in the Joint Development Zone necessary for carrying out such activities; or

(d) The subzones with respect to which such concessionaires are authorized.

2. Each Party (including local authorities) may impose taxes and other charges upon its concessionaires with respect to:

(a) Exploration or exploitation activities in the Joint Development Zone;

(b) The possession of fixed assets in the Joint Development Zone necessary for carrying out such activities; and

(c) The subzones with respect to which such concessionaires are authorized.

Article XVIII

In the application of the laws and regulations of each Party on customs duties, imports and exports:

(1) The introduction of equipment, materials and other goods necessary for exploration or exploitation of natural resources in the Joint Development Zone (hereinafter referred to as "equipment") into the Joint Development Zone, the subsequent use of equipment therein or the shipment of equipment therefrom shall not be regarded as imports or exports;

(2) The shipment of equipment from areas under the jurisdiction of one Par-

ty to the Joint Development Zone shall not be regarded as imports or exports by that Party;

(3) The users of equipment in the Joint Development Zone which has been introduced into the Joint Development Zone from areas under the jurisdiction of either Party may be required to submit reports to that Party on the use of such equipment;

(4) Notwithstanding the provisions of (1) of this article, the shipment of the equipment referred to in (3) of this article from the Joint Development Zone to areas other than those under the jurisdiction of that Party shall be regarded as exports by that Party.

Article XIX

Except where otherwise provided in this Agreement, the laws and regulations of one Party shall apply with respect to matters relating to exploration or exploitation of natural resources in the subzones with respect to which that Party has authorized concessionaires designated and acting as operators.

Article XX

The Parties shall agree on measures to be taken to prevent collisions at sea and to prevent and remove pollution of the sea resulting from activities relating to exploration or exploitation of natural resources in the Joint Development Zone.

Article XXI

1. When damage resulting from exploration or exploitation of natural resources in the Joint Development Zone has been sustained by nationals of either Party or other persons who are resident in the territory of either Party, actions for compensation for such damage may be brought by such nationals or persons in the court of one Party (a) in the territory of which such damage has occurred, (b) in the territory of which such nationals or persons are resident, or (c) which has authorized the concessionaire designated and acting as the operator in the subzone where the incident causing such damage has occurred.

2. The court of one Party in which actions for compensation for such damage have been brought under paragraph 1 of this article shall apply the laws and regulations of that Party.

3. (1) When damage referred to in paragraph 1 of this article has been caused by digging operations of seabed and subsoil, or discharging of mine water or used water:

(a) Concessionaires of both Parties who have exploration right or exploitation right with respect to the subzone concerned at the time of occurrence of such damage,

(b) In case no concessionaire has exploration right or exploitation right with respect to the subzone concerned at the time of occurrence of such damage, the concessionaires who had exploration right or exploitation right most recently with respect to the subzone concerned or

(c) In case only one concessionaire has exploration right or exploitation right with respect to the subzone concerned at the time of occurrence of such damage, such concessionaire and the former concessionaire as defined in paragraph 1 of article XV, shall be jointly and severally liable for the compensation for such damage in accordance with the laws and regulations applicable under paragraph 2 of this article.

(2) For the purposes of (1) of this paragraph, when exploration right or exploitation right has been transferred after the occurrence of the damage referred to in (1) of this paragraph, the concessionaire who has transferred exploration right or exploitation right and the concessionaire who has obtained exploration right or exploitation right by such transfer shall be jointly and severally liable for the compensation.

Article XXII

1. Each Party shall, when assigning a frequency or frequencies to a radio station on a fixed installation for exploration or exploitation of natural resources in the Joint Development Zone, inform as soon as possible prior to such assignment the other Party of such frequency or frequencies, class of emission, antenna power, location of the station and other particulars deemed necessary. Each Party shall likewise inform the other Party of any subsequent changes in the above particulars.

2. The Parties shall hold consultations at the request of either Party for nec-

essary coordination concerning the above particulars.

Article XXIII

1. If any single geological structure or field of natural resources extends across any of the lines specified in paragraph 1 of article II and the part of such structure or field which is situated on one side of such lines is exploitable, wholly or in part, from the other side of such lines, concessionaires and other persons authorized by either Party to exploit such structure or field (hereinafter referred to as "concessionaires and other persons") shall, through consultations, seek to reach agreement as to the most effective method of exploiting such structure or field.

2. (1) If concessionaires and other persons fail to reach agreement as to the method referred to in paragraph 1 of this article within six months after such consultations have started, the Parties shall, through consultations, endeavour to make a joint proposal concerning such method to concessionaires and other persons within a reasonable period of time.

(2) When agreement concerning such method is reached among all or some of concessionaires and other persons, the agreement (including modifications thereof) shall enter into force upon approval by the Parties. Such agreement shall provide for details relating to the sharing, in accordance with paragraph 3 of this article, of natural resources and expenses.

3. In cases of exploitation under the agreement referred to in paragraph 2 (2) of this article, natural resources extracted from such structure or field and expenses reasonably attributable to exploitation of such natural resources shall be shared among concessionaires and other persons in proportion to the quantities of producible reserves in the respective parts of such structure or field which are situated in the area with respect to which they have been authorized by either Party.

4. The provisions of the foregoing paragraphs of this article shall apply mutatis mutandis with respect to exploitation of a single geological structure or field of natural resources extending across lines bounding the subzones of the Joint Development Zone.

5. (1) For the purposes of article XVI, the share of natural resources ex-

tracted in the Joint Development Zone to which persons (other than concessionaires) authorized by one Party are entitled under paragraph 3 of this article and the agreement referred to in paragraph 2 (2) of this article shall be regarded as the share of natural resources to which concessionaires of that Party are entitled.

(2) For the purposes of article XVII, persons (other than concessionaires) authorized by one Party who are parties to the agreement referred to in paragraph 2 (2) of this article shall be regarded as concessionaires of that Party.

(3) Neither Party (including local authorities) shall impose taxes or other charges upon concessionaires of the other Party with respect to:

(a) Exploitation activities carried out outside the Joint Development Zone in accordance with the agreement referred to in paragraph 2 (2) of this article;

(b) Income derived from such activities; or

(c) The possession of fixed assets necessary for carrying out such activities.

Article XXIV

1. The Parties shall establish and maintain the Japan – Republic of Korea Joint Commission (hereinafter referred to as "the Commission") as a means for consultations on matters concerning the implementation of this Agreement.

2. The Commission shall be composed of two national sections, each consisting of two members appointed by the respective Parties.

3. All resolutions, recommendations and other decisions of the Commission shall be made only by agreement between the national sections.

4. The Commission may adopt and amend, when necessary, rules of procedure for its meetings.

5. The Commission shall meet at least once each year and whenever requested by either national section.

6. At its first meeting, the Commission shall select its Chairman and Vice – Chairman from different national sections. The Chairman and the Vice – Chairman shall hold office for a period of one year. Selection of the Chairman and the Vice – Chairman from the national sections shall be made in such a manner as will provide in turn each Party with representation in these offices.

7. A permanent secretariat may be established under the Commission to car-

ry out the clerical work of the Commission.

8. The official languages of the Commission shall be Japanese, Korean and English. Proposals and data may be submitted in any official language.

9. In case the Commission decides that joint expenses are necessary, such expenses shall be paid by the Commission through contributions made by the Parties as recommended by the Commission and approved by the Parties.

Article XXV

1. The Commission shall perform the following functions:

(a) To review the operation of this Agreement and, when necessary, deliberate on and recommend to the Parties measures to be taken to improve the operation of this Agreement;

(b) To receive technical and financial reports of concessionaires, which shall be submitted annually by the Parties;

(c) To recommend to the Parties measures to be taken to settle disputes incapable of solution by concessionaires;

(d) To observe operations of operators and installations and other facilities for exploration or exploitation of natural resources in the Joint Development Zone;

(e) To study problems, including those relating to the application of laws and regulations of the Parties, unexpected at the time of entry into force of this Agreement, and, when necessary, recommend to the Parties appropriate measures to solve such problems;

(f) To receive notices concerning the laws and regulations promulgated by the Parties relating to exploration or exploitation of natural resources in the Joint Development Zone, which shall be submitted by the Parties;

(g) To discuss any other matter relating to the implementation of this Agreement.

2. The Parties shall respect to the extent possible recommendations made by the Commission under paragraph 1 of this article.

Article XXVI

1. Any dispute between the Parties concerning the interpretation and implementation of this Agreement shall be settled, first of all, through diplomatic channels.

2. Any dispute which fails to be settled under paragraph 1 of this article shall be referred for decision to an arbitration board composed of three arbitrators, with each Party appointing one arbitrator within a period of thirty days from the date of receipt by either Party from the other Party of a note requesting arbitration of the dispute, and the third arbitrator to be agreed upon by the two arbitrators so chosen within a further period of thirty days or the third arbitrator to be appointed by the government of a third country agreed upon within such further period by the two arbitrators, provided that the third arbitrator shall not be a national of either Party.

3. If the third arbitrator or the third country is not agreed upon between the arbitrators appointed by each Party within a period referred to in paragraph 2 of this article, the Parties shall request the President of the International Court of Justice to appoint the third arbitrator who shall not be a national of either Party.

4. At the request of either Party, the arbitration board may in urgent cases issue a provisional order, which shall be respected by the Parties, before an award is made.

5. The Parties shall abide by any award made by the arbitration board under this article.

Article XXVII

Exploration and exploitation of natural resources in the Joint Development Zone shall be carried out in such a manner that other legitimate

activities in the Joint Development Zone and its superjacent waters such as navigation and fisheries will not be unduly affected.

Article XXVIII

Nothing in this Agreement shall be regarded as determining the question of sovereign rights over all or any portion of the Joint Development Zone or as prejudicing the positions of the respective Parties with respect to the delimitation of the continental shelf.

Article XXIX

Upon the request of either Party, the Parties shall hold consultations regarding the implementation of this Agreement.

Article XXX

The Parties shall take all necessary internal measures to implement this Agreement.

Article XXXI

1. This Agreement shall be ratified. The instruments of ratification shall be exchanged at Tokyo as soon as possible. This Agreement shall enter into force as from the date on which such instruments of ratification are exchanged.

2. This Agreement shall remain in force for a period of fifty years and shall continue in force thereafter until terminated in accordance with paragraph 3 of this article.

3. Either Party may, by giving three years' written notice to the other Party, terminate this Agreement at the end of the initial fifty - year period or at any time thereafter.

4. Notwithstanding the provisions of paragraph 2 of this article, when either Party recognizes that natural resources are no longer economically exploitable in the Joint Development Zone, the Parties shall consult with each other whether to revise or terminate this Agreement. If no agreement is reached as to the revision or termination of this Agreement, this Agreement shall remain in force during the period as provided for in paragraph 2 of this article.

IN WITNESS WHEREOF, the undersigned, being duly authorized by their respective Governments, have signed this Agreement.

DONE in duplicate at Seoul in the English language, this thirtieth day of January of the year one thousand nine hundred and seventy - four.

For Japan: TORAO USHIROKU
For the Republic of Korea: DONG - JO KIM

Appendix

The Subzones shall be those areas of the Joint Development Zone bounded respectively by straight lines connecting the following points in the sequence given below:

Subzone Ⅰ

Point 1	32°57.0′N	127°43.0′E
Point 2	32°39.5′N	127°32.6′E
Point 3	32°39.6′N	127°39.2′E
Point 4	32°38.6′N	127°39.2′E
Point 5	32°39.1′N	128°18.0′E
Point 6	32°57.0′N	128°18.0′E
Point 1	32°57.0′N	127°43.0′E

Subzone Ⅱ

Point 1	32°57.0′N	127°41.1′E
Point 2	32°53.4′N	127°36.3′E
Point 3	32°48.1′N	127°30.0′E
Point 4	32°39.5′N	127°30.0′E
Point 5	32°39.5′N	127°32.6′E
Point 6	32°57.0′N	127°43.0′E
Point 1	32°57.0′N	127°41.1′E

Subzone Ⅲ

Point 1	32°48.1′N	127°30.0′E
Point 2	32°46.2′N	127°27.8′E
Point 3	32°40.2′N	127°20.8′E
Point 4	32°40.3′N	127°25.7′E
Point 5	32°39.4′N	127°25.7′E
Point 6	32°39.5′N	127°30.0′E
Point 1	32°48.1′N	127°30.0′E

Subzone Ⅳ

Point 1	32°39.5′N	127°30.0′E
Point 2	32°35.0′N	127°30.0′E
Point 3	32°39.5′N	127°32.6′E
Point 1	32°39.5′N	127°30.0′E

(四) 1974年日本与韩国共同开发东海大陆架案

Subzone Ⅴ

Point 1	32°40.2′N	127°20.8′E
Point 2	32°33.6′N	127°13.1′E
Point 3	32°10.5′N	126°51.5′E
Point 4	30°53.1′N	126°00.0′E
Point 5	30°35.2′N	126°00.0′E
Point 6	30°33.3′N	126°00.8′E
Point 7	30°31.0′N	126°01.5′E
Point 8	30°31.0′N	126°43.0′E
Point 9	31°56.0′N	127°07.0′E
Point 10	32°35.0′N	127°30.0′E
Point 11	32°39.5′N	127°30.0′E
Point 12	32°39.4′N	127°25.7′E
Point 13	32°40.3′N	127°25.7′E
Point 1	32°40.2′N	127°20.8′E

Subzone Ⅵ

Point 1	30°53.1′N	126°00.0′E
Point 2	30°46.2′N	125°55.5′E
Point 3	30°35.2′N	126°00.0′E
Point 1	30°53.1′N	126°00.0′E

Subzone Ⅶ

Point 1	32°39.5′N	127°32.6′E
Point 2	32°35.0′N	127°30.6′E
Point 3	31°56.0′N	127°07.0′E
Point 4	30°31.0′N	126°43.0′E
Point 5	30°31.0′N	126°01.5′E
Point 6	30°18.2′N	126°05.5′E
Point 7	29°38.6′N	126°41.8′E
Point 8	29°39.7′N	127°45.4′E
Point 9	31°47.0′N	128°32.6′E
Point 10	31°47.0′N	128°14.0′E

Point 11	32°12.0′N	127°50.0′E
Point 12	32°27.0′N	127°56.0′E
Point 13	32°27.0′N	128°18.0′E
Point 14	32°39.1′N	128°18.0′E
Point 15	32°38.6′N	127°39.2′E
Point 16	32°39.6′N	127°39.2′E
Point 1	32°39.5′N	127°32.6′E

Subzone VIII

Point 1	31°47.0′N	128°32.6′E
Point 2	29°39.7′N	127°45.4′E
Point 3	29°38.6′N	126°41.8′E
Point 4	28°56.6′N	127°19.6′E
Point 5	29°08.9′N	127°32.6′E
Point 6	29°09.0′N	127°40.1′E
Point 7	29°21.4′N	127°58.3′E
Point 8	29°47.2′N	127°57.9′E
Point 9	30°16.8′N	128°16.2′E
Point 10	30°16.9′N	128°32.0′E
Point 11	30°57.4′N	129°01.5′E
Point 12	31°13.0′N	128°50.0′E
Point 13	31°47.0′N	128°50.0′E
Point 1	31°47.0′N	128°32.6′E

Subzone IX

Point 1	30°57.4′N	129°01.5′E
Point 2	30°16.9′N	128°32.0′E
Point 3	30°16.8′N	128°16.2′E
Point 4	29°47.2′N	127°57.9′E
Point 5	29°21.4′N	127°58.3′E
Point 6	29°09.0′N	127°40.1′E
Point 7	29°08.9′N	127°32.6′E
Point 8	28°56.6′N	127°19.6′E

(四) 1974 年日本与韩国共同开发东海大陆架案

Point 9	28°36.0′N	127°38.0′E
Point 10	29°19.0′N	128°00.0′E
Point 11	29°43.0′N	128°38.0′E
Point 12	30°19.0′N	129°09.0′E
Point 13	30°54.0′N	129°04.0′E
Point 1	30°57.4′N	129°01.5′E

3. 《日本和大韩民国关于共同开发邻接两国的大陆架南部的协定的会议纪要》

(1974年1月30日订于汉城)

邓妮雅译，黄文博校

日本和大韩民国政府代表愿意记录以下共识，这些共识是双方于今日签订《日本和大韩民国关于共同开发邻接两国的大陆架南部的协定》（以下称"协定"）的谈判过程中达成的。

1. 协定中的"法律和法规"应该被解释为包括大韩民国政府与其特许权持有人之间签订的特许权协议，除非有相反的规定。

2. 协定第2条第1款以及协定附录所指的地理坐标，应根据日本海洋安全机构1955年12月新版第210号地图来确定。

3. （1）不论单一风险方是不是经营者，第5条第1款所指的单一风险经营应该由相关分区的经营者进行。

（2）通过单一风险经营开采的自然资源，相关的特许权持有人应当按照第9条平等分享。

（3）非单一风险方应当向单一风险方支付相当于单一风险红利一半的自然资源部分的合理价款、与此部分份额出售产生的较少费用以及有关的税收和其他费用。

4. 第5条第1款提到的"渔业利益的调整"，双方政府应当对各自特许权持有人给予行政指导，以促使特许权持有人在其得到授权的分区内进行自然资源的勘探或开发前，尽一切努力关切该方相关国民的渔业利益。

5. 关于第5条第2款，双方政府应当通知对方经营协议提交该方政府的日期，以及一方准备批准或者不批准经营协议的日期。

6. 关于第6条，双方应努力确保对经营者的指定尽最大可能在公平的基础上做出。

7. 第9条第2款所指的"勘探或开发自然资源的合理费用"应当包括协定生效之前共同开发区内为调查的目的而产生的费用。

8. 第9条第2款不适用于单一风险经营产生的费用。

9. 关于第10条第3款，勘探权延期的申请，应当至少于届期之前6个月提出。

10. 关于第10条第4款，双方政府经过协商之后，应当在相同的日期授予双方各自的特许权持有人开采权。

11. 关于第10条第5款，新的特许权持有人可以根据第10条第3款申请延期。

12. 依第12条的规定，单一风险经营应当视为由双方的特许权持有人施行。

13. 双方的特许权持有人由于不可避免的原因，无法遵守第12条的规定时，应当向授权的政府提交一项声明，陈述引起经营活动迟延或者停止的原因、期限，以获得准许。双方政府应当在批准前与对方进行协商。

14. 第15条第1款所指的政府的批准，无正当理由不得被保留。

15. 关于第15条第2款，现存的特许权持有人，按照其与第15条第1款所指的前特许权持有人签订的资源勘探或开发的合同，在不是经营者的情形下，现存的租让权持有人在其特许权存续期间，应当被视为对方的特许权持有人，并作为经营者行事。

16. 按照第15条第2款，对收入征收的税不应当包括矿区使用费。

17. 按照第17条第2款，征收的税收和其他费用包括：

（1）日本：

（a）矿产税，

（b）固定资产费，以及

（c）矿区税；

（2）大韩民国：

（a）矿区使用费，

（b）财产税，以及

（c）租金。

18. （1）第21条第3款所指的由海床和底土的挖掘作业引起的损害，

包括石油或天然气引起的爆炸。

（2）第 21 条第 3 款所指的"矿水"，是指为勘探和开采自然资源，在钻井过程中流出的水，以及与这些水一起流出的石油或其他物质。

19．第 21 条第 3 款（1）（a）应当适用于，一方的特许权持有人根据第 15 条第 1 款进行自然资源勘探和开采的情形。在这种情形下，不再适用第 21 条第 3 款（1）（c）的规定。

20．有关第 23 条第 2 款第（1）项，各方政府应当在权力范围内，采取必要措施，以促使其特许权持有人和其他人，在第 23 条第 2 款第（1）项所指的 6 个月内或双方政府为提出共同建议的协商期间，不对单一地质构造或油田单独进行勘探。

21．一方特许权持有人不应达成第 23 条第 2 款第（2）项所指的协议，除非同一分区内的其他特许权持有人达成了此种协议。

首尔，1974 年 1 月 30 日。

日本政府代表　　　　　大韩民国政府代表
后宫虎郎　　　　　　　金东祚

4. Agreed Minutes to the Agreement between Japan and the Republic of Korea Concerning Joint Development of the Southern Part of the Continental Shelf Adjacent to the Two Countries

The representatives of the Government of Japan and the Government of the Republic of Korea wish to record the following understanding which has been reached during the negotiations for the Agreement between Japan and the Republic of Korea concerning joint development of the southern part of the continental shelf adjacent to the two countries signed today (hereinafter referred to as "the Agreement"):

1. "The laws and regulations" referred to in the Agreement shall be construed, unless the context otherwise requires, to include concession agreements between the Government of the Republic of Korea and its concessionaires.

2. The geographical coordinates as specified in paragraph 1 of article II and the appendix to the Agreement are based on Japan Maritime Safety Agency Chart No. 210 of December 1955, New Edition.

3. (1) Regardless of whether the sole risk party is the operator, sole risk operations referred to in paragraph 1 of article V shall be carried out by the operator of the subzone concerned.

(2) Natural resources extracted through sole risk operations shall be equally shared between the concessionaires concerned in accordance with article IX.

(3) The non-sole risk party shall pay in money to the sole risk party the reasonable price for the portion of natural resources equal to the half of the sole risk bonus, less expenses incurred in connection with the sale of such portion and

tax or other charges paid in connection with such portion.

4. As regards "adjustment of fisheries interests" referred to in paragraph 1 of article Ⅴ, the Government of each Party shall give administrative guidance to its concessionaires so that they will, before operations for exploration or exploitation of natural resources begin in the subzones with respect to which they have been authorized, endeavour to adjust fisheries interests of nationals concerned of that Party.

5. As regards paragraph 2 of article Ⅴ, the two Governments shall notify each other of the date on which the operating agreement was submitted to them and the date on which they intend to approve or disapprove the operating agreement.

6. As regards article Ⅵ, the two Governments shall endeavour to ensure that the designation of operators be made in such a way as to be equitable to the greatest possible extent.

7. "Expenses reasonably attributable to exploration and exploitation" referred to in paragraph 2 of article Ⅸ shall include expenses incurred for the purposes of survey in the Joint Development Zone prior to the date of entry into force of the Agreement.

8. The provisions of paragraph 2 of article Ⅸ shall not apply to expenses incurred by sole risk operations.

9. As regards paragraph 3 of article Ⅹ, application for an extension of the period of exploitation right shall be made at least six months prior to the expiration of each of such periods.

10. As regards paragraph 4 of article Ⅹ, the two Governments shall, after consultations, grant exploitation right respectively to concessionaires of both Parties on the same date.

11. As regards paragraph 5 of article Ⅹ, the new concessionaire may apply for an extension of the period of exploitation right under paragraph 3 of article Ⅹ.

12. For the purposes of article Ⅻ, sole risk operations shall be regarded as having been carried out by concessionaires of both Parties.

13. When concessionaires of both Parties are unable to comply with the provisions of article XII for unavoidable reasons, they shall submit for approval a statement setting forth reasons for, and the period of, such delay or suspension to the respective Governments authorizing them. The two Governments shall consult with each other before giving such approval.

14. The approval of the Party referred to in paragraph 1 of article XV shall not be withheld without justifiable reasons.

15. As regards paragraph 2 of article XV, when the remaining concessionaire of one Party who was not the operator under the operating agreement to which such concessionaire and the former concessionaire were parties carries out exploration or exploitation of natural resources under paragraph 1 of article XV, such concessionaire shall be regarded as the concessionaire of the other Party designated and acting as the operator, while retaining its own concessionaireship.

16. As regards paragraph 2 of article XV, taxes on income shall not include royalty.

17. Taxes and other charges to be imposed under paragraph 2 of article XVII include

(1) For Japan:

(a) Mineral product tax,

(b) Fixed assets tax and

(c) Mine lot tax;

(2) For the Republic of Korea:

(a) Royalty,

(b) Property tax and

(c) Rental.

18. (1) "Damage caused by digging operations of seabed and subsoil" referred to in paragraph 3 of article XXI include damage caused by blow-out of oil or natural gas.

(2) "Mine water" referred to in paragraph 3 of article XXI means water flowing out in the course of drilling wells for exploration or exploitation of natural resources, and oil and other substances flowing out together with such water.

19. The provisions of paragraph 3 (1) (a) of article XXI shall apply when a concessionaire of one Party carries out exploration or exploitation of natural resources under paragraph 1 of article XV. In such a case, the provisions of paragraph 3 (1) (c) of article XXI shall not apply.

20. As regards paragraph 2 (1) of article XXIII, each Government shall take, within its powers, necessary measures so that its concessionaires and other persons will not exploit independently the structure or field referred to in paragraph 1 of article XXIII during the six - month period referred to in paragraph 2 (1) of article XXIII or during the period in which the two Governments hold consultations for the purpose of making a joint proposal.

21. A concessionaire shall not enter into the agreement referred to in paragraph 2 (2) of article XXIII unless the other concessionaire authorized with respect to the same subzone also enters into such agreement.

Seoul, January 30, 1974.

For the Government of Japan: TORAO USHIROKU

For the Government of the Republic of Korea: DONG - JO KlM

（五）1974 年法国与西班牙划界与共同开发案

1.《法兰西共和国政府与西班牙王国政府划分两国在比斯开湾大陆架的公约》

（1974 年 1 月 29 日订于巴黎）

黄文博译，邓妮雅、杨泽伟校

法兰西共和国与西班牙王国政府，考虑到 1958 年 4 月 29 日在日内瓦签订的《大陆架公约》，兹决定划定两国在比斯开湾的大陆架分界线，以便两国在各自区域行使对自然资源勘探和开发的主权权利，

达成如下约定。

第一条

本公约适用于比斯开湾至 12 海里以内的海域，即由法国和西班牙基线量起，连接西班牙奥特加尔角和法国拉兹岬角之间的线段所围成的海域。

第二条

（1）两国大陆架界线为一条连接 Q、R、T 点的线段。

（a）Q 点是根据法国与西班牙于 1974 年 1 月 29 日签订的，划分两国在比斯开湾的领海与毗连区的公约之第 2 条第 1 款 b 项所确定的点。

根据最新的测绘图，Q 点的坐标为：

北纬 43°35′43″　　　　西经 1°48′08″

（b）QR 线原则上是一条由距离法国和西班牙各自基线距离相等的点组成

的线。为本条的实施，QR 线由连接如下各点坐标的大圆弧线的测地线构成：

Q1	北纬 43°39′40″	西经 1°51′30″
Q2	北纬 43°43′45″	西经 1°55′30″
Q3	北纬 43°48′00″	西经 2°02′40″
Q4	北纬 43°53′25″	西经 2°11′25″
Q5	北纬 44°00′00″	西经 2°16′00″
Q6	北纬 44°06′30″	西经 2°20′30″
Q7	北纬 44°13′00″	西经 2°25′30″
Q8	北纬 44°19′10″	西经 2°31′00″
Q9	北纬 44°24′40″	西经 2°36′19″
Q10	北纬 44°30′00″	西经 2°42′30″
Q11	北纬 44°35′45″	西经 2°50′27″
Q12	北纬 44°39′50″	西经 2°57′00″
Q13	北纬 44°45′25″	西经 3°03′50″
R	北纬 44°52′00″	西经 3°10′20″

（c）T 点的坐标为：

北纬 45°28′30″　　　　西经 6°41′4″

RT 线由连接如下各点坐标的大圆弧线的测地线构成。

（2）该界线按照上述标准和数据划定，并标注于法国于 1972 年更新的 5381 号海洋图中，此图见本公约附件一。

第三条

（1）当事国为授予许可证进行区域内自然资源的勘探和开发，同意适用附件二规定的补充程序。该区域为连接如下点的测地线所构成的区域：

Z1	北纬 45°30′00″	西经 5°40′00″
Z2	北纬 45°30′45″	西经 5°00′00″
Z3	北纬 45°00′30″	西经 5°00′00″
Z4	北纬 45°00′30″	西经 5°40′00″

（2）该区域的界线标明于本公约第二条第 2 款提及的海洋图表中。

第四条

（1）如果自然资源矿藏横跨两国大陆架边界线，且位于边界线一侧的资源矿藏通过位于边界线另一侧的设备可部分或全部开采，当事国应当尽最大努力与开发证的持有者（如果存在开采证的持有者），就该矿藏的开发条件达成一项安排，使此种开发具有最大的经济效益，并且使各方当事国保留其在本国大陆架内自然资源上的所有权利。该程序特别适用于位于边界线一侧的部分矿藏的开发模式会影响另一侧部分矿藏的开发条件的情形。

（2）若位于大陆架界线任意一侧矿藏的自然资源已被开采，当事国应当与所有开发证的持有者（如果存在开采证的持有者），就适当补偿达成一致。

第五条

（1）因本公约的解释或适用引起的争端，当事国应通过外交途径尽快予以解决。

（2）任何争端，若在一方当事国发出其意图启动上款程序的通知后4个月内，仍未解决，任意当事方可请求将该争端提交仲裁庭裁决。

（3）仲裁庭应通过如下方式组成：双方各任命一名仲裁员，由该两名仲裁员共同任命第三名仲裁员，且第三名仲裁员不能为任意一方当事国国民；第三名仲裁员担任仲裁庭主席。若当事国发出其意图将争端提交仲裁的通知后的2个月内，仍未任命仲裁员，或第二名仲裁员任命后一个月内，当事方任命的仲裁员不能就第三名仲裁员的任命达成一致时，任一方当事国均可请求国际法院主席做出必要任命。若国际法院主席为一方当事国国民，或因其他原因不能任命，则由国际法院副主席任命。若副主席仍为一方当事国国民，或因其他原因不能任命，则由非双方当事国国民的国际法院高级法官任命。

（4）每一当事国应负担其各自仲裁员费用，并负担一半的其他费用。若当事国自第三名仲裁员任命后两个月内没有决定仲裁程序规则，则由仲裁庭自己决定。

（5）仲裁庭应采取多数票决。裁决对当事国双方具有法律效力。

（6）仲裁庭可依据一方当事国的请求采取保全措施。

第六条

本公约的任何规定都不影响上覆水域和领空的法律地位。

第七条

双方当事国应尽力保证比斯开湾大陆架的勘探和自然资源的开发,不会对生态平衡和海洋环境合法利用造成不利影响,且双方应为此目的进行协商。

第八条

若当事国间生效的多边条约,对 1958 年 4 月 29 日在日内瓦签订的《大陆架公约》做出了修改,并且会影响本公约的内容,当事国应就本公约的修改迅速进行必要的协商。

第九条

任一当事国完成了公约生效必要的国内宪法程序后,应通知对方。本公约应于最后书面通知之日起生效。

下列签署人,经其各自政府正式授权,在本协定上签字,以昭信守。

1974 年 1 月 29 日签订于巴黎,签订法语和西班牙语各一份,两份文本均具有同等效力。

法兰西共和国政府代表:卡伯尔特(J. P. Cabouat)

西班牙王国政府代表:波希(A. Poch)

附件二 适用于本公约第三条所确定的开发区的条款

1. 双方当事国鼓励开发开发区资源,并进行资源的平均分配。

2. 依据此原则,任一合同当事国应依据本国矿产法,鼓励公司间就区域内开发的许可证的申请达成协议,以使具有另一当事国国籍的公司能在平等合作和依据出资比例经营的基础上,参与资源的开发。

3. 为此目的,任意一方当事国收到在其海域内进行开发的许可证申请后,应通知另一当事方。被通知的当事方可在 6 个月内指派具有本国国籍的公司,与其他申请者一起参与许可证授权程序。

4. 若申请人在指派后一年内未达成协议,在未达成协议的海域享有管辖权的当事国,做出任何其他的授权许可证的决定前,应与另一当事国协商。

5. 享有勘探和开发许可证的公司,以及区域内签订了合作协议的公司,应当向将其对协议做出的任何修改通知双方当事国。为此目的,在任意当事国的请求下,为了研究修改的范围和对本附件第 1 条目标的影响的,当事方应当进行磋商。

6. 对一方当事国为勘探和开发区域内自己一侧海域而颁发的许可证拟议的任何修改,应当通知另一当事方,若有必要,另一方可在 3 个月内提出意见和建议。若对拟议的修改有任何分歧,双方应依据本公约第五条的程序予以处理。

7. 当事国应就上述第二条规定的鼓励达成合作协议制定合适的程序,还应就一方当事国任命的公司在区域内他方当事国一侧开发所获得的产品出口至本国制定有关程序。

外交信件 I

1974 年 1 月 29 日于巴黎

尊敬的阁下,

今日签订的《法兰西共和国政府与西班牙王国政府划分两国在比斯开湾大陆架的公约》第二条第 1 款 b 项规定 "QR 线原则上是一条由距离法国和西班牙各自基线距离相等的点组成的线"。为了该原则的实施,公约该条在 Q 点和 R 点之间的中间线上,确立了一些坐标点。

在我们谈判的过程中,我们承认在确定公约第二条第 1 款 b 项的点中所使用的大地坐标系、制图数据和技术在将来可能会得到改进。然而,我们也同意,这种情况不影响双方在不同解决方案的后续协定中,在 Q 点和 R 点之间的法国和西班牙的大陆架界线,应当继续由连接本公约中坐标列出各点的大圆弧线的测地线构成。

如果您表示同意,我提议本信和您的回复应构成两国政府对协定第二条第 6 款解释的协议,该协议从回复之日起生效。

II

1974 年 1 月 29 日于巴黎

尊敬的阁下,

我荣幸地确认收悉阁下于今日致我方的外交信件,其内容如下:

[参见外交信件 I]

我荣幸地通知您,西班牙政府同意上述内容。

2. Convention Between the Government of the French Republic and the Government of the Spanish State on the Delimitation of the Continental Shelves of the Two States in the Bay of Biscay

The Government of the French Republic and The Government of the Spanish State,

Taking into consideration the Convention on the Continental Shelf, done at Geneva on April 29, 1958,

Having resolved to establish the dividing line between the portions of the continental shelf in the Bay of Biscay over which the two States exercise their respective sovereign rights for purposes of exploration and exploitation of their natural resources,

Have agreed on the following provisions:

Article 1

This Convention applies to the Bay of Biscay beyond the 12 – mile limit, from the French and Spanish base line up to a line joining Cape Ortegal in Spain to Pointe du Raz in France.

Article 2

1. The dividing line between the two States' continental shelves is the line joining points Q, R, and T.

(a) Point Q is the point defined in Article 2 (1, a) of the Convention of January 29, 1974 between France and Spain on the delimitation of the territorial sea and contiguous zone in the Bay of Biscay.

(五) 1974 年法国与西班牙划界与共同开发案

The coordinates of point Q, according to the most recent surveys, are as follows:

Latitude: 43°35′43″N. Longitude: 1°48′08″W. (GR)

(b) Up to point R, defined below, the line QR is, in principle, the line whose points are all equidistant from the French and Spanish baselines. In application of the foregoing, line QR consists of the geodetic lines following the great-circle arcs joining the points having the following coordinates:

Latitude N.	Longitude W.	(GR)
Q1	43°39′4″	1°51′30″
Q2	43°43′59″	1°55′30″
Q3	43°48′00″	2°02′40″
Q4	43°53′25″	2°11′25″
Q5	44°00′00″	2°16′00″
Q6	44°06′30″	2°20′30″
Q7	44°13′00″	2°25′30″
Q8	44°19′10″	2°31′00″
Q9	44°24′40″	2°36′19″
Q10	44°30′00″	2°42′30″
Q11	44°35′45″	2°50′27″
Q12	44°39′50″	2°57′00″
Q13	44°45′25″	3°03′50″
R	44°52′00″	3°10′20″

(c) Point T is defined by the following coordinates:

Latitude: 45°28′30″N.

Longitude: 6041′14″W.

Line RT is the geodetic line following the great-circle arc joining points R and T.

2. The dividing line is indicated, in conformity with the criteria and data given above, on French marine chart No. 5381 published in 1972, attached to this Convention (Annex 1).

Article 3

1. The contracting parties agree to apply the supplementary procedures provided in Annex II for the awarding of rights to prospect for and exploit natural resources in the zone defined by the geodetic lines joining the points having the following coordinates:

Latitude	N	Longitude W (GR)
Z1	45°30′00″	5°40′00″
Z2	45°30′00″	5°00′00″
Z3	45°00′00″	5°00′00″
Z4	45°00′00″	5°40′00″

2. The boundaries of this zone are indicated on the marine chart referred to in Article 2 (2) of this Convention.

Article 4

1. If a deposit of a natural resource lies across the continental shelves' dividing line, and if the portion of the deposit on one side of the dividing line is wholly or partially exploitable by means of installations located on the other side of the line, the Contracting Parties, acting in conjunction with the holders of the exploitation rights, if such exist, shall seek an agreement on terms for exploiting the deposit so that such exploitation may be as profitable as possible and in such manner that each of the Parties shall preserve all its rights over the natural resources of its continental shelf. This procedure is particularly applicable if the method for exploiting the portion of the deposit located on one side of the dividing line affects conditions for exploiting the other portion of the deposit.

2. In the event that the natural resources of a deposit lying across the dividing line have already been exploited, the Contracting Parties, acting in conjunction with the holders of exploitation rights, if such exist, shall seek an agreement on appropriate compensation.

Article 5

1. The Contracting parties shall seek to settle any disagreement arising with regard to interpretation or application of this Convention as quickly as possible,

through diplomatic channels.

2. In the event that a disagreement is not settled within four months of notification by one Contracting Party of its intention to initiate the procedure referred to in the preceding paragraph, it shall be submitted to an arbitral court by request of either party.

3. The arbitral court shall be constituted in each instance as follows: Each Party shall appoint an arbiter and these two arbiters shall jointly appoint a third, who is not a national of either Party; the third arbiter shall preside over the arbitral court. If the arbiters are not appointed within two months following notification by one Contracting State of its intention to refer the matter to the court, or if the arbiters appointed by the two Parties do not reach an agreement, within one month of the appointment of the second of them, on the appointment of the third arbiter, either Party may request the President of the International Court of Justice to make the necessary appointments. If the President of the Court is a national of either Party, or is unable to act for any reason, the Vice President of the Court shall make the appointments. If the President is also a national of one of the two Parties, or is unable to act for any reason, the Court's senior judge who is not a national of either Party shall make the appointments.

4. Each Contracting Party shall cover its arbiter's costs and one – half of all other costs. The arbitral court shall establish its own rules of procedure if the Parties do not establish them within two months following the appointment of the second arbiter.

5. The arbitral court shall adopt decisions by majority vote. These decisions shall be binding upon the Parties.

6. The arbitral court may adopt precautionary measures at the request of either Party.

Article 6

None of the provisions of this Convention shall affect the rules governing superjacent waters and air space.

Article 7

The Contracting Parties shall attempt to prevent the explorations of the continental shelf of the Bay of Biscay and the exploitation of its natural resources from threatening the ecological balance and legitimate uses of the marine environment, and shall consult with each other to this end.

Article 8

In the event that a multilateral treaty which modifies the Convention on the Continental Shelf done at Geneva on April 29, 1958 and which would be capable of affecting the provisions of this Convention enters into force between the Contracting Parties, they shall consult with each other immediately with a view to agreeing on such amendments to the provisions of this Convention as appear necessary.

Article 9

Each Contracting Party shall notify the other of completion of the constitutional procedures necessary for the Convention's entry into force. The Convention shall enter into force upon the date of the final notification.

In witness whereof, the undersigned plenipotentiaries, duly authorized for this purpose by their respective Governments, have signed this Convention.

Done at Paris on January 29, 1974 in two copies, each in French and Spanish, both texts being equally authentic.

For the Government of the French Republic: J. P. Cabouat

For the Government of the Spanish State: A. Poch

ANNEX II Provisions Applicable to the Zone Defined in Article 3 of This Convention

1. The Contracting Parties encourage exploitation of the zone conducive to equal distribution of its resources.

2. Consistent with this principle, each Contracting Party, acting in accordance with its mining regulations, undertakes to encourage agreements between companies applying for prospecting rights in the zone in order to permit companies having the nationality of the other Party to participate in such prospecting on an equal partnership basis, with financing of operations proportional to each company's interest.

3. To this end, any application for prospecting rights in one Contracting Party's sector must be communicated to the other Party. The latter Party shall

have six months in which to designate one or more companies of its nationality to participate in the rights – awarding procedure with the other applicants.

4. If the applicant companies do not reach an agreement within one year following their designation, the Contracting Party with jurisdiction over the sector in question shall consult with the other Contracting Party before making any decision to award rights.

5. Companies holding prospecting and exploitation rights and linked by partnership agreements concerning the zone must notify the Parties of any changes they may make in these agreements. In this instance, and at the request of one of them, the parties would confer in order to examine the significance of the change and its effects on the objective referred to in Paragraph 1 of this Annex.

6. Any draft amendment of the rights granted by one Contracting Party for prospecting and exploitation of its sector of the zone shall be communicated to the other Contracting Party, which shall have three months in which to submit comments and proposals, if it so desires. In the event of disagreement on the proposed amendment, the Parties may have recourse to the procedures provided for in Article 5 of this Convention.

7. The Contracting Parties shall agree on appropriate procedures for encouraging the partnership agreements referred to in Paragraph 2 above, and also on the system for exporting to one Party the products obtained from the exploitation in the other Party's sector by the company or companies designated by the first Party.

EXCHANGE OF LETTERS

I

Pairs, 29 January 1974

Sir,

Article 2 (b) of the Convention signed this day between the Government of the Spanish State and the Government of the French Republic on the dilimitation of the continental shelves of the two States in the Bay of Biscay stipulates that "line QR is, in principle, the line which at every point is equidistant from the French and Spanish baselines". In implementation of this principle, the same article of the Convention establishes the co‑ordinates of a certain number of points, situated on this equidistant line, between points Q and R.

During the course of our negotiations, we recognized that the geodetic and cartographic data and be improved in the future. We nevertheless agreed that, even in such a case, and without prejudice to any subsequent agreement between the Parties concerning a different solution, the line dividing the Spanish and French continental shelves between points/Q/and/R should continue to be determined by the geodetic lines following the arcs of a great circle joining the points having the co‑ordinates set forth in the Convention.

If you agree with the above, I propose that this letter and your reply shall constitute an Agreement between our two Governments on the interpretation of article 2 (b) of the Convention, such Agreement to take effect on the date of your reply.

II

Paris, 29 January 1974

Sir,

I have the honour to acknowledge receipt of your letter of today's date, the text of wihich in translation reads as follows: [See letter I]

I have the honour to inform you that the Spanish Government agrees with the above.

（六）1976年英国与挪威共同开发弗里格天然气案

1.《关于开发弗里格气田并向联合王国输送天然气的协定》

（1976年5月10日订于伦敦）

邓妮雅译，黄文博校

大不列颠及北爱尔兰联合王国政府与挪威王国政府，考虑到属于联合王国的大陆架和属于挪威王国的大陆架，经勘探发现存在天然气田，现将该天然气田命名为弗里格气田。该气田跨越了两国于1965年3月10日签订的关于两国大陆架划界协定确定的分界线。

上述划界协定中第4条规定，两国政府应当在与许可证持有人协商后，就这类气田最有效的开发方式和收益分配方式达成一致。

双方愿意在开始生产前，将弗里格气田作为一个单一整体，为其开发做好准备，并且调控某些为了将弗里格气田的天然气，通过为运输目的即将建立的两条管道，输送至联合王国所产生的问题。

因此，做出如下规定。

第一部分 弗里格气田的开发

第一条

（1）弗里格气田的天然气以及由天然气产生的碳氢化合物（不包括天然气层下的石油，以及其他地层中的天然气和石油），依本协定称"弗里格天然气"，应当作为一个单一整体，通过本协定附件 A 中所列的设备进行开发。除了在同一地点为了同一目的对设备进行更换外，双方政府应要求，没有两国政府的事先同意，不得使用任何其他设备。

（2）每个政府应要求，在本协定签字之日，本国的许可证持有人之间，以及与另一国的许可证持有人间，按照本协定达成的协议管理开发事宜。这种协议应当得到两国政府的批准，并确保此类协议与本协定冲突时以本协定条款优先。许可证持有人可以在会计、运营以及其他开发的专门事项上，达成补充协议。所有补充协议应于达成 45 日内，或于符合本协定规定的日期通知两国政府。两国政府一致同意为了共同开发的必要，也可以要求对这种协议进行修改或重新订立协议。

（3）许可证持有人应提交关于本条第（2）款所指的协议的修正案，以获得两国的事先批准。如修正条款提交双方政府 45 日内，未收到一方或双方政府的否定性通知，则被视为已获批准。

第二条

（1）双方政府应当以双方同意的方式，共同勘定 1965 年 3 月 10 日协定规定的分界线。继而为了有效履行本协定，双方应共同决定与边界线有关的每个设备的位置。

（2）双方政府应当就弗里格气田的界线、预估总储量，以及联合王国和挪威王国有关大陆架上天然气的分配达成一致。为此目的，许可证持有人应当向双方政府提交有关这些决定的建议。

（3）双方政府应当在弗里格气田开始生产前，尽最大努力就该气田的分配达成一致；如无法达成一致，则在此期间应当以许可证持有人对储量分配的建议为临时依据进行生产；如果没有此种建议，应将平均分配作为临时依据。这种临时性的分配不应当影响任何一方政府的地位。当双方就分配方案达成一致时，应被视为依据第三条做出的修改，由其代替临时分配方案。

（4）如果从生产开始后 12 个月内，双方政府无法就本条第（2）款的事项达成一致，有关问题应根据第 28 条的规定解决。

（5）基于安全要求，为了确定弗里格气田的界线、总储量或气田分配方案，一方政府的许可证持有人，按照第一条第（2）款所述的许可证持有人间的协议提出钻探申请时，任意一方政府不得拒绝批准。

第三条

（1）根据第二条一致同意或决定的，弗里格气田的界线、总储量、储量的分配，或者其他事项，经任意一方政府要求可在如下时间进行审查：

（a）在弗里格气田开始生产之日；

（b）生产开始后，每隔4年期满之日；

（c）被证明存在自然产生的含气储层，其气体在开始生产时就有可能流入弗里格气田，且提出要求的政府认为此种情形足以证明有复查的必要。

（2）如依第二条的决定或本条的修订，弗里格气田的界线内包含了一块大陆架区域，该区域内存在非第一条提及的协议合同方，但在决定或审查做出之日持有生产许可证的第三方，该第三方应当与这些协定的合同方，在政府规定的时间内达成一项协议，协议的条款应当与第一条第（2）款保持一致，并得到双方政府的批准。

（3）根据第二条规定可以适用的事项，第二条第（2）和第（4）款的规定适用于本条所做的审查。许可证持有人应进行每一次审查所必需的操作，保证每次弗里格气田停止生产时，联合王国政府的许可证持有人和挪威王国的许可证持有人享有的份额，均应与气田最终的分配份额保持一致。生产开始前，所有的审查应该基于弗里格气田的特性做出。当产生了气田总储量新的分配方案时，许可证持有人应就此新的分配方案制定条款，保证联合王国和挪威王国的许可证持有人分别接收了弗里格气田的天然气，弥补审查做出之前根据现有分配产生的缺额或盈余。所有的审查应自双方政府一致同意的审查之日或通过仲裁裁决之日起生效，视情况而定。

（4）在任何时候，如果有不属于弗里格气田的气体经证明流入气田，这些气体应该被视为弗里格天然气，并根据本协定进行开发。在这种情形下，双方政府应一致协商决定：

（a）弗里格气田的总储量、这种额外的气体及其分配；

（b）开发这种额外气体所必须做出的后续安排；以及

（c）许可证持有人和持有额外气体生产许可证人之间，在气体开发问题上所需要做出的后续安排。

第四条

（1）每个政府应要求其各自的许可证持有人，提交一份为保证弗里格气田的高效运行而保护气田的计划，包括间隔不超过4年的审查条款，以及审查结果应当提交两国政府批准的条款。

（2）政府应当保证任何批准的计划得到执行。

第五条

为了保证弗里格气田按照本协定进行开发，双方许可证持有人应当协商，并经两国政府同意，指定一个联合经营人。

第六条

（1）根据安全需要，为了开发弗里格气田，任意一方政府应当保证所有设备间人员和物资的自由流动。

（2）根据安全需要，所有设备上的着陆设施（包括管道运行中的中间平台），应根据有关当局所做的安排，供船舶自由使用，也为了开展与开发弗里格有关的活动，供具备任意一国国籍的航空器使用。

第七条

（1）双方政府应当与另一方政府就每个设备恰当的安全措施进行协商，应该尽可能保证所有设备符合统一的安全和建设标准。

（2）根据第二十九条管辖权的规定，各自政府都享有采取安全措施来管理设备的最终决定权。关于穿过设备之间的管道，双方政府应当在协商之后，制定统一的安全措施，并责成各方的许可证持有人遵守。

（3）弗里格气田的无线通信设备的建立、运行以及设备的控制，应按照有关电信机构间的协议来进行。

第八条

（1）为了保证第七条的安全和建设标准得到遵守，双方政府同意进行协商并采取一切实现该目的的必要措施，包括授予观察员以监督实施各项设备安全和建设标准的职权；对建立在另一国大陆架上的设施，则按照本条第（3）和第（4）款的规定进行。

（2）每个政府应当保证观察员，包括另一国的观察员进入设备、设施，并向观察员提供对另一国在弗里格气田利益产生影响的所有相关信息。

（3）一国的观察员应当与另一国的观察员进行合作和协商，以保证每个设备的安全和建设标准得到遵守。特别是对于安装在另一国大陆架上的设备，一国的观察员应要求该国的观察员在必要时行使其权利以保证标准得到遵守。如果两国的观察员之间存在分歧，或一国观察员拒绝另一国观察员采取行动的请求，所涉问题应该提交两国主管当局解决。

（4）为了避免人员丧生或危害生命的伤亡或其他事故的发生，无论危险是否紧急，或为了减少这种伤亡或事故的后果，而此时间和情形不允许两国的观察员进行协商，在任意一方政府的观察员认为必要或适当时，可以要求立即停止弗里格油气田内的部分或全部作业。同时，需要立即向两国主管当局报告这一命令的情况和原因，主管当局应随后就安全和迅速恢复作业的必要措施进行协商。

（5）两国政府的主管当局应该就执行本条的方法进行协商。

第九条

（1）每个政府应当依据本国的税法，对本国授权的许可证持有人在弗里格气田中获得的全部利润，按照下述原则进行征税，不论其是否产自他国大陆架。但是，不能对他国的许可证持有人获得的利润征税。

（2）对在弗里格气田获得的利润进行征税应当基于以下原则：各国政府对许可证持有人的征税，应在气田的生产期内，按照第3款确定的最终分配方案，依据本条约获得的天然气总产量和其他碳氢化合物方面的收入进行。在任何会计期内，各自政府对许可证持有人的征税，应当仅依据许可证持有人在天然气和其他碳氢化合物方面的实际产量所获的收入来征税，但征税前应考虑会计周期内，许可证持有人间按照第三条规定程序对过高或过低产量进行的调整。

（3）参照天然气产量和价值征收的特许权使用费、应缴款和税费，应当由每国政府按照本条第（1）和第（2）款的原则进行计算。

（4）每国政府可以对本国许可证持有人所有或部分所有的，用于弗里格气田勘探的固定设施和设备征收资产税，即使这种设施位于另一国的大陆架上。但是，对于一国许可证持有人部分所有，另一国许可证持有人部分所有的资产，每国只能对本国许可证持有人所占比重的那部分价值征税。两国政府都不得对他国许可证持有人完全所有的、用于勘探弗里格气田的固定设施和设备征收资产税。

（5）每国政府可以对本国的许可证持有人，处分其用于弗里格气田勘探的，全部或部分所有的固定设施和设备所获收入征税，即使这种设施位于另一国的大陆架上。但是，对于一国许可证持有人部分所有，另一国许可证持有人部分所有的资产，每国只能对本国许可证持有人处分其所占比重的部分征税。两国政府都不得对他国许可证持有人处分其完全所有的、用于勘探弗里格气田的固定设施和设备的收益征税。

（6）根据第五条担任联合经营人的公司，所获的任何利润和所拥有的任何资本，只能由为其颁发许可证的国家对其征税。

第十条

每个政府都应当保证其许可证持有人不转让与其获得的与弗里格气田任何部分的生产许可有关的权利，也不能未经授权政府事先同意而授予其他人类似的权利。在给予这种同意前，授权国家应当与另一国进行协商。

第十一条

（1）在弗里格气田任何部分的任何生产许可，或者许可证的任何部分，在期满、放弃或撤销的情形下，颁发许可证的国家应当保证，弗里格气田的勘探仍应按照本协定的规定继续进行，第一条所指的许可证持有人之间的，在期满、放弃或撤销之前的协议继续有效。特别是相关国家应当采取以下步骤：

（a）授予新的许可，取代期满、放弃或撤销的许可；或

（b）该国政府作为许可证持有人从事勘探工作；或

（c）采取两国同意的其他方式，继续勘探弗里格天然气。

（2）政府采取本条第（1）款规定的措施，应保证第一条规定的许可证持有人之间达成的协议符合补充协议的规定，此补充协议为采取这种措施的必要后果。

第十二条

（1）任意一方政府，在与另一方协商后，可以允许使用任何设备勘探弗里格气田之外的油气矿床，只要对按照本规定对弗里格天然气的开发活动不产生不利影响。

（2）本协定的任何规定不应妨碍政府要求其许可证持有人以实物缴纳特许权使用费。

第二部分　从弗里格气田输出天然气

第十三条

（1）向联合王国输送天然气，应当使用联合王国和挪威王国的管道。

(2) 挪威的管道应当由依据挪威法律成立，且住所位于挪威的法律实体所有。在民事和刑事诉讼、法庭选择和执行问题上，挪威王国管道的所有人应当受挪威法律和管辖权的约束。这也适用于挪威王国管道及与之有关的事项；同时，这也不应当排除根据联合王国冲突法的规定，联合王国法院的共享管辖权和联合王国法律的适用。

(3) 挪威王国管道的路线应当得到两国政府的批准。

(4) 联合王国政府应当依据联合王国法律的规定，对涉及挪威王国管道的事项授予必要的许可和给予必要的同意。

(5) 一国对与联合王国管道或挪威王国管道有关的事项给予许可证或同意时，该国应当将许可证或同意的副本送交另一国政府。

(6) 在与另一国进行事先协商之前，一国政府不得对涉及联合王国管道或挪威王国管道授予的许可证或转让许可证的同意进行任何实质性的变更或修改。

第十四条

两国政府应当采取一切公开措施，确保本协定签订之日，管道的所有者之间达成一项协议来管理天然气的运输。这种协议需要两国政府的批准，并且列入如果该协议与本协定发生冲突，本协定规定优先的条款。管道的所有者可以在中间平台、陆上终端、会计程序以及其他天然气运输的特定事项上达成补充协定。双方政府可以要求在协议签订45日内，或本协定规定的其他日期，管道所有者将协议的内容通知两国政府，并可以要求在它们认为必要时制定协议的修正条款。双方政府可以要求，管道所有者将本条中提到的任何协议的任何修正案，通知政府以获得双方政府的事先批准。凡需两国政府批准的协议或修正条款，在管道所有者向两国政府提出后45日内，如果没有收到一方或双方政府相反的通知，则视为已经被批准。

第十五条

为了保证联合王国管道和挪威王国管道的运行、维护和安全符合本协定规定，联合王国和挪威王国管道的所有人，应当经两国政府批准，任命一个管道经营者。

第十六条

(1) 双方政府应当采取措施保证，联合王国和挪威王国管道的所有人，在大陆架不同部分所产天然气的输送优先性条款，纳入第十四条所指的协议中，包括给予弗里格气田第一优先的条款，以及作为抵消特许权使用费的天然气，享有与已经按实物缴纳特许权使用费区域的天然气一样的输送优先权。

（2）联合王国政府和挪威王国政府可以各自给予本国管道的所有人指令，要求所有人输送或不输送弗里格以外的碳氢化合物，但是每个政府在没有与另一政府协商之前不得下达此种指令。

第十七条

（1）双方政府应当就两条管道共同的建设和安全标准进行协商，并要求管道所有者遵守该标准。

（2）两条管道相关的无线通信设施的建设、运行和设备的控制，应遵守主管电信当局达成的协议。与两条管道相关的其他通信系统，应当尽可能遵守共同的设计标准。如果无法实施共同标准，双方政府的标准应当协调一致。

（3）在联合王国管道建设期间安装的，供联合王国和挪威王国管道使用或者将供两国使用的设备，或者仅供挪威王国管道使用的设备，联合王国政府应当与挪威王国政府协商确定适用该设备的安全标准。

第十八条

（1）联合王国政府和挪威王国政府应当各自指派人员作为观察员协助各自政府确保管道建设和安全运营的标准得到执行。

（2）联合王国政府和挪威王国政府应当采取步骤，保证另一国政府指定的观察员可以进入联合王国管道和挪威王国管道。

（3）为了避免人员丧生或危害生命的伤亡或其他事故的发生，无论危险是否紧急，或为了减少这种伤亡或事故的后果，而时间和情形不允许两国的观察员进行协商，在任意一方政府的观察员认为必要或适当时，可以要求立即停止联合王国或/和挪威王国管道的部分或全部作业。同时，需要立即向两国主管当局报告这一命令的情况和原因，主管当局应随后就安全和迅速恢复作业的必要措施进行协商。

（4）第八条第（3）和第（5）款适用于本条对管道的监督，就如它们适用于第8条下对设备的监督。

第十九条

（1）两国政府愿意就对于除本条第（2）款所指的许可证持有人以外

的人，所享有的弗里格天然气，在公平的商业关税的基础上，通过管道进行运输。如果此种气体是从挪威王国大陆架上开采而通过联合王国管道输送，或者从联合王国大陆架上开采而通过挪威王国管道输送，双方政府应采取公开措施，保证管道所有者遵守两国政府批准的关税政策。

（2）本条第（1）款所指的许可证持有人是指：道达尔海上石油有限公司（Total Oil Marine Limited），爱尔夫石油勘探开发（联合王国）有限公司〔Elf Oil Exploration and Production (UK) Limited〕，阿奎泰恩石油（联合王国）有限公司〔Aquitaine Oil (UK) Limited〕（联合王国政府的许可证持有人），Elf Norge A/S, Aquitaine Norge A/S, Total Marine Norsk A/S, Norsk Hydro Produksjon a. s. and Den norske stats oljeselskap a. s. （挪威政府的许可证持有人）以及其继任者。

第二十条

两国政府应当就通过两条管道输送弗里格天然气所得的利润、两条管道所代表的资本以及处分管道和财产所产生的所得或收益的征税事宜，做出一致的安排。

第二十一条

（1）管道的任何许可证在期满、放弃或撤销的情形下，颁发许可证的政府应当保证，若两国政府一致同意所涉管道有继续使用和运营的必要，相关管道的继续使用和运营仍应符合本协定的规定，并遵守管道所有人依第十四条规定的在期满、放弃或撤销之前签订的协议。特殊情况下相关政府应当采取以下步骤：

（a）授予新的许可，取代期满、放弃或撤销的许可；或

（b）该国政府自行使用和运营管道；或

（c）采取两国政府同意的其他方式，继续使用和运营管道。

（2）政府采取本条第（1）款规定的措施后，管道所有人根据第十四条规定达成的协议，应为补充协议，作为政府采取措施后产生的必要后果。

（3）如果联合王国管道所属的联合王国政府，或者挪威王国管道所属的挪威王国政府，认为由于技术、经济或者其他因素，管道的继续运营不再可行，则需要与另一国政府协商；并保证尽最大努力保证此种情形下，另一国政府在公平的基础和条件上，有权接管其认为碳氢化合物运输所必

需的那部分管道的运行。

（4）根据本条第（3）款，接管全部管道或部分管道的政府应当保证，管道所有人或其他人应当移除或隔离不再使用的管道，以及两国政府一致同意需要移除或隔离的管道。

第三部分 一般规定

第二十二条

（1）测量弗里格气田生产的天然气的数量和容积，以及确定碳氢化合物组成的系统，应当能够分别测量运输至陆上的天然气和液体的数量，气田和个别泵站上消耗的数量，火炬平台上燃烧或排除的数量。这个系统应由两国主管当局协商一致。这个测量系统的设计、安装和运行的方式应当告知许可证持有人。两国政府有关主管当局应当就测量系统的设计、安装和运行的监督事项，制订一个共同计划；且为此目的，有关当局的代表应有权进入这个系统的所有部分。

（2）两国政府应当就对测量系统进行经常性的调试达成一致，并且应当在双方同意的间隔期间，交换第二条第（1）款所指的边界线两侧弗里格气田的生产记录，以及经核实的输送至陆地的气量记录。

第二十三条

双方政府应当在协商后，共同或分别地尽一切努力确保弗里格气田的开发，或者开发中任何设备和管道的运行，不会引起海洋环境污染，或因污染损害任何国家的海岸线、海洋设备或设施，或者渔船、渔具。

第二十四条

（1）双方政府应当采取措施保证自然人雇佣合同，无论是联合经营人签订的有关开采弗里格气田的，或者管道经营人签订的有关管道建设、维护和运营的，都应受许可证持有人为雇佣者的国家法律的管辖，但是不影响雇员选择其他法律的自由。

（2）双方政府应保证，所有的雇员都享有社会保险福利，且每个雇员只属于一种社会福利体系。

（3）双方政府应保证，关于雇员保护和福利的其他法律，符合弗里格气田作为单一整体的开发的目的，并符合本协定规定的管道的运营。

（4）对于弗里格气田或任何管道，在社会安全、雇员福利以及劳动关系领域内，涉及共同利益管理的事项，双方政府可以做出个别安排。

（5）本条的任何规定不损害或影响在本协定签订之日既存的本条第（4）款所涉事项的相关安排。

第二十五条

（1）在许可证适当限制的范围内，一国政府可向另一国政府公开许可证持有人向政府提供的本协定中许可经营的信息。如果提供给政府的信息是保密的，政府应当视为保密信息，任何进一步的披露应当遵守相关许可的限制性规定。但是，为编制弗里格气田内活动的综合报告，每个政府有权在任何时候使用这些信息。

（2）一国政府公布的综合报告或声明的复印件（包括新闻稿），应该至少在公布日期之前送达另一国政府。

第二十六条

本协定或者第一条和第十四条所指协议的任何内容，都不应当影响一国政府行使或两国政府共同行使，在国内和国际紧急情况发生时的特别权力。两国政府应当尽早进行协商，对采取合适的联合措施达成一致意见，使紧急情况不损害它们在最有效开发弗里格天然气上的共同利益。

第二十七条

为了促进本协定的实施，双方政府应各指派三个人，共六人组成委员会，并命名为弗里格气田咨询委员会，以促进本协定的实施。委员会的职能应包括审议两国政府提交的问题，委员会程序性的规则由两国政府一致同意的后续安排来规定。

第二十八条

（1）任何与本协定解释和适用有关争端，或者依第一条第（2）款和第十四条所指的许可证持有人间的协议提交两国政府解决的其他事项，应当通过弗里格气田咨询委员会解决，或者两国政府协商解决。

（2）如果争端无法通过这种方式解决，或者通过两国政府同意的其他程序解决，应当在任何一国的要求下，将争端提交仲裁庭解决。仲裁庭组成如下。

每个政府指定一名仲裁员，这两名仲裁员选定第三名仲裁员。第三名仲裁员不能是联合王国或挪威王国的国民或居民，且应作为仲裁主席。如果仲裁要求提出后 3 个月内,任意一国政府没有指定一名仲裁员,任意一国政府可以请求国际法院主席指定一名仲裁员。如果在第二名仲裁员指定后一个月内,没有选出第三名仲裁员,则适用同样的程序。仲裁庭应当决定自己的程序规则,在无法全体一致达成决议时,仲裁决议应由仲裁庭成员的多数票达成。仲裁庭的决议对两国政府具有约束力,为了达成本协定的目的,决议应当被视为两国政府间协议。

第二十九条

(1) 本协定的任意条款不应当解释为,影响每个国家按照国际法对本国的大陆架享有的管辖权。特别是,位于联合王国大陆架上的设备应属于联合王国管辖,位于挪威大陆架上的设备应属于挪威王国管辖。

(2) 本协定的任何内容不应被解释为,影响或限制任何一国法律的适用,或任何一国的法庭按照国际法行使管辖权。

第三十条

依本协定,除非有其他相反的规定:

(1) "弗里格气田"是指,在海底约 1955 米深处,海床下较低的始新世时代,自然产生的含天然气砂岩地层。气田位于北纬 59°53′纬线和 1965 年 3 月 10 日两国关于大陆架划界协定中规定的边界线的交叉点处。气田共有附件 B 中的 4 个油井,并包括在开始生产时,可以流入以上含天然气砂岩地层的其他含气地层。

(2) "设备"是指,在弗里格气田开发活动中,在海床上安装的任何结构或装置,包括管道。设备不包括下文规定的挪威王国管道和联合王国管道。

(3) "许可证持有人"包括:联合王国政府的许可证持有人——Total Oil Marine Limited, Elf Oil Exploration and Production (UK) Limited, Aquitaine Oil (UK) Limited;挪威政府的许可证持有人——Elf Norge A/S, Aquitaine Norge A/S, Total Marine Norsk A/S, Norsk Hydro Produksjon a. s. and Den norske stats oljeselskap a. s.,以及它们的继任者。除上述外,这包括任意一国政府为了开发某一部分弗里格气田而不时授予的许可证持有人,以及代替上述部分或全部的许可证持有人的法人。

(4) "挪威管道"指该管道从挪威大陆架上弗里格气田平台上的入口

法兰,延伸直至圣弗格斯的陆地测量仪器,并包括中间平台上为管道提供服务的相关设备。

(5)"联合王国管道"指的是即将建造并运行的管道,该管道从联合王国大陆架上弗里格气田平台上的入口法兰,延伸至圣弗格斯的陆地测量仪器,并包括中间平台上为管道提供服务的相关设备。

(6)"联合经营人"和"管道经营人",包括根据第一条和第十四条所指的协议行事的公司。

第三十一条

(1)本协定应于双方政府互相通知对方政府本国国内所有条件已成就时生效。

(2)双方政府可以在任何时候经一致同意修改或终止本协定。

下列签署人,经其各自政府正式授权,在本协定上签字,以昭信守。

1976年5月10日于伦敦签订,签订英文和挪威文文本各一份,两种文本具有同等效力。

大不列颠及北爱尔兰联合王国代表:安东尼·韦奇伍德·本
约翰·汤姆林森
挪威王国政府:奥拉夫·C. 穆勒

附件 A
设备

1. 在挪威王国的大陆架上:
(a) 一个钻井平台
(b) 一个综合的处理和压缩平台
2. 在联合王国的大陆架上:
(a) 一个钻井平台
(b) 一个处理平台
(c) 一个宿舍平台
(d) 一个火炬塔

附件 B

国家	钻井编号	地理位置
挪威	25/1－1	北纬 59°53′17.09″，东经 02°04′42.7″
挪威	25/1－2	北纬 59°56′08″，东经 02°04′54.6″
挪威	25/1－3	北纬 59°54′05″，东经 02°10′08″
英国	10/1－1A	北纬 59°50′10.5″，东经 02°00′34.5″

2. Agreement Relating to the Exploitation of the Frigg Field Reservoir and the Transmission of Gas therefrom to the United Kingdom

London, 10 May 1976

[The agreement entered into force on 22 July 1977]

The Government of the United Kingdom of Great Britain and Northern Ireland and the Government of the Kingdom of Norway;

CONSIDERING that the drilling in the Continental Shelf appertaining to the United Kingdom and in the Continental Shelf appertaining to the Kingdom of Norway has proved the existence of a gas reservoir, now named the Frigg Field Reservoir, which extends across the dividing line as defined in the Agreement of 10 March 1965 between the two Governments relating to the delimitation of the Continental Shelf between the two countries;

HAVING REGARD TO Article 4 of the said Agreement under which the two Governments have undertaken, in consultation with the licensees, to seek agreement as to the manner in which any such field shall be most effectively exploited and the manner in which the proceeds deriving therefrom shall be apportioned;

DESIRING, before production commences, to make provision for the exploitation of the Frigg Field Reservoir as a single unit, and to regulate certain further questions which will arise in connection with the transmission of the gas from the Frigg Field Reservoir to the United Kingdom by two pipelines to be built for this purpose;

HAVE AGREED as follows:

PART I EXPLOITATION OF THE FRIGG FIELD RESERVOIR

Article 1

(1) The gas in the Frigg Field Reservoir and the hydrocarbons produced with or from the gas (excluding oil underlying the gas and gas and oil in other horizons), referred to in this Agreement as "Frigg Gas", shall be exploited as a single unit by means of installations specified in Annex A to this Agreement, and except that those installations may be replaced from time to time by installations for a similar purpose on a similar location, the Governments shall require that no other installations are used without prior consent of both Governments.

(2) Each Government shall require those who are its licensees at the date of sig nature of this Agreement to enter into agreements between themselves and the licensees at that date of the other Government to regulate the exploitation in accordance with this Agreement of Frigg Gas, which agreements require the approval of the two Governments, and incorporate provisions to ensure that in the event of a conflict between any of those agreements and this Agreement the terms of this Agreement shall prevail. The licensees may supplement the agreements so concluded by agreements in respect of accounting, operating and other specialized aspects of the exploitation, and the terms of all such supplementary agreements shall be notified to the two Governments within 45 days of their conclusion or the date of this Agreement as the case may be and the two Governments may require amendments or such further agreements to be made as the Governments agree to be necessary properly to secure the exploitation of Frigg Gas.

(3) The licensees shall be required to submit any proposed amendment to any of the agreements mentioned in paragraph (2) of this Article for the prior approval of the two Governments, which approval may be deemed to have been given unless the licensees have been notified to the contrary by one or both Governments within 45 days of the submission to both Governments.

Article 2

(1) The Governments shall jointly demarcate, in a manner to be agreed, the dividing line defined in the Agreement of 10 March 1965, and shall thereafter

jointly determine the position of each installation when in place in relation to the dividing line, with conclusive effect for the purposes of this Agreement.

(2) The two Governments shall consult with a view to agreeing a determination of the limits and estimated total reserves of the Frigg Field Reservoir and an apportionment of the reserves therein as between the Continental Shelf appertaining to the United Kingdom and the Continental Shelf appertaining to the Kingdom of Norway. For this purpose the licensees shall be required to submit to the Governments a proposal for such determinations.

(3) The two Governments shall endeavour to agree the apportionment of the reserves of the Frigg Field Reservoir before production of the reserves commences. If they are not able to do so, then pending such agreement, the production shall proceed on the provisional basis of a proposal for the apportionment submitted by the licensees, or, if there is none, on the provisional basis of equal shares. Such provisional apportionment shall be without prejudice to the position of either Government. When the apportionment is agreed, the agreed apportionment shall be substituted for the provisional apportionment as if the agreed apportionment were a revision made under Article 3.

(4) If the two Governments are unable to reach agreement on any of the matters which fall to be agreed under paragraph (2) of this Article within 12 months from the date of the commencement of production, the question shall be settled in accordance with the provisions of Article 28.

(5) Subject to requirements of safety, neither Government shall withhold a permit for the drilling of wells by, or on account of, licensees of the other Government, in conformity with those agreements mentioned in paragraph (2) of Article 1 between the licensees, for purposes related to the determination of the limits of the Frigg Field Reservoir, the total amount of reserves therein or the apportionment of the reserves.

Article 3

(1) The limits of the Frigg Field Reservoir and the total amount of the reserves and the apportionment of the reserves or any of them when agreed or determined under Article 2 shall be reviewed if either Government so requests:

(a) At the date of commencement of production of Frigg Gas;

(b) At the expiry of every period of four years after that date;

(c) At any other time when naturally occurring gas – bearing reservoirs are proved to contain gas which was capable of flowing into the Frigg Field Reservoir at the start of production, and the Government making the request considers that the circum stances are of sufficient importance to justify a revision.

(2) If, as a result of a determination under Article 2 or a revision under this Article, the limits of the Frigg Field Reservoir include an area of the Continental Shelf in respect of which a person not a party to any agreements mentioned in Article 1 subsisting at the date of the determination or revision, as the case may be, holds a production licence, that person and the licensees who are parties to those agreements shall be required to enter into an agreement, within such time as the Governments shall stipulate, the terms of which shall conform to the provisions of paragraph (2) of Article 1 and shall be subject to the approval of the two Governments.

(3) The provisions of paragraphs (2) and (4) of Article 2 shall apply to revisions under this Article as those provisions apply to matters to be agreed pursuant to Article 2. The licensees shall be required to conduct all operations necessary for each revision and to secure that at the time the production from the Frigg Field Reservoir ceases the share in the total volume of Frigg Gas received by the licensees of the Government of the United Kingdom and the share thereof received by the licensees of the Government of the Kingdom of Norway shall each correspond to the final apportionment of the reserves in place. All revisions shall be based upon the characteristics of the Frigg Field Reservoir before commencement of production. Whenever a revision results in a new apportionment of the total amount of the reserves, such revisions shall make such provision as between the licensees as will ensure that the licensees of the Governments of the United Kingdom and Norway respectively receive deliveries of Frigg Gas such that any surplus or deficiency resulting from deliveries made under the apportionment in force immediately before such revision is made good. All revisions shall have effect from the date that revision has been agreed by both Governments or settled

by arbitration, as the case may be.

(4) If, at any time, gas which is not part of the Frigg Field Reservoir is proved to be flowing into the Reservoir, such gas shall be exploited under the provisions of this Agreement as if it were Frigg Gas. In these circumstances the two Governments shall consult with a view to determining:

(a) The total amount of the reserves of the Frigg Field Reservoir and such other gas and the apportionment thereof;

(b) Any consequential arrangements which need to be made for the exploitation of such other gas; and

(c) Any consequential arrangements which need to be made between the licensees and the persons who hold production licences relating to such other gas, regarding its exploitation.

Article 4

(1) Each Government shall require its licensees to submit for the approval of the two Governments a scheme to secure the conservation of the Frigg Field Reservoir for productive operations, with provision for review at intervals of not more than four years, the results of which shall be submitted to the two Governments for approval.

(2) The Governments shall ensure that any approved scheme is implemented.

Article 5

For the purposes of the exploitation of Frigg Gas in accordance with this Agreement, a Unit Operator shall be appointed by agreement between the licensees, subject to the approval of the two Governments.

Article 6

(1) Subject to the requirements of safety, each Government shall ensure the free movement of all persons and materials between all installations for the purposes of the exploitation of Frigg Gas.

(2) Subject to the requirements of safety, the landing facilities on every installation (including intermediate platforms involved in the operation of the pipelines) shall be freely available to vessels and, in accordance with any arrange-

ments which may be concluded between the competent authorities, available to aircraft of the nationality of either State for the purposes of activities connected with the exploitation of Frigg Gas.

Article 7

(1) The two Governments shall consult one another with a view to agreeing appropriate safety measures for each installation and with a view to ensuring that all installations are as far as possible subject to uniform safety and construction standards.

(2) Each Government shall have the final right to determine the safety measures which are to govern the installations under its jurisdiction as set out in Article 29. With respect to pipelines crossing the dividing line between installations, the two Governments shall, after consultations, formulate joint safety measures and shall require compliance therewith by their respective licensees.

(3) The establishment, operation, and control of equipment for radio communications for the Frigg Field Reservoir shall be subject to agreement between the competent telecommunications authorities.

Article 8

(1) With a view to ensuring compliance with the safety and construction standards referred to in Article 7, the Governments agree to consult and to take all necessary steps to that end, including the conferment on their inspectors of functions with respect to such safety and construction standards on or about the installations; their powers in respect of installations located on the Continental Shelf appertaining to the other State being those specified in paragraphs (3) and (4) of this Article.

(2) Each Government shall procure access for such inspectors including the inspectors of the other Government to installations and equipment, and production to those inspectors of all relevant information affecting the interest of the other Government in the Frigg Field Reservoir.

(3) The inspectors of each Government shall act in co-operation and consult with inspectors of the other Government with a view to achieving compliance with the safety and construction standards applicable to each installation and in

particular an inspector of one Government may, with regard to an installation located on the Continental Shelf appertaining to the other State, request an inspector of the Government of that other State to exercise his powers to ensure such compliance whenever it appears that circumstances so warrant. In the event of any disagreement between the inspectors of the two Governments or the refusal of the inspector of the one Government to take action at the request of the inspector of the other, the matter shall be referred to the competent authorities of both Governments.

(4) If it appears to an inspector of either Government to be necessary or expedient for the purpose of averting a casualty or other accident involving loss of life or danger to life suffered by a person, whether the danger is immediate or not, or minimising the consequences of such a casualty or other accident, and time and circumstances do not permit consultation between the inspectors of the two Governments, that inspector may order the immediate cessation of any or all operations in the Frigg Field provided the fact of such an order and the reason therefor is reported immediately to the competent authorities of both Governments who shall then consult to consider the actions necessary for the safe and speedy resumption of operations.

(5) The competent authorities of the two Governments shall consult with each other to agree on methods to implement this Article.

Article 9

(1) Each Government may charge tax, in accordance with the tax law of that Government, on the whole of the profits arising by virtue of its own licences from the exploitation of the Frigg Field Reservoir in accordance with the principles set out in the following paragraph, regardless of whether this refers to production carried out on the Continental Shelf of the other State, but shall not charge to tax any such profits arising by virtue of the licences of the other Government.

(2) The taxation of the profits derived from the exploitation of the Frigg Field Reservoir shall be based on the principle that over the production life of the field the licensees of each Government shall be charged to tax by reference to

their income from so much of the total production of gas and other hydrocarbons covered by this Agreement as is attributed to them under the final apportionment of the Frigg Field Reservoir made in accordance with Article 3. In any accounting period, however, the licensees of each Government shall be charged to tax only by reference to the income from so much of the actual quantities of gas and other hydrocarbons lifted in that period as is attributed to them under the apportionment in force in that period after taking account of any adjustments made in that period between the licensees for overliftings and underliftings in previous periods in accordance with the adjustment procedure referred to in Article 3.

(3) Royalties, dues and taxes, calculated by reference to the quantity or value of production, shall be calculated as regards each Government in accordance with the principles set out in paragraphs (1) and (2) of this Article.

(4) Each Government may charge capital taxes on those fixed installations and equipment used for the exploitation of the Frigg Field Reservoir which are owned or partly owned by its own licensees, even though situated on the Continental Shelf of the other State, but, where such assets are owned partly by the licensees of one Government and partly by the licensees of the other Government, each Government may charge capital taxes only on such part of the cost or value of those assets as is proportional to the interest of its own licensees in them. Neither Government shall charge capital taxes on fixed installations and equipment used for the exploitation of the Frigg Field Reservoir which are wholly owned by the other Government's licensees.

(5) Each Government may charge tax on gains realised on the disposal of those fixed installations and the equipment used for the exploitation of the Frigg Field Reservoir which are owned or partly owned by its own licensees even though situated on the Continental Shelf of the other State, but where such assets are owned partly by the licensees of one Government and partly by the licensees of the other Government, each Government may charge tax only on such part of the gains as is proportional to the interest of its own licensees in those assets. Neither Government shall charge tax on gains realised on the disposal of those fixed installations and the equipment used for the exploitation of the Frigg Field Reservoir

which are wholly owned by the other Government's licensees.

(6) Any profits derived or any capital owned by a company in its capacity as a Unit Operator in accordance with Article 5 shall be taxable only in the State of which the Unit Operator is a licensee.

Article 10

Each Government shall ensure that its licensees shall not transfer any of the rights granted by virtue of any production licence relating to any part of the Frigg Field Reservoir and shall not grant the like rights to any other person without the prior consent of the licensing Government. Before granting its consent, the licensing Government shall consult with the other Government.

Article 11

(1) In the event of the expiration, surrender or revocation of any production licence or any part of such a licence relating to any part of the Frigg Field Reservoir, the Government which issued the licence shall ensure that the exploitation of Frigg Gas is continued in accordance with the terms of this Agreement and the agreements between the licensees referred to in Article 1 subsisting immediately before such expiration, surrender or revocation. In particular the Government concerned shall take one of the following steps:

(a) Issue a new licence in replacement of the licence which has expired, been surrendered or revoked; or

(b) Itself conduct such exploitation as if it were a licensee; or

(c) Take such other action to continue the exploitation of the Frigg Gas as the two Governments may agree.

(2) The Government taking action as described in paragraph (1) of this Article shall procure that the agreements between the licensees referred to in Article 1 shall be the subject of such supplementary agreements as are necessary consequent upon the action taken.

Article 12

(1) Either Government may, after consultation with the other, permit the use of any installations for the exploitation of petroleum deposits not comprised in the Frigg Field Reservoir, provided that such use does not adversely affect the ex-

ploitation of Frigg Gas in accordance with this Agreement.

(2) Nothing in this Agreement shall preclude either Government from requiring of their licensees that royalty be paid in kind.

PART II TRANSMISSION OF GAS FROM THE FRIGG FIELD RESERVOIR

Article 13

(1) For the transmission of Frigg Gas to the United Kingdom, use shall be made of the United Kingdom Pipeline and the Norwegian Pipeline.

(2) The Norwegian Pipeline shall be owned by Norwegian legal entities incorporated under the law of the Kingdom of Norway and having their domicile in Norway. The owners of the Norwegian Pipeline shall be subject to Norwegian law and jurisdiction as regards civil and criminal proceedings, forum and enforcement. This shall also apply in relation to the Norwegian Pipeline and incidents pertaining thereto; it being understood, however, that this shall not exclude the concurrent jurisdiction of the United Kingdom Courts and the application of the laws of the United Kingdom subject to the rules of the laws of the United Kingdom governing the conflict of laws.

(3) The route of the Norwegian Pipeline shall be subject to the approval of both Governments.

(4) The Government of the United Kingdom shall, in accordance with and subject to the laws of the United Kingdom, grant any necessary licences and give any necessary consents concerning the Norwegian Pipeline.

(5) A Government shall on granting a licence or giving a consent in relation to either the United Kingdom Pipeline or the Norwegian Pipeline make available a copy of that licence or consent to the other Government.

(6) A Government shall not substantially alter or modify a licence or consent to the assignment of a licence relating to the United Kingdom Pipeline or the Norwegian Pipeline without prior consultation with the other Government.

Article 14

The two Governments shall take whatever measures are open to them with the aim of securing that the owners of the pipelines at the date of signature of this Agreement enter into an agreement between themselves to regulate the transmission of gas, and that such agreement requires the approval of the two Governments, and incorporates provisions to ensure that in the event of a conflict between that agreement and this Agreement the terms of this Agreement shall prevail. The owners of the pipelines may supplement the agreement so concluded by agreements in respect of the intermediate platform (s), the onshore terminal, accounting procedure and other specialized items relating to the transmission of gas. The two Governments may request to be notified of the terms of such supplementary agreements within 45 days of their conclusion or the date of this Agreement as the case may be and may request that amendments or such further agreements be made as they agree to be necessary. The two Governments may request to be notified of any proposed amendments to any of the agreements mentioned in this Article for prior approval by the two Governments. Where any approval is required of the two Governments the same shall be deemed to have been given unless the owners have been notified to the contrary by one or both Governments within 45 days of the submission to both Governments.

Article 15

For the purposes of the operation of the United Kingdom Pipeline and the Norwegian Pipeline in accordance with this Agreement and their maintenance and safety, a pipeline Operator shall be appointed by agreement between the owners of the United Kingdom Pipeline and the owners of the Norwegian Pipeline, subject to the approval of the two Governments.

Article 16

(1) The two Governments shall take measures to secure that the owners of the United Kingdom Pipeline and the owners of the Norwegian Pipeline include in the agreements referred to in Article 14 provisions regarding priorities in the transmission of gas originating in different parts of the Continental Shelf, including provisions for giving first priority to Frigg Gas and securing that royalty gas taken in kind is given the same priority of transmission as gas from the field from which royalty is taken in kind.

(2) The Government of the United Kingdom may give to the owners of the United Kingdom Pipeline, and the Government of the Kingdom of Norway may give to the owners of the Norwegian Pipeline, directions requiring such owners to transmit or refrain from transmitting hydrocarbons other than Frigg Gas but no direction shall be given by either Government without prior consultation with the other.

Article 17

(1) The two Governments shall consult one another with a view to agreeing common construction and safety standards for the two pipelines and shall require the owners of the pipelines to comply with those standards.

(2) The establishment, operation and control of equipment for radio communications relating respectively to the two pipelines shall be subject to agreement between the competent telecommunications authorities. Other communications systems relating to the two pipelines shall as far as possible be subject to common standards of design. Where it is not possible to impose common standards, the standards imposed by each Government shall be compatible.

(3) If equipment is installed during the construction of the United Kingdom Pipeline and serves or is intended to serve both the United Kingdom Pipeline and the Norwegian Pipeline, or serves the Norwegian Pipeline only, the Government of the United Kingdom shall consult the Government of the Kingdom of Norway on the safety standards which are to apply to that equipment.

Article 18

(1) The Government of the United Kingdom and the Government of the Kingdom of Norway shall each appoint persons to be inspectors for the purpose of assisting their respective Governments in securing compliance with the standards for the proper construction and safe operation of pipelines.

(2) The Government of the United Kingdom and the Government of the Kingdom of Norway shall take such steps as are available to them to secure for inspectors appointed by the other, access to the United Kingdom Pipeline and the Norwegian Pipeline respectively.

(3) If it appears to an inspector of either Government to be necessary or ex-

pedient for the purposes of averting a casualty or other accident involving loss of life or danger to life suffered by a person, whether the danger is immediate or not, or minimising the consequences of such a casualty or other accident, and time and circumstances do not permit consultation between the inspectors of the two Governments, that inspector may order the immediate cessation of any or all operations in relation to the United Kingdom Pipeline or the Norwegian Pipeline or both, provided the fact of such an order and the reason therefor is reported immediately to the competent authorities of both Governments who shall then consult to consider the actions necessary for the safe and speedy resumption of operations.

(4) Paragraphs (3) and (5) of Article 8 apply to the inspection of pipelines under this Article as they apply to the inspection of installations under Article 8.

Article 19

(1) It is the intention of the two Governments that Frigg Gas belonging to persons other than the licensees referred W in paragraph (2) of this Article shall be transmitted through the pipelines at fair commercial tariffs, and if such gas having been extracted from the Continental Shelf appertaining to the Kingdom of Norway is transmitted through the United Kingdom Pipeline, or having been extracted from the Continental Shelf appertaining to the United Kingdom is transmitted through the Norwegian Pipeline, the two Governments shall take such measures as are open to them to ensure that tariffs approved by the two Governments are observed by the owners of the pipelines.

(2) The licensees referred to in paragraph (1) of this Article are Total Oil Marine Limited, Elf Oil Exploration and Production (UK) Limited, Aquitaine Oil (UK) Limited (being licensees of the United Kingdom Government), Elf Norge A/S, Aquitaine Norge A/S, Total Marine Norsk A/S, Norsk Hydro Produksjon a. s. and Den norske stats oljeselskap a. s. (being licensees of the Norwegian Government) and their successors.

Article 20

The Governments shall make agreed arrangements regarding the taxation of profits arising from the transmission of Frigg Gas through the two pipelines and of capital represented by the pipelines and of capital gains arising from the disposal of the pipelines or an interest therein.

Article 21

(1) In the event of the expiration, surrender or revocation of any licence relating to a pipeline, the Government which issued the licence shall ensure that if the two Governments are agreed that there is need for the continued use and operation of the pipeline in question, such use and operation is continued in accordance with the terms of this Agreement and the agreements between the owners of the pipelines referred to in Article 14 subsisting immediately before such expiration, surrender or revocation. In particular the Government concerned shall take one of the following steps:

(a) Issue a new licence in replacement of the licence which has expired, been surrendered or revoked; or

(b) Itself conduct such use and operation; or

(c) Take such other action to continue such use and operation as the two Governments may agree.

(2) The Government taking action as described in paragraph (1) of this Article shall procure that the agreements between the owners of the pipelines referred to in Article 14 shall be the subject of such supplementary agreements as are necessary consequent upon the action taken.

(3) If the Government of the United Kingdom in relation to the United Kingdom Pipeline or the Government of the Kingdom of Norway in relation to the Norwegian Pipeline considers the continued operation of the pipeline for technical, economic or other reasons not to be practicable, it shall consult with the other Government and shall use its best endeavours to procure in such circumstances for that other Government the right to take over on fair terms and conditions the operation of that part of the pipeline which it considers necessary for transmission of hydrocarbons.

(4) Subject to paragraph (3) of this Article, the Government which takes over the operation of the pipeline or part thereof shall ensure the removal or isola-

tion whether by the owners of the pipeline or otherwise, of any part of the pipeline which is no longer in use and which both Governments agree should be removed or isolated.

PART III   GENERAL PROVISIONS

Article 22

(1) The system for metering the quantity of gas and liquid volumes and determination of the composition of hydrocarbons produced from the Frigg Field Reservoir shall be capable of separately metering the quantities of gas and liquids landed ashore, consumed on the field and at individual pumping stations, and discharged from or burnt off on flare platforms. Such system shall be the subject of agreement between the competent authorities of the two Governments. The licensees shall be instructed as to the manner in which the metering system is to be designed, installed and operated. The competent authorities of the two Governments shall agree a joint scheme for the supervision of the designing, installation and operation of the metering system, and for this purpose the representatives of those authorities shall have access to all parts of the system.

(2) The two Governments shall agree on regular calibration of the metering systems and shall exchange at agreed intervals certified production records of the Frigg Field Reservoir relating to production from each side of the dividing line mentioned in paragraph (1) of Article 2 together with certified records of landed volume.

Article 23

The two Governments undertake to make every endeavour, jointly and severally, after consultations, to ensure that the exploitation of Frigg Gas or the operation of any installation or pipeline involved in that exploitation shall not cause pollution of the marine environment or damage by pollution to the coast – line, shore facilities or amenities, or vessels or fishing gear of any country.

Article 24

(1) The Governments shall take steps to procure that all contracts of employment of natural persons by the Unit Operator in connection with the exploita-

tion of the Frigg Field Reservoir or by the Pipeline Operator in connection with the construction, maintenance or operation of pipelines are governed by the law of the State of which the employer is a licensee but without prejudice to the freedom of any employee to choose another law.

(2) The two Governments shall endeavour to ensure that all employees are covered with regard to social security benefits and that each employee need comply only with one social security system.

(3) The two Governments shall endeavour to ensure that other legislation for the protection and welfare of employees is applied consistently with the exploitation of the Frigg Field Reservoir as a single unit and with the operation of the pipelines in accordance with this Agreement.

(4) The Governments may from time to time conclude separate arrangements for the regulation of matters of common interest in the field of social security, employee welfare and labour relations in respect of the Frigg Field Reservoir or any pipeline.

(5) Nothing in this Article shall prejudice or affect any arrangements concerning matters referred to in paragraph (4) of this Article existing at the date of signature of this Agreement.

Article 25

(1) A Government may, subject where appropriate to any restrictions in a licence, disclose to the other Government information in respect of licensed operations covered by this Agreement which a licensee has supplied to its Government. Where information is given to a Government in confidence, that Government shall treat it as confidential and any further disclosure shall be subject to any restrictions in the licence in question. Each Government shall nevertheless be entitled at any time to make use of the information for the purpose of preparing general reports on activities in respect of the Frigg Field Reservoir.

(2) Copies of all such general reports or statements (including press releases) published by one Government shall be transmitted to the other Government not later than the date of publication.

Article 26

Nothing in this Agreement or in the agreements referred to in Article 1 and Article 14 shall prejudice the exercise by each Government or by the two Governments jointly of special powers in the case of national or international emergency. Consultations shall be held at the earliest opportunity in order that the two Governments may agree on appropriate joint measures to reconcile the urgency of the situation with their common interest in the most effective exploitation of the Frigg Gas.

Article 27

A commission shall be established consisting of six persons of whom each Government shall appoint three persons, to be known as the Frigg Field Consultative Commission, for the purpose of facilitating the implementation of this Agreement. The functions of the Commission, which shall include that of considering matters referred to it by the Governments, and its procedures shall be subject to such further arrangements which may be agreed by the two Governments from time to time.

Article 28

(1) Any dispute about the interpretation or application of this Agreement, or any other matter referred to the Governments for settlement under the agreements between the licensees mentioned in paragraph (2) of Article 1 and Article 14 shall be resolved through the Frigg Field Consultative Commission or by negotiation between the two Governments.

(2) If any such dispute cannot be resolved in this manner or by any other procedure agreed to by the two Governments, the dispute shall be submitted, at the request of either Government, to an Arbitral Tribunal composed as follows: Each Government shall designate one arbitrator, and the two arbitrators so designated shall elect a third, who shall be the Chairman and who shall not be a national of or habitually reside in the United Kingdom or in the Kingdom of Norway. If either Government fails to designate an arbitrator within three months of a request to do so, either Government may request the President of the International Court of Justice to appoint an arbitrator. The same procedure shall apply if, within one month of the designation or appointment of the second arbitrator, the third

arbitrator has not been elected. The Tribunal shall determine its own procedure, save that all decisions shall be taken, in the absence of unanimity, by a majority vote of the members of the Tribunal. The decisions of the Tribunal shall be binding upon the two Governments and shall, for the purposes of this Agreement, be regarded as agreements between the two Governments.

Article 29

(1) Nothing in this Agreement shall be interpreted as affecting the jurisdiction which each State has under international law over the Continental Shelf which appertains to it. In particular, installations located on the Continental Shelf appertaining to the United Kingdom shall be under the jurisdiction of the United Kingdom, and installations located on the Continental Shelf appertaining to the Kingdom of Norway shall be under the jurisdiction of the Kingdom of Norway.

(2) Nor shall anything in this Agreement be interpreted as prejudicing or restricting the application of the laws of either State or the exercise of jurisdiction by their Courts, in conformity with international law.

Article 30

For the purpose of this Agreement, unless the context otherwise requires:

(1) "Frigg Field Reservoir" means the naturally occurring gas-bearing sand formations of the lower Eocene age beneath the sea bed but immediately above the subsea level of approximately 1955 metres located in the vicinity of the intersection of the line of latitude 59°53′ North and of the dividing line which is defined in the Agreement of 10 March 1965 between the two Governments relating to the delimitation of the Continental Shelf between the two States, and encountered by the four wells described in Annex B and includes all other gas-bearing strata from which gas at the start of the production is capable of flowing into the above-mentioned gas-bearing sand formations.

(2) "Installation" means any structure or device installed in or on the sea bed, including a pipeline, which is involved in the exploitation of the Frigg Field Reservoir. Installation does not include the Norwegian Pipeline or the United Kingdom Pipeline hereinafter defined.

(3) "The licensees" means Total Oil Marine Limited, Elf Oil Exploration

and Production (UK) Limited, Aquitaine Oil (UK) Limited (being licensees of the United Kingdom Government), Elf Norge A/S, Aquitaine Norge A/S, Total Marine Norsk A/S, Norsk Hydro Produksjon a. s. and Den norske stats oljeselskap a. s. (being licensees of the Norwegian Government) and their successors and such other persons as may from time to time be licensees of either Government for the exploitation of any part of the Frigg Field Reservoir in addition to, or in substitution for, all or any of the above – named persons.

(4) "Norwegian Pipeline" means the pipeline to be built and operated from the inlet flange of the pipeline at a Frigg Field Reservoir platform situated on the Continental Shelf appertaining to the Kingdom of Norway up to and including metering instruments on – shore at St. Fergus, and also including associated installations serving this pipeline on an intermediate platform or platforms.

(5) "United Kingdom Pipeline" means the pipeline to be built and operated from the inlet flange of the pipeline at a Frigg Field Reservoir platform situated on the Continental Shelf appertaining to the United Kingdom up to and including metering instruments on – shore at St. Fergus, and also including associated installations serving this pipeline on an inter mediate platform or platforms.

(6) References to "Unit Operator" and "Pipeline Operator" include references to the company or companies for the time being acting as such pursuant to the agreements referred to in Articles 1 and 14.

Article 31

(1) This Agreement shall enter into force on the date on which the two Governments shall have informed each other that all necessary internal requirements have been fulfilled.

(2) The two Governments may amend or terminate this Agreement at any time by agreement.

IN WITNESS WHEREOF the undersigned, duly authorised by their respective Governments, have signed this Agreement.

DONE in duplicate at London this 10th day of May 1976, in the English and Norwegian languages, both texts being equally authoritative.

For the Government of the United Kingdom of Great Britain and Northern

Ireland:

ANTHONY WEDGWOOD BENN

JOHN TOMLINSON

For the Government of the Kingdom of Norway:

OLUF C. MüLLER

ANNEX A
INSTALLATIONS

1. On the Continental Shelf appertaining to the Kingdom of Norway:

   (a) One drilling platform.

   (b) One combined treatment and compressor platform.

2. On the Continental Shelf appertaining to the United Kingdom:

   (a) One drilling platform

   (b) One treatment platform.

   (c) One quarters platform.

   (d) One flare column.

ANNEX B

Country	Well No.	Geographical Location
Norway	25/1 – 1.	59°53′17.09″N 02°04′42.7″E
Norway	25/1 – 2.	59°56′08″ N 02°04′54.6″E
Norway	25/1 – 3.	59°54′05″ N 02°10′08″ E
UK	10/1 – 1A.	59°50′10.5″ N 02°00′34.5″E

3.《大不列颠及北爱尔兰联合王国政府与挪威王国政府关于修改 1976 年 5 月 10 日有关开发弗里格气田并向联合王国输送天然气的协定的协定》

(1998 年 8 月 25 日订于斯塔万格)

邓妮雅译,黄文博校

1976 年 5 月 10 日签订的,大不列颠及北爱尔兰联合王国与挪威王国,关于开发弗里格气田并向联合王国输送天然气的协定继续有效,后文附件中的修正案应纳入该协定中。

本协定应于双方政府互相通知对方政府国内必需的条件已经成就时生效。

下列签署人,经其各自政府正式授权,在本协定上签字,以昭信守。

1998 年 8 月 25 日于斯塔万格签订,签订英文和挪威文文本各一份,两种文本具有同等效力。

大不列颠及北爱尔兰联合王国代表:约翰·巴特尔
挪威王国政府:玛丽特·阿恩斯塔

附件
《大不列颠及北爱尔兰联合王国政府与挪威王国政府关于修改 1976 年 5 月 10 日有关开发弗里格气田以及为开发和输送碳氢化合物而使用设施和管道的协定的协定》

大不列颠及北爱尔兰联合王国政府与挪威王国政府,考虑到在联合王国的大陆架和挪威王国的大陆架上,经勘探发现存在天然气田,现将该天然气田命名为弗里格气田，由于田跨越了两国于 1965 年 3 月 10 日签订的两国大陆架划界协定确定的分界线；

上述划界协定中第四条规定，两国政府应当在与许可证持有人协商后，就这类气田最有效的开发方式和收益分配方式达成一致；

双方愿意在开始生产前，将弗里格天然气田作为一个整体，为弗里格气田的开发做好准备，并且调控某些为了将弗里格气田的天然气，通过以运输为目的即将建设的两条管道，输送至联合王国所产生的问题；

希望促进弗里格设备和两条管道在弗里格气田停产后继续使用；

希望对管道放弃做出规制；

遂达成如下约定。

第一部分　弗里格气田的开发及相关设备的使用

第一条

1. 弗里格气田的天然气以及由天然气产生的碳氢化合物（不包括天然气层下的石油，以及其他地层中的天然气和石油），在本协定中称"弗里格天然气"，应当作为一个整体，通过本协定附件 A 种所列的设备进行开发。除了在同一地点为了同一目的对设备进行更换外，双方政府应要求，没有两国政府的事先同意，不得使用任何其他设备。

2. 每个政府应要求，在本协定签字之日，本国的许可证持有人之间，以及其与另一国的许可证持有人之间，按照本协定达成协议管理开发事宜。这种协议应当得到两国政府的批准，并确保此协议与本协定冲突时本协定条款优先。许可证持有人可以在会计、运营以及其他开发专门事项上，达成补充协议。所有补充协议应于达成 45 日内，或于符合本协定规定的日期通知两国政府。两国政府一致同意为了共同开发的必要，也可以要求对这种协议进行修改或订立新协议。

3. 许可证持有人应提交关于本条第 2 款所指的协议的修正案，以获得两国的事先批准。如修正条款提交双方政府 45 日内，未收到一方或双方政府的否定性通知，则视为已获批准。

第二条

1. 双方政府应当以双方同意的方式，共同勘定 1965 年 3 月 10 日协定规定的分界线。继而为了有效实现本协定，双方应共同决定与边界线有关的每个设备的位置。

2. 双方政府应当就弗里格气田的界线、预估总储量，以及联合王国和挪威王国大陆架上天然气的分配达成一致。为此目的，许可证持有人应当向双方政府提交有关这些决定的建议。

3. 双方政府应该在弗里格气田开始生产前，尽最大努力就该气田的分配达成一致；如无法达成一致，则在此期间应当以许可证持有人对储量分配的建议为临时依据进行生产；如果没有此种建议，应将平均分配作为临时依据。这种临时性分配不应当影响任何一方政府的地位。当分配方案达成一致时，应被视为依据第三条做出的修改，代替临时分配方案。

4. 如果从生产开始后 12 个月内，双法政府无法就本条第 2 款的事项达成一致，有关问题应根据第二十八条的规定解决。

5. 基于安全要求，为了确定弗里格气田的界线、总储量或气田分配方案，一方政府的许可证持有人，按照第一条第 2 款所述的许可证持有人间的协议提出钻探申请时，任意一方政府不得拒绝批准。

第三条

1. 根据第二条一致同意或决定的，弗里格气田的界线、总储量、储量的分配，或者其他事项，经任意一方政府要求可在如下时间进行审查：

（d）在弗里格气田开始生产之日；

（e）生产开始后，每隔 4 年期满之日；

（f）被证明存在自然产生的含气储层，其气体在开始生产时就有可能流入弗里格气田，且提出要求的政府认为此种情形足以证明有复查的必要。

2. 如依第二条的决定或本条的修订，弗里格气田的界线内包含了一块大陆架区域，该区域内存在非第一条提及的协议合同方，但在决定或审查做出之日持有生产许可证的第三方，该第三方应当与这些协定的合同方在政府规定的时间内达成一项协议，协议的条款应当与第一条第 2 款保持一致，并得到双方政府的批准。

3. 根据第二条规定可以适用的事项，第二条第 2 和第 4 款的规定适用于本条所做的审查。许可证持有人应进行每一次审查所必需的操作，保证每次弗里格气田停止生产时，联合王国政府的许可证持有人和挪威王国许可证持有人享有的份额，均应与气田最终的分配份额保持一致。生产开始前，所有的审查应该基于弗里格气田的特性做出。当产生了气田总储量新的分配方案时，许可证持有人应就此新的分配方案制定条款，保证联合王国和挪威王国的许可证持有人分别接收弗里格气田的天然气，填补审查做出之前根据现有分配方案产生的缺额或盈余。所有的审查应自双方政府一致同意的审查之日或通过仲裁裁决之日起生效，视情况而定。

4. 在任何时候，如果有不属于弗里格气田的气体经证明流入气田，这些气体应该被视为弗里格天然气，根据本协定进行开发。在这种情形下，双方政府应一致协商决定：

（d）弗里格气田的总储量、这种额外的气体及其分配；

（e）开发这种额外气体所必须做出的后续安排；以及

（f）许可证持有人和持有额外气体生产许可证人之间，在气体开发问题上所需要做出的后续安排。

第四条

（1）每个政府应要求其各自的许可证持有人，提交一份为保证弗里格气田的高效运行而保护气田的计划，包括间隔不超过4年的审查条款，以及审查结果应当提交两国政府批准的条款。

（2）政府应当保证任何批准的计划得到执行。

第五条

为了保证弗里格气田按照本协定进行开发，双方许可证持有人应当协商，并经两国政府同意，指定一个联合经营人。

第六条

1. 根据安全需要，为了开发弗里格气田，任意一方政府应当保证所有设备间人员和物资的自由流动。

2. 根据安全需要，所有设备上的着陆设施（包括管道运行中的中间平台），应根据有关当局所做的安排，供船舶自由使用，也为了开展与开发弗里格有关活动，供具备任意一国国籍的航空器使用。

第七条

1. 双方政府应当与另一方政府就每个设备恰当的安全措施进行协商，应该尽可能保证所有设备达成统一的安全和建设标准。

2. 根据第二十九条管辖权的规定，各自政府都享有采取安全措施管理设备的最终决定权。关于穿过设备的管道，双方政府应当在协商之后，制定统一的安全措施,并责成各方的许可证持有人遵守。

3. 弗里格气田的无线通信设备的建立、运行以及设备的控制,应按照有关电信机构间的协议来进行。

第八条

1. 为了保证第七条的安全和建设标准得到遵守,双方政府同意进行协商并采取一切实现该目的的必要措施,包括授予观察员以监督实施各项设备安全和建设标准的职权;对建立在另一国大陆架上的设施,则按照本条第 3 和第 4 款进行。

2. 每个政府应当保证观察员包括另一国的观察员进入设备、设施,并向观察员提供对另一国在弗里格气田利益产生影响的所有相关信息。

3. 一国的观察员应当与另一国的观察员进行合作和协商,以保证每个设备的安全和建设标准得到遵守。特别是对于安装在另一国大陆架上的设备,一国的观察员应要求该国的观察员,在必要时行使其权利以保证标准得到遵守。如果两国的观察员之间存在分歧,或一国观察员拒绝另一国观察员采取行动的请求,所涉问题应提交两国主管当局解决。

4. 为了避免人员丧生或危害生命的伤亡或其他事故的发生,无论危险是否紧急,或为了减轻这种伤亡或事故的后果,而此时间和情形不允许两国的观察员进行协商,在任意一方政府的观察员认为必要或适当时,可以要求立即停止弗里格油气田内的部分或全部作业。同时,需要立即向两国主管当局报告这一命令的情况和原因,主管当局应随后就安全和迅速恢复作业必要的措施进行协商。

5. 两国政府的主管当局应就执行本条的方法进行协商。

第九条

如下所得的利润、收益和资本:

(a) 弗里格气田的开发;

(b) 用于开发弗里格气田的固定装置和设备;以及

(c) 使用或处置这种固定装置和设备;

应当按照以下法律征税——相应的联合王国的法律和挪威王国的法律;1985 年 10 月 3 日在奥斯陆签订的,避免双重征税以及防止所得税和资本税逃税漏税的公约;未来可能签订的该公约的修正案或者替代性公约。

第十条

每个政府都应当保证其许可证持有人不转让与其获得的与弗里格气田任何部分的生产许可有关的权利，也不能未经授权政府事先同意而授予其他人类似的权利。在给予这种同意前，授权国家应当与另一国进行协商。

第十一条

1. 在弗里格气田任何部分的任何生产许可，或者许可证的任何部分，期满、放弃或撤销的情形下，颁发许可证的国家应当保证，弗里格气田的勘探仍应按照本协定的规定继续进行，第一条所指的许可证持有人之间的，在期满、放弃或撤销之前的协议继续有效。特别是相关国家应当采取以下步骤：

（a）授予新的许可，取代期满、放弃或撤销的许可；或

（b）该国政府作为许可证持有人从事勘探工作；或

（c）采取两国同意的其他方式，继续勘探弗里格天然气。

2. 政府采取本条第1款规定的措施，应保证第一条规定的许可证持有人之间达成的协议符合补充协议的规定，此补充协议为采取这种措施的必要后果。

第十二条

1. 依据本协定，运用设备开发其他的碳氢化合物，不应对弗里格气田的开发活动产生有害影响。

2. 本协定的任何规定不应妨碍政府要求其许可证持有人以实物缴纳特许权使用费。

第二部分　管道的使用

第十三条

1. 向联合王国输送天然气，应当使用联合王国和挪威的管道。

2. 挪威的管道应当由依据挪威法律成立且住所位于挪威的法律实体所有。在民事和刑事诉讼、法庭选择和执行问题上，挪威管道的所有人应当受挪威法律和管辖权的约束。这也适用于挪威管道，及位于联合王国大陆架上发生的管道事故；同时，这也不应当排除根据联合王国冲突法的规定，联合王国法院的共享管辖权和联合王国法律的适用。

3. 位于联合王国领海、内水和陆地领土上的挪威管道部分，应该受联

合王国法律和管辖权约束。联合王国不能用不公平或歧视性收费或其他方式，或者施加会对运输产生实际妨害的要求，阻碍碳氢化合物通过挪威管道从挪威大陆架输送至联合王国。

4. 挪威管道的路线应当得到两国政府的批准。

5. 联合王国政府应当依据联合王国法律的规定，对涉及挪威管道的事项授予必要的许可和给予必要的同意。

6. 一国对与联合王国管道或挪威管道有关的事项给予许可证或同意时，该国应当将许可证或同意的副本送交另一国政府。

7. 在与另一国进行事先协商之前，一国政府不得对涉及联合王国管道或挪威管道授予的许可证或转让许可证的同意进行任何实质性的变更或修改。就与联合王国相关的挪威管道部分，联合王国不能授予任何许可证、同意或实质性变更、修改许可及同意，以防止损害挪威管道作为一个整体的统一的所有权、运行和安全安排。

第十四条

两国政府应当采取一切公开措施，确保本协定签订之日，管道的所有者之间达成一项协议来管理天然气的运输。这种协议需要两国政府的批准，并且列入如果该协议与本协定发生冲突，本协定规定优先的条款。管道的所有者可以在中间平台、陆上终端、会计程序以及其他天然气运输的特定事项上达成补充协定。双方政府可以要求在协议签订45日内，或本协定规定的其他日期，管道所有者将协议的内容通知两国政府，并可以要求在它们认为必要时制定协议的修正条款。双方政府可以要求，管道所有者将本条中提到的任何协议的任何修正，通知政府以获得双方政府的事先批准。凡需两国政府批准的协议或修正条款，在管道所有者向两国政府提出后45日内，如果没有收到一方或双方政府相反的通知，则被视为已获批准。

第十五条

为了保证联合王国管道和挪威王国管道的运行、维护和安全符合本协定规定，联合王国和挪威王国管道的所有人，应当经两国政府批准，任命一个管道经营者。

第十六条

1. 两国政府应当鼓励管道的最佳使用。在这方面，两国政府同意就关税和挪威管道使用的其他事项上的决定,应当基于对管道或部分管道使用的综合建议。关税和其他事项应仅由相关政府,在碳氢化合物进入全部或部分管道用于运输之时,批准或同意。

2. 两国政府同意,依照本条以下几款规定,可以使用管道输送其他碳氢化合物。

3. 双方政府应当采取措施,保证联合王国和挪威管道的所有人,在大陆架不同部分所产碳氢化合物的输送优先性条款,纳入第十四条所指的协议中,包括给予弗里格气田第一优先的条款,保证以实物偿付的特许权使用费,将给予弗里格气田中的碳氢化合物一样的输送优先权。

4. 为了促进本条第1、2、3款目的的实现,每国政府应当采取可能的措施帮助希望连接管道的人,或者希望进入任一管道以利用闲置输送能力的人,尽管此类连接和进入不应妨碍,运输一定数量的碳氢化合物管道的有效运行,包括那些通过连接点进入管道的碳氢化合物,只要其相应的所有人签署了运输合同。

5. 如果有人(以下称"申请人")想使用挪威管道的闲置输送能力,运输从联合王国大陆架上的气田生产的碳氢化合物,或者使用联合王国管道运输挪威大陆架上的气田生产的碳氢化合物,但是无法与管道所有人就使用管道的公平商业条款达成一致,申请人可以向相关国家申请使用管道。

6. 对于按照本条第5款提出的申请,相关国家应当与另一国协商,达成一个双方都能接受的对申请的回复。在对这项申请进行审议时,相关国家应当按照本条第3款,适用对所有相关方的非歧视和公平原则。双方政府在协商使用管道的问题时,应当全面处理和适当考虑:

(a) 管道和岸上终端可用的闲置输送能力,还要考虑所有者既存的合同义务和所有者在合理预期内可得到的使用权;

(b) 通过管道运输的碳氢化合物和承诺运输的碳氢化合物,技术上的兼容性;

(c) 相关的经济因素,包括拟议合同相关的费用、类似关税以及其他管道使用的情形;

(d) 应采取措施以防止危及供应安全,或对安全和环境带来不利影响;

（e）申请人的技术能力和经济能力；

（f）相关国家提出的其他相关事项。

7. 相关国家进行这种协商之后，在申请者认为其对管道使用的申请遭到了不合理的拒绝或者是没有向申请人提供公平的商业条件时，政府应当要求管道的所有者，在其指明的条款和条件下，运送申请者的碳氢化合物。按照本条第 6 款进行协商后，相关政府应至少于向申请者传达其决定 21 日前，向另一国政府传达其准备做出的决定。

8. 如果两国政府无法就对申请人的答复，达成相互接受的一致，任意一方政府有权依据第二十八条，就相关政府是否履行本条，尤其是本条第 6 和第 7 款下的义务，提交仲裁裁决。

第十七条

1. 双方政府应当就两条管道共同的建设和安全标准进行协商，并要求管道所有者遵守该标准。

2. 两条管道相关的无线通信设施的建设、运行和设备的控制，应遵守主管电信当局达成的协议。与两条管道相关的其他通信系统，应当尽可能遵守共同的设计标准。如果无法实施共同标准，双方政府的标准应当协调一致。

3. 在联合王国管道建设期间安装的，供联合王国和挪威王国管道使用，或者将供两国使用的设备，或者仅供挪威王国管道使用的设备，联合王国政府应当与挪威王国政府协商确定适用该设备的安全标准。

第十八条

1. 联合王国政府和挪威王国政府应当各自指派人员作为观察员，协助各自政府确保管道建设和安全运行的标准得到执行。

2. 联合王国政府和挪威王国政府应当采取步骤，保证另一国政府指定的观察员可以进入联合王国管道和挪威王国管道。

3. 为了避免人员丧生或危害生命的伤亡或其他事故的发生，无论危险是否紧急，或为了减少这种伤亡或事故的后果，而时间和情形不允许两国的观察员进行协商，在任意一方政府的观察员认为必要或适当时，可以要求立即停止联合王国或/和挪威王国管道的部分或全部作业。同时，需要立即向两国主管当局报告这一命令的情况和原因，主管当局应随后就安全和迅速恢复作业必要的措施进行协商。

4. 第八条第 3 和第 5 款适用于本条对管道的监督，就如它们适用于第 8 条下对设备的监督。

第十九条

1. 两国政府愿意就对于除本条第 2 款所指的许可证持有人以外的人，所享有的弗里格天然气，在公平的商业关税的基础上，通过管道进行运输。如果此种气体是从挪威王国大陆架上开采而通过联合王国管道输送，或者从联合王国大陆架上开采而通过挪威王国管道输送，双方政府应采取公开措施，保证管道所有者遵守两国政府批准的关税政策。

2. 本款第 1 款所指的许可证持有人是指：道达尔海上石油有限公司（Total Oil Marine Limited），爱尔夫石油勘探开发（联合王国）有限公司（Elf Oil Exploration and Production (UK) Limited），阿奎泰恩石油（联合王国）有限公司（Aquitaine Oil (UK) Limited），（联合王国政府的许可证持有人），Elf Norge A/S, Aquitaine Norge A/S, Total Marine Norsk A/S, Norsk Hydro Produksjon a. s. and Den norske stats oljeselskap a. s. （挪威政府的许可证持有人）以及他们的继任者。

第二十条

就如下事项获得的利润、收益和资本：

（a）通过管道运输碳氢化合物；

（b）管道；以及

（c）处分管道或与之相关的利益；

应当按照以下法律征税——相应的联合王国的法律和挪威王国的法律；包括 1985 年 10 月 3 日在奥斯陆签订的，避免双重征税以及防止所得税和资本税逃税漏税的公约，或未来可能签订的该公约的修正案或者替代性公约。

第二十一条

1. 管道的任何许可证在期满、放弃或撤销的情形下，颁发许可证的国家应当保证，两国政府同意所涉管道应继续使用和运行。此种使用和运行，根据本协定及本协定第十四条规定的管道所有人之间协议，在期满、放弃或撤销之前，继续进行。特别是相关政府应当采取以下步骤：

（a）授予新的许可，取代期满、放弃或撤销的许可；或

（b）该国政府自行使用和运行管道；或

（c）采取两国同意的其他方式，继续使用和运行管道。

2. 政府采取本条第1款的措施后，应保证作为这种措施的必要后果，第十四条所指的管道所有人之间的协议应作为补充协议。

3. 如果联合王国管道所属的联合王国政府，或者挪威管道所属的挪威王国政府，认为由于技术、经济或者其他原因，管道的继续运行不再可行，则需要与另一国政府协商；并尽最大努力保证此种情形下，另一国政府在公平的基础和条件上，有权接管其认为碳氢化合物运输所必需的那部分管道的运行。

4. 根据本条第3款，接管管道或部分管道的政府应当保证，管道所有人或其他人应当移除或隔离两国政府一致同意移除或隔离的，不再使用的某部分管道。根据本条规定，按照本条接管运行的管道或部分管道的国家，应当被看作相关国家。关于以后放弃全部或部分管道，应当比照本条第5~12款适用。

5. 根据本条第3和第5款，管道所有人应该至少于拟开始放弃两年前，向相关政府联合提交一个计划（以下简称"计划"），列明应当采取的与管道放弃或部分放弃有关的措施。

6. 不影响本条第5款一般性原则的前提下，计划应当包括：

（a）拟议措施费用评估；

（b）列明关于拟议措施和采取措施时间的细节，或者是决定如何确定时间的条款。

7. 考虑到管道间的相互联系和位置的邻近，需要采取一个一致的方法来处理放弃事宜，相关的政府在对提交的计划做出决定之前，应当与另一个政府进行协商，达成相互接受的对拟议措施的回复。双方政府在进行与全部或部分管道放弃有关的协商时，应全面处理和适当考虑：

（a）可获取的最佳的符合成本效益的技术；

（b）经济因素；

（c）可适用的国际标准和指导规则；

（d）与放弃有关的安全隐患，包括相关的运输和处置；

（e）航行安全；

（f）拟议措施对环境的影响；

（g）拟议措施对海上其他活动的影响；

(h) 放弃的时间表；

(i) 拟议措施对其他管道继续运行和放弃的影响；

(j) 相关政府提出的其他事项。

8. 相关政府可以批准计划，可以修改也可以不做修改，可以附条件也可不附条件。在批准修改的计划或附条件的计划前，相关政府应当给予提交计划的所有人机会，对拟做的修改或条件进行陈述。

9. 对于位于联合王国领海、内水以及陆地领土上的挪威管道，联合王国政府应当确保，其对于提交的计划做出的任何决定带来的经济上的影响，对于挪威政府来说都是可接受的。

10. 相关政府对其是否批准或拒绝计划，以及批准是否要求实施的事项，应该不予延迟地做出决定。

11. 如果计划不被接受，相关政府应当通知所有者拒绝的原因。在此情形下，所有者应当被要求在双方政府接受的特定时间内，提交一份修改计划。

12. 如果两国政府无法就对申请人的答复达成相互接受的一致，任意一方政府有权依据二十八条，就相关政府是否履行本条，特别是第7款下的义务，提交仲裁裁决。

第三部分　一般条款

第二十二条

1. 在弗里格气田产生的，以及依据本协定在其他碳氢化合物的开发中产生的天然气气体量、液体量以及确定碳氢化合物组成的测量系统，应当能够分别测量运输至陆上的天然气和液体的量，气田和个别泵站上消耗的量，火炬平台上燃烧或排出的量。这个系统应当遵守两国政府相关当局间的协议。这个系统的设计、安装和运行的方式应当告知许可证持有人。两国政府有关当局应当就测量系统的设计、安装和运行的监督事项，制订一个共同计划且为此目的，有关当局的代表应有权进入这个系统的所有部分。

2. 如果双方政府在决定使用设备上的设施运输碳氢化合物的量，或者允许进入管道的制度上享有合法利益，这种制度应该由两国政府的有关当局达成一致。

3. 两国政府应当就对测量系统进行经常性调试达成一致，并且应当在双方确定的间隔期间，交换第二条第 1 款所指的边界线两侧与生产有关的弗里格气田和其他开采的碳氢化合物的生产记录，以及输送至陆地的气量记录。

第二十三条

双方政府应当在协商后，共同或分别地尽一切努力确保任何设备和管道的运行，不会引起海洋环境的污染，或因污染损害任何国家的海岸线、海洋设备或设施，或者渔船、渔具。双方政府的有关当局应该制定紧急情况下执行本条的程序。

第二十四条

1. 双方政府应当采取措施保证自然人雇佣合同，无论是联合经营人还是管道经营人依据本协定为任何目的签订的，应受许可证持有人为雇佣者的国家法律的管辖，但是不影响雇员选择其他法律的自由。

2. 双方政府应保证，所有的雇员都享有社会保险福利，且每个雇员只享受守一种社会福利体系。

3. 双方政府应保证，关于雇员保护和福利的其他法律，适用于弗里格气田作为单一整体的开发，以及按照本协定进行的设备和管道的运行。

4. 对于弗里格气田或任何设备和管道，在社会安全、雇员福利以及劳动关系领域内，对涉及共同利益管理的事项，双方政府可以做出个别安排。

5. 本条的任何规定不损害或影响，在本协定签订之日已经存在的，本条第 4 款所涉事项的相关安排。

第二十五条

1. 在许可证适当限制的范围内，一国政府可以不向另一国政府提供许可证持有人向政府提供的本协定中许可经营的信息。如果提供给政府的信息是保密的，政府应当视为保密信息，任何进一步的披露应当符合相关许可的限制。但是，为安排弗里格气田内活动，以及为开采和运输碳氢化合物而使用设备和管道情况的综合报告，每个政府有权在任何时候使用这些信息。

2. 一国政府发表的综合报告或声明的复印件（包括新闻稿），应该至少在公布日期之前送达另一个政府。

第二十六条

本协定或者第一条和第十四条所指协议的任何内容,都不应当影响一国政府行使或两国政府共同行使,在国内和国际紧急情况发生时的特别权力。两国政府应当尽早进行协商,以达成合适的共同措施,使紧急情况下不损害它们在最有效开发弗里格天然气以及利用设备和管道上的共同利益。

第二十七条

为了促进本协定的实施,两国政府各指派三个人共六人组成委员会,并命名为弗里格气田咨询委员会,以促进本协定的实施。委员会的职能应包括审议两国政府提交的问题,委员会程序性的规则由两国政府一致同意的后续安排来规定。

第二十八条

1. 任何与本协定解释和适用有关争端,或者依第一条第 2 款和第十四条所指的许可证持有人间的协议提交两国政府解决的其他事项,应当通过弗里格咨询委员会解决,或者由两国政府协商解决。

2. 如果争端无法通过这种方式解决,或者通过两国政府同意的其他程序解决,应当在任何一国的要求下,将争端提交仲裁庭解决。仲裁庭组成如下:

每个政府指定一名仲裁员,这两名仲裁员选定第三名仲裁员。第三名仲裁员不能是联合王国或挪威王国的国民或居民,且应作为仲裁主席。如果仲裁要求提出后三个月内,任意一国政府没有指定一名仲裁员,任意一国政府可以请求国际法院主席指定一名仲裁员。如果在第二名仲裁员指定后一个月内,没有选出第三名仲裁员,则适用同样的程序。仲裁庭应当决定自己的程序规则,在无法全体一致达成决议时,仲裁决议应由仲裁庭成员的多数票达成。仲裁庭的决议对两国政府具有约束力,为了实现本协定的目的,决议应当被视为两国政府间协议。

第二十九条

1. 本协定的任意条款不应当解释为,影响每个国家按照国际法对本国的大陆架享有的管辖权。特别是,位于联合王国大陆架上的设备应属于联合王国管辖,位于挪威大陆架上的设备应当属于挪威管辖。

2. 本协定的任何内容也不应当解释为,影响或限制任何一国法律的适用，或任何一国的法庭按照国际法行使管辖权。

第三十条

根据本协定规定，除非另有要求：

1. "弗里格气田"是指，在海底约 1955 米深处，海床下较低的始新世时代，自然产生的含天然气砂岩地层。气田位于北纬 59°53′纬线和 1965 年 3 月 10 日两国关于大陆架划界协定中规定的边界线的交叉点处。气田共有附件 B 中的 4 个油井，并包括在开始生产时，可以流入以上含天然气砂岩地层的其他含气地层。

2. "设备"是指，在弗里格气田开发活动中，在海床上安装的任何结构或装置，包括管道。设备不包括下文规定的挪威管道和联合王国管道。"设备"指两个或多个设备。

3. "许可证持有人"包括：联合王国政府的许可证持有人——Total Oil Marine Limited，Elf Oil Exploration and Production（UK）Limited，Aquitaine Oil（UK）Limited；挪威政府的许可证持有人——Elf Norge A/S，Aquitaine Norge A/S，Total Marine Norsk A/S，Norsk Hydro Produksjon a. s. and Den norske stats oljeselskap a. s.，以及它们的继任者。除上述外，还包括任意一国政府为了开发某一部分弗里格气田而不时授予的许可证持有人，以及代替上述部分或全部的许可证持有人的法人。

4. "其他的碳氢化合物"是指产生于弗里格气田之外的石油层的任何气态或液态的碳氢化合物，除了本协定第三条第 4 款所指的其他气体。

5. "联合经营人"和"管道经营人"包括根据第一条、第五条、第十四条所指的协议行事的公司。

6. "挪威管道"指的是即将建造并运行的管道，该管道从挪威大陆架上弗里格气田平台上的入口法兰，延伸至圣弗格斯的陆地测量仪器，并包括中间平台上服务于管道的相关设备。

7. "联合王国管道"指的是即将建造并运行的管道，该管道从联合王国大陆架上弗里格气田平台上的入口法兰，延伸至圣弗格斯的陆地测量仪器，并包括中间平台上为管道提供服务的相关设备。

8. "管道"是指挪威管道或联合王国管道。所有管道是指挪威管道和联合王国管道。

9. "相关国家"是指与挪威和联合王国大陆架上，与部分挪威管道所有事项有关的挪威王国政府,以及与(a)联合王国管道;(b)位于联合王国领海、内水和陆地领土上的部分挪威管道,所有事项有关的联合王国政府。

第三十一条

1. 本协定应于双方政府相互通知本国国内所有条件已成就时生效。

2. 双方政府可以在任何时候经一致同意修改或终止本协定。任何一方政府可以在任何时候,要求就本协定的修正进行协商。应在要求提出后两个月内开始协商,且应迅速而有效地进行。为了在最短的时间内达成双方都可接受的解决方案,双方政府的这种协商应当全面处理和适当考虑修正建议案。

附件 A
设备

3. 在挪威王国的大陆架上:

(c) 一个钻井平台

(d) 一个综合的处理和压缩平台

4. 在联合王国的大陆架上:

(e) 一个钻井平台

(f) 一个处理平台

(g) 一个宿舍平台

(h) 一个火炬塔

附件 B

国家	钻井编号	地理位置
挪威	25/1-1	北纬59°53′17.09″ 东经02°04′42.7″
挪威	25/1-2	北纬59°56′08″ 东经02°04′54.6″
挪威	25/1-3	北纬59°54′05″ 东经02°10′08″
英国	10/1-1A	北纬59°50′10.5″ 东经02°00′34.5″

4. Agreement between the Government of the United Kingdom of Great Britain and Northern Ireland and the Government of the Kingdom of Norway Relating to the Amendment of the Agreement of 10 May 1976 Relating to the Exploitation of the Frigg Field Reservoir and the Transmission of Gas therefrom to the United Kingdom

The Agreement of 10 May 1976 between the Government of the United Kingdom of Great Britain and Northern Ireland and the Government of the Kingdom of Norway relating to the Exploitation of the Frigg Field Reservoir and the Transmission of Gas therefrom to the United Kingdom shall continue in force subject to the amendments incorporated into the revised text which is set out in the Schedule hereto.

This Agreement shall enter into force on the date on which the two Governments shall have informed each other that all necessary internal requirements have been fulfilled.

In witness whereof the undersigned, duly authorised by their respective Governments, have signed this Agreement.

Done in duplicate at Stavanger this 25th day of August 1998 in the English and Norwegian languages, both texts being equally authoritative.

For the Government of the United Kingdom of Great Britain and Northern Ireland:

JOHN BATTLE

For the Government of the Kingdom of Norway:

MARIT ARNSTAD

Agreement between the Government of the United Kingdom of Great Britain and Northern Ireland and the Government of the Kingdom of Norway Relating to the Amendment of the Agreement of 10 May 1976 Relating to the Exploitation of the Frigg Field Reservoir and the Use of the Installations and Pipe – lines for the Exploitation and Transmission of Hydrocarbons

The Government of the United Kingdom of Great Britain and Northern Ireland and the Government of the Kingdom of Norway;

Considering that the drilling in the Continental Shelf appertaining to the United King – dom and in the Continental Shelf appertaining to the Kingdom of Norway has proved the existence of a gas reservoir, now named the Frigg Field Reservoir, which extends across the dividing line as defined in the Agreement of 10 March 1965 between the two Governments relating to the Delimitation of the Continental Shelf between the two countries;

Having regard to Article 4 of the said Agreement under which the two Governments have undertaken, in consultation with the licensees, to seek agreement as to the manner in which any such field shall be most effectively exploited and the manner in which the proceeds deriving therefrom shall be apportioned;

Desiring, before production commences, to make provision for the exploitation of the Frigg Field Reservoir as a single unit, and to regulate certain further questions which will arise in connection with the transmission of the gas from the Frigg Field Reservoir to the United Kingdom by two pipelines to be built for this purpose;

Desiring to facilitate the continued use of the Frigg installations and the two Pipelines after the cessation of production from the Frigg Field Reservoir;

Desiring to make provision for the abandonment of the two Pipelines; Have agreed as follows:

PART I EXPLOITATION OF THE FRIGG FIELD RESERVOIR AND USE OF FRIGG INSTALLATIONS

Article 1

1. The gas in the Frigg Field Reservoir and the hydrocarbons produced with or from the gas (excluding oil underlying the gas and gas and oil in other horizons), referred to in this Agreement as "Frigg Gas", shall be exploited as a single unit by means of installations specified in Annex A to this Agreement, and except that those installations may be replaced from time to time by installations for a similar purpose on a similar location, the Governments shall require that no other installations are used without prior consent of both Governments.

2. Each Government shall require those who are its licensees to enter into agreements between themselves and the licensees of the other Government to regulate in accordance with this Agreement the exploitation of Frigg Gas and the use of the Installations for other hydrocarbons, which agreements require the approval of the two Governments, and incorporate provisions to ensure that in the event of a conflict between any of those agreements and this Agreement the terms of this Agreement shall prevail. The licensees may supplement the agreements so concluded by agreements in respect of accounting, operating and other matters, and the terms of all such supplementary agreements shall be notified to the two Governments within 45 days of their conclusion or the date of this Agreement as the case may be and the two Governments may require amendments or such further agreements to be made as the Governments agree to be necessary.

3. The licensees shall be required to submit any proposed amendment to any of the agreements mentioned in paragraph (2) of this Article for the prior approval of the two Governments which approval may be deemed to have been given unless the licensees have been notified to the contrary by one or both Governments within 45 days of the submission to both Governments.

Article 2

1. The Governments shall jointly demarcate, in a manner to be agreed, the dividing line defined in the Agreement of 10 March 1965, and shall thereafter jointly determine the position of each Installation when in place in relation to the dividing line, with conclusive effect for the purposes of this Agreement.

2. The two Governments shall consult with a view to agreeing a determination of the limits and estimated total reserves of the Frigg Field Reservoir and an apportionment of the reserves therein as between the Continental Shelf appertaining to the United Kingdom and the Continental Shelf appertaining to the Kingdom of Norway. For this purpose the licensees shall be required to submit to the Governments a proposal for such determinations.

3. The two Governments shall endeavour to agree the apportionment of the reserves of the Frigg Field Reservoir before production of the reserves commences. If they are not able to do so, then pending such agreement, the production shall proceed on the provisional basis of a proposal for the apportionment submitted by the licensees, or, if there is none, on the provisional basis of equal shares. Such provisional apportionment shall be without prejudice to the position of either Government. When the apportionment is agreed, the agreed apportionment shall be substituted for the provisional apportionment as if the agreed apportionment were a revision made under Article 3.

4. If the two Governments are unable to reach agreement on any of the matters which fall to be agreed under paragraph (2) of this Article within 12 months from the date of the commencement of production, the question shall be settled in accordance with the provisions of Article 28.

5. Subject to requirements of safety, neither Government shall withhold a permit for the drilling of wells by, or on account of, licensees of the other Government, in conformity with those agreements mentioned in paragraph (2) of Article 1 between the licensees, for purposes related to the determination of the limits of the Frigg Field Reservoir, the total amount of reserves therein or the apportionment of the reserves.

(六) 1976 年英国与挪威共同开发弗里格天然气案

Article 3

1. The limits of the Frigg Field Reservoir and the total amount of the reserves and the apportionment of the reserves or any of them when agreed or determined under Article 2 shall be reviewed if either Government so requests:

(a) at the date of commencement of production of Frigg Gas;

(b) at the expiry of every period of four years after that date;

(c) at any other time when naturally occurring gas – bearing reservoirs are proved to contain gas which was capable of flowing into the Frigg Field Reservoir at the start of production, and the Government making the request considers that the circumstances are of sufficient importance to justify a revision.

2. If, as a result of a determination under Article 2 or a revision under this Article, the limits of the Frigg Field Reservoir include an area of the Continental Shelf in respect of which a person not a party to any agreements mentioned in Article 1 subsisting at the date of the determination or revision, as the case may be, holds a production licence, that person and the licensees who are parties to those agreements shall be required to enter into an agreement, within such time as the Governments shall stipulate, the terms of which shall conform to the provisions of paragraph (2) of Article 1 and shall be subject to the approval of the two Governments.

3. The provisions of paragraphs (2) and (4) of Article 2 shall apply to revisions under this Article as those provisions apply to matters to be agreed pursuant to Article 2. The licensees shall be required to conduct all operations necessary for each revision and to secure that at the time the production from the Frigg Field Reservoir ceases the share in the total volume of Frigg Gas received by the licensees of the Government of the United Kingdom and the share thereof received by the licensees of the Government of the Kingdom of Nor – way shall each correspond to the final apportionment of the reserves in place. All revisions shall be based upon the characteristics of the Frigg Field Reservoir before commencement of production. Whenever a revision results in a new apportionment of the total amount of the reserves, such revisions shall make such provision as between the licensees as will ensure that the licensees of the Governments of the United King-

dom and Norway respectively receive deliveries of Frigg Gas such that any surplus or deficiency resulting from deliveries made under the apportionment in force immediately before such revision is made good. All revisions shall have effect from the date that revision has been agreed by both Governments or settled by arbitration, as the case may be.

4. If, at any time gas which is not part of the Frigg Field Reservoir is proved to be flowing into the Reservoir, such gas shall be exploited under the provisions of this Agreement as if it were Frigg Gas. In these circumstances the two Governments shall consult with a view to determining:

(a) the total amount of the reserves of the Frigg Field Reservoir and such other gas and the apportionment thereof;

(b) any consequential arrangements which need to be made for the exploitation of such other gas; and

(c) any consequential arrangements which need to be made between the licensees and the persons who hold production licences relating to such other gas, regarding its exploitation.

Article 4

1. Each Government shall require its licensees to submit for the approval of the two Governments a scheme to secure the conservation of the Frigg Field Reservoir for productive operations, with provision for review at intervals of not more than four years, the results of which shall be submitted to the two Governments for approval.

2. The Governments shall ensure that any approved scheme is implemented.

Article 5

For the purposes of the exploitation of Frigg Gas and other hydrocarbons in accordance with this Agreement a Unit Operator shall be appointed by agreement between the licensees, subject to the approval of the two Governments.

Article 6

1. Subject to the requirements of safety, each Government shall ensure the free movement of all persons and materials between all Installations for the purposes of the exploitation and transmission of Frigg Gas and other hydrocarbons under

this Agreement.

2. Subject to the requirements of safety, the landing facilities on every Installation (including intermediate platforms involved in the operation of the Pipelines) shall be freely available to vessels and, in accordance with any arrangements which may be concluded between the competent authorities, available to aircraft of the nationality of either State for the purposes of activities connected with the exploitation and transmission of Frigg Gas and other hydrocarbons under this Agreement.

Article 7

1. The two Governments shall consult one another with a view to agreeing appropriate safety measures for each Installation and with a view to ensuring that all Installations are as far as possible subject to uniform safety and construction standards.

2. Each Government shall have the final right to determine the safety measures which are to govern the Installations under its jurisdiction as set out in Article 29. With respect to pipelines crossing the dividing line between Installations, the two Governments shall, after consultations, formulate joint safety measures and shall require compliance therewith by their respective licensees.

3. The establishment, operation and control of equipment for radio communications for the Frigg Field Reservoir and for the use of the Installations for any purpose under this Agreement, shall be subject to agreement between the competent authorities.

Article 8

1. With a view to ensuring compliance with the safety and construction standards referred to in Article 7, the Governments agree to consult and to take all necessary steps to that end, including the conferment on their inspectors of functions with respect to such safety and construction standards on or about the Installations; their powers in respect of Installations located on the Continental Shelf appertaining to the other State being those specified in paragraphs (3) and (4) of this Article.

2. Each Government shall procure access for such inspectors including the

inspectors of the other Government to Installations and equipment, and production to those inspectors of all relevant information affecting the interest of the other Government in the Frigg Field Reservoir or in the exploitation of other hydrocarbons under this Agreement.

3. The inspectors of each Government shall act in co – operation and consult with inspectors of the other Government with a view to achieving compliance with the safety and construction standards applicable to each Installation and in particular an inspector of one Government may, with regard to an Installation located on the Continental Shelf appertaining to the other State, request an inspector of the Government of that other State to exercise his powers to ensure such compliance whenever it appears that circumstances so warrant. In the event of any disagreement between the Inspectors of the two Governments or the refusal of the inspector of the one Government to take action at the request of the inspector of the other, the matter shall be referred to the competent authorities of both Governments.

4. If it appears to an inspector of either Government to be necessary or expedient for the purpose of averting a casualty or other accident involving loss of life or danger to life suffered by a person, whether the danger is immediate or not, or minimising the consequences of such a casualty or other accident, and time and circumstances do not permit consultation between the inspectors of the two Governments, that inspector may order the immediate cessation of any or all operations in the Frigg Field or in relation to the exploitation of other hydrocarbons on the Installations provided the fact of such an order and the reason therefor is reported immediately to the competent authorities of both Governments who shall then consult to consider the actions necessary for the safe and speedy resumption of operations.

5. The competent authorities of the two Governments shall consult with each other to agree on methods to implement this Article.

Article 9

Profits, gains and capital in respect of:

(a) the exploitation of the Frigg Field Reservoir;

(b) fixed installations and equipment used for the exploitation of the Frigg Field Reservoir; and

(c) the disposal or use of such fixed installations and equipment shall be taxed in accordance with the laws of the United Kingdom and the Kingdom of Norway respectively, including the Convention for the Avoidance of Double Taxation and the Prevention of Fiscal Evasion with respect to Taxes on Income and Capital signed at Oslo on 3rd October 1985 and any Protocol or Protocols to that Convention or any Convention replacing that Convention as may be signed in the future.

Article 10

Each Government shall ensure that its licensees shall not transfer any of the rights granted by virtue of any production licence relating to any part of the Frigg Field Reservoir and shall not grant the like rights to any other person without the prior consent of the licensing Government. Before granting its consent, the licensing Government shall consult with the other Government.

Article 11

1. In the event of the expiration, surrender or revocation of any production licence or any part of such a licence relating to any part of the Frigg Field Reservoir, the Government which issued the licence shall ensure that the exploitation of Frigg Gas is continued in accordance with the terms of this Agreement and the agreements between the licensees referred to in Article 1 subsisting immediately before such expiration, surrender or revocation. In particular the Government concerned shall take one of the following steps:

(a) issue a new licence in replacement of the licence which has expired, been surrendered or revoked; or

(b) itself conduct such exploitation as if it were a licensee; or

(c) take such other action to continue the exploitation of the Frigg Gas as the two Governments may agree.

2. The Government taking action as described in paragraph (1) of this Article shall procure that the agreements between the licensees referred to in Article 1 shall be the subject of such supplementary agreements as are necessary conse-

quent upon the action taken.

Article 12

1. The use of any Installation for the exploitation of other hydrocarbons shall not adversely affect the exploitation of Frigg Gas in accordance with this Agreement.

2. Nothing in this Agreement shall preclude either Government from requiring of their licensees that royalty be paid in kind.

PART II USE OF THE PIPELINES

Article 13

1. For the transmission of Frigg Gas to the United Kingdom, use shall be made of the United Kingdom Pipeline and the Norwegian Pipeline.

2. The Norwegian Pipeline shall be owned by Norwegian legal entities incorporated under the law of the Kingdom of Norway and having their domicile in Norway. The owners of the Norwegian Pipeline shall be subject to Norwegian law and jurisdiction as regards civil and criminal proceedings, forum and enforcement. This shall also apply in relation to the Norwegian Pipeline and incidents pertaining thereto in respect of those parts of the Norwegian Pipeline located on the Continental Shelf appertaining to the United Kingdom; it being understood, however, that this shall not exclude the concurrent jurisdiction of the United Kingdom Courts and the application of the laws of the United Kingdom subject to the rules of the laws of the United Kingdom governing the conflict of laws.

3. Those parts of the Norwegian Pipeline located in the territorial sea, internal waters and on the land territory of the United Kingdom shall be subject to United Kingdom law and jurisdiction. The United Kingdom shall neither impede by means of an unfair or discriminatory charge or in any other way, nor impose any requirements which have the practical effect of hampering the transmission of hydrocarbons from the Norwegian Continental Shelf to the United Kingdom through the Norwegian Pipeline.

4. The route of the Norwegian Pipeline shall be subject to the approval of both Governments.

5. The Government of the United Kingdom shall, in accordance with and subject to the laws of the United Kingdom, grant any necessary licences and give any necessary consents concerning the Norwegian Pipeline.

6. A Government shall on granting a licence or giving a consent in relation to either the United Kingdom Pipeline or the Norwegian Pipeline make available a copy of that licence or consent to the other Government.

7. A Government shall not substantially alter or modify a licence or consent to the assignment of a licence relating to the United Kingdom Pipeline or the Norwegian Pipeline without prior consultation with the other Government. In respect of that part of the Norwegian Pipeline for which it is the relevant Government, the Government of the United Kingdom shall not grant any licenses or consents or substantially alter or modify a licence or consent so as to prevent there being unified ownership, operating and safety arrangements for the Norwegian Pipeline as a whole.

Article 14

The two Governments shall take whatever measures are open to them with the aim of securing that the owners of the Pipelines enter into an agreement between themselves to regulate in accordance with this Agreement the transmission of hydrocarbons, and that such agreement requires the approval of the two Governments, and incorporates provisions to ensure that in the event of a conflict between that agreement and this Agreement the terms of this Agreement shall prevail. The owners of the Pipelines may supplement the agreement so concluded by agreements in respect of the intermediate platform (s), the onshore terminal, accounting procedure and other matters relating to the transmission of hydrocarbons. The two Governments may request to be notified of the terms of such supplementary agreements within 45 days of their conclusion or the date of this Agreement as the case may be and may request that amendments or such further agreements be made as they agree to be necessary. The two Governments may request to be notified of any proposed amendments to any of the agreements mentioned in this Article for prior approval by the two Governments. Where any approval is required of the two Governments the same shall be deemed to have been given unless the owners have been notified to the contrary by one or both Governments within 45 days of the submission to both Governments.

Article 15

For the purposes of the operation of the United Kingdom Pipeline and the Norwegian Pipeline in accordance with this Agreement and their maintenance and safety, a Pipeline Operator shall be appointed by agreement between the owners of the United Kingdom Pipeline and the owners of the Norwegian Pipeline, subject to the approval of the two Governments.

Article 16

1. The two Governments shall encourage the optimal use of the Pipelines. In this respect, the Governments agree that any decision they make on tariffs and other terms for the use of the Norwegian Pipeline shall be based on integrated proposals for the use of that Pipeline or part thereof, as appropriate, and that tariffs and other terms may only be determined or approved by the relevant Government at the point of entry of hydrocarbons into that Pipeline for their transmission throughout the whole length of the Pipeline or part thereof.

2. The two Governments agree that, subject to the following paragraphs of this Article, other hydrocarbons may be transmitted through the Pipelines.

3. The two Governments shall take measures to secure that the owners of the Pipelines include in the agreements referred to in Article 14 provisions regarding priorities in the transmission of other hydrocarbons, including provisions for giving first priority to Frigg Gas and securing that royalty taken in kind is given the same priority of transmission as hydrocarbons from the field from which royalty is taken in kind.

4. In furtherance of the aims set out in paragraphs (1), (2) and (3) of this Article, each Government shall take such measures as may be available to it to assist persons wishing to connect pipelines or otherwise obtain access to either of the Pipelines to make use of any spare capacity, provided that any such connection or access shall not prejudice the efficient operation of the Pipeline (s) for the transmission of quantities of hydrocarbons, including those entering the Pipeline (s) through connections, which their respective owners have at any

time contracted to carry.

5. Where a person desires to use spare capacity in the Norwegian Pipeline for landing hydrocarbons produced from reservoirs on the United Kingdom Continental Shelf or to use the United Kingdom Pipeline in relation to hydrocarbons produced from reservoirs on the Norwegian Continental Shelf (hereinafter referred to as the "applicant"), but is unable to agree fair commercial terms for the use of the Pipeline with the owner of the Pipeline, the applicant may apply to the relevant Government requesting access.

6. When an application is made under paragraph (5) of this Article, the relevant Government shall consult the other Government with a view to agreeing a mutually acceptable response to such an application. When considering such an application the relevant Government shall, subject to paragraph (3) of this Article, apply the principles of nondiscrimination and fairness for all parties concerned. In undertaking consultation concerning such access to the Pipelines the Governments shall address fully and take proper account of:

(a) the spare capacity available in the Pipeline and at the onshore terminal, allowing for the owner's existing contractual obligations and usage which the owners may reasonably be expected to require;

(b) the technical compatibility of hydrocarbons proposed for transmission through the Pipeline with the hydrocarbons contracted for transmission therein;

(c) relevant economic factors including costs relevant to the contract proposed, comparable tariffs and other conditions applied to the use of the Pipeline;

(d) the need not to endanger security of supply or prejudice safety and environmental measures;

(e) the technical capability and financial viability of the applicant;

(f) other relevant matters raised by the relevant Government.

7. If after such consultation the relevant Government is satisfied that capacity in the Pipeline has been unreasonably refused or that fair commercial terms have not been offered to the applicant, that Government shall require the owner to convey the applicant's hydrocarbons subject to such terms and conditions as it may specify. Following the consultation provided for in paragraph (6) of this Ar-

ticle, and at least 21 days before conveying its decision to the applicant, the relevant Government shall communicate to the other Government the response it intends to make to the applicant.

8. If the two Governments are unable to agree a mutually acceptable response to an application, either Government shall have the right to submit to arbitration in accordance with Article 28 the question of whether or not the relevant Government has met its obligations under this Article, particularly paragraphs (6) and (7).

Article 17

1. The two Governments shall consult one another with a view to agreeing common construction and safety standards for the Pipelines and shall require the owners of the Pipelines to comply with those standards.

2. The establishment, operation and control of equipment for radio communications relating respectively to the Pipelines shall be subject to agreement between the competent authorities. Other communications systems relating to the two Pipelines shall as far as possible be subject to common standards of design. Where it is not possible to impose common standards, the standards imposed by each Government shall be compatible.

3. If equipment is installed during the construction of the United Kingdom Pipeline and serves or is intended to serve both the United Kingdom Pipeline and the Norwegian Pipeline, or serves the Norwegian Pipeline only, the Government of the United Kingdom shall consult the Government of the Kingdom of Norway on the safety standards which are to apply to that equipment.

Article 18

1. The Government of the United Kingdom and the Government of the Kingdom of Norway shall each appoint persons to be inspectors and agree a joint scheme for the purpose of assisting their respective Governments in securing compliance with the standards for the proper construction and safe operation of Pipelines.

2. The relevant Government shall take such steps as are available to it to secure for inspectors appointed by the other, assess to the Pipelines.

3. If it appears to an inspector of either Government to be necessary or expedient for the purposes of averting a casualty or other accident involving loss of life or danger to life suffered by a person, whether the danger is immediate or not, or minimising the consequences of such a casualty or other accident, and time and circumstances do not permit consultation between the inspectors of the two Governments, that inspector may order the immediate cessation of any or all operations in relation to the United Kingdom Pipeline or the Norwegian Pipeline or both, provided the fact of such an order and the reason therefor is reported immediately to the competent authorities of both Governments who shall then consult to consider the actions necessary for the safe and speedy resumption of operations.

4. Paragraphs (3) and (5) of Article 8 apply to the inspection of Pipelines under this Article as they apply to the inspection of Installations under Article 8.

Article 19

1. It is the intention of the two Governments that Frigg Gas belonging to persons other than the licensees referred to in paragraph (2) of this Article shall be transmitted through the Pipelines at fair commercial tariffs, and if such gas having been extracted from the Continental Shelf appertaining to the Kingdom of Norway is transmitted through the United Kingdom Pipeline, or having been extracted from the Continental Shelf appertaining to the United Kingdom is transmitted through the Norwegian Pipeline, the two Governments shall take such measures as are open to them to ensure that tariffs approved by the two Governments are observed by the owners of the Pipelines.

2. The licensees referred to in paragraph (1) of this Article are Total Oil Marine Limited, Elf Oil Exploration and Production (UK) Limited, Aquitaine Oil (UK) Limited (being licensees of the United Kingdom Government), Elf Norge A/S, Aquitaine Norge A/S, Total Marine Norsk A/S, Norsk Hydro Produksjon a. s. and Den norske stats oljeselskap as (being licensees of the Norwegian Government) and their successors.

Article 20

Profits, gains and capital in respect of: (a) the transmission of hydrocarbons through the Pipelines; (b) the Pipelines; and (c) the disposal of the

Pipelines or an interest therein shall be taxed in accordance with the laws of the United Kingdom and the Kingdom of Norway respectively, including the Convention for the Avoidance of Double Taxation and the Prevention of Fiscal Evasion with respect to Taxes on Income and Capital signed at Oslo on 3 October 1985 and any Protocol or Protocols to that Convention or any Convention replacing that Convention as may be signed in the future.

Article 21

1. In the event of the expiration, surrender or revocation of any licence relating to a Pipeline, the Government which issued the licence shall ensure that if the two Governments are agreed that there is need for the continued use and operation of the Pipeline in question, such use and operation is continued in accordance with the terms of this Agreement and the agreements between the owners of the Pipeline referred to in Article 14 subsisting immediately before such expiration, surrender or revocation. In particular the Government concerned shall take one of the following steps:

(a) issue a new licence in replacement of the licence which has expired, been surrendered or revoked; or

(b) itself conduct such use and operation; or

(c) take such other action to continue such use and operation as the two Governments may agree.

2. The Government taking action as described in paragraph (1) of this Article shall procure that the agreements between the owners of the Pipelines referred to in Article 14 shall be the subject of such supplementary agreements as are necessary consequent upon the action taken.

3. If the relevant Government considers the continued operation of the Pipeline or part thereof for technical, economic or other reasons not to be practicable, it shall consult with the other Government as to whether that Government wishes in consultation with the owners of the Pipeline to take steps to ensure the continued operation on fair terms and conditions of the Pipeline or part thereof. Subject to safety and environmental considerations, the relevant Government shall not prevent the other Government from securing the continued operation of the Pipe-

line or part thereof on such terms and conditions.

4. Subject to paragraph (3) of this Article, if the other Government takes over the operation of the Pipeline or part thereof it shall ensure the removal or isolation of any part of the Pipeline which is no longer in use and which both Governments agree should be removed or isolated. The Government which takes over the operation of the Pipeline or part thereof according to this paragraph shall thereafter be considered to be the relevant Government for the purpose of this Agreement. In regard to future abandonment of the Pipeline or part thereof, paragraphs (5) to (12) of this Article shall apply, mutatis mutandis.

5. Subject to paragraphs (3) and (4) of this Article, the owners of the Pipeline shall be required to submit jointly to the relevant Government at least two years in advance of the proposed commencement of the abandonment a plan (hereinafter referred to as the "plan") setting out the measures to be taken in connection with the abandonment of the Pipeline or part thereof.

6. Without prejudice to the generality of paragraph (5) of this Article, the plan shall include:

(a) an estimate of the cost of the measures proposed in it;

(b) details of the times at or within which the measures proposed in it are to be taken or make provision as to how those times are to be determined.

7. Recognising that the interdependence and proximity of the Pipelines makes desirable a consistent approach to their abandonment, the relevant Government shall, before it makes its decision on the plan submitted, consult the other Government with a view to agreeing a mutually acceptable response to the measures proposed in the plan. In undertaking consultation concerning abandonment of the Pipeline or part thereof the two Governments shall address fully and take proper account of:

(a) best available costeffective techniques;

(b) economic factors;

(c) applicable international standards or guidelines;

(d) safety hazards associated with abandonment, including where relevant transport and disposal;

(e) safety of navigation;

(f) the environmental impact of the measures proposed in the plan;

(g) the impact of the measures proposed on other uses of the sea;

(h) the timetable for abandonment;

(i) the impact of the measures proposed on the continued operation and abandonment of the other Pipeline;

(j) other relevant matters raised by the relevant Government.

8. The relevant Government may approve the plan with or without modifications and either subject to conditions or unconditionally. Before approving the plan with modifications or subject to conditions, the relevant Government shall give the owners who submitted the plan an opportunity to make representations about the proposed modifications or conditions.

9. In addition, in respect of the Norwegian Pipeline located in the territorial sea, internal waters and on the land territory of the United Kingdom, the United Kingdom Government shall ensure that the financial implications of whatever decision it makes on the plan submitted to it are acceptable to the Norwegian Government.

10. The relevant Government shall act without unreasonable delay in reaching a decision as to whether to approve or reject the plan and if approved require its implementation.

11. If the plan is rejected, the relevant Government shall inform the owners of the reasons for doing so. The owners shall in such circumstances be required to submit a revised plan within a specific time limit acceptable to both Governments.

12. If the two Governments are unable to agree a mutually acceptable response to an application, either Government shall have the right to submit to arbitration in accordance with Article 28 the question of whether or not the relevant Government has met its obligations under this Article, particularly paragraph 7.

PART III GENERAL PROVISIONS

Article 22

1. The system for metering the quantity of gas and liquid volumes and deter-

mination of the composition of hydrocarbons produced from the Frigg Field Reservoir and from the exploitation of other hydrocarbons in accordance with this Agreement shall be capable of separately metering the quantities of gas and liquids landed ashore, consumed on the field and at individual pumping stations, and discharged from or burnt off on flare platforms. Such system shall be the subject of agreement between the competent authorities of the two Governments. The licensees shall be instructed as to the manner in which the metering system is to be designed, installed and operated. The competent authorities of the two Governments shall agree a joint scheme for the supervision of the designing, installation and operation of the metering system, and for this purpose the representatives of those authorities shall have access to all parts of the system.

2. When both Governments have a legitimate interest in the system for determining the quantities of other hydrocarbons using facilities on an Installation or being admitted into the Pipelines, such system shall be subject to agreement between the competent authorities of the two Governments.

3. The two Governments shall agree on regular calibration of the metering systems and shall exchange at agreed intervals production records of the Frigg Field Reservoir and from the exploitation of other hydrocarbons in accordance with this Agreement relating to production from each side of the dividing line mentioned in paragraph 1 of Article 2 together with records of landed volume.

Article 23

The two Governments undertake to make every endeavour, jointly and severally, after consultations, to ensure that the operation of any Installation or Pipeline shall not cause pollution of the marine environment or damage by pollution to the coastline, shore facilities or amenities, or vessels or fishing gear of any country. The competent authorities of the two Governments shall develop procedures for the implementation of this Article in an emergency.

Article 24

1. The Governments shall take steps to procure that all contracts of employment of natural persons by the Unit Operator or by the Pipeline Operator for any purpose under this Agreement are governed by the law of the State of which the

employer is a licensee but without prejudice to the freedom of any employee to choose another law.

2. The two Governments shall endeavour to ensure that all employees are covered with regard to social security benefits and that each employee need comply only with one social security system.

3. The two Governments shall endeavour to ensure that other legislation for the protection and welfare of employees is applied consistently with the exploitation of the Frigg Field Reservoir as a single unit and with the operation of the Installations and Pipelines in accordance with this Agreement.

4. The Governments may from time to time conclude separate arrangements for the regulation of matters of common interest in the field of social security, employee welfare and labour relations in respect of the Frigg Field Reservoir or any Installation or Pipeline.

5. Nothing in this Article shall prejudice or affect any arrangements concerning matters referred to in paragraph 4 of this Article existing at the date of signature of this Agreement.

Article 25

1. A Government may, subject where appropriate to any restrictions in a licence, disclose to the other Government information in respect of licensed operations covered by this Agreement which a licensee has supplied to its Government. Where information is given to a Government in confidence, that Government shall treat it as confidential and any further disclosure shall be subject to any restrictions in the licence in question. Each Government shall nevertheless be entitled at any time to make use of the information for the purpose of preparing general reports on activities in respect of the Frigg Field Reservoir and the use of the Installations and Pipelines for the exploitation and transmission of hydrocarbons.

2. Copies of all such general reports or statements (including Press releases) published by one Government shall be transmitted to the other Government not later than the date of publication.

Article 26

Nothing in this Agreement or in the agreements referred to in Article 1 and

Article 14 shall prejudice the exercise by each Government or by the two Governments jointly of special powers in the case of national or international emergency. Consultations shall be held at the earliest opportunity in order that the two Governments may agree on appropriate joint measures to reconcile the urgency of the situation with their common interest in the most effective exploitation of the Frigg Gas and the use of the Installations and Pipelines.

Article 27

A commission shall be established consisting of six persons of whom each Government shall appoint three persons, to be known as the Frigg Consultative Commission, for the purpose of facilitating the implementation of this Agreement. The functions of the Commission, which shall include that of considering matters referred to it by the Governments, and its procedures shall be subject to such further arrangements which may be agreed by the two Governments from time to time.

Article 28

1. Any dispute about the interpretation or application of this Agreement, or any other matter referred to the Governments for settlement under the agreements between the licensees mentioned in paragraph (2) of Article 1 and Article 14 shall be resolved through the Frigg Consultative Commission or by negotiation between the two Governments.

2. If any such dispute cannot be resolved in this manner or by any other procedure agreed to by the two Governments, the dispute shall be submitted, at the request of either Government, to an Arbitral Tribunal composed as follows:

Each Government shall designate one arbitrator, and the two arbitrators so designated shall elect a third, who shall be the Chairman and who shall not be a national of or habitually reside in the United Kingdom or in the Kingdom of Norway. If either Government fails to designate an arbitrator within three months of a request to do so, either Government may request the President of the International Court of Justice to appoint an arbitrator. The same procedure shall apply if, within one month of the designation or appointment of the second arbitrator, the third arbitrator has not been elected. The Tribunal shall determine its own procedure, save that all decisions shall be taken, in the absence of unanimity, by a majority vote of the members of the Tribunal. The decisions of the Tribunal shall be binding upon the two Governments and shall, for the purposes of this Agreement, be regarded as agreements between the two Governments.

Article 29

1. Nothing in this Agreement shall be interpreted as affecting the jurisdiction which each State has under international law over the Continental Shelf which appertains to it. In particular, Installations located on the Continental Shelf appertaining to the United Kingdom shall be under the jurisdiction of the United Kingdom, and Installations located on the Continental Shelf appertaining to the Kingdom of Norway shall be under the jurisdiction of the Kingdom of Norway.

2. Nor shall anything in this Agreement be interpreted as prejudicing or restricting the application of the laws of either State or the exercise of jurisdiction by their Courts, in conformity with international law.

Article 30

For the purpose of this Agreement, unless the content otherwise requires:

1. "Frigg Field Reservoir" means the naturally occurring gas – bearing sand formations of the lower Eocene age beneath the sea bed but immediately above the sub – sea level of approximately 1955 meters located in the vicinity of the intersection of the line of latitude 59°53′ North and of the dividing line which is defined in the Agreement of 10 March 1965 between the two Governments relating to the Delimitation of the Continental Shelf between the two States, and encountered by the four wells described in Annex B and includes all other gas – bearing strata from which gas at the start of the production is capable of flowing into the above mentioned gas – bearing sand formations.

2. "Installation" means any structure or device installed in or on the sea bed, including a pipeline, which is or has been involved in the exploitation of the Frigg Field Reservoir. Installation does not include the Norwegian Pipeline or the United Kingdom Pipeline hereinafter defined. "Installations" means two or more such Installations.

3. "the licensees" means Total Oil Marine Limited, Elf Oil Exploration and Production (UK) Limited, Aquitaine Oil (UK) Limited (being licensees of the

(六) 1976 年英国与挪威共同开发弗里格天然气案

United Kingdom Government), Elf Norge A/S, Aquitaine Norge A/S, Total Marine Norsk A/S, Norsk Hydro Produksjon a. s. and Den norske stats oljeselskap a. s. (being licensees of the Norwegian Government) and their successors and such other persons as may from time to time be licensees of either Government for the exploitation of any part of the Frigg Field Reservoir in addition to, or in substitution for, all or any of the above – named persons.

4. "other hydrocarbons" means any gaseous or liquid hydrocarbons originating from other petroleum deposits than the Frigg Field Reservoir save for such other gas as referred to in Article 3 paragraph (4) of this Agreement.

5. References to "Unit Operator" and "Pipeline Operator" include references to the company or companies for the time being acting as such pursuant to the agreements referred to in Articles 1, 5 and 14.

6. "Norwegian Pipeline" means the pipeline to be built and operated from the inlet flange of the pipeline at a Frigg Field Reservoir platform situated on the Continental Shelf appertaining to the Kingdom of Norway up to and including metering instruments onshore at St. Fergus, and also including associated installations serving this pipeline on an intermediate platform or platforms.

7. "United Kingdom Pipeline" means the pipeline to be built and operated from the inlet flange of the pipeline at a Frigg Field Reservoir platform situated on the Continental Shelf appertaining to the United Kingdom up to and including metering instruments onshore at St. Fergus, and also including associated installations serving this pipeline on an intermediate platform or platforms.

8. "Pipeline" means either the Norwegian Pipeline or the United Kingdom Pipeline. "Pipelines" means both the United Kingdom Pipeline and the Norwegian Pipeline.

9. "relevant Government" means the Government of the Kingdom of Norway in all matters relating to those parts of the Norwegian Pipeline on the Continental Shelves of the Kingdom of Norway and the United Kingdom and the Government of the United Kingdom in all matters relating to (a) the United Kingdom Pipeline, and (b) those parts of the Norwegian Pipeline located in the territorial sea, internal waters and on the land territory of the United Kingdom.

Article 31

1. This Agreement shall enter into force on the date on which the two Governments shall have informed each other that all necessary internal requirements have been fulfilled.

2. The two Governments may amend or terminate this Agreement at any time by agreement. Either Government may at any time request that consultations are initiated with a view to considering amendments to this Agreement. Such consultations shall commence within two months of the request, and shall be conducted expeditiously. In such consultations the two Governments shall consider fully and take proper account of the proposals for amendment with the aim of reaching a mutually acceptable solution within the shortest possible time.

ANNEX A

Installations

1. On the Continental Shelf appertaining to the Kingdom of Norway:

(a) One drilling platform.

(b) One combined treatment and compressor platform.

2. On a Continental Shelf appertaining to the United Kingdom:

(a) One drilling platform.

(b) One treatment platform.

(c) One quarters platform.

(d) One flare column.

ANNEX B

Country	Well No.	Geographical Location
Norway	25/1 - 1	59°53′17. 09″ N 02° 04′ 42. 7″E
Norway	25/1 - 2	59° 56′ 08″ N 02° 04′ 54. 6″E
Norway	25/1 - 3	59° 54′05″ N 02°10′08″E
UK	10/1 - 1A	59°50′10. 5″ N 02° 00′ 34. 5″E

（七）1979年泰国与马来西亚有关泰国湾的共同开发案

1. 《马来西亚和泰王国为开发泰国湾两国大陆架划定区域内海床资源而设立联合管理局的谅解备忘录》

（1979年2月21日订于清迈）

王晓梅译，邓妮雅校

马来西亚和泰王国，愿意进一步加强两国间既存的传统友谊；承认作为两国在泰国湾大陆架边界线重叠主张的结果，两国在相邻的大陆架上存在一块重叠区域；注意到两国正在进行的关于划分泰国湾大陆架边界的谈判可能会持续一段时间，考虑到对重叠海域海床资源尽快进行开发符合两国的最佳利益，以及确信此种开发活动需要两国彼此间的合作，双方达成以下协议。

第一条

双方同意作为两国就泰国湾大陆架边界线重叠主张的结果，泰国湾存有一块重叠海域，该区域由下列坐标点以直线连接而成：

A	北纬 6°50′00″	东经 102°21′02″
B	北纬 7°10′25″	东经 102°29′00″
C	北纬 7°49′00″	东经 103°02′05″
D	北纬 7°22′00″	东经 103°42′05″

E	北纬 7°20′00″	东经 103°39′00″
F	北纬 7°03′00″	东经 103°06′00″
G	北纬 6°53′00″	东经 102°34′00″

该区域由附后的英国海军航海图 1967 年版，第 2414 号相关部分标示。

第二条

双方都同意按照国际法原则和国际惯例，特别是遵照泰马两国于 1978 年 2 月 27 日至 3 月 1 日举行的，关于划分马来西亚和泰国在泰国湾和南海大陆架划界的官方会议所达成的协议备忘录中的条款，本着合作原则，以两国的安全利益为重，采取协商谈判或双方同意的其他和平手段，来解决两国在泰国湾的大陆架的划界问题。

第三条

（1）双方将建立"马泰联合管理局"（以下简称"联管局"），旨在勘探和开发重叠区域内海床和底土中的非生物自然资源。期限为 50 年，自备忘录生效之日起算。

（2）联管局应代表双方享有和承担勘探及开发重叠区域（以下称"共同开发区"）内，海床和底土非生物自然资源事宜所有的权利和义务，以及共同开发区域内开发、控制和管理的所有权利和义务。联管局的这种权利和义务不得以任何方式影响或减损任何一方迄今授予的特许权、已签发的许可证、协定或安排的有效性。

（3）联管局组成如下：

（A）两名联合主席，每国各一名，以及

（B）每国相同数量的成员。

（4）根据本备忘录的条款规定，联管局将代表双方行使，与共同开发区内勘探和开发海床及底土非生物自然资源，所必需的、有关的或附带的所有权利。

（5）联管局在共同开发区活动所产生的费用，以及由此获得的利润，应由两国平等分担和分享。

（6）如果任何单一的地质石油或天然气构造或油气田，或其他任何类型的矿床延伸至本备忘录第一条所规定的共同开发区界线外，联管局和合同方应该就此交换所有信息，并就最有效地开发该构造、油气田和矿藏的

(七) 1979年泰国与马来西亚有关泰国湾的共同开发案

方式达成一致安排，所有因此所需的费用及由此而获得的利润应该公平地分担与分享。

第四条

（1）任意一方国内当局在渔业、航行、水文和海洋勘测，防止和控制海洋污染及其他类似事项上，所赋予或行使的权利（也包括与此相关的执行的权力）都应沿用于共同开发区，而且这些权利应得到联管局的承认和尊重。

（2）双方在共同开发区内应做出一项协调一致的安全安排。

第五条

共同开发区内，马来西亚的刑事司法管辖范围应于以直线依次连接下列坐标点的区域内行使：

A	北纬 6°50′00″	东经 102°21′02″
X	北纬 7°35′00″	东经 103°23′00″
D	北纬 7°22′00″	东经 103°42′05″
E	北纬 7°20′00″	东经 103°39′00″
F	北纬 7°03′00″	东经 103°06′00″
G	北纬 6°53′00″	东经 102°34′00″

共同开发区内，泰王国的刑事司法管辖范围应于以直线依次连接下列坐标点的区域内行使：

A	北纬 6°50′0″	东经 102°21′2″
B	北纬 7°10′25″	东经 102°29′0″
C	北纬 7°49′0″	东经 103°02′0″
X	北纬 7°35′0″	东经 103°23′0″

本条款关于刑事司法管辖范围的规定，既不构成依据第二条确定的共同开发区内两国的大陆架界线，也不应损害任何一方在共同开发区内的主权权利。

第六条

（1）虽然有第三条的规定，但是若双方在规定的50年期限届满之前，对大陆架划界问题达成了满意的解决方案，那么联管局应解散，其所管辖的资产应该双方平均分享，其所有的债务也应双方对等分担。但是，若双方同意也可做出一项新的安排。

（2）若两国在规定的 50 年内未能就大陆架划界问题达成满意的解决方案，则现存的安排在期满后继续有效。

第七条

对在本备忘录条款的解释或执行中所产生的分歧或争端，双方应通过协商或谈判的方式和平解决。

第八条

本备忘录自双方互换批准文书之日起生效。

本备忘录于 1979 年 2 月 21 日在清迈用泰语、马来语和英语三种语言文本写成。三种文本若存在不一致，应以英文文本为准。

马来西亚	泰王国
侯赛因·奥恩	江萨·乔马南将军
马来西亚总理	泰王国总理

2. Memorandum of Understanding between Malaysia and the Kingdom of Thailand on the Establishment of the Joint Authority for the Exploitation of the Resources of the Sea Bed in a Defined Area of the Continental Shelf of the Two Countries in the Gulf of Thailand

Adopted in Chiang Mai, Thailand on 21 February 1979

Malaysia and the Kingdom of Thailand,

DESIRING to strengthen further the existing bonds of traditional friendship between the two countries;

RECOGNISING that as a result of overlapping claims made by the two countries regarding the boundary line of their continental shelves in the Gulf of Thailand, there exists an overlapping area on their adjacent continental shelves;

NOTING that the existing negotiations between the two countries on the delimitation of the boundary of the continental shelf in the Gulf of Thailand may continue for some time;

CONSIDERING that it is in the best interests of the two countries to exploit the resources of the sea – bed in the overlapping area as soon as possible; and

CONVINCED that such activities can be carried out jointly through mutual cooperation,

HAVE AGREED AS FOLLOWS:

Article I

Both parties agree that as a result of overlapping claims made by the two countries regarding the boundary line of their continental shelves in the Gulf of Thailand, there exists an overlapping area, which is defined as that area bounded by straight lines joining the following coordinated points:

(A)	N 6°50'.0	E 102°21'.2
(B)	N 7°10'.25	E 102°29'.0
(C)	N 7°49'.0	E 103°02'.5
(D)	N 7°22'.0	E 103°42'.5
(E)	N 7°20'.0	E 103°39'.0
(F)	N 7°03'.0	E 103°06'.0
(G)	N 6°53'.0	E 102°34'.0

And shown in the relevant part of the British Admiralty Chart No: 2414 Edition 1967, annexed hereto.

Article II

Both Parties agree to continue to resolve the problem of the delimitation of the boundary of the continental shelf in the Gulf of Thailand between the two countries by negotiations or such other peaceful means as agreed to by both Parties, in accordance with the principles of international law and practice especially those agreed to in the Agreed Minutes of the Malaysia – Thailand Officials' Meeting on Delimitation of the Continental Shelf Boundary Between Malaysia and Thailand in the Gulf of Thailand and in the South China Sea, 27 February – 1 March 1978 and in the spirit of friendship and in the interest of mutual security.

Article III

(1) There shall be established a Joint Authority to be known as "Malaysia-Thailand Joint Authority" (thereafter referred to as "the Joint Authority") for the purpose of the exploration and exploitation of the non – living natural resources of the sea – bed and subsoil in the overlapping area for a period of fifty years commencing from the date this Memorandum comes into force.

(2) The Joint Authority shall assume all rights and responsibilities on behalf of both Parties for the exploration and exploitation of the non – living natural resources of the sea – bed and subsoil in the overlapping area (hereinafter referred

to as the joint development area) and also for the development, control and administration of the joint development area. The assumption of such rights and responsibilities by the Joint Authority shall in no way affect or curtail the validity of concessions or licences hitherto issued or agreements or arrangements hitherto made by either Party.

(3) The Joint Authority shall consist of:

(a) two joint-chairmen, one from each country, and

(b) an equal number of members from each country.

(4) Subject to the provisions of this Memorandum, the Joint Authority shall exercise on behalf of both Parties all the powers necessary for, incidental to or connected with the discharge of its functions relating to the exploration and exploitation of the non-living natural resources of the sea-bed and subsoil in the joint development area.

(5) All costs incurred and benefits derived by the Joint Authority from activities carried out in the joint development area shall be equally borne and shared by both Parties.

(6) If any single geological petroleum or natural gas, structure or field, or other mineral deposit of whatever character, extends beyond the limit of the joint development area defined in Article I, the Joint Authority and the Party or Parties concerned shall communicate to each other all information in this regard and shall seek to reach agreement as to the manner in which the structure, field or deposit will be most effectively exploited; and all expenses incurred and benefits derived therefrom shall be equitably shared.

Article IV

(1) The rights conferred or exercised by the national authority of either Party in matters of fishing, navigation, hydrographic and oceanographic surveys, the prevention and control of marine pollution and other similar matters (including all powers of enforcement in relation thereto) shall extend to the joint development area and such rights shall be recognized and respected by the Joint Authority.

(2) Both Parties shall have a combined and coordinated security arrangement in the joint development area.

Article V

The criminal jurisdiction of Malaysia in the Joint Development Area shall extend over that area bounded by straight lines joining the following coordinated points:

(A)	N6°50'.0	E 102°21'.2
(X)	N7°35'.0	E103°23'.0
(D)	N7°22'.0	E103°42'.5
(E)	N7°20'.0	E103°39'.0
(F)	N7°03'.0	E103°06'.0
(G)	N6°53'.0	E102°34'.0

The criminal jurisdiction of the Kingdom of Tbailand in the joint development area shall extent over that area bounded by straight lines joining the following coordinated points:

(A)	N6°50'.0	E102°21'.2
(B)	N7°10'.25	E102°29'.0
(C)	N7°49'.0	E103°02'.5
(X)	N7°35'.0	E103°23'.0

The areas of criminal jurisdiction of both Parties defined under this Article shall not in any way be construed as indicating the boundary line of the continental shelf between the two countries in the joint development area, which boundary is to be determined as provided for by Article II, nor shall such definition in any way prejudice the sovereign rights of either Party in the joint development area.

Article VI

(1) Notwithstanding Article III, if both Parties arrive at a satisfactory solution on the problem of the delimitation of the boundary of the continental shelf before the expiry of the said fifty-year period, the Joint Authority shall be wound up and all assets administered and liabilities incurred by it shall be equally shared and borne by both Parties. A new arrangement may, however, be concluded if both Parties so decide.

(2) If no satisfactory solution is found on the problem of the delimitation of the boundary of the continental shelf within the said fifty-year period, the existing arrangement shall continue after the expiry of the said period.

Article VII

Any difference or dispute arising out of the interpretation or implementation of the provisions of this Memorandum shall be settled peacefully by consultation or negotiation between the Parties.

Article VIII

This Memorandum shall come into force on the date of exchange of instruments of ratification.

DONE in duplicate at *Chiang Mai the Twenty-first day of February* in the year One Thousand Nine Hundred and Seventy-Nine in the Malay, Thai and English Languages.

In the event of any conflict among the texts, the English text shall prevail.

For Malaysia	For the Kingdom of Thailand
Datuk Hussein Onn	General Kriangsak Chomanan
Prime Minister	Prime Minister

3. 《马来西亚政府和泰王国政府关于设立马来西亚—泰国联合管理局及其他事项的 1990 年协定》

(1990 年 5 月 30 日订于吉隆坡)

王晓梅译，邓妮雅校

马来西亚政府和泰王国政府（以下简称"政府"），旨在执行 1979 年 2 月 21 日签订的《马来西亚和泰王国为开发泰国湾两国大陆架划定区域内海床资源而建立联合管理局的谅解备忘录》（以下简称《1979 年谅解备忘录》），双方已达成一致建立马来西亚泰国联合管理局（以下简称"联管局"），联管局应依据以下条款运行。

第一章　法律地位和组成

第一条　法律人格和能力

（1）联管局应当具备法律人格和相应的能力，马来西亚政府和泰国政府也应分别颁布建立联管局的议会法令（以下简称"法令"）。

（2）第一条第一款所指的法令草案分别作为附件 A 和附件 B 附于本协定后，并构成本协定不可分割的一部分。

第二条　目的

（1）成立联管局的目的是在《1979 年谅解备忘录》有效期内，负责勘探和开发该备忘录规定的共同开发区内海床和底土的非生物自然资源，尤其是石油资源。

（2）在本协定中，"石油"是指任何矿物油，或在自然条件下存在的相关碳氢化合物和天然气，以及井口凝析油，包括沥青页岩和其他可以提炼出石油的层状沉积物。

第三条　成员组成

（1）联管局应当包含

（a）两名联合主席，双方政府各指派一名；以及

（b）双方政府各指派相同数量的成员，不包含联合主席在内，双方政府各指派六名初始成员。

（2）为了本协定的目的，除非文本中有其他要求，"成员"应当包括联合主席。

第四条　程序

（1）联合主席应在联管局会议中轮流行使主席职责。若一方缺乏联合主席，联管局成员应当从代表该政府的成员中选出一名作为相应的联合主席。一旦当选，该成员拥有主席的所有权力。

（2）联管局的任何会议法定人数不得少于 10 人，会议决定应当由联合主席共同做出。

第五条　个人责任

联管局的所有成员对于其在管理联管局事务中的行为或过失所造成的损失和损害，不必承担任何个人责任，除非该损失和损害是其不法行为、重大过失或失职引起的。

第六条　薪资

联管局成员的薪资和其他津贴由联管局决定，并经双方政府核准。

第二章　权力和职能

第七条　权力和职能

（1）联管局应当管控共同开发区内所有勘探和开发非生物自然资源的活动，也应负责制定政策。

（2）在不影响前述条文一般性原则的前提下，联管局的权力和职能应当包括以下内容：

（a）在政府批准前提下，决定联管局的组织结构；

（b）依据上述（a）项，任命联管局的首席执行官和其他职员，但是首席执行官和副首席执行官的任命需得到政府的批准；

（c）决定联管局首席执行官和其他职员服务的条款和条件；

（d）决定共同开发区的作业计划和管理工作计划；

（e）在政府批准的前提下，准许其实施和缔结与共同开发区勘探和开发非生物自然资源相关的交易或合同；

（f）关于（e）项所指的石油勘探和开发合同，应包括

（i）批准和延长勘探和开发期限；

（ii）批准承包商的工作计划和预算；以及

（iii）批准承包商的生产计划，包括生产成本，条件和生产时间安排；

（g）关于（f）项中涉及的承包商，应包括

（i）审查和审计共同开发区与作业相关的承包商的簿册及账目；

（ii）定期清查作业者在石油作业中获取的财产和资产；以及

（iii）接收，整理和储存作业者提供的，与其在共同开发区作业相关的所有数据；

（h）批准和授予与共同开发区进行石油作业所需商品和服务相关的标书和合同；

（i）任命联管局行政管理所必需的委员会、小组委员会或独立专家和顾问团；

（j）管理联管局、委员会和小组委员会的会议活动；以及

（k）履行其职责必需的或附带的其他事项。

第八条　产品分成

（1）为了第七条第（2）款第（f）项的目的，依据法案第三部分第十四条规定授予的，共同开发区内任何石油勘探和开发合同，应当为产品分成合同。

（2）在不影响本条第三款的前提下，本条第一款所指的产品分成合同应当包括法令第三部分第十四条确定的如下条款和条件：

（a）合同的有效期不应超过35年，也不应超出本协定的有效期；

（b）承包商应向联管局缴纳石油总产量的10%，作为特许权使用费，支付方式和时间可在合同中详细说明；

（c）承包商应将石油总产量的50%用于维护石油作业的费用；

（d）在扣除（b）（c）项之后，石油总产量的剩余部分应作为利润油，由联管局和承包商平均分配；

（e）石油作业的所有费用应由承包商承担，根据（c）项，该费用可以从产量中补偿；

(f) 联管局和承包商可以协商，承包商在石油作业中的最低花费应作为最低承诺；

(g) 承包商应向联管局支付石油总产量的 0.5%，作为研究经费，该经费用于研究第（c）项下成本回收以及第（d）项承包商利润油的分享，支付的方式和时间由联管局决定，但该费用不能从产量中进行补偿；

(h) 双方因该订约产生的任何争端或分歧若不能和平地解决，则应该把该争议提交由 3 名仲裁员组成的仲裁小组仲裁。其中双方各自指派一名仲裁员，双方共同指派第三名仲裁员。若双方在一定的时间内不能就第三名仲裁员的人选达成一致，则应请求联合国国际贸易委员会指派一名仲裁员。仲裁程序应当依据联合国国际贸易委员会规则进行。仲裁地点应为曼谷或吉隆坡或双方一致同意的其他地点。

(3) 除了第（2）款明确指明的条款，联管局可在产品分成合同中选持性纳入下列条款：

(a) 第（2）款（a）项所指的期间应适用如下规定：

(i) 石油（不包括天然气）合同的勘探期和开发期均不得超过 5 年，生产期不得超过 25 年；以及（ii）天然气合同的勘探期、天然气市场的确定和进入期，以及开发期均不得超过 5 年，生产期不得超过 20 年；但是（a）(i) 项和（a）(ii) 项规定的期间，联管局可以根据现实需要做出变更，如果这种变更影响了原有合约，则仅能与承包商之间通过协议做出变更。

同时，在期限届满之前，如果（A）石油（不包括天然气）实现了初次商业化生产，则开发阶段的剩余期限应当并入生产期；（B）在天然气市场的确定和进入期以及开发期届满之前，天然气实现了初次商业化生产，则这些阶段的剩余期间均应并入生产期。

(b) 承包商因石油作业而购买或取得的设备或资产上的权利，应转移至联管局；

(c) 联管局对石油作业产生的所有原始数据（原始的，加工的或解释的），享有全部权利，包括但不限于地质、地理、岩芯样本、石油物理、完井报告、工程、其他数据报告以及由承包商收集和汇编的其他实际采样；

(d) 承包商应当从泰国和马来西亚购买或收购技术和经济上可行的设

备、设施、物资、材料、补给，包括专业或非专业服务和研究设施。

（4）联管局可以在获得政府批准后，变更合同中第（2）款第（c）（d）（g）项的数量；但若未经承包商同意，不能对既有合同中规定的数量做任何改变。

（5）为了本条的目的——

（a）与石油（不包括天然气）相关的"第一个商业化生产"日期是指，继第一次生产井测试完成后并持续生产24小时的日期；与天然气有关的"第一个商业化生产"日期是指，第一个60天内累计售出10^6千兆焦耳（约9470亿英制热量单位）的日期，如果60天内累计未售出10^6千兆焦耳天然气，则是指第60天后累计售出达到该量的日期；

（6）根据该协议第十六条和第十七条，承包商应从其分享的利润油支付出口税和石油所得税。

第三章 财务规定

第九条 财务

（1）联管局在共同开发区所有活动产生的支出和获得的收益，应由两国政府平等承担和分享。

（2）直到联管局拥有足够的收入负担其年度运营支出，两国政府应当商定并每年向联管局缴纳相等数额的经费，建立马来西亚—泰国联合管理基金（以下简称"基金"）。

（3）若达到第（2）款的要求，除非双方政府另做决定，应停止这种政府的年度缴费。

第十条 账目和记录

（1）联管局应当依照一般会计原则，建立交易和相关事务适当的账目和其他记录，同时联管局应尽其所能确保适当记录其所有收入，以及基金所有支出，包括薪资支付、联管局成员和雇员的酬金和其他货币利益，是经过适当授权的，并且对资产进行适当维护或使资产处于联管局监管下。

（2）双方政府在任何时候均可要求提供账目或记录，联管局应当遵从其指示。

第十一条 预算

联管局的年度预算应当在相关政府财政年度之前提交给两国政府，以获得批准。

第十二条　审计

（1）联管局的财政年度应当从1月1日起。

（2）联管局账目应当由联管局指定且双方政府批准之审计员进行年度审计。

（3）联管局应当在每个财政年度结束之后6个月内完成其账目审计，并提交给双方政府，同时提交审计员对联管局任何声明或账目观察报告的副本，和联管局上一年度活动的年度报告副本。

第四章　有关法律以及联管局与其他机构的关系

第十三条　法规

为了法令第15部分的目的，联管局可对政府管理的任何事项提交法律建议，以供政府参考。

第十四条　联管局与其他机构的关系

为了实现其宗旨，联管局可与任何政府或组织合作，为此，联管局可在获得政府批准后，与其他政府和组织签订协议或安排。

第五章　法令

第十五条　法令的修改

为了促进本协议的有效管理和运行，双方政府同意，除非双方政府事先达成一致，不能对法令进行修改。

第六章　关税、消费税和税收

第十六条　关税事项

（1）为了法案第十部分的目的

（a）依据本款b项（ii）的规定，承包商将分享的利润油销售至马来西亚和泰王国之外的地方，应支付10%的出口税；

（b）海关和税务当局应根据马来西亚和泰王国的既有法规，继续行使其与共同开发区进出口货物流动管理有关的所有权力。如下另有规定的除外：

（i）由联管局或其授权的任何人进口的海关核准的用于共同开发区的

物品、设备和材料应当免收关税；如果一方政府要对这些海关核准的物品、设备和材料征收关税或其他税项，与另一方政府磋商之后才可征收；

（ii）泰马两国根据其本国立法各自征收其相关的关税和其他税项赋税，但应当将适用的税率降低50%；

（iii）若进入共同开发区的货物来源于：

（A）来自第三方国家，或马来西亚和泰王国任何一方的保税仓库和保税区，应当视为进口；以及

（B）若为海关核准的用于共同开发区的货物、设备和材料，则应视为境内流动；

（iv）共同开发区内生产的任何货物进入泰王国、马来西亚或第三方国家，应当视为出口；

（v）进入共同开发区的任何货物，符合本款第（b）（iii）（B）项规定的，若要进入马来西亚或者泰王国，则应依据具体情形适用马来西亚或泰王国法律；

（vi）依据马来西亚和泰王国的法律，属于双方违禁品清单上的任何货物，不能进入共同开发区；

若确有需要进口违禁货物，则须由另一方国家的主管当局同意做出例外规定；

（vii）出售共同开发区没收货物所得的收益，应由马来西亚和泰王国两国平均分享；

（c）为了本款（b）（iii）和（iv）规定货物进口、出口和境内流动的目的，海关和税务当局应当适用共同关税条款；以及

（d）若有联合关税办公室，联管局总部所在的国家应当授予另一方国家海关和税务当局官员清关的权力，包括征收关税和其他税务的权力；

（2）虽然法案第18部分适用于海关和税务事项，但下列安排也应适用：

（a）共同开发区内的某项行为仅违反了一方国家的法律，则该国家可对该指控的行为行使司法管辖权；

（b）上述（a）项行为若违反了两国法律，对被指控之行为人首先实施逮捕或拘留的国家应被推定为享有管辖权的国家；

（c）上述（a）项行为若违反了两国法律，且两国的海关和税务当局

同时实施了逮捕或拘留，则司法管辖权应由两国相关当局协商决定。

（3）为了本条之目的——

（a）"两个国家"是指马来西亚和泰王国，若使用单数则应根据上下文判定为马来西亚或者泰王国；

（b）"海关核准的货物"是指根据马来西亚和泰国两国与关税相关的法律，免除海关关税的货物；

（c）"海关和税务当局"，是指马来西亚的皇家海关和税务局，以及泰王国的泰国海关部门，若使用的是复数则指前述两者；

（d）"联合海关委员会"是指为了协调共同开发区内关税和其他税务法律的管理而建立的委员会，由双方海关和税务当局的官员组成；以及

（e）"联合海关办公室"是指为了协调共同开发区内关税和其他税务法律的管理，而建立于联管局总部的联合海关委员会的办公室。

第十七条　税收

1. 为了法令第十部分的目的，政府税收当局根据下列条款，依据马来西亚和泰王国既有的税收立法，对共同开发区的收入征收税款，具体如下：

（a）根据联管局授予的合同，在共同开发区有权勘探和开发石油资源的任何人，应按照下列税率征税：

最初 8 年生产期；应纳所得税为 0；

随后 7 年生产期，应纳所得税税率为 10%；

剩余生产期内，应纳所得税税率为 20%；

同时，各政府征税税率降低应征税率的 50%；

如果一方政府每年所征税款超过另一方政府所征税款，超出部分应由两国平均分享，同时联管局应根据法案第十部分（d）款项对支付的费用做适当调整；

（b）对在共同开发区内或者在联合管理局工作的马来西亚或泰国国民，其所得税的征收应依据其住所决定；以及

（c）除本条（a）（b）项之外的其他人的所得税，应依据马来西亚和泰王国的法律法规征收。若两国对相同收入均应征税，则两国均应将其应征税率降低 50%。

（2）双方政府同意一般销售税性质的税收法律，包括对共同开发区内

物品和服务的征税，不适用于共同开发区。

（3）马来西亚和泰王国不应对联管局征税。

（4）双方政府的税收当局，应对共同开发区税收法律的实施与管理，保持交流和协商。

第七章　杂项条款

第十八条　生效和终止

（1）本协定自交换批准文书之日起生效，除非双方政府另达成一致，本协定有效期与《1979年谅解备忘录》有效期一致。

（2）本协定终止后，联管局应按照双方政府批准的清算程序解散。

第十九条　适用

本协定条款的解释与适用，应与《1979年谅解备忘录》的精神与条款保持一致。

第二十条　修改

本协定的修改可由联合主席共同决定，并经双方政府批准。

第二十一条　争端处理

在本协定条款的解释或适用中产生的任何分歧或争端，应由双方政府通过协商或谈判和平解决。若3个月内仍未能解决争端，任何一方政府可将争端提交至马来西亚首相和泰王国总理，两国首相应共同决定该争端的解决方式。

第二十二条

本协议于1990年5月30日在马来西亚首都吉隆坡签订，英文文本一式两份。

马来西亚政府	泰国政府
拿督·哈吉·阿布·哈桑·哈吉·阿布（音）	马歇尔·西提·赛维特西罗（音）
外交部长	外交部长

4. 1990 Agreement between the Government of Malaysia and the Government of the Kingdom of Thailand on the Constitution and Other Matters Relating to the Establishment of the Malaysia – Thailand Joint Authority

Adopted in Kuala Lumpur, Malaysia on 30 May 1990

THE GOVERNMENT OF MALAYSIA AND THE GOVERNMENT OF THE KINGDOM OF THAILAND, hereinafter referred to as "the Governments",

DESIRING to implement the Memorandum of Understanding between Malaysia and the Kingdom of Thailand on the Establishment of a Joint Authority for the Exploitation of the Resources of the Sea – bed in a Defined Area of the Continental Shelf of the Two Countries in the Gulf of Thailand dated 21 February 1979, hereinafter referred to as "the Memorandum of Understanding, 1979",

HAVE HEREBY AGREED on the establishment of the Malaysia – Thailand Joint Authority, hereinafter referred to as "the Joint Authority", which shall operate in accordance with the following provisions:

CHAPTER I   LEGAL STATUS AND ORGANIZATION

Article 1   JURISTIC PERSONALITY AND CAPACITY

(1) The Joint Authority shall have a juristic personality and such capacities as shall be provided for in the Acts of Parliament to be enacted by the Government of Malaysia and the Government of the Kingdom of Thailand, respectively, for the establishment of the Joint Authority, hereinafter referred to as "the Acts".

(2) The drafts of the Acts, referred to in paragraph (1) and attached hereto

as Appendix A and Appendix B respectively, shall form an integral part of this Agreement.

Article 2　PURPOSE

(1) The purpose of the Joint Authority shall be the exploration and exploitation of the non-living natural resources of the sea-bed and subsoil, in particular petroleum, in the Joint Development Area as defined in the Memorandum of Understanding, 1979 for the period of validity of the Memorandum of Understanding, 1979.

(2) In this Agreement, "petroleum" means any mineral oil or relative hydrocarbon and natural gas existing in its natural condition and casinghead petroleum spirit, including bituminous shales and other stratified deposits from which oil can be extracted.

Article 3　MEMBERSHIP

(1) The Joint Authority shall comprise

(a) two Co-Chairmen, one each to be appointed by the respective Governments; and

(b) an equal number of members to be appointed by each Government, provided that the initial number of members, excluding the Co-Chairmen, to be appointed by each Government shall be six.

(2) The word "member" shall, for the purposes of this Agreement, and unless the context otherwise requires, include a Co-Chairman.

Article 4　PROCEDURE

(1) The Co-Chairmen shall alternate to perform the functions of a Chairman at meetings of the Joint Authority. In the absence of a Co-Chairman during his chairmanship, the members of the Joint Authority shall elect a Chairman from amongst the members representing the same Government as the corresponding Co-Chairman. When so elected, he shall have all the powers of the Chairman.

(2) The quorum for any meeting of the Joint Authority shall not be less than ten. Decisions shall be taken jointly at a meeting by the Co-Chairmen.

Article 5　PERSONAL LIABILITY

No member of the Joint Authority shall incur any personal liability for any loss or damage caused by any act or omission in the administration of the affairs of the Joint Authority unless such loss or damage is occasioned by a wrongful act, gross negligence or omission on his part.

Article 6　EMOLUMENTS

The members of the Joint Authority shall be paid such emoluments and other allowances as the Joint Authority may determine with the approval of the Governments.

CHAPTER Ⅱ　POWERS AND FUNCTIONS

Article 7　POWERS AND FUNCTIONS

(1) The Joint Authority shall control all exploration and exploitation of the non-living natural resources in the Joint Development Area and shall be responsible for the formulation of policies for the same.

(2) Without prejudice to the generality of the foregoing, the powers and functions of the Joint Authority shall include the following:

(a) to decide, with the approval of the Governments, on the organizational structure of the Joint Authority;

(b) subject to subparagraph (a), to appoint the chief executive officer and other officers of the Joint Authority, provided that the appointment of the chief executive officer and the deputy chief executive officer shall require the approval of the Governments;

(c) to decide on the terms and conditions of service of the chief executive officer and other officers of the Joint Authority;

(d) to decide on the plan of operation and the working programme for the administration of the Joint Development Area;

(e) to permit operations and to conclude transactions or contracts for or relating to the exploration and exploitation of the non-living natural resources in the Joint Development Area subject to the approval of the Governments;

(f) in respect of any contract referred to in subparagraph (e) for the exploration and exploitation of petroleum

(i) to approve and extend the period of exploration and exploitation;

(ii) to approve the work programmes and budgets of the contractor; and

(iii) to approve the production programmes of the contractor, including the production costs, conditions and schedules of the production;

(g) in respect of an operator of any contract referred to in subparagraph (f)

(i) to inspect and audit the operator's books and accounts relating to its operations in the Joint Development Area;

(ii) to take periodic inventories of the properties and assets procured by the operator for petroleum operations; and

(iii) to receive, collate and store all data supplied by the operator relating to its operations in the Joint Development Area;

(h) to approve and award tenders and contracts relating to goods and services required in carrying out petroleum operations in the Joint Development Area;

(i) to appoint committees, sub-committees or independent experts and consultants where necessary for the administration of the Joint Authority;

(j) to regulate any meeting of the Joint Authority, any committee and sub-committee thereof; and

(k) to do any other thing incidental to or necessary for the performance of any of its functions.

Article 8　PRODUCTION SHARING

(1) For the purpose of paragraph (2) (f) of Article 7, any contract awarded to any person for the exploration and exploitation of petroleum in the Joint Development Area shall, in accordance with subsection (3) of section 14 of the Acts, be a production sharing contract.

(2) A production sharing contract referred to in paragraph (1) shall include, without prejudice to paragraph (3), the terms and conditions specified in subsection (3) of section 14 of the Acts as follows:

(a) the contract shall be valid for a period not exceeding thirty-five years but shall not exceed the period of validity of this Agreement;

(b) payment in the amount of ten per centum of gross production of petroleum by the contractor to the Joint Authority as royalty in the manner and at such times as may be specified in the contract;

(c) fifty per centum of gross production of petroleum shall be applied by the contractor for the purpose of recovery of costs for petroleum operations;

(d) the remaining portion of gross production of petroleum, after deductions for the purposes of subparagraphs (b) and (c), shall be deemed to be profit petroleum and be divided equally between the Joint Authority and the contractor;

(e) all costs of petroleum operations shall be borne by the contractor and shall, subject to subparagraph (c), be recoverable from production;

(f) a minimum amount that the contractor shall expend on petroleum operations under the contract as a minimum commitment as may be agreed to by the Joint Authority and the contractor;

(g) payment of a research cess [sic] by the contractor to the Joint Authority in the amount of one half of one per centum of the aggregate of that portion of gross production which is applied for the purpose of recovery of costs under subparagraph (c) and the contractor's share of profit petroleum under subparagraph (d) in the manner and at such times as may be determined by the Joint Authority, provided that such payment shall not be recoverable from production; and

(h) any disputes or differences arising out of or in connection with the contract which cannot be amicably settled shall be referred to arbitration before a panel consisting of three arbitrators, one arbitrator to be appointed by each party, and a third to be jointly appointed by both parties. If the parties are unable to concur on the choice of a third arbitrator within a specified period, the third arbitrator shall be appointed upon application to be United Nations Commission of International Trade Law (UNCITRAL). The arbitration proceedings shall be conducted in accordance with the rules of UNCITRAL. The venue or arbitration shall be either Bangkok or Kuala Lumpur, or any other place as may be agreed to by the parties.

(3) In addition to the matters specified in paragraph (2), production sharing contract may, at the option of the Joint Authority, include the following:

(a) the period referred to under subparagraph (a) of paragraph (2) shall be applied as follows:

(i) in respect of a contract for petroleum (other than gas), the periods for the purposes of exploration, development and production shall not exceed five years, five years and twenty – five years, respectively; and

(ii) in respect of a contract for gas, the periods for the purposes of exploration, the identification and nomination of the gas market, development and production shall not exceed, in respect of the first three periods, five years each, and in respect of the fourth period, twenty years:

Provided that any period referred to in subparagraphs (a) (i) and (a) (ii) may be varied by the Joint Authority from time to time as may be necessary on condition that where any such variation affects a subsisting contract it shall only be made with the agreement of the contractor:

Provided further that where the first commercial production occurs, in the case of

(A) petroleum (other than gas), before the expiry of the development period, the balance of that development period shall be added to the production period; and

(B) gas, before the expiry of the period for the identification and nomination of the gas market or the development period, the balance of either of those periods shall be added to the production period;

(b) title to any equipment or assets purchased or acquired by the contractor for the purpose of petroleum operations shall pass to the Joint Authority upon such purchase or acquisition;

(c) the Joint Authority shall have title to all original data (raw, processed or interpreted) resulting from petroleum operations, including but not limited to geological, geophysical, core samples, petro – physical, well completion reports, engineering and other data reports and actual samples as the contractor may collect and compile; and

(d) the contractor shall purchase or acquire equipment, facilities, goods, materials, supplies, including services and research facilities, professional or otherwise, from sources in Malaysia or the Kingdom of Thailand where technically and economically feasible.

(4) The Joint Authority may vary any of the amounts referred to in subparagraphs (c), (d) and (g) of paragraph (2) in respect of any contract with the ap-

proval of the Governments:

Provided that there shall be no variation of any of these amounts in respect of a subsisting contract without the agreement of the contractor.

(5) For the purpose of this Article –

(a) "first commercial production" in relation to petroleum (other than gas) means the date that production has continued for a period of twenty – four hours following completion of testing from the first production well, and, in relation to gas, means the date within the first sixty days on which a cumulative 106 Giga Joule (approximately 947 billion BTU) of gas is first sold or, the sixtieth day after the gas is first sold if the cumulative sale within the first sixty days does not exceed 106 Giga Joule; and

(b) "gross production" with reference to gas means gross proceeds of sale of gas.

(6) The contractor shall pay export duty on its share of profit oil and petroleum income tax in accordance with Article 16 and Article 17 of this Agreement, respectively.

CHAPTER III   FINANCIAL PROVISIONS

Article 9   FINANCE

(1) All costs incurred and benefits derived by the Joint Authority from activities carried out in the Joint Development Area shall be equally borne and shared by the Governments.

(2) Until such time as the Joint Authority shall have sufficient income to finance its annual operational expenditure, the Governments shall annually provide the Joint Authority with the agreed amounts of money in equal shares to be paid into the Malaysia – Thailand Joint Authority Fund, hereinafter referred to as "the Fund".

(3) Thereupon, as specified in paragraph (2), and unless otherwise decided by the Governments, all such annual government contributions shall cease.

Article 10   ACCOUNTS AND RECORDS

(1) The Joint Authority shall cause proper accounts and other records of its

transactions and affairs to be kept in accordance with generally accepted accounting principles and shall do all things necessary to ensure that all incomes are properly accounted for all that all expenditures out of the Fund including payments of salaries, remuneration and other monetary benefits to members of the Joint Authority and its employees, are properly authorized and that adequate control is maintained over the assets of or in the custody of the Joint Authority.

(2) Either Government may at any time direct any account or records to be made available to it and the Joint Authority shall comply with such direction.

Article 11　BUDGET

The annual budget of the Joint Authority shall be submitted to the Governments well in advance before the financial year of the respective Governments for their approval.

Article 12　AUDIT

(1) The Joint Authority shall have a financial year beginning on the first day of January.

(2) The accounts of the Joint Authority shall be audited annually by an auditor appointed by the Joint Authority with the approval of the Governments.

(3) The Joint Authority shall, within six months after the end of each financial year, have its accounts audited and transmitted to both Governments together with a copy of any observations made by the auditor on any statement or on the accounts of the Joint Authority and a copy of the annual report dealing with the activities of the Joint Authority in the preceding year.

CHAPTER IV　REGULATIONS AND RELATIONS WITH OTHER ORGANIZATIONS

Article 13　REGULATIONS

The Joint Authority may, in accordance with and for the purpose of section 15 of the Acts, submit recommendations on regulations in respect of any matter falling thereunder to the Governments for consideration.

Article 14　RELATIONS WITH OTHER ORGANIZATIONS

In order to fulfill its purpose, the Joint Authority may cooperate with any government or organization, and, to this end, may, subject to the approval of the Governments, conclude any agreement or arrangement with such government or organization.

CHAPTER V   THE ACTS

Article 15   AMENDMENT OF THE ACTS

In order to facilitate the efficient management and operation of this Agreement, the Governments agree that the Acts shall not be amended without prior agreement between the Governments.

CHAPTER VI   CUSTOMS AND EXCISE, AND TAXATION

Article 16   CUSTOMS MATTERS

(1) For the purpose of Part X of the Acts

(a) the rate of export duty payable by the contractor in respect of the contractor's share of profit oil sold outside Malaysia and the Kingdom of Thailand shall be ten per centum subject to the provision of subparagraph (b) (ii);

(b) the Customs and Excise Authorities shall continue to exercise all powers in relation to all matters relating to the regulation of the movement of goods imported into or exported from the Joint Development Area in accordance with the existing legislation of Malaysia or the Kingdom of Thailand, as the case may be, subject to the following:

(i) customs approved goods, equipment and materials for use in the Joint Development area shall be accorded duty exemption if they are imported by the Joint Authority or any person authorized by it;

Provided that where one of the Governments proposes to impose any duties or taxes on any such customs approved goods, equipment and materials, it may impose such duties or taxes after consultation with the other Government;

(ii) Malaysia and the Kingdom of Thailand shall collect their respective duties and taxes collectible under their respective legislation but shall reduce the applicable rates by fifty per centum;

(iii) any goods entering the Joint Development Area from:

(A) a third country, any licensed warehouse or bonded are of either Malaysia or the Kingdom of Thailand shall be deemed an import; and

(B) Malaysia or the Kingdom of Thailand, shall be deemed an internal movement, provided they are customs approved goods, equipment and materials for use in the Joint Development Area;

(iv) any goods produced in the Joint Development Area entering Malaysia or the Kingdom of Thailand or a third country shall be deemed an export;

(v) any goods which has entered the Joint Development Area under the situation described in subparagraph (b) (iii) (B) and is to be moved into Malaysia or the Kingdom of Thailand shall be subject to the laws of Malaysia or the Kingdom of Thailand, as the case may be;

(vi) any goods falling within the category of goods appearing in both the lists of prohibited goods made in accordance with the laws of Malaysia and the Kingdom of Thailand, respectively, shall not be permitted to be brought into the Joint Development Area;

Provided that where an exception is required in respect of any specific importation, such an exception may be made with the agreement of the competent authorities of the other Country;

(vii) proceeds from any sale of forfeited goods which are the produce of the Joint Development Area shall be equally shared by Malaysia and the Kingdom of Thailand;

(c) the Customs and Excise Authorities shall use common customs forms for the purposes of import, export and internal movement of goods in the Joint Development Area as specified in subparagraphs (b) (iii) and (iv); and

(d) the Country where the headquarters of the Joint Authority is located shall empower the officers of the Customs and Excise Authority of the other Country to exercise their authority with regard to customs clearance, including the collection of duties and taxes, within the premises of the Joint Customs Office.

(2) Notwithstanding section 18 of the Acts, and insofar as it applies to cus-

toms and excise matters, the following arrangements shall apply:

(a) where an act is committed in the Joint Development Area and that act is an offence under the laws of one of the Countries only, such Country whose laws are alleged to have been breached may assume jurisdiction over such alleged offence;

(b) where the act referred to in subparagraph (a) is an offence under the laws of the Countries, the Country which may assume jurisdiction over the act shall be that whose officer first makes an arrest or seizure in respect of the alleged offence; and

(c) where the act referred to in subparagraph (a) is an offence under the laws of the Countries and in respect of which there are simultaneous arrests or seizures by the Customs and Excise Authorities, the jurisdiction over the alleged offence shall be determined through consultation between such Authorities.

(3) For the purpose of this Article –

(a) "Countries" means Malaysia and the Kingdom of Thailand, and when used in the singular means Malaysia or the Kingdom of Thailand, as the context requires;

(b) "customs approved goods" means goods in respect of which customs duties are exempted under both the laws of Malaysia and the Kingdom of Thailand relating to customs;

(c) "Customs and Excise Authority" in relation to Malaysia means the Royal Customs and Excise, Malaysia and in relation to the Kingdom of Thailand means the Customs Department of Thailand, and when used in the plural means both such Authorities;

(d) "Joint Customs Committee" means the committee comprising officers of the Customs and Excise Authorities established for the purpose of the coordination of the administration of customs and excise laws in the Joint Development Area; and

(e) "Joint Customs Office" means the office of the Joint Customs Committee established in the headquarters of the Joint Authority for the purpose of the coordination of the administration of the customs and excise laws in the Joint Development Area.

Article 17　TAXATION

(1) For the purpose of Part X of the Acts, the Revenue Authorities of the Governments shall, subject to the following, continue to impose and collect taxes in respect of income from the Joint Development Area in accordance with the existing tax legislation of Malaysia and the Kingdom of Thailand, as the case may be:

(a) the taxation of such income of any person who holds the right to explore and exploit any petroleum in the Joint Development Area under a contract awarded by the Joint Authority shall be in accordance with the following rates:

First 8 years of production	0% of taxable income
Next 7 years	10% of taxable income
Subsequent years	20% of taxable income:

Provided that the tax chargeable by each of the Governments shall be reduced to fifty per centum of the amount so chargeable:

Provided further that where the tax chargeable for each year by one of the Governments exceeds that chargeable by the other Government, such excess shall be shared equally by the two Governments and shall be effected by the Joint Authority through appropriate adjustments of payments made under paragraph (d) of section 10 of the Acts;

(b) the taxation of such income of a person who is a Malaysian or Thai national exercising employment in the Joint Development Area or with the Joint Authority shall be based on his residence; and

(c) the taxation of such income of any person other than a person mentioned in subparagraphs (a) and (b) shall be in accordance with the laws and regulations of Malaysia and the Kingdom of Thailand, provided that where the same income is subject to tax in both countries, the tax chargeable in each country shall be reduced by fifty per centum of the amount so chargeable.

(2) The Governments agree that any law for taxation which is in the nature of general sales tax, including any tax imposed on the provision of goods and services in the Joint Development Area, shall not be applicable to the Joint Development

Area.

(3) The Joint Authority shall be exempt from taxation in Malaysia and the Kingdom of Thailand.

(4) The Revenue Authorities of the Governments shall continue to communicate with and consult each other in respect of the implementation and administration of any tax law in the Joint Development Area.

CHAPTER VII   MISCELLANEOUS AND PROVISIONS

Article 18   ENTRY INTO FORCE AND TERMINATION

(1) The Agreement shall enter into force upon the exchange of instruments of ratification, and, unless otherwise agreed to by the Governments, shall remain in force for the period of validity of the Memorandum of Understanding, 1979.

(2) Upon termination of this Agreement, the Joint Authority shall be wound up in accordance with a liquidation procedure as may be approved by the Governments.

Article 19   APPLICATION

The application and interpretation of the provisions of this Agreement shall be consistent with the spirit and provisions of the Memorandum of Understanding, 1979.

Article 20   AMENDMENT

This Agreement may be amended by a joint decision of the Co－Chairman with the approval of the Governments.

Article 21   SETTLEMENT OF DISPUTES

Any differences or disputes arising out of the interpretation or application of the provisions of this Agreement shall be settled peacefully by consultation or negotiation between the Governments. In the event that no settlement is reached within a period of three months either Government may refer the matter to the Prime Minister of Malaysia and the Prime Minister of the Kingdom of Thailand who shall jointly decide on the mode of settlement for the purpose of the particular matter referred to them.

Article 22

This Agreement is made in duplicate at Kuala Lumpur, Malaysia, on the Thirtieth day of May, in the year One thousand Nine hundred and Ninety, in the English Language.

FOR THE GOVERNMENT OF
MALAYSIA

Dato' Haji Abu Hassan bin Haji Omar
Minister of Foreign Affairs

FOR THE GOVERNMENT
OF THE KINGDOM OF THAILAND

Air Chief Marshal Siddhi Savetsila
Minister of Foreign Affairs

5.《泰国—马来西亚联合管理局第 2533 号法令（1990）》

普密蓬·阿杜德陛下于执政第 45 年，8 月 29 日颁布第 2533 号法令（1990）

王晓梅译，邓妮雅校

尊敬的普密蓬·阿杜德陛下发布皇家命令，宣布，

鉴于有必要颁布一项有关马来西亚—泰国联合管理局的法律，

根据国民议会的建议和同意，最英明的国王陛下通过如下法律。

第一条

本法令命名为"泰国—马来西亚联合管理局第 2533 号法令（1990）"。

第二条

本法令自政府公报公布之日起生效。

第三条

其他现行法律、法规和规章的规定与本法令不一致或冲突的，应以本法令规定为准。

第四条

在本法令中，除非文本另有规定；

"《1979 年谅解备忘录》（B. E. 2522）"是指 1979 年 2 月 21 日签订的，《泰王国和马来西亚为开发泰国湾两国大陆架划定区域内海床资源而建立联合管理局的谅解备忘录》（B. E. 2522）；

"协定"是指泰王国政府和马来西亚于 1990 年 5 月 30 日，在马来西亚首都吉隆坡签订的《关于建立马来西亚—泰国联合管理局及其他事项的协定》（B. E. 2533）；

"政府"是指泰王国政府和马来西亚政府；

"联合管理局"是指泰国—马来西亚联合管理局；

"基金"是指第十二部分所指的泰国—马来西亚联合管理局基金；

"共同开发区"是指第九部分所指的，位于泰国湾泰国和马来西亚大陆架上的划定区域；

"管辖分界线"是指下面两点连接的直线：

（A） 北纬 6°50′00″　　东经 102°21′02″

（X） 北纬 7°35′00″　　东经 103°23′00″

该管辖分界线划分了共同开发区内的民事和刑事管辖范围；

"自然资源"是指所有的非生物自然资源，包括任何矿物质、矿物油和金属质；

"石油"是指任何矿物油，或在自然条件下存在的相关碳氢化合物和天然气，以及井口凝析油，包括沥青页岩和其他可以提炼出石油的层状沉积物；

"部长"是指负责和管控本法案执行的部长。

第五条

工业部部长应负责和管控本法案的执行，有权任命主管官员，发布有关执行的部门规章。

该部门规章自政府公报公布之日起生效。

第一部分　泰国—马来西亚联合管理局

第六条

成立泰国—马来西亚联合管理局（以下简称"联管局"）。

联管局应当具备法律人格，住所位于泰王国和马来西亚。

为了本法令的目的，联管局应可以订立合约，有权收购、购买、取得、持有和使用除土地以外的任何动产和不动产，可以运输、分配、放弃、收取、抵押、转让、转移或以其他方式处分动产和不动产，以及任何归属于联管局的财产。

第七条

联管局应享有依据本法令，履行其职责、行使其权利和特权所必需的权力和职能。

第八条

联管局被赋予和承担关于勘探和开发共同开发区的自然资源,尤其是石油资源的专属性权利、权力、自由和特权。

第二部分　共同开发区

第九条

共同开发区是由依次连接以下点的直线所构成的区域:

A	北纬 6°50′00″	东经 102°21′02″
B	北纬 7°10′025″	东经 102°29′00″
C	北纬 7°49′00″	东经 103°02′05″
D	北纬 7°22′00″	东经 103°42′05″
E	北纬 7°20′00″	东经 103°39′00″
F	北纬 7°03′00″	东经 103°06′00″
G	北纬 6°53′00″	东经 102°34′00″

该区域在英国海军航海图 1967 年版第 2414 号(B. E. 2510)相关部分标示,该区域的复制图附于本法令附件地图中。

第三部分　特许权使用费

第十条

联管局应按照部门规章规定的时间和方式,向双方政府各缴纳石油总产量5%的特许权使用费。

第四部分　财务规定

第十一条

联管局在共同开发区的活动所产生的费用应由双方政府平等分担,所获收益也由双方政府平等分享。

运行期间,联管局若没有足够的收入负担其年度运营支出,泰王国和马来西亚国政府应当依据协定,向基金内支付相等数额的年度经费。

第五部分　泰国—马来西亚联合管理局基金

第十二条

为了本法令和协定的目的，成立泰国—马来西亚联合管理局基金（本法令中简称"基金"），该基金由联合管理局监管。

基金的资产应当包括：

（1）依据第十一条后半部分和协定，双方政府缴纳的捐资；

（2）任何由基金资助的项目、计划和企业的运营所取得的资金；

（3）联管局购入或属于联管局的任何财产、投资、抵押或收费孳生的资金；

（4）联管局为履行义务和职责所借的资金；

（5）其他与联管局权力和职责相关的，应支付给或归属于联管局的资金或财产。

第十三条

基金可用于：

（1）依据第十八条制定的部门规章，联管局按照批准的预算内容，支付为履行职责和行使权力而产生的费用；

（2）归还联管局根据第15部分第1款第（3）项的借款，包括借款产生的利息和费用；

（3）联管局根据政府的批准而进行的投资；以及

（4）根据第十四条规定，扣除本条第（1）和第（2）款的费用，以及其他经政府同意的花费，将联管局的收入以平等份额支付给双方政府。

第十四条

联管局应依据双方政府共同决定的条款和条件，在基金内部建立和管理一个储备基金。

第十五条

未经双方政府事先批准，联管局不应从事以下行为：

（1）通过购买股权、债券或以贷款、预付款、经费或其他方式，给予任何企业、团体和个人以经济援助；

（2）以购买、出售、包销或其他方式购入任何国有或私有公司的股票和债券；

(3) 借款，或进行任何具有经济责任的担保或赔偿；

授权允许从事本条第（1）款的行为时，双方政府应共同决定施加其认为合适的条款和条件。

第十六条

本法案在任何情况下都不应为泰王国政府和马来西亚政府创设任何责任，或使其承担联管局的任何违法责任。

第六部分　勘探和开发合同

第十七条

尽管有其他成文法规定，在共同开发区内除了联管局外，任何人都不能进行任何自然资源，包括石油的勘探和开发，除非其与联管局签订了勘探和开发自然资源的合同。

以上所指的合同应有双方政府的事先批准。

根据第（4）款的规定，第（1）款所指的石油的勘探和开采合同应为产品分成合同，除其他事项外还应包含以下条款和条件：

（1）根据第十条，承包商应向联管局缴纳石油总产量的10%作为特许经营税费，支付方式和时间可在合同中详细说明；

（2）承包商应将石油总产量的50%用于维护石油作业的费用；

（3）在扣除第（1）和第（2）项之后，石油总产量的剩余部分应作为利润油，由联管局和承包商平均分配；

（4）合同的有效期不应超过35年，也不应超过协定的有效期；

（5）石油作业的所有费用应由承包商承担，根据第（2）项，该费用可以从产量中补偿；

（6）联管局和承包商可以协商，确定承包商在石油作业中的最低花费应作为最低承诺；

（7）承包商应向联管局支付总石油总产量的0.5%，作为研究经费，该经费用于研究第（2）项成本回收以及第（3）项承包商利润油的分享，支付的方式和时间由联管局决定，但该费用不能从产量中进行补偿；

（8）双方因合同产生的任何分歧或争端若不能和平地解决，则应该把该争议提交由3名仲裁员组成的仲裁小组裁决。其中双方各自指定一名仲裁员，并共同指定第三名仲裁员。若双方在一定时间内不能就第三名仲裁员的人选达成一致，则应请求联合国国际贸易委员会指派一名仲裁员。仲裁程序应当依据联合国国际贸易委员会规则进行。仲裁地点应为曼谷或吉隆坡或双方一致同意的其他地点。联管局可以在获得政府批准后，变更合同中第（2）款第（c）（d）（g）项所指的数量；但在承包商同意的情形下，不能对既有合同中规定的数量做任何改变。

为了本条之目的，天然气的总产量是指天然气的出售总额。

第七部分 规章

第十八条

经双方政府同意，部长可就以下事项制定部门规章：

（1）有关共同开发区内自然资源勘探和开采的商业或服务行为；

（2）联管局根据第十条和第十三条第（4）项支付给双方政府的任何费用；

（3）联管局联合主席和其他成员的任命、薪酬、差旅费和生活津贴的条款和条件；

（4）依据本法令第十七条产品分成合同的招标与中标程序，以及产品分成合同中可能包括的条款和条件；

（5）依据一般会计原则，对联管局的交易和其他事务进行妥善保存和记录；

（6）准备年度账目报表和按照本法案条款进行利润分配；

（7）审计账目并提交给双方政府；

（8）准备年度预算并提交双方政府；

（9）在共同开发区勘探和开采的规则和程序；

（10）影响本法令实施效果的其他事项。

涉及上述第（1）、（4）、（5）、（6）、（7）、（8）和（9）之事项的部门规章，应事先与联管局进行协商。

第八部分 官员和法院司法管辖权

第十九条

所有联管局成员，官员、工人以及联管局的代理人，以及部长根据第五条指定的主管人员，均属于刑法上的特定公职人员。

第二十条

尽管有其他成文法规定，宋卡省法院、民事法院或刑事法院，对本法案或部门规章规定的事项具有管辖权。

对违反本法令或其第十八条规定的部门规章的行为，实施管辖权时，应适用第二十一条第2款和第二十一条第6款第（2）和第（4）项的规定。

第九部分　司法管辖

第二十一条

根据第（2）和第（3）款规定，泰国应继续在共同开发区行使管辖权。

（1）泰国在共同开发区内的民事和刑事管辖权范围，延伸至连接下列坐标点的直线构成的区域：

A	北纬6°50′00″	东经102°21′02″
B	北纬7°10′25″	东经102°29′00″
C	北纬7°91′00″	东经103°02′05″
X	北纬7°35′00″	东经103°23′05″

（2）马来西亚在共同开发区内的民事和刑事管辖权范围，延伸至连接下列坐标点的直线构成的区域：

A	北纬6°50′00″	东经102°21′02″
X	北纬7°35′00″	东经103°23′00″
D	北纬7°22′00″	东经103°42′05″
E	北纬7°20′00″	东经103°39′00″
F	北纬7°03′00″	东经103°06′00″
G	北纬6°53′00″	东经102°34′00″

本法令的任何内容不影响泰王国在共同开发区的主权权利，本条下任何管辖权的放弃，在协议到期之后，不具有任何效力和影响。泰王国对马来西亚在第（2）款第（2）项区域内行使民事和刑事管辖权，以及共同开发区内对海关、税务和税收事务管辖权的同意，应基于互惠承认，马来西

亚也同意泰国在第（2）款第（1）项规定之区域内享有同等管辖权。

马来西亚和泰国依据本条，在共同开发区内享有的管辖权，不得超出一般国际法承认的，与大陆架制度有关的法律所规定的事项。为了本条之目的：

（a）"民事和刑事管辖权"不包括对关税、消费税和其他税收有关事项的管辖权；

（b）对发生在横跨管辖权界线，或为勘探和开采共同开发区海床和底土的自然资源而建造的钻井平台或设施上的犯罪行为，其刑事管辖权应仅由该钻井平台或设施设立国马来西亚或泰国来行使；

（c）在决定横跨管辖权分界线，或为勘探和开采共同开发区海床和底土的自然资源而建造的钻井平台或设施，适用泰国还是马来西亚的民事程序或由泰国还是马来西亚行使民事管辖权，应根据该钻井平台或设施是马来西亚还是泰国设立的来决定；以及

（d）第（2）和第（3）项所指钻井平台或设施的设立国是泰国或马来西亚，应根据最具体的位置原则来决定。

第十部分　上覆水域的权利

第二十二条

本法令的条款，既不调整泰国或马来西亚根据1979年《谅解备忘录》（B. E. 2522）第四条在共同开发区上覆水域，包括与渔业相关的任何权益、权利和特权，也不影响对该上覆水域的任何主张。

第十一部分　违法行为和处罚

第二十三条

根据第二十五条，任何人，包括法人团体的董事或主管，若违反了第十七条第1项规定应被判处5年以下有期徒刑，或不超过50万泰铢的罚款，或两者并罚；若犯罪仍持续进行，则应在判决宣布后第一天后、犯罪持续期间，另处每天（不足一天按一天算）不超过1万泰铢的罚款；罚没任何用于或准备用于犯罪的设备、工具、赃物、建造物及其他财产或物品。

第二十四条

根据第二十三和第二十五条，任何人，包括法人团体的董事或主管，

若违反本法案或依据第十八条制定的部门规章，应判处两年以下有期徒刑，或不超过20万泰铢的罚款，或两者并罚；若犯罪持续进行，则在判决宣布后第一天后、犯罪持续期间，另处每天（不足一天按一天算）不超过2000泰铢的罚款。

第二十五条

若法人团体实施第二十三或第二十四条的犯罪行为，则仅按照规定处以罚款。

第二十六条

若法人团体违反了本法令或依据第十八条制定的部门规章，违法行为发生时担任该法人团体的董事或主管者应被共同定罪处罚，除非该法人团体的董事或主管可以证明其不知情或已采取合理措施阻止违法犯罪行为的发生，否则该董事或主管会则被推定有罪。

第二十七条

若本人代理人的行为违反了本法令或依据第十八条制定的部门规章，本人负有和代理人同样的责任，除非本人能证明已采取合理措施阻止代理人的行为或疏忽的发生。

6. Thailand – Malaysia Joint Authority Act, B. E. 2553 (1990)

Given on the 29th August, B. E. 2553 (1990)

Being the 45th Year of Present Regin

Bhumibol Adulyadej P. R.

By Royal Command of His Majesty King Bhumibol Adulyadej, it is hereby proclaimed that;

Whereas it is deemed proper to enact a law on Thailand – Malaysia Joint Authority;

Be it, therefore, enacted by the King's most Excellent Majesty, by and with the advice and consent of National Assembly, as follows:

Section 1

This Act shall be called the "Thailand – Malaysia Joint Authority Act, B. E. 2553 (1990)".

Section 2

This Act comes into force as from the day following the date of its publication in the Government Gazette.

Section 3

Those provisions of all other laws, regulations and rules in as so far as they are stipulated herein or are contrary to or inconsistent with the provisions hereof shall be replaced hereby.

Section 4

In this Act, unless the context otherwise requires;

"Memorandum of Understanding, 1979 (B. E. 2522)" means the Memorandum of Understanding between the kingdom of Thailand and Malaysia on the Establishment of the Joint Authority for the Exploitation of the Resources of the Sea Bed in a Defined Area of the Continental Shelf of the Two Countries in the Gulf of Thailand, signed on the 21 February 1979 (B. E. 2522);

"Agreement" means Agreement on the Constitution and Other Matters Relating to the Establishment of the Malaysia – Thailand Joint Authority signed by the Government of the Kingdom of Thailand and the Government of Malaysia on 30 May B. E. 2553, at Kuala Lumpur, Malaysia;

"Governments" means the Government of the Kingdom of Thailand and the Government of Malaysia;

"Joint Authority" means Thailand – Malaysia Joint Authority;

"Funds" means Thailand – Malaysia Joint Authority Fund referred to under Section 12;

"Joint Development Area" means the defined area of the continent shelf of Kingdom of Thailand and Malaysia in the Gulf of Thailand described under Section 9;

"Line Dividing Jurisdiction" means the straight line joining the following coordinated points;

(A)　N 6°50′.0　　　　E 102°21′.2
(X)　N 7°35′.0　　　　E 103°23′.0

which divides civil and criminal jurisdiction in the Joint Development Area;

"natural resources" means any non – living natural resources including any minerals, mineral oils and metals;

"petroleum" means any mineral oil or relative hydrocarbon and natural gas existing in its natural condition and casing head petroleum spirit, including bituminous shales and other stratifies deposits from which oil can be extracted;

"Minster" means the Minister having charge and control the execution of this Act.

Section 5

The Minister of Industry shall have charge and control of the charge of the execution of this Act and shall have the power to appoint competent officers and to issue Ministerial Regulations for the execution thereof.

Such Ministerial Regulations shall come into force after their publication in the Government Gazette.

PART I THAILAND – MALAYSIA JOINT AUTHORITY

Section 6

There is hereby established a body by the name of Thailand – Malaysia Joint Authority (referred to in this Act as "the joint Authority").

The joint authority shall have a juristic personality and shall be domiciled in the Kingdom of Thailand and Malaysia.

Subject to and for the purpose of this Act, the joint Authority is empowered to enter into contracts, and to acquire, purchase, take, hold and enjoy any movable and immovable property of every description, excluding the holding of title of land, and is empowered to convey, assign, surrender, charge, mortgage, reassign, transfer or otherwise dispose of, or deal with, any movable or immovable property or any interest therein vested in the joint Authority upon such terms as it deems appropriate.

Section 7

The joint Authority shall have such powers and perform such functions as are necessary for the performance of its duties and the enjoyment of its rights and privileges under, and to the extent not inconsistent with, this Act.

Section 8

The joint Authority is hereby vested with and assumes the exclusive rights, powers, liberties and privileges of exploring and exploiting the natural resources, in particular petroleum, in the Joint Development Area.

PART II THE JOINT DEVELOPMENT AREA

Section 9

The joint Development Area shall be the area bounded by of straight lines joining the following coordinated points:

A	N6°50′.0	E102°21′.2
B	N7°10′.25	E102°29′.0
C	N7°49′.0	E103°02′.5
D	N7°22′.0	E103°42′.5
E	N7°20′.0	E103°39′.0
F	N7°03′.0	E103°06′.0
G	N6°53′.0	E102°34′.0

and shown in the relevant part of the British Admiralty Chart No. 2414, Edition 1967 (B.E. 2510), a reproduction of which is as in the map annexed to this Act.

PART III ROYALTY

Section 10

The Joint Authority shall pay royalty to each of the Government in the account of five per centum of gross production of petroleum, in the manner and at such times as may be prescribed by Ministerial Regulations.

PART IV FINANCIAL PROVISIONS

Section 11

All cost incurred and benefits derived by the joint Authority from activities carried out in the joint Development Area shall be equally borne and shared by the Governments.

During the period which the joint Authority does not have sufficient income to finance its annual operational expenditure, the Government of the Kingdom of Thailand shall pay to the Fund annual payments as may be determined in accordance with the Agreement, subject to equal payments being made by the Government of Malaysia.

PART V THE THAILAND – MALAYSIA JOINT AUTHORITY FUND

Section 12

For the purpose of this Act and the Agreement, there is hereby established a

Fund called the Thailand – Malaysia Joint Authority Fund (referred to this Act as "the Fund") to be administered and controlled by the joint Authority.

The assets of the Funds shall include:

(1) contributions as may be provided by the Governments under the Agreement, and referred to under Section 11, paragraph 2;

(2) monies earned by the operation of any projects, schemes or enterprises financed from the Fund;

(3) monies earned or arising from any properties, investments, mortgages, or charges acquired by or vested in the joint Authority;

(4) monies borrowed by the joint Authority for the purposes of meeting any of its obligations or discharging any of its duties; and

(5) any other monies or properties which may in any manner become payable to or vested in the joint Authority in respect of any matters incidental to its powers and duties.

Section 13

The Fund may be used for:

(1) defraying such expenditures as the Joint Authority may incur in carrying out its functions and exercising its powers in accordance with the approved budgetary provisions and subject to any Minister Regulation issued under Section 18;

(2) setting any monies borrowed by the Joint Authority under Section 15 paragraph 1 (3), including interests and other charges incidental to the borrowing;

(3) investments as the Joint Authority may decide subject to the approval of the Government; and

(4) subject to Section 14, payment of monies in equal amounts to the Government out of income accruing to the Joint Authority after deducting the expenditures referred to in (1) and (2) including such other expenditures as may be agreed to by the Governments.

Section 14

The Joint Authority shall establish and manage a reserve fund within the Fund in accordance with such terms and conditions as the Governments may jointly decide.

Section 15

The Joint Authority shall not undertake the following actions unless it has received prior approval from the Governments

(1) to give financial assistance to any company, body or person by the taking up of shares or debentures or by way of loan, advance, grant or otherwise;

(2) to purchase, dispose, underwrite, or otherwise acquire any stocks and shares in any public or private company; or

(3) to borrow money, or enter into any guarantee or indemnity involving financial liability.

In giving any consent under paragraph 1 the Governments may jointly impose terms and conditions as they may deem appropriate.

Section 16

The provisions of this Act shall not create any responsibility whatsoever for the Government of the Kingdom of Thailand or the Government of Malaysia in respect of any liability of the Joint Authority.

PART VI CONTRACT FOR EXPLORATION AND EXPLORATION

Section 17

Notwithstanding the provisions of any other written law, no person, except the Joint Authority, shall carry out any business of exploration and exploitation of any natural resources, including petroleum, in the Joint Development Area unless there is a contract entered into between the Joint Authority and such person to explore and exploit such natural resources.

A contract referred to under paragraph 1 shall require the prior approval of the Governments.

Subject to the provisions of paragraph 4, in the case where a contract referred to under paragraph 1 is the contract for exploration and exploitation of petroleum, such contract shall be a production sharing contract and shall include, amongst others, the following terms and conditions:

(1) for the purpose of section 10, the contractor shall pay royalty in the amount of ten per centum of gross production of petroleum to the Joint Authority in the manner and at such times as may be specified in the contract;

(2) the contractor shall apply fifty per centum of gross production of petroleum for the purpose of recovery of costs for petroleum operations;

(3) the remaining portion of gross production of petroleum, after deductions for the purpose of (1) and (2), shall be deemed to be profit petroleum and be divided equally between the Joint Authority and the contractor;

(4) the contract shall be valid for a period not exceeding thirty – five years but shall not exceed the period of validity of the Agreement;

(5) all costs of petroleum operations shall be borne by the contractor and shall, subject to (2), be recoverable from production;

(6) a minimum amount that the contractor shall expend on petroleum operations under the contract as a minimum commitment as may be agreed to by the Joint Authority and the contractor;

(7) the contractor shall pay a research cess to the Joint Authority in the amount of one half of one per centum of the aggregate of the portion of gross production which is applied for the purpose of recovery of the costs under (2) and the contractor's share of profit petroleum under (3) in the manner and at such times as may be determined by the Joint Authority, provided that such payment shall not be recoverable from production; and

(8) any disputes or differences arising out of or in connection with the contract which cannot be amicably settled shall be referred to arbitration before a panel consisting of three arbitrators, one arbitrator to be pointed by each party, and a third to be jointly appointed by both parties. If the parties are unable to

concur on the choice of a third arbitrator within a specified period, the third arbitrator shall be appointed upon application to the United Nations Commission of International Trade Law (UNCITRAL). The arbitration proceedings shall be conducted in accordance with the rules of UNCITRAL. The venue of arbitration shall be either Bangkok or Kuaka Lumpur, or any other place as may be agreed to by the parties. The Joint Authority may vary any of the amounts referred to in (2), (3) and (7) of paragraph 3 in respect of any contract with the approval of the Governments; provided that there shall be no variation of any of these amounts in respect of a subsisting contract without the agreement of the contractor.

For the purpose of this section, "gross production" with reference to gas means gross proceeds of sale of gas.

PART VII REGULATIONS

Section 18

The Minister, with the approval of the Governments, shall have the power to issue Ministerial Regulations in respect of the following:

(1) the conduct of or the carrying on of any business or service relating to the exploration and exploitation of the natural resources in the Joint Development Area;

(2) the payment of any monies due to the Governments from the Joint Authority under Section 10 and Section 13 (4);

(3) the terms and conditions of the appointment of, and the emoluments, traveling and subsistence allowance payable to, the Co-Chairman and other members of the Joint Authority;

(4) the procedure for the tender and award of any contract that may be entered into under Section 17, including the terms and conditions that may be included in such contract;

(5) the keeping of proper accounts and other records of the transactions and affairs of the Joint Authority in accordance with generally accepted accounting principles;

(6) the preparation of annual statements of accounts and, subject to the provisions of this Act, the allocation of;

(7) the audit of accounts and its subsequent submission to the Governments;

(8) the preparation and submission of the annual budget to the Governments;

(9) the rules and procedures for the exploration and exploitation of petroleum in the Joint Development Area; and

(10) any other matters for the purpose of carrying into effect the provisions of this Act.

Provided that in respect of the Minister Regulations relating to matters referred to under (1), (4), (5), (6), (7), (8) and (9) above, such regulations may be made after consultations with the Joint Authority.

PART VIII OFFICERS AND JURISDICTIONG OF COURTS

Section 19

Any member, officer, servant, and agent of the Joint Authority and any competent officer who has been appointed by the minister under Section 5 shall be the officer – designated under the Criminal Code.

Section 20

Notwithstanding the provision of any other written law, the Provincial Court of Songkhla, the Civil Court or the Criminal Court shall have jurisdiction to try and adjudicate on any case under this Act or Ministerial Regulations issued thereunder.

For the purpose of the exercise of jurisdiction over any offence committed under this Act or Ministerial Regulations issued under Section 18, the provision of Section 21 paragraph 2 and Section 21 paragraph 6 (2) and (4) shall apply.

PART IX JURISDICTION

Section 21

Subjected to paragraph 2 and paragraph 2, the Kingdom of Thailand shall continued to have and exercise jurisdiction over the joint Development Area.

The civil and criminal jurisdiction of

(七) 1979年泰国与马来西亚有关泰国湾的共同开发案

(1) The Kingdom of Thailand in the joint Development Area shall extend over the area bounded by straight lines joining the following coordinated points:

A	N6°50′.00	E102°21′.2
B	N7°10′.25	E102°29′.0
C	N7°91′.00	E103°02′.5
X	N7°35′.00	E103°23′.5

(2) Malaysia in the joint Development Area shall extend over the area bounded by straight lines joining the following coordinated points:

A	N6°50′.0	E102°21′.2
X	N7°35′.0	E103°23′.0
D	N7°22′.0	E103°42′.5
E	N7°20′.0	E103°39′.0
F	N7°03′.0	E103°06′.0
G	N6°53′.0	E102°34′.0

The provisions of this Act shall not in any way effect the sovereign rights of the Kingdom of Thailand over the joint Development Area, and any waiver of jurisdiction under this section shall have no force and effect beyond the period of validity of the Agreement. The consent by the Kingdom of Thailand to the exercise of civil and criminal jurisdiction over matters relating to customs and exercise, and taxation in the joint Development Area shall be conditional upon a reciprocal recognition of the Kingdom of Thailand's rights under (1) of paragraph 2.

Any jurisdiction that may be vested in the Kingdom of Thailand or Malaysia under this section in respect of the joint Development Area shall only be over matters and to the extent provided for in any law relating to the continental shelf and as recognized under international law. For the purpose of this section:

(1) "civil and criminal jurisdiction" shall not include jurisdiction over matters relating to customs and exercise, and taxation;

(2) criminal jurisdiction over an offence committed on a platform or an in-

stallation which straddles the line dividing jurisdiction and constructed for the purposes of exploration and exploitation of the natural resources of the sea – bed and subsoil in the joint Development Area is to be assumed exclusively by the Kingdom of Thailand or Malaysia in accordance with the designation of such platform or installation as Thai or Malaysian;

(3) the determination of whether a platform or an installation which straddles the line dividing jurisdiction and constructed for the purposes of exploration and exploitation of the natural resources of the sea – bed and subsoil in the joint Development Area is part of the Kingdom of Thailand or Malaysia in relation to any question that falls to be determined in any civil proceedings or for the purpose of the assumption or exercise of civil jurisdiction by the Kingdom of Thailand or Malaysia shall be in accordance with the designation of such platform or installation as Thai or Malaysian; and

(4) the designation of a platform or an installation as Thai or Malaysian under (2) and (3) shall be determined according to the principle of most substantial location.

PART X RIGHTS IN SUPERJACENT WATERS

Section 22

The provisions of this Act shall neither regulate any rights, Rights and privileges, including to those relating to fishing, nor effect any claims thereof, that the Kingdom of Thailand or Malaysia may have over the superjacent waters of the joint Development Area by virtue fi Article IV of the Memorandum of Understanding, 1979 (B. E. 2522).

PART XI OFFENCES AND RENALTY

Section 23

Subject to Section 25, any person, including a director or officer of a body corporate, who violates Section 17 paragraph 1, shall be liable to imprisonment for a term not exceeding five years or to a fine not exceeding five hundred thousand Baht or to both; and, in the case of a continuing offence, shall be liable to a further fine not exceeding ten thousand Baht per day or part of a day during which the offence continues after the first day of pronouncement of the judgment; and any machinery, tools, plants, buildings and other properties or things used or intended to be used in the commission of the offence shall be forfeited.

Section 24

Subjection to Section 23 and Section 25, any person, including a director or officer of a body corporate, who violates any provision of this Act or Ministerial Regulation issued under Section 18 shall be liable to imprisonment for a term not exceeding two years or to a fine five years or to a fine not exceeding two hundred thousand Baht or to both; and, in the case of a continuing offence, shall be liable to a further fine not exceeding two thousand Baht per day or part of a day during which the offence continues after the first day of pronouncement of the judgment.

Section 25

Where a person convicted in respect of any offence referred to under Section 23 or Section 24 is a body corporate, it shall only be liable to the imposition of any fine provided therein.

Section 26

Where a person charged with an offence under this Act or any Ministerial Regulation issued under Section 18 is a body corporate every person who, at the time of the commission of the offence, is a director or officer of the body corporate may be charged jointly in the same proceedings with the body corporate, and where the body corporate is convicted of the offence charged, every such director or officer shall be deemed to be guilty of that offence unless he can prove that the offence was committed without his knowledge or that he took reasonable precautions to prevent its commission.

Section 27

If an agent of a person commits the offences under this Act or Ministerial Regulation issued under Section 18, that person shall also be deemed to be liable to the same penalty as his agent, unless he can prove that he has taken reasonable precautions to prevent the doing or omission of the thing.

7.《马来西亚和泰国联合管理局第 440 号法令（1991）》

王晓梅译，邓妮雅校

序　言

本法令旨在执行建立和运行马来西亚—泰国联合管理局的协议，并制定相关规定。

1991 年 1 月 23 日

本法令依据马来西亚和泰王国政府于 1979 年 2 月 21 日签订的《马来西亚和泰王国为开发泰国湾两国大陆架划定区域内海床资源而建立联合管理局的谅解备忘录》，以及 1990 年于马来西亚首都吉隆坡签订的《马来西亚和泰王国政府关于建立马来西亚—泰国联合管理局及其他事项的 1990 年协定》而制定。

因此，本法令由尊敬的马来西亚国王陛下根据马来西亚上议院和下议院的建议和许可以及授权，颁布如下。

第一部分　初步措施

第一条　简称及生效

（1）本法令名称为《马来西亚—泰国联合管理局 1990 年法令》。

（2）本法令自部长公布于指定的政府公报之日起生效。

第二条　解释

在本法令中，除非文中另有规定，

"协定"是指 1990 年 5 月 30 日于马来西亚首都吉隆坡签订的《马来西亚和泰王国政府关于建立马来西亚—泰国联合管理局及其他事项的 1990 年协定》；

"基金"是指第九部分提到的马来西亚和泰国联合管理局基金；

"政府"是指马来西亚政府和泰王国政府；

"联管局"是指马来西亚—泰国联合管理局；

"共同开发区"是指第六部分所指的马来西亚和泰王国位于泰国湾大陆架的指定区域；

"管辖分界线"是连接指下面两点的直线：

（A） 北纬 6°50′00″　　　东经 102°21′02″

（X） 北纬 7°35′00″　　　东经 103°23′00″

管辖分界线划分了共同开发区内的民事和刑事管辖范围；

"1979 年谅解备忘录"是指于 1979 年 2 月 21 日签订的《马来西亚和泰王国为开发泰国湾两国大陆架划定区域内海床资源而建立联合管理局的谅解备忘录》；

"部长"是指负责管理石油资源的部长；

"自然资源"是指包括任何矿物质、矿物油和金属质的非生物自然资源；

"石油"是指任何矿物油，或在自然条件下存在的相关碳氢化合物和天然气，以及井口凝析油，包括沥青页岩和其他可以提炼出石油的层状沉积物。

第二部分　马来西亚—泰国联合管理局

第三条　马来西亚—泰国联合管理局的成立

（1）成立马来西亚和泰国联管局（本法令中简称"联管局"）。

（2）联管局应当具备法律人格，且住所应位于马来西亚和泰王国。

（3）联管局应当是一个法人团体，根据本法令的目的，依据本法令，可以订立合约，有权收购、购买、取得、持有和使用除土地以外的任何动产和不动产，可以运输、分配、放弃、收取、抵押、转让、转移或以其他方式处分动产和不动产，以及任何归属于联管局的财产。

第四条　联管局的权力和职能

联管局应享有依据本法令履行其职责、行使其权力和特权所必需的权力和职能。

第五条　自然资源的勘探和开采

联管局被赋予和承担有关勘探和开发共同开发区的自然资源，尤其是石油资源的专属性权利、权力、自由和特权。

第三部分　共同开发区

第六条　共同开发区

共同开发区是由连接以下点的直线所构成的区域：

A	北纬 6°50′00″	东经 102°21′02″
B	北纬 7°10′25″	东经 102°29′00″
C	北纬 7°49′00″	东经 103°02′05″
D	北纬 7°22′00″	东经 103°42′05″
E	北纬 7°20′00″	东经 103°39′00″
F	北纬 7°03′00″	东经 103°06′00″
G	北纬 6°53′00″	东经 102°34′00″

该区域在英国海军航海图 1967 年版第 2414 号（B. E. 2510）相关部分标示，该区域的复制图附于本法令附件地图中。

第四部分　特许权使用费

第七条　特许权使用费

联管局应按照法规规定的时间和方式，向双方政府各缴纳石油总产量 5% 的特许权使用费。

第五部分　财务事项

第八条　费用、收益和年费

（1）联管局在共同开发区的活动所产生的费用应由双方政府平等分担，获得的收益也由双方政府平等分享。

（2）联管局若没有足够的收入负担其年度运营支出，马来西亚和泰国国政府应当依据协定，向基金内支付相等数额的年度经费。

第六部分　马泰联管基金

第九条　基金的成立

（1）根据协定和本法令的立法目的，成立马泰联管基金（在本法令中简称"基金"），该基金由联管局监管。

（2）基金的资产应当包括——

（a）依据本法令第八条第2款和协定，双方政府缴纳的捐资；

（b）任何由基金资助的项目、计划和企业的运营所取得的资金；

（c）联管局购入或属于联管局的任何财产、投资、抵押或收费孳生的资金；

（d）联管局为履行义务和职责所借的资金；

（e）其他与联管局权力和职责相关的，应支付给或归属于联管局的资金或财产。

第十条　基金的用途

基金可用于——

（a）依据第十五条制定的规章，联管局按照批准的预算内容，支付为履行职责和行使权力而产生的费用；

（b）归还联管局根据第十二条第（1）款第c项的借款，包括借款产生的利息和费用；

（c）联管局根据政府的批准而进行的投资；以及

（d）根据第十一条的规定，扣除第（a）和第（b）项中的费用，以及其他经政府同意的花费，将联管局的收入以平等份额支付给双方政府。

第十一条　储备基金

联管局应依据双方政府共同决定的条款和条件，在基金内部建立和管理一个储备基金。

第十二条　金融交易的限制

（1）未经双方政府同意，联管局不应做出以下行为——

（a）通过占有股权、债券或以贷款、预付款、拨款等其他方式给予任何企业、团体和个人以财政资助；

（b）以购买、出售、包销或其他方式购入任何国有或私有公司的股票和债券；

（c）借款，或进行任何具有经济责任的担保或赔偿。

（2）授权允许从事第（1）款的行为时，双方政府应共同决定施加其认为合适的条款和条件。

第十三条　政府不承担联管局的违法责任

本法令在任何情况下都不应为马来西亚政府和泰国政府创设任何责任，使其承担联管局的任何违法责任。

第七部分　勘探和开采合同

第十四条　勘探和开采自然资源必须签订合同

（1）尽管有其他成文法规定，在共同开发区内除了联管局外，任何人都不能进行任何自然资源包括石油的勘探和开发，除非其与联管局签订了勘探和开发自然资源的合同。

（2）上述第（1）款所指的合同应有双方政府的事先批准。

（3）根据第（4）款的规定，第（1）款所指的石油的勘探和开采合同应为产品分成合同，除其他事项外还应包含以下条款和条件：

（a）根据第7条，承包商应向联管局缴纳石油总产量的10%作为特许经营税费，支付方式和时间可在合同中详细说明；

（b）承包商应将石油总产量的50%用于维护石油作业的费用；

（c）在扣除第（a）和第（b）项之后，石油总产量的剩余部分应作为利润油，由联管局和承包商平均分配；

（d）合同的有效期不应超过35年，也不应超过协定的有效期；

（e）石油作业的所有费用应由承包商承担，根据（b）项，该费用可以从产量中补偿；

（f）联管局和承包商可以协商，确定承包商在石油作业中的最低花费应作为最低承诺；

（g）承包商应向联管局支付石油总产量的0.5%，作为研究经费，该经费用于研究第（b）项成本回收以及第（c）项承包商利润油的分享，支付的方式和时间由联管局决定，但该费用不能从产量中进行补偿；

（h）双方因合同产生的任何分歧或争端若不能和平地解决，则应该把该争议提交由3名仲裁员组成的仲裁小组裁决。其中双方各自指定一名仲裁员，并共同指定第三名仲裁员。若双方在一定的时间内不能就第三名仲裁员的人选达成一致，则应请求联合国国际贸易委员会指派一名仲裁员。仲裁程序应当依据联合国国际贸易委员会规则进行。仲裁地点应为曼谷或吉隆坡或双方一致同意的其他地点。

(4) 联管局可以在获得政府批准后,变更合同中依据第(3)款第(b)(c)(g)项所指的数量;但未经承包商同意,不能对既有合同中规定的数量做任何改变。

(5) 为了本条的目的,天然气的"总产量"是指天然气的销售总额。

第八部分 规章

第十五条 部长制定规章的权力

经双方政府同意,部长可就以下事项制定部门规章:

(a) 共同开发区内任何有关自然资源勘探和开采的商业或服务行为;

(b) 联管局根据第七条和第十条第(d)项支付给双方政府的任何费用;

(c) 联管局联合主席和其他成员的任命、薪酬、差旅费和生活津贴的条款和条件;

(d) 依据第十四条产品分成合同的招标与中标程序,以及产品分成合同中可能包括的条款和条件;

(e) 依据一般会计原则,对联管局交易和其他事务进行妥善保存和记录;

(f) 准备年度账目报表和按照本法令条款进行利润分配;

(g) 审计账目并提交给双方政府;

(g) 准备年度预算并提交双方政府;

(i) 共同开发区内石油勘探和开采的标准;

(j) 影响本法令实施效果的其他事项;涉及上述第(a),(d),(e),(f),(g),(h)和(i)项的规章,应事先与联管局进行协商。

第九部分 官员和法庭的管辖权

第十六条 公职人员

联管局的所有成员,或其他官员、工人以及联管局的代理人,以及部长根据第五条指定的主管人员,均属于刑法上的特定公职人员。

第十七条 地方法院司法管辖权

(1) 尽管有其他成文法的相反规定,地方法院对违反本法令或其他法规的犯罪行为有管辖权,有权进行处罚。

（2）为了对任何违反本法令或根据第十五条制定规章的犯罪行为行使管辖权，应适用第十八条第（2）款和第（6）款第（b）和第（d）项的规定。

第十部分　司法管辖

第十八条　共同开发区内的司法管辖

（1）根据第（2）和第（3）款的规定，马来西亚应在共同开发区内继续享有和行使管辖权。

（2）民事和刑事管辖

（a）马来西亚在共同开发区内的民事和刑事管辖权范围，延伸至连接下列坐标点的直线构成的区域：

A	北纬 6°50′00″	东经 102°21′02″
X	北纬 7°35′00″	东经 103°23′00″
D	北纬 7°22′00″	东经 103°42′05″
E	北纬 7°20′00″	东经 103°39′00″
F	北纬 7°03′00″	东经 103°06′00″
G	北纬 6°53′00″	东经 102°34′00″

（b）泰国在共同开发区内的民事和刑事管辖权范围，延伸至连接下列坐标点的直线构成的区域：

A	北纬 6°50′00″	东经 102°21′02″
B	北纬 7°10′25″	东经 102°29′00″
C	北纬 7°91′00″	东经 103°02′05″
X	北纬 7°35′00″	东经 103°23′05″

（3）本法令的任何内容不影响马来西亚在共同开发区的主权权利，本条下任何管辖权的放弃在协议到期之后，不具有任何效力和影响。

（4）马来西亚对泰王国在第（2）款第（b）项区域内行使民事和刑事管辖权，以及共同开发区内对海关、税务和税收事务管辖权的同意，应基于互惠承认，泰王国也同意马来西亚在第（2）款第（a）项区域内享有同等管辖权。

(5) 马来西亚和泰国依据本条,在共同开发区内享有的管辖权,不得超出一般国际法承认的,与大陆架制度有关的法律所规定的事项。

(6) 为了本条的目的——

(a) 民事和刑事管辖权不包括海关、税务和税收事务;

(b) 对发生在横跨管辖权界线,或为勘探和开采共同开发区海床和底土的自然资源而建造的钻井平台或设施上的犯罪行为,其刑事管辖权应仅由该钻井平台或设施设立国马来西亚或泰国来行使;

(c) 在决定横跨管辖权分界线,或为勘探和开采共同开发区海床和底土的自然资源而建造的钻井平台或设施,适用泰国还是马来西亚的民事程序或由泰国还是马来西亚行使民事管辖权时,应根据该钻井平台或设施是马来西亚还是泰国设立的来决定;以及

(d) 第(b)和第(c)项所指钻井平台或安装设施的设立国是泰国或马来西亚,应根据最实质性的位置原则来决定。

第十一部分　在上覆水域的权利

第十九条　在上覆水域的权利、自由或特权

本法令的条款,既不调整马来西亚或泰国根据1979年谅解备忘录(B. E. 2522)第四条在共同开发区上覆水域,包括与渔业相关的任何权益、权利和特权,也不影响对该上覆水域的任何主张。

第十二部分　违法行为和处罚

第二十条　违反第4款第(1)项

根据第二十二条,任何人,包括法人团体的董事或高管,若违反了第14款第(1)项的规定,应判处5年以下有期徒刑或不超过5万林吉特的罚款,或两者并罚;若犯罪持续进行,则应在判决宣布后第一天后、犯罪持续期间,另处每天(不足一天按一天算)不超过1000林吉特的罚款;并罚没任何用于或准备用于犯罪的设备、工具、赃物、建造物及其他财产或物品。

第二十一条　其他犯罪

根据第二十条和二十二条,任何人,包括法人团体的董事或高管,若违反本法令或依据第十五条制定的规章,应判处两年以下有期徒刑,或不

超过 20 万林吉特的罚款，或两者并罚；若犯罪持续进行，则在判决宣布后第一天后、犯罪持续期间，另处每天（不足一天按一天算）不超过 200 林吉特的罚款。

第二十二条　法人团体犯罪

若法人团体实施第二十条或二十一条规定的犯罪行为，则仅按照规定处以罚款。

第二十三条　共同指控法人团体和董事或高管

若法人团体违反本法令或依据第十五条制定的规章，违法行为发生时担任该法人团体的董事或主管应被共同定罪处罚，除非该法人团体的董事或主管可以证明其不知情或已采取合理措施阻止违法犯罪行为的发生，否则该董事或主管会被推定有罪。

第二十四条　代理人的行为或疏忽引起的犯罪的处罚

若本人代理人的行为违反了本法令或依据第十五条制定的规章，本人负有和代理人同样的责任，除非本人能证明已采取合理措施阻止代理人行为或疏忽的发生。

第十三部分　一般规定

第二十五条　本法令优于其他法律

若本法令条款与其他法律条款存在冲突或不一致，应优先适用本法令的规定。

第二十六条　法令的执行

部长应监管本负责依据第十五条制定的规章的执行，并有权任命负责执行的官员。

8. Malaysia – Thailand Joint Authority Act 440

Preamble

An Act to give effect to an agreement on the establishment and operation of the Malaysia – Thailand Joint Authority and to make provisions connected therewith.

[23 January 1991.]

WHEREAS pursuant to the Memorandum of Understanding between Malaysia and the Kingdom of Thailand on the Establishment of a Joint Authority for the Exploitation of the Resources of the Sea – bed in a Defined Area of the Continental Shelf of the Two Countries in the Gulf of Thailand dated 21 February 1979, the Agreement on the Constitution and Other Matters Relating to the Establishment of the Malaysia – Thailand Joint Authority was signed on 30 May 1990, at Kuala Lumpur, Malaysia, between the Government of Malaysia and the Government of the Kingdom of Thailand;

NOW THEREFORE, BE IT ENACTED by the Duli Yang Maha Mulia Seri Paduka Baginda Yang di – Pertuan Agong, with the advice and consent of the Dewan Negara and Dewan Rakyat in Parliament assembled, and by authority of the same, as follows:

PART I PRELIMINARY

1. Short title and commencement.

(1) This Act may be cited as the Malaysia – Thailand Joint Authority Act 1990.

(2) This Act shall come into force on such date as the Minister may, by notification in the Gazette, appoint.

2. Interpretation.

In this Act, unless the context otherwise requires –

"Agreement" means Agreement on the Constitution and Other Matters Relating to the Establishment of the Malaysia – Thailand Joint Authority signed by the Government of Malaysia and the Government of the Kingdom of Thailand on 30 May 1990, at Kuala Lumpur, Malaysia;

"Fund" means the Malaysia – Thailand Joint Authority Fund referred to under section 9; "Governments" means the Government of Malaysia and the Government of the Kingdom of Thailand;

"Joint Authority" means the Malaysia – Thailand Joint Authority;

"Joint Development Area" means the defined area of the continental shelf of Malaysia and the Kingdom of Thailand in the Gulf of Thailand described under section 6;

"line dividing jurisdiction" means the straight line joining the following co-ordinated points:

(A) N 6272 50′. 0 E 102272 21′. 2

(X) N 7272 35′. 0 E 103272 23′. 0

which divides civil and criminal jurisdiction in the Joint Development Area;

"Memorandum of Understanding, 1979" means the Memorandum of Understanding between Malaysia and the Kingdom of Thailand on the Establishment of a Joint Authority for the Exploitation of the Resources of the Sea – Bed in a Defined Area of the Continental Shelf of the Two Countries in the Gulf of Thailand, signed on 21 February 1979;

"Minister" means the Minister charged with the responsibility for petroleum;

"natural resources" means any non – living natural resources including any minerals, mineral oils and metals;

"petroleum" means any mineral oil or relative hydrocarbon and natural gas existing in its natural condition and casinghead petroleum spirit, including bituminous shales and other stratified deposits from which oil can be extracted.

PART II MALAYSIA – THAILAND JOINT AUTHORITY

3. Establishment of Malaysia – Thailand Joint Authority.

(1) There is hereby established a body by the name of the Malaysia – Thailand Joint Authority (referred to in this Act as "the Joint Authority").

(2) The Joint Authority shall have a juristic personality and shall be domiciled in Malaysia and the Kingdom of Thailand.

(3) The Joint Authority shall be a body corporate and, subject to and for the purposes of this Act, may enter into contracts, and may acquire, purchase, take, hold and enjoy any movable and immovable property of every description, excluding land, and may convey, assign, surrender, charge, mortgage, reassign, transfer or otherwise dispose of, or deal with, any movable or immovable property or any interest therein vested in the Joint Authority upon such terms as it deems appropriate.

4. Powers and functions of Joint Authority.

The Joint Authority shall have such powers and perform such functions as are necessary for the performance of its duties and the enjoyment of its rights and privileges under, and to the extent not inconsistent with, this Act.

5. Exploration and exploitation of natural resources.

The Joint Authority hereby is vested with and assumes the exclusive rights, powers, liberties and privileges of exploring and exploiting the natural resources, in particular petroleum, in the Joint Development Area.

PART III THE JOINT DEVELOPMENT AREA

6. The Joint Development Area. The Joint Development Area shall be the area bounded by straight lines joining the following coordinated points:

(A) N 6272 50'. 0 E 102272 21'. 2

(B) N 7272 10'. 25 E 102272 29'. 0

(C) N 7272 49′. 0 E 103272 02′. 5

(D) N 7272 22′. 0 E 103272 42′. 5

(E) N 7272 20′. 0 E 103272 39′. 0

(F) N 7272 03′. 0 E 103272 06′. 0

(G) N 6272 53′. 0 E 102272 34′. 0

and shown in the relevant part of the British Admiralty Chart No. 2414, Edition 1967, a reproduction of which is as in the Schedule.

PART IV   ROYALTY

7. Royalty.

The Joint Authority shall pay to each of the Governments royalty in the amount of five per centum of gross production of petroleum, in the manner and at such times as may be prescribed by regulations.

PART V   FINANCIAL PROVISIONS

8. Cost, benefit and annual payment.

(1) All costs incurred and benefits derived by the Joint Authority from activities carried out in the Joint Development Area shall be equally borne and shared by the Governments.

(2) Until such time as the Joint Authority shall have sufficient income to finance its annual operational expenditure, the Government of Malaysia shall pay to the Fund such annual payments as may be determined in accordance with the Agreement subject to equal payments being made by the Government of the Kingdom of Thailand.

PART VI   THE MALAYSIA THAILAND JOINT AUTHORITY FUND

9. Establishment of Fund.

(1) For the purposes of this Act and the Agreement, there is hereby established a fund called the Malaysia – Thailand Joint Authority Fund (referred to in

this Act as "the Fund") to be administered and controlled by the Joint Authority.

(2) The assets of the Fund shall include –

(a) such contributions as may be provided by the Governments under the Agreement, and referred to under subsection (2) of section 8;

(b) monies earned by the operation of any projects, schemes or enterprises financed from the Fund;

(c) monies earned or arising from any properties, investments, mortgages, or charges acquired by or vested in the Joint Authority;

(d) monies borrowed by the Joint Authority for the purposes of meeting any of its obligations or discharging any of its duties; and

(e) any other monies or properties which may in any manner become payable to or vested in the Joint Authority in respect of any matters incidental to its powers and duties.

10. Application of Fund.

The Fund may be used for –

(a) defraying such expenditures as the Joint Authority may incur in carrying out its functions and exercising its powers in accordance with the approved budgetary provisions and subject to any regulation made under section 15;

(b) settling any monies borrowed by the Joint Authority under paragraph (c) of subsection (1) of section 12, including interests and other charges incidental to the borrowing;

(c) such investments as the Joint Authority may decide subject to the approval of the Governments; and

(d) subject to section 11, payment of monies in equal amounts to the Governments out of income accruing to the Joint Authority after deducting the expenditures referred to in paragraphs (a) and (b) including such other expenditures as may be agreed to by the Governments.

11. Reserve Fund.

The Joint Authority shall establish and manage a reserve fund within the Fund in accordance with such terms and conditions as the Governments may jointly decide.

12. Restriction on financial dealings.

(1) The Joint Authority shall not, without the prior approval of the Governments –

(a) give financial assistance to any company, body or person by the taking up of shares or debentures or by way of loan, advance, grant or otherwise;

(b) purchase, underwrite or otherwise acquire any stocks and shares in any public or private company; or

(c) borrow money, or enter into any guarantee or indemnity involving financial liability.

(2) In giving any consent under subsection (1) the Governments may jointly impose such terms and conditions as they may deem appropriate.

13. Liability of Joint Authority not the responsibility of Governments. Nothing in this Act shall be construed as creating any responsibility whatsoever for the Government of Malaysia or the Government of the Kingdom of Thailand in respect of any liability of the Joint Authority.

PART VII CONTRACT FOR EXPLORATION AND EXPLOITATION

14. Prohibition on exploration or exploitation of natural resources without contract.

(1) Notwithstanding the provisions of any other written law, no business of exploration and exploitation of any natural resources, including petroleum, may be carried out in the Joint Development Area by any person other than the Joint Authority unless there is in respect of any such business a contract entered into between the Joint Authority and such person to explore and exploit such natural resources.

(2) A contract referred to under subsection (1) shall require the prior approval of the Governments.

(3) Subject to the provisions of subsection (4), a contract referred to under subsection (1) for the purpose of the exploration and exploitation of petroleum shall be a production sharing contract and shall include, amongst others, the

following terms and conditions:

(a) for the purpose of section 7, payment in the amount of ten per centum of gross production of petroleum by the contractor to the Joint Authority as royalty in the manner and at such times as may be specified in the contract;

(b) fifty per centum of gross production of petroleum shall be applied by the contractor for the purpose of recovery of costs for petroleum operations;

(c) the remaining portion of gross production of petroleum, after deductions for the purposes of paragraphs (a) and (b), shall be deemed to be profit petroleum and be divided equally between the Joint Authority and the contractor;

(d) the contract shall be valid for a period not exceeding thirty – five years but shall not exceed the period of validity of the Agreement;

(e) all costs of petroleum operations shall be borne by the contractor and shall, subject to paragraph (b), be recoverable from production;

(f) a minimum amount that the contractor shall expend on petroleum operations under the contract as a minimum commitment as may be agreed to by the Joint Authority and the contractor;

(g) payment of a research cess by the contractor to the Joint Authority in the amount of one half of one per centum of the aggregate of that portion of gross production which is applied for the purpose of recovery of costs under paragraph (b) and the contractor's share of profit petroleum under paragraph (c) in the manner and at such times as may be determined by the Joint Authority, provided that such payment shall not be recoverable from production; and

(h) any disputes or differences arising out of or in connection with the contract which cannot be amicably settled shall be referred to arbitration before a panel consisting of three arbitrators, one arbitrator to be appointed by each party, and a third to be jointly appointed by both parties. If the parties are unable to concur on the choice of a third arbitrator within a specified period, the third arbitrator shall be appointed upon application to the United Nations Commission of International Trade Law (UNCITRAL). The arbitration proceedings shall be conducted in accordance with the rules of UNCITRAL. The venue of arbitration shall be either Bangkok or Kuala Lumpur, or any other place as may be agreed to by the parties.

(4) The Joint Authority may vary any of the amounts referred to in paragraphs (b), (c) and (g) of subsection (3) in respect of any contract with the approval of the Governments: Provided that there shall be no variation of any of these amounts in respect of a subsisting contract without the agreement of the contractor.

(5) For the purposes of this section, "gross production" with reference to gas means gross proceeds of sale of gas.

PART VIII REGULATIONS

15. Power of Minister to make regulations. The Minister may, with the approval of the Governments, make regulations in respect of the following:

(a) the conduct of or the carrying on of any business or service relating to the exploration and exploitation of the natural resources in the Joint Development Area;

(b) the payment of any monies due to the Governments from the Joint Authority under section 7 and paragraph (d) of section 10;

(c) the terms and conditions of the appointment of, and the emoluments, travelling and subsistence allowances payable to, the Co – Chairmen and other members of the Joint Authority;

(d) the procedure for the tender and award of any contract that may be entered into under section 14, including the terms and conditions that may be included in such contract;

(e) the keeping of proper accounts and other records of the transactions and affairs of the Joint Authority in accordance with generally accepted accounting principles;

(f) the preparation of annual statements of accounts and, subject to the provisions of this Act, the allocation of profits;

(g) the audit of accounts and its subsequent submission to the Governments;

(h) the preparation and submission of the annual budget to the Governments;

(i) the standards for the exploration and exploitation of petroleum in the Joint Development Area; and

(j) any other matters for the purposes of carrying into effect the provisions of this Act: Provided that in respect of the matters referred to under paragraphs (a), (d), (e), (f), (g), (h) and (i), such regulations may be made after consultations with the Joint Authority.

PART IX　OFFICERS AND JURISDICTION OF COURTS

16. Public servants.

Any member of the Joint Authority or any officer, servant or agent of the Joint Authority shall be deemed to be a public servant within the meaning of the Penal Code.

17. Jurisdiction of Sessions Court.

(1) Notwithstanding anything contained in any other written law to the contrary, a Sessions Court shall have jurisdiction to try any offence under this Act or any regulation made thereunder and, on conviction, to impose the full penalty prescribed therefor.

(2) For the purpose of the exercise of jurisdiction over any offence committed under this Act or any regulation made under section 15, subsection (2), and paragraphs (b) and (d) of subsection (6) of section 18 shall apply.

PART X　JURISDICTION

18. Jurisdiction over Joint Development Area.

(1) Subject to subsections (2) and (3), Malaysia shall continue to have and exercise jurisdiction over the Joint Development Area.

(2) The civil and criminal jurisdiction of –

(a) Malaysia in the Joint Development Area shall extend over the area bounded by straight lines joining the following coordinated points:

(A) N 6272 50'.0 E 102272 21'.2

(X) N 7272 35'.0 E 103272 23'.0
(D) N 7272 22'.0 E 103272 42'.5
(E) N 7272 20'.0 E 103272 39'.0
(F) N 7272 03'.0 E 103272 06'.0
(G) N 6272 53'.0 E 102272 34'.0; and

(b) the Kingdom of Thailand in the Joint Development Area shall extend over the area bounded by straight lines joining the following coordinated points:

(A) N 6272 50'.0 E 102272 21'.2
(B) N 7272 10'.25 E 102272 29'.0
(C) N 7272 49'.0 E 103272 02'.5
(X) N 7272 35'.0 E 103272 23'.0

(3) Nothing in this Act shall in any way affect the sovereign rights of Malaysia over the Joint Development Area, and any waiver of jurisdiction under this section shall have no force and effect beyond the period of validity of the Agreement.

(4) The consent by Malaysia to the exercise of civil and criminal jurisdiction by the Kingdom of Thailand under paragraph (b) of subsection (2) and the continued exercise of jurisdiction over matters relating to customs and excise, and taxation in the Joint Development Area are conditional upon a reciprocal recognition of Malaysia's rights under paragraph (a) of subsection (2).

(5) Any jurisdiction that may be vested in Malaysia or the Kingdom of Thailand under this section in respect of the Joint Development Area shall only be over matters and to the extent provided for in any law relating to the continental shelf as recognised under international law.

(6) For the purpose of this section –

(a) "civil and criminal jurisdiction" shall not include jurisdiction over matters relating to customs and excise, and taxation;

(b) criminal jurisdiction over an offence committed on a platform or an installation which straddles the line dividing jurisdiction and constructed for the purposes of exploration and exploitation of the natural resources of the sea – bed and subsoil in the Joint Development Area is to be assumed exclusively by Malaysia or the Kingdom of Thailand in accordance with the designation of such platform or installation as Malaysian or Thai;

(c) the determination of whether a platform or an installation which straddles the line dividing jurisdiction and constructed for the purposes of exploration and exploitation of the natural resources of the sea – bed and subsoil in the Joint Development Area is part of Malaysia or the Kingdom of Thailand in relation to any question that falls to be determined in any civil proceedings or for the purpose of the assumption or exercise of civil jurisdiction by Malaysia or the Kingdom of Thailand shall be in accordance with the designation of such platform or installation as Malaysian or Thai; and

(d) the designation of a platform or an installation as Malaysian or Thai under paragraphs (b) and (c) shall be determined according to the principle of most substantial location.

PART XI RIGHTS IN SUPERJACENT WATERS

19. Right, liberty or privilege in superjacent waters.

Nothing in this Act shall in any way regulate, or affect any claims in respect of, any rights, liberties and privileges, including but not limited to those relating to fishing, that Malaysia or the Kingdom of Thailand may have over the superjacent waters of the Joint Development Area by virtue of Article IV of the Memorandum of Understanding, 1979.

20. Contravention of subsection (1) of section 4.

Subject to section 22, any person, including a director or officer of a body corporate, who acts in contravention of the provision of subsection (1) of section 14 shall be guilty of an offence and shall, on conviction, be liable to imprisonment for a term not exceeding five years or to a fine not exceeding fifty thousand ringgit or to both, and, in the case of a continuing offence, be liable to a further fine not exceeding one thousand ringgit for each day or part of a day during which the offence continues after the first day in respect of which the conviction is recorded; and any machinery, tools, plants, buildings and other properties or things used or intended to be used in the commission of the offence shall be liable to forfeiture.

21. Other offences.

Subject to sections 20 and 22, any person, including a director or officer of a body corporate, who acts in contravention of any provision of this Act or regulation made under section 15 shall be guilty of an offence and shall, on conviction, be liable to imprisonment for a term not exceeding two years or to a fine not exceeding twenty thousand ringgit or to both, and, in the case of a continuing offence, shall be liable to a further fine not exceeding two hundred ringgit for each day or part of a day during which the offence continues after the first day in respect of which the conviction is recorded.

22. Offence by body corporate.

Where a person convicted in respect of any offence referred to under section 20 or 21 is a body corporate, it shall only be liable to the imposition of any fine provided therein.

23. Director and officer of body corporate may be charged jointly with body corporate.

Where a person charged with an offence under this Act or any regulation made under section 15 is a body corporate every person who, at the time of the commission of the offence, is a director or officer of the body corporate may be charged jointly in the same proceedings with the body corporate, and where the body corporate is convicted of the offence charged, every such director or officer shall be deemed to be guilty of that offence unless he proves that the offence was committed without his knowledge or that he took reasonable precautions to prevent its commission.

24. Penalty for offence due to anything done or omitted by agent.

Any person who would be liable under this Act or any regulation made under section 15 to any penalty for anything done or omitted if the thing had been done or omitted by him personally, shall be liable to the same penalty if the thing had been done or omitted by his agent, unless he proves that he took reasonable precautions to prevent the doing or omission of the thing.

PART XII GENERAL

25. This Act to prevail over other laws.

Where any provision of this Act is in conflict or is inconsistent with any provision of any other law, the provision of this Act shall prevail.

26. Charge and control of this Act.

The Minister shall have charge and control of the execution of this Act and any regulation made under section 15, and shall have the power to appoint officials for the execution thereof.

9.《马来西亚—泰国联合管理局石油作业准则》

邓妮雅译，黄文博校

第一部分　前言

引述

1. 这些规定可以被称为《马来西亚—泰国联合管理局（石油作业准则）1997年条例》。

解释

2. 在这些规定中，除非文本中有相反要求——

"承包人"是指为了在共同开发区内勘探和生产，依据马来西亚—泰国联合管理局1990年法令第十四条，与联合管理局签订产品分享合同的任何个人，应包括其指定的经营者、分包人、被许可的指派人以及机构。

"合同区域"是指依据马来西亚—泰国联合管理局1990年法令第十四条第（3）款签订的合同中所指明的区域。

"石油作业"是指在合同区域内为勘探和/或开发合同区内的石油资源而签订的产品分享合同规定的所有的作业活动，包括油田和石油产品的开发活动。

第二部分　勘探和钻探

提交勘探活动的信息以获批准

3.（1）依据产品分享合同，按照联合管理局批准的工作计划和预案在合同区域内进行任何开发活动之前，合同方应当至少提前72小时，书面提交联合管理局关于此种活动的充分的信息，包括但不限于以下内容：

（a）勘探的方法；

（b）工作的时间和期限；

（c）合同方机构的姓名和联系地址；

（d）勘探活动相关的必要信息。

（2）联合管理局可指示合同方提交，其认为必要的关于此种活动的进一步的信息，且合同方应遵守该指示。

石油作业的限制

4. 承包人不得在任何合同区域内，开展任何可能无端影响合同区域内渔业或航行，或者影响海洋生物资源保育的石油作业活动。

防止泄露等措施

5. 承包人应采取与优良的石油工业实践相一致的所有的必要预防措施，以：

（a）防止石油泄露或渗漏至海洋或海床；

（b）防止有毒的液体或有毒的化学物质溢入海洋；

（c）防止对浅水层或地下含水层造成损害；

（d）防止对含油层或结构造成损害；及

（e）防止水体从油井流入含油层或构造，但用于第二生产阶段或为了维持油田压力的水流除外。

适用回旋钻钻探方法钻井

6. 适用回旋钻钻探方法钻井时，承包人应：

（a）遵循优良的石油工业实践，在必要时安装防止井喷的设备和可操控的控制面板；

（b）在进行钻探工程时，要对这种防止井喷的设备进行合理和周期性的测试，保证其处于良好的工作状态；并且

（c）保证钻探全程钻井平台上有足够数量和重量的钻井液，以平衡地下构造液压，防止地下结构内液体的喷发。

钻井方案等获批的限制条件

7. （1）承包人的钻井和钻井路径不得超过合同区域的垂直边界。

（2）除非联合管理局事先同意，不应在距离合同区垂直边界 125 米的合同区域内钻井。

为了获批应提交的钻井方案等

8. （1）承包人应提前或在任何情况下不少于 72 小时，向联合管理局

书面提交每口井的钻探方案和计划,以供审阅和批准。

(2) 没有联合管理局事先的书面批准,承包人不应当:

(a) 在任何合同区内开始任何钻井工作;或

(b) 重新开始任何已经暂停的钻井工作。

第三部分 放弃

油井的放弃

9. (1) 承包人不应当放弃任何油井,除非:

(a) 按照规定填补油井,并且

(b) 经联合管理局的事先书面批准。

(2) 任何油井的填补应遵循:

(a) 联合管理局批准的该油井或该类油井或该油井从属的一系列油井所适用的规范;及

(b) 良好的石油工业实践。

第四部分 安全

钻探机等的安置及安全区的设立

10. (1) 任何钻探机、平台或者其他离岸设施的安置,应当依照通行的石油行业的做法,与其他钻探机、平台、离岸设施、灯塔、航行标识、海底电缆和管道以及其他可能的设施,保持一段安全距离。

(2) 承包人应当——

(a) 经联合管理局事先的书面批准,在钻探机、平台或者其他离岸设施周围设立一个合理的安全区;

(b) 应保证钻探机、平台或者其他离岸设施周围建立的安全区的半径,不超过500米;

(c) 采取一切必要措施保证安全区内航行以及钻探机、平台或者其他离岸设施的安全;

(d) 对安全区的范围做出适当的公开通告。

承包人提供可靠的通信系统

11. 承包人应保证所有使用或参与的船舶、航空器、钻探机、平台或其他离岸设施,应按照良好的石油工业实践,在石油作业中配备了可靠的通信系统。这种通信系统可以从陆地上的承包人办公处接收信息或消息，也可向陆地上的承包人办公处发送信息或消息。承包人或政府当局也可在紧急情况下使用此通信系统。

钻探机等的安全

12. 在石油作业中，承包人应当采取一切必要步骤，保证每个使用或参与的钻探机、平台及其他离岸设施等的安全。

灭火设施的设置

13.（1）在石油作业中，承包人应当保证在所有使用或参与的作业船、航空器、钻探机、平台或其他离岸设施中，设置了必要的、足够的和可靠的灭火设施。

（2）要适当维护所有的灭火设施，并保证其处于可操作状态，以备在任何情况下即刻使用。

意外或事故的通报

14.（1）石油作业中发生的或与之有关的任何意外或事故，造成了人员丧生或重伤或对财产和环境造成了损害的，承包人应当通报联合管理局。

（2）这种通报应于意外或事故发生后72小时内迅速做出，通报内容应当包括：

（a）意外和事故的详情，包括性质、损害和损失；及

（b）承包人采取的及时的处理措施。

工作人员的防护制服

15. 承包人应当保证在钻探机、平台或者其他离岸设施上工作的人员，均配备且正确穿着了合适的防护服，包括安全头盔、靴子、手套、眼镜和其他必要的防护用具。

急救设施

16. 承包人应当保证每个可操作的钻探机、平台及其他离岸设施都配备了急救必需的药品、医疗设施和接受过训练的医疗人员，以为生病或者在事故中受伤的工作人员提供及时的医疗救护。

承包人提供食宿等

17. 承包人应当为钻探机、平台及其他离岸设施上的工作人员，提供充足干净的生活区域、安全健康的食物、饮用水和其他用水、灯管和卫生

的盥洗室。

保有个人信息登记簿

18.（1）承包人应当：

（a）保有最新的在每个钻探机、平台及其他离岸设施上工作的人员的个人信息登记簿。

（b）该登记簿应当包括但不限于工作人员的名字、身份、联系地址、年龄、国籍和亲属关系。

（2）承包人应当：

（a）保证登记簿上，每个钻探机、平台或者其他离岸设施上工作或离开的工作人员的名字和记录及时更新。

（b）将登记簿保存在安全的地方，定期将复印本传送给承包人陆上办公室，并保证可以应联合管理局要求随时查看。

救生船、救生筏和其他救生用具

19.（1）承包人应当保证在每个可操作的钻探机、平台及其他离岸设施上，为其工作人员都配备了在紧急情况下使用的救生船、救生筏和其他救生设施。

（2）救生船、救生筏和其他救生设施应当合理保存并定期测试，保证其处于可操作状态，以备在任何情况下即刻使用。

第五部分　检查

检查

20. 联合管理局依据马来西亚—泰国联合管理局1990年法令任命的任何官员，为了检查和确定承包人是否遵守该法令和相关法规，有权利进入任何承包人在共同开发区内石油作业中使用的钻探机、平台或其他离岸设施和设备，以及承包人的陆地设施。

10. Malaysia – Thailand Joint Authority Standards of Petroleum Operations

PART I   PRELIMINARY

Citation.

1. These regulations may be cited as the Malaysia – Thailand Joint Authority (Standards of Petroleum Operations) Regulations 1997.

Interpretation.

2. In these Regulations, unless the context otherwise requires –

"Contractor" means any person who has entered into a production sharing contract with the Joint Authority under section 14 of the Malaysia – Thailand Joint Authority Act 1990 for the purpose of exploration and production in the joint development Area and shall include its designated operator, subcontractor, permitted assign, and agent;

"Contract Area" means an area described in any contract entered into pursuant to subsection 14 (3) of the Malaysia – Thailand Joint Authority Act 1990;

"Petroleum Operations" means all operations under a production sharing contract for exploration and/or exploitation of petroleum in a Contract Area, including development of petroleum fields and production of petroleum.

PART II   EXPLORATION ANS DRILLING

Submission of information on exploration activity for approval.

3. (1) Before conduction any exploration activity in any Contract Area according to the Work Programme and Budget that has received approval of the Joint Authority pursuant to the production sharing contract, the Contractor shall, in

advance and in any case not less than 72 hours, submit in writing to the Joint Authority for approval, sufficient information on such activity which sha ll include, but not limited to –

(a) method of exploration;

(b) timing and duration of work;

(c) name and contact address of the Contractor's agent;

(d) essential details concerning exploration activity.

(2) The Joint Authority may direct the Contractor to submit further information on such activity as it may deem necessary, and the Contractor shall comply with such direction.

Restriction on Petroleum Operation.

4. The Contractor shall not carry out any Petroleum Operations in any Contract Area in a manner that would interfere unjustifiably with navigation or fishing in? the waters of the Contract Area or with the conversation of living resources of the sea.

Prevention of leakage, etc.

5. The Contractor shall take all necessary precautions, in accordance with good petroleum industry practice, to –

(a) prevent leakage or seepage of petroleum into the sea or on the sea – bed;

(b) prevent spilling of toxic fluids or toxic chemicals into the sea;

(c) prevent damage to shallow fresh – water – bearing strata or subsurface water aquifer;

(d) prevent damage to petroleum – bearing strata or formations; and

(e) prevent entrance of water through wells to petroleum strata or formation, except where water is used in second stage production or for the purpose of maintaining the pressure at petroleum deposits.

Drilling of any well using rotary drilling method.

6. In drilling any well, using rotary – drilling method, the Contractor shall –

(a) install a blowout – preventer equipment and its readily accessible control panel, where necessary in accordance with good petroleum industry practice;

(b) properly and periodically test and maintain such blowout preventer in good working condition at all times while drilling is in progress; and

(c) ensure that there is, at all times while drilling, adequate quantity and weight of, as well as good quality, drilling fluid in the well or available on the rig so as to balance against fluid pressure in underground formations and prevent blowout of formation fluids from underground.

Restriction of drilling proposal, etc. for approval.

7. (1) The Contractor shall not drill any well the well – path of which goes beyond or outside the vertical boundary of the Contract Area.

(2) No well shall be drilled, except with the prior written approval of the Joint Authority, inside ant Contract Area so that any part of the well is less than one hundred and twenty – five (125) metres away from the vehicle boundary of the Contract Area.

Submission of drilling proposal, etc. for approval.

8. (1) The Contractor shall, in advance and in any case not less than 72 hours, submit in writing to the Joint Authority for review and approval, drilling proposal and programme of each well.

(2) The Contractor shall not, without the prior written approval of the Joint Authority –

(a) commence drilling of any well in any Contract Area; or (b) recommence drilling of any well that has been suspended.

PART Ⅲ ABANDONMENT

Abandonment of well.

9. (1) The Contractor shall not abandon any well without –

(a) plugging it in accordance with these Regulations; and

(b) prior written approval of the Joint Authority.

(2) The plugging of any well shall be carried out in accordance with –

(a) specifications approved by the Joint Authority applicable to that well or to wells generally or to a class of wells to which that well belongs; and

(b) good petroleum industry practice.

PART Ⅳ SAFETY

Location of drilling rig, etc. and establishment of safety zone.

10. (1) Any drilling rig, platform, or other offshore installation shall be located at a safe distance in accordance with good petroleum industry practice from other drilling rigs, platforms, offshore installations, lighthouse, navigation marks, subsea cables and pipelines, as the case may be.

(2) The Contractor shall –

(a) with prior written approval of the Joint Authority establish a reasonable safety Zone around the drilling rigs, platforms or other offshore installations;

(b) ensure that the radius of such safety zone shall not exceed a distance of five hundred (500) metres around the drilling rigs, platforms or other offshore installations;

(c) take all necessary measures to ensure within such safety zone safety of navigation and of the drilling rigs, platforms or other offshore installations; and

(d) give due public notification of the extent of such safety zone.

Contractor to provide reliable communication system.

11. The Contractor shall ensure that all vessels, aircrafts, drilling rigs, platforms or other offshore installations used or engaged, as the case may be, in Petroleum Operations are equipped with reliable communication system, in accordance with good petroleum industry practice, which is capable of relaying information or messages to and from the Contractor's onshore office, and that can be used by the Contractor or governmental authorities as a means of communications in case of an emergency.

Safety at drilling rig etc.

12. The contractor shall take all necessary steps to ensure safety at every drilling rig, platform and other offshore installations used or engaged, as the case may be, in Petroleum Operations.

Installation of fire fighting system.

13. (1) The Contractor shall ensure that necessary, adequate and reliable

fire fighting system is installed on well vessels, aircrafts, drilling rigs, platforms or other offshore installations used or engaged, as the case may be, in Petroleum Operations.

(2) All fire fighting equipment shall be properly maintained and kept in operable condition ready for immediate use at all times.

Notification of any accident or incident.

14. (1) The Contractor shall notify the Joint Authority of ant accident or incident arising from or in relation to Petroleum Operations that has resulted in a serious injury or loss of human life, or damage to properties or to the environment.

(2) Such notice shall be made promptly within 72 hours of the happening of the accident or incident, and such notice shall include –

(a) adequate details of the accident or incident including their nature, damages and loss; and

(b) immediate measures being taken by the Contractor to deal with the situation.

Suitable protective working uniforms for workers.

15. The contractor shall ensure that all workers working on all drilling rigs, platforms, or other offshore installations are provided with, and property wear, suitable protective working uniform including safety helmet, boots, gloves, glasses and other necessary protective materials.

First Aid Facilities.

16. The Contractor shall ensure that all the medicine, medical equipment, and trained medical personnel necessary for First Aid treatments are provided at every manned drilling rig, platform and other offshore installation to render immediate First Aid to workers who are involved in accidents or who fall sick.

Contractor to provide accommodation, meals, etc.

17. The Contractor shall provide adequate clean living quarters, safe and whilom food and drinking water and water for other sues, lights and hygienic toilets for workers at every manned drilling rig, platform and other offshore installation.

Maintenance of register of personnel records.

18. (1) The Contractor shall –

(a) maintain an up – to – date register of personnel records on board every manned drilling rig, platform and other offshore installation; and

(b) in such register include but not limited to, records of workers' names identification, contact address, age, nationality, and next – of – kin.

(2) The Contractor shall –

(a) ensure that any worker entering or leaving such drilling rig, platform or other offshore installations has his name and record updated promptly in the register; and

(b) keep such register in safe place with a copy transmitted regularly to the contractor's onshore office, and ensure that they shall be made available for inspection upon request by the Joint Authority.

Survival crafts, life rafts and other saving appliances.

19. (1) The Contractor shall ensure that every manned drilling rig, platform and other offshore installation is provided on board with survival crafts, life rafts and other life – saving appliances having sufficient capacity to all persons on such drilling rig, platform and other offshore installation for use in case of emergency.

(2) Such survival crafts, life rafts and other life – saving appliances shall be properly maintained and regularly tested, and kept in operable condition ready for immediate at all times.

PART V   INSPECTION

Inspection

20. Any officer of Joint Authority appointed under the Malaysia – Thailand Joint Authority Act 1990 shall have the power to enter into any of the Contractor's drilling rigs, platforms or other offshore installations and equipment used or to be used in Petroleum Operations in the Joint Development Area or Contractor's onshore facilities for the purpose of inspecting and determining whether they are being carried out in compliance with the Malaysia – Thailand Joint Authority Act 1990 and these Regulations.

（八）1981年冰岛与挪威扬马延岛共同开发案

1.《关于冰岛和扬马延岛之间的大陆架协定》

（1981年10月22日订于奥斯陆）

宗吕谦译，黄文博校

冰岛和挪威政府为了确定冰岛与扬马延岛之间区域的大陆架边界，

根据冰岛与扬马延岛之间于1980年5月28日达成的有关渔业及大陆架问题的协议，双方同意在扬马延岛与冰岛间距离不足400海里的海域，将冰岛的经济区扩展至200海里，

根据上述1980年协议第九条的规定，双方同意共同任命一个调解委员会，就冰岛与扬马延岛间划界问题提出建议，并且该委员会已获任命。

1981年5月调解委员会一致同意一份建议书，大意为：冰岛与扬马延岛之间的两国大陆架界线，应当与界线两侧的位于冰岛与扬马延岛之间勘探和开发碳氢化合物资源的特定区域相连。

双方发现实施委员会的建议是可行的，遂达成以下共识。

第一条

双方在冰岛和扬马延岛之间的大陆架界线与双方的经济区界线一致。

第二条

第三条到第九条适用由以下坐标划定的区域：

北纬70°35′

北纬 68°00′

西经 10°30′

西经 6°30′

第三条

在第一个探测阶段，针对第二条中系统的地质测绘所划区域，两国需共同进行地震测量且在必要时进行地磁测量。在两国专家共同制订方案的基础上，由挪威石油部门实际执行。挪威石油部门和挪威政府在无另拟协议的情况下分担测量费用。两国专家在平等的基础上均有机会参与测量及进行数据评估。数据和评估报告需要提交两国政府当局，且应保密，除非两国另有约定。

向公司或组织出售地震或地磁数据所获得的纯利润，应依两国约定进行分配。

第四条

若第三条涉及的测量结果显示需要在区域内的特定领域进行更详细的调查，包括更为细致的地震测量工作、着手钻探、涉及特定领域的任何排他的专业勘探和生产许可，需基于联合经营合同的形式，除非两国对合同形式另有约定。两国可允许官方或非官方石油公司参与。

第五条

在第二条划定的两国经济区边界以北的海域（约 32750 平方千米），冰岛有权参与第四条涉及的石油活动，并能分享 25% 的利润。挪威通过与外部官方或非官方石油公司协商，应力图与之达成协议，使挪威和冰岛因石油活动所产生的费用由相关公司（或公司组）承担，直到开采出具有商业价值的石油。

若无法达成上述由相关公司（企业）承担费用的协议，两国需启动谈判，寻求达成联合经营，双方各自承担自己的费用或一起分担费用。若冰岛不愿在此基础上参与，挪威可以单独进行。如有商业发现，在此阶段，冰岛有权参与，并以其份额偿还挪威的花费，偿还的份额等同于最初挪威进行勘探到现阶段冰岛参与期间原本双方合作冰岛应该承担的费用。

挪威有关油气活动管理、安全措施和环境保护的法律法规、石油政策适用于本条第一款中所提及区域的油气活动。挪威当局也应负责执行和管理上述区域。

第六条

在第二条划定的两国经济区边界以南（约 12720 平方千米）的海域，挪威有权参与第四条涉及的石油活动，并能分享 25% 的利润。经与外部官方或非官方石油公司协商，冰岛无须确保达成让相关公司（或公司组）承担挪威相关油气活动费用的协议。

冰岛有关油气活动管理、安全措施和环境保护的法律法规、石油政策适用于本条第一款规定区域的油气活动。冰岛当局也应负责执行法律法规及政策，并管理上述区域。

第七条

有商业发现之后，在后续开发中，双方应按照有关合同各自承担与之份额成比例的费用。

第八条

若碳氢化合物储藏位于两国经济区分界线两侧，或位于边界南侧但超出第二条规定的坐标区域，则适用通常的联合开发原则。如需适用更详尽的规则需双方同意。

若碳氢化合物储藏位于边界北侧但超出第二条规定坐标区域，则此碳氢化合物储藏被视为位于坐标区域内，其适用规则参见第五条、第六条和第七条。

第九条

若一国认为第五条和第六条所规定的安全措施和环境保护有关规定不能对第二条所划区域内的勘探和生产活动提供足够的保护，双方应协商，参见 1980 年 5 月 28 日有关渔业和大陆架问题的协议之第十条的规定。若双方在磋商中未达成一致，相关问题应该提交至由三人组成的调解委员会。在调解委员会给出建议之前，双方在没有重大理由的情况下不应着手或继续相关的开发。

两国各任命一名委员会成员，主席由两国共同任命。

委员会的建议应该尽早提交双方政府。建议对两国不具有约束力，但在后续讨论中，双方政府应当对建议予以合理尊重。

第十条

本协定在双方交换照会，互相通知业已完成所需要的法律程序时生效。

全权代表签在此签名，以资证明。

1981年10月22日签署于奥斯陆，使用冰岛语和挪威语两种语言，两种文本具有同等效力。

　　冰岛政府代表　　　　　　挪威政府代表

　　乔纳森·奥拉芬　　　　　　斯文·斯特雷

2. Agreement on the Continental Shelf Between Iceland and Jan Mayen

22 October 1981

The Governments of Iceland and of Norway,

Desiring to determine the delimitation line on the continental shelf in the area between Iceland and Jan Mayen,

Having agreed, by entering into the Agreement of May 28, 1980 on fishery and continental shelf questions, on the extension of the economic zone of Iceland to 200 nautical miles also in those areas between Iceland and Jan Mayen where the distance between the baselines is less than 400 nautical miles,

Having agreed in Article 9 of the above – mentioned Agreement that the Parties should jointly appoint a Conciliation Commission to submit recommendations with regard to the dividing line for the shelf area between Iceland and Jan Mayen and having jointly appointed such a Commission,

Having in May 1981 received the Conciliation Commission's unanimous recommendations to the effect that the delimitation line between the two Parties' parts of the continental shelf in the area between Iceland and Jan Mayen shall coincide with the delimitation line for the economic zones, and that co – operation between the two Parties be established in connection with the exploration for and exploitation of hydrocarbon resources in a specified area between Iceland and Jan Mayen on both sides of the delimitation line, and

Finding it possible to proceed on the basis of the Commission's recommendations,

Have agreed as follows:

Article 1

The delimitation line between the Parties' parts of the continental shelf in the area between Iceland and Jan Mayen shall coincide with the delimitation line for the Parties' economic zones.

Article 2

The provisions in Articles 3 to 9 apply in an area defined by the following co－ordinates:

70° 35′ N
68° 00′N
10° 30′ W
6° 30′ W

Article 3

In the first exploration phase, aimed at a systematic geological mapping of the area defined in Article 2, the Parties shall jointly carry out seismic and, if necessary, magnetic surveys. The practical implementation of these surveys shall be the task of the Norwegian Petroleum Directorate on the basis of plans elaborated by the two Parties' experts jointly. The costs of the surveys shall be borne by the Petroleum Directorate/The Norwegian State, unless the Parties otherwise agree. Norwegian and Icelandic experts shall have the opportunity to participate in the surveys and in the assessment of the resulting data on an equal footing. The data and their assessment shall be submitted to the authorities of the two Parties. They shall be treated as confidential, unless the Parties otherwise agree.

If there is any net profit from the sale of seismic or magnetic data to companies or organizations, such net profit shall be shared by the two Parties on a basis agreed between them.

Article 4

If the surveys mentioned in Article 3 indicate that it is desirable to carry out more detailed surveys of special fields in the area, including more detailed seismic work and the commencement of drilling, any exclusive exploration and production licences in respect of such special fields shall be based on joint venture contracts, unless the Parties agree on some other form of contract. The Parties may agree to allow governmental or non‑governmental petroleum companies to participate in such contracts.

Article 5

In the part of the area defined in Article 2 north of the delimitation line between the two Parties' economic zones (approximately 32 750 sq. km.), Iceland shall be entitled to participate with a share of 25 per cent in such petroleum activities as are referred to in Article 4. In negotiations with outside governmental or non‑governmental petroleum companies, Norway shall seek to arrive at an arrangement whereby both the Norwegian and the Icelandic percentage of the costs of such petroleum activities are carried by the company (or companies) concerned up to the stage where commercial finds have been declared.

If it is not possible to obtain an arrangement whereby the two Parties' costs are carried by the company (or companies) concerned, the Parties shall initiate negotiations on the possibility of conducting the operations as a joint venture where each of them carries its own costs, or where they share the costs. If Iceland does not wish to participate on this basis, Norway may proceed on its own. If commercial finds are declared, Iceland shall be entitled, at this stage, to enter into participation with its share in return for reimbursing Norway for that share of the costs incurred up to this juncture which would correspond to Iceland's share if Iceland had participated from the outset.

Norwegian legislation, Norwegian petroleum policy and Norwegian regulations relating to the control of such activities, safety measures and environmental protection shall apply to the activities in the area referred to in the first paragraph. The Norwegian authorities shall also be responsible for enforcement and administration in the said area.

Article 6

In the part of the area defined in Article 2 south of the delimitation line between the two Parties' economic zones (approximately 12 720 sq. km.), Norway shall be entitled to participate with a share of 25 per cent in such petroleum activities as are referred to in Article 4. In negotiations with outside governmental or non‑governmental petroleum companies, Iceland shall not be bound to seek to arrive at an arrangement whereby the Norwegian percentage of the costs of such petroleum activities are carried by the company (or companies) concerned.

Icelandic legislation, Icelandic petroleum policy and Icelandic regulations relating to the control of such activities, safety measures and environmental protection shall apply to the activities in the area referred to in the first paragraph. The Icelandic authorities shall also be responsible for enforcement and administration in the said area.

Article 7

After a find has been declared commercial, each of the Parties shall carry its costs in the further development of the field in proportion to its share under the contract concerned.

Article 8

If a hydrocarbon deposit lies on both sides of the delimitation line between the two Parties' economic zones, or lies in its entirety south of the delimitation line, but extends beyond the co-ordinates stated in Article 2, the usual unitization principles for the distribution and exploitation of the deposit shall apply. The more detailed rules to be applied in such cases shall be agreed between the Parties.

If a hydrocarbon deposit lies in its entirety north of the delimitation line, but extends beyond the co-ordinates stated in Article 2, the deposit shall in its entirety be considered to lie within the co-ordinates, cf. Articles 5, 6 and 7.

Article 9

If one of the Parties considers that the regulations relating to safety measures and environmental protection referred to in Articles 5 and 6 fail to provide adequate protection when exploration or production operations are carried out in the area defined in Article 2, the Parties shall consult each other, cf. Article 10 in the Agreement of 28 May 1980 on fishery and continental shelf questions. If, during such consultations, the Parties fail to agree, the question shall be referred to a Conciliation Commission consisting of three members. The Parties shall not commence or continue such operations before the Conciliation Commission's recommendation is available, unless there are weighty grounds for so doing.

Each of the Parties shall appoint one member of the Commission. The chairman of the Commission shall be appointed by the Parties jointly.

The Commission's recommendations shall be submitted to the two Governments at the earliest opportunity. The recommendations are not binding on the Parties, but during their further discussions the Parties shall pay reasonable regard to them.

Article 10

This Agreement shall enter into force when the Parties, by an exchange of notes, have notified each other that the necessary constitutional procedures have been completed.

IN WITNESS WHEREOF the undersigned plenipotentiaries have signed this Agreement.

DONE at Oslo on October 22, 1981, in duplicate in the Icelandic and Norwegian languages, both texts being equally authoritative.

For the Government of Iceland:	For the Government of Norway:
Olafur Johannesson (sign.)	Svenn Stray (sign.)

(九) 1989年澳大利亚与印度尼西亚共同开发案

1. 《澳大利亚与印度尼西亚共和国在印度尼西亚东帝汶省与澳大利亚北部之间的区域设立合作区的条约》

(1989年12月11日订于堪培拉)

董世杰译，黄文博校

澳大利亚和印度尼西亚共和国，

鉴于1982年12月10日在蒙特哥湾签署的《联合国海洋法公约》，尤其是第83条要求海岸相向国家，基于谅解和合作的精神，尽一切努力做出实际性的临时安排，不危害或阻碍最后协议的达成。渴望对印度尼西亚东帝汶省与澳大利亚北部之间的区域石油资源进行勘探开发，是缔约国之间永久性大陆架划界的主题。意识到有必要鼓励和促进本区域石油资源的开发，期望石油资源的勘探开发不被迟延，承认缔约国之间现有的大陆架划界协定。为了两国人民的相互利益，决定进一步推进开发大陆架资源，是缔约国之间大陆架永久性划界的主题。通过现有的协定及安排，维护、更新以及进一步强化两国之间相互尊重、友好合作的关系，同时也促进建设性友好睦邻合作政策的推进。铭记两国作为近邻基于合作、友谊、善意精神，而共同享有的利益。坚信允许在区域内勘探和开发石油资源的共同安排将深化两国政府的交流与合作，并惠及两国人民，

遂达成如下协议。

第一章 合作区

第1条 定义

1. 根据本条约规定，

（a）"合同"或者"产品分成合同"是指，联合当局与公司之间，基于《范式产品分成合同》，并依本条约第8条以及《石油开采规则》第三章的规定而签订的合同。

（b）"合同区域"是指合同中明确规定，且未退回或放弃的区块。

（c）"承包商"是指与联合当局签订合同的公司，并根据《石油开采规则》第38条登记为承包商。

（d）"承包商的所得税"是指根据印度尼西亚1983所得税法第7条，和1983年一般税收条款和程序法第6条（不时进行修改）所规定的税种。

（e）"刑法"是指缔约国内有效的任何有关犯罪，或者有关犯罪侦查或起诉，或者有关对罪犯的惩处（其中包括执行法院判处的刑罚）的实体或程序法。"调查"包括进入A区的设施，对嫌疑犯进行搜查、质问以及逮捕。

（f）"良好的油田实践"是指在石油作业过程中，被广泛认可为良好且安全的实践经验。

（g）"范式产品分成合同"是指附件C中的范式合同，关于A区的产品分成合同应该以其为基础进行缔结，部长理事会可以根据本条约第6条第1款c项对范式合同进行适时修改。

（h）"石油"是指：（a）任何自然产生的碳氢化合物，无论是气态、液态还是固态；（b）任何自然产生的碳氢化合物的混合物，无论是气态、液态或者固态；（c）上述a、b项中定义为石油的物质，返回到合同区域的储油层中。

（i）"石油开采规则"是指附件B中规定的，规范A区内与石油资源勘探开发有关的活动的"合作区内A区的石油开采规则"。部长理事会可以根据本条约第6条第1款b项对其进行适时修改。

（j）"石油作业"是指生产石油的所有活动，包括勘探、开发、矿场处理、生产、管道作业，以及根据产品分成合同进行市场授权或市场规划。

（k）"资源租赁税"是指根据澳大利亚 1987 年的《资源租赁税法案》所征收的税款（会不时进行修改）。

（l）"构造"是指用于石油作业的装置或结构。

（m）"税收规则"是指附件 D 中规定的，用于避免对 A 区有关的活动进行双重征税的规则。

（n）"税法"是指本条约所适用的，不时生效的，澳大利亚关于税收的联邦法律，或者印度尼西亚共和国关于税收的法律。但不包括缔约国之间缔结的，或者缔约国一方与第三国缔结的税收协定。

（o）"条约"就是指本条约，包括附件 A、B、C、D。

（p）"合作区"是指附件 A 中所划定的并以地图标明的区域，包括附件中提及的 A、B、C 三个区域。

2. 基于本条约第 10 条和《税收规则》，缔约国居民是指：

（a）就澳大利亚而言，一个人因为是澳大利亚税法中的澳大利亚居民而向澳大利亚纳税；

（b）就印度尼西亚而言，一个人因为是印度尼西亚税法中的印度尼西亚居民而向印度尼西亚纳税；

但是不包括在一缔约国内因资源获得收入，而向该缔约国纳税的人。

3. 鉴于本条第 2 款之规定，如果一个人是缔约国双方的居民，该人的地位应按以下方法确立：

（a）在一缔约国拥有永久性居所，视为该缔约国居民。

（b）在两缔约国均有永久性居所，或都没有永久性居所，日常居所地仅在一缔约国的，为该缔约国居民。

（c）如果在两缔约国均有日常居所，或者都没有，其人身和经济关系仅与一缔约国更为紧密的，则为该缔约国居民。

4. 鉴于本条第 2 款之规定，除了作为缔约国双方的居民的自然人以外，其他非自然人的机构仅受一缔约国的有效管理，则视为该缔约国的居民。

第 2 条　区域

1. 合作区位于印度尼西亚东帝汶省与澳大利亚北部之间的区域，由 A、B、C 三个区域组成。

2. 合作区内的有关石油资源勘探开发活动以下述条件为基础：

（a）根据本条约之规定，A 区内石油资源勘探开发活动，应由缔约国双方共同管理，以期获得最大商业利用，以及缔约国之间的同等分配；

（b）在 B 区内，澳大利亚应当通知印度尼西亚共和国一些信息，并与之分享其根据本条约第 4 条之规定从 B 区石油生产中收取的"资源租赁税"；

（c）在 C 区内，印度尼西亚共和国应当通知澳大利亚一些信息，并与之分享其根据本条约第 4 条之规定从 C 区石油生产中收取的"承包商所得税"。

3. 本条约内的任何内容以及条约生效后的任何行为，不得被解释为有损任一缔约国对于合作区永久性大陆架划界的立场，条约中的任何内容不得认为会影响缔约国对于合作区所主张的主权权利。

4. 尽管缔结了本条约，但是缔约国双方应继续努力以期就合作区内大陆架的永久性划界达成一致。

第二章　合作区内的勘探和开发

第 3 条　A 区

1. 关于对 A 区石油资源的勘探和开发，两缔约国的权利和责任由部长理事会和联合当局依本条约规定行使。A 区的石油作业应该根据产品分成合同予以实施。

2. 联合当局应该与为此合同而设立的有限责任公司，订立一份产品分成合同。这一规定同样适用于该公司的继承者或者代理人。

第 4 条　B 区和 C 区

1. 有关 B 区石油资源的勘探和开发，澳大利亚应当：

（a）通知印度尼西亚共和国关于权利的授予、更新、放弃、期满和取消，以及澳大利亚授予的开发许可、保留租约和生产许可；以及

（b）将其从 B 区石油生产公司获得的毛资源租赁税的 10%（相当于净资源租赁税的 16%）支付给印度尼西亚共和国。以一般公司税的最高税率为基础进行计算。

2. 有关 C 区石油资源的勘探和开发，印度尼西亚共和国应当：

（a）通知澳大利亚关于权利的授予、更新、放弃、期满和取消，以及印度尼西亚共和国授予的开发许可、保留租约和生产许可；

（b）将其从 C 区石油生产公司获得的承包商所得税的 10% 支付给澳大利亚。

3. 一旦澳大利亚改变资源租赁税或一般公司税的计算基础，或者印度尼西亚共和国改变承包商所得税计算基础，缔约国双方应当审查本条第 1 款 b 项和第 2 款 b 项所规定的比例。缔约国双方应就新的比例达成一致，确保每一缔约国将其从 B 或 C 区石油生产公司所得税款支付给另一缔约国的相对份额不变。

4. 一旦任一缔约国相关税收制度发生变化，缔约国双方应当审查本条第 1 款 b 项和第 2 款 b 项所规定的税收制度，并就新的税收制度达成一致，确保每一缔约国将其从 B 和 C 区石油生产公司所得的税款支付给另一缔约国的相对份额不变。

5. 关于 B 区和 C 区，缔约国应该缔结必要的行政协议，使本条第 1 款 b 项和第 2 款 b 项所规定的两国间分享协议，在任何一片区域开始投产时，得以实行。尤其是规定一缔约国向另一缔约国支付份额的方式。一缔约国向另一缔约国支付份额时，应当提供计算该份额的信息。

6. 缔约国双方应当采取必要措施，确保 B、C 区石油资源得到及时有效的利用。

第三章　部长理事会

第 5 条　部长理事会

1. 合作区的部长理事会据此设立。

2. 部长理事会由缔约国任命的部长组成，在任何时候缔约国双方任命的部长人数应当相同。

3. 部长理事会每年召开一次会议，或者应要求召开会议。

4. 部长理事会通常应当在澳大利亚或印度尼西亚共和国轮流召开会议。会议由每一缔约国任命的部长轮流主持。

5. 部长理事会做出决定时要求协商一致。部长理事会应当制定休会时的决策程序。

第 6 条　部长理事会的职能

1. 部长理事会全面负责与合作区中的 A 区域有关的石油资源的勘探开发，以及缔约国授予的其他与石油资源的勘探开发有关的职能。部长理事会的职能包括：

（a）指导联合当局履行职能；

（b）自行决定或者根据联合当局的建议，以一种符合条约目的的方式，修订《石油开采规则》，促进 A 区石油生产；

（c）自行决定或者根据联合当局的建议，以一种符合条约目的的方式，修订《范式产品分成合同》以促进 A 区石油生产；

（d）批准联合当局计划与公司签订的产品分成合同；

（e）批准终止联合当局与公司之间的产品分成合同；

（f）经承包商同意后，批准变更产品分成合同的如下条款：

（ⅰ）联合当局或者承包商的产品份额；

（ⅱ）作业成本收回条款；

（ⅲ）合同期限；

（ⅳ）合同区域退回条款；

（g）批准对年度合同服务费的变更；

（h）在部长理事会规定的决定的情形，批准联合当局销售部分或全部石油产品；

（i）批准承包商将其权利和责任转让为其他将成为承包商的公司；

（j）批准源自 A 区产品分成合同收益，在澳大利亚和印度尼西亚共和国之间的分配；

（k）通过协商，解决联合当局内部的争端；

（l）批准联合当局收支的财政预算；

（m）批准联合当局有效运行所需的规则、规定和程序，其中包括人事规则；

（n）审查本条约的运行情况，向缔约国建议，部长理事会考虑修改本条约的必要性；

（o）任命联合当局的执行董事；

（p）应部长理事会成员的要求，检查和审计部长理事会的账簿和账户；

（q）批准联合当局对承包商账簿和账户检查和审计的结果；

（r）审议和采纳联合当局的年度报告；

（s）审查 A 区石油作业的支出在印度尼西亚共和国、澳大利亚以及第三国之间的分担。

2. 部长理事会在履行职能时，应当确保根据良好油田实践以及环境实践，实现 A 区石油资源的最大商业化利用。

3. 部长理事会应当授权联合当局采取一切必要措施，确保在本条约生效后，A 区石油资源的勘探和开发立即开始。

第四章 联合当局

第7条 联合当局

1. 联合当局据此设立。

2. 联合当局具有法律人格，该能力对于其行使权力和履行职能是必要的。尤其是联合当局必须有缔约，接受和处置动产和不动产，以及提起诉讼和应诉的能力。

3. 联合当局对部长理事会负责。

4. 联合当局的执行董事做出决定应当协商一致。如果没有协商一致，问题应该提交部长理事会。

5. 除非部长理事会另有决定，联合当局应在印度尼西亚共和国设有总部，在澳大利亚设有办公室，均由一名执行董事领导。

6. 联合当局自条约生效后开始履行职能。

第8条 联合当局的职能

联合当局遵循部长理事会的指示，根据条约，特别是《石油开采规则》和《范式产品分成合同》，负责 A 区石油资源勘探和开发的管理。其管理职能主要包括：

（a）将 A 区分为若干合同区块，在合同区块招标之前，发布勘探许可及委托进行环境调查；进行合同区块招标，评估适用情况，就产品分成合同的适用向部长理事会提出建议；

（b）根据部长理事会的批准，与公司缔结产品分成合同，根据《石油开采规则》以及《产品分成合同》中的条款，监督承包商的活动；

（c）如果承包商未能满足《产品分成合同》所规定的条款和条件，向部长理事会建议终止产品分成合同；

（d）与承包商协商一致终止《产品分成合同》；

（e）向部长理事会建议，批准承包商将其权利和责任转让给其他将成为承包商的公司；

（f）经部长理事会批准，收取联合当局在石油产品分成合同中的份额，并在缔约国之间分配收益；

（g）编制联合当局收支年度预算并提交部长理事会，联合当局的任何支出，应当符合部长理事会批准的预算或者符合部长理事会批准的规范和程序；

（h）管理用于石油资源勘探和开发的船只、飞机、建筑物和其他设备进出 A 区，根据第二十三条之规定，授权承包商和分包商雇员以及其他人员进入 A 区；

（i）根据国际法建立安全区和限制区，以确保石油作业和航行的安全；

（j）根据《石油开采规则》就有关石油作业的监督管理问题（包括健康、安全、环保、评估以及工作实践）发布规范和命令；

（k）根据本条约的规定，向部长理事会建议修订《石油开采规则》和《范式产品分成合同》；

（l）根据条约要求澳大利亚和印度尼西亚相关当局采取下列行动：

（ⅰ）在 A 区进行搜索和营救；

（ⅱ）阻止针对 A 区内从事石油作业的船只及设施的恐怖威胁；

（m）要求澳大利亚、印度尼西亚相关当局，或者其他机构或个人，就防止污染的措施、设备以及程序予以援助；

（n）编制向部长理事会提交的年度报告；

（o）经部长理事会批准，与承包商就变更产品分成合同的以下内容达成一致：

（ⅰ）联合当局或者承包商的产品份额；

（ⅱ）运行成本回收条款；

（ⅲ）合同期限；

（ⅳ）合同区域的退回条款；

（p）经部长理事会批准，变更年度合同服务费；

（q）除了本条 o、p 项外，经与承包商协商一致，变更产品分成合同的其他条款；

（r）经部长理事会批准，在部长理事会规定的情形下，销售部分或全部石油产品；

（s）每年检查和审计承包商与产品分成合同有关的账簿和账户；

（t）监督 A 区石油作业的支出在印度尼西亚共和国、澳大利亚以及第三国之间的分配，并向部长理事会报告；

（u）部长理事会授予的其他职能。

第 9 条 联合当局的结构

1. 联合当局的构成如下：

（a）部长理事会任命执行董事，由每一缔约国指派的相同数量的人员组成；

（b）以下三个理事会对执行董事负责：

（ⅰ）技术理事会负责涉及石油资源的勘探和开发作业，其中包括第 8 条第 a 项提及的职能；

（ⅱ）财政理事会负责收取费用以及出售联合当局产品份额后的收入；

（ⅲ）法律理事会负责就产品分成合同有关的任何法律问题，以及在 A 区的法律适用提供建议；以及

（c）公司服务理事会为执行董事和其他三个理事会提供行政支持，以及为部长理事会会议提供服务。

2. 联合当局的人员，由执行董事根据规定联合当局适当职能的条款和条件，以及 A 区内不时进行的自然资源勘探开发的性质，从缔约国提名的人选中任命。四名理事领导四个理事会，执行董事必须从每一缔约国提名的人选中任命两名理事。如果印度尼西亚的提名人选被任命为技术理事会的理事，那么澳大利亚的提名人选应当被任命为财政理事会的理事，反之亦然。

3. 除非部长理事会另有决定，技术理事会必须在位于澳大利亚的联合当局所在地。

4. 执行董事和四名理事构成执行董事会。

5. 执行董事和联合当局的其他人员，不得与 A 区石油资源勘探和开发有关的任何活动，存在经济利益。

第 10 条 对联合当局及其公务人员的捐税

1. 对联合当局免征以下税款：

（a）在澳大利亚，根据澳大利亚联邦法律征收的所得税；

（b）在印度尼西亚，根据印度尼西亚共和国法律征收的所得税。

除了现有税种外,还包括在本条约签署之后所征收的相同或大体类似的税收;或者在本条约签署之后所征收的相同或大体类似的税收,以取代现有税种。

2. 联合当局的执行董事和其他公务人员:

(a)对联合当局支付的,与他们为联合当局服务有关的工资、津贴和其他报酬,予以免税,而不是出于征税的目的,将他们视为本条约第1条所规定的居民,根据缔约国的法律予以征税;

(b)依据本条约第1条之规定,公务人员不属于该缔约国公民,而联合当局位于该缔约国内。他们第一次任职时,为了个人使用或居住而进口的家具,以及他们所有或订购的家庭用品和个人物品免征关税和其他费用(服务费除外)。这些物品应当在公务人员第一次入境后的6个月内予以进口,除非缔约国政府允许延长时间。公务人员所取得或进口,并且根据本项之规定免于纳税的物品,不得赠送、出卖、出借、出租或者以其他方式处置,除非事先与公务人员所在国政府达成一致。

3. 部长理事会可以建议缔约国,授予联合当局或其工作人员另外的特权,如果这些特权对促进联合当局有效运作是必要的。这些特权只能根据缔约国之间的协定授予。

第11条 财政

1. 联合当局的资金,来源于根据《石油开采规则》第五章所征收的费用。其规定,如果缔约国共同决定有必要使联合当局开始运作,可预先提供这些资金。

2. 一旦联合当局不能履行,针对产品分成合同争端而做出的裁决中的义务,缔约国双方应当公平提供必要资金促使联合当局履行义务。

第五章 关于A区相关事项的合作

第12条 监督

1. 根据本条约规定,缔约国双方有权对A区的活动进行监督。

2. 缔约国之间应根据本条第1款之规定,就任何监督活动进行合作和协调。

3. 缔约国之间应根据本条第1款之规定,交换从监督活动中获得的信息。

第 13 条　安全措施

1. 缔约国之间应就与 A 区石油资源勘探和开发有关的威胁或安全事件交换信息。

2. 缔约国之间应就 A 区安全事件的应对做出安排。

第 14 条　搜索和营救

经考虑广泛接受的国际法规则，以及相关国际组织制定的规范和程序，缔约国之间应就 A 区搜索和营救安排进行合作。

第 15 条　空中交通服务

经考虑广泛接受的国际法规则，以及相关国际组织制定的规范和程序，缔约国之间应就 A 区提供空中交通服务进行合作。

第 16 条　水文和地震勘测

1. 缔约国双方均有权在 A 区进行水文勘测以促进石油作业。缔约国双方应就下列事项进行合作：

（a）实施水文勘测，包括提供必要的岸上设施；

（b）交换与 A 区石油作业相关的水文信息。

2. 根据本条约规定，缔约国双方应当在促进 A 区内地震勘测方面进行合作，包括提供必要的岸上设施。

第 17 条　海洋科学研究

在对缔约国双方主张的 A 区海洋科学研究相关国际法权利不予损害的情况下，一缔约国收到请求在 A 区开展有关大陆架非生物资源的海洋科学研究的申请时，应该与另一缔约国就该研究是否与 A 区石油资源的勘探开发有关，进行协商。如果缔约国双方认为该研究与石油资源的勘探开发联系密切，应该征求联合当局的意见。根据联合当局的意见，缔约国共同决定规则、授权和研究行为，包括向两国和联合当局提供数据、样本和此次研究的结果，以及缔约国双方共同参与该研究项目。

第 18 条　海洋环境保护

1. 缔约国之间应当就防止和减少 A 区石油资源勘探开发产生的污染进行合作，尤其是以下方面：

（a）缔约国应当对联合当局根据本条约第 8 条 m 款提出的请求提供帮助；

（b）如果 A 区内产生的污染溢出 A 区，缔约国应当在防止、减轻和消除污染方面进行合作。

2. 根据本条约第 8 条 j 款之规定，联合当局应当发布规范保护 A 区的海洋环境，应当制订防控 A 区石油作业污染的应急计划。

第 19 条　承包商对海洋环境污染的责任

承包商对于 A 区石油作业产生的海洋环境污染所造成的损失或花费，应根据其与联合当局的合同规定，以及对损害或费用提出主张的国家的法律，承担责任。

第 20 条　对 A 区和超出 A 区部分的联合经营

如果任何一个单一的石油聚集，超越了本条约第 1 条和附件 A 所划定的 A 区界线，并且位于界线另一边的石油聚集，可以从 A 区进行部分或者全部开发，缔约国之间应就石油聚集最为高效开发的方式，以及就开发所获利益进行公平分配，努力达成一致。

第 21 条　设施建设

一旦在 A 区勘探开发石油资源，需要在 A 区以外的地方建设设施和提供服务，缔约国应向承包商和联合当局提供所有帮助，推动设施的建设和运作以及提供服务。这些设施的建设和运行以及服务的提供，应该遵循相关缔约国的法律法规以及缔约国设定的条件。

第六章　适用的法律

第 22 条　产品分成合同适用的法律

产品分成合同所适用的法律，应在合同中具体规定。

第 23 条　关税、移民和检疫适用的法律

1. 根据本条第 3、第 5 款之规定，缔约国有权对从本国前往 A 区，或者自 A 区进入本国的人、设备和货物，适用自己的关税、移民和检疫法。缔约国应做出必要的安排，便利这种进出。

2. 承包商应当确保，除非得到缔约国的授权，否则没有首先进入澳大利亚或者印度尼西亚共和国的人员、设备和货物，不得进入 A 区的构筑物内。承包商应当确保，承包商的雇员和分包商的雇员进入 A 区有联合当局的授权。

3. 出于控制这些人员、设备或货物的转移之目的，一缔约国可以要求与另一国就特定人员、设备和货物进入 A 区进行协商。

4. 本条规定不得损害缔约国对未获得任何一方缔约国授权进入 A 区的人员、设备和货物，适用其关税、移民和检疫法。缔约国之间应就适用安排进行协调以协调行使这一权利。

5. （a）与 A 区石油作业有关的进入 A 区的货物和设备，无须缴纳关税。

（b）与石油作业相关的基于进入 A 区的目的，而离开或途经一缔约国的货物和设备，无须缴纳关税。

（c）为永久性的运往一缔约国而离开 A 区的货物和设备，应该向该国缴纳关税。

第 24 条 雇佣

1. 缔约国应采取适当措施确保 A 区优先雇用澳大利亚和印度尼西亚共和国的永久性居民，在产品分成合同存续期间，雇用两国永久性居民的人数相同，但要适当考虑有效运行和良好油田实践。

2. A 区设施所雇用人员的待遇和劳动条件，应由劳动合同或者集体协议规定。包括有关工伤保险赔偿条款，其中应有死亡或伤残抚恤金；还可能规定适用任一缔约国现有的赔偿制度。待遇和劳动条件还应该包括劳动报酬、劳动时间或者加班时间、休假和合同终止。A 区雇员的待遇和劳动条件应该不低于澳大利亚和印度尼西亚共和国国内类似职业的用工标准。

3. 与 A 区石油作业相关的用于地震勘测、钻井、补给和服务的船只所雇用的人员，无论船只国籍如何，均适用本条第 2 款之规定。

4. 对本条第 2、第 3 款所适用的人员提供相关的设施和机会时，不得基于国籍予以歧视。

5. 雇主和雇员之间的争端首先应当通过谈判解决。如果争端无法通过谈判解决，应当寻求一个三方争端解决委员会进行解决，三方争端解决委员会由雇主代表、雇员代表以及缔约国任命的人员组成；或者寻求缔约国内可用的调解和仲裁机制解决。

6. 在劳动合同或集体协议谈判中，以及在调解仲裁程序中，缔约国法律承认的雇主联合会和职工联合会分别代表雇主和雇员。

7. 劳动合同或者集体协议，应该规定其适用哪一方缔约国的法律，同时根据本条第 5 款之规定，规定适用的争端解决机制。根据缔约国的法律，任何裁决一经做出即具有强制性。

第 25 条　工作人员的健康和安全

联合当局应当制定 A 区雇员的职业健康和安全标准和规程，并且不低于澳大利亚和印度尼西亚共和国国内相似职业相关人员所适用的标准和规程。承包商应当适用这一标准和规程。联合当局应当根据本条，在考虑缔约国法律中的现有制度后，通过职业健康安全标准和规程。

第 26 条　油轮

除了本条约另有规定外，参与石油作业的船只应当遵守作为其国籍国的缔约国的法律（除非拥有另一缔约国国籍），以及作业港口所属缔约国的法律，法律涉及安全、作业标准和船员管理。这些船只进入 A 区且不在任一缔约国港口作业的，应当根据缔约国双方的法律适用相关的国际安全和作业标准。

第 27 条　刑事管辖权

1. 根据本条第 3 款之规定，一缔约国的公民或永久性居民，在 A 区内进行与石油资源勘探开发相关的作为或不作为，适用该国的刑法；如果是一缔约国的永久性居民，同时也是另一缔约国的公民，适用后一国的刑法。

2. （a）根据本条第 3 款之规定，非任一缔约国永久性居民的第三国公民，在 A 区内进行与石油资源勘探开发相关的作为或不作为，适用缔约国双方的刑法。如果一人因同一作为或不作为，已经根据一缔约国的法律，受到该国主管法庭审判并且认定无罪或免除刑事责任，或者已经受到处罚，或者主管当局根据本国法律，基于公共利益，不对该人的行为提起公诉，那么该人在另一缔约国就无须遭受刑事追诉。缔约国双方应相互咨询以确定将要适用的刑事法律，考虑受害人国籍以及被影响的缔约方的利益。

（b）在上述 a 项所提情形下，必要时，缔约国双方应相互咨询以确定将要适用的刑事法律，并要考虑受害人国籍以及受影响的缔约国之利益。

3. 对于 A 区内航行的船只（包括地震勘测船或者钻井船）上发生的作为或不作为，适用船旗国刑法；对于飞越 A 区的飞机上发生的作为或不作为，适用国籍国刑法。

4. （a）为了执行本条所规定的刑法，包括获得证据和信息，缔约国之间应当互助合作，包括通过适当的协定或安排进行。

(b) 当一缔约国公民是所控罪行的受害者时，另一缔约国须承认其利益，并在法律允许的范围内，将针对所控罪行所采取的措施告知该缔约国。

5. 缔约国之间应做出安排，允许一缔约国公务人员协助另一缔约国执行刑法。如果这一协助需要对本条第 1 款所列的由另一缔约国进行管辖的人员进行拘留，拘留只能持续到将相关人员能移交给另一缔约国的相关公务人员为止。

第 28 条 民事行为

由于 A 区内的活动造成的损害而产生的主张或赔偿，可以向受害人或者加害人的国籍国或者永久性居所地所在的缔约国提出。受理诉讼的法院应当适用该缔约国的法律和法规。

第 29 条 税法适用

1. 鉴于税法与下列事项直接或间接相关：

（a） A 区石油的勘探开发活动；

（b） 与任何勘探开发活动相关，或产生于勘探开发活动的行为、问题和情形；

A 区应被每一缔约国视为自己的一部分。

2. 税法适用于：

（a） A 区；

（b） 承包商支付的利益；

（c） 承包商支付的特许权使用费。

根据《税收规则》，每一缔约国都应该避免双重征税。

3. 对于下列事项，一缔约国不得征收《税收规则》未规定的税收：

（a） A 区内石油的勘探和开发；

（b） A 区内实施的与石油勘探开发相关的活动。

除非另一缔约国同意其征收这一税收。

第七章 争端解决

第 30 条 争端解决

1. 任何有关条约适用或解释的争端，应该由缔约国之间通过协商或谈判解决。

2. 联合当局缔结的每一份产品分享合同，应该包含有关产品分成合同的解释或适用的任何争端，应提交给一个有拘束力的特殊形式的商业仲裁的争端解决机制的内容。缔约国应该促进各自法院执行仲裁裁决。

第八章　最后条款

第 31 条　修正

1. 任何时候，经缔约国双方达成一致可对条约进行修改。

2. 根据本条约第 6 条第 1 款 b 项之规定，部长理事会通过决议对《石油开采规则》进行修改或修正；根据本条约第 6 条第 1 款 c 项之规定，部长理事会通过决议对《范式产品分成合同》进行修改或修正。修正和修改与《石油开采规则》《范式产品分成合同》具有同等地位。

第 32 条　生效

在缔约国以书面形式相互通知对方，各自关于条约生效的要求均已完成之日起满 30 日条约生效。

第 33 条　条约期限

1. 自条约生效之日起，条约有效期为 40 年。

2. 除非缔约国双方有相反约定，否则条约在最初的 40 年期满后，顺延 20 年；除非在每个期限届满时（包括最初的 40 年期），缔约国双方就合作区所覆盖的大陆架永久性划界缔结协定。

3. 如果在本条第 1、第 2 款所提及的任何一个期限届满前 5 年，缔约国未就合作区覆盖的大陆架永久划界缔结协定，缔约国双方的代表，应基于永久性大陆架划界的目的，进行会晤。

4. 本条之规定不损害本条约第 34 条持续有效。

第 34 条　承包商的权利

1. 一旦出现下列情形：

（a）如果由于缔约国之间在合作区达成永久性大陆架划界协定，使得本条约失效；

（b）在本条约即将失效之前，所存在的与联合当局缔结的产品分成合同，

将继续适用于每个当事国，或者当事国任命的取代联合当局的其他人员，产品分成合同将在每个缔约国领土管辖范围内执行。每一缔约国，对

在其领土管辖内履行合同的承包商所适用的制度，不能比本条约和相关产品分成合同中的规定繁重。

2. 缔约国双方在缔结永久性划界协定时，做出必要安排来实施本条第1款之规定。

本条约由双方政府授权的代表签署，以昭信守。

1989 年 12 月 11 日，两原始文本以英语作成。

澳大利亚	印度尼西亚共和国
加雷斯·埃文斯	阿利·阿拉塔斯
外交事务和贸易部长	外交部长

2. Treaty between Australia and the Republic of Indonesia on the Zone of Cooperation in an Area between the Indonesian Province of East Timor and Northern Australia

AUSTRALIA AND THE REPUBLIC OF INDONESIA

TAKING INTO ACCOUNT the United Nations Convention on the Law of the Sea done at Montego Bay on 10 December 1982 and, in particular, Article 83 which requires States with opposite coasts, in a spirit of understanding and cooperation, to make every effort to enter into provisional arrangements of a practical nature which do not jeopardize or hamper the reaching of final agreement on the delimitation of the continental shelf;

DESIRING to enable the exploration for and exploitation of the petroleum resources of the continental shelf of the area between the Indonesian Province of East Timor and northern Australia yet to be the subject of permanent continental shelf delimitation between the Contracting States;

CONSCIOUS of the need to encourage and promote development of the petroleum resources of the area;

DESIRING that exploration for and exploitation of these resources proceed without delay;

AFFIRMING existing agreements on the delimitation of the continental shelf between their two countries;

DETERMINED to cooperate further for the mutual benefit of their peoples in the development of the resources of the area of the continental shelf yet to be the subject of permanent continental shelf delimitation between their two countries;

FULLY COMMITTED to maintaining, renewing and further strengthening the mutual respect, friendship and cooperation between their two countries through existing agreements and arrangements, as well as their policies of promoting constructive neighbourly cooperation;

MINDFUL of the interests which their countries share as immediate neighbours, and in a spirit of cooperation, friendship and goodwill;

CONVINCED that this Treaty will contribute to the strengthening of the relations between their two countries; and

BELIEVING that the establishment of joint arrangements to permit the exploration for and exploitation of petroleum resources in the area will further augment the range of contact and cooperation between the Governments of the two countries and benefit the development of contacts between their peoples;

HAVE AGREED as follows:

PART I ZONE OF COOPERATION

Article 1 Definitions

1. For the purposes of this Treaty,

(a) "contract" or "production sharing contract" means a contract between the Joint Authority and corporations, concluded on the basis of the Model Production Sharing Contract, entered into under Article 8 of this Treaty and in accordance with Part III of the Petroleum Mining Code;

(b) "contract area" means the area constituted by the blocks specified in the contract that have not been relinquished or surrendered;

(c) "contractor" means a corporation or corporations which enter into a contract with the Joint Authority and which is registered as a contractor under Article 38 of the Petroleum Mining Code;

(d) "Contractors' Income Tax" means tax imposed by the Indonesian Laws No. 7 of 1983 on Income Tax and No. 6 of 1983 on General Tax Provisions and Procedures as amended from time to time;

(e) "criminal law" means any law in force in the Contracting States, whether substantive or procedural, that makes provision for or in relation to offences or for or in relation to the investigation or prosecution of offences or the punishment of offenders, including the carrying out of a penalty imposed by a court. For this purpose "investigation" includes entry to a structure in Area A, the exercise of powers of search and questioning and the apprehension of a suspected offender;

(f) "good oilfield practice" means all those things that are generally accepted as good and safe in the carrying on of petroleum operations;

(g) "Model Production Sharing Contract" means the model contract as appears in Annex C, on the basis of which production sharing contracts for Area A should be concluded, as may be modified from time to time by the Ministerial Council in accordance with paragraph 1 (c) of Article 6 of this Treaty;

(h) "petroleum" means

(a) any naturally occurring hydrocarbon, whether in a gaseous, liquid or solid state;

(b) any naturally occurring mixture of hydrocarbons, whether in a gaseous, liquid or solid state; or

(c) any petroleum as defined by sub-paragraph (a) or (b) of this paragraph that has been returned to a reservoir in the contract area;

(i) "Petroleum Mining Code" means the "Petroleum Mining Code for Area A of the Zone of Cooperation" to govern operational activities relating to exploration for and exploitation of the petroleum resources in Area A of the Zone of Cooperation contained in Annex B, as amended from time to time by the Ministerial Council in accordance with paragraph 1 (b) of Article 6 of this Treaty;

(j) "petroleum operations" means activities undertaken to produce petroleum and includes exploration, development, field processing, production and pipeline operations, and marketing authorized or contemplated under a production sharing contract;

(k) "Resource Rent Tax" means tax imposed by the Petroleum Resource Rent Tax Act 1987 of Australia as amended from time to time;

(l) "structure" means an installation or structure used to carry out petroleum operations;

(m) "Taxation Code" means the "Taxation Code for the Avoidance of Double Taxation in Respect of Activities Connected with Area A of the Zone of Cooperation", contained in Annex D;

(n) "taxation law" means the federal law of Australia or the law of the Republic of Indonesia, from time to time in force, in respect of taxes to which this Treaty applies but shall not include a tax agreement between the Contracting States and a tax agreement of either Contracting State with a third country;

(o) "Treaty" means this Treaty including Annexes A, B, C and D;

(p) "Zone of Cooperation" refers to the area so designated and described in Annex A and illustrated in the maps forming part of that Annex, which consists of the whole of the area embraced by Areas A, B and C designated in that Annex.

2. For the purposes of Article 10 of this Treaty and the Taxation Code, resident of a Contracting State means:

(a) in the case of Australia, a person who is liable to tax in Australia by reason of being a resident of Australia under the tax law of Australia; and

(b) in the case of the Republic of Indonesia, a person who is liable to tax in the Republic of Indonesia by reason of being a resident of the Republic of Indonesia under the tax law of the Republic of Indonesia,

but does not include any person who is liable to tax in that Contracting State in respect only of income from sources in that Contracting State.

3. Where by reason of the provisions of paragraph 2 of this Article, an individual is a resident of both Contracting States, then the status of the person shall be determined as follows:

(a) the person shall be deemed to be a resident solely of the Contracting State in which a permanent home is available to the person;

(b) if a permanent home is available to the person in both Contracting States, or in neither of them, the person shall be deemed to be a resident solely of the Contracting State in which the person has an habitual abode;

(c) if the person has an habitual abode in both Contracting States, or if the person does not have an habitual abode in either of them, the person shall be deemed to be a resident solely of the Contracting State with which the person's personal and economic relations are the closer.

4. Where by reason of the provisions of paragraph 2 of this Article a person other than an individual is a resident of both Contracting States, then it shall be deemed to be a resident solely of the Contracting State in which its place of effective management is situated.

Article 2　The Zone

1. A Zone of Cooperation is hereby designated in an area between the Indonesian Province of East Timor and northern Australia, which comprises Areas A, B and C.

2. Within the Zone of Cooperation activities in relation to the exploration for and exploitation of petroleum resources shall be conducted on the following basis:

(a) In Area A, there shall be joint control by the Contracting States of the exploration for and exploitation of petroleum resources, aimed at achieving optimum commercial utilization thereof and equal sharing between the two Contracting States of the benefits of the exploitation of petroleum resources, as provided for in this Treaty;

(b) In Area B, Australia shall make certain notifications and share with the Republic of Indonesia Resource Rent Tax collections arising from petroleum production on the basis of Article 4 of this Treaty; and

(c) In Area C, the Republic of Indonesia shall make certain notifications and share with Australia Contractors' Income Tax collections arising from petroleum production on the basis of Article 4 of this Treaty.

3. Nothing contained in this Treaty and no acts or activities taking place while this Treaty is in force shall be interpreted as prejudicing the position of either Contracting State on a permanent continental shelf delimitation in the Zone of Cooperation nor shall anything contained in it be considered as affecting the respective sovereign rights claimed by each Contracting State in the Zone of Cooperation.

4. Notwithstanding the conclusion of this Treaty, the Contracting States shall

continue their efforts to reach agreement on a permanent continental shelf delimitation in the Zone of Cooperation.

PART II EXPLORATION AND EXPLOITATION IN THE ZONE OF COOPERATION

Article 3   Area A

1. In relation to the exploration for and exploitation of petroleum resources in Area A, the rights and responsibilities of the two Contracting States shall be exercised by the Ministerial Council and the Joint Authority in accordance with this Treaty. Petroleum operations in Area A shall be carried out through production sharing contracts.

2. The Joint Authority shall enter into each production sharing contract with limited liability corporations specifically established for the sole purpose of the contract. This provision shall also apply to the successors or assignees of such corporations.

Article 4   Area B and Area C

1. In relation to the exploration for and exploitation of petroleum resources in Area B Australia shall:

(a) notify the Republic of Indonesia of the grant, renewal, surrender, expiry and cancellation of titles made by Australia being exploration permits, retention leases and production licences; and

(b) pay to the Republic of Indonesia ten (10) per cent of gross Resource Rent Tax collected by Australia from corporations producing petroleum from Area B equivalent to sixteen (16) per cent of net Resource Rent Tax collected, calculated on the basis that general company tax is payable at the maximum rate.

2. In relation to exploration for and exploitation of petroleum resources in Area C the Republic of Indonesia shall:

(a) notify Australia of the grant, renewal, surrender, expiry and cancellation of petroleum exploration and production agreements made by the Republic of Indonesia; and

(b) pay to Australia ten (10) per cent of Contractors' Income Tax collected by the Republic of Indonesia from corporations producing petroleum from Area C.

3. In the event that Australia changes the basis upon which the Resource Rent Tax or general company tax is calculated or that the Republic of Indonesia changes the basis upon which Contractors' Income Tax is calculated, the Contracting States shall review

the percentages set out in paragraphs 1 (b) and 2 (b) of this Article and agree on new percentages, ensuring that the relative shares paid by each Contracting State to the other in respect of revenue collected from corporations producing petroleum in Area B and Area C remain the same.

4. In the event of any change occurring in the relevant taxation regimes of either Contracting State, the Contracting States shall review the formulation set out in paragraphs 1 (b) and 2 (b) of this Article and agree on a new formulation, ensuring that the relative shares paid by each Contracting State to the other in respect of revenue collected from corporations producing petroleum in Area B and Area C remain the same.

5. With regard to Area B and Area C, the Contracting States shall enter into necessary administrative arrangements to give effect to the sharing arrangements in the two Areas as provided in paragraph 1 (b) and paragraph 2 (b) of this Article at the time that production from either Area commences. In particular, the arrangements shall provide for the manner in which such a share shall be paid from one Contracting State to the other Contracting State. A Contracting State when making a payment to the other Contracting State shall provide information on the basis on which the relevant payment was calculated.

6. The Contracting States shall take necessary measures to ensure the timely and optimum utilization of the petroleum resources in Area B and Area C.

PART III THE MINISTERIAL COUNCIL

Article 5 The Ministerial Council

1. A Ministerial Council for the Zone of Cooperation is hereby established.

2. The Ministerial Council shall consist of those Ministers who may from time to time be designated for that purpose by the Contracting States provided that, at

any one time, there shall be an equal number of Ministers designated by each Contracting State.

3. The Ministerial Council shall meet annually or as often as may be required.

4. The Ministerial Council shall normally meet alternately in Australia or in the Republic of Indonesia. Its meetings shall be chaired alternately by a Minister nominated by each Contracting State.

5. Decisions of the Ministerial Council shall be arrived at by consensus. The Ministerial Council may establish procedures for taking decisions out of session.

Article 6　Functions of the Ministerial Council

1. The Ministerial Council shall have overall responsibility for all matters relating to the exploration for and exploitation of the petroleum resources in Area A of the Zone of Cooperation and such other functions relating to the exploration for and exploitation of petroleum resources as the Contracting States may entrust to it. The functions of the Ministerial Council shall include:

(a) giving directions to the Joint Authority on the discharge of its functions;

(b) of its own volition or on recommendation by the Joint Authority, in a manner not inconsistent with the objectives of this Treaty, amending the Petroleum Mining Code to facilitate petroleum operations in Area A;

(c) of its own volition or on recommendation by the Joint Authority, in a manner not inconsistent with the objectives of this Treaty, modifying the Model Production Sharing Contract to facilitate petroleum operations in Area A;

(d) approving production sharing contracts which the Joint Authority may propose to enter into with corporations;

(e) approving the termination of production sharing contracts entered into between the Joint Authority and corporations;

(f) approving the variation of the following provisions of a production sharing contract, with the agreement of the contractor:

(i) the Joint Authority's or the contractor's production share;

(ii) the operating cost recovery provisions;

(iii) the term of the contract; and

(iv) the contract area relinquishment provisions;

(g) approving the variation of the annual contract service fee;

(h) giving approval to the Joint Authority to market any or all petroleum production in circumstances determined by the Ministerial Council;

(i) approving the transfer of rights and responsibilities by contractors to other corporations that will then become contractors;

(j) approving the distribution to Australia and the Republic of Indonesia of revenues derived from production sharing contracts in Area A;

(k) through consultation, settling disputes in the Joint Authority;

(l) approving financial estimates of income and expenditure of the Joint Authority;

(m) approving rules, regulations and procedures for the effective functioning of the Joint Authority including staff regulations;

(n) reviewing the operation of this Treaty and making recommendations to the Contracting States that the Council may consider necessary for the amendment of this Treaty;

(o) appointment of the Executive Directors of the Joint Authority;

(p) at the request of a member of the Ministerial Council inspecting and auditing the Joint Authority's books and accounts;

(q) approving the result of inspections and audits of contractors' books and accounts conducted by the Joint Authority;

(r) considering and adopting the annual report of the Joint Authority; and

(s) reviewing the distribution among the Republic of Indonesia, Australia and third countries, of expenditure on petroleum operations related to Area A.

1. The Ministerial Council in exercising its functions shall ensure the achievement of the optimum commercial utilization of the petroleum resources of Area A consistent with good oilfield and sound environmental practice.

2. The Ministerial Council shall authorize the Joint Authority to take all necessary steps to enable the commencement of exploration for and exploitation of the petroleum resources of Area A as soon as possible after the entry into force of this Treaty.

PART IV   THE JOINT AUTHORITY

Article 7   The Joint Authority

1. A Joint Authority is hereby established.

2. The Joint Authority shall have juridical personality and such legal capacities under the law of both Contracting States as are necessary for the exercise of its powers and the performance of its functions. In particular, the Joint Authority shall have the capacity to contract, to acquire and dispose of movable and immovable property and to institute and be party to legal proceedings.

3. The Joint Authority shall be responsible to the Ministerial Council.

4. Decisions of the Executive Directors of the Joint Authority shall be arrived at by consensus. Where consensus cannot be reached, the matter shall be referred to the Ministerial Council.

5. Unless otherwise decided by the Ministerial Council, the Joint Authority shall have its head office in the Republic of Indonesia and an office in Australia, each of which shall be headed by an Executive Director.

6. The Joint Authority shall commence to function on entry into force of this Treaty.

Article 8   Functions of the Joint Authority

The Joint Authority, subject to directions from the Ministerial Council, shall be responsible for the management of activities relating to exploration for and exploitation of the petroleum resources in Area A in accordance with this Treaty, and in particular the Petroleum Mining Code and with production sharing contracts. These management functions shall be:

(a) dividing Area A into contract areas, issuing prospecting approvals and commissioning environmental investigations prior to contract areas being advertised, advertising of contract areas, assessing applications, and making recommendations to the Ministerial Council on applications for production sharing contracts;

(b) entering into production sharing contracts with corporations, subject to Ministerial Council approval, and supervising the activities of the contractor pursuant to the requirements of the Petroleum Mining Code, including regulations and directions thereunder, and the terms and conditions set out in the contract;

(c) recommending to the Ministerial Council the termination of production sharing contracts where contractors do not meet the terms and conditions of those contracts;

(d) terminating production sharing contracts by agreement with contractors;

(e) recommending to the Ministerial Council the approval of transfer of rights and responsibilities by contractors to other corporations that will then become contractors;

(f) collecting and, with approval of the Ministerial Council, distributing between the two Contracting States the proceeds of the Joint Authority's share of petroleum production from contracts;

(g) preparation of annual estimates of income and expenditure of the Joint Authority for submission to the Ministerial Council. Any expenditure shall only be made in accordance with estimates approved by the Ministerial Council or otherwise in accordance with regulations and procedures approved by the Council;

(h) controlling movements into, within and out of Area A of vessels, aircraft, structures and other equipment employed in exploration for and exploitation of petroleum resources; and, subject to Article 23, authorizing the entry of employees of contractors and their subcontractors and other persons into Area A;

(i) establishment of safety zones and restricted zones, consistent with international law, to ensure the safety of navigation and petroleum operations;

(j) issuing regulations and giving directions under the Petroleum Mining Code on all matters related to the supervision of and control of petroleum operations including on health, safety, environmental protection and assessments and work practices, pursuant to the Petroleum Mining Code;

(k) making recommendations to the Ministerial Council to amend the Petroleum Mining Code and to modify the Model Production Sharing Contract consistent with the objectives of this Treaty;

(l) requesting action by the appropriate Australian and Indonesian authorities consistent with this Treaty

(i) for search and rescue operations In Area A; and

(ii) in the event of terrorist threat to the vessels and structures engaged in petroleum operations in Area A;

(m) requesting assistance with pollution prevention measures, equipment and procedures from appropriate Australian or Indonesian authorities or other bodies or persons;

(n) preparation of annual reports for submission to the Ministerial Council;

(j) with the approval of the Ministerial Council, the variation of the following provisions of a production sharing contract with the agreement of the contractor:

(1) the Joint Authority's or the contractor's production share;

(ii) the operating cost recovery provisions;

(iii) the term of the contract; and

(iv) the contract area relinquishment provisions;

(p) with the approval of the Ministerial Council, the variation of the annual contract service fee;

(q) variation, with the agreement of the contractor, of provisions in the production sharing contract other than those in paragraphs (o) and (p) of this Article;

(r) with the approval of the Ministerial Council, the marketing of any or all petroleum production in circumstances determined by the Ministerial Council;

(s) inspecting and auditing contractors' books and accounts relating to the production sharing contract for any calendar year;

(t) monitoring and reporting to the Ministerial Council the distribution among the Republic of Indonesia, Australia and third countries, of expenditure on petroleum operations related to Area A; and

(u) such other functions as may be conferred on it by the Ministerial Council.

Article 9   Structure of the Joint Authority

1. The Joint Authority shall consist of:

(a) Executive Directors appointed by the Ministerial Council comprising an equal number of persons nominated by each Contracting State;

(b) the following three Directorates responsible to the Executive Directors:

(i) a Technical Directorate responsible for operations involving exploration for and exploitation of petroleum resources including operations in respect of functions referred to in paragraph (1) of Article 8;

(ii) a Financial Directorate responsible for collecting fees and proceeds from the sale of the Joint Authority's share of production; and

(iii) a Legal Directorate responsible for providing advice on any legal issues relating to production sharing contracts and on the operation of law applying in Area A; and

(c) a Corporate Services Directorate, to provide administrative support to the Executive Directors and the three other Directorates and to service the meetings of the Ministerial Council.

2. The personnel of the Joint Authority shall be appointed by the Executive Directors under terms and conditions that have regard to the proper functioning of the Joint Authority and the nature of the exploration for and exploitation of petroleum resources being undertaken from time to time in Area A from amongst individuals nominated by each Contracting State. Of the four Directors heading the Directorates, the Executive Directors shall appoint two from each Contracting State. If an Indonesian nominee is appointed to head the Technical Directorate, then an Australian nominee shall be appointed to head the Financial Directorate, and vice versa.

3. Unless otherwise decided by the Ministerial Council, the Technical Directorate shall be in the Joint Authority office located in Australia.

4. The Executive Directors and the four Directors shall constitute the Executive Board.

5. The Executive Directors and personnel of the Joint Authority shall have no financial interest in any activity relating to exploration for and exploitation of petroleum resources in Area A.

Article 10　Taxation of the Joint Authority and its officers

1. The Joint Authority shall be exempt from the following existing taxes:

(a) in Australia, the income tax imposed under the federal law of Australia;

(b) in Indonesia, the income tax (Pajak – Penghasilan) imposed under the law of the Republic of Indonesia,

as well as any identical or substantially similar taxes which are imposed after the date of signature of this Treaty in addition to, or in place of, the existing taxes.

2. The Executive Directors and other officers of the Joint Authority:

(a) shall be exempt from taxation of salaries, allowances and other emoluments paid to them by the Joint Authority in connection with their service with the Joint Authority other than taxation under the law of the Contracting State in which they are deemed under the provisions of Article 1 of this Treaty to be resident for taxation purposes; and

(b) shall, at the time of first taking up a post with the Joint Authority located in the Contracting State in which they are not resident under the provisions of Article 1 of this Treaty, be exempt from customs duties and other such charges (except payments for services) in respect of imports of furniture and other household and personal effects in their ownership or possession or already ordered by them and intended for their personal use or for their establishment; such goods shall be imported within six months of an officer's first entry but in exceptional circumstances an extension of time shall be granted by the Government of the Contracting State; goods which have been acquired or imported by officers and to which exemptions under this sub-paragraph apply shall not be given away, sold, lent, hired out, or otherwise disposed of except under conditions agreed in advance with the Government of the Contracting State in which the officer is located.

3. The Ministerial Council may recommend to the Contracting States that additional privileges be conferred on the Joint Authority or its officers, if that is necessary to promote the effective functioning of the Joint Authority. Such privileges shall be conferred only following the agreement of the two Contracting States.

Article 11　Financing

1. The Joint Authority shall be financed from fees collected under Part VI of the Petroleum Mining Code, provided that the Contracting States shall advance such funds as they jointly determine to be necessary to enable the Joint Authority to commence operations.

2. In the event that the Joint Authority cannot meet an obligation under an arbitral award arising from a dispute under a production sharing contract, the Contracting States shall contribute the necessary funds in equal shares to enable the Joint Authority to meet that obligation.

PART V COOPERATION ON CERTAIN MATTERS IN RELATION TO AREA A

Article 12 Surveillance

1. For the purposes of this Treaty, both Contracting States shall have the right to carry out surveillance activities in Area A.

2. The Contracting States shall cooperate on and coordinate any surveillance activities carried out in accordance with paragraph 1 of this Article.

3. The Contracting States shall exchange information derived from any surveillance activities carried out in accordance with paragraph 1 of this Article.

Article 13 Security measures

1. The Contracting States shall exchange information on likely threats to, or security incidents relating to, exploration for and exploitation of petroleum resources in Area A.

2. The Contracting States shall make arrangements for responding to security incidents in Area A.

Article 14 Search and rescue

The Contracting States shall cooperate on arrangements for search and rescue in Area A taking into account generally accepted international rules, regulations and procedures established through competent international organizations.

Article 15 Air traffic services

The Contracting States shall cooperate on the provision of air traffic services in Area A taking into account generally accepted international rules, regulations and procedures established through competent international organizations.

Article 16 Hydrographic and seismic surveys

1. Both Contracting States shall have the right to carry out hydrographic surveys to facilitate petroleum operations in Area A. Both Contracting States shall co-

operate on:

(a) the conduct of such surveys, including the provision of necessary on-shore facilities; and

(b) exchanging hydrographic information relevant to petroleum operations in Area A.

2. For the purposes of this Treaty, the Contracting States shall cooperate in facilitating the conduct of seismic surveys in Area A, including in the provision of necessary onshore facilities.

Article 17   Marine scientific research

Without prejudice to the rights under international law in relation to marine scientific research in Area A claimed by the two Contracting States, a Contracting State which receives a request for consent to conduct marine scientific research into the non-living resources of the continental shelf in Area A shall consult with the other Contracting State on whether the research project is related to the exploration for and exploitation of petroleum resources in Area A. If the Contracting States decide that the research is so related they shall seek the views of the Joint Authority on the research project and, in the light of such views, mutually decide on the regulation, authorization and conduct of the research including the duty to provide data, samples and results of such research to both Contracting States and the Joint Authority and participation by both Contracting States in the research project.

Article 18   Protection of the marine environment

1. The Contracting States shall cooperate to prevent and minimize pollution of the marine environment arising from the exploration for and exploitation of petroleum in Area A. In particular:

(a) the Contracting States shall provide such assistance to the Joint Authority as may be requested pursuant to paragraph (m) of Article 8 of this Treaty; and

(b) where pollution of the marine environment occurring in Area A spreads beyond Area A, the Contracting States shall cooperate in taking action to prevent, mitigate and eliminate such pollution.

2. Pursuant to paragraph (j) of Article 8 of this Treaty the Joint Authority shall issue regulations to protect the marine environment in Area A. It shall establish a contingency plan for combating pollution from petroleum operations in that Area.

Article 19　Liability of contractors for pollution of the marine environment

Contractors shall be liable for damage or expenses incurred as a result of pollution of the marine environment arising out of petroleum operations in Area A in accordance

with contractual arrangements with the Joint Authority and the law of the State in which a claim in respect of such damage or expenses is brought.

Article 20　Unitization between Area A and areas outside Area A

If any single accumulation of petroleum extends across any of the boundary lines of Area A of the Zone of Cooperation as designated and described in Article 1 and Annex A of this Treaty, and the part of such accumulation that is situated on one side of a line is exploitable, wholly or in part, from the other side of the line, the Contracting States shall seek to reach agreement on the manner in which the accumulation shall be most effectively exploited and on the equitable sharing of the benefits arising from such exploitation.

Article 21　Construction of facilities

In the event that exploration for and exploitation of petroleum resources in Area A necessitates the construction of facilities and provision of services outside Area A, the Contracting States shall provide every assistance to contractors and the Joint Authority to enable the construction and operation of those facilities, and the provision of those services. Construction and operation of such facilities and provision of such services shall be subject to the law and regulations of the relevant Contracting State and any terms and conditions set by the Contracting States.

PART VI　APPLICABLE LAWS

Article 22　Law applicable to production sharing contracts

The law applicable to a production sharing contract shall be specified in that contract.

Article 23　Application of customs, migration and quarantine laws

1. Each Contracting State may, subject to paragraphs 3 and 5 of this Article, apply customs, migration and quarantine laws to persons, equipment and goods entering its territory from, or leaving its territory for, Area A. The Contracting States may adopt arrangements to facilitate such entry and departure.

2. Contractors shall ensure, unless otherwise authorized by the Contracting States, that persons, equipment and goods do not enter structures in Area A without first entering Australia or the Republic of Indonesia, and that their employees and the employees of their subcontractors are authorized by the Joint Authority to enter Area A.

3. One Contracting State may request consultations with the other Contracting State in relation to the entry of particular persons, equipment and goods to structures in Area A aimed at controlling the movement of such persons, equipment or goods.

4. Nothing in this Article prejudices the right of either Contracting State to apply customs, migration and quarantine controls to persons, equipment and goods entering Area A without the authority of either Contracting State. The Contracting States may adopt arrangements to coordinate the exercise of such rights.

5. (a) Goods and equipment entering Area A for purposes related to petroleum operations shall not be subject to customs duties.

(b) Goods and equipment leaving or in transit through a Contracting State for the purpose of entering Area A for purposes related to petroleum operations shall not be subject to customs duties.

(c) Goods and equipment leaving Area A for the purpose of being permanently transferred to a part of a Contracting State may be subject to customs duties of that Contracting State.

Article 24　Employment

1. The Contracting States shall take appropriate measures to ensure that preference is given in employment in Area A to nationals or permanent residents of Australia and the Republic of Indonesia, and to their employment in equivalent

numbers over the term of a production sharing contract, but, with due regard to efficient operations and to good oilfield practice.

2. The terms and conditions under which persons are employed on structures in Area A shall be governed by employment contracts or collective agreements. The terms and conditions shall include provisions on insurance and compensation in relation to employment injuries, including death or disability benefits, and may provide for use of an existing compensation system established under the law of either Contracting State. The terms and conditions shall also include provisions in relation to remuneration, periods of duty or overtime, leave and termination. The terms and conditions shall be no less favourable than those which would apply from time to time to comparable categories of employment in both Australia and the Republic of Indonesia.

3. Paragraph 2 of this Article shall also apply to persons employed on seismic, drill, supply and service vessels regularly engaged in activities related to petroleum operations in Area A, regardless of the nationality of the vessel.

4. In relation to the provision of facilities and opportunities, there shall be no discrimination on the basis of nationality amongst persons to which paragraphs 2 and 3 of this Article apply.

5. Disputes arising between employers and employees shall be settled by negotiation in the first instance. Disputes which cannot be settled by negotiation shall be settled either by recourse to a tripartite dispute settlement committee, comprising representatives of employers, employees and persons nominated by the Contracting States, or by recourse to a conciliation and arbitration system available in either Contracting State.

6. Employer and employee associations recognised under the law of either Contracting State may respectively represent employers and employees in the negotiation of contracts or collective agreements and in conciliation and arbitration proceedings.

7. An employment contract or collective agreement shall provide that it shall be subject to the law of one or other Contracting State and shall identify, consistent with paragraph 5 of this Article, the applicable dispute settlement mecha-

nism. Any arbitration decision shall be enforceable under the law of the Contracting State under which it is made.

Article 25 Health and safety for workers

The Joint Authority shall develop, and contractors shall apply, occupational health and safety standards and procedures for persons employed on structures in Area A that are no less effective than those standards and procedures that would apply in relation to persons employed on similar structures in both Australia and the Republic of Indonesia. The Joint Authority may adopt, consistent with this Article, standards and procedures taking into account an existing system established under the law of either Contracting State.

Article 26 Petroleum industry vessels

Except as otherwise provided in this Treaty, vessels engaged in petroleum operations shall be subject to the law of the Contracting State whose nationality they possess and, unless they are a vessel with the nationality of the other Contracting State, the law of the Contracting State out of whose ports they operate, in relation to safety and operating standards, and crewing regulations. Such vessels that enter Area A and do not operate out of either Contracting State shall be subject to relevant international safety and operating standards under the law of both Contracting States.

Article 27 Criminal jurisdiction

1. Subject to paragraph 3 of this Article a national or permanent resident of a Contracting State shall be subject to the criminal law of that State in respect of acts or omissions occurring in Area A connected with or arising out of exploration for and exploitation of petroleum resources, provided that a permanent resident of a Contracting State who is a national of the other Contracting State shall be subject to the criminal law of the latter State.

2. (a) Subject to paragraph 3 of this Article, a national of a third State, not being a permanent resident of either Contracting State, shall be subject to the criminal law of both Contracting States in respect of acts or omissions occurring in Area A connected with or arising out of the exploration for and exploitation of petroleum resources.

Such a person shall not be subject to criminal proceedings under the law of one Contracting State if he or she has already been tried and discharged or acquitted by a competent tribunal or already undergone punishment for the same act or omission under the law of the other Contracting State or where the competent authorities of one Contracting State, in accordance with its law, have decided in the public interest to refrain from prosecuting the person for that act or omission.

(b) In cases referred to in sub-paragraph (a) of this paragraph, the Contracting States shall, as and when necessary, consult each other to determine which criminal law is to be applied, taking into account the nationality of the victim and the interests of the Contracting State most affected by the alleged offence.

3. The criminal law of the flag State shall apply in relation to acts or omissions on board vessels including seismic or drill vessels in, or aircraft in flight over, Area A.

4. (a) The Contracting States shall provide assistance to and cooperate with each other, including through agreements or arrangements as appropriate, for the purposes of enforcement of criminal law under this Article, including the obtaining of evidence and information.

(b) Each Contracting State recognizes the interest of the other Contracting State where a victim of an alleged offence is a national of that other State and shall keep that other State informed to the extent permitted by its law of action being taken with regard to the alleged offence.

5. The Contracting States may make arrangements permitting officials of one Contracting State to assist in the enforcement of the criminal law of the other Contracting State. Where such assistance involves the detention of a person who under paragraph 1 of this Article is subject to the jurisdiction of the other Contracting State that detention may only continue until it is practicable to hand the person over to the relevant officials of that other Contracting State.

Article 28　Civil actions

Claims for damages or restitution of expenses as a result of activities in Area A may be brought in the Contracting State which has or whose nationals or permanent residents have suffered the damage or incurred the expense. The court in which the action is brought shall apply the law and regulations of that State.

Article 29　Application of taxation law

1. For the purposes of the taxation law related directly or indirectly to:

(a) the exploration for or the exploitation of petroleum in Area A; or

(b) acts, matters, circumstances and things touching, concerning, arising out of or connected with any such exploration or exploitation,

Area A shall be deemed to be, and be treated by, each Contracting State as part of that Contracting State.

2. In the application of the taxation law:

(a) in Area A;

(b) to interest paid by a contractor; or

(c) to royalties paid by a contractor,

each Contracting State shall grant relief from double taxation in accordance with the Taxation Code.

3. A Contracting State shall not impose a tax not covered by the provisions of the Taxation Code in respect of or applicable to:

(a) the exploration for or exploitation of petroleum in Area A; or

(b) any petroleum exploration or exploitation related activity carried on in Area A, unless the other Contracting State consents to the imposition of that tax.

PART VII　SETTLEMENT OF DISPUTES

Article 30　Settlement of disputes

1. Any dispute arising between the Contracting States concerning the interpretation or application of this Treaty shall be resolved by consultation or negotiation between the Contracting States.

2. Each production sharing contract entered into by the Joint Authority shall contain provisions to the effect that any dispute concerning the interpretation or application of such contract shall be submitted to a specified form of binding commercial arbitration. The Contracting States shall facilitate the enforcement in their respective courts of arbitral awards made pursuant to such arbitration.

PART VIII FINAL CLAUSES

Article 31 Amendment

1. This Treaty may be amended at any time by agreement between the Contracting States.

2. The Petroleum Mining Code, in accordance with paragraph 1 (b) of Article 6 of this Treaty and the Model Production Sharing Contract, in accordance with paragraph 1 (c) of Article 6 of this Treaty, may also be amended or modified by decision of the Ministerial Council. Such amendments or modifications shall have the same status as the Petroleum Mining Code and the Model Production Sharing Contract.

Article 32 Entry into force

This Treaty shall enter into force thirty (30) days after the date on which the Contracting States have notified each other in writing that their respective requirements for entry into force of this Treaty have been complied with.

Article 33 Term of this treaty

1. This Treaty shall remain in force for forty (40) years from the date of entry into force of this Treaty.

2. Unless the two Contracting States agree otherwise, this Treaty shall continue in force after the initial forty (40) year term for successive terms of twenty (20) years, unless by the end of each term, including the initial term of forty years, the two Contracting States have concluded an agreement on a permanent continental shelf delimitation in the area covered by the Zone of Cooperation.

3. Where the Contracting States have not concluded an agreement on a permanent continental shelf delimitation in the area covered by the Zone of Cooperation five years prior to the end of any of the terms referred to in paragraphs 1 or 2 of this Article, representatives of the two Contracting States shall meet with a view to reaching agreement on such permanent continental shelf delimitation.

4. This Article shall be without prejudice to the continued operation of Article 34 of this Treaty.

Article 34 Rights of contractors

1. In the event that

(a) this Treaty ceases to be in force following conclusion of an agreement between the Contracting States on permanent continental shelf delimitation in the area of the Zone of Cooperation; and

(b) there are in existence immediately prior to the date on which this Treaty ceases to be in force, production sharing contracts with the Joint Authority,

production sharing contracts shall continue to apply to each Contracting State or some other person nominated by the Contracting State concerned, in place of the Joint Authority, in so far as the contract is to be performed within the territorial jurisdiction of each Contracting State, having regard to the agreement on delimitation. Each Contracting State shall apply to contractors performing contracts within its territorial jurisdiction a regime no more onerous than that set out in this Treaty and the relevant production sharing contract.

2. The two Contracting States shall at the time of the conclusion of the permanent delimitation agreement make arrangements to give effect to paragraph 1 of this Article.

IN WITNESS WHEREOF the undersigned, being duly authorized thereto by their respective Governments, have signed this Treaty.

DONE over the Zone of Cooperation on this eleventh day of December, one thousand nine hundred and eighty nine, in two originals in the English language.

FOR AUSTRALIA:	FOR THE REPUBLIC OF INDONESIA:
[Signed:]	[Signed:]
GARETH EVANS	ALI ALATAS
Minister for Foreign Affairs and Trade	Minister for Foreign Affairs

（十）1992年马来西亚与越南共同开发案

1.《马来西亚与越南社会主义共和国关于两国大陆架划定区域内石油勘探和开采的谅解备忘录》

（1992年6月5日订立吉隆坡）

邓妮雅译，黄文博校

马来西亚和越南社会主义共和国，为了进一步加强两国间的合作，承认在马来西亚西部的东北部海岸和越南的西南部海岸的大陆架边界线主张存在重叠；遵守双方领导人仅在两国间重叠海域合作方面达成的协议；鉴于两国领导人决定在适当的时机和平解决两国间所有涉及多方的主张重叠问题；考虑到搁置两国在马来西亚西部的东北部海岸和越南西南部海岸的大陆架划界，达成在重叠海域进行石油勘探和开采的临时安排，符合两国最大利益；确信勘探和开采活动可以通过相互合作来实现，达成如下协议。

第一条

（1）两国一致同意，由于双方在位于马来西亚西部的东北部海岸和越南西南部海岸的大陆架边界线主张存在重叠，产生了重叠海域（划定区域），该区域由以下坐标相连的直线围成：

A	北纬 7°22′00″	东经 103°42′30″
B	北纬 7°20′00″	东经 103°39′00″

C	北纬 7°18′18.6″	东经 103°35′42.6″
D	北纬 7°03′00″	东经 103°52′00″
E	北纬 6°05′48″	东经 105°49′12″
F	北纬 6°48′15″	东经 104°30′00″
A	北纬 7°22′00″	东经 103°42′30″

该区域由附后的 1967 年版英国海军航海图第 2414 号标示，见附件。

（2）本条第（1）款所指的点在海上的实际位置，应该由双方主管当局以互相同意的方式确定。马来西亚的主管当局为马来西亚国家测绘局及其授权的个人，越南社会主义共和国的主管当局为地理制图部和海军地理制图部门及其授权的个人。

第二条

（1）双方同意，搁置"划定区域"内大陆架的最终划界，通过相互合作，在本谅解备忘录的有效期内，按照备忘录的相关规定，勘探和开发区域内的石油资源。

（2）一块油田如果部分位于"划定区域"内，部分位于马来西亚或者越南社会主义共和国的大陆架范围内，在这种情形下，双方需要达成互相接受的勘探和开发该油田的条款。

（3）双方应平等分担"划定区域"内石油勘探和开采产生的所有费用，平等分享其产生的收益。

第三条

依本谅解备忘录，

（a）马来西亚和越南社会主义共和国同意，分别授权马来西亚国家石油公司（PETRONAS）和越南国家石油公司（PETROVIETNAM）代表各自利益在"划定区域"内进行石油勘探和开采活动；

（b）马来西亚和越南社会主义共和国应当分别责成马来西亚国家石油公司和越南国家石油公司就"划定区域"内的石油勘探和开采达成商业安排。该安排的条款和条件应由马来西亚政府和越南社会主义共和国政府批准；

（c）双方同意考虑"划定区域"内已经产生的重大开支，尽一切努力保证"划定区域"内的早期勘探活动继续进行。

（十）1992 年马来西亚与越南共同开发案

第四条

本谅解备忘录的任何条款都不应当以任何方式做如下解释：

（a）影响任何一方对"划定区域"的立场和主张；及

（b）在不影响第三条规定的情形下，授予任何非当事国的任何人在"划定区域"内与石油资源相关的任何权利、利益或者特权。

第五条

本谅解备忘录需要双方在一定时间内通过外交换文的方式进一步细化。

第六条

因本谅解备忘录条款的解释或履行而产生的争端，需要双方通过协商或谈判的方式和平解决。

第七条

本谅解备忘录的生效日期为双方互换外交换文的日期。

第八条

依本备忘录，

（a）"划定区域"是指本备忘录第一条第（1）款所指的区域；

（b）"石油"是指任何自然状态下的矿物石油或者相关的碳氢物和天然气，包括沥青页岩和其他可以提炼出石油的积层；

（c）"油田"是指由单一储油层或者多层储油层构成的区域，但后者具有或者有相关的单一地质构造的特征，或者具有石油商业开发的地质条件；

（d）"PETRONAS"是马来西亚国家石油公司（马来语：Petroliam Nasional Berhad）的缩写，该公司根据 1965 年《马来西亚公司法》成立；而且

（e）"PETROVIETNAM"是越南国家石油和天然气公司的缩写，该公司根据 1990 年 7 月 6 日 No. 250/HDBT 法令成立。

本备忘录于 1992 年 6 月 5 日在吉隆坡签订，文本以英语作成，一式两份。

马来西亚政府	越南社会主义共和国
艾哈迈德·卡米勒·加法尔　阁下	武宽　阁下
马来西亚外交部秘书长	越南社会主义共和国外交部副部长

2. 1992 Memorandum of Understanding between Malaysia and the Socialist Republic of Vietnam for the Exploration and Exploitation of Petroleum in A Defined Area of the Continental Shelf Involving the Two Countries

Adopted in Kuala Lumpur, Malaysia on 5 June 1992

MALAYSIA AND THE SOCIALIST REPUBLIC OF VIETNAM,

DESIRING to further strengthen the cooperation between the two countries;

RECOGNIZING that as a result of overlapping claims made by the two countries regarding the boundary lines of their continental shelves located off the northeast coast of West Malaysia and off the southwest coast of Vietnam, there exists an overlapping area of their continental shelves;

CONSISTENT with the agreement reached by the leaders of the two countries to cooperate in that part of the overlapping area involving the two countries only;

MINDFUL of the decision by the leaders of the two countries to resolve peacefully the question of all overlapping claims involving multiple parties with the parties concerned at an appropriate time;

CONSIDERING that it is in the best interests of both countries, pending delimitation of their continental shelves located off the northeast coast of West Malaysia and off the southwest coast of Vietnam, to enter into an interim arrangement for the purpose of exploring and exploiting petroleum in the seabed in the overlapping area;

CONVINCED that such activities can be carried out through mutual cooperation;

HAVE AGREED AS FOLLOWS:

Article 1

(1) Both parties agree that as a result of overlapping claims made by the two countries regarding the boundary lines of their continental shelves located off the northeast coast of West Malaysia and off the southwest coast of Vietnam, there exists an overlapping area (the Defined Area), being that area bounded by straight lines joining the following coordinated points:

A	N7°22.0′	E103°42.5′
B	N7°20.0′	E103°39.0′
C	N7°18.31′	E103°35.71′
D	N7°03.0′	E103°52.0′
E	N6°05.8′	E105°49.2′
F	N6°48.25′	E104°30.0′
A	N7°22.0′	E103°42.5′

and shown in the relevant part of the British Admiralty Chart No: 2414, Edition 1967, annexed hereto.

(2) The actual location at sea of the points referred to in Clause (1) of this Article shall be determined by a method to be mutually agreed upon by the competent authorities of both parties. The competent authorities in relation to Malaysia means the Directorate of National Mapping Malaysia and includes any person authorized by it and in relation to the Socialist Republic of Vietnam means the Department of Geo - Cartography and the Navy Geo - Cartography Section and includes any person authorized by them.

Article 2

(1) Both parties agree, pending final delimitation of the boundary lines of their continental shelves pertaining to the Defined Area, through mutual cooperation, to explore and exploit petroleum in that area in accordance with the terms of, and for a period of the validity of this Memorandum of Understanding.

(2) Where a petroleum field is located partly in the Defined Area and part-

ly outside that area in the continental shelf of Malaysia or the Socialist Republic of Vietnam, as the case may be, both parties shall arrive at mutually acceptable terms for the exploration and exploitation of petroleum therein.

(3) All costs incurred and benefits derived from the exploration and exploitation of petroleum in the Defined Area shall be borne and shared equally by both parties.

Article 3

For the purpose of this Memorandum of Understanding –

(a) Malaysia and the Socialist Republic of Vietnam agree to nominate PETRONAS and PETROVIETNAM, respectively, to undertake, on their respective behalves, the exploration and exploitation of petroleum in the Defined Area;

(b) Malaysia and the Socialist Republic of Vietnam shall cause PETRONAS and PETROVIETNAM, respectively, to enter into a commercial arrangement as between them for the exploration and exploitation of petroleum in the Defined Area provided that the terms and conditions of that arrangement shall be subject to the approval of the Government of Malaysia and the Government of the Socialist Republic of Vietnam;

(c) both parties agree, taking into account the significant expenditures already incurred in the Defined Area, that every effort shall be made to ensure continued early exploration of petroleum in the Defined Area.

Article 4

Nothing in this Memorandum of Understanding shall be interpreted so as to in any way –

(a) prejudice the position and claims of either party in relation to and over the Defined Area; and

(b) without prejudice to the provisions of Article Ⅲ, confer any rights, interests or privileges to any person not being a party hereto in respect of any petroleum resources in the Defined Area.

Article 5

This Memorandum of Understanding shall continue for a period to be specified by an exchange of Diplomatic Note between the two parties.

Article 6

Any dispute arising out of the interpretation or implementation of the provisions of this Memorandum of Understanding shall be settled peacefully by consultation or negotiation between both parties.

Article 7

This Memorandum of Understanding shall come into force on the date to be specified by an exchange of Diplomatic Notes between the two parties.

Article 8

For the purpose of this Memorandum of Understanding –

(a) 'Defined Area' means the area referred to in Article I (1) of this Memorandum of Understanding;

(b) 'petroleum' means any mineral oil or relative hydrocarbon and natural gas existing in its natural condition and casinghead petroleum spirit, including bituminous shales and other stratified deposits from which oil can be extracted;

(c) 'petroleum field' means an area consisting of a single reservoir or multiple reservoirs all grouped on, or related to, the same individual geological structural feature, or stratigraphic conditions from which petroleum may be produced commercially;

(d) 'PETRONAS' is the short form of Petroliam Nasional Berhad, a company incorporated under the Malaysia Companies Act 1965; and

(e) 'PETROVIETNAM' is the short form of Vietnam National Oil and Gas Company established by the Decree of No. 250/HDBT of 6 July 1990.

DONE in duplicate at Kuala Lumpur the 5th day of June in the year One Thousand Nine Hundred and Ninety Two in the English Language.

For Malaysia	For the Socialist Republic of Vietnam
H. E. Datuk Ahmad Kamil Jaafar	H. E. Vu Khoan
Secretary – General, Ministry of Foreign Affairs, Malaysia	Vice Minister of Foreign Affairs Socialist Republic of Vietnam

（十一）1993年哥伦比亚与牙买加共同开发案

1.《牙买加与哥伦比亚共和国海域划界条约》

（1993年11月12日订于金斯顿）

宗吕谦译，黄文博校

牙买加政府和哥伦比亚共和国政府，鉴于两国之间的友谊；承认两国在合理开发、管理和保护两国共同海域方面的共同利益，包括在开发生物资源相关的事宜方面的共同利益；承认缔结海洋划界条约对双方的利益；考虑到最近海洋法的发展趋势；欲在相互尊重、主权平等以及有关国际法原则的基础上划定两国之间海域；达成以下约定。

第一条

牙买加和哥伦比亚共和国之间的海洋分界线为以下坐标点连接而成的测地线：

坐标点	纬度（北）	经度（西）
1.	14°29′37″	78°38′00″
2.	14°15′00″	78°19′30″
3.	14°05′00″	77°40′00″
4.	14°44′10″	74°30′50″

5. 从第四点向坐标为北纬15°02′00″、西经73°27′30″的方向划界，至

牙买加与海地之间的分界线，截断哥伦比亚与海地之间的分界线。

第二条

若在第一条规定的分界线两侧发现碳氢化合物或天然气矿床或油田，从此矿床或油田开采的量需与分界线两侧发现的油气储藏量成一定比例。

第三条

1. 在两国在以下指定区域的管辖权界线无法确定的情况下，双方同意在该区域确立一个联合管理、支配、勘探和开发生物及非生物资源的区域，以下简称"联合区"。

（1）联合区是由下列坐标点按顺序连接的测地线形成的闭合区域，若两坐标之间连线非测地线则会特别做出说明。

坐标点	纬度（北）	经度（西）
1.	16°04′15″	79°50′32″
2.	16°04′15″	79°29′20″
3.	16°10′10″	79°29′20″
4.	16°10′10″	79°16′40″
5.	16°04′15″	79°16′40″
6.	16°04′15″	78°25′50″
7.	15°36′00″	78°25′50″
8.	15°36′00″	78°38′00″
9.	14°29′37″	78°38′00″
10.	15°30′10″	79°56′00″
11.	15°46′00″	80°03′55″

再以坐标北纬15°47′50″、西经79°51′20″为圆心，以12海里为半径作出圆弧，这样弧线穿过小赛拉纳沿岸礁群西部至坐标北纬15°58′40″、西经79°56′40″。然后连接到坐标点1，形成闭合的区域。

（2）联合区不包括小赛拉纳岛周边群岛周围的海域，最外界线是以坐标北纬15°47′50″、西经79°51′20″为圆心，12海里为半径的圆弧，弧线经过坐标北纬15°46′00″、西经80°03′55″以及北纬15°58′40″、西经79°56′40″。

（3）联合区也不包括巴霍努埃沃礁周边群岛周围海域，最外界线是以坐标北纬 15°51′00″、西经 78°38′00″为圆心，以 12 海里为半径作出的圆弧。

2. 两国可在联合区开展以下活动：

（1）勘探及开采自然资源，包括上覆水域、海床、底土的生物资源与非生物资源，以及联合区的其他经济开发和勘探活动；

（2）建造和使用人工岛屿、设施和建筑；

（3）海洋科学研究；

（4）保护和保持海洋环境；

（5）养护海洋生物资源；

（6）可通过本条约授权或者双方另行协商等措施，确保本条约确立的制度得到遵守和执行。

3. 勘探和开发非生物资源相关活动，以及上文第 2 款第（3）项、第（4）项规定的活动，需经双方同意后进行。

4. 缔约国不得授权第三国、国际组织或此类国家的船舶及机构进行第（2）款中涉及的任何活动。但不排除缔约国签署或授权租赁、许可、合资和技术援助有关的协议，促进第（2）款中权利严格按照第四条规定程序行使。

5. 缔约国同意，两国可在联合区对其自己的国民以及悬挂其国旗的船只行使管辖权，或根据国际法行使管辖权执行管理。

在任何情况下，缔约一方指控另一方国民或船只违反本条约规定及两国实施本条约采取的措施，指控一方应提醒被指控一方注意，随后两国应立即进行磋商，以期在 14 日内达成和解。

收到指控不影响被指控一方在以上条款提及的磋商中的结果。

（1）对于违反规定的指控，违规行为已经做出的，需保证此类活动以及指控的内容不再发生；

（2）对于违反规定的指控，违规行为正在做出的，需确保停止此类活动。

6. 缔约国同意采取措施，确保第三国的国民及船只遵守两国为进行第 2 款规定活动制定的各项规定及采取的各项措施。

第四条

1. 缔约国同意成立一个联合委员会，以下称"联合委员会"，以详细说明第三条第 2 款规定的活动、第三条第 6 款规定采取的措施如何实施和执行，以及执行缔约国分配其执行的有利于实现本条约目的的其他工作。

2. 两国各自委任一名联合委员会代表，在必要时可配备相关顾问协助。

3. 联合委员会产生的决议需获一致通过，且决议只能作为建议告知缔约两国。联合委员会的建议一旦被缔约两国采纳，即对双方均具有约束力。

4. 除缔约两国特殊约定外，联合委员会在本条约生效时立即开始工作，并在工作开始后 6 个月内完成本条第 1 款所规定的任务。

第五条

大地测量数据基于世界地心坐标系（1984）。

第六条

仅作说明目的，美国国防部制图处 402 号测绘图展示了该分界线及联合区，见附件。若测绘图与坐标发生冲突，以坐标为准。

第七条

缔约两国在解释和适用本条约时产生的争端，由双方依照国际法规定达成协议，和平解决。

第八条

本条约需经正式批准。

第九条

本条约在批准书交换之日生效。

第十条

英语和西班牙语文本一式两份，两文本具有同等效力。

两国外交部长在此签字，以资证明。

于 1993 年 11 月 12 日签署于金斯顿。

2. Maritime Delimitation Treaty between Jamaica and the Republic of Colombia

12 November 1993

The Government of Jamaica and the Government of the Republic of Colombia;

Considering the bonds of friendship existing between both countries;

Recognizing the common interests of both countries in considering issues related to the rational exploitation, management and conservation of the maritime areas between them, including questions relating to the exploitation of living resources;

Acknowledging the interests which both countries have in concluding a maritime delimitation treaty;

Taking into account recent developments in the law of the sea;

Desirous of delimiting the maritime areas between both countries on the basis of mutual respect, sovereign equality and the relevant principles of international law;

Agree as follows:

Article 1

The maritime boundary between Jamaica and the Republic of Colombia is constituted by geodesic lines drawn between the following points:

	Latitude (North)	Longitude (West)
1.	14° 29′37″	78° 38′00″
2.	14° 15′00″	78° 19′30″

3.	14°05′00″	77°40′00″
4.	14°44′10″	74°30′50″

5. From point 4, the delimitation line proceeds by a geodesic line in the direction to another point with coordinates 15°02′00″N, 73°27′30″W, as far as the delimitation line between Colombia and Haiti is intercepted by the delimitation line to be decided between Jamaica and Haiti.

Article 2

Where hydrocarbon or natural gas deposits, or fields are found on both sides of the delimitation line established in article 1, they shall be exploited in a manner such that the distribution of the volumes of the resource extracted from said deposits or fields is proportional to the volume of the same which is correspondingly found on each side of the line.

Article 3

1. Pending the determination of the jurisdictional limits of each Party in the area designated below, the Parties agree to establish therein a zone of joint management, control, exploration and exploitation of the living and non-living resources, hereafter called "The Joint Regime Area".

(a) The Joint Regime Area is established by the closed figure described by the lines joining the following points in the order in which they occur. The lines so joining the listed points are geodesic lines unless specifically stated otherwise.

Point	Latitude (North)	Longitude (West)
1.	16°04′15″	79°50′32″
2.	16°04′15″	79°29′20″
3.	16°10′10″	79°29′20″
4.	16°10′10″	79°16′40″
5.	16°04′15″	79°16′40″
6.	16°04′15″	78°25′50″
7.	15°36′00″	78°25′50″
8.	15°36′00″	78°38′00″
9.	14°29′37″	78°38′00″

| 10. | 15°30′10″ | 79°56′00″ |
| 11. | 15°46′00″ | 80°03′55″ |

The limit of the Joint Regime Area then continues along the arc of 12 nautical miles radius centred on a point at 15°47′50″N, 79°51′20″W, such that it passes to the west of Serranilla Cays to a point at 15°58′40″N, 79°56′40″W. The figure is then closed by the geodesic line to point 1.

(b) The Joint Regime Area excludes the maritime area around the cays of Serranilla Bank comprised within the outermost arc of the circle of 12 nautical miles radius centred at a point 15°47′50″N, 79°51′20″W, such that it passes to through points 15°46′00″N, 80°03′55″W and 15°58′40″N, 79°56′40″W.

(c) The Joint Regime Area will also exclude the maritime area around the cays of Bajo Nuevo comprised within the outermost arc of the circle of 12 nautical miles radius centred at the point 15°51′00″N, 78°38′00″W.

2. In the Joint Regime Area, the Parties may carry out the following activities:

(a) Exploration and exploitation of the natural resources, whether living or non-living, of the waters superjacent to the seabed and the seabed and its subsoil, and other activities for the economic exploitation and exploration of the Joint Regime Area;

(b) The establishment and use of artificial islands, installations and structures;

(c) Marine scientific research;

(d) The protection and preservation of the marine environment;

(e) The conservation of living resources;

(f) Such measures as are authorized by this Treaty, or as the Parties may otherwise agree for ensuring compliance with and enforcement of the regime established by this Treaty.

3. Activities relating to exploration and exploitation of non-living resources, as well as those referred to in paragraph 2 (c) and (d), will be carried out on a joint basis agreed by both Parties.

4. The Parties shall not authorize third States and international organizations

or vessels of such States and organizations to carry out any of the activities referred to in paragraph 2. This does not preclude a Party from entering into, or authorizing arrangements for leases, licences, joint ventures and technical assistance programmes in order to facilitate the exercise of the rights pursuant to paragraph 2, in accordance with the procedures established in article 4.

5. The Parties agree that in the Joint Regime Area, each Party has jurisdiction over its nationals and vessels flying its flag or over which it exercises management and control in accordance with international law.

Provided that in any case where it is alleged by one Party that nationals or vessels of the other Party have breached, or are breaching the provisions of this Treaty and any measures adopted by the Parties for their implementation, the Party alleging the breach shall bring it to the attention of the other Party, following which both Parties shall forthwith commence consultations with a view to arriving at an amicable settlement within 14 days.

On receipt of the allegation, the Party to whose attention the allegation has been brought shall, without prejudice to the consultations referred to in the above paragraph:

(a) In relation to an allegation that a breach has been committed, ensure that the activities, the subject – matter of the allegation, do not recur;

(b) In relation to an allegation that a breach is being committed, ensure that the activities are discontinued.

6. The Parties agree to adopt measures for ensuring that nationals and vessels of third States comply with any regulations and measures adopted by the Parties for implementing the activities set out in paragraph 2.

Article 4

1. The Parties agree to establish a Joint Commission, hereinafter called "The Joint Commission", which shall elaborate the modalities for the implementation and the carrying out of the activities set out in paragraph 2 of article 3, the measures adopted pursuant to paragraph 6 of article 3, and carry out any other functions which may be assigned to it by the Parties for the purpose of implementing the provisions of this Treaty.

2. The Joint Commission shall consist of one representative of each Party, who may be assisted by such advisers as is considered necessary.

3. Conclusions of the Joint Commission shall be adopted by consensus and shall be only recommendations to the Parties. Conclusions of the Joint Commission when adopted by the Parties shall become binding on the Parties.

4. The Joint Commission shall begin its work immediately on the entry into force of this Treaty and shall, unless the Parties agree otherwise, conclude the tasks identified in paragraph 1 of this article within six months from the commencement of its work.

Article 5

Geodetic data are based on the World Geodetic System (1984).

Article 6

For illustrative purposes only, the delimitation line and the Joint Regime Area are shown on a United States Defence Mapping Agency Chart 402, which is attached. In the event of conflict between the coordinates and the Chart, the coordinates will prevail.

Article 7

Any dispute between the Parties on the interpretation or application of this Treaty shall be settled by agreement between the two countries in accordance with the means for the peaceful settlement of disputes provided for by international law.

Article 8

This Treaty shall be subject to ratification.

Article 9

This Treaty shall enter into force on the date of exchange of instruments of ratification.

Article 10

Done in English and Spanish, each text being equally authentic.

IN WITNESS WHEREOF, the Ministers for Foreign Affairs of both countries have signed the present Treaty.

DONE at Kingston this 12th day of November 1993.

（十二）1993年几内亚比绍与塞内加尔共同开发案

1.《几内亚比绍共和国与塞内加尔共和国管理和合作协定》[*]

（1993年10月14日订于达喀尔）

黄文博译，邓妮雅校

塞内加尔共和国政府为一方，几内亚比绍政府为另一方，为进一步发展两国睦邻友好关系，深化双边合作，达成如下约定。

第一条

双方应当共同开发从罗克舍（Roxo）岬角268°到220°方位角间的海域。

共同开发区域不包括几内亚比绍和塞内加尔两国的领海。然而，在共同开发区域内和在268°到220°方位角间的领海内，乘坐独木舟进行的非工业性捕鱼应当被允许。

第二条

共同开发区域内的资源应当做出下分配：

渔业资源：塞内加尔50%，几内亚比绍50%；

大陆架资源：塞内加尔85%，几内亚比绍15%。

如果发现了新资源，以上百分比必须进行根据发现资源的数量进行

---

[*] 依据协定第七条，在达喀尔通过外交换文的方式，于1995年12月21日生效。

修订。

第三条
双方为勘探区域内的石油而从国家基金中支付的花费,将根据其各自享有的比例进行偿还,并按照本协定生效之前,确定的条件和程序来实施。

第四条
双方同意建立国际管理局对共同开发区进行开采。

管理局的组织和运作,应当在本协定签字后 12 个月内,由双方达成共同协定来做出安排。

第五条
管理局建立后,由该管理局继承双方签订的协议中所规定的,与共同开发区资源开采相关的权利与义务。

第六条
依据本协定,当事国应该联合行使各自权利,不损害各方依法先前取得的、经司法裁决确认的权利,以及在区域划定前的主张。

第七条
国际管理局建立和运作的协定一经达成,并由双方互换批准文书后,本协定生效。

第八条
本协定有效期为 20 年且可自动续期。

第九条
因本协定或国际管理局的协定而产生的争端,应首先经过直接谈判解决,若在 6 个月内仍不能解决,则可诉诸仲裁庭或国际法庭。

如果本协定暂停执行或期满,双方当事国可以通过直接谈判、仲裁或诉诸国际法庭,来解决未决的划界问题。

1993 年 10 月 14 日于达喀尔签署。

塞内加尔共和国政府	几内亚比绍共和国政府
狄奥尤·阿卜杜	维拉·贝纳多·乔奥
共和国总统	共和国总统

2. Agreement on Management and Cooperation between the Republic of Guinea – Bissau and the Republic of Senegal

The Government of the Republic of Senegal on the one hand,

The Government of Guinea – Bissau, on the other,

Desirous of further developing relations of good neighbourliness and cooperation between the two countries, have agreed as follows:

Article 1

The Parties shall jointly exploit a maritime area between azimuths 268° and 220° from Cape Roxo.

The territorial seas of Guinea – Bissau and Senegal shall be excluded from the Area of joint exploitation. However, non – industrial fishing from pirogues shall be permitted within the Area and within the parts of the territorial seas lying between azimuths 268° and 220°.

Article 2

Resources from the exploitation of the Area shall be shared in the following proportions:

Fishery resources

Fifty percent to Senegal,

Fifty percent to Guinea – Bissau;

Resources from the continental shelf

Eighty – five percent to Senegal,

Fifteen percent to Guinea – Bissau.

In the event of new discoveries, these proportions shall be revised, and such revision shall depend on the quantity of resources discovered.

Article 3

The expenditures already effected from State funds by the Parties for petroleum prospecting in the Area shall be reimbursed to each State in proportion to the size of its share, under such conditions and according to such procedures as are determined before the entry into force of this Agreement.

Article 4

The two Parties agree to establish an international Agency to exploit the Area.

The organization and operation of the Agency shall be the subject of a joint agreement within a maximum of 12 months from the date of signature of the present instrument.

Article 5

Upon its establishment, the Agency shall succeed Guinea – Bissau and Senegal in the rights and obligations deriving from the Agreements concluded by each State and relating to the exploitation of the resources in the Area.

Article 6

Under this Agreement, the Parties shall pool the exercise of their respective rights, without prejudice to the rights in law previously acquired by each Party and confirmed by judicial decisions, or to any claims previously formulated by them in respect of areas that have not been delimited.

Article 7

This Agreement shall enter into force upon the conclusion of the agreement on the establishment and operation of the international Agency and with the exchange of the instruments of ratification of the two agreements by both States.

Article 8

This Agreement shall remain in force for a period of 20 years and shall be automatically renewable.

Article 9

Disputes in respect of this Agreement or the Agreement on the International Agency shall be resolved initially by direct negotiations and, in the event of failure, after six months, by arbitration or by the International Court of Justice.

In the event that this Agreement is suspended or upon its expiration, both States shall have recourse to direct negotiation, arbitration or the International Court of Justice for such parts of the delimitations as have not been settled.

DONE at Dakar on 14 October 1993.

For the Government	For the Government
of the Republic of Senegal:	of the Republic of Guinea – Bissau:
ABDOU DIOUF	JOÃO BERNARDO VIEIRA
President of the Republic	President of the Republic

3. 《几内亚比绍共和国与塞内加尔共和国关于通过 1993 年 10 月 14 日协定设立的管理和合作局的组织和运作的协定的议定书》

(1995 年 6 月 12 日订于比绍)

黄文博译，邓妮雅校

概　要

　　本文件为了回应并延续 1994 年 1 月的里斯本会议，在此次会议上两国政府间代表对 1993 年 10 月 14 日协定要求建立的管理局的形式、组织和运作，首次交换了意见。

　　本草案第一部分第二节介绍了管理局的形式和目的；第二部分介绍管理局本身，它包括两个机构：其一为高级委员会，高级委员会由国家元首或政府首脑或其代表以及管理局的秘书处组成；其二为企业，管理局通过企业执行 1993 年《协定》授予的所有职能。

　　高级委员会是政策制定机关，企业是决策执行机构，并管理开发区内的资源。

　　企业是一个根据私法建立的公开的责任有限公司，由一个董事会、一名由两个负责两大主要区域内活动的董事协助的董事长，以及一名行政和财务的董事组成。

　　高级委员会主席在其任期内同时兼任董事会主席。

　　第四节包括高级委员会的运作和职责；第五节包括秘书处的职责。

　　董事会的权力和特权将规定于与企业有关的条款中。

　　第三部分界定了当事国与管理局之间广泛的合作领域。

第四部分规定了对区域内资源的勘探、开发和开采活动,以及争端解决应适用的法律。

第五部分规定了议定书生效后,管理局开始运作和企业组成之前的过渡安排。

第六部分是最后条款,比如对本议定书的修订及其生效日期的规定。

这就是本案文的架构。

序　言

议定书是关于依据几内亚比绍共和国与塞内加尔共和国在1993年10月14日于达喀尔签订的协定第4条,有关共同开发从罗克舍(RoXo)岬角268°到220°方位角间的海域而设立的管理局的组织及其运作。

第一部分

第一节　定义

第1条

为本议定书之目的,

1.1. "渔业协定"指由企业与一方当事国,或企业与一方或多方当事国之间签订的文件及附件而组成的合同,以及当事国为设定获取区域内渔业资源的条件、规范区域内可能实施的渔业勘察、探测和开发活动,而批准的其他附加协议或修正案。

1.2. "采矿或采油活动"指除石油产品的提炼和分配外,包括勘探、定位、评估、开发、生产、提取或开采、运输与出售矿产和石油资源(包括原油和天然气),以及天然气加工的一切活动。

1.3. "管理局"指依据1993年10月14日在达喀尔签订的《几内亚比绍共和国和塞内加尔共和国管理和合作协议》,就共同开发从罗克舍(Roxo)岬角268°到220°方位角间的海域而建立的管理和合作局。

1.4. "渔业合同"指由企业与一个或多个公司之间签订的文件及附件而组成的合同,以及当事国为设定前述公司获取区域内渔业资源的条件、规范区域内可能实施的渔业勘察、探测和开发活动,而批准的其他附加协议或修正案。

1.5. "协定"指由企业与一个或多个公司之间签订的文件及附件而组

成的合同，以及当事国为规范区域内的所有采矿或采油活动而批准的其他附加协议或修正案。

1.6. "可适用的法律"指当事国批准的所有文件与附件，以及任何附加协议或修正案，包括适用于本议定书第 5 条规定的活动，并与 1993 年 10 月 14 日协定或本议定书不相冲突的规则、法规或程序。

1.7. "企业"指执行管理局依 1993 年 10 月 14 日协定授予的所有职能的机构。

"一个企业"或"多个企业"指附属于企业，或由管理局为多元化经营而建立的一个或多个法人。

1.8. "一方当事国"或"双方当事国"指 1993 年 10 月 14 日协定的双方当事国，即几内亚比绍共和国和/或塞内加尔共和国。

1.9. "单一第三国"或"多方第三方国"指除上述 1.8 条以外的一个或多个主权国家。

1.10. "渔业许可"指企业授予一国船主、公司或公司团体，在区域内法律规定的特定时期内、用特定船只并以特定方式捕鱼的权利。

1.11. "采矿或采油许可"指企业依程序，授予公司或公司团体或子企业在协定附件 A 限定区域内的排他采矿权或石油勘探权。

1.12. "共享比例"指企业内实体持有的或与企业共同持有的，在开发区内勘探、开发和开采活动中获得的共享利润的比例。

1.13. "附加石油税"指依协定向企业缴纳的与石油活动有关的税费，税费的数额依据从上述活动中获取的利润比例确定。

1.14. "特许权使用费"指：

（a）在矿产或石油资源开发中，按产量比例以现金或以实物支付的税；缴纳的数额和评估的规则以及收取的办法，应在协定中详细规定，并附于采矿或采油许可证之后；

（b）在渔业资源开发中，船主根据渔业协定或渔业合同缴纳的，作为企业对船只授予渔业许可补偿的数额；授予此类许可的价格、条件和程序，应当符合区域内有效的法律规定。

1.15. "一个公司"或"多个公司"指与企业签署协定，或渔业协定，或矿产与石油开发合同的一个或多个法人，或者依据法律规定利润可转让的、具有公司地位的法人。

1.16. "区域税"指在采矿许可所覆盖的区域内，公司向企业缴纳的每平方千米的年税。

1.17. "矿产或石油权利"指管理局根据 1993 年 10 月 14 日的协定，在区域内所有的矿产或石油权利；管理局授权企业对这种权利进行管理。

1.18. "区域"指 1993 年 10 月 14 日协定第 1 条规定的合作区域。

第二节　名称、注册办公地、形式和目的

第 2 条　名称

管理局被命名为"管理和合作局"。

第 3 条　名称以下类推

管理局的注册办公地在达喀尔，但可转移至比绍。

第 4 条　形式

管理局是一个通过企业或其子公司或其他公司，负责管理区域内资源的国际组织。

管理局同时也负责促进两国之间的双边合作。

第 5 条　目的

管理局负责：

（a）在矿产与石油方面

——开展或引发地质学和地球物理学方面的研究及钻探工作，或为探查、勘探或开发区域内矿产或石油资源而开展的各种活动；

——促进区域内矿产或石油资源的探查、勘探或开发；

——销售归其所有的全部或部分矿物或石油产品。

（b）在海洋渔业方面

——独自或通过与其他国家或部门合作，执行渔业资源的评估和管理，以及监控海洋生态系统与区域内渔业资源的开发；

——尤其通过确定或执行渔业资源获取和开采的条件，来行使或授权行使捕鱼权。

——推动区域内渔业资源的探查、勘探或开发；

——销售归其所有的全部或部分渔业产品。

（c）一般职责

——控制区域内资源的理性开发。

——根据本议定书第 16 条和第 23 条的规定，与双方当事国及相关国际组织开展合作，确保区域内：

——安全；

——资源探查、勘探和开发活动的常规管理与监督；

——海洋环境的保护；

——污染预防与控制。

基于以上目的，管理局应当在区域内单独开展行动，或与其他公司或国际组织合作开展行动。

第二部分

第三节 管理局

第 6 条 权力

管理局对区域内的矿产和石油以及渔业资源享有排他的权利。

企业为此目的可获取此项权利。

企业：

——企业可自己执行，或由其授权的采矿与采油或捕鱼许可证的持有者，来执行已决的工作或活动，并对此类工作或活动进行监督；

——必须采取所有可能的措施提高其活动所需的财政支持；

——对区域内的探查、勘探和开采运营，必须协助各国的采矿与采油以及渔业协定、合同或许可证持有者实施行政管理。

——必须采取推动措施，吸引更多的公司参与该地区的资源探查、勘探及开采活动。

第 7 条 组织

管理局应包括：高级委员会和秘书处；其各自的运行及权限规定如后。

第 8 条 特权与豁免

当事国应赋予管理局及其人员和企业，以国际组织及其机构普遍享有的特权与豁免，

第四节 高级委员会

第 9 条 运行

高级委员会必须由国家元首或政府首脑或其授权的代表组成。

高级委员会主席由国家元首或政府首脑或其授权的代表轮流担任。

高级委员会主席任期两年。

第一任高级委员会主席由东道国元首或政府首脑出任；第一届高级委员会会议在东道国举行。

高级委员会根据需要举行会议，并且应每年至少举行一次会议，会议在当事国间轮流举行。

高级委员会应建立必要的议事规则以确保做出决议。

高级委员会主席在其任期内，兼任企业董事会主席。

管理局秘书长兼任高级委员会秘书长，负责组织高级委员会会议。

高级委员会主席可邀请任何有资质的人对所讨论的事项发表意见。

第 10 条　职责

10.1. 高级委员会确定管理局的总方针；

10.2. 高级委员会应每年举行一次例行会议，研究和批准秘书长提出的一般管理与合作政策；

10.3. 高级委员会应当任命秘书长和副秘书长；

10.4. 高级委员会的职能包括：

（a）为企业或企业运作提供指导；

（b）以与本议定书和 1993 年 10 月 14 日协定相符的方式，经企业董事会建议，修改区域内有关资源探查、勘探、开发，以及监管和科学研究方面的规则和规定；

（c）监督本议定书、1993 年 10 月 14 日协定，以及企业适用的规则的执行情况，就必要的修订向企业董事会提出建议；

（d）行使区域内的警察权并决定行使的方式。

10.5. 高级委员会在履行职能时，须确保区域内资源探查、勘探及开采的最优化，符合良好的采矿与采油实践，并注重海洋环境保护及渔业资源的养护。

第五节　秘书处

第 11 条　职责

11.1. 管理局秘书长应是由高级委员会任命的自然人代表，享有一般行政职能和适当的管理权力，并由副秘书长协助其履行职责。

11.2. 在高级委员会规定的权限内,秘书长有权签订合同、获取和处置动产与不动产,代表管理局参与诉讼程序。

11.3. 秘书长应执行高级委员会给予的任务,并向高级委员会报告。

11.4. 秘书长有责任管理区域内资源的探查、勘探和开发活动,包括:

(a) 评估投标,就缔结协定和渔业协议向董事会提出建议;

(b) 董事会同意后,经高级委员会批准,缔结协定或渔业协议。渔业合同的签订无须按此程序;

(c) 监督各个公司依据区域内的规则而进行的采矿、采油和捕鱼活动;

(d) 确保依据区域内适用规则与规定,颁布的法规和指导方针得到适用,以及合理地执行了协定、渔业协议和合同;

(e) 公司或船主不遵守相关规定的,中止或取消渔业合同;

(f) 经董事会事先同意和高级委员会批准,终止协定及渔业协议;

(g) 根据1993年10月14日协定规定,确定当事方从开发活动中获取的收益份额;

(h) 在适当情况下管控或在当事国的协助下管控区域内用于资源探查、勘探及开采的船只、飞机、设备和其他设施的进入或活动。

(i) 依国际法设定安全和限制进入的区域,以确保区域内航行和探查、勘探及开采活动的安全;

(j) 依区域内资源探查、勘探和开采规则,就监督和管理探查、勘探和开采有关的一切问题,制定规则并提供指导;

(k) 依据区域内卫生、安全、环境保护、环境影响评估和劳工活动方面的规则和规定,指定规则并提供指导;

(l) 为了实现本议定书及1993年协定的目的,向高级委员会提出建议,修改有关探查、勘探和开发区域内资源的法律法规,以及协定和渔业协定;

(m) 要求高级委员会遵守本议定书、1993年10月14日协定,以及区域内可适用的法律和法规的规定,就如下情形采取措施:

——区域内的搜查、监视和营救行动;

——用于区域内资源探查、勘探及开采活动的船只、设备、平台或人工岛出现险情时;

（n）请求当事国或其他组织及人员提供协助，以防止或治理任何影响环境或资源的污染或灾难出现；

（o）经当事国或相关利益公司的要求或同意，并经董事会接受和高级委员会批准，修改协定或渔业协议中有关合同特许权使用费、酬金和/或许可证数量的规定。

第六节　企业

第 12 条　结构

企业通过如下机构管理：

董事会，由大会任命 3~11 位代表组成，这些代表从如下人员中选取：

——一方面，从任职于高级委员会的当事国代表中选取；

——另一方面，从自然人或法人股东中选取。

执行局，负责企业的行政、组织和管理工作。如下三个理事会应协助执行局：

——一个是负责矿产和石油探查、勘探和开发活动的理事会；

——一个是负责捕鱼、监督和调查的理事会；

——一个是负责行政和财务事项的理事会。

各理事会会长应经执行局总干事与董事会商议后任命。

总干事由董事会根据高级委员会的建议任命。

总干事的职责包括：

（a）批准公司向其他公司（上述 1.15 款规定的公司）转让权利和义务；

（b）编制企业临时预算；

（c）准许企业雇员、分包商和其他人员进入开发区；

（d）必要时，出售企业在已决项目中享有的全部或部分矿产、石油和渔业产品；

（e）执行高级委员会和董事会委托的，与 1993 年 10 月 14 日协定或本议定书不相冲突的其他职责。

第 13 条　资本

企业核定资本为 10 万美元，全部由双方当事国出资。

第 14 条 资本的分配

企业资本股的分配比例为：

——塞内加尔占 67.5%；

——几内亚比绍占 32.5%。

其中 51% 的股份为 A 股，将被分配给双方当事国且不可以转让；其余的 49% 为 B 股，可以转让给私人实体。

在每一项销售中，共享收益的 67.5% 归属于塞内加尔共和国的资本收益，32.5% 归属于几内亚比绍共和国。

有关此类分配的形式和特性被规定在与企业有关的条款中。

第 15 条 收入来源

除了从开发活动中获取的自有资本（资金捐赠，股东预付款，当事国的捐赠和补贴），管理局的收入还来源于：

（a）在矿产和石油方面：

——征收矿区税；

——征收矿产品从价税；

——征收石油产品特许权使用费；

——对企业因开发区域内矿产和石油资源获得的利润征税；

——征收附加的石油税；

——分享管理局在区域内进行资源开采所获的矿产品和石油（原油和天然气）产品的销售利润。

（b）在渔业方面：

——鱼产品的销售所得；

——收取许可费；

——因监督收取的罚款；

——根据协定或合同获得的补偿金；

——因紧急降落获得的补偿金；

——企业在捕鱼活动中设定的所有专项收费、税款或税费。

（c）在培训和科研方面：

——根据石油或海洋渔业企业与涉及科学探矿、石油或海洋渔业研究的国际合作组之间签订的条约、协定和合同，对企业的培训和调查工作收取的费用；

(d) 一般性收入

——管理局在政策框架内，与当事国和/或国际合作组织或金融机构或类似的组织或国家实体开展合作，而获得的所有资金来源；

——企业因投资所得的所有经济利润。

第三部分

第七节 合作

第 16 条 合作的义务

根据本议定书的意图，当事国与管理局应就区域内科研安全、监督、营救、海洋环境保护和运输展开合作。为此，当事国应就从下述领域的活动中获得的相关信息开展定期交流。

第 17 条 安全

17.1. 作为安全运营的一部分，当事国有权在区域内代表管理局行使治安和管控的权利。

17.2. 当事国与管理局应当就与区域内资源探查、勘探和开发活动有关的事项，以及可能对开发活动安全产生不利影响的事件交换信息。

第 18 条 监督

当事国与管理局应开展合作以监督区域内的活动。

第 19 条 搜寻与营救

当事国与管理局应开展合作，以对区域内开展的搜寻与营救活动做出安排。

第 20 条 运输服务

当事国与管理局应开展合作在区域内提供运输服务。

第 21 条 文献、文件与数据库

21.1. 在符合保密规定的情况下，应管理局的请求，当事国应向管理局免费提供区域内的所有现存文件和文献资料，特别是地质学和地球物理学数据，包括油田形状、钻井数据和渔业资源与海洋环境方面的数据，但管理局应承担提供复制品的费用。

21.2. 在符合保密规定的情况下，当事国应当保证管理局免费地获取上述数据不受限制。

第 22 条　科学与海洋研究

22.1. 当事国和管理局应当直接地，或者在国际组织内部，在区域内的科学、技术以及技术研究方面开展合作，并在这些领域协调双方的活动。

22.2. 当事国应向管理局提供由管理局单方面，或联合其他国家、组织或公司开展科学研究的机会。

22.3. 作为回报，根据有关此类研究的保密条款的规定，经当事国的请求，管理局应向当事国提供在此类研究中获取的数据、样本和/或结论。

第 23 条　海洋环境保护

23.1. 当事国应当与管理局合作，防止或减少因区域内资源探查、勘探和开发活动引发的污染，或其他任何形式的海洋环境退化，特别是：

（a）当事国应就本议定书第 11 条第（m）和（n）款的事项的要求，向管理局提供帮助；

（b）当海洋环境污染超出了区域范围或有超出的危险（洋流、风暴及流向），当事国应当开展合作以防止、减轻或消除污染。

23.2. 根据本议定书第 11 条（j）款、（k）款、（l）款、（m）款和（n）款的规定，管理局应当制定法规来保护区域内的海洋环境。管理局应确定一项应急方案或管理方案，以抵御因区域内的资源探查、勘探和开发活动而引发的污染和退化。

23.3. 根据已生效的法律规定，因区域内的资源探查、勘探和开发活动引发的海洋环境污染和任何形式的退化而产生的损害和支出，公司应承担责任。

第四部分

第八节　法律适用和争端的解决

第 24 条　法律适用

24.1. 对于矿产和石油资源探查、勘探和开发活动，矿层与油层进行的监督和科学研究，应当适用塞内加尔的法律，以及依 10.4（b）款修正或修改的法律，在本议定书签署之日起适用。

24.2. 对于渔业资源的探查、勘探和开发活动，以及渔业监管和渔业科学研究，应当适用几内亚比绍的法律，在本议定书签署之日起适用。

24.3. 高级委员会应根据本议定书第 11 条第 1 款和 1993 年 10 月 14 日协定的目标，建议当事国对上述法律和规范做出修改或修正。

第 25 条　争端的解决

25.1. 当事国之间就本议书的解释或适用有关的任何争端，应根据 1993 年 10 月 14 日的管理和合作协定第 9 条的规定解决。

25.2. 管理局与一方当事国就本议定书解释或适用产生的争端，应通过直接谈判解决。若争端在 3 个月内仍未解决，可提交仲裁。

25.3. 当事国有义务履行仲裁裁决。

25.4. 企业达成的所有条约和渔业协定与合同，应包括对其解释或适用争端设立解决程序的特别条款。

第五部分

第九节　暂行规定

第 26 条　预付款

当事国应为管理局的运转提供一年的必要资金。

预付款的金额为 25 万美元，其中塞内加尔共和国提供 67.5%，几内亚比绍共和国提供 32.5%。在秘书长的建议下，高级委员会可将期限延长。

预付款金额应在秘书长提交年度预算的基础上确定。

缴费应按照如下进程缴纳：

——在本议定书第 28 条规定的生效日起 60 日内，双方分别缴纳 50%；

——余下的 50% 在本议定书生效之日起 6 个月内缴纳。

资金应做如下安置：

——要么作为股东的预付款，与企业资本整合，直到达到当事国的分配比例，余下的作为一项长期贷款，自企业开始运行之年算起，每五年为一个年度分期。

——或作为一项长期贷款，或作为每五年为一个年度分期贷款的设立成本，其首批分期付款最迟应在企业开始运行之日起第五年支付。

第六部分

第十节 最后条款

第 27 条 修订

27.1. 本议定书为 1993 年 10 月 14 日协定的组成部分,双方当事国可进行修订。

27.2. 任何修订或修改不影响管理局获得的、未被附加收入包含的任何收费。

第 28 条 生效

本议定书在当事国交换批准文书后生效。

1995 年 1 月 12 日签署于比绍。

几内亚比绍共和国政府	塞内加尔共和国政府
乔奥·贝纳多·维拉	阿卜杜·狄奥尤
共和国总统	共和国总统

4. Protocol to the Agreement between the Republic of Guinea – Bissau and the Republic of Senegal Concerning the Organization and Operation of the Management and Cooperation Agency Established By the Agreement of 14 October 1993

SUMMARY

The present document attempts to reflect, as part of the follow – up to the January 1994 meeting in Lisbon, the initial exchanges of views between the delegations of the two States Parties to the Agreement of 14 October 1993 as to the form, organization and operation of the Agency set up under that Agreement.

Part One of this draft covers, in its title II, the form and the purpose of the Agency; Part Two covers the Agency itself, which comprises two bodies:

The High Authority, composed of heads of State or Government or persons delegated by them, and the Secretariat of the Agency; and

The Enterprise, the body through which the Agency carries out the mission conferred on it by the Agreement of 14 October 1993.

The High Authority is the policy – making organ; the Enterprise is the instrument for implementing that policy and managing the resources in the Area.

The Enterprise is a public limited liability company constituted under private law, having a Board of Directors and a Directorate – General assisted by two directorates corresponding to the two main areas of activity, and an administrative and financial directorate.

The President of the High Authority is also Chairman of the Board of Directors during his term of office at the head of the High Authority.

Title IV covers the operation and responsibilities of the High Authority; Title V covers the responsibilities of the Secretary – General.

The powers and prerogatives of the Board of Directors shall be defined in the articles of association of the Enterprise.

Part Three gives the broad outlines of the various areas of cooperation between the States Parties and the Agency.

Part Four deals with the law to be applied to prospecting, exploration and exploitation of resources in the Area and with the settlement of disputes.

Part Five deals with the interim provisions allowing the Agency to begin operating when this Protocol enters into force and before the Enterprise is definitively constituted.

Part Six contains the final articles, i. e., provisions for amending this Protocol and for its date of entry into force.

Such is the organization of the text.

PROTOCOL TO THE AGREEMENT

PREAMBLE

This Protocol concerns the organization and operation of the Agency as provided for under article 4 of the Agreement concluded at Dakar on 14 October 1993 between the Republic of Guinea – Bissau and the Republic of Senegal in respect of the joint exploitation of the maritime area between azimuths 268° and 220°from Cape Roxo.

PART ONE

TITLE I DEFINITIONS

Article 1

For the purposes of this Protocol:

1.1. "Fisheries agreement" means the instrument and its annexes constituting a contract between the Enterprise and either of the States Parties or between the Enterprise and one or more third States and any addition or amendment thereto that may be approved by the Parties for the purpose of regulating conditions for access to the fishery resources of the Area by the said States and any fishery prospecting, exploration and exploitation activities which they may carry out therein.

1.2. "Mining or petroleum activities" means all operations in respect of prospecting, locating, evaluating, developing, producing, extracting or exploiting, transporting and marketing mineral and petroleum (crude oil and natural gas) resources, including natural gas processing, to the exclusion of petroleum product refining and distribution.

1.3. "Agency" means the Management and Cooperation Agency established pursuant to the Agreement on Management and Cooperation between the Government of the Republic of Guinea – Bissau and the Government of the Republic of Senegal, done at Dakar on 14 October 1993, in respect of the joint exploitation of the maritime area between azimuths 268°and 220°from Cape Roxo.

1.4. "Fisheries contract" means the instrument and its annexes constituting a contract between the Enterprise and a company or group of companies and any addition or amendment thereto that may be approved by the Parties for the purpose of regulating access to the fishery resources of the Area by the said companies and any fishery prospecting, exploration and exploitation activities which they may carry out therein.

1.5. "Convention" means the instrument and its annexes constituting a contract between the Enterprise and one or more companies and any addition or amendment thereto that may be approved by the Parties for the purpose of regulating all mining or petroleum activities in the Area.

1.6. "Applicable law" means all texts and their annexes and any addition or amendment thereto approved by the Parties containing rules, regulations or procedures applicable to the activities defined in article 5 of this Protocol and not incompatible with either the Agreement of 14 October 1993 or with this Protocol.

1.7. "Enterprise" means the body through which the Agency carries out the mission conferred on it by the Agreement of 14 October 1993.

"Enterprise" or "Enterprises" means one or more legal person (s) subsidiary to the Enterprise or established by the Agency as part of the diversification of its activities.

1.8. "State Party" or "States Parties" means the Republic of Guinea – Bissau and/or the Republic of Senegal, Parties to the Agreement of 14 October 1993.

1.9. "Third State" or "third States" means a State or States other than those referred to in paragraph 1.8 above.

1.10. "Fisheries licence" means a permit to fish, awarded by the Enterprise to shipowners appertaining to a State, a company or group of companies, for a specific length of time, a specific vessel and a given type of fishing in accordance with the rules and regulations applicable in the Area.

1.11. "Mining or petroleum permit" means the exclusive mineral or petroleum prospecting licence which the Enterprise awards to a company or group of companies or to a subsidiary enterprise in accordance with the procedures established to that end for an area whose limits are defined in an annex A of the Convention relating thereto.

1.12. "Percentage share" means the percentages of joint interests held by any entity in the Enterprise or in association with the Enterprise in prospecting, exploration and exploitation activities in the Area.

1.13. "Additional petroleum levy" means a levy on petroleum activities which is paid to the Enterprise under a convention, the amount of which rises in proportion to the profitability of the said activities.

1.14. "Royalties" means:

(a) In mineral or petroleum resource exploitation, the percentage (s) of production to be paid in cash or in kind; the amount thereof and the rules for its assessment and collection shall be specified in the convention attached to the mineral or petroleum exploitation concession;

(b) In fisheries resource exploitation, the amounts to be paid by shipowners acting under a fisheries agreement and/or fisheries contracts as compensation for the fisheries licences granted by the Enterprise to their vessels; rates, conditions and procedures for issuing such licenses shall be set in accordance with the rules and regulations in force in the Area.

1.15. "Company" or "companies" means a legal person or persons concluding a convention or fisheries contract or mineral or petroleum exploitation contract with the Enterprise, or any legal person having company status under applicable law to which an interest may be transferred.

1.16. "Area tax" means the annual tax per square kilometre that a company pays to the Enterprise for the area covered by its mining permit.

1.17. "Mining or petroleum title" means all mining or petroleum rights in the Area held by the Agency under the Agreement of 14 October 1993; the management of those rights is delegated to the Enterprise by the Agency.

1.18. "Area" means the area of cooperation defined in article 1 of the Agreement of 14 October 1993.

TITLE II   NAME, REGISTERED OFFICE, FORM AND PURPOSE

Article 2   NAME

The Agency shall be named "Management and Cooperation Agency".

Article 3   REGISTERED OFFICE

The Agency shall have its registered office in Dakar, but may be transferred to Bissau.

Article 4   FORM

The Agency shall be an international organization responsible for managing the resources of the Area, directly through the Enterprise or its subsidiaries or through other companies.

The Agency shall also be responsible for promoting cooperation between the States.

Article 5   PURPOSE

The Agency shall be responsible:

(a) In the mining and petroleum area

— For undertaking or causing to be undertaken any geological and geophysical studies, any drilling work, or any activities with the aim of prospecting, exploring or exploiting the mineral or petroleum resources in the Area;

— For promoting mineral or petroleum resource prospecting, exploration or exploitation activities in the Area;

— For marketing all or part of the mining or petroleum production falling to it;

(b) In the marine fishing area

— For carrying out, alone or in cooperation with other States or other bodies, the

evaluation and management of fisheries resources, the monitoring of the marine

ecosystem and the development of the fisheries in the Area;

— For exercising or authorizing the exercise of the right to fish, in particular by determining and implementing conditions for accessing and exploiting the fisheries resources in the Area;

— For promoting prospecting, exploration and exploitation of the fisheries resources in the Area;

— For marketing all or part of the fisheries production falling to it;

(c) More generally

— For controlling the rational exploitation of the resources in the Area;

— For cooperating with the States Parties and with the relevant international organizations to ensure within the Area, in accordance with the terms of articles 16 and 23 of this Protocol:

— Security;

— Regulatory control and surveillance of resource prospecting, exploration and exploitation activities;

— Protection of the marine environment;

— Pollution prevention and control.

For these purposes, the Agency may act alone or in association with other companies or with international organizations in any activity in the Area.

PART TWO

TITLE Ⅲ THE AGENCY

Article 6 POWERS

The Agency shall have exclusive rights to mining and petroleum titles and to fishing in the Area.

The Enterprise shall be available to it for these purposes.

The Enterprise:

— May itself carry out, or cause to be carried out by holders of any mining or petroleum permits or fisheries licences which it has granted, such work or activities as shall have been decided, and shall monitor the conduct of such work or activities;

— Shall take all possible steps to raise the financial backing needed for its activities;

— Shall assist the holders of mining or petroleum permits and fisheries agreements, contracts or licences in their administrative approaches to each State Party with a view to carrying out their prospecting, exploration and exploitation operations in the Area;

— Shall carry out all promotion missions undertaken to interest other companies in any resource prospecting, exploration and exploitation activities in the Area.

Article 7 ORGANIZATION

The Agency shall compromise:

— The High Authority and the Secretariat; their respective operations and areas of competence are defined hereinafter.

Article 8 PRIVILEGES AND IMMUNITIES

The States Parties shall afford the Agency and its personnel and the Enterprise the privileges and immunities generally afforded international organizations and their agents.

TITLE IV   THE HIGH AUTHORITY

Article 9   OPERATION

The High Authority shall be composed of the heads of State or Government, or such persons as they may delegate.

The High Authority shall be presided over, alternately, by the heads of State or Government or their representatives.

The term of office of the President of the High Authority shall be two years.

The first presidency of the High Authority shall be filled by the High Authority's host State; likewise, the first meeting of the High Authority shall take place in the host State.

The High Authority shall meet when necessary and at least once a year, alternately, in one or the other State Party.

The High Authority shall establish as necessary the rules of procedure enabling it to take decisions.

The President of the High Authority, for the length of his term of office, shall also serve as Chairman of the Board of Directors of the Enterprise.

The Secretary – General of the Agency shall serve as secretariat for the High Authority and shall be responsible for organizing the meetings of the High Authority.

The President of the High Authority may invite any person qualified and able to do so to provide an opinion on a matter under discussion.

Article 10   RESPONSIBILITIES

10. 1. he High Authority defines the Agency's general policy.

10. 2. he High Authority shall meet in ordinary session once a year to study and approve the general management and cooperation policies proposed by the Secretary – General.

10. 3. he High Authority shall appoint the Secretary – General and his deputy.

10. 4. he High Authority's functions shall include the following:

(a) Providing the Enterprise with guidance or guidelines for the conduct of its operations;

(b) Amending, on the recommendation of the Board of Directors of the Enterprise, in a way that is not incompatible with the objectives of this Protocol and of the Agreement of 14 October 1993, the rules and regulations applicable to resource prospecting, exploration and exploitation in the Area and to surveillance and scientific research;

(c) Supervising the implementation of this Protocol, the Agreement of 14 October 1993 and the rules and regulations applicable to the Enterprise, and making recommendations to the Board of Directors for it to make any necessary amendments;

(d) Exercising policing powers in the Area and determining the forms thereof。

10.5. n carrying out its functions, the High Authority shall ensure that resource prospecting, exploration and exploitation in the Area are carried out optimally, in accordance with good mining or petroleum practice, with care for the marine environment and for the preservation of fisheries resources.

TITLE V   THE SECRETARIAT

Article 11   RESPONSIBILITIES

11.1. he Secretary-General of the Agency, who shall be a natural person and an authorized representative appointed by the High Authority, shall be vested with general executive functions and appropriate management power. In carrying out his duties, he shall have the assistance of a Deputy Secretary-General.

11.2. ithin the limits set by the High Authority, the Secretary-General shall have the power to contract, acquire and dispose of movable and immovable property and to represent the Agency in any judicial proceedings.

11.3. he Secretary-General shall report to the High Authority on the execution of the tasks entrusted to him by that body.

11.4. he Secretary-General shall be responsible for managing resource prospecting, exploration and exploitation activities in the Area, including the following:

(a) Evaluating bids and making recommendations to the Board of Directors with a view to concluding conventions and fisheries agreements;

(b) Concluding conventions and fisheries agreements subject to approval by the High Authority on receipt of a favourable opinion from the Board of Directors. The conclusion of fisheries contracts shall not be subject to this procedure;

(c) Supervising companies'activities under the rules and regulations applicable in the Area to the exploitation of mineral, petroleum and fisheries resources;

(d) Ensuring that the regulations and guidelines promulgated under the rules and regulations applicable in the Area are applied and that conventions, fisheries agreements and contracts are properly executed;

(e) Suspending or rescinding fisheries contracts in the event that companies or shipowners do not observe the terms thereof;

(f) Terminating conventions and fisheries agreements, subject to prior acceptance by the Board of Directors and upon approval by the High Authority;

(g) Settling the shares of the States Parties in the profits of resource exploitation activities in the Area under the terms of the Agreement of 14 October 1993;

(h) Controlling, where appropriate, or participating with the assistance of the States Parties in controlling, entries into and movements within the Area of vessels, aircraft, structures and other matériel used in resource prospecting, exploration and exploitation activities in the Area;

(i) Establishing safe and restricted – access areas, in accordance with international law, so as to ensure the safety of navigation and of prospecting, exploration and exploitation operations in the Area;

(j) Setting forth rules and providing guidelines under the rules and regulations covering prospecting, exploration and exploitation of the resources in the Area, on all issues relating to the oversight and management of prospecting, exploration and exploitation operations;

(k) Setting forth rules and providing guidelines under the rules and regulations in force in the areas of health, safety, environmental protection, environmental impact assessment and labour practices;

(l) Recommending to the High Authority, in keeping with the objectives of this Protocol and the Agreement of 14 October 1993, amendments to the rules and regulations covering prospecting, exploration and exploitation of the resources in the Area, and to conventions and fisheries agreements;

(m) Requesting the High Authority to take steps compatible with this Protocol and the Agreement of 14 October 1993 and with the rules and regulations applicable in the Area:

— For search, surveillance and rescue operations in the Area;

— In the event of threats against vessels, structures, platforms or artificial islands used in resource prospecting, exploration and exploitation operations in the Area;

(n) Requesting the assistance of the States Parties or other bodies or persons with a view to preventing or combating pollution or any disaster affecting the environment or resources;

(o) Amending, at the request or with the agreement of the States or of interested companies, the provisions of the relevant convention or fisheries agreement concerning contractual royalties or considerations and/or volume of permits subject to prior acceptance by the Board of Directors and approval by the High Authority.

TITLE VI THE ENTERPRISE

Article 12 STRUCTURE

The Enterprise shall be administered by:

— A Board of Directors composed of a minimum of three and a maximum of 11 members appointed by the General Assembly and drawn:

— On the one hand, from the representatives of the States Parties serving on the High Authority;

— On the other hand, from the shareholders, be they natural or legal persons; and

— A Directorate – General responsible for the administrative, organizational and management functions of the Enterprise. The Directorate – General shall be assisted by the following three directorates:

— A directorate responsible for mining and petroleum prospecting, exploration and exploitation activities;

— A directorate responsible for fisheries, surveillance and research;

— An administrative and financial directorate.

The heads of the directorates shall be appointed by the Director – General after consultation with the Board of Directors.

The Director – General shall be appointed by the Board of Directors on the proposal of the High Authority.

The Director – General's responsibilities shall include the following:

(a) Approving the transfer of rights and obligations by companies to other companies which thereupon become Companies within the meaning of paragraph 1.15 above;

(b) Establishing the Enterprise's provisional budgets;

(c) Authorizing entry into the Area by employees of enterprises, by their subcontractors and by other persons;

(d) Where necessary, marketing all or part of the mineral, petroleum or fisheries production falling to the Enterprise under the programmes decided upon;

(e) Carrying out any other functions that the High Authority or the Board of Directors may entrust to him which are not incompatible with either the Agreement of 14 October 1993 or the terms of this Protocol.

Article 13　CAPITAL

The authorized capital of the Enterprise shall be set at US $ 100,000 and shall be wholly paid up by the two States.

Article 14　ALLOCATION OF CAPITAL

The percentage shares in the capital of the Enterprise shall be allocated as follows:

— Republic of Senegal　　　　　　　67.5 percent;

— Republic of Guinea – Bissau　　　32.5 percent.

Fifty – one percent of the shares shall be A shares assigned to the States and may not be transferred.

Forty – nine percent of the shares shall be B shares and may be transferred to the private sector.

On each sale, 67. 5 per cent of the shares sold shall pertain to the capital of the Republic of Senegal and 32. 5 per cent shall pertain to that of the Republic of Guinea – Bissau.

The forms and prerogatives related to these shares are defined in the articles of association of the Enterprise.

Article 15　RESOURCES

In addition to its equity capital (capital endowment, shareholders' "advances", contribution from States, subsidy) resulting from exploitation, the Agency's other resources shall be:

(a) In respect of mining and petroleum:

— The area tax;

— The ad valorem royalties on mineral production;

— The royalties on petroleum production;

— The tax on profits owed by the enterprises exploiting the mineral and petroleum resources of the Area;

— The additional petroleum levy;

— The share of the Agency's revenues derived from marketing mineral and petroleum (crude oil and natural gas) products in the exploitation of the resources of the Area.

(b) In respect of fisheries:

— Any revenues from marketing fishery products;

— Licence fees;

— Fines resulting from inspections;

— Compensation under agreements or contracts;

— Compensation for forced landings;

— Any specific charges, taxes or levies which the Enterprise may establish in connection with fisheries.

(c) In respect of training and scientific research:

— The contributions made under signed conventions, agreements and contracts by petroleum or marine fishing enterprises and international cooperation organizations involved in scientific mining, petroleum or marine fishing research, to the Enterprise's training and research efforts;

(d) In general:

— Any financial resources which the Agency may obtain within the framework of cooperation policies with States and/or international cooperation or financial agencies, similar organizations or State bodies;

— Any financial profit from investment of the sums available to the Enterprise.

PART THREE

TITLE VII COOPERATION

Article 16 OBLIGATION TO COOPERATE

For the purposes of this Protocol, the States Parties and the Agency undertake to cooperate in respect of scientific research security, surveillance, rescue, protection of the marine environment, and transport in the Area. To this end, the Parties shall regularly exchange the information they obtain in the course of any activities they may carry out in the spheres listed below.

Article 17 SECURITY

17.1. s part of their security operations, the States Parties have policing and control rights in the Area on behalf of the Agency.

17.2. he States Parties and the Agency shall exchange information on any matter liable to affect prospecting, exploration and exploitation of the resources in the Area and on incidents that may adversely affect the safety of their activities.

Article 18 SURVEILLANCE

The States Parties and the Agency shall cooperate in surveillance activities in the Area.

Article 19 SEARCH AND RESCUE

The States Parties and the Agency shall cooperate in order to make arrangements for search and rescue operations to be carried out in the Area.

Article 20 TRANSPORT SERVICES

The States Parties and the Agency shall cooperate to provide transport services in the Area.

Article 21 BIBLIOGRAPHY, DOCUMENTATION AND DATA BANKS

21.1. he States Parties shall provide the Agency, free of charge and on condition of confidentiality, with all existing documentation on the Area and a bibliography thereof, in particular geological and geophysical data, including field tapes, drilling data and data on fishery resources and the marine environment, at the request of the Agency, which shall meet the cost of reproduction.

21.2. he States Parties grant the Agency unrestricted access to the aforementioned data free of charge and on condition of confidentiality.

Article 22 SCIENTIFIC AND MARINE RESEARCH

22.1. The States Parties and the Agency shall cooperate directly or within international organizations on scientific, technical and technological research in the Area and shall coordinate their activities in this sphere.

22.2. The States Parties shall also afford the Agency the opportunity to conduct scientific studies and research for itself, alone or in association with other States, organizations or companies.

22.3. In return, the Agency undertakes to provide the States Parties, at their request, subject to the confidentiality clauses pertaining to such studies, with the data, samples and/or results obtained in the course of such research.

Article 23 PROTECTION OF THE MARINE ENVIRONMENT

23.1. The States Parties shall cooperate with the Agency to prevent or minimize pollution or any other type of degradation in the marine environment resulting from resource prospecting, exploration and exploitation activities in the Area. In particular:

(a) The States Parties shall provide the Agency with such assistance as may be requested of them under article 11, subparagraphs (m) and (n), of this Protocol;

(b) When pollution of the marine environment within the Area extends beyond it or there is a risk of its doing so (currents, winds, direction), the

States Parties shall cooperate in order to take steps to prevent, mitigate or eliminate such pollution.

23.2. In accordance with article 11, subparagraphs (j), (k), (I), (m) and (n), of this Protocol, the Agency shall lay down regulations to protect the marine environment in the Area. It shall establish an emergency plan or management plan to combat pollution and any degradation arising from resource prospecting, exploration and exploitation activities in the Area.

23.3. Companies shall be responsible for damage and expenditures incurred by pollution and any form of degradation of the marine environment arising out of their resource prospecting, exploration and exploitation activities in the Area in accordance with the rules and regulations in force.

PART FOUR

TITLE Ⅷ APPLICABLE LAW AND DISPUTE SETTLEMENT

Article 24 APPLICABLE LAW

24.1. The law applicable to mineral and petroleum resource prospecting, exploration and exploitation activities and to surveillance and scientific research in the mining and petroleum sphere shall be the law of Senegal, amended or modified in accordance with paragraph 10.4 (b) above, in force on the date of signature of this Protocol.

24.2. The law applicable to fisheries resource prospecting, exploration and exploitation activities and to surveillance and scientific research in the sphere of fisheries shall be the law of Guinea – Bissau in force on the date of signature of this Protocol.

24.3. The High Authority may, in accordance with article 11, paragraph 1, of this Protocol and with the objectives of the Agreement of 14 October 1993, propose to the States Parties modifications or amendments to the above rules and regulations.

Article 25 DISPUTE SETTLEMENT

25.1. Any dispute between the States Parties concerning the interpretation or implementation of this Protocol shall be settled in accordance with article 9 of the Agreement on Management and Cooperation of 14 October 1993.

25. 2. Any dispute between the Agency and a contracting State concerning the interpretation or implementation of this Protocol shall be resolved initially by direct negotiations.

If the dispute has not been resolved after three months, it shall be settled by arbitration.

25. 3. The States Parties are responsible for enforcement of arbitral awards.

25. 4. All conventions and fisheries agreements and contracts concluded by the Enterprise must contain specific provisions setting out procedures for the settlement of disputes concerning the interpretation or implementation of the said conventions and fisheries agreements and contracts.

PART FIVE

TITLE IX INTERIM PROVISIONS

Article 26 ADVANCES OF FUNDS

The States Parties undertake to provide the Agency with the necessary funds for it to operate for a period of one (1) year.

The amount of the advances shall be set at $ US 250, 000, 67. 5 per cent for the Republic of Senegal and 32. 5 per cent for the Republic of Guinea – Bissau. The said period may be extended by the High Authority at the request of the Secretary – General.

The amount of the advances shall be set on the basis of an annual budget submitted by the Secretary – General.

Contributions shall be paid in accordance with the following schedule:

— Fifty percent of the share of each State Party, to be paid sixty (60) days from the date of entry into force of this Protocol as established in article 28 below;

— The balance, i. e. 50 per cent, to be paid six (6) months from the date of entry into force of this Protocol.

The funds shall be posted:

— Either as a shareholders' advance to be consolidated into the capital of the

Enterprise up to the percentage shares of the States Parties, with the residue being considered as a long-term loan repayable in five (5) equal annual instalments from the year of entry into operation of the Enterprise;

— Or as a long-term loan or initial set-up costs repayable in five (5) equal annual instalments, the first instalment of which shall be paid at the latest during the fifth year from the date of entry into operation of the Enterprise.

PART SIX

TITLE X FINAL ARTICLES

Article 27 AMENDMENT

27.1. This Protocol, which shall be an integral part of the Agreement of 14 October 1993, may be amended by the States Parties.

27.2. Amendments and modifications may not have the effect of incurring to the Agency any charges that are not covered by additional resources.

Article 28 ENTRY INTO FORCE

This Protocol shall enter into force on the date of exchange of the instruments of ratification.

DONE at Bissau on 12 June 1995

For the Government of the Republic of Guinea-Bissau:	For the Government of the Republic of Senegal:
JOAO BERNARDO VIEIRA	ABDOU DIOUF
President of the Republic	President of the Republic

国家领土主权与海洋权益协同创新中心

武汉大学边界与海洋问题研究丛书
海洋文库·研究丛书

武汉大学边界与海洋问题研究丛书编委会

主　编　胡德坤
副主编　易显河　余敏友

委　员（按姓氏笔画排序）
丁　煌　孔令杰　匡增军　关培凤　杨泽伟　李仁真
李　斐　余敏友　张　彬　易显河　周茂荣　胡德坤
秦天宝　谈广鸣　彭敦文　韩永利

海上共同开发协定汇编（汉英对照）

International Agreements on the Joint Development of Marine Resources

(Chinese – English Bilingual Version)

（下）

杨泽伟　主编
邓妮雅　黄文博　副主编

社会科学文献出版社
SOCIAL SCIENCES ACADEMIC PRESS (CHINA)

三

海上共同开发的平稳阶段

（十三）2001年尼日利亚与圣多美和普林西比共同开发案

1.《尼日利亚联邦共和国与圣多美和普林西比民主共和国共同开发两国专属经济区的石油及其他资源的条约》

（2001年2月21日订于阿布贾）

张慧芬译，邓妮雅校

尼日利亚联邦共和国与圣多美和普林西比民主共和国考虑到1982年12月10日于蒙特哥湾缔结的《联合国海洋法公约》，尤其是其第74条第3款，要求海岸相向国家在专属经济区的划界协议达成之前应基于谅解与合作精神，尽一切努力做出实际的临时安排，并在此过渡期间，不危害或阻碍最后协议的达成；充分致力于维持、重建和进一步加强两国间的互信、友谊与合作关系，并且促进建设性的睦邻合作；承认在各自专属经济区内存在主张重叠的海域（区域）；决定寻求共同经济和战略利益；注意到区域内可能存在石油和其他资源；希望能够立即有序地进行资源勘探和开采；念及两国近邻关系，双方应本着合作、友好和善意的精神分享利益；确信该条约能够有助于深化双边关系；相信允许勘探和开采石油和其他资源共同安排的建立，能够进一步扩大两国政府间联系与合作的范围，并惠及民间交往；决定在不影响依国际法对海域的最终划界的前提下，根据本条约在此区域建立共同开发区；并重申本条约未规定的问题将继续由国际法规则调整；达成协议如下：

前 言

第一条 定义

为本条约的目的：

1. "可适用的法律"是指本条约以及本条约确定的区域内所适用的法律原则和规则；

2. "管理局"是指按照本条约第三部分建立的联合管理局；

3. "董事会"是指在本条约第十条中所指的联合管理局董事会；

4. "合同区"是指开发合同中的共同开发区域，其中不包括已被承包商放弃的区域；

5. "承包商"是指联合管理局之外的开发合同缔约方；

6. "委员会"是指按照本条约第二部分建立的联合部长委员会；

7. "开发活动"是指区域内或与区域相关的所有经济活动，包括石油活动、渔业活动、为开发或开采其他矿物或生物资源进行的所有其他活动，以及与上述活动相关的一切形式的勘探和研究活动；

8. "开发合同"是指联合管理局和承包商间订立的，涉及开发活动的所有协议（包括租赁、许可、产品分成合同和特许）；

9. "专属海域"指共同开发区外，依国际法属于一方当事国的大陆架或专属经济区的任何区域；

10. "财务条款"包括所有税收性质（无论是基于生产还是收入）的义务，和包括特许权使用费、实物偿付、产品分成安排和资源租赁在内的其他财务上的义务；

11. "渔业活动"是指与捕获和开采开发区内的生物自然资源相关的任何活动；

12. "设施"是指安装在海床上方、内部、表面或下方，用于进行开发活动的任何建筑物、设备或人工岛屿，包括原地钻探船；

13. "国民"是指根据一方当事国的法律拥有该国国籍的自然人或法人；

14. "国家机构"是指对其领土或水域的活动负责的，当事国的一个部门、官方或半官方的行政或技术机构；

15. "运营协议"是指由两个或两个以上承包商，旨在区域内进行开发活动而缔结的合同；

16. "运营者"是指运营协议指定并担任运营者的承包商；

17. "石油"是指：

（a）任何在海底自然生成的碳氢化合物或碳氢化合物的混合物，不论其为气体、液体或固体；

（b）以上（a）所界定且已返回至储油层中的石油；以及

（c）与上述多种物质衍生的所有其他矿物；

18. "石油活动"是指勘探与开采区域内石油的全部活动；

19. "石油承包商"是指相关石油开发合同的承包商；

20. "石油开发合同"是指与石油有关的开发合同；

21. "污染"是指进入海洋环境（包括港湾）的物质或能源，会造成或可能造成对生物资源和海洋生物的损害，危害人类健康，损害海水的利用质量或者降低舒适度；

22. "秘书处"是指本条约第十四条中提到的联合管理局秘书处；

23. "特别制度区"是指在附录第一款中特别规定的区域；

24. "当事国"是指尼日利亚联邦共和国与圣多美和普林西比民主共和国；

25. "区域"是指第五条和第三十一条第 5 款规定的，依据第二条所建立的共同开发区域，包括海床、底土及其上覆水域；

26. "区域计划"是指依据本条约第七部分达成的或由委员会采用的，为区域内活动指定的开发计划。

第一部分　共同开发区

第二条　共同开发区的建立

2.1　共同开发区是双方当事国根据本条约，为实现本条约之目的而建立的共同开发区域。

2.2　共同开发区所覆盖区域如下：

（a）由下表所标明的，运用 WGS 84 基准确定的点而连成的测地线所组成的区域；以及

（b）其海床、底土和上覆水域。

纬度	经度
北纬 03°02′22″	东经 07°07′31″
北纬 02°50′00″	东经 07°25′52″
北纬 02°42′38″	东经 07°36′25″
北纬 02°20′59″	东经 06°52′45″
北纬 01°40′12″	东经 05°57′54″
北纬 01°09′17″	东经 04°51′38″
北纬 01°13′15″	东经 04°41′27″
北纬 01°21′29″	东经 04°24′14″
北纬 01°31′39″	东经 04°06′55″
北纬 01°42′50″	东经 03°50′23″
北纬 01°55′18″	东经 03°34′33″
北纬 01°58′53″	东经 03°53′40″
北纬 02°02′59″	东经 04°15′11″
北纬 02°05′10″	东经 04°24′56″
北纬 02°10′44″	东经 04°47′58″
北纬 02°15′53″	东经 05°06′03″
北纬 02°19′30″	东经 05°17′11″
北纬 02°22′49″	东经 05°26′57″
北纬 02°26′21″	东经 05°36′20″
北纬 02°30′08″	东经 05°45′22″
北纬 02°33′37″	东经 05°52′58″
北纬 02°36′38″	东经 05°59′00″
北纬 02°45′18″	东经 06°15′57″
北纬 02°50′18″	东经 06°26′41″
北纬 02°51′29″	东经 06°29′27″
北纬 02°52′23″	东经 06°31′46″
北纬 02°54′46″	东经 06°38′07″
北纬 03°00′24″	东经 06°56′58″
北纬 03°01′19″	东经 07°01′07″
北纬 03°01′27″	东经 07°01′46″

北纬 03°01′44″　　　　　　东经 07°03′07″

北纬 03°02′22″　　　　　　东经 07°07′31″

2.3　为说明之目的，附图描述了共同开发区所覆盖区域。联合管理局可为其宗旨，以适当比例尺在一张或多张图表上对此区域的界线进行更精确的描述。

第三条　共同开发的原则

3.1　在开发区内，应由双方当事国共同管控资源的勘探和开发，旨在实现最大限度的商业利用。双方当事国应依据本条约，对开发区内由开发活动所产生的所有收益和责任做如下分配：尼日利亚占60%，圣多美和普林西比占40%。

3.2　除非依据本条约，在开发区内的其他任何开发活动都是被禁止的。

3.3　双方当事国对区域开发的权利和义务，应该由联合部长委员会和联合管理局依本条约行使。

3.4　区域内的石油和其他资源应依本条约，考虑到对海洋环境的保护，并借鉴公认的良好油田和渔业开发实践，进行高效开发。

3.5　依据上述第4款，在本条约生效后，联合部长委员会和联合管理局应当采取一切必要措施，确保在开发区内尽快开始勘探和开发活动。

第四条　不放弃开发区的权利主张

4.1　不得将本条约的内容解释为任一当事国放弃对部分或整个区域的权利或主张，也不能将其解释为承认另一方当事国对部分或整个区域的任何权利或主张的立场。

4.2　本条约及其实施引起的任何行为或活动，以及依据本条约在此区域实施的任何法律，都不得构成主张、支持或否认任一当事国对部分或整个区域权利或主张所持的立场的根据。

第五条　特别制度

5.1　本条约的规定（除本条、第一条、第二条、第四条、第五十条、第五十一条、第五十二条第2款以及附录外）不适用于特别制度区，涉及此区域的，应依本条的规定理解和解释。

5.2　在协议有效期间，特别制度区按照附录所载规定管理。

第二部分　联合部长委员会

第六条　委员会的构成

6.1　建立联合部长委员会。

6.2　委员会应由2到4位部长，或由各国元首指定的相同级别的代表组成。

6.3　委员会不具有独立的法律人格。

6.4　向秘书处书面通知后，委员会的任一成员可任命一位代表，参加委员会的一个或多个会议。依任命规则，每位代表都应有权在该成员缺席时，行使其作为委员会成员的任何权利或职责，包括计入法定人数。

6.5　担任委员会秘书长的执行董事，同时也担任联合管理局秘书长。

第七条　委员会的会议和决议

7.1　委员会有效会议的法定人数应当过半数，其中包括至少一位由当事国各自指定的代表。

7.2　委员会一年应至少召开两次会议，会议应在尼日利亚与圣多美和普林西比轮流举行。首次会议应当在本条约生效后60日内举行。

7.3　会议主席由主办国任命的成员担任。

7.4　委员会的所有决定都应经过协商一致通过。

7.5　委员会可以建立其自身的程序，包括会外决策程序。

7.6　委员会的决定只有通过书面记录，并在双方当事国至少一名成员签字后才有效。

第八条　委员会的职能和权力

8.1　委员会全面负责与共同开发区资源的勘探和开采有关的所有问题，并履行双方当事国赋予的其他职能。

8.2　委员会的职能应包括如下内容：

（a）指导联合管理局履行协议中规定的职能；

（b）批准使联合管理局有效运作的规则、条例（包括工作人员条例）和程序；

（c）审批联合管理局的审计账目和审计报告；

（d）审批联合管理局的年度报告；

（e）检查协议的执行情况，并就与协议运行或修订相关的任何事项，向协议双方提出建议；

（f）核准联合管理局与承包商签订的开发合同；

（g）核准联合管理局与承包商开发合同的终止；

（h）根据第十八条第 2 款的规定，批准国家对区域内开发合同中获得收益和产品进行的分配；

（i）审批联合管理局的年度预算；

（j）核准联合管理局开设银行账户；

（k）修改根据本条约条款对联合管理局施加的任何时间限制；

（l）通过协商解决联合管理局内的争议；

（m）为联合管理局委任外聘审计师并核准其报酬。

8.3 双方当事国都有权查看联合部长委员会和联合管理局的所有文件。

8.4 委员会、委员会成员及其秘书长，在必要情况下为履行协议的职能，应有权使用联合管理局秘书处的服务。

第三部分　联合管理局

第九条　建立、职能和权力

9.1 建立联合管理局。

9.2 联合管理局在国际法、当事国的法律框架下均具有法人资格，并且在双方当事国的法律框架下行使权力和履行职能时具有必要的法律能力。特别是，联合管理局有订立合同的能力，获得并处置动产和不动产的能力，以及提起并参与法律诉讼的能力。

9.3 联合管理局应该对委员会负责。

9.4 除非委员会另有决定，联合管理局所在地应该设在尼日利亚首都阿布贾，并在圣多美和普林西比首都圣多美设立办事处。

9.5 联合管理局在本条约生效后即开始运作。

9.6 依据本条约，该机构应当在委员会的指导下，管理责任区域内与资源勘探和资源开发相关的活动。联合管理局的职能尤其应包括以下内容：

（a）将共同开发区划分为合同区域，以及就该区域的合同进行协商、招标、签署和监督；

（b）根据委员会的批准，与承包商签订开发合同；

（c）对承包商的活动进行监督和管理；

（d）向委员会建议终止开发合同；

（e）根据委员会批准，终止开发合同；

（f）根据第十八条第 2 款的规定和委员会的批准，收取联合机构从开发合同中获得的收益和产品，并在双方当事国间进行分配；

（g）编制联合管理局预算并提交委员会，其开支应按照委员会核准的预算或估算来进行，或按照委员会批准的规定和程序进行；

（h）控制船舶、飞行器、建筑物、设备和人员进出区域和在区域内活动；

（i）依照国际法建立安全区域和限制区域，确保航行、石油开采、捕鱼和其他一切开发活动的安全，以及开发区的有效管理；

（j）就与监督和控制运行相关的所有事项，包括卫生、安全和环境保护等，颁布规定并给予指导；

（k）海洋科学研究的管理；

（l）准备向联合委员会提交年度报告；

（m）检查和审计任意日历年，有关承包商开发合同的账簿和账目；

（n）就促进共同开发区内的资源开发所必需的法律适用以及法律修正，向双方当事国提出建议；

（o）依据开发区内可适用的国际法规则来维持海洋环境；

（p）搜集和交换与开发区及其资源相关的科研、技术和其他数据；

（q）除执行董事外，任命和解雇管理局的技术和其他人员；

（r）根据本条约，就如下事项，要求当事国有关当局采取行动：

（i）开发区内的搜索和救援行动；

（ii）制止或打击恐怖主义，或其他对开发区内用于开采的船舶和设施的威胁；以及

（iii）污染的防止和补救；

（s）审议由委员会或当事国提交的事项；

（t）委员会赋予的其他职能。

9.7 联合管理局的工作语言为英语。

第十条　董事会

10.1　根据本条约及委员会的指令，联合管理局应由四个执行董事组成的董事会管理。其中两名（可随时更换）应当由尼日利亚政府首脑在具有资质和经验的国民中选派，另外两名（可随时更换）应当由圣多美和普林西比政府首脑在具有资质和经验的国民中选派。所有这些任命在书面通知对方当事国首脑后生效。执行董事的任职期限应由任命的政府首脑决定，一般情况下期限为6年，可延期一次，或直到委派了接替人员。

10.2　执行董事由委员会指派到管理局的不同部门中担任长官，任期3年，包括担任管理局秘书长和秘书处长官。

10.3　董事会应委员会、一方当事国或任何执行董事的要求举行会议，或为履行其职能在必要时举行会议。

10.4　董事会有效会议的法定人数为至少有两位执行董事。

10.5　管理局执行董事的决议应当经全体一致同意。不能一致同意的事项将被提交给委员会。

10.6　除非董事会另有决议，会议应在联合管理局所在地举行。

10.7　除非有书面决议且有两位执行董事签名，其中至少有一位执行董事由当事国指派，否则董事会的决议无效。

10.8　考虑到管理局的正常运作，管理局的人员由董事会根据情况和条件任免，并经委员会批准。

10.9　除非委员会另有决议，应指派一位执行董事担任管理局主席和董事会主席，任期一年。

10.10　董事会根据本条约和委员会的指导决定其程序。

第十一条　负责制

11.1　管理局在各方面应向委员会负责，遵守委员会做出的所有指令。

11.2　管理局的秘书处和其他所有行政机构或组织，以及技术或其他委员会，都应在各方面向董事会负责。

11.3　联合管理局应按照委员会指令，以其活动和区域内进展为内容制作年度报告，并提交委员会审批。

第十二条　特权与豁免

12.1　联合管理局对本条约下的活动应免除一切形式的征税。这不影响在一方当事国领土内对管理局活动，征收该国国内机构开展同等活动而征收的非歧视性费用或服务费用。

12.2 联合管理局应享有当事国法院或法庭的司法豁免，除非涉及：

(a) 一方当事国领土内的商业交易，且该交易不属于第四十七条争端解决调整；

(b) 一方当事国国内机构在其领土内，同等情况下做出的，应当审查的强制性决定。

12.3 管理局的执行董事、官员和其他人员，如果属于一方或另一方当事国国民，须由其所属国就其依据本条约提供的服务而获得的酬劳而被征税，而不考虑其服务的地点。

12.4 为了本条约的目的，若一个人具有双方当事国国籍，应该选择其中一个国籍且该选择有效。

第十三条 服务的提供

13.1 依据本条约和第三条所确定的原则，为实现其职能，联合管理局可使用当事国已有的技术装置和其他服务。不同实体可请求不同的服务。

13.2 被委托的实体应对联合管理局负责。

13.3 联合管理局依据第十二条第1款和第2款所享有的豁免，应适用于实体履行本条所授权职能而做出的各项活动。

13.4 本条第1款的授权在规定期限内有效，直到董事会撤回委派。

13.5 为了信息和专业知识的培训和交换，任何被在第1款下被授权的实体都应接受当事国临时调任适当资历的，或者是当事国任命的外部员工，并应使这些员工充分履行被授权的职责。

13.6 第5款提到的人员的人数和配置由双方当事国的协议决定，应考虑到行使职能的范围，以及不属于实体的当事国人员的发展和培训的需要。

13.7 根据机构同意的条件和情况，行使委派职能而产生的成本及其他花费，包括劳务支出，都是可补偿的。

13.8 联合管理局（包括秘书处）的人员或被雇佣的人员应当，在确保圣多美和普林西比的国民或居民不超过40%的基础上，进行选择。

第四部分 行政服务

第十四条 秘书处和其他服务

14.1 管理局应当设立秘书处，由执行董事轮流担任秘书长，任期3

年，负责委员会和管理局的行政工作。

14.2 董事会对秘书处的所有任命，应依据委员会制定的限制条件和程序。

14.3 秘书处官员和工作人员应依据联合管理局批准的条件招聘，高层人员任命应该由委员会批准。这些官员和工作人员可以但非必须，从当事国政府的官员或雇员、前官员或前雇员中选任。

第五部分　工作人员的职责

第十五条　公正和利益冲突

15.1 董事会成员、管理局的官员和其他人员，以其身份行事时应只考虑联合管理局自身的利益，秉持公正的态度，不以损害一方当事国为代价而支持另一方。此项原则应当同样适用于执行第十三条委派职能的国内机构或其他实体及工作人员。

15.2 除非被委员会另行明确批准，管理局的任何执行董事、官员及人员都不得在开发区内享有直接或间接的经济利益。

15.3 执行董事、管理局的官员和其他人员在履职之前，应以委员会批准的方式做出书面宣誓，详述一切与第 2 款规定相关的，可能被合理认为相当于经济利益的直接或间接利益。

第十六条　保密

16.1 董事会成员、管理局的官员和其他工作人员，以及双方当事国，都应该对为本条约之目的制作或接收的所有机密文件和信息的内容保密，非经双方当事国或特殊情形下一方当事国当局授权，不得进一步披露或公布任何前述文件或信息。

16.2 执行董事、管理局的官员和其他工作人员，在其任期内和任期结束后都不应披露联合管理局知悉或拥有的任何工业机密或专有数据，或任何其他因为在联合管理局履职而知悉的机密信息。

16.3 本条款不减损关于实质或潜在的违反保密事项上个人的其他义务，以及管理局或对一方当事国可采取补救措施的义务。

第六部分　财政

第十七条　预算、账目和审计

17.1 管理局的经费源于开发活动获得的收入。当事国应预付双方共同决定开始运作的必要的款项。

17.2 联合管理局所持的向其付或应付的经费,都应该存放在按照第八条第2款(j)项建立的账户。

17.3 联合管理局应该依据良好的国际会计实践和委员会的指令,制定和保留完整的、正规的以及最新的账户信息、资产负债表、预算和现金流预测。

17.4 委员会、联合管理局及其各自的成员和工作人员的一切费用和开支,都应由联合管理局支付。

17.5 本条约生效后5个月内,管理局应建立预算和会计体系,并经委员会批准。所有成本和支出都应遵从该体系。

17.6 所有预算、费用和开支,以及联合管理局的所有其他收支和款项,都应该由委员会认可的外部审计师进行年度审计。

17.7 每一会计期核准预算的差额,按尼日利亚60%、圣多美和普林西比40%的比例承担。除非委员会另行决定,本款规定的预算缴费应是对联合管理局的无息贷款,自联合管理局在后续会计期产生第一次盈余时开始偿还。

17.8 联合管理局应遵守有效的预算程序,并应该有效利用其可用的资源。

第十八条 盈余的用途

18.1 联合管理局可在委员会批准后建立稳健的储备基金。

18.2 在储备基金建立后,所有支出之外的盈余不得被扣减或预扣,应该立即以尼日利亚60%、圣多美和普林西比40%的比例支付给两国,当储备基金持有的任何款项不再必需时也做上述处理。

第七部分 区域计划

第十九条 区域计划的准备和批准

19.1 本条约一旦生效,联合管理局应尽快召开会议,按照本条约第三条规定的原则起草一份区域计划草案,以便制订一套高效、经济且迅速开采区域资源的方案。

19.2 为实现第一款之目的,双方当事国应相互提供区域内现有的和预期的、与经济活动有关的信息材料。

19.3 区域计划应提交委员会审批，委员会可修改后批准或不经修改而批准，也可退回联合管理局，并附加进一步工作建议或改进意见。

19.4 委员会批准的区域计划，应由联合管理局和双方当事国以适当的方式发布。

19.5 区域计划中没有涉及的内容应依照本条约规定；本条约没有规定的，由委员会做出决议或由双方当事国签署补充协定规定。

第二十条 区域计划的定期检查

20.1 除非委员会另行指示，联合管理局应该至少每3年检查和修改区域计划，并将修改建议提交给委员会通过。

20.2 在修改建议被采纳之前，原先批准的区域计划继续有效。

20.3 第十九条第3款和第5款应适用于任何提交的区域计划或获批准的修改建议。

第八部分 区域内石油制度

第二十一条 石油活动的监管和税收制度

21.1 在本条约生效后3个月内，联合管理局应制定一套符合本条约的管理和税收制度，并由委员会批准，该制度适用于开发区内的石油勘探和开采活动。

21.2 在本条约生效后6个月内，管理和税收制度草案由委员会合理修改后采纳。经采纳后，该制度（依据第五条）适用于开发区内的石油活动，并由管理局执行。

21.3 一经采纳，联合管理局就应立即颁布监管和税收制度。

21.4 委员会在任何时候都可以对如前建立的监管和税收制度进行其认为适当的修订，而该修订应该立即在区域内适用，并由联合管理局执行。

21.5 联合管理局应当立即公布对管理和税收制度进行的修改。

第二十二条 海关和关税豁免

22.1 除非委员会另有决定，对区域内石油设备的进口、使用或出口都不应征收任何关税或其他税收。当石油设备在区域内不再使用后，本条款不影响一方当事国为原产地或目的地的出口或进口设备的权利。

22.2 就本条款而言，"石油设备"包括进行区域内石油活动必需的装置、厂房和设备（包括钻探设备）、任何材料和其他物品。

22.3 从区域内采出的石油运输到两当事国管辖区域内应该免除一切税款，有相关开发合同的财务条款规定的除外。

第二十三条 石油开发合同的一般制度

23.1 只有依照联合管理局与一个或多个承包商订立的石油开发合同，才能在区域内从事石油活动。

23.2 依据委员会为招投标制定的规程，除非委员会另行决定，签订石油开发合同，必须持有石油招标证书。

第二十四条 石油开发合同的财务制度

24.1 开发区内承包商对管理局有关区域内石油活动的财税（包括财政）义务，应当由本款批准的石油开发合同中的财税条款做出排他规定。

24.2 为平衡下述需求，除了依照第二十一条建立的监管和税收制度中的财务条款，联合管理局还可制定与前述条款不抵触的其他条款：

（a）通过对资源的商业开发，为管理局和双方当事国保有最大限度的利益；

（b）鼓励商业开采和激励投资；

（c）确保经营的透明度和确定性；

（d）尽可能确保承包商在财务条款下的纳税能够免除双重征税，包括在第三国的征税在内；

（e）确保开发区内的部分或全部油田，在开发期限内得到最大限度的利用。

24.3 双方当事国应在其本国法律框架内，采取一切适当措施确保财务条款的执行。

24.4 除本条约规定以外，双方当事国不应对区域内开发活动或由此产生的收益征税。本款规定不影响，双方当事国对超过了原油销售必要的初步处理之外，对石油进行加工或做进一步处理获得的利润，进行征税的权利。

第二十五条 承包商的权利和义务

25.1 在相应的石油发展合同期限内，根据其条款和适用的法律，承包商对开采活动享有排他的权利。

25.2 承包商可以处置依据相关开发合同获得的石油，仅受管理局施加的在登陆、购买者身份和容量核查方面的非歧视性限制的管制。

第二十六条　取消或暂停联合承包商的石油开发合同的影响

26.1　如果因一个承包商违约，联合管理局取消一份由多个承包商共同签订的石油开发合同后，应向所有未违约承包商，在原区域发出一份新合同的要约，并尽可能与原合同保持一致。

26.2　要约可规定：

（a）要求受要约人对违约的后果采取补救措施；

（b）受要约人接受联合管理局认同或接受的替代承包商。

26.3　本条不影响在原石油开发合同下，其他承包商应承担的责任。

第二十七条　承包商权利的转让

未经联合管理局许可，承包商在石油开发合同中的权利和义务不得转让。当拟受让人满足了管理局经济、技术上和其他要求的资质时，管理局不得无理拒绝批准转让。

第二十八条　石油开发承包商在区域外双方当事国领土内的运营

在任意一方当事国的领土内，承包商可以依照相关当事国的法律和规章，取得、建造、维护、使用和处理建筑、平台、油罐、管道、终端和其他区域内石油活动必需的设施。

第二十九条　开展运营

29.1　按照本条约第三条提出的共同开发的原则，任一当事国有权：

（a）无歧视地考虑其国民的石油开发合同申请；

（b）对区域内石油开发活动进展情况进行监督和定期报告；

（c）在本条约第十六条的保密义务和其他义务下，获取地质数据；

（d）独立地计量、检查或监督所有石油活动（包括为开展计量、监督或检查而进入设施的权利）。

29.2　联合管理局和/或双方当事国应采取专门的产量检测程序，以确保就石油产量达成一致。

第三十条　监督权

30.1　联合管理局应自己或通过一个国家机构或第三方检查石油活动、相关设施和管道，并对区域内这些管道和设施上实施的作业进行监督。

30.2　联合管理局应决定依第 1 款开展活动时，监督人员所应遵循的认证程序。

30.3 如果当事国在检视后,认为区域内相关法律没有得到遵守,可书面通知要求联合管理局采取补救措施。

30.4 若经一方当事国要求,联合管理局未能或拒绝采取行动,当事国可以将问题提交委员会。

30.5 除非另有指令,在必要或紧急情况下,第1款所指的检查人员有权下令立即停止区域内任何或所有石油作业:

(a) 为避免可能导致丧失生命或危害生命的事故发生;

(b) 为避免遭受实际损害或损害危险;

(c) 为保护任一方当事国的海岸或其他海洋利益(包括渔业利益),免遭实际的或潜在的污染;

(d) 由于不可抗力灾害或预计会造成重大有害后果的紧急情况;或

(e) 将这种伤亡事故或其他事故的后果减至最小。

30.6 上述指示的内容和依据应该立即上报给董事会。

30.7 董事会随后应立即召开会议,考虑为安全快速地恢复作业应采取的必要行动。

第三十一条 石油联合经营

31.1 如果经钻探证实存在跨越区域和一方当事国专属海域的分界线的单一的地质石油构造或油田,而位于界线一侧的这种构造或油田可以从界线的另一侧进行全部或部分的开采,当事国应通知对方,考虑本条约第三条所确立的原则和分界线两侧石油量的比例,尽力在公平、合理的基础上对该构造或油田的联合开发达成协议。如果发出通知后在9个月内没有达成协议,应根据上述方法对这种构造或油田中开采出的石油做出公平合理的分配。若在钻探核实后当事方已经做出了合理的迅速通知,该分配应追溯到生产开始时。

31.2 如果经钻探证实存在跨越区域内合同区域分界线的单一的地质石油构造或油田,而位于界线一侧的这种构造或油田可以从界线的另一侧进行全部或部分的开采,委员会应依据最有效开发该石油构造或油田的原则和财政收入分配比例的方式,并且考虑本条约第三条所确立的原则和分界线两侧石油量的比例,促使双方达成协议。

31.3 如果经钻探证实存在跨越区域和第三国专属海域的分界线的单

一的地质石油构造或油田，而位于界线一侧的这种构造或油田可以从界线的另一侧进行全部或部分的开采，联合管理局有责任本着能够最有效开发该石油构造或区域的原则和财政收入分配比例的方式，并且考虑到分界线两侧石油资源比例、双方的权利以及第三条规定的分配原则，寻求与第三国达成协议。联合管理局与第三国达成的协议必须经过联合部长委员会的批准。

31.4 联合管理局应采取一切必要措施与承包商进行协商，以使上述第 1 款、第 2 款和第 3 款达成的协议得以生效。

31.5 据本条的规定，特殊制度区域应当被视为在开发区之外，且仅尼日利亚专属海域之内的区域。

第九部分　区域内的其他资源

第三十二条　区域计划中的非石油资源条款

区域计划可在联合管理局认为合适的范围或经委员会指令，为区域内非石油资源开发活动订立规则。

第三十三条　管理制度和税收制度

经区域计划要求或委员会认为适当时，联合管理局应制定并向委员会提交适用于开发区内非石油开发活动的管理和税收制度的建议书。

第三十四条　缺乏非石油资源开发活动的管理制度和税收制度时的安排

34.1 第三十三条的特殊制度缺失时，经委员会批准，当事国应运用本国专属经济区相关法律来管理开发区内本国国民的活动，但应避免将本国法律适用于另一方的国民。

34.2 双方当事国应依照本国法律，接受非本国国民在区域内从事非石油资源开发活动的申请，但应将申请立即通知对方当事国。如果对方当事国在一个月内未做出合理反对，收到申请的当事国可以根据本身情况决定申请结果。

34.3 尽管在第 2 款中受到另一当事国反对，如果收到申请的当事国认为该申请还是应该获得准许，应将申请提交委员会决定。

34.4 在处理本条款规定的申请时，双方当事国和委员会应考虑下列因素：

（a）本条约第三条设立的原则；

（b）联合国海洋法公约和其他相关的公约所规定的各项义务；

（c）对于海洋生物资源，委员会对有关期间区域内最大捕获量的规定。

34.5 依据本条中得到允许在区域内从事非石油资源开发活动的人，应依据有权当事国的法律和在其专属管理下，进行开发活动。

第三十五条 信息和检查

35.1 双方当事国应通过联合管理局，定期通知对方当事国本国国民和非本国国民提交的非石油资源开发活动申请的结果。

35.2 对依据本部分进行的开发活动的结果，联合管理局可要求提供进一步的信息。双方当事国应当遵守有关此项的合理请求。

第十部分 其他事项

第三十六条 雇佣和培训

36.1 为了以下目的，联合管理局应就开发区内承包商应遵守的雇佣和培训政策，制定指导方针：

（a）提高双方当事国国民的雇佣机会，并有效、安全地开展石油和其他资源开发活动；

（b）切实可行地协助双方当事国公平地分享雇佣和培训的利益。

36.2 开发合同的条款应遵守上述指导方针。

36.3 双方当事国应在移民管理和劳工法方面进行合作，为区域内开发合同所需的签证和工作许可证问题提供便利。

第三十七条 卫生和安全

37.1 联合管理局应采取一切合理措施确保开发活动从业人员的健康和安全，以及区域内石油设施和管道的安全，以及立即向委员会建议适用与离岸开发活动相关的卫生安全方面的法律、法规和方针。

37.2 双方当事国应根据联合管理局的建议，采用行政程序，以交换关于第1款涉及事项的信息。

第三十八条 污染的防治及海洋环境的保护

38.1 联合管理局应采取一切合理措施，以确保区域内石油活动不会也不可能引起或带来污染或其他危害海洋环境的风险。

38.2　依照第 1 款，双方当事国应根据联合管理局的建议，对预防和补救区域内开发活动造成海洋环境污染的必要措施和程序达成一致。

38.3　为促进对区域石油活动对环境影响的有效监督，双方当事国应定期向委员会提供，双方从其承包商或检查员处获取的，有关石油排放等级和污染程度的信息，特别是发生下述事件时，双方须立即报告联合管理局：

（a）任何石油泄漏或可能造成污染的类似事故，而且需要的补救措施超出运营者的能力范围；

（b）大量石油从装置或管道内向海洋排放；

（c）海上碰撞引发的装置或管道损坏；

（d）因不可抗力、危难或其他紧急情况，人员从设施上疏散。

报告应当包括已采取的措施，或根据事件情况建议采取的措施。

38.4　就实际损害或威胁，本条约不应损害一方当事国采取措施或双方当事国联合采取措施的权利，以保护各自海岸线或专属海域免遭污染或污染的危险，以免造成严重损害后果。

第三十九条　私法的适用

根据本条约第三条，在开发区内适用的私法未依据本条约或本条约的其他部分确定的情况下，联合管理局应当向委员会建议立即适用一方当事国的私法。

第四十条　刑法和刑事管辖权

40.1　根据本条第 3 款，一国国民或永久居民在开发区内的作为或不作为，应当适用其本国刑法，若一国的永久居民拥有另一方当事国国籍，将适用另一方当事国刑法。拥有双方当事国国籍的国民应适用两国的刑法。

40.2　非双方当事国永久居民的第三国国民，在区域内的作为或不作为应适用两国的刑法。若该国民依据另一国法律，已经经法庭审判、释放或宣告无罪，或因同一作为或不作为已受处罚，则该国民不得适用另一国的刑事程序。

40.3　双方当事国应互助和合作，包括通过适当的协议或安排，以实施本条款规定的刑事法律，包括获取证据和信息。

40.4　当被指控罪行的受害人是另一方当事国的国民时，每个当事国应承认另一当事国的利益,并在其法律允许范围内,把对该指控罪行采取的处罚通知另一方当事国。

40.5 一方当事国可做出安排,允许执行其本国刑法时由另一方当事国的官员协助。如果这种协助涉及另一方当事国按照本条款规定,拘留一个属于另一方当事国管辖的人时,则这一拘留只能进行到可以将此人转交给该当事国的有关官员为止。

40.6 本条不影响双方当事国行使刑事管辖权的任何基础。

第四十一条 遵守和实施

41.1 区域开发活动应遵照相关可适用的法律进行。

41.2 双方当事国应在其国家法律制度范围内,采取一切适当措施来实施可适用的法律。

41.3 双方当事国应提供一切必要合理的协助和支持,以确保承包商遵守可适用的法律。

第四十二条 民事和行政管辖

42.1 除非本条约另有规定,任一当事国可对开发区内与开发活动有关的事项,或者对实施开发活动的个人,行使民事或行政管辖权,如同该当事国在其专属经济区内对相关活动和人员行使管辖权一样。

42.2 在根据第1款行使管辖权时,双方当事国应实施相关可适用法律。

42.3 本条不损害任一当事国行使民事或行政管辖权的任何基础。

第四十三条 区域安全和治安

43.1 除非委员会有另行指示,双方当事国应为协议目的和各自防卫治安需要,在适当的情况下在区域内共同进行防卫或治安活动(治安活动是为了实施可适用法律)。这些活动的开支应该由双方当事国按照本条约第三条第1款规定的比例承担。

43.2 如果限于且仅限于任一当事国未能遵守第1款规定的义务,或拒绝参与共同防卫或治安活动,不影响另一方当事国可能有的任何其他权益,本条约将不禁止另一方当事国在其认为必须或适当时单独进行这些活动。

43.3 双方当事国应根据需求相互协商,以确保本条约得到高效有序的实施,和正在进行的和计划进行的开发活动的安全。

43.4 本条不损害任一当事国依据国际法开展的防卫或治安活动的基础。

第四十四条 审查适用的法律和执行安排

在必要的限度内,联合管理局有权随时向委员会对适用法律或执行安排提出修改建议。

第四十五条 第三国的权利

45.1 在依据本条约行使权利和权力时,当事国应当考虑其他国家依据普遍接受的国际法原则,在开发区内享有的权利和自由。

45.2 如果第三方提出,与当事国依据本条约享有的权利不相符的权利主张,当事国应当通过恰当的渠道协商解决。

第四十六条 与开发区有关的第三人地位

46.1 双方当事国间应以公平的方式解决,一方当事国在本条约谈判期间,在区域内的任何部分与第三人进行的先前交易(该交易已经向另一方当事国披露)引发的问题。

46.2 对于一方当事国在本条约谈判过程中,没有向另一方当事国披露的问题,应该由该当事国单方承担,但不影响为了解决开发区内,当事国与第三人先前交易引发的问题,另一当事国合作和帮助的权利。

第十一部分 僵局和争端的解决

第四十七条 联合管理局与私营企业之间争端的解决

47.1 联合管理局与承包商之间,或联合承包商与联合承包商之间,或联合承包商与经营者之间,就某个开发合同或运营协议解释和使用有关的争端,除非双方另有约定,应按照相关的开发合同或经营协议中事先规定的条款,提交商业仲裁。

47.2 除非双方达成其他一致,仲裁应依据联合国国际贸易委员会仲裁规则(UNCITRAL)在拉各斯进行,并由拉各斯的国际商业争端解决AACCL中心管理。

47.3 对依据第1款涉及仲裁的案件实质内容,管理局享有法庭诉讼的豁免权。

第四十八条 联合管理局或委员会工作中产生的争端的解决

48.1 考虑到本条约的目的和宗旨,第三条中所设立的原则以及双方当事国友好的兄弟关系的精神，本条约的运行引起的任何争端应由董事会解决。

48.2 董事会不能解决的争端，如果其会继续影响或有可能影响本条约实际的或未来的实施，该争端应提交委员会。

48.3 委员会应尽一切努力，本着折中的精神，在不损害双方当事国地位的前提下，解决争端。

48.4 依据第2款提交至委员会的争端，若在收到后12个月内，或者在国家元首决定的其他期限内，没有得到解决，委员会或任何当事方都可以将争端提交至国家元首，请求其做出决定。

第四十九条　国家间未解决争端的解决

49.1 第五十二条的规定应适用于下列情况：

（a）双方国家元首以书面方式承认，根据第四十八条向其提交的争端涉及的政策或行政问题，且在国家元首收到后12个月内，或者在国家元首同意的其他期限内，争端没有得到解决；或者

（b）根据下面第2款的仲裁程序，基于（无论明示或暗示）该争端涉及政策问题或行政问题的原因，没有解决双方之间的实质性争议。

49.2 对第1款（a）项以外的情况，若国家元首在接到依据第四十八条第4款向其提交的争端后，6个月内依然没有解决，除非双方达成其他一致，那么任何一方都可以通知对方将争端提交仲裁法庭。

49.3 仲裁法庭应以下述方式组成：

（a）双方当事国应在提交仲裁后60天内各指定一名仲裁员，在第二位仲裁员指定后60天内，两位仲裁员应指定一名第三国国民作为仲裁员，并担任仲裁法庭庭长；

（b）如果一方当事国在提交仲裁法庭后60天内未能指定一位仲裁员，或第二位仲裁员指定后60天内，两位仲裁员未能指定第三位仲裁员，任一方当事国可以请求国际法院院长来指定一名第三国国民作为仲裁员填补空缺；

（c）如果国际法院院长是一方当事国的国民或常住居民，或因其他原因无法指定仲裁员，则应由仅次于院长的、非为当事国国民的高级法官来指定；

（d）除非当事国另有约定，仲裁庭应当适用联合国国际贸易委员会仲

裁规则，此规则未规定的内容，由仲裁法庭根据自己的规则决定；

（e）在最终裁决之前，仲裁庭可根据任一当事国的请求，采取临时性措施来保证双方的权利或阻止争端的加剧和扩大；

（f）除非当事国另有约定，仲裁法庭应位于海牙，仲裁的管理当局为常设仲裁法庭的秘书处。

49.4 仲裁法庭的裁决是最终裁决，对双方当事国都具有约束力。

49.5 双方当事国应善意地执行仲裁法庭的所有裁决，包括临时措施在内的任何指令。对执行裁决的任何问题可以提交给仲裁法庭，若该仲裁法庭不再存在且不能重组，将根据本条第3款组成新的仲裁法庭。

第十二部分　生效和其他问题

第五十条　生效

50.1 本条约在双方当事国互换批准书后立即生效。

50.2 在互换批准文书后3个月内，任一当事国为了实施本条约必需的法律和法规，应在其法律框架内通过立法程序使其生效。此项法律或法规应当发送给对方当事国。

50.3 协议生效后，本条约应立即提交联合国秘书长登记。

第五十一条　期限和终止

51.1 双方当事国应在30年内审查本条约。除非另有协议或依据第五十二条终止，本条约应从生效之日起45年内有效。

51.2 如双方当事国同意，协议在45年后可继续有效。

51.3 除非另有协议，协议期满或终止不应影响终止期限晚于协定终止或期满日期的开发合同，仅为了管理合同和维持共同开发制度的目的，本条约的规定应在必要范围内继续有效。在最后一项合同期满或提前终止时，协议中的未决准备金也应立即终止。

51.4 相应的，除非双方当事国达成其他一致，委员会和联合管理局在协议期满或终止后，为了继续履行余下的开发合同，应继续行使必要的职能。

51.5 除非双方当事国达成其他一致，期满或终止不应影响在协议终止前双方当事国依据本条约享有的财政权利和义务。

第五十二条　在某些情况下终止的特殊规定

52.1 本条款适用于下列情况：

（a）属于第四十九条第 1 款规定的争端未解决的情形；

（b）一方当事国在根据第四十九条组成仲裁庭做出判决 180 天后，依然存在重大违约事实。

52.2 在第五十二条第 1 款（a）项的情形下，任一当事国可通知对方将于 6 个月之后终止协议。根据第五十二条第 1 款（b）项，受损害方可行使此项权利。

第五十三条 协议的语言

本条约以英语和葡萄牙语作成，两种文本具有同等效力。

本条约由各自政府授权的代表签署。

2001 年 2 月 21 日订于阿布贾。

尊敬的杜布姆·昂来雅	尊敬的乔丘姆·拉斐尔·布兰克
外交国务大臣	外交和合作部长
尼日利亚联邦共和国政府	圣多美和普林西比民主共和国政府

附录 特别制度区

1. 特别制度区如下：

（a）运用 WGS 84 基准，下面各点按顺序连接而成的线围成的类似三角形的海域：

A：北纬 3°00′28″　　　东经 6°57′16″

B：北纬 2°56′23″　　　东经 6°57′17″

C：北纬 2°56′22″　　　东经 6°43′27″

AB 和 BC 线是两条定向线段，AC 线沿着开发区边缘呈西北走向。

（b）其海床、底土和上覆水域。

2. 虽然本条约有任何其他规定，尼日利亚应该在协议有效期内，对特别制度区有排他性的管理权和管辖权，包括为其自身利益进行资源的开采和开发。

3. 尼日利亚将通过开展一些开发项目保障圣多美和普林西比的利益，这些项目将由单独的谅解备忘录规定，并为本条约的一部分。谅解备忘录的内容不损害两国间为加强合作在未来制定的其他安排。

2. Treaty between The Federal Republic of Nigeria and The Democratic Republic of São Tomé e Príncipe on the Joint Development of Petroleum and other Resources, in Respect of Areas of the Exclusive Economic Zone of the Two States

THE FEDERAL REPUBLIC OF NIGERIA

and

THE DEMOCRATIC REPUBLIC OF SÃO TOMÉ E PRÍNCIPE,

TAKING INTO ACCOUNT the United Nations Convention on the Law of the Sea done at Montego Bay on 10 December 1982 and, in particular, Article 74 (3) which requires States with opposite coasts, in a spirit of understanding and co‐operation, to make every effort, pending agreement on delimitation, to enter into provisional arrangements of a practical nature which do not jeopardize or hamper the reaching of final agreement on the delimitation of their exclusive economic zones;

FULLY COMMITTED to maintaining, renewing and further strengthening the mutual respect, friendship and co‐operation between their two countries, as well as promoting constructive neighbourly co‐operation;

ACKNOWLEDGING THE EXISTENCE of an area of overlapping maritime claims as to the exclusive economic zones lying between their respective territories ("the Area");

DETERMINED to pursue their common economic and strategic interests;

NOTING the possibility that petroleum and other resources may exist in the Area;

DESIRING to enable the exploration for and exploitation of those resources without delay and in an orderly fashion;

MINDFUL of the interests which their countries share as immediate neighbours, and in a spirit of co-operation, friendship and goodwill;

CONVINCED that this Treaty will contribute to the strengthening of the relations between their two countries; and

BELIEVING that the establishment of joint arrangements to permit the exploration for and exploitation of petroleum and other resources in the Area will further augment the range of contact and co-operation between the Governments of the two countries and benefit the development of contacts between their peoples;

HAVING DECIDED ACCORDINGLY TO CONSTITUTE by the present Treaty a Joint Development Zone for the Area, without prejudice to the eventual delimitation of their respective maritime zones by agreement in accordance with international law;

REAFFIRMING that the rules of international law will continue to govern questions not regulated by the provisions of this Treaty;

HAVE AGREED AS FOLLOWS:

PRELIMINARY

Article 1 DEFINITIONS

For the purpose of this Treaty:

1. "applicable law" means this Treaty, and the principles and rules of law applicable in the Zone by virtue of this Treaty;

2. "Authority" means the Joint Authority established by Part Three of this Treaty;

3. "Board" means the Board of the Authority, as referred to in Article 10;

4. "contract area" means a part of the Zone which is the subject of a development contract, but excluding areas which have been relinquished by the

contractor;

5. "contractor" means a party to a development contract other than the Authority;

6. "Council" means the Joint Ministerial Council established under Part Two of this Treaty;

7. "development activity" means any economic activity in or concerning the Zone, including petroleum activity, fishing activity, all other activities for the development or exploitation of other mineral or living resources of the Zone, and all forms of exploration and research relating to any of the foregoing;

8. "development contract" means any agreement (including leases, licences, production sharing contracts and concessions) from time to time entered into between the Authority and a contractor in relation to a development activity;

9. "exclusive maritime area" means any area of continental shelf or exclusive economic zone, outside the Zone, which pertains to one or other of the States Parties under international law;

10. "financial terms" includes all obligations in the nature of taxation (whether production or income based) and any other financial obligations including royalties, payments in kind, production sharing arrangements and resource rentals;

11. "fishing activity" means any activity concerning the harvesting and exploitation of the living natural resources of the Zone;

12. "installation" means any structure, device or artificial island utilised in development activities, installed above, in, on or under the seabed including drilling vessels in situ;

13. "national" means a natural or juridical person having the nationality of a State Party in accordance with the laws of that State Party;

14. "national body" means a Ministry or a governmental or quasi-governmental administrative or technical organ of a State Party responsible for activities in or in the waters of that State Party;

15. "operating agreement" means a contract concluded between two or more contractors for the purpose of carrying out development activities in the Zone;

16. "operator" means a contractor appointed and acting as operator under the terms of an operating agreement;

17. "petroleum" means:

(a) any hydrocarbon or mixture of hydrocarbons, whether in a gaseous, liquid or solid state, naturally occurring beneath the seabed; and

(b) any petroleum as defined by sub-paragraph (a) that has been returned to a reservoir; and

(c) any other minerals which are produced in association with them;

18. "petroleum activities" means all activities of exploration for and exploitation of the petroleum in the Zone;

19. "petroleum contractor" means a contractor in respect of a petroleum development contract;

20. "petroleum development contract" means a development contract relating to petroleum;

21. "pollution" means the introduction of substances or energy into the marine environment, including estuaries, which results or is likely to result in deleterious effects such as harm to living resources and marine life, hazards to human health, impairment of quality for use of sea water or reduction of amenity;

22. "Secretariat" means the secretariat of the Authority as referred to in Article 14;

23. "Special Regime Area" means the area more particularly defined in paragraph 1 of the Appendix;

24. "States Parties" means the Federal Republic of Nigeria and the Democratic Republic of São Tomé e Príncipe;

25. "Zone" means, subject to Article 5 and paragraph 5 of Article 31, the area of seabed and subsoil, together with the superjacent waters, established as a joint development zone under Article 2;

26. "Zone Plan" means the development plan or plans from time to time adopted by the Council, pursuant to Part Seven of this Treaty, for activities in the Zone.

PART ONE – THE JOINT DEVELOPMENT ZONE

Article 2 ESTABLISHMENT OF JOINT DEVELOPMENT ZONE

2. 1. The Zone is hereby established as an area of joint development by the States Parties in accordance with, and for the purposes set out in, this Treaty.

2. 2. The area covered by the Zone shall be as follows:

(a) the area of the sea which is bounded by geodesic lines joining the following points using the WGS 84 Datum in the order listed below; and

(b) the seabed, subsoil and the superjacent waters thereof.

DEGREES	MINUTES	SECONDS		DEGREES	MINUTES	SECONDS	
03	02	22	N	07	07	31	E
02	50	00	N	07	25	52	E
02	42	38	N	07	36	25	E
02	20	59	N	06	52	45	E
01	40	12	N	05	57	54	E
01	09	17	N	04	51	38	E
01	13	15	N	04	41	27	E
01	21	29	N	04	24	14	E
01	31	39	N	04	06	55	E
01	42	50	N	03	50	23	E
01	55	18	N	03	34	33	E
01	58	53	N	03	53	40	E
02	02	59	N	04	15	11	E
02	05	10	N	04	24	56	E
02	10	44	N	04	47	58	E
02	15	53	N	05	06	03	E
02	19	30	N	05	17	11	E
02	22	49	N	05	26	57	E
02	26	21	N	05	36	20	E

DEGREES	MINUTES	SECONDS		DEGREES	MINUTES	SECONDS	
02	30	08	N	05	45	22	E
02	33	37	N	05	52	58	E
02	36	38	N	05	59	00	E
02	45	18	N	06	15	57	E
02	50	18	N	06	26	41	E
02	51	29	N	06	29	27	E
02	52	23	N	06	31	46	E
02	54	46	N	06	38	07	E
03	00	24	N	06	56	58	E
03	01	19	N	07	01	07	E
03	01	27	N	07	01	46	E
03	01	44	N	07	03	07	E
03	02	22	N	07	07	31	E

2.3. The area covered by the Zone is depicted for illustrative purposes on the attached map. The Authority may for its purposes more accurately depict the boundaries of the Zone on a chart or charts of appropriate scale.

Article 3 PRINCIPLES OF JOINT DEVELOPMENT

3.1. Within the Zone, there shall be joint control by the States Parties of the exploration for and exploitation of resources, aimed at achieving optimum commercial utilization. The State Parties shall share, in the proportions Nigeria 60 percent, São Tomé e Príncipe 40 percent, all benefits and obligations arising from development activities carried out in the Zone in accordance with this Treaty.

3.2. No development activities shall be conducted or permitted in the Zone except in accordance with this Treaty.

3.3. The rights and responsibilities of the States Parties to develop the Zone shall be exercised by the Council and the Authority in accordance with this Treaty.

3.4. The petroleum and other resources of the Zone shall be exploited efficiently in accordance with this Treaty having due regard to the protection of the marine environment, and in a manner consistent with generally accepted good oilfield and fisheries practice.

3.5. Subject to paragraph 4, the Council and the Authority shall take all necessary steps to enable the commencement of exploration for and exploitation of the petroleum resources of the Zone as soon as possible after the entry into force of this Treaty.

Article 4   NO RENUNCIATION OF CLAIMS TO THE ZONE

4.1. Nothing contained in this Treaty shall be interpreted as a renunciation of any right or claim relating to the whole or any part of the Zone by either State Party or as recognition of the other State Party's position with regard to any right or claim to the Zone or any part thereof.

4.2. No act or activities taking place as a consequence of this Treaty or its operation, and no law operating in the Zone by virtue of this Treaty, may be relied on as a basis for asserting, supporting or denying the position of either State Party with regard to rights or claims over the Zone or any part thereof.

Article 5   SPECIAL REGIME

5.1. The provisions of this Treaty (except this Article, Articles 1, 2, 4, 50, 51, paragraphs 2 of Article 52 and the Appendix) shall not apply to the Special Regime Area, and references therein to the Zone shall be read and construed accordingly.

5.2. The Special Regime Area shall for the duration of this Treaty be administered in accordance with the provisions of the Appendix.

PART TWO: THE JOINT MINISTERIAL COUNCIL

Article 6   COMPOSITION OF THE COUNCIL

6.1. A Joint Ministerial Council for the Zone is hereby established.

6.2. The Council shall comprise not less than two nor more than four Ministers or persons of equivalent rank appointed by the respective Heads of State of each State Party.

6.3. The Council does not have separate legal personality.

6.4. Any member of the Council may by written notice to the Secretariat nominate a representative to participate on his or her behalf at one or more meetings of the Council. Subject to the specific terms of the nomination, every such representative shall be entitled, in the absence of the designating member, to exercise any power or function of that member as a member of the Council, including counting towards a Quorum.

6.5. The Executive Director acting as Secretary of the Authority shall also act as Secretary of the Council.

Article 7 MEETINGS AND DECISIONS OF THE COUNCIL

7.1. The quorum for a valid meeting of the Council shall be at least half the members, including at least one appointed by each of the States Parties.

7.2. The Council shall meet at least twice a year and as often as may be required, alternately in Nigeria and in São Tomé e Príncipe. The first meeting shall be held not later than 60 days after the entry into force of this Treaty.

7.3. Meetings shall be chaired by a member nominated by the host State Party.

7.4. All decisions of the Council shall be adopted by consensus.

7.5. The Council may establish its own procedures, including procedures for taking decisions out of session.

7.6. No decision of the Council shall be valid unless it is recorded in writing and signed by at least one member from each State Party.

Article 8 FUNCTIONS AND POWERS OF THE COUNCIL

8.1. The Council shall have overall responsibility for all matters relating to the exploration for and exploitation of the resources in the Zone, and such other functions as the States Parties may entrust to it.

8.2. The functions of the Council shall include the following:

(a) to give directions to the Authority on the discharge of its functions under this Treaty;

(b) to approve rules, regulations (including staff regulations) and procedures for the effective functioning of the Authority;

(c) to consider and approve the audited accounts and audit reports of the

Authority;

(d) to consider and approve the Annual Report of the Authority;

(e) to review the operation of this Treaty and to make recommendations to the States Parties on any matter concerning the functioning or amendment of this Treaty as may be appropriate;

(f) to approve development contracts which the Authority may propose to enter into with any contractor;

(g) to approve the termination of development contracts entered into between the Authority and contractors;

(h) subject to the provisions of paragraph 2 of Article 18, to approve the distribution to the States Parties of revenues or products derived from development contracts in the Zone;

(i) to consider and approve the annual budget of the Authority;

(j) to approve the opening of bank accounts by the Authority;

(k) to vary any time limit imposed upon the Authority under the terms of this Treaty;

(l) through consultation, to settle disputes in the Authority;

(m) to appoint the external auditors for the Authority and approve their remuneration.

8.3. Each of the States Parties shall have full access on request to all papers of the Council and the Authority.

8.4. The Council, its members and its Secretary shall be entitled to use the services of the Secretariat of the Authority as necessary for the discharge of their functions under this Treaty.

PART THREE: THE JOINT AUTHORITY

Article 9 ESTABLISHMENT, FUNCTIONS AND POWERS

9.1. The Authority is hereby established.

9.2. The Authority shall have juridical personality in international law and under the law of each of the States Parties and such legal capacities under the law of both States Parties as are necessary for the exercise of its powers and the performance of its functions. In particular, the Authority shall have the capacity to contract, to acquire and dispose of movable and immovable property and to institute and be party to legal proceedings.

9.3. The Authority shall be responsible to the Council.

9.4. Unless and until the Council otherwise decides, the seat of the Authority shall be at Abuja, Nigeria, with a subsidiary office in São Tomé, São Tomé e Príncipe.

9.5. The Authority shall commence functioning on entry into force of this Treaty.

9.6. The Authority, subject to directions from the Council, shall be responsible for the management of activities relating to exploration for and exploitation of the resources in the Zone, in accordance with this Treaty. In particular, the Authority shall have the following functions:

(a) the division of the Zone into contract areas, and the negotiation, tendering for and issue and supervision of contracts with respect to such areas;

(b) entering into development contracts with contractors, subject to the approval of the Council;

(c) oversight and control of the activities of contractors;

(d) recommending to the Council the termination of development contracts;

(e) terminating development contracts, subject to the approval of the Council;

(f) subject to paragraph 2 of Article 18, collecting and, with the approval of the Council, distributing between the two States Parties the proceeds or products of the Authority's share of production from development contracts;

(g) preparation of budgets of the Authority for submission to the Council. Expenditure shall be incurred in accordance with budgets or estimates approved by the Council or otherwise in accordance with regulations and procedures approved by the Council;

(h) controlling the movements into, within and out of the Zone of vessels, aircraft, structures, equipment and people;

(i) the establishment of safety zones and restricted zones, consistent with international law, to ensure the safety of navigation, petroleum activities, fishing activities and other development activities and the effective management of the Zone;

(j) issuing regulations and giving directions on all matters related to the supervision and control of operations, including on health, safety and environmental issues;

(k) the regulation of marine scientific research;

(l) preparation of Annual Reports for submission to the Council;

(m) inspecting and auditing contractors' books and accounts relating to development contracts, for any calendar year;

(n) making recommendations to the States Parties on any issues arising as to the applicable law, and on any changes to that law which may be necessary to promote the development of the resources of the Zone;

(o) the preservation of the marine environment, having regard to the relevant rules of international law applicable to the Zone;

(p) the collection and exchange of scientific, technical and other data concerning the Zone and its resources;

(q) the appointment and dismissal of technical and other staff of the Authority other than Executive Directors;

(r) requesting action by the appropriate authorities of the States Parties consistent with this Treaty, in respect of the following matters:

(i) search and rescue operations in the Zone;

(ii) deterrence or suppression of terrorist or other threats to vessels and structures engaged in development activities in the Zone; and

(iii) the prevention or remedying of pollution;

(s) consideration of matters from time to time specifically referred to it by the Council or by either State Party; and

(t) such other functions as may be conferred to it by the Council.

9.7. The working language of the Authority shall be English.

Article 10 THE BOARD

10.1. Subject to this Treaty and to any direction of the Council, the Authority shall be governed by a Board consisting of four Executive Directors. Two (and their replacements from time to time) shall be appointed by the Head of State of Nigeria from among Nigerian nationals of suitable qualifications and experience, and two (and their replacements from time to time) shall be appointed by the Head of State of São Tomé e Príncipe from among nationals of São Tomé e Príncipe, of suitable qualifications and experience. All such appointments shall be effected by notice in writing served upon the Head of the other State Party. Executive Directors shall hold office for such period as the appointing Head of State shall determine, normally for a period of six years once renewable or until a replacement is appointed.

10.2. Executive Directors may from time to time be assigned by the Council, on a three year basis, to head various departments of the Authority, including to act as Secretary of the Authority and Head of the Secretariat.

10.3. The Board shall meet on the request of the Council, either State Party or any Executive Director, or otherwise, as often as necessary for the discharge of its functions.

10.4. The quorum for a valid meeting of the Board shall be at least two Executive Directors, including at least one appointed by each State Party.

10.5. Decisions of the Executive Directors of the Authority shall be arrived at by consensus. Where consensus cannot be reached, the matter shall be referred to the Council.

10.6. Unless the Board otherwise decides, it shall meet at the seat of the Authority.

10.7. No decision of the Board shall be valid unless recorded in writing and signed by two Executive Directors, including at least one appointed by each State Party.

10.8. The personnel of the Authority shall be appointed by the Board under terms and conditions, approved by the Council, that have regard to the proper functioning of the Authority.

10.9. Unless the Council otherwise decides, it shall appoint one of the Executive Directors to act as Chairman of the Authority and of the Board, such appointments to be for a one year period.

10.10. Subject to this Treaty and to any direction of the Council, the Board may determine its own procedures.

Article 11 ACCOUNTABILITY

11.1. The Authority shall in all respects be responsible and accountable to the Council and shall comply with all directions from time to time given to it by the Council.

11.2. The Secretariat and all other administrative agencies or organs and technical or other committees of the Authority shall in all respects be responsible and accountable to the Board.

11.3. The Authority shall produce an Annual Report on its activities and on the progress made in the Zone, in accordance with any directions of the Council, and shall submit it to the Council for approval.

Article 12 PRIVILEGES AND IMMUNITIES

12.1. The Authority shall be immune from all forms of taxation in respect of its activities under this Treaty. This is without prejudice to the application of non–discriminatory fees or charges for services in respect of activities of the Authority on the territory of a State Party, to the extent that a national authority of that State Party would be subject to corresponding fees or charges in respect of equivalent activities.

12.2. The Authority shall be immune from the jurisdiction of any court or tribunal of a State Party except as concerns:

(a) commercial transactions entered into on the territory of the State Party in question, to the extent that such transactions are not subject to dispute resolution under Article 47;

(b) non–discretionary decisions which would be reviewable if they were made in equivalent circumstances by a national authority on the territory of the State Party in question.

12.3. The Executive Directors, officers and other personnel of the Authority who are nationals of one or other State Party shall be subject to taxation in respect of any remuneration for services performed under this Treaty only by the State

Party of their nationality, irrespective of where the services in question are performed.

12.4. A person who is a national of both States Parties shall be required to elect which of the two nationalities is to be treated as effective for the purposes of this Treaty.

Article 13   SUPPLY OF SERVICES

13.1. Subject to this Treaty and in accordance with the principles set out in Article 3, for the accomplishment of its functions, the Authority may use technical structures and other

services already existing in the States Parties. Different services may be requested from different entities.

13.2. The entities to which such delegation is made shall be accountable to the Authority.

13.3. The immunities of the Authority under paragraphs 1 and 2 of Article 12 shall apply to the activities of any entity exercising delegated functions under the present Article.

13.4. A delegation under paragraph 1 of this Article remains in force in accordance with its terms until it is revoked by the Board.

13.5. Any entity to which functions are delegated under paragraph 1 shall accept the secondment to its staff, at appropriate levels of seniority, of nominees of any State Party not already involved in the entity, for the purposes of training and exchange of information and expertise, and shall involve those persons to the fullest extent in the exercise of the delegated functions.

13.6. The number and placement of the persons referred to in paragraph 5 are subject to agreement between the States Parties, having regard to the extent of the functions to be performed and the needs for personnel development and training of the State Party not already involved in the entity.

13.7. Costs and other expenses, including personnel costs and expenses, incurred in the exercise of delegated functions, are reimbursable, subject to the terms and conditions agreed upon with the Authority.

13.8. The staff of or retained by the Authority (including the Secretariat) shall be selected on a basis which ensures that the maximum percentage of such staff who are nationals or residents of São Tomé e Príncipe does not exceed 40 percent.

PART FOUR: ADMINISTRATIVE SERVICES

Article 14   SECRETARIAT AND OTHER SERVICES

14.1. The Authority shall establish a Secretariat, headed by one of the Executive Directors as Secretary on a three year rotating basis, to carry out the administrative work of the Council and the Authority.

14.2. All appointments to the Secretariat shall be made, by the Board, within the limits and subject to any procedures laid down by the Council.

14.3. The officers and staff of the Secretariat shall be recruited on such terms as the Authority approves. Senior appointments shall be subject to approval by the Council. Such officers and staff may but need not be selected from amongst the officials or employees, or former officials or employees, of the government of either State Party.

PART FIVE: DUTIES OF PERSONNEL

Article 15   IMPARTIALITY AND CONFLICTS OF INTEREST

15.1. Members of the Board, officers and other staff of the Authority in their capacities as such shall have regard to the interests of the Authority alone, and shall act with impartiality and without favouring either of the States Parties at the expense of the other. This principle shall apply equally to a national body or other entity and its personnel in respect of the exercise by it of delegated functions under Article 13.

15.2. Unless otherwise expressly approved by the Council, no Executive Director, officer or other staff member of the Authority may have any direct or indirect financial interest in development activities in the Zone.

15.3. Executive Directors, officers and other staff members of the Authority shall, before assuming their functions, make a written declaration under oath, in a form approved by the Council, detailing any direct or indirect interest which might reasonably be considered to amount to a financial interest as referred to in paragraph 2.

Article 16　CONFIDENTIALITY

16.1. Members of the Board, officers and other staff of the Authority, as well as each State Party, shall treat the contents of all confidential papers and information produced or received for the purposes of or pursuant to this Treaty as confidential, and shall not further disclose or publish any such document or information without the authority of both State Parties or as the case may be of the other State Party.

16.2. No Executive Director or officer or other staff member of the Authority shall disclose, during or after the termination of their functions, any industrial secret or proprietary data which comes to the knowledge or into the possession of the Authority, or any other confidential information coming to his or her knowledge by reason of his or her holding a position in the Authority.

16.3. This Article does not derogate from any other obligation upon a person, or any remedy available to the Authority or to a State Party, in respect of any actual or potential breach of confidentiality.

PART SIX　FINANCE

Article 17　BUDGETS, ACCOUNTS AND AUDIT

17.1. The Authority shall be financed from revenues collected as a result of its activities. The States Parties shall advance such funds as they jointly determine to be necessary to enable the Authority to commence its operations.

17.2. All funds paid or payable to the Authority shall be held by the Authority in such accounts as it shall establish, in accordance with sub–paragraph 2 (j) of Article 8.

17.3. The Authority shall prepare and maintain full, proper and up–to–date accounts, balance sheets, budgets and cash flow projections, in accordance with good international accountancy practice and with any directions of the Council.

17.4. All costs and expenses from time to time incurred by the Council, the

Authority and their respective members and other personnel shall be paid by the Authority.

17.5. All such costs and expenses shall be subject to a budgetary and accounting system to be established by the Authority and approved by the Council within five months of the entry into force of this Treaty.

17.6. All budgets, costs and expenses, and in addition all other receipts and payments by the Authority, and all accounts of the Authority, shall be audited annually by external auditors approved by the Council.

17.7. Any shortfall in the approved budget for any accounting period shall be borne by the States Parties in the proportions Nigeria 60 percent, São Tomé e Príncipe 40 percent. Unless the Council otherwise decides, budgetary contributions under this paragraph shall constitute interest – free loans to the Authority, repayable as first charges on the surplus of the Authority in any subsequent accounting period.

17.8. The Authority shall comply with the budgetary procedures in force and shall make efficient use of its available resources.

Article 18 APPLICATION OF SURPLUSES

18.1. The Authority may with the approval of the Council establish such reserve funds as it considers prudent.

18.2. All surpluses of revenue over expenditure shall, after the establishment of such reserve funds, be promptly paid, without deduction or withholding, to the national treasuries of the States Parties in the proportions Nigeria 60 percent, São Tomé e Príncipe 40 percent, as shall any sum held in a reserve fund which is no longer required.

PART SEVEN THE ZONE PLAN

Article 19 PREPARATION AND APPROVAL OF THE ZONE PLAN

19.1. As soon as practicable following the entry into force of this Treaty the Authority shall meet in order to prepare an initial Zone Plan in accordance with the principles set out in Article 3, so as to establish ways in which the resources of the Zone may be developed in an efficient, economical and expeditious manner.

19. 2. For the purposes of paragraph 1, the States Parties have provided each other with all material information available to them in respect of economic activity, actual or prospective, within the Zone.

19. 3. The Zone Plan is subject to the approval of the Council, which may approve it with or without amendment or refer it back to the Authority with recommendations for further work or instructions for change.

19. 4. The Zone Plan as approved by the Council shall be published in an appropriate manner by the Authority and the States Parties.

19. 5. Matters which are not included in the Zone Plan shall be governed by this Treaty, or in the absence of any provision in this Treaty by decisions of the Council or supplemental agreement between the States Parties.

Article 20 PERIODIC REVIEW OF THE ZONE PLAN

20. 1. Unless otherwise directed by the Council, the Authority shall review and revise the Zone Plan at least every three years and submit any proposed revisions to the Council for adoption.

20. 2. Pending adoption of any revised Zone Plan the previously approved Zone Plan shall remain in force.

20. 3. Paragraphs 3 to 5 of Article 19 apply to any proposed or approved revision of the Zone Plan.

PART EIGHT REGIME FOR PETROLEUM IN THE ZONE

Article 21 REGULATORY AND TAX REGIME FOR PETROLEUM ACTIVITIES

21. 1. As soon as practicable following the entry into force of this Treaty and in any event within a three month period, the Authority shall prepare for the approval of the Council a regulatory and tax regime consistent with this Treaty, which shall be the applicable law relating to the exploration for and exploitation of petroleum in the Zone.

21. 2. Within six months of the entry into force of this Treaty, the draft regulatory and tax regime shall be adopted by the Council with such modifications as

the Council considers appropriate. By virtue of such adoption the regime shall (subject to Article 5) become legally applicable to petroleum activity throughout the Zone, and shall be enforced accordingly by the Authority.

21.3. Upon its adoption, the regulatory and tax regime shall be promptly published by the Authority.

21.4. The Council may at any time adopt such modifications as it thinks fit to the regulatory and tax regime so established, and any such modification shall immediately become legally applicable in the Zone and enforced by the Authority.

21.5. The Authority shall promptly publish every such modification to the regulatory and tax regime.

Article 22 CUSTOMS AND DUTY EXEMPTIONS

22.1. Petroleum equipment shall not be subject to any customs duties or other taxes and duties in respect of its import into, use in or export from the Zone unless and to the extent the Council otherwise decides. Nothing in this Article shall affect a State Party's rights in respect of export or import, following the completion of its use in the Zone of petroleum equipment having the territory of that State Party as its country of, respectively, origin or destination.

22.2. For the purposes of this Article "petroleum equipment" includes installations, plant and equipment (including drilling rigs) and any materials and other goods necessary for the conduct of petroleum activities in the Zone.

22.3. The shipment of petroleum extracted from the Zone to areas within the jurisdiction of the States Parties shall be free of all taxes and duties other than those provided for in the financial terms of the relevant development contract.

Article 23 GENERAL REGIME FOR PETROLEUM DEVELOPMENT CONTRACTS

23.1. No petroleum activities may be undertaken in the Zone other than pursuant to a petroleum development contract between the Authority and one or more contractors.

23.2. Unless the Council otherwise decides, and in accordance with procedures laid down by the Council for tendering, the principle of holding licensing rounds must be followed prior to the signature of any petroleum development contract.

Article 24 FINANCIAL REGIME FOR PETROLEUM DEVELOPMENT CONTRACTS

24.1. The financial (including fiscal) obligations of contractors to the Authority in respect of petroleum activities in the Zone shall be exclusively determined by the financial terms of petroleum development contracts approved under this Article.

24.2. In addition to the financial terms imposed by the regulatory and tax regime established pursuant to Article 21, the Authority may impose such other terms, not inconsistent with the foregoing, as it may formulate, having regard to the requirement to balance the following needs:

(a) to obtain optimum revenues for the Authority and through the Authority the State Parties from commercial exploitation of the resources;

(b) to encourage commercial exploitation and provide incentives for investment;

(c) to ensure clarity and certainty of operation;

(d) to ensure as far as possible that contractors' tax payments under the financial terms qualify for double taxation relief, including in third States;

(e) to ensure optimum utilisation of any fields wholly or partly within the Zone over the life of those fields.

24.3. The States Parties shall take all appropriate measures within their national legal systems to ensure that the financial terms are enforced.

24.4. Neither State Party shall tax development activities in the Zone or the proceeds deriving therefrom except in accordance with this Article. This does not affect the States Parties' rights to tax any profits arising from the processing or further treatment of petroleum beyond the initial treatment necessary to effect its sale as a raw Material.

Article 25 RIGHTS AND DUTIES OF CONTRACTORS

25.1. A contractor shall have exclusive rights to carry out the activities authorised under its respective petroleum development contract for the duration of the latter, subject to compliance with its terms and the applicable law.

25. 2. A contractor may dispose of any petroleum to which it is entitled under the relevant development contract, subject only to any non – discriminatory restrictions the Authority may impose on landing, identity of the purchaser and verification of the volumes concerned.

Article 26　EFFECT OF CANCELLATION OR SUSPENSION OF PETROLEUM DEVELOPMENT CONTRACTS ON CO – CONTRACTORS

26. 1. If following a contractor's default the Authority cancels a petroleum development contract held jointly by more than one contractor, the Authority shall offer a new contract for that area to any contractor (s) not in default, as far as possible on similar terms to those of the previous contract.

26. 2. The offer may be subject to:

(a) a requirement that the offeree (s) remedy any consequences of the default;

(b) the acceptance by the offeree (s) of a suitable replacement contractor identified by or acceptable to the Authority.

26. 3. This Article is without prejudice to any obligations to which the other contractor (s) may be liable under the original petroleum development contract.

Article 27　ASSIGNMENT OF CONTRACTORS' RIGHTS

A contractor's rights and obligations under a petroleum development contract shall not be transferred without the consent of the Authority. The Authority shall not unreasonably withhold its consent where the proposed transferee is financially and technically qualified and otherwise meets any requirements maintained by the Authority.

Article 28　OPERATIONS BY PETROLEUM CONTRACTORS IN THE TERRITORY OF THE STATES PARTIES OUTSIDE THE ZONE

Within the territory of either State Party petroleum contractors may acquire, construct, maintain, use and dispose of buildings, platforms, tanks, pipelines, terminals and other facilities necessary for petroleum activities in the Zone in accordance with the laws and regulations of the State Party concerned.

Article 29 ACCESS TO OPERATIONS

29. 1. In accordance with the principles of joint development set out in Article 3 each State Party is entitled to:

(a) the benefit of non-discriminatory consideration of its nationals' applications for petroleum development contracts;

(b) monitor, and be kept regularly informed as to the progress of, petroleum development activities in the Zone;

(c) obtain access to geological data, subject to obligations of confidentiality under Article 16 or otherwise;

(d) independently meter, monitor or inspect any petroleum activities (including the right of access to installations in order to carry out such metering, monitoring or inspection).

29. 2. The Authority and/or the States Parties shall adopt procedures in respect of metering production designed to ensure agreement on the quantities of petroleum uplifted.

Article 30 INSPECTION RIGHTS

30. 1. The Authority, acting either itself or through a national body or third party, shall have responsibility for the inspection of petroleum activities, related installations and pipelines pipelines, and for the supervision of operations carried out on such and pipelines installations situated in the Zone.

30. 2. The Authority shall decide upon the certification procedures to be followed by the inspectors carrying out the activities referred to in paragraph 1.

30. 3. Where, in the opinion of a State Party, it appears to it, following an inspection, that applicable laws are not being observed in the Zone, that State Party may by written notice request the Authority to remedy the situation.

30. 4. If the Authority fails or refuses to take action at such request by one of the States Parties, that State Party may refer the matter to the Council.

30. 5. Unless otherwise directed, the inspectors referred to in paragraph 1 may order the immediate cessation of any or all petroleum operations in the Zone if such a course appears necessary or expedient:

(a) for the purpose of avoiding an accident involving loss of life or danger to life;

(b) for the purpose of avoiding actual or threatened damage;

(c) to protect the coastline or other maritime interests of either State Party, including fishing interests, against actual or potential pollution;

(d) due to force majeure distress or an emergency which may give rise to reasonable fears of major harmful consequences; or

(e) to minimise the consequences of such a casualty or other accident.

30.6. The content of and justification for any such order must be reported immediately to the Board.

30.7. The Board shall thereafter meet promptly to consider the actions necessary for the safe and speedy resumption of operations.

Article 31　PETROLEUM UNITISATION

31.1. If any single geological petroleum structure or petroleum field exists, verified by drilling to extend across the dividing line between the Zone and an exclusive maritime area of one of the States Parties, and part of such structure or field which is situated on one side of the dividing line is exploitable, wholly or in part, from the other side of the said dividing line, either of the States Parties may give notice thereof to the other, whereupon the States Parties shall endeavour to reach agreement upon a fair and reasonable basis for the unitisation of such structure or field, having regard to the principles set out in Article 3 and the respective proportion of the petroleum located on each side of the dividing line. If such agreement is not reached within nine months following the giving of such notice, a fair and reasonable apportionment shall be made, having regard as aforesaid, of the petroleum to be taken from the structure or field. Such apportionment shall be with retrospective effect back to the start of production provided that the State Party which has given notice did so with reasonable promptitude after the verification by drilling.

31.2. If any single geological petroleum structure or petroleum field exists, verified by drilling to extend across the dividing line between any contract areas within the Zone, and the part of such structure or field which is situated on one side of the dividing line is exploitable, wholly or in part, from the other side of the said dividing line, the Council shall seek to reach agreement as to the manner in which the structure or field can most effectively be exploited and the manner in which the fiscal returns should be apportioned, having regard to the principles set out in Article 3 and to the respective proportion of the resource located on each side of the dividing line.

31.3. If any single geological petroleum structure or petroleum field exists, verified by drilling to extend across the dividing line between the Zone and an exclusive maritime area of a third State, and the part of such structure or field which is situated on one side of the dividing line is exploitable, wholly or in part, from the other side of the said dividing line, then the Authority shall consider whether to seek to reach agreement with the third State as to the manner in which the structure or field can most effectively be exploited and the manner in which the fiscal returns shall be apportioned, having regard to the respective proportions of the resource located on each side of the dividing line and, so far as concerns the rights of the States Parties, to the principles set out in Article 3. No such agreement with a third State shall be reached without the approval of the Council

31.4. The Authority shall take any necessary steps, in consultation with any contractors, to give effect to any agreement reached under paragraphs 1, 2 and 3.

31.5. For the purposes of this Article 31, the Special Regime Area shall be treated as if it were outside the Zone and exclusively within the exclusive maritime area of Nigeria.

PART NINE – OTHER RESOURCES OF THE ZONE

Article 32　PROVISION IN THE ZONE PLAN FOR NON – PETROLEUM RESOURCES

The Zone Plan may make provision for non – petroleum development activities within the Zone, to such extent as the Authority considers appropriate or the Council may direct.

Article 33　DEVELOPMENT OF REGULATORY AND TAX REGIME

As and when required by the Zone Plan or otherwise considered appropriate by the Council, the Authority shall prepare and submit to the Council proposals for regulatory and tax regimes applicable to non－petroleum development activities within the Zone.

Article 34 ARRANGEMENTS IN THE ABSENCE OF A REGULATORY AND TAX REGIME FOR NON－PETROLEUM DEVELOPMENT ACTIVITIES

34.1. In the absence of any special regime proposed under Article 33 and approved by the Council, the States Parties shall apply the provisions of their own laws relating to the exclusive economic zone to the activity of their own nationals in the Zone, but shall refrain from applying those laws to the conduct of persons who are nationals of the other State Party.

34.2. Each State Party may accept, in accordance with its own laws, applications by nonnationals to engage in non－petroleum development activity in the Zone, but shall forthwith inform the other State Party of each such application. In the absence of a reasonable objection from that State Party within one month, the State Party applied to may consider the application on its merits and decide upon it.

34.3. If the State Party applied to considers that, notwithstanding an objection under paragraph 2, the application ought nonetheless to be approved, it shall refer the application to the Council for a decision.

34.4. In dealing with applications under this Article, States Parties and the Council shall take into account:

(a) the principles set out in Article 3;

(b) their respective obligations under the United Nations Convention on the Law of the Sea and under any Convention in force related thereto;

(c) in the case of living marine resources, any determination by the Council of the allowable catch within the Zone for the period in question.

34.5. A person to whom permission to engage in a non－petroleum development activity in the Zone is given under this Article may carry out that activity, subject to the laws of the authorising State Party and to its exclusive administration.

Article 35 INFORMATION AND MONITORING

35.1. Each State Party shall, through the Authority, periodically inform the other of the outcome of applications made, whether by nationals or non-nationals, in respect of non-petroleum development activity in the Zone.

35.2. The Authority may request further information as to the consequences of development activities carried out pursuant to this Part. The States Parties shall comply with all reasonable requests in this regard.

PART TEN MISCELLANEOUS

Article 36 EMPLOYMENT AND TRAINING

36.1. The Authority may issue guidelines in respect of the employment and training policies to be followed by contractors in the Zone for the purposes of:

(a) enhancing the employment opportunities of nationals of the States Parties consistent with the safe and efficient conduct of petroleum and other development activities;

(b) assisting to the extent practicable the equitable division of employment and training benefits between the States Parties.

36.2. The terms of development contracts shall comply with such guidelines.

36.3. The States Parties shall co-operate in the administration of their immigration and employment laws so as to facilitate the issue of visas and work permits for the purposes of development contracts in relation to the Zone.

Article 37 HEALTH AND SAFETY

37.1. The Authority shall take all reasonable steps to secure the health and safety of personnel engaged in development activities and the safety of the installations and pipelines in the Zone, and shall promptly propose to the Council, for adoption as part of the applicable law, laws, regulations and guidelines for health and safety in relation to off-shore development activity.

37.2. The States Parties shall, on the recommendation of the Authority, adopt administrative procedures for the exchange of information concerning the matters referred to in paragraph 1.

Article 38 PREVENTION OF POLLUTION AND PROTECTION OF THE MARINE ENVIRONMENT

38.1. The Authority shall take all reasonable steps to ensure that development activities in the Zone do not cause or create any appreciable risk of causing pollution or other harm to the marine environment.

38.2. In accordance with paragraph 1, the States Parties on the recommendation of the Authority shall agree necessary measures and procedures to prevent and remedy pollution of the marine environment resulting from development activities in the Zone.

38.3. In order to facilitate the effective monitoring of the environmental impact of petroleum activities in the Zone both States Parties shall regularly provide the Authority with such relevant information as they obtain from contractors or inspectors concerning levels of petroleum discharge and contamination. In particular the States Parties shall immediately inform the Authority of the occurrence of the following events:

(a) any petroleum spillage or event likely to cause pollution and requiring remedial measures beyond the capacity of the operator;

(b) discharge into the sea of large quantities of petroleum from an installation or pipeline;

(c) collisions at sea involving damage to an installation or pipeline;

(d) evacuation of personnel from an installation due to force majeure, distress or other emergency.

The notification shall include any measures taken or proposed with respect to such events.

38.4. Nothing in this Treaty shall prejudice the taking or enforcement by each State Party or by the States Parties jointly of measures in the Zone proportionate to the actual or threatened damage to protect their coastline or exclusive maritime areas from pollution or threat of pollution which may reasonably be expected to result in major harmful consequences.

Article 39 APPLICABLE PRIVATE LAW

In accordance with Article 3, the Authority shall propose to the Council for immediate adoption as part of the applicable law, to the extent that the private law of the Zone is not determined by or pursuant to other parts of this Treaty, the private law of one of the States Parties.

Article 40　CRIMINAL LAW AND JURISDICTION

40.1. Subject to paragraph 3 of this Article a national or permanent resident of a State Party shall be subject to the criminal law of that State Party in respect of acts or omissions occurring in the Zone provided that a permanent resident of a State Party who is a national of the other State Party shall be subject to the criminal law of the latter State Party. A national of both States Parties shall be subject to the criminal law of both.

40.2. A national of a third State, not being a permanent resident of either State Party, shall be subject to the criminal law of both States Parties in respect of acts or omissions occurring in the Zone. Such a person shall not be subject to criminal proceedings under the law of one State Party if he or she has already been tried and discharged or acquitted by a competent tribunal or already undergone punishment for the same act or omission under the law of the other State Party.

40.3. The States Parties shall provide assistance to and co – operate with each other including through agreements or arrangements as appropriate, for the purposes of enforcement of criminal law under this Article, including the obtaining of evidence and information.

40.4. Each State Party recognises the interest of the other where a victim of an alleged offence is a national of that other State Party, and shall keep that other State Party informed to the extent permitted by its law of action being taken with regard to the alleged offence.

40.5. A State Party may make arrangements permitting officials of the other State Party to assist in the enforcement of the criminal law of the first State Party. Where such assistance involves the detention by the other State Party of a person who under the foregoing provisions of this Article is subject to the jurisdiction of the first State Party, that detention may continue only until it is practicable to hand the person over to the relevant officials of the first State Party.

40.6. This Article is without prejudice to any other basis for the exercise of the criminal jurisdiction of either of the States Parties.

Article 41　COMPLIANCE AND ENFORCEMENT

41.1. Development activities in the Zone shall be carried on in accordance with the relevant applicable law.

41.2. The States Parties shall take all appropriate measures within their national legal systems to enforce the applicable law.

41.3. The States Parties shall render all necessary and reasonable assistance and support in ensuring that contractors comply with the applicable law.

Article 42　CIVIL AND ADMINISTRATIVE JURISDICTION

42.1. Unless otherwise provided in this Treaty, each of the States Parties may exercise civil or administrative jurisdiction in relation to development activities in the Zone, or persons present in the Zone for the purposes of those activities, to the same extent as they may do so in relation to activities and persons in their own exclusive economic zone.

42.2. In the exercise of jurisdiction under paragraph 1, the States Parties shall give effect to the relevant applicable law.

42.3. This Article is without prejudice to any other basis for the exercise of civil or administrative jurisdiction by either of the States Parties.

Article 43　SECURITY AND POLICING IN THE ZONE

43.1. The States Parties shall to the extent from time to time appropriate having regard to the purposes of this Treaty and their respective defence and police needs, jointly conduct defence or police activities throughout the Zone (in the case of police activities for the purposes of enforcing the applicable law), except to the extent that the Council may from time to time otherwise direct. The costs of such activities shall be borne by the States Parties in the proportions set out in paragraph 1 of Article 3.

43.2. If and to the extent that either State Party shall fail to comply with its obligations set out in paragraph 1 or otherwise refuse to participate in proposed joint defence or police activities then without prejudice to any other rights the other State Party may have, nothing in this Treaty shall prevent that other State Party from separately carrying on such activities to such extent as it considers necessary or appropriate.

43.3. The States Parties shall consult with each other as required with a view to ensuring the effective and orderly enforcement of this Treaty and the security of the Zone for the purposes of development activities, ongoing or proposed.

43.4. This Article is without prejudice to any other basis for the conduct of defence or police activities which either State Party may have under international law.

Article 44   REVIEW OF APPLICABLE LAW AND ENFORCEMENT ARRANGEMENTS

The Authority may at any time recommend to the Council any changes in the applicable law or in the arrangements for its enforcement, to the extent that these may be necessary.

Article 45   RIGHTS OF THIRD STATES

45.1. In the exercise of their rights and powers under this Treaty, the States Parties shall take into account the rights and freedoms of other States in respect of the Zone as provided under generally accepted principles of international law.

45.2. If any third party claims rights inconsistent with those of the States Parties under this Treaty then the States Parties shall consult through appropriate channels with a view to coordinating a response.

Article 46   POSITION OF THIRD PERSONS IN RELATION TO THE ZONE

46.1. The States Parties shall co-operate with a view to resolving in an equitable manner as between themselves any issues arising in respect of prior dealings by either State Party with any third person in respect of any part of the Zone that have been disclosed to the other State Party in the course of negotiating the present Treaty.

46.2. However, in respect of any matter not disclosed by a State Party to the other State Party in the course of the negotiation of the present Treaty, it shall be a matter for the non-disclosing State Party alone, without any right to the co – operation or assistance of the other State Party, to resolve any issues arising in respect of prior dealings by it with any third person in respect of any part of the Zone.

PART ELEVEN   RESOLUTION OF DEADLOCKS AND SETTLEMENT OF DISPUTES

Article 47   SETTLEMENT OF DISPUTES BETWEEN THE AUTHORITY AND PRIVATE INTERESTS

47.1. Disputes between the Authority and a contractor or between joint contractors and/or operators concerning the interpretation or application of a development contract or operating agreement, shall unless otherwise agreed between the parties thereto be subject to binding commercial arbitration pursuant to the terms of the relevant development contract or operating agreement.

47.2. Unless otherwise agreed, the arbitration shall be held in Lagos pursuant to the UNCITRAL Arbitration Rules and administered by the AACCL Centre for International Commercial Dispute Settlement, Lagos.

47.3. The Authority shall be immune from suit in any court in respect of the merits of any dispute referable to arbitration in accordance with paragraph 1.

Article 48   RESOLUTION OF DISPUTES ARISING IN THE WORK OF THE AUTHORITY OR THE COUNCIL

48.1. Any dispute that arises with respect to the functioning of this Treaty shall be sought to be resolved by the Board having regard to the objects and purposes of this Treaty, the principles set out in Article 3 and the spirit of amicable fraternal relations between the two States Parties.

48.2. If a dispute cannot be resolved by the Board and its continuance affects or threatens to affect the actual or future implementation of this Treaty, it shall be referred to the Council.

48.3. The Council shall make every effort to resolve the dispute in a spirit of compromise, and without prejudice to any underlying position of either State Party.

48.4. If the dispute has not been resolved by the Council within 12 months of being referred to the Council under paragraph 2, or such other period as the

Heads of State may decide, the Council or either State Party may refer it to the Heads of State for their decision.

Article 49 **SETTLEMENT OF UNRESOLVED DISPUTES BETWEEN THE STATES PARTIES**

49.1. The provisions of Article 52 shall apply

(a) if the Heads of State agree in writing that a dispute referred to them under paragraph 48 concerns a matter of policy or administration and the dispute has not been resolved by the Heads of State within 12 months of its referral to them, or such additional time as they agree; or

(b) if arbitral proceedings under paragraph 2 below leave a substantial dispute between the parties unresolved by reason, either expressly or implicitly, of the fact that such dispute concerns a matter of policy or administration.

49.2. In any case not covered by sub-paragraph 1 (a), if the dispute has not been resolved by the Heads of State within six months of the reference under paragraph 4 of Article 48, and unless the States Parties have otherwise agreed, either State Party may give notice to the other State Party (the "referral") to refer the dispute to an arbitral tribunal ("the Tribunal") for resolution.

49.3. The Tribunal shall be constituted in the following manner:

(a) Each State Party shall, within 60 days of the referral, appoint one arbitrator and the two arbitrators so appointed shall within 60 days of the appointment of the second arbitrator appoint a national of a third State as third arbitrator who shall act as President of the Tribunal;

(b) If a State Party fails to appoint an arbitrator within 60 days of the referral, or the two arbitrators fail to appoint a third arbitrator within 60 days of the appointment of the second, either State Party may request the President of the International Court of Justice to fill the vacancy by appointing a national of a third State;

(c) If the President of the International Court of Justice is a national of or habitually resident in the territory of a State Party or is otherwise unable to act, the appointment shall be made by the next most senior judge of the Court who is not a national of either State Party and who is available to act;

(d) The Tribunal shall apply the UNCITRAL Rules, and on any point not covered by those Rules shall determine its own procedure, unless the States Parties have otherwise agreed;

(e) The Tribunal pending its final award may on the request of a State Party issue an order or orders indicating the interim measures which must be taken to preserve the respective rights of either State Party or prevent the aggravation or extension of the dispute;

(f) Unless the States Parties otherwise agree, the Tribunal shall sit at The Hague and the administering authority for the arbitration shall be the Secretariat of the Permanent Court of Arbitration.

49.4. Decisions of the Tribunal shall be final and binding on the States Parties.

49.5. The States Parties shall carry out in good faith all decisions of the Tribunal including any orders for interim measures. Any question as to the implementation of a decision may be referred to the Tribunal, or if the same tribunal is no longer in existence and cannot be reconstituted, to a new Tribunal constituted in accordance with paragraph 3.

PART TWELVE　ENTRY INTO FORCE AND OTHER MATTERS

Article 50　ENTRY INTO FORCE

50.1. This Treaty shall enter into force on the exchange of instruments of ratification by both States Parties.

50.2. Within three months of the exchange of ratifications, each State Party shall procure the enactment by its own constitutional processes of any legislation or regulations necessary to implement this Treaty in its legal system. The text of any such legislation or regulations shall be promptly forwarded to the other State Party.

50.3. Upon entry into force, this Treaty shall be registered with the Secretary-General of the United Nations.

Article 51 DURATION AND TERMINATION

51.1. This Treaty shall, be reviewed by the States Parties in year thirty (30), and unless otherwise agree or terminated pursuant to Article 52, shall remain in force for forty-five (45) years from the date of entry into force.

51.2. If the two States Parties agree, this Treaty shall be continued in force after the initial forty-five (45) year term.

51.3. Unless otherwise agreed, the expiry or other termination of this Treaty shall not affect development contracts with an expiry date after such expiry or other termination and the provisions of this Treaty shall remain in force for the sole purpose of administering such contracts and maintaining the joint development regime to the extent necessary. On the expiry or earlier termination of the last remaining such contract the outstanding provisions of this Treaty shall terminate forthwith.

51.4. Accordingly, unless the States Parties otherwise agree, the Council and the Authority shall, following expiry or other termination of this Treaty, continue to exercise such residual functions as may be necessary in respect of the continuing administration of existing development contracts, and shall continue in being for that purpose.

51.5. Unless the States Parties otherwise agree, such expiry or other termination shall not affect the financial rights and obligations of the States Parties accrued under or pursuant to this Treaty prior to expiry or termination.

Article 52 SPECIAL PROVISION FOR TERMINATION IN CERTAIN CASES

52.1. This Article applies:

(a) in any case of a dispute which falls under paragraph 1 of Article 49;

(b) in any case in which a State Party remains for more than 180 days in material breach of an award by a tribunal constituted pursuant to Article 49.

52.2. In the case referred to in sub-paragraph 1 (a) of this Article 52, either State Party may give six months notice of termination of this Treaty, and in the case referred to in subparagraph 1 (b) the aggrieved State Party may do so.

Article 53 LANGUAGE OF TREATY

This Treaty is executed in the English and Portuguese languages, both versions having equal authority.

IN WITNESS WHEREOF the undersigned, being duly authorised thereto by their respective Governments, have signed this Treaty.

Done at Abuja the 21st day of February 2001.

Hon. Dubem Onyia	Hon. Joaquim Rafael Branco
Minister of State for Foreign Affairs	Minister for Foreign Affairs and Cooperation
for the Government of	for the Government of
the Federal Republic of Nigeria	the Democratic Republic of São Tomé e Príncipe

Appendix

Special Regime Area

1. The Special Regime Area is as follows:

(a) The approximately triangular area of the sea which is bounded by lines joining the following points using the WGS 84 Datum in the order listed:

A   3°00′28″   N6°57′16″E
B   2°56′23″   N6°57′17″E
C   2°56′22″   N6°43′27″E

The lines from A to B and B to C being lines of constant bearing and the line from A to C follwoing the north – west edge of the Zone; and

(b) The seabed, subsoil and the superjacent waters thereof.

2. Notwithstanding any other provision of this Agreement, Nigeria shall throughout the duration of this Agreement tave the exclusive right to administer the Special Regime Area and exercise jurisdiction over it, including the right to exploit and develop its resources for its own benefit.

3. Nigeria will safeguard the interest of São Tome and Principe by undertaking some development projects, which will be governed by a separate Memoran-

dum of Understanding that will form an integral part of this Treaty. The provisions of this Memorandum of Understanding are without prejudice to any other arrangements in the future that will enhance the joint cooperation between the two countries.

3. 2003年《尼日利亚与圣多美和普林西比共同开发管理局石油法规》

黄文博译,邓妮雅校

鉴于尼日利亚联邦共和国与圣多美和普林西比民主共和国,为专属经济区之间重叠海域的共同开发已于2001年2月21日签订了条约,上述条约已于2003年1月16日互换批准文书,已经建立了共同开发管理局,条约第三条和第九条授权联合管理局对区域内资源勘探和开发有关的开发活动进行控制和管理,依据条约第二十一条第1款的规定及条约赋予的职能,联合管理局向联合部长委员会提交了两份草案,即《2003年石油法规》(即本文件)和《2003年税收法规》,这两项法案共同构成了开发区内有关活动的石油管理与税收制度。条约第二十一条第2款授予联合部长委员会,有权批准和采纳上述管理和税收制度,联合部长委员会依据条约第八条第2款(b)项的规定,批准并采纳上述两份草案。

2003年4月4日,上述两份文件在此再次被批准并被采纳。

第一部分 引言

第一条 简称与生效

本法规被命名为《2003年石油法规》,立即生效。

第二条 定义

基于本法规的目的和安排,作如下理解:

"可适用的法律"指条约和依据条约而在开发区内适用的原则与规则;

"条款"指条约的条款;

"桶"指容积为42美国加仑的桶;

"董事会"指条约第十条规定的联合管理局董事会;

"承包商"指除了联合管理局之外开发合同中的另一当事方；

"合同区域"指 OPL 区域或从 OML 派生的区域；

"委员会"指据条约第二部分建立的联合部长委员会；

"原油"指在被提炼或处理（排除水分或其他杂质）以前，以自然状态呈现的矿物石油；

"开发活动"指在开发区内或与开发区相关的任何经济活动，包括石油活动、渔业活动、开发区域内矿物或生物资源的所有开发或开采活动，以及所有与前述相关的所有形式的勘探和研究活动；

"开发合同"指在联合管理局与其他一方或多方当事人之间生效的，与任何与石油开发活动（包括非限制性租赁、许可、产品分享合同和特许权）相关的协定；

"勘探"与石油有关，指通过航空测量、表面地质学和地球物理的方法开展的一项前期调查，包括钻井和钻孔；

"财务安排"包括所有税务性质的义务（不论基于产出还是收入）和其他一切财务义务，包括特许权使用费、实物偿付、产品分享安排和资源租金；

"在公报上发表"指在双方当事国政府公报上发表，并/或管理局认为合适的，在当事国的其他刊物上发表；

"设施"是指安装在海床上方、内部、表面或下方的用于进行开发活动的任何建筑物、设备或人工岛屿，包括就地安置的钻探船；

"共同开发管理局"或"管理局"指依据条约第三部分建立的联合管理局；

"共同开发区"或"开发区"指第五条和第三十一条第 5 款规定的，依据第二条所建立的共同开发区域，包括海床、底土及其上覆水域；

"租约"指石油采矿租约（OML）；

"承租人"指持有石油采矿租约的承租人，但对于产品分享合同，产品分享合同的承租人将被根据本法规第九条第 3 款和第九条第 4 款的规定的持有人所替代；

"许可"指一项勘探许可（EL）或一项石油勘探许可（OPL）；

"许可证持有人"指持有 EL 或 OPL 的人，但对于产品分享合同，产品分享合同的承包商将被根据本法规第九条第 3 款和第九条第 4 款的规定的持有人所替代；

"国民"指根据双方当事国法律,拥有一方当事国国籍的自然人或法人;

"国家机构"是指对其领土或水域的活动负责的,当事国的一个部门、官方或半官方的行政或技术机构;

"天然气"指从钻孔或钻井中获取的,主要由石油碳氢化合物组成的气体;

"OML"或"石油采矿租约"指第八条规定的石油采矿租约;

"开放面积"指在特定时间内不属于 OPL、OML 或 PSC 区域的面积;

"运营协议"是指由两个或两个以上承包商,为在区域内进行开发活动而缔结的合同;

"运营者"是指由运营协议指定并担任运营方的承包商;

"OPL"或"石油勘探许可"指第七条规定的石油勘探许可;

"石油"是指:

(a) 任何在海底自然生成的碳氢化合物或碳氢化合物的混合物,不论其为气体、液体或固体;

(b) 以上 (a) 所界定并被返还于油层的任何石油;以及

(c) 与上述多种物质产生的所有其他矿物;但不包括煤或其他可通过干馏提取的石油成层矿藏;

"石油活动"指开发区内所有勘探和开发石油的活动;

"石油承包商"指石油开发合同的一方当事人;

"石油开发合同"指有关石油的开发合同;

"污染"是指进入海洋环境(包括港湾)的物质或能源,这些物质会造成或可能造成对生物资源和海洋生物的损害,危害人类健康,损害海水的利用质量或者降低舒适度;

"勘探"与石油有关,指通过各种地质学和地球物理学方法所做的各项调查,包括钻井和地震工作;

"PSC"指第九条规定的产品分享合同;

"PSC 合同方"指除了管理局或其附属机构外,PSC 中的一个或多个缔约方;

"法规"是指本文件规定的条款,包括法规所允许的安排,也包括根据《尼日利亚联邦共和国与圣多美和普林西比民主共和国关于共同开发两国专属经济区石油资源和其他资源的条约》第二十一条第 4 款之规定得以通过而生效的修改，以及其他所有此类修改；

"租金"指对依据本法规授权的许可，按年度或按其他期限收取的费用；

"安排"指对本法规的安排；

"签约定金"指投标协议的受让人在签署协议时支付的资金；

"当事国"指尼日利亚联邦共和国与圣多美和普林西比民主共和国，以及法案中规定的两国领土；

"投标协议"指第十条第2款规定的协议；

"条约"指2001年2月21日双方当事国签订的，关于共同开发两国专属经济区的石油及其他资源的条约；

"区域计划"是指依据《尼日利亚联邦共和国与圣多美和普林西比民主共和国关于共同开发两国专属经济区石油资源和其他资源的条约》第七部分达成的或由委员会采用的，为区域内活动指定的开发计划。

第二部分 许可、租赁与合同

第三条 一般条款

3.1. 除非依据和遵守法规的许可、租赁与合同条款，否则不得在开发区内开展任何石油活动。

3.2. 共同开发区的总面积，包括依据石油勘探许可和所有石油采矿租约获得的面积，应当由共同开发管理局代表当事国进行确定。

3.3. 共同开发管理局：

（a）应当对本法规授予的所有与许可、租赁和合同有关的事项进行全面监管；

（b）为了监督经营活动的开展和法案的实施，监督本法规授予的许可或租赁项下的规定和条件，共同开发联合管理局应当能够随时进入勘探许可、石油勘探许可和石油采矿租约所涉及的区域，以及本法和其他法律规定的设施；

（c）书面通知本法规授予的许可证或租赁的持有者，以及任何为这些持有者工作的合同方（或任何服务人员或持有者的机构或合同方），在适合的时间和地点出现，以通知他们关于许可、租赁或合同运营相关的信息，所有出席的人员均应遵守此项通知，并通报相关信息；

（d）书面指令本法规授予的许可、租赁或合同持有者，为避免对生命或财产造成威胁，而暂停相关运营活动；

（e）指令任何经营者在不符合良好石油领域实践行事的情况下，停止经营行为；

（f）书面指令暂停任何违反或可能违反本法规或其他规范的经营行为；

（g）应当有逮捕的权力。

第四条 划分开发区块

4.1. 为了促进开发区内石油开发活动的许可，管理局应将开发区划分为若干合适的区块，以便授予第七条规定的石油勘探许可。每一区块应标明识别数字。

4.2. 除了为了与开发区边界线应保持必要的一致，每一区块的界线应这样划定：经线参照格林尼治子午线，以五分的整数倍划定，纬线参照赤道，以五分的整数倍划定。

4.3. 前述规定不影响第五条第 6 款的规定。

第五条 许可、租赁和产品分享合同

5.1. 根据本法规规定并经委员会批准，管理局可授予：

（a）一项勘探许可（EL）；

（b）一项石油勘探许可（OPL）；

（c）一项石油采矿租约（OML）；

（d）产品分享合同（PSC）。

5.2. 勘探许可包括获得投机性质的地质勘探。

5.3. 除非委员会另有指令，EL、OPL、OML 和 PSC 应仅被授予：

（a）在尼日利亚或圣多美和普林西比成立的公司，或依尼日利亚或圣多美和普林西比法律成立的公司；或者

（b）依据在尼日利亚或圣多美和普林西比法律，在该国注册的公司。

5.4. 在 OPL 或 OML 有效期间，区块内的活动应受许可证或租赁以及石油分享合同项下的条款规范。

5.5. OPL 和 OML 所包含的区域，应当由第四条规定的一系列坐标（经度与纬度）标明，形成一个紧凑的完整区块。

5.6. 若从 OPL 中创设一项 OML，管理局应该重新指定区块，以创设一个与 OML 区域完全一致的区块。

5.7. 如果在许可或租约中规定允许退回或放弃相关区域的一部分，这种退回或放弃应当使得剩余部分，正如本条第 4、5 款所规定的那样，构成完整区块；并且在向管理局提出退回或放弃申请之前，被许可人、承租人或者承包人应当就剩余区域的形状和面积获得管理局的事先同意。

第六条 勘探许可

6.1. 一项勘探许可证持有者，有在许可区域内获取投机性地质勘查资料的权利。勘探许可另有明确保留，在任何区域内授予一项勘探许可不应排除在相同区域或其他部分授予其他许可或租赁。

6.2. 一项勘探许可的期限、终止及更新由许可证项下条款规制。

6.3. 一项勘探许可不应授予一项 OPL 或一项 OML 授予的权利。

6.4. 许可证持有人依据一项勘探许可开展活动，应当受一位有资历的人员的持续监督，并且监督的执行应让管理局满意。

第七条 石油勘探许可

7.1. 一项石油勘探许可（OPL）的许可证持有人在许可区域内有排他性的勘探和探查的权利。OPL 的许可证持有人可运输或处置，依 OPL 项下条款而获得的石油，并应全面履行 OPL 条款、本法规及石油税法规，或其他适用的法规的义务。

7.2. OPL 的最长期限为 8 年。这一年限可被划分为若干子期间，并与相应的 PSC 的规定保持一致。

7.3. OPL 的许可证持有者，至少在许可届期前 6 个月内，有权向管理局书面申请续期。

第八条 石油采矿租约

8.1. 一项石油采矿租约（OML）使承租人在租赁区域内对出口或发现石油享有排他性的勘探、生产和运输的权利。

8.2. OML 的期限不超过 20 年，但可根据相应的 PSC 续期。

第九条 产品分享合同

9.1. 经联合部长委员会批准，管理局可签订 PSC。管理局仅能与在尼日利亚或圣多美和普林西比成立或注册的公司，签订该 PSC。

9.2. 根据下面的第九条第 3 款，一项 PSC 应依据其条款授予承包商在 OPL 区域内，开展石油活动的排他性权利和义务。

9.3. 在 PSC 终止之前，每一承包商都应遵守管理局的指令，根据本法规遵守和履行与相关的许可或租赁有关的所有义务，遵守相关法律法规（包括但不限于当前的法规以及许可或租赁条款）。

9.4. 每一 PSC 应包含承包商对管理局的明确保证，保证遵守并行使所有义务，若保证条款缺失，此种保证应为 PSC 隐含之义务。

9.5. 任何时候，与 PSC 相关的任何许可或租赁，若发生重大事件，不论是否违背此项许可或租赁或相关的 PSC 条款，管理局都有权依据本法规或其他条款采取行动，或采取措施，以对抗许可证持有者、承租人或承包商。管理局也可根据本条规定，采取相同或相应行动，或采取相同或相应的步骤，以对抗 PSC 承包商。

9.6. 除非联合部长委员会做出相反同意，除了依据第十条规定的，遵守许可竞标相关联的竞标程序以外，管理局不得签订 PSC。

9.7. 联合部长委员会批准的 PSC 样本，构成管理局签订的 PSC 的基础。

第十条　许可与投标程序

10.1. 所有投标协定应按照如下第十一条至第十五条之规定，遵守许可的竞标程序。

10.2. 本条"投标协定"指：

（a）由管理局持有的 OPLs 所授予的 PSCs；

（b）根据第十六条第 2 款规定而授予的 OMLs。

第十一条　投标邀请书

11.1 招标程序，应首先由管理局发布招标邀请书。邀请书应详细说明如下事项：

（a）区块或区块内授予的权利；

（b）适用的投标体系；

（c）评价投标的基础；

（d）将签订的投标协定的细节，包括的双方权利义务；以及

（e）申请的期限。

11.2. 邀请书的所有细节，应在双方当事国国家日报上公布，或以管理局决定的其他方式公布。

11.3. 管理局可向预期的投标者提供整套招标书，并收取一定费用（整套招标书费或申请费），也可收取对整套招标书的评标费（手续费）。

第十二条 对申请者的审查

12.1. 在宣传相关的投标时，投标协定应符合管理局公布的标准。

12.2. 管理局应对投标制订正式的指导方针。这些方针将特别包括审查申请者的依据和申请者应当满足的相关标准。

12.3. 管理局应依法规规定，对面积报价制订指导方针，并经联合部长委员会批准。此方针在被管理局修改或替换前应一直适用。

12.4. 审查申请者的主要原则标准应是技术能力和经济能力、工作计划承诺和拟议的签约定金。

12.5. 管理局满意的投标协议授予的条件应为，申请者应当具备必要的经济能力和必要的技术知识与能力，符合投标协定、本法规及其他法律规定的条件和要求，以进行石油活动。

第十三条 竞标申请形式

13.1. 每一份竞标协议的申请应以适当的书面形式提交给管理局，并附有整套招标书。

13.2. 每一份申请书应附带如下内容：

(a) 第二十三条规定的手续费（此项费用在任何情况下不退还）；

(b) 申请者的资金状况和技术能力的证明材料；

(c) 申请者准备实施的工作详情或招标方承担最小责任的方案；

(d) 申请者提供的签约定金；

(e) 申请者在申请区域内拟支出的年度开销明细；

(f) 在相关的投标协定授权后开始运营的日期；

(g) 对当事国国民进行雇佣和培训的详细计划；

(h) 申请者在此前三年的石油勘探和生产活动的年度报告；以及

(i) 管理局以通知或其他方式要求提供的其他信息。

13.3. 申请者应根据管理局的要求，就第十三条第2款规定的内容提供更多证明信息。

第十四条 申请的撤回

经书面通知管理局，申请者可随时撤回投标协议申请。

第十五条 投标协定的授予或否决

15.1. 管理局应就与成功申请者或申请团达成投标协定获得委员会的事先批准。

15.2. 经批准，管理局应当向成功申请者（或申请团）提供书面要约，要约应特别载明签订投标协定的条款和条件。

15.3. 收到要约的申请者应在管理局发出要约的15日内，以书面形式决定接受或拒绝要约。若在此期限内没有表示接受，则该要约自动失效。

15.4. 投标协议达成之前双方应满足相关的条件，以及符合第十五条第2款中要约规定的限制和其他规定，则管理局与申请者可达成投标协议。

15.5. 与管理局达成一项投标协议的承包商，应自协议签订之日起30日内支付签约定金。

15.6. 若申请者在30日内未能支付签约定金，则依据第十五条第4款，协议自动终止。

第十六条 OPL转换为OML

16.1. 一项OPL可被授予OPL的许可证持有人，该许可证持有人应：

（a）满足OPL的所有规定和条件，本法规或其他适用的法律法规规定的所有其他要求；

（b）发现了大量具有商业价值的石油，并获得管理局认可。

16.2. 若一项OML因废除、放弃或其他原因而终止，不论是部分或全部终止，在此情况下，管理局要在参照第十一条至第十五条规定的基础上，通过管理局的招标程序，授予一项新的OML。

第十七条 许可、租赁及PSCs的公布

管理局应当在公报上刊载所有ELs、OPLs、和OMLs的授权和续期，以及签订的PSCs。管理局也应当在公报上刊载所有放弃、终止、撤销及分配事项，并附上持有者名称及相关区域的位置。

第十八条 投标协议登记簿的持有与监督

管理局应当持有本法规中投标协议的登记簿，并列明如下事项：

（a）每个投标协定生效的区域；

（b）每个投标协定的协议双方、各自的参股权益和运营者（如果有的话）；

（c）运营者（如果有的话）或/和当事方相应参股权益的变动；

（d）让渡或放弃的区域；

（e）运营者（如果有的话）和其他当事方的名称及地址的变动。

第十九条　申请分配

19.1. 未经管理局及委员会的事先同意，投标协议的持有者不得分配其协议，或协议项下的任何权利、权力或利益。

19.2. 依据本条规定申请分配需交纳规定的费用，缴纳这种费用和/或保费后，管理局可根据其决定的条款和条件同意进行分配。在特殊情况下，若分配至公司组中的一个公司，且分配者属于公司组成员，管理局可放弃收取这种费用或/和保费。

19.3. 管理局不应同意一项分配，除非其满足以下条件：

（a）拟被分配人有良好的信誉，或者是信誉良好的公司组中的成员，或者其所有者是信誉良好的公司；

（b）拟被分配人（通过其自身财产，或通过其所属公司组的其他公司，或其他）具有充足的技术知识、经验、资金，可以确保其高效地开展依据相关协定所分配的项目，并得到管理局的认可；

（c）拟被分配人获得管理局和委员会的接受。

第二十条　OPL 或 OML 的终止

20.1. OPL 或 OML 的持有者，在任何情况下，经书面通知管理局，可终止 OPL 或 OML。终止前通知的时限，OPL 不得少于 6 个月，OML 不得少于 12 个月。

20.2. 若根据前项规定做出通知，不退还已支付的租金，并且终止不影响 OPL 或 OML 在终止前施加的或其项下规定的或与之相关的责任或义务。

第二十一条　OPLs 和 OMLs 的撤销

21.1. 若许可证持有者、承租人或 PSC 承包商具有如下情形，则管理局可撤销 OPL、OML 或 PSC：

（a）没有按照良好的石油行业实践，积极地、高效地、连续地开展运营活动；或

（b）不遵守本法规或其他规定或指令，或者不履行许可证项下或租赁条款规定的义务；

（c）在本法规规定的时限内，未交纳到期租金或特许权使用费，不论管理局是否做出此种要求；

（d）不提供管理局依法要求提供的运营报告。

21.2. 管理局应当通知许可证持有者、承租人或 PSC 承包商撤销的理据。若管理局认为必要，可邀请许可证持有者、承租人或 PSC 承包商做出解释。

21.3. 若管理局认可上述解释，管理局可要求许可证持有者、承租人或 PSC 承包商在特定时间内对所诉问题做出改进。

21.4. 管理局可撤销许可、租赁或 PSC，如果：

（a）许可证持有者、承租人或 PSC 承包商未做解释或所做解释不充分；

（b）未在特定时期内对所诉问题做出改进。

21.5. 若许可、租赁或 PSC 被撤销，则管理局应向许可证、承租人或 PSC 承包商最后提供的地址，或向其在尼日利亚或圣多美和普林西比的法定代表人，充分告知撤销许可证、租赁或 PSC 的相关事项，并在报上刊载。

21.6. 撤销不影响许可证持有者、承租人或 PSC 承包商的任何责任，也不影响其对管理局做出的任何主张。

第三部分　费用、租金和特许权使用费

第二十二条　费用、租金和特许权使用费

22.1　应根据第二十三条第 1 款和第 2 款的规定，支付许可，费用与租金。

22.2　应当依据第 23 条之规定，即根据相关许可或租约的具体期限和条件而确定的不同比例支付特许权使用费；或者根据管理局作为代表发出通知，要求以实物的形式支付而确立的具体比例，来支付特许权使用费。

第二十三条　费用、租金和特许权使用费的比例

23.1. 在其他费用做出规定前，应支付如下费用（以美元为单位）：

（a）OPL（整套招标书）申请费：$ 15000

（b）OPL 申请手续费：$ 10000

（c）OML 申请费：$ 1000000

（d）申请对 OPL 或 PSC 的资助：$ 500000

（e）申请对 OML 或 PSC 的资助：$ 1000000

（f）申请终止 OPL、OML 或 PSC：$ 100000

（g）申请许可运营钻探设备费：$ 100000

（h）许可运营钻探设备费（按年计）：$ 50000

（i）输出用作分析费的样本许可费（按井数计）：$ 10000

23.2. 以下是 OPL 或 OML 应交纳的年租金，除非许可或租赁协议另有声明：

（a）对 OPL，每平方千米或每等份：$ 200

（b）对 OML，每平方千米或每等份

（i）在前 10 年间：$ 500

（ii）10 年后：$ 200

23.3. 许可证持有者、承租人或 PSC 承包商应向管理局缴纳，在开发区相关期内生产原油和套管溶剂油所需的特许权使用费。除非管理局另有指令，该特许权使用费应在每一季度的最后一个月内缴纳（包括许可或租赁生效的季度）。

23.4. 在共同开发区内开发天然气，不需缴纳特许权使用费。

23.5. 在共同开发区内，对原油和套管溶剂油生产缴纳的特许权使用费，应根据如下递进表收取：

P < 20　　　　　　　　R = 0

20 ≤ P ≤ 70　　　　　　R = 5% {1 − [（70 − P）／（70 − 20）]}

P > 70　　　　　　　　R = 5

其中，P 代表产量（千桶/天），R 代表特许权使用费率。

23.6. 因特许权使用费而引发的争端，在争端解决之前应足额缴纳数额。

第四部分　运营和生产许可证持有者、承租人和承包商的权利与义务

第二十四条　许可证持有者、承租人和承包商的权利

24.1. OPL、OML 或 PSC 持有者应当有权进入或保有许可区域或承租区域，并行使许可或租赁授予的类似权利。

24.2. 根据法律和管理局的书面批准，许可证持有者、承租人和承包商依据本法规，对如下事项享有包括建造、携带、保持、更换、运营、拆

除或移除的权力和权利：

（a）装置，包括钻井平台、引擎、动力装置、流水线、储油罐、装货码头、起重机；

（b）通信工具，包括电话线路和无线电台；

（c）船舶和航空设施；

（d）许可证持有者、承租人和承包商为雇员和工作人员提供的居住舱和便利设施；

（e）其他设施、工程、动产和财物。

24.3. 许可证持有者、承租人和承包商可通过其机构或独立承包商行使权利或权力（遵守且不影响第九条第3款的规定），其机构或独立承包商应向管理局负责。

第二十五条 保留

25.1. 管理局或其授权的人员，除了许可或租约已授予被许可人或承租人的事项外，可以基于任何目的，有权进入相关区域从事调查、钻探和开采活动，并可以获得除石油以外的任何物质。

25.2. 本法规授予的权力不应阻碍或影响，或允许任何人或任何机构，阻碍或影响许可证持有者、承租人和承包商的权利和权力。

第二十六条 捕鱼权

若许可证持有者、承租人和承包商，行使许可、租约或合同授予的权利，若对管理局或一方当事国授予的捕鱼权造成不合理的干扰，则应对此行使上述权利造成的人身伤害给予充分赔偿，数额由管理局确定。

第二十七条 监督权

管理局任命的任何人，有权在合理时间进入许可证持有者、承租人和承包人开发区的任何区域，或任何地点、经营场所、建筑，或开发区外的营业处所，以在相关区域开展如下活动或为该活动提供便利：

（a）检查或核实法规授予许可证持有者、承租人和承包商的执行、安装、建造或占有的一切事项；

（b）监督并摘录或复印法规要求许可证持有者、承租人和承包商制定或持有的日志、记录、地图、账户或其他资料。

第二十八条 赔款

许可证持有者、承租人和承包商在任何情况下，应对第三方对与本法规有关的行为或事情，所做出或产生的行动、费用、指控、主张和要求做出赔偿，并使管理局及其官员和雇员（包括其机构）免受其责。

安全与安全保障

第二十九条 航行安全

被许可人、承租人或承包人所建立的任何工程或设施，应当以一种在任何时候和任何条件下可以为相关区域的船舶航行预留安全便捷的航道的方式，进行建设、安装、标识、设浮标、配备和维护；在不损害前述一般性规定的前提下，依据管理局的批准或国际公约的要求，应当安装可以视听的航行辅助设施，并以管理局认可的方式进行维护。

第三十条 安全区域

30.1. 不影响第三十二条的前提下，管理局可在开发区内特殊建筑物周围宣布设立安全区域，并可要求许可证持有者、承租人和承包商安装、保持或提供导航、驱雾、照明、传声及其他必要的装置与设备，以确保石油运营活动的安全。安全区域可从建筑物的边缘最远延伸 500 米。未经授权的船只不得进入安全区域。

30.2. 此外，应设立一个限制区域，该区域从安全区域或管道的边缘起不超过一千二百五十（1250）米，在此区域内，未经授权的勘探和开采石油资源的船只不得停泊或操控。

第三十一条 建筑安全

31.1. 开发区内船舶、钻探设备和建筑物的运营者，应当负责对其的管控；为安全区域或进港通道提供充分的监督；与有关当局建立通信联系，在发生事故或发生对生命安全造成威胁的事件时，由适当当局采取处置措施。

31.2. 为帮助运营者履行责任，管理局应指派办公地的常驻人员，负责与尼日利亚及圣多美和普林西比相关当局保持联络。

第三十二条 雇员及其他人员的安全

许可证持有者、承租人和承包商应当采取必要措施，保证参与石油活动的相关人员的安全、卫生和福利。尤其是但不限于，许可证持有者、承租人和承包商应当遵守与有关许可、租约、合同的运营有关的或参与人员的安全、健康、卫生的，既有的和未来的安全法律，以及管理局发出的书面指令。

环　　境

第三十三条　环境保护和预防污染

33.1. 许可证持有者、承租人和承包商应当保护许可、租赁或合同区域内或有关的环境。

33.2. 许可证持有者、承租人和承包商应当遵守既有和未来的环境法律，以及管理局的其他书面指令。

33.3. 在不损害本条第1款规定的情况下，许可证持有者、承租人或承包商应采取一切可行的预防措施，包括经管理局批准而采用最新设备，来预防因石油、污泥或其他污染水体的液体或物质，对海洋或海岸线造成污染，或对海洋生物造成伤害，并对任何污染采取迅速措施予以控制、消除和补救。

第三十四条　排污

许可证持有者、承租人和承包商应当将从贮存罐、钻孔和井中排出的废油、盐水、烂泥或垃圾排放到依安全法规或其他相关法规而建造的合适的容器中。许可证持有者、承租人和承包商经采用管理局批准的方式，或依其他法律规定的方式，处置前述废弃物。

第三十五条　财产的转移

35.1. 依管理局的指令，许可证持有者、承租人和承包商应当转移许可、租赁或合同区域内的所有财产，并根据法律规定和指令控制和清除污染。

35.2. 若许可证持有者、承租人和承包商转移财产，或清除污染，未获管理局认可或未采取保护和保存海洋环境的必要措施，则管理局应当指令其采取管理局认为必要的补救措施。若许可证持有者、承租人和承包商不遵守此项指令，将承担管理局采取修复措施而产生的所有费用。

勘探和钻井

第三十六条　开始勘探

每一位许可证持有者、承租人和承包商：

（a）考虑到管理局合理的预期，应当运用地质、地球物理和其他一切可行的方法，来探明区域内可能存在的石油，直到对区域已进行了充分勘探；

(b) 应当在许可、租赁或合同授权后 6 个月内，开始着手地震勘测，直到相关区域已获得充分勘测。

第三十七条 开始钻探

在 OPL 授权之日起不超过 18 月内，许可证持有者、承租人和承包商应当开始钻探工作。许可证持有者、承租人或承包商应当遵守与管理局达成的工作计划承诺中的钻探要求。

第三十八条 钻孔和钻井

38.1. 钻孔或钻井活动停止 6 个月后，未经管理局书面允许，任何钻孔或钻井活动都不得开始或重新开始。

38.2. 一旦确定了钻孔或钻井地点，许可证持有者、承租人或承包商应依据如下规定，书面通知管理局拟定的地点：

（a）如果探孔或者任何钻孔穿透先前未被钻探的构造、地层或者石油层，应向管理局通知如下信息：

（i）通过表 1 标明油田的名称或拟定的名称；

（ii）拟定位置的初步坐标；

（iii）拟定油井的最大井深；

（iv）被勘测结构的地震图或方案，以及钻探预计日期（从通知之日起不得少于 21 天）；以及

（v）许可证持有者、承租人或承包商提供的，与钻探、装入、测试、黏结和完成项目相关的信息，和管理局任何时候书面要求提供的其他信息。

（b）如果开发井、详探井或者油井，仅穿透先前的钻探过的构造、地层或者石油层，有关先前钻探过的构造、地层或石油层的地震地图或计划，之前就已经提交给了管理局。此时的通知应当包括经批准的油田的名称，以及代表代表时间顺序的序号，油井钻探的时间顺序与探井有关，同时还包括以下因素：

（i）计划开钻井的日期；

（ii）初步坐标；

（iii）计划钻井的最大深度；

（iv）预计钻井的日期（应当自通知之日起 20 天以后）；

（v）有关钻探、套管、测井、注入水泥、试油和完成项目的信息，以及管理局不时地以书面通知的形式要求提供的其他信息。

38.3. 管理局若对通知的方案满意，应当书面批准开始钻井，并做出其期望做出的监测和评论。

38.4. 管理局若对通知的方案不满意，应当保留许可，但应当向许可证持有者、承租人或承包商说明否决的理由。

第三十九条　钻井与油田

39.1. 许可证持有者、承租人或承包商经管理局事先书面同意，对每一油井应当用特定名称进行识别。

39.2. 油井的名称一般应包括油井所属油田的名称，其后为反映油田钻井时间顺序的一系列数字。

39.3. 所有油田应当用尼日利亚或圣多美和普林西比本国语言命名，并能大体上反映其中一国的地理、地形或其他方面的特征，这些命名可取自其国家的植物、动物的名字或当地的数字。

39.4. 油井的命名不能仅因部分油井偏离、转移或倾斜，或为钻井只实现了较低的目标而进行更改。

39.5. 若一个原孔被回填和废弃，但其他钻孔被定位为其他目标区域，若新孔底部距原孔底部至少 100 米，则新的定位孔应当有一个特殊序号。

39.6. 新的定位孔可经管理局的批准，在任何油井的名字上附加其他的前缀、后缀或附加的字母或特征（有附加的必要性）。

39.7. 许可证持有者、承租人或承包商在未获得管理局书面批准的情况下，不得擅自更改油井或油田的命名、地位或分类。

39.8. 本条中"油田"包括现存的油田和拟开发的油田。

第四十条　钻探设备

40.1. 未获得管理局授权的合法许可，任何人不得运营钻探设备。

40.2. 依据本法规授予的许可应遵守如下规定：

（a）许可应当在被授予的下一个 12 月 31 日终止，但在届期前两个月内可书面申请续期；

（b）在规定的期限内，若油井的运营不遵守相关法令，或其所有者及运营者不遵守管理局的指令，许可将被撤回或暂停；

（c）许可不得转让；

（d）许可证的复印件应当在钻井上列明，原件应当在接受钻井检查时提供。

40.3. 依据本法规授予许可证的申请，以及授权的许可，应符合本条规定的适当形式。

油田开发

第四十一条　发出特定指令的权利

管理局应当在其认为必要的时候发出指令，以确保正确开发石油，并在所有许可、租赁或合同区域内鼓励良好的保护实践，许可证持有者、承租人或承包商也应遵守这些指令。

第四十二条　常驻经理

OPL、OML 和 PSC 的持有者应确保运营者能：

（a）在双方当事国中委派一位常驻经理，监督许可、租赁和合同的运行；

（b）向管理局通告常驻经理的姓名和地址（及其变更），以及许可证持有者、承租人或承包商被要求提供的信息，若向驻店经理所在地址递送或邮寄上述信息，应充分告知。

第四十三条　设备的保持和运营的实施

在作业过程中使用的设备和机械，以及所有产油的油井，被许可人、承租人或承包人应当保证它们得到妥善维护并处于良好状态。此外，被许可人、承租人或承包人还应当根据相关法规以及被管理局视为良好油田实践的方法和实践，以一种恰当而娴熟的方式进行所有的作业。并不损害前述的一般规定，依据这些实践，采取可行的步骤：

（a）控制石油的流动，防止在相关区域发现或获取的石油泄漏，或避免浪费；

（b）防止损害邻接的含油层；

（c）除了管理局批准为了二次采油的目的，防止水流通过钻孔或油井流向含油层；

（d）防止石油流向海洋。

第四十四条　油田开发计划

44.1. 所有油田、构造、油气储藏及其他油圈闭的开发及生产，应当严格按照油田开发计划，该计划应提交并获得管理局的事先批准，应包括如下内容：

（a）油池的预估大小；

（b）在起草计划时已知的油气储藏或构造的物理参数；

（c）欲采用的钻井模式（如果有的话）；

（d）产量或排水模式；以及

（e）预计的动力机制。

44.2. 有下列情况的，在评估油田构造、矿藏或石油层，以及钻探油井的初步阶段，不需要向管理局提交油田开发计划。

（a）同一油池中产油的油井距离少于 800 米；

（b）除了与下一个批准的油田开发计划相一致，非从同一个油池产油的油井间距离不得少于 400 米。

第四十五条　天然气的可行性研究

天然气利用的可行性研究应当同油田开发计划一并提交管理局。

第四十六条　石油生产的批准

未经管理局批准，许可证持有者、承租人和承包商不得开发石油或建造任何生产设施。管理局不得不合理地保留批准。

第四十七条　原油和天然气的生产

对任何油池或油气储藏中原油或天然气的开发，承租人或承包商应当运用管理局批准的方法和管理局接受的行业实践，特别是要采取一切必要的措施：

（a）获取储油层的原始物理特征以及储油层的参数（例如温度、压力、油气比例、泡点压力、气孔、黏度、有关液体饱和度的相对渗透率、液体重力等），详细的数据和结果，以及对数据和结果的分析，应当在任何一个储油层或矿藏开始投产前提交管理局，或者在投产后立即提交管理局。

（b）获取根据本条（a）项规定，且每隔一段时间由管理局批准的，需要获得的数据的阶段性信息。

（c）使每一油池内的每一口井，在承租人决定的最佳效率潜能或比例内进行生产，并每隔 6 个月向管理局提交其决定。

第四十八条　石油生产工作

除非承租人或承包人同管理局另有约定，在永久构筑物上进行石油生产作业，应当在 OML 被授权后 6 个月内开始。

第四十九条　生产率

管理局可对石油生产的开始日期和石油生产的特殊比例做出指令和规定，在做出指令和规定时，管理局应参考良好的油田实践。

第五十条　石油限制

为了限制对从油气储藏、气孔、管道、输油管或其他为此目的建造的区域中，获取利益的欲望，承租人或承包商应当运用管理局批准的方法和接受的实践方式进行生产。

第五十一条　压力降低

51.1. 在实现油池或石油储层压力在最初的储层压力10%的递减率时/前（考虑到平均的当前储层压力视情况而定），承租人或承包商应当开始研究以确定进行二次采油的经济实用性，或压力维持计划及其建议的时限。

51.2. 在实现上款所指的压力递减后，应尽快向管理局提交研究结果报告（任何情况下不得超过6个月）。

第五十二条　样本和样品

52.1. 许可证持有者、承租人和承包商可转移其在运营过程中发现的岩石和石油样本和样品，以进行分析与实验。

52.2. 管理局通过其授权的代表，可在任何时候获得样本。

52.3. 应管理局要求，在不超过转移的一半样本或样品的范围内，应向管理局提供特殊的有代表性的样本或样品。

52.4. 除非经管理局书面同意，并符合规定条件，任何许可证持有者、承租人和承包商不得出口样本或样品至国外。

52.5. 被许可人、承租人或承包人对下列样本应当正确标识，并保存两年以备参考：

（a）被许可人、承租人或承包人从任何钻孔或钻井中取得的，或经管理局要求而从任何钻孔或钻井中取得的，关于地层或水的典型样本；

（b）在相关区域发现的石油或其他液体的样本。

第五十三条　共同开发方案

53.1. 在许可、租赁或合同项下：

（a）管理局，在与许可证持有者、承租人和承包商（指受让人）协商后，在许可、租赁或合同生效的区域，对油床或单一的地质储油层（指油田）的任何部分，同意受让人依据良好的油田开发实践，将油田作为一个整体进行开发；

（b）管理局认为基于当事国双方的利益，油田任何部分的受让人、被许可人、承租人或承包人（被许可人或承租人在本法规中被称作其他当事方）为了确保最终石油回收的最大化，油田必须作为整体，通过所有持有油田任何部分的许可或租约的当事方之间相互合作的方式进行开发，同时也应遵守五十三条第2、第3和第4款之规定。

53.2. 经管理局书面通知其他方，受让人与其他方为了将油田作为一个整体进行合作开发，受让人应当与其他方合作制订方案（即本条规定的"开发方案"），并共同向管理局提交开发方案以便审核批准。

53.3. 上述通知应当包括通过地图对应管理局要求提交给其批准的开发方案中的区域进行描述的文件，还应包括开发方案提交的期限。

53.4. 若开发方案在通知规定的期限内未提交到管理局，或依第五十三条第3款提交的开发方案未获得管理局批准，管理局应当根据对受让人和其他方公平和平等的原则，制订一项开发方案。

53.5. 当开发方案已经：

（a）依据第五十三条第3款提交并被批准，

（b）被管理局依据第五十三条第4款而制订，

则受让人和其他方应当履行并遵守其所有规定和条件。

第五十四条 抛弃、封堵等

54.1. 未经管理局书面同意，所有钻孔或钻井都不得被二次钻探、封堵或抛弃，所有注水泥套管或其他永久套管都不得从拟抛弃的钻孔或钻井中被撤回。

54.2. 许可证持有者、承租人和承包商意图抛弃的每一个钻孔或钻井，除非经管理局书面同意，应当由许可证持有者、承租人和承包商进行安全封堵，以防止水流通过钻孔进入地层或从地层流出，并应严格按照管理局批准或同意的抛弃方案进行处理。

54.3. 除了紧急情况外，管理局可指令钻孔或钻井不得被封堵，或者不得进行作业，除非管理局任命的官员在场。

第五十五条 终止

55.1. 许可证持有者、承租人和承包商，应当在许可、租赁或合同终止后6个月内（或管理局批准的更长的时间内）：

（a）向管理局交付状况良好的、修理完善的并且适合进一步作业的，所有生产性钻孔或钻井（除非管理局书面要求、书面指令或依法律规定，许可证持有者、承租人和承包商将其封堵），连同钻孔和钻井的所有套管和其他配件，井口采油装置和不能移动的装置，以及移动会钻孔和钻井造成损害的装置；

（b）采取合理措施将相关区域修复至原状。

55.2. 许可、租赁或合同终止后6个月内（或管理局批准的更长时间内），若管理局要求，许可证持有者、承租人和承包商应当依管理局的指示和管理局指定的方式封堵每一个钻孔。

55.3. 许可、租赁或合同终止后，许可证持有者、承租人和承包商应当尊重相关区域或部分区域权利享有者，转移所有装置、工程、动产和财物，或由许可证持有者、承包商带来的与运营相关的财物的权利，管理局可以指定相关的装置、工事、动产或财物，并按合理的折价购买。

55.4. 如果有关许可、租约或合同的区域有一部分被放弃，那么基于本法规之目的，被放弃的部分区域不得再被视为许可、租约或合同的相关区域的一部分。

第五部分　报告、账户和记录

第五十六条　钻孔和钻井记录

56.1. 许可证持有者、承租人和承包商，应当按管理局批准的方式记录所有与钻孔和钻井有关的情况，记录应特别包括每一个钻孔或钻井的：

（a）钻孔和钻井经过的地层、底土和最终埋深；

（b）钻孔的海深；

（c）钻孔或钻孔内安装的套管及其附属装置；

（d）发现的所有石油、水流、矿藏；

（e）许可证持有者、承租人和承包商或其代表，对石油、水流、矿藏的分析，或者本条规定的或依本条获取的其他数据；

（f）对油井（包括最小电阻率测井套件和最小孔隙度测井套件）各种形式的记录；

（g）所有钻井调查和测试结果（包括油井上采取的或要求采取的生产测试和压力测试）；

（h）管理局于任何时候要求记录的其他事项。

第五十七条　发现报告

许可证持有者、承租人和承包商一旦发现石油或含油层，应立即向管理局报告。

第五十八条　原油和天然气的测量和称重

58.1. 许可证持有者、承租人和承包商，应当将容积和重力校正到华氏60度，采取管理局书面批准的方式来测量和称重：

（a）所有从相关区域开采的原油和套管石油溶剂；

（b）所有出售的天然气。

58.2. 不论进行测量或称重的时间或地点，均应当有管理局授权的官员在场。

58.3. 当对原油或天然气进行测量和称重所使用的设备或器具，进行校准、重新校准、测试、对比、测量或称重，所采用的标准与管理局批准的标准不符时，应当采用管理局批准的标准，管理局授权的官员应一直在场；所有校准应当采取管理局接受的方法并采用经管理局事先批准的程序。

58.4. 若任何测量或称重器具，被认为错误或不合理或不精确的范围超过1%：

（a）该器具被认为在发现之前3个月内，就已经呈现上述状态，除非许可证持有者、承租人和承包商能向管理局证明，此错误在那段时间不可能发生，或者距离上次该器具被检查或测试的时间段内，误差已经消失或减小；

（b）对器具存在误差期间，所收取的特许权使用费应做适当调整。

58.5. 未经第一时间通知管理局，许可证持有者、承租人和承包商对测量或称重设备或工具，或管理局批准的测量或称重方法，不得修理、维修或做任何替换；确需进行修理、维修或替换的，需有管理局任命的人员或其代表在场。

58.6. 管理局及其任命的代表不论是否事先通知许可证持有者、承租人和承包商，均有权指定测量和称重工具校正或测试的频率；不管是否事先通知许可证持有者、承租人和承包商，有权在任何时候测试或证明工具或设备的准确度。

第五十九条　账户和详细资料

许可证持有者、承租人和承包商，在相关区域应以管理局批准的方式，就如下相关内容保持一项完整准确的账户：

（a）在相关区域获取及开采的原油和石油溶剂的数量；

（b）对原油进行物理测试所采用的方法和结果；

（c）开发区内出售或出口原油和套管石油溶剂的数量，以及出售和出口的详细资料；

（d）处置的原油数量及处置的方式；

（e）出售的天然气的数量和价格；

（f）用于钻井或抽水以便存储或重新注入地层的原油和套管石油溶剂的数量；

（g）用于钻井、生产或燃料或重新注入地层的天然气的数量；

（h）管理局随时要求的，与运营有关的进一步的详细资料或数据。

每一季度结束后的一个月内，应当以管理局批准的形式，向管理局提交一份有关上一季度会计账户的摘录，以及一份相同形式的、对所有上季度内缴纳的特许权使用费所做的声明。

第六十条　进度报告

60.1. 许可证持有者、承租人和承包商应在每个月结束后 21 天内，以管理局批准的形式，向管理局提交进度报告，包括法规要求记录的内容的详细资料，以及许可证持有者、承租人和承包商在开发区实施的所有地质学或地球物理学工作和工作记录的附加声明。

60.2. 许可证持有者、承租人和承包商，应当在每一季度结束后一个月内，以管理局批准的形式，向管理局提交报告，内容包括每一季度在相关海域内实施的运营活动，对下一季度工作的预报，以及管理局批准的展示钻孔或钻井位置、规模的计划。

60.3. 许可证持有者、承租人和承包商，应当在每一日历年结束后两个月内，或管理局延长的其他期限内，向管理局提交报告，包括在管理局指定年限内在相关区域的与工作进度相关的信息。

第六十一条 与记录有关的其他规定

61.1 许可证持有者、承租人和承包商应当对地质和地下方案、地图、表格、章节以及其他恰当的地质学进行准确记录（包括一项评估，对每一日历年年终获取的信息的修正，包括在评估或修正之日对可能储藏量和石油发掘量的合理预期），对年度报告的摘录或复印件，这些文件构成年度报告的组成部分，年度报告应提交与之相关的但未提交的信息。

61.2 第1款所要求的信息，应当包括在上款规定的年度报告中，可以独立卷形式提交。

61.3 许可证持有者、承租人和承包商应当向管理局提交在相关区域内与运营进度有关的地图、计划和信息，包括在相关海域进行的地质学和地球物理学调查的报告。

61.4 许可证持有者、承租人和承包商在每一项记录或对每口钻井或钻孔调查完成后，且在任何情况下不超过一个月（或管理局许可的较长期限内），应当尽早地向管理局提交记录或调查的复印件。

61.5 许可证持有者、承租人和承包商应当向管理局提交在相关区域获得的地震图和其他地球物理学记录的复印件，包括：

（a）管理局指令许可证持有者、承租人和承包商代为保管的记录；以及

（b）管理局要求提交的任何记录。

61.6 所有地震调查结果，包括相关的地震图，应当提交给管理局。

61.7 许可证持有者、承租人和承包商在运营过程中获取的各种航空照片的底片和电子档复印件，以及卫星图像的复印件，应被提交给管理局。管理局有权保留这些底片和复印件，并在其认为适当的时候使用这些底片和复印件，以及从中获取的信息。

61.8 许可证持有者、承租人和承包商应当在其许可或租赁期限届满前3个月内向管理局提交报告，包括：

（a）相关区域的地质情况记录；

（b）记录地层和结构情况，地质学、结构和其他地下地图，以及地图和图表的设计图和节选；以及

（c）包括相关区域内所有的不动产、设备、机械、构筑物以及其他类似设施。

61.9. 法律规定应当提交的，与相关海域和运营工作或运营进度有关的信息，不得基于保密或解释条款而有所保留。

第六十二条 对合同方账簿和账户的审计

合同方的账簿和账户应当由管理局按年度审计，管理局应对此制定规章和指令。

第六十三条 许可证持有者、承租人和承包商承担记录开支

所有要求提交的记录、报告、计划、地图、图表、账户和信息所产生的开支，依本条及其他法律规定，由许可证持有者、承租人和承包商负担。

第六十四条 保密条款

许可证持有者、承租人和承包商提供的所有信息（除非法律另有规定），管理局及其官员应当将其作为保密信息；管理局就开发区内的石油运营活动准备累计收益或综合报告时，或在与许可证持有者、承租人和承包商进行仲裁或诉讼时，有权利用这些信息。

第六十五条 信息与数据的发布

65.1. 管理局可利用提交给其的汇报、报告或其他文件中的信息和数据，即使这些信息和数据在保密条款规定的期限届满之前不是公开的。

65.2. 与许可或租赁区域内，与石油运营活动有关的基础信息和数据，可在提交给管理局5年后发布，或者与这些信息和数据有关的区域不是许可或租赁区时可发布。然而，基于此类全部或部分信息和数据所得的结论和意见，直到其被提交给管理局10年后才可被发布。

65.3. 若许可证持有者、承租人和承包商或代表其行事的主体，已经发布了这些信息和数据，管理局则不再受保密条款的限制。

65.4. 与地震勘探或者其他地球化学和地球物理勘探相关的信息和数据，应当在勘探基本完成后的6个月内提交。有关油井的信息和数据，应当在钻探基本完成后的3个月内提交。

65.5. 获取与一项特殊的许可、租赁或合同有关且未发布的信息，应依据管理局与相关合同方的双边协定。

65.6. 管理局可自行利用让渡和放弃与区块有关的信息和数据，或者与许可或租赁区外其他区块有关的信息和数据，包括将其公布给任何一方。

65.7. 当事国的政府官员可依据相关法律，获取提交给管理局的信息，这些官员也应遵守管理局适用的本法规的规定。

第六十六条　特殊条款

管理局可对许可证持有者或承租人施加与本法规相符的特殊条款和条件，包括（在不损害前述一般原则的前提下）涉及管理局许可参与的条款和条件，租赁或 PSC 的风险的条款，管理局与许可证或租赁申请者之间的协商条款，以及适用于发现的天然气申请的特殊条款，包括：

（a）对许可证持有者、承租人和承包商的与原油一起产生的天然气，管理局有权利免费获得或以协议价格购买，但无须缴纳特许权使用费；

（b）许可证持有者、承租人和承包商销售天然气（管理局没有获得的天然气）的价格，应获得管理局批准的义务；

（c）对天然气的生产和销售，许可证持有者、承租人和承包商应当交纳特许权使用费。

第六部分　当事国国民的雇佣和培训

第六十七条　培训方案

67.1. 石油勘探许可的被许可人或运营人在许可证授予后 12 个月内，石油采矿租约的承租人在租赁授予后 12 个月内，应当向管理局提交一份详细的对当事国国民的雇佣和培训方案，并由管理局批准。

67.2. 方案应当包括在石油运营各阶段对国民的培训，不论该阶段由承租人还是由其机构和承包商负责。

第六十八条　奖学金计划

被许可人、承租人或承包人准备的所有奖学金计划，以及提议发放的任何奖学金（不论与被许可人、承租人或承包人的作业是否相关，或者与石油产业是否存在一般性关联），都应当提交管理局批准。

第六十九条　更改

一旦第六十七条规定的方案和第六十八条规定的计划经管理局批准，则没有管理局的书面同意，不得更改。

第七十条　报告

对第六十九条提到的方案的执行报告，应当由许可证持有者、承租人和承包商在每一日历年的 6 月底和 12 月底提交。

第七十一条 指标

石油采矿租约的持有人应当确保：

（a）自租赁授予后 10 年内，当事国雇佣的管理人员、专业人员和监管级别（或其他以管理局批准的方式任命的相应级别）人员中，当事国国民的数量至少应达到雇佣总人数的 75%；

（b）依据（a）款之规定应当雇佣的当事国国民的人数，应当依据《尼日利亚联邦共和国与圣多美和普林西比民主共和国关于共同开发两国专属经济区石油资源和其他资源的条约》之规定，尽可能地在尼日利亚与圣多美和普林西比的国民之间，进行合理可行的分配。

（c）自租赁授予后 10 年内，每一级别的当事国国民数量应不少于 60%；

（d）应为当事国国民的所有技术人员、半技术人员以及非技术人员，应当依据《尼日利亚联邦共和国与圣多美和普林西比民主共和国关于共同开发两国专属经济区石油资源和其他资源的条约》之规定，尽可能地在两国之间进行合理可行的分配。

第七部分　其他条款

第七十二条　基准

为了本法规的目的，确定任何区块边界、计算面积、识别区域内的任何地点或任何其他与大地测量位置有关的活动，应采用 WGS 84 基准。

第七十三条　保险

73.1. 管理局应当要求每一位许可证持有者、承租人和承包商，自许可、租赁或合同生效之日起，依据严格责任购置保险，金额由管理局和许可、租赁申请者协商。管理局也应与许可证持有者、承租人和承包商协商确定赔偿机制。保险应当覆盖所有与石油开发活动有关的开支或责任，以及有关许可或租赁区石油运营和其他活动而产生的其他特定事项，包括为预防及处理石油泄漏而产生的开支。

73.2. 许可证持有者和承租人应当确保，从开发区内大批石油的运输应由根据相关国际协定购买保险的油轮承担。

第七十四条　对许可证持有者、承租人和承包商的干扰和侵害

74.1. 任何人如果干扰或阻挠许可证或租约持有者行使被授予的权利、

权力或自由，将被视为犯罪，且将面临一项不超过 20 万美元的罚款或不超过 6 个月的监禁，或二者同时采用。

74.2. 任何人：

（a）未获石油勘探许可而勘探石油或

（b）不按照 2003 年石油法规授予的一项许可或租赁进行石油活动，

（c）未经许可实施任何依据本法规需要获得许可的行为，

将面临有罪指控，并面临不超过 20 万美元的罚款。

74.3. 若一人因石油或石油产品，而依第七十四条第 2 款规定被认为有罪，除了第七十四条第 2 款规定的惩罚，法院还可：

（a）判令没收石油或石油产品，或者

（b）判令其向管理局支付与石油或石油产品等值的金钱。

第七十五条　进一步规定和立法权

根据委员会的批准，管理局可对如下事项制订指导方针：

（a）规定基于本法规之目的需要规范的任何事项；

（b）依本法确定与许可和租赁有关的一般事项及活动，包括：

（i）安全工作；

（ii）石油资源的保存；

（iii）海洋和大气污染的防治；

（iv）制定汇报和报告（包括事故报告）；

（v）对事故的调查；

（vi）记录、账簿、数据、账户和计划的保存和监督；

（vii）产品的测量；

（c）根据本法规和其他法规规定，规范设施的建造、保持和运营；

（d）规范石油的储存，特别是（不影响前述一般规定）：

（i）定义危险石油；

（ii）管理石油及石油产品的装载、卸载和运输；

（iii）提供与石油有关的检查和测试，规定探知燃点的测试及测试的方法；

（iv）规定石油和石油产品运输的数量、存储的方式、运输的油轮和装载的容器及数量，并对所有油轮进行搜查和监督；

（e）授予或对公职人员施加本法规规定之外的权力和责任；

（f）若（a）项不适用，则可规定：

（i）为本法规目的规定适用的形式；

（ii）为执行这些条款收取的费用（在不损害前述一般规定的情况下，包括部长委员会的许可费、文件或信息的提供费、检查和执行其他事项的费用）；

（g）为了法案的生效必须规定的其他事项。

第七十六条 法规的公布

本法规及其他根据条约第二十一条第4款进行的修正，一经管理局采纳，应依条约第二十一条第3款和第5款规定，由管理局立即公布。

第七十七条 争端的解决

77.1 因本法规的任何规定或其他规定产生的问题或争端，应当依条约的规定提交仲裁。

77.2 与所有许可或租赁有关的，属于管理局与许可证持有者、承租人或承包商之间的问题或争端（包括所有费用、租金或特许权使用费的缴纳产生的争端），应通过仲裁解决，除非属于仲裁明确排除的事项或管理局享有裁量权的事项。

第七十八条 超出控制的情况

78.1 许可证持有者或承租人，不能依本法规履行许可或租赁项下的条款或条件时，若违反是因许可证持有者、承租人和承包商所不能控制的原因，管理局不能主张（除非许可或租赁另有规定）许可证持有者、承租人和承包商违反许可或租赁。

78.2 如果在此情况下，被许可人、承租人或承包人延迟履行其许可或租约中的任何条款或条件，或者延迟履行本法规的任何条款，那么应在原本规定的履行条款或条件所需期限上，加上迟延的时间。

4. Nigeria – Sao Tome and Principe Joint Development Authority Petroleum Regulations 2003

WHEREAS the Treaty of 21 February 2001 between the Federal Republic of Nigeria and the Democratic Republic of São Tomé e Príncipe provides for the Joint Development of an overlapping maritime area between their Exclusive Economic Zones

WHEREAS instruments of ratification of the said Treaty were exchanged on 16 January 2003;

WHEREAS by virtue of the Treaty a Joint Development Authority was established;

WHEREAS Articles 3 and 9 of the Treaty empower the Authority to amongst other things control and manage the development activities relating to the exploration for and exploitation of the resources in the zone,

WHEREAS in accordance with Article 21.1 and pursuant to its powers under the Treaty, the Authority has submitted to the Joint Ministerial Council two draft documents entitled "Petroleum Regulations 2003" (being the present document) and the other entitled "Tax Regulations 2003", which documents, taken together, constitute the Regulatory and Tax Regimes for petroleum related activities within the Zone.

WHEREAS under Article 21.2 of the Treaty the Joint Ministerial Council is empowered to approve and adopt a Regulatory and Tax Regime as aforesaid.

THE JOINT MINISTERIAL COUNCIL, pursuant to Article 8.2 (b) of the said Treaty

HEREBY APPROVES AND ADOPTS

the afore mentioned documents, this 4th day of April 2003.

PART ONE INTRODUCTORY

Regulation 1 Short title and Entry into force

The present Regulations shall be called the "Petroleum Regulations 2003". They shall enter into force with immediate effect.

Regulation 2 Definitions

For the purposes of these Regulations and of the Schedules, wherever the context permits:

"applicable law" means the Treaty and the principles and rules of law applicable in the Zone by virtue of the Treaty;

"Article" means an Article of the Treaty;

"barrel" means a barrel of forty-two United States gallons;

"Board" means the Board of the Authority, as referred to in Article 10 of the Treaty;

"contractor" means a party to a development contract other than the Authority;

"Contract Area" means the area of an OPL or any OML derived therefrom;

"Council" means the Joint Ministerial Council established under Part Two of the Treaty;

"crude oil" means mineral petroleum oil in its natural state before it is refined or treated (excluding water and other foreign substances);

"development activity" means any economic activity in or concerning the Zone, including petroleum activity, fishing activity, all other activities for the development or exploitation of other mineral or living resources of the Zone, and all forms of exploration and research relating to any of the foregoing;

"development contract" means any agreement relating to a development activity concerning petroleum (including without limitation leases, licences, production sharing contracts and concessions) entered into, from time to time, between, on the one hand, the Authority and, on the other hand, one or more other parties;

"explore", in relation to petroleum, means to make a preliminary search by aerial survey, surface geological and geophysical methods, including the drilling of wells and boreholes;

"financial terms" includes all obligations in the nature of taxation (whether production or income based) and any other financial obligations including royalties, payments in kind, production sharing arrangements and resource rentals;

"gazetted" means published in the Official Gazettes of both States Parties; and/or such other publications in the States Parties as the Authority may determine to be appropriate;

"installation" means any structure, device or artificial island utilised in development activities, installed above, in, on or under the seabed, including drilling vessels in situ;

"Joint Development Authority" or "Authority" means the Joint Authority established by Part Three of the Treaty;

"Joint Development Zone" or "Zone" means, subject to Article 5 and paragraph 5 of Article 31 of the Treaty, the area of seabed and subsoil, together with the superjacent waters, established as a joint development zone under Article 2 of the Treaty;

"Lease" means an Oil Mining Lease (OML);

"Lessee" means the holder from time to time of an OML, but so that in relation to PSCs the PSC Contractor shall be substituted for the holder in the manner and to the extent provided for in Regulations 9.3 and 9.4;

"Licence" means an Exploration Licence (EL) or an Oil Prospecting Licence (OPL);

"Licensee" means the holder from time to time of an EL or an OPL, but so that in relation to PSCs the PSC Contractor shall be substituted for the holder in the manner and to the extent provided for in Regulations 9.3 and 9.4;

"national" means a natural or juridical person having the nationality of either of the States Parties in accordance with the laws of that States Parties;

"national body" means a Ministry or a governmental or quasi-governmental administrative or technical organ of any of the States Parties responsible for activities in or in the waters of that States Parties;

"natural gas" means gas obtained from boreholes and wells and consisting primarily of petroleum hydrocarbons;

"OML" or "Oil Mining Lease" means an Oil Mining Lease of the kind referred to in Regulation 8;

"open acreage" means acreage of the Zone not subject at the relevant time to an OPL, OML or PSC;

"operating agreement" means a contract concluded between two or more contractors for the purpose of carrying out development activities in the Zone;

"operator" means a contractor appointed by the Authority and acting as operator under the terms of an operating agreement;

"OPL" or "Oil Prospecting Licence" means an oil prospecting licence of the kind referred to in Regulation 7;

"petroleum" means

(a) any hydrocarbon or mixture of hydrocarbons, whether in a gaseous, liquid or solid state, naturally occurring beneath the seabed; and

(b) any petroleum as defined by sub-paragraph (a) that has been returned to a reservoir; and

(c) any other minerals which are produced in association with them; but shall not include coal or other stratified deposits from which oil can be extracted by destructive distillation;

"petroleum activities" means all activities of exploration for and development of petroleum in the Zone;

"petroleum contractor" means a contractor in respect of a petroleum development contract;

"petroleum development contract" means a development contract relating to petroleum;

"pollution" means the introduction of substances or energy into the marine environment, including estuaries, which results or is likely to result in deleterious effects such as harm to living resources and marine life, hazards to human health, impediment of quality for use of sea water or reduction of amenity;

"prospect", in relation to petroleum, means search for by all geological and geophysical methods, including drilling and seismic operations;

"PSC" means a production sharing contract of the kind referred to in Regulation 9.

"PSC Contractor" means one or more parties together constituting all the parties to a PSC other than the Authority or it's subsidiaries;

"Regulation" and "Regulations" means the provisions laid down in the present document, including wherever the context permits its Schedules, and further modifications including with effect from the adoption of each modification thereof pursuant to paragraph 4 of Article 21 of the Treaty, any and all such modifications;

"rent" includes any annual or other periodic charge made in respect of a Licence granted under these Regulations;

"Schedule" means a Schedule to the present Regulations;

"signature bonus" means a bonus paid by the grantee of a Tender Agreement upon signing of that agreement;

"States Parties" means the Federal Republic of Nigeria and the Democratic Republic of São Tomé e Príncipe, and, wherever the context so requires, their respective territories;

"Tender Agreement" has the meaning set out in Regulation 10.2;

"Treaty" means the Treaty signed on 21 February 2001 by the States Parties on the joint development of petroleum and other resources in respect of areas of the Exclusive Economic Zones of the two States;

"Zone Plan" means the development plan or plans from time to time adopted by the Council pursuant to Part Seven of the Treaty, for activities in the Zone;

PART TWO LICENSING, LEASING AND CONTRACTS

Regulation 3 General Provisions

3.1 No petroleum activities may be undertaken in the Zone except pursuant to and in accordance with the provisions of the Licences, leases and contracts in these Regulations.

3.2 All acreage in the Joint Development Zone including Oil Prospecting Licences and all Oil Mining Leases derived there from within the Zone shall be held on behalf of the States Parties by the Joint Development Authority.

3.3 The Joint Development Authority:

(a) Shall exercise general supervision over all operations carried on under licences, leases and contrtacts granted under these Regulations;

(b) Shall have access at all times to the areas covered by exploration licences, oil prospecting licences and oil mining leases, and to installations which are subject to these and any other regulations, for the purpose of inspecting the operations conducted therein and enforcing the provisions of and any regulations made there under and the conditions of any licences or leases granted under these Regulations;

(c) May by notice in writing require the holder of a licence or lease granted under these Regulations or any contractor working for the holder (or any servant or agent of the holder or the contractor) to appear before it at a reasonable time and place to give such information as it may require about the operations being conducted under the licence, lease or contract, and every person so required to appear shall be legally bound to comply with the notice and give the information;

(d) May direct in writing that operations under a licence, lease or contract granted under these Regulations be suspended in any area until arrangements have been made which in its opinion are necessary to prevent danger to life or property;

(e) May direct in writing the suspension of any operations which in its opinion are not being conducted in accordance with good oil field practice;

(f) May direct in writing the suspension of any operations where in its opinion a contravention of these Regulations or any other regulations has been or may have been or is likely to be committed; and

(g) Shall have powers of arrest.

Regulation 4 Division of the Zone into Blocks

4.1 In order to facilitate the licensing of petroleum development activities in the Zone, the Zone shall be divided by the Authority into a series of Blocks of appropriate dimensions for the grant of OPLs as specified in Regulation 7. Each such Block shall be allocated a discrete identifying number.

4.2 Except where necessary in order to correspond to the boundaries of the Zone, the boundaries of each such Block shall be defined by meridians of longitude of integral multiples of 5 minutes (reference the meridian of Greenwich) and by parallels of latitude of integral multiples of 5 minutes (reference the Equator).

4.3 The foregoing provisions of this Regulation shall be without prejudice to the provisions of paragraph 6 of Regulation 5.

Regulation 5　Licences, Leases and Production Sharing Contracts

5.1 Subject to these Regulations and the approval of the Council, the Authority may grant:

(a) An Exploration Licence (EL)

(b) An Oil Prospecting Licence (OPL);

(c) An Oil Mining Lease (OML);

(d) Production Sharing Contract (PSC).

5.2 Exploration Licenses cover the acquisition of speculative geophysical surveys.

5.3 Unless the Council otherwise directs, an EL, OPL, OML or PSC may be granted under these Regulations only to:

(a) A company incorporated in and under the laws of either Nigeria or São Tomé e Príncipe; or

(b) A company registered in and under the laws of either Nigeria or São Tomé e Príncipe.

5.4 Activities in the Block in question shall, for the duration of such OPL or OML, be governed by such Licence or Lease and a Production Sharing Contract.

5.5 The area of an OPL and any OML derived there from shall be defined by a series of coordinates (latitude, longitude) as specified in Regulation 4 and shall form a compact unit.

5.6 In creating an OML from an OPL the Authority may redesignate Blocks for the purpose of creating a unit specifically corresponding to the area of the OML.

5.7 Where there is provision for the relinquishment or surrender of part of the relevant area of a Licence or Lease, the relinquishment or surrender shall be such that the retained part is a compact unit as provided in paragraphs 4 and 5 of this Regulation; and the Licensee, Lessee or Contractor shall obtain the prior agreement of the Authority as to the shape and area of the retained part before an application for the relinquishment or surrender is made to the Authority.

Regulation 6　Exploration Licences

6.1 An Exploration Licence (EL) grants rights to the Licensee to undertake acquisition of speculative geophysical surveys in the area of the Licence. Save where the Exploration Licence expressly provides otherwise, the grant of an Exploration Licence in respect of any area shall not preclude the grant of another Licence or Lease over the same area or any part thereof.

6.2 Duration, termination and renewal of an Exploration Licence shall be governed by its terms.

6.3 An Exploration Licence shall not confer any right to the grant of an OPL or OML.

6.4 The Licensee shall procure that at all times its activities under an Exploration Licence shall be supervised continuously by a qualified personnel and shall be carried out to the satisfaction of the Authority.

Regulation 7　Oil Prospecting Licences

7.1 An Oil Prospecting Licence (OPL) grants the Licensee the exclusive right to explore and prospect for petroleum within the area of his Licence. The Licensee of an OPL may carry away and dispose of petroleum won during the term of the OPL, subject to the fulfilment of all obligations imposed upon it by or under the terms of the OPL, these Regulations, the Petroleum Tax Regulations or any other applicable law or regulation.

7.2 OPLs shall have a maximum period of 8 years. This period is divided into sub-periods that can be entered into in accordance with the provisions of the respective PSC.

7.3 The Licensee of an OPL shall be entitled to apply in writing to the Authority, not less

then six months before the expiration of the Licence, for its renewal.

Regulation 8 Oil Mining Leases

8.1 An Oil Mining Lease (OML) grants the Lessee the exclusive right, within the leased area, to explore, produce and carry away for export or otherwise petroleum discovered.

8.2 The term of an OML shall not exceed 20 years, but may be renewed in accordance with the respective PSC.

Regulation 9 Production Sharing Contracts

9.1 The Authority may, with the approval of the Joint Ministerial Council, enter into a PSC. Such a PSC may be entered into only with a Contractor which is a company incorporated or registered in Nigeria or in São Tomé e Príncipe.

9.2 Subject to sub-paragraph 9.3 below, a PSC shall in accordance with its terms confer upon the PSC Contractor the exclusive right and responsibility to undertake petroleum activities in the area of the OPL in question.

9.3 Each Contractor shall be under a direct obligation to the Authority, by virtue of this Regulation, to observe and perform all obligations accruing, prior to the termination of the PSC, in respect of the relevant Licence or Lease, under all relevant laws and regulations (including without limitation the present Regulations and the terms of such Licences or Leases).

9.4 Every PSC shall contain express undertakings by the Contractor to the Authority to observe and perform all such obligations, but in the absence of any such provision such express undertakings shall be implied.

9.5 Whenever, in relation to any Licence or Lease to which a PSC relates, an event occurs which, whether or not a breach of the terms of such Licence or Lease or the related PSC, entitles the Authority by virtue of these Regulations or any other provision to do any act or thing, or take any step against the Licensee, Lessee or Contractor, the Authority shall by virtue of this paragraph be entitled to do the same or a corresponding act or thing, or take the same or a corresponding step, against the relevant PSC Contractor in respect of the PSC.

9.6 Unless the Joint Ministerial Council otherwise consents no PSC shall be entered into by the Authority except following a process of competitive tendering associated with a licensing round, as provided for in Regulation 10.

9.7 A model PSC as approved by the Joint Ministerial Council shall form the basis for any PSC to be entered into by the Authority.

Regulation 10　Licensing Rounds and Tendering Processes

10.1 All Tender Agreements shall be subject to a process of competitive bidding in licensing rounds, in accordance with Regulations 11 to 15 below.

10.2 For the purposes of this Regulation "Tender Agreement" means:

(i) PSCs awarded in respect of OPLs held by the Joint Development Authority; and;

(ii) OMLs awarded pursuant to paragraph 2 of Regulation 16.

Regulation 11　Invitations to Bid

11.1 The tender process shall begin by the Authority inviting tenders. The invitation for applications shall specify:

(a) The Block or Blocks over which rights are to be granted;

(b) The bidding system to apply;

(c) The basis on which bids shall be assessed;

(d) Details of the Tender Agreement to be entered into, including the rights and responsibilities of the parties thereto; and

(e) The period within which applications may be made.

11.2 Details of the invitation for applications shall be published in the national daily press in both States Parties and in such other ways, if any, as the Authority decides.

11.3 The Authority may make a charge for supplying the bid package to prospective bidders (bid package or application fee) and may also charge for the evaluation of bid packages (processing fee).

Regulation 12　Consideration of Applications

12.1 Tender Agreements shall be offered in accordance with the published criteria stated by the Authority at the time of publicising the relevant bidding round.

12.2 The Authority shall set out formal guidelines for tendering. Those guidelines will include, inter alia, information as to the basis on which applications will be considered and the relevant criteria which applicants will be expected to meet.

12.3 Guidelines for acreage bidding in accordance with these regulations shall be prepared by the Authority and approved by the Joint Ministerial Council. These Guidelines shall apply unless and until revised or substituted by the Authority.

12.4 The principal criteria for the consideration of applications shall be technical and financial capability, work programme commitment and the proposed signature bonus.

12.5 It shall accordingly be a condition of the award of any Tender Agreement that the Authority is satisfied that the applicant has the necessary financial capability, and also the necessary technical knowledge and ability, to carry out petroleum operations in a manner consistent with the terms and conditions of the Tender Agreement, these Regulations and all other applicable laws and regulations.

Regulation 13 Form of Applications by Competitive Tender

13.1 Every application for a Tender Agreement shall be made to the Authority in writing on the appropriate form supplied with the bid package.

13.2 Every application shall be accompanied by:

(a) The prescribed processing fee as set out in Regulation 23 (the fee in question not being refundable under any circumstances);

(b) Evidence of the financial status and technical competence of the applicant;

(c) Details of the work which the applicant is prepared to undertake or a programme for carrying out any minimum working obligations imposed;

(d) The signature bonus offered by the applicant;

(e) Details of the annual expenditure which the applicant is prepared to make in the area applied for;

(f) The date on which he is prepared to begin operations after the grant of the Tender Agreement to which the application relates;

(g) Details of a specific scheme for the recruitment and training of nationals of the States Parties;

(h) Annual reports in respect of the applicant's (or its technical partner's) oil exploration and production activities in the preceding three years; and

(i) Any other information which the Authority may call for by notice or otherwise.

13.3 The applicant shall furnish such further evidence relating to the matters mentioned in sub-paragraph 13.2 of this Regulation as the Authority may require.

Regulation 14   Withdrawal of Applications

An applicant may at any time withdraw his application for a Tender Agreement by notifying the Authority in writing accordingly.

Regulation 15   Grant or Refusal of Tender Agreements

15.1 The Authority shall seek prior approval from the Council to enter into a Tender Agreement with the successful applicant or group of applicants.

15.2 Following that approval, the Authority shall offer in writing to the successful applicant (or group of applicants) to enter into the Tender Agreement upon the terms and subject to the conditions specified in the offer.

15.3 The applicant to whom any offer is made shall have fifteen (15) days from the date on which the Authority despatched the offer to accept or refuse the offer in writing. In the absence of acceptance within that time, the offer shall automatically lapse.

15.4 Upon the Authority being satisfied that any other conditions precedent to the entry by the parties into the Tender Agreement have been satisfied in accordance with the time limits and other terms of the offer referred to in paragraph 2, the Authority and the Applicant shall enter into the Tender Agreement.

15.5 The Contractor with whom the Authority enters into a Tender Agreement shall have a period of 30 days from the date of the signing of the agreement to pay the signature bonus.

15.7 If by the end of the said 30 days the Applicant has not paid the signature bonus, the agreement referred to in paragraph 4 shall automatically terminate.

Regulation 16　Conversion of an OPL into an OML

16.1 An OML may be granted to the Licensee of an OPL who has:

(a) Satisfied all the terms and conditions of the OPL and all other requirements under or pursuant to these Regulations or any other applicable law or regulation, and

(b) Demonstrated to the satisfaction of the Authority that it has discovered oil in commercial quantities.

16.2 Where an OML terminates by revocation, surrender or any other reason, and whether in whole or in part, the Authority may grant another OML over the whole or as the case may be such part, on such terms as the Authority considers appropriate, through a tender process carried out by the Authority upon the same basis, mutatis mutandis, as under Regulations 11 to 15.

Regulation 17　Publication of Licences, Leases and PSCs

The Authority shall gazette all grants and renewals of ELs, OPLs and OMLs, and of PSCs entered into. The Authority shall also gazette all surrenders, determinations, revocations or assignments thereof, with the name of the holder and the situation of the relevant acreage.

Regulation 18　Keeping and Inspection of Register of Tender Agreements

The Authority shall maintain a register of Tender Agreements as defined in the preceding Regulation, setting out summary details of:

(a) The areas over which each Tender Agreements is in force;

(b) The parties to each Tender Agreement and their participating interests and the operator (if any);

(c) Changes to the operator (if any) and/or the respective participating interests of the parties;

(d) Areas relinquished or surrendered; and

(e) Changes in names and addresses of the operator (if any) and the other parties.

Regulation 19　Applications for Assignment

19.1　Without the prior consent of the Authority and the Council, the holder of a Tender Agreement shall not assign his agreement, or any right, power or interest therein or hereunder.

19.2　The prescribed fee shall be paid on an application for an assignment under this Regulation, and the Authority's consent for the assignment may be given on payment of such other fee or such premium, or both, and upon such terms and subject to such other conditions, as it may decide, PROVIDED that in any specific case the Authority may waive payment of that other fee or that premium, or both, if it is satisfied that the assignment is to be made to a company in a group of companies of which the assignor is also a member.

19.3　The Authority shall not consent to an assignment unless it is satisfied that:

(a) The proposed assignee is of good reputation, or is a member of a group of companies of good reputation, or is owned by a company or companies of good reputation;

(b) There is likely to be available to the proposed assignee (from his own resources or through other companies in the group of which he is a member, or otherwise) sufficient technical knowledge and experience and sufficient financial resources to enable him effectively to carry out a programme satisfactory to the Authority in respect of operations under the Relevant Agreement which is to be assigned; and

(c) The proposed assignee is in all other respects acceptable to the Authority and the Council.

Regulation 20　Termination of an OPL or OML

20.1　The holder of an OPL or OML may, at any time, terminate the OPL or OML, by giving notice to the Authority. The period of the notice preceding the termination shall not be less than six months for an OPL and twelve months for an OML.

20.2 Where notice is given under the preceding paragraph, no rent paid shall be refundable, and the termination shall otherwise be without prejudice to any obligation or liability imposed by or incurred under or in relation to the OPL, OML before the effective date of termination.

Regulation 21　Revocation of OPLs and OMLs

The Authority may revoke an OPL, OML or PSC, if in its opinion the Licensee, Lessee or relevant PSC Contractor:

(a) Is not conducting operations continuously and in a vigorous and businesslike manner and in accordance with good oil field practice; or

(b) Has failed to comply with any provision of these Regulations or any further regulation or direction given there under or is not fulfilling his obligations under the special conditions of his Licence or Lease; or

(c) Fails to pay his due rent or royalties, whether or not they have been demanded by the Authority, within the period specified by or in pursuance of these Regulations; or

(d) Has failed to furnish such reports on his operations as the Authority may lawfully require.

21.2 The Authority shall inform the Licensee, Lessee or as the case may be PSC Contractor of the grounds on which the revocation is contemplated and shall invite the Licensee, Lessee or PSC Contractor to make any explanation if it so desires.

21.3 If the Authority is satisfied with the explanation, it may invite the Licensee, Lessee or PSC Contractor to rectify the matter complained of within a specified period.

21.4 The Authority may revoke the Licence, Lease or PSC, if:

(a) The Licensee, Lessee or PSC Contractor provides no or insufficient explanation; or

(b) Does not rectify the matter complained of within the specified period.

21.5 A notice sent to the last known address of the Licensee, Lessee or PSC Contractor, or its legal representative in Nigeria or São Tomé e Príncipe, and gazetted, shall, for all purposes, be sufficient notice to it of the revocation of the Licence, Lease or PSC.

21.6 The revocation shall be without prejudice to any liabilities, which the Licensee, Lessee or PSC Contractor may have incurred, or to any claim against it which may have accrued to the Authority.

PART THREE FEES, RENTS AND ROYALTIES

Regulation 22 Fees, Rents and Royalties

22.1 There shall be paid in respect of Licences and Leases the fees and rents set out in Regulation 23.1 and 23.2.

22.2 Royalties shall be paid at rates prescribed in Regulation 23 or, where different rates are specified in special terms and conditions attached to the relevant Licence or Lease, at the rates so specified: PROVIDED that the Authority may, on giving notice in that behalf, call for and receive any royalty (or part thereof) in kind.

Regulation 23 Rates of Fees, Rents and Royalties

23.1 The following fees (all expressed in United States dollars) shall be payable until other fees are prescribed:

(a) On an application for an OPL (bid package) $ 15000

(b) Processing fee for an OPL application $ 10000

(c) On an application for an OML $ 1000000

(d) On an application to assign a stake in an OPL or related PSC $ 500000

(e) On an application to assign a stake in an OML or related PSC $ 1000000

(f) On an application to terminate an OPL, OML or related PSC $ 100000

(g) On an application for a licence to operate a drilling rig $ 100000

(h) For a licence to operate a drilling rig (annually) $ 50000

(i) For a permit to export samples for analysis (per well) $ 10000

23.2 The following annual rents shall be payable on an OPL or OML unless otherwise stated in the special conditions of the Licence or Lease

(a) On an OPL for each square kilometre or part thereof $ 200

(b) On an OML, for every square kilometre or part thereof

(i) during the first ten years of the term $ 500

(ii) thereafter $200

23.3 The Licensee, Lessee or Contractor shall pay to the Authority Royalties on the production of crude Oil and Casinghead Petroleum Spirit in the Area over the relevant period. This Royalty shall be payable not more than one month after the end of every Quarter (including the Quarter in which its Licence or Lease becomes effective) or otherwise as the Authority may direct.

23.4 There shall be no Royalties payable for the production of Natural Gas in the Joint Development Zone.

23.5 The applicable Royalties payable in the Joint Development Zone for Crude Oil and Casinghead Petroleum Spirit shall be according to the following sliding scale table:

$P < 20 \quad R = 0$

$20 <= P <= 70 \quad R = 5\% \{1 - [(70 - P) / (70 - 20)]\}$

$P > 70 \quad R = 5$

where: P = production in thousands of barrels/day

R = royalty rate

23.6 In the event of a dispute on royalties, the said amount under dispute shall be fully paid before settlement of the dispute.

PART FOUR   OPERATIONS AND PRODUCTION

Rights and obligations of licensees, lessees and Contractors

Regulation 24   Rights of Licensees, Lessees and Contractors

24.1 The holder of an OPL, OML or PSC shall have a general right to enter and remain on the licensed or leased areas and do such things as are authorised by the Licence or Lease.

24.2 The rights and powers conferred on Licensees, Lessees and Contractors under these Regulations shall include the right, subject to applicable regulations and the approval in writing of the Authority and to such conditions as it may impose to construct, bring, maintain, alter, operate, dismantle or remove:

(a) Installations, including drilling platforms, engines, power plants, flow lines, storage tanks, loading terminals, derricks,

(b) Means of communication, including telephone lines and wireless stations,

(c) Facilities for shipping and aircraft,

(d) Living accommodation and amenities for the employees and workmen of the Licensee, Lessee or relevant contractors, and

(e) Other facilities, works, chattels and effects.

24.3 The Licensee, Lessee or Contractor may exercise any of his rights or powers through agents or independent contractors and subject and without prejudice to subparagraph 9.3, shall be responsible to the Authority for all the actions of the agents and contractors in question.

Regulation 25   Reservations

25.1 The Authority or any person authorised by it, shall have the right to enter the relevant area to search for, dig, work and get any substance other than petroleum, and generally for any purposes other than those for which a licence or lease has been granted.

25.2 The powers conferred by this Regulation shall not be exercised in such a way as to hinder or interfere with or to allow any person or body to hinder or interfere with the rights and powers of the Licensee, Lessee or Contractor.

Regulation 26   Fishing Rights

If the Licensee, Lessee or Contractor exercises the rights conferred by his Licence, Lease or Contractor in such a manner as to unreasonably interfere with the exercise of any fishing rights, granted by the Authority or either of the States Parties, it shall pay adequate compensation thereof to any person injured by the exercise of those afore mentioned rights, the amount thereof to be determined by the Authority.

Regulation 27   Rights of Inspection

Any person or persons designated by the Authority shall be entitled at all reasonable times to enter into and upon any part of the Zone or any location, premises, structure or business place outside the Zone occupied by the Licensee, Lessee or Contractor for the purpose of carrying out or facilitating the carrying out of his operations in the relevant area:

(a) To examine or check anything which the Licensee, Lessee or Contractor is authorised by these and other Regulations to perform, install, construct or take possession of; or

(b) To inspect and make abstracts or copies of any logs, records, maps, accounts or other document which the Licensee, Lessee or Contractor is required to make or keep in accordance with these and other Regulations.

Regulation 28　Indemnity

The holder of a Licence, Lease or Contract shall at all times indemnify and keep harmless the Authority and its officers and employees (and their agents) against all actions, costs, charges, claims and demands whatsoever which may be made or brought by any third party in relation to any matter or thing done or purported to be done pursuant to these Regulations.

Safety and security

Regulation 29　Safety of Navigation

Any works or installations erected by the Licensee, Lessee or Contractor shall be of such a nature and shall be so constructed, placed, marked, buoyed, equipped and maintained as to leave at all times and in any conditions safe and convenient channels for shipping in the relevant area; and, without prejudice to the generality of the foregoing, it shall install such audible or visual navigational aids as may be approved or required by the Authority and International Conventions and shall maintain the same in a manner satisfactory to the Authority.

Regulation 30　Safety zones

30.1　Without prejudice to the provisions of Regulation 32, the Authority may declare a safety zone around any specified structure in the Zone, and may require the Licensee, Lessee or Contractor to install, maintain or provide thereon, navigation, fog and illumination lighting, acoustic and other devices and equipment necessary for the safety of the petroleum operations. A safety zone may extend up to five hundred (500) metres from the extremities of the structure. Unauthorized vessels shall be prohibited from entering the safety zone.

30.2　Additionally, a restricted zone of one thousand two hundred and fifty

(1250) metres may be declared around the extremities of safety zones and pipelines within which area unauthorized vessels employed in exploration for and exploitation of petroleum resources are prohibited from laying anchor or manoeuvring.

Regulation 31　Security of Structures

31. 1　Operators of vessels, drilling rigs and structures in the Zone shall be responsible for controlling access to their facilities; providing adequate surveillance of safety zones and their approaches; and establishing communications with, and arranging action by, the appropriate authorities in the event of an accident or incident involving threat to life or security.

31. 2　To assist operators in meeting these responsibilities, the Authority shall appoint persons, to be stationed at the office of the Authority, responsible for liasing with appropriate authorities of Nigeria and São Tomé e Príncipe.

Regulation 32　Safety of Employees and Others

The licensee, lessee or Contractor shall take the necessary action to secure the safety, health and welfare of persons engaged in petroleum operations in or about the area of the Licence, Lease or Contract. In particular but without limitation, the Licensee, Lessee or Contractor shall comply with all existing and future safety regulations and all such instructions as may, from time to time, be given in writing by the Authority for security, health and safety of persons engaged on or in connection with operations under its Licence, Lease or Contract.

Environment

Regulation 33　Protection of Environment and Prevention of Pollution

33. 1　The Licensee, Lessee or Contractor shall protect the environment in and about the area of the licence, lease or Contract.

33. 2　The Licensee, Lessee or Contractor shall comply with existing and future environmental regulations and all such instructions as may, from time to time, be given in writing by the Authority.

33. 3　Without prejudice to paragraph 1 of this Regulation, the Licensee Lessee or Contractor shall adopt all practicable precautions including the provision

of up-to-date equipment approved by the Authority, to prevent the pollution of sea areas by oil, mud or other fluids or substances which might contaminate the water or shore line or which might cause harm or destruction to marine life, and where any such pollution occurs or has occurred, shall take prompt steps to control, terminate and remediate.

Regulation 34　Drainage of Waste

The Licensee, Lessee or Contractor shall drain all waste oil, brine and sludge or refuse from all storage vessels, boreholes and wells into proper receptacles constructed in compliance with safety regulations made under these or any other applicable regulations, and shall dispose thereof in a manner approved by the Authority or as provided by any other applicable regulations.

Regulation 35　Removal of Property

35.1　As directed by the Authority, the Licensee, Lessee or Contractor shall remove all property brought into the area of the Licence, Lease or Contract and comply with regulations and directions concerning the containment and clean-up of pollution.

35.2 In the event that the Licensee, Lessee or Contractor does not remove property or pollution to the satisfaction of the Authority or take such other action as is necessary for the conservation and protection of the marine environment, the Authority may direct it to take such remedial action as the Authority deems necessary. If it does not comply with that direction, it shall be liable for any costs incurred by the Authority in rectifying the matter.

Exploration and drilling

Regulation 36　Commencement of Exploration

Every Licensee, Lessee or Contractor:

(a) Shall explore the relevant area using geological, geophysical and any other acceptable method of examination for the purpose of ascertaining what petroleum prospects exist, until the area has been adequately explored for that purpose, giving in this respect due regard to the reasonable wishes of the Authority; and

(b) Shall, within six months of the date of the grant of the Licence, Lease or Contract, commence (in so far as the work has not already begun) seismic investigations which shall continue until the relevant area has been fully investigated.

Regulation 37 Commencement of Drilling

Not later than eighteen months from the date of the grant of an OPL, the Licensee, Lessee or Contractor shall begin drilling operations. The Licensee, Lessee or Contractor shall comply with the drilling requirements in the work programme commitment entered into with the Authority.

Regulation 38 Boreholes and Wells

38.1 No borehole or well shall be commenced or re – entered after work has been stopped for six months, without the written permission of the Authority.

38.2 As soon as the site of any borehole or well has been decided, the Licensee, Lessee or Contractor shall notify the Authority in writing of the proposed site in accordance with the following provisions:

(a) In the case of an exploration hole or any hole penetrating any previously undrilled structure, strata or pool, the notification to the Authority shall contain;

(i) the name or proposed name of the field followed by the figure 1,

(ii) the preliminary co – ordinates of the proposed location;

(iii) the total depth of the proposed well;

(iv) a seismic map or plan of the structure or structures to be investigated and the estimated date of spudding (which shall not be less than twenty – one days from the date of the notification), and

(v) information as to the drilling, casing, testing, cementation and completion programmes proposed by the Licensee, Lessee or Contractor and all such other information as the Authority may by notice in writing require from time to time;

(b) In the case of a development or appraisal well or a well penetrating only previously drilled structures, strata or pools, the seismic maps or plans of which have already been submitted to the Authority, the notification shall contain the approved name of the field and its number which shall represent the chronological sequence in which the well is to be drilled relative to the exploration well (which shall always commence by the figure 1) together with:

(i) the proposed spud date of the well;

(ii) its preliminary co-ordinates;

(iii) the total depth of the proposed well;

(iv) its estimated date of spudding (which shall not be less than twenty-one days from the date of the notification), and

(v) information as to the drilling, casing, logging, cementation, testing and completion programmes and all such other information as the Authority may by notice in writing require from time to time.

38.3　Where it is satisfied with the programme notified to it, the Authority shall give its written approval to the drilling of the well together with such observations and comments as it may wish to make.

38.4　If it is not satisfied with the programme, the Authority may withhold its permission, but it shall convey to the Licensee, Lessee or Contractor the reasons for its refusal.

Regulation 39　Wells and Fields

39.1　Every well shall be identified by a unique designation for which the Licensee, Lessee or Contractor shall obtain the prior approval in writing of the Authority.

39.2　The designation of a well shall in general consist of the name of the field in which the well is to be drilled, followed by the serial number which indicates the chronological order in the drilling sequence for the field.

39.3　All fields shall bear names in a Nigerian or Sao Tomean vernacular language which shall in general refer to any geographical, topographical or other general features in either State, and may be chosen from the names of national flora and fauna in either State, or from any local numerals.

39.4　The designation of a well may not be altered simply because a part of the well was deviated or sidetracked/whipstocked or because the well was re-drilled to a lower target.

39.5　Where an original hole has been plugged back and abandoned but another hole is drilled directionally to another target area, the new directional hole shall have a unique number if the new bottom is at least one hundred meters from the bottom of the original hole.

39.6 The new directional hole may with the approval of the Authority, have other prefixes, suffixes or any other additional letters or characters (which shall first be satisfied of the necessity for the addition) appended to the designation of any well.

39.7 The Licensee, Lessee or Contractor shall not change the designation, status or classification of a well or field without the approval in writing of the Authority.

39.8 In this Regulation "field" includes an existing field and a proposed field.

Regulation 40 Drilling Rigs

40.1 No person shall operate a drilling rig without a valid licence granted by the Authority.

40.2 The following provisions shall apply in respect of a licence granted under this regulation:

(a) The licence shall expire on the 31st December next following the date on which it was granted, but may be renewed upon application in writing made at least two months before the expiry;

(b) The licence may be withdrawn or suspended for a stated period if the rig is operated in contravention of any enactment, or if the owners or operators thereof do not comply with instructions issued by the Authority;

(c) The licence shall not be transferable;

(d) A copy of the current licence shall be displayed on the rig and the original shall be available for inspection at all times on the rig.

40.3 Applications for a licence to be granted under this Regulation, and any licences so granted, shall be in the appropriate form to these Regulations.

Field Development

Regulation 41 Power to give certain Directives

The Authority may give such directives as may in its opinion be necessary from time to time, to ensure the proper exploitation of petroleum and to encourage good conservation practices in any licensed, leased or Contract Area; and the Licensee, Lessee or Contractor shall comply with any such directions which affect him.

Regulation 42　Resident Manager

The holder of an OPL, OML or PSC shall ensure that the operator:

(a) Appoints a manager resident in either of the States Parties to supervise operations under the Licence, Lease or Contract; and

(b) Notifies the name and address of the said manager (and changes therein) to the Authority, and any notices required to be served on the Licensee, Lessee or Contractor shall be sufficiently served if delivered or posted to the manager at the address notified.

Regulation 43　Maintenance of Apparatus and Conduct of Operations

The Licensee, Lessee or Contractor shall maintain all apparatus and appliances in use in his operations, and all boreholes and wells capable of producing petroleum, in good repair and condition, and shall carry out all its operations in a proper and workmanlike manner in accordance with these and other relevant regulations and methods and practices accepted by the Authority as good oilfield practice; and without prejudice to the generality of the foregoing it shall, in accordance with those practices, take all steps practicable:

(a) To control the flow and to prevent escape or avoidable waste of petroleum discovered in or obtained from the relevant area;

(b) To prevent damage to adjoining petroleum‐bearing strata;

(c) To prevent, except for the purpose of secondary recovery as authorised by the Authority, the entrance of water through boreholes and wells to petroleum-bearing strata;

(d) To prevent the escape of petroleum into any sea area.

Regulation 44　Field Development Programme

45.1 All fields, structures, reservoirs and other oil traps shall be developed and produced in strict compliance with a field development programme, which shall be submitted for the prior approval of the Authority and shall give details of the following:

(a) Estimated size of the pool,

(b) The known physical parameters of the pools reservoirs or structures at the time of drawing up the programme,

(c) The intended drilling pattern (if any),

(d) The production or drainage pattern, and

(e) The anticipated drive mechanism.

45.2 No such field development programme shall be required to be submitted during the initial phase when the extent of a field structure, reservoir or pool is being appraised and wells are being drilled:

(a) Not closer than 800 metres, where the wells are likely to produce from the same pool; or

(b) Not closer than 400 metres, where the wells will not at any one time produce from the same pool except in conformity with the subsequently approved field development programme.

Regulation 45 Natural Gas Feasibility Study

Feasibility studies for the utilization of Natural Gas shall be submitted to the Authority with all field development proposals.

Regulation 46 Approval to Produce Petroleum

A Licensee, Lessee or Contractor shall not produce petroleum nor construct any production structures without the approval of the Authority. The Authority shall not unreasonably withhold such approvals.

Regulation 47 Production of Crude Oil and Natural Gas

The Lessee or Contractor shall use approved methods and practices acceptable to the Authority for the production of crude oil or natural gas from any pools or reservoir, and shall in particular take all necessary steps:

(a) To obtain the initial physical characteristics of the reservoir fluids and reservoir parameters (such as temperatures, pressures, gas oil ratios, bubble point pressures, porosities, viscosities, relative permeabilities in relation to fluid saturations, fluid gravities and the like), the detailed data and results and analyses of which shall be submitted to the Authority prior to, or as soon as possible after, the commencement of production from any such pool or reservoir;

(b) To obtain periodical information on the data required to be obtained by paragraph (a) of this regulation, at intervals approved by the Authority;

(c) To cause every pool in each well to produce within the limits of its maximum efficient potential or rate as may be determined from time to time by the Lessee, and to submit the results of his determinations to the Authority every six months.

Regulation 48　Petroleum Production Work

Unless otherwise agreed between the Lessee or Contractor and the Authority, work on a permanent structure to produce petroleum shall commence within six (6) months of the grant of an OML.

Regulation 49　Rates of Production

The Authority may direct and make regulations on the commencement of petroleum production and the specific rates of petroleum production. In giving such directives and in making such regulations the Authority shall take account of good oilfield practice.

Regulation 50　Confinement of Petroleum

The Lessee or Contractor shall use approved methods and practices acceptable to the Authority for confining the petroleum obtained from the relevant area in tanks, gasholders, pipes, pipelines or other receptacles constructed for that purpose.

Regulation 51　Pressure Decline

51.1　Prior to or upon the attainment of a 10 per cent decline in the initial reservoir pressure of a pool or reservoir (determined by the consideration of the average current reservoir pressure weighted as appropriate), the Lessee or Contractor shall commence or cause to be commenced a study to determine the economic practicability of instituting a secondary recovery or pressure maintenance project and its recommended timing.

51.2　A full report of the result of the study shall be submitted to the Authority as soon as possible (and in any case not more than six months) after the attainment of the pressure decline mentioned in sub-paragraph 51.1.

Regulation 52　Samples and Specimens

52.1　The holder of any Licence or Lease or Contract may remove for examination and analysis samples and specimens of rock and petroleum found by him in the course of his operations.

52.2　The Authority, through its authorised representatives shall have access to the samples at all times.

52.3　The Authority shall be given particulars of all such samples and specimens and provided, if it so requests, with representative samples and specimens not exceeding one half of the samples and specimens removed.

52.4　The holder of any Licence/Lease or Contract may not export samples or specimens abroad except with the written permission of the Authority and subject to such conditions as it may prescribe.

52.5　The Licensee, Lessee or Contractor shall correctly label and preserve for reference for a period of two years:

(a) Any characteristic samples which it takes, or is required by the Authority to take, of the strata or water encountered in any borehole or well; and

(b) Samples of petroleum or other fluids found in the relevant area.

Regulation 53　Joint Development Schemes

53.1　If at any time during the term of a Licence, Lease or Contract:

(a) The Authority, after consultation with the Licensee, Lessee or Contrator (referred to in this Regulation as "the grantee"), is satisfied that an oil accumulation or any part thereof forms part of a single geological petroleum reservoir (referred to in this Regulation as "the oilfield") in respect of other parts of which any other Licence, Lease or Contract is in force and that the oilfield is susceptible of being developed as a unit in accordance with good oilfield practice; and

(b) The Authority considers that it is in the interests of the States Parties, the grantee and the Licensees, Lessees or Contractors of any other part of the oilfield (those Licensees or Lessees being referred to in this regulation as "the other parties") in order to secure the maximum ultimate recovery of petroleum that the oilfield should be worked and developed as a unit in co-operation with all those who hold a Licence, Lease or Contract over any part thereof, sub‑paragraphs 53.2, 53.3 and 53.4 shall apply.

53.2 The grantee shall, upon being so required by the Authority by a notice in writing specifying the other parties, co‑operate with each other in the preparation of a scheme (referred to in this regulation as "the development scheme") for the working and development of the oilfield as a unit by the grantee and the other parties in co‑operation, and they shall jointly submit the development scheme for the approval of the Authority.

53.3 The said notice shall contain a description, by reference to a map, of the area in respect of which the Authority requires the development scheme to be submitted for its approval, and shall state the period within which the development scheme is required to be so submitted.

53.4 If the development scheme is not submitted to the Authority within the period limited in that behalf by the said notice, or if the development scheme on being submitted in pursuance of sub‑paragraph 53.3 is not approved by the Authority, the Authority shall prepare the development scheme in a manner which in its opinion is fair and equitable to the grantee and the other parties.

53.5 When the development scheme has been:

(a) Submitted under sub‑paragraph 53.3 and duly approved; or

(b) Prepared by the Authority under sub‑paragraph 53.4,

the grantee and the other parties shall perform and observe all the terms and conditions thereof.

Regulation 54　Abandonment, Plugging, etc.

54.1 No borehole or existing well shall be re‑drilled, plugged or abandoned, and no cemented casing or other permanent form of casing shall be withdrawn from any borehole or existing well which is proposed to be abandoned, without the written permission of the Authority.

54.2 Every borehole or existing well which the Licensee, Lessee or Contractor intends to abandon shall, unless the Authority otherwise permits in writing, be securely plugged by the Licensee, Lessee or Contractor so as to prevent ingress and egress of water into and from any portion or portions of the strata bored through and shall be dealt with in strict accordance with an abandonment programme approved or agreed to by the Authority.

54.3 Except in an emergency, the Authority may, in any case direct that no borehole or well may be plugged, or no works be executed, save in the presence of a designated officer of the Authority.

Regulation 55　Termination

55.1 The Licensee, Lessee or Contractor shall within six months (or such further period as the Authority may approve) after the termination of its Licence, Lease or Contract:

(a) Deliver to the Authority, in good order, repair and condition and fit for further working, all productive boreholes or wells (unless the Authority requires the Licensee, Lessee or Contractor in writing to plug them as it may direct or as provided by these Regulations) together with all casings and other appurtenances to the boreholes and wells which are below the Christmas tree and cannot be moved without causing injury to the said boreholes or wells;

(b) To the like extent take reasonable steps to restore the relevant area as far as possible to its original condition.

55.2 Within six months (or such further period as the Authority may approve) after the termination of its Licence, Lease or Contract, the Licensee, Lessee or Contractor shall, if so required by the Authority, plug every borehole which the Authority may indicate in the manner specified by the Authority.

55.3 On the termination of its Licence, Lease or Contract, the Licensee, Lessee or Contractor shall, subject to the rights of any person in the relevant area or any part of it, remove all installations, works, chattels and effects erected or brought by the Licensee, Lessee or Contractor upon the relevant area for or in connection with its operations PROVIDED that, subject as aforesaid, the Authority may specify any such installations, works, chattels or effects, and shall then be entitled to take the same at a price bearing a reasonable relationship to the written down value thereof.

55.4 Where part of the relevant area of a Licence, Lease or Contract is surrendered, it shall be deemed for the purposes of this Regulation to have terminated as regards that part of the relevant area.

PART FIVE REPORTING, ACCOUNTS AND RECORDS

Regulation 56 Records of Boreholes and Wells

56.1 The Licensee, lessee or Contractor shall keep a record of all boreholes and wells in a form from time to time approved by the Authority, and the records shall contain particulars in respect of each borehole or well, as the case may be, of:

(a) The strata and subsoil through which the borehole or well was drilled and the final depth;

(b) The depth of the sea where the borehole was drilled;

(c) The casing inserted in the borehole or well and any alterations thereto;

(d) Any petroleum, water, mineral deposits encountered;

(e) The results of any analyses, by or on behalf of the Licensee, Lessee or Contractor, of any such petroleum, water, mineral deposits or of any other data required to be obtained by or under this regulation;

(f) Logs of all types taken in the well (in every case including a minimum of one resistivity log suite and porosity log suite),

(g) Results of all borehole surveys and tests (including production tests and pressure tests taken or required to be taken on the well); and

(h) Such other matters as the Authority may from time to time require.

Regulation 57 Discovery Reports

The Licensee, Lessee or Contractor shall immediately report to the Authority the discovery of petroleum or petroleum – bearing strata.

Regulation 58 Measurement and Weighing of Crude Oil and Natural Gas

58.1 The Licensee, Lessee or Contractor shall, with volume and gravity correction to sixty degrees Fahrenheit and by a method or methods approved by the Authority in writing, measure or weigh:

(a) All crude oil won and saved and casinghead petroleum spirit recovered from the relevant area; and

(b) All natural gas sold.

58.2 An officer authorised by the Authority shall have the right to be present whenever any such measurement or weighing takes place.

58.3 An officer authorised by the Authority shall at all times be present when equipment or an appliance for measuring or weighing crude oil or gas is being calibrated, recalibrated, tested, compared, measured or weighed against a standard approved by the Authority; and any such calibration shall be in accordance with accepted methods and procedures previously agreed to by the Authority.

58.4 If any measuring or weighing appliance is at any time found to be false or unjust or inaccurate to the extent of more than 1 per cent:

(a) The appliance shall be deemed to have existed in that condition during the period of three months prior to the discovery unless the Licensee, Lessee or Contractor can prove to the reasonable satisfaction of the Authority that such an error could not have possibly occurred over that period or the period that has elapsed since the last occasion upon which the appliance was examined or tested, whichever is less; and

(b) The royalties payable in respect of the period during which the appliance is deemed to have so existed shall be adjusted accordingly.

58.5 The Licensee, Lessee or Contractor shall not repair, maintain, or make any alterations in the measuring or weighing equipment or appliances or in the method or methods of measurement or weighing approved by the Authority without first informing the Authority; and in every case any such repairs, maintenance or alterations shall be carried out in the presence of an authorised person of the Authority or its representative.

58.6 The Authority and its authorised representatives shall, have the right to specify the frequency at which all measuring and weighing instruments shall be calibrated or tested, and notwithstanding any such specification, may test or demonstrate the accuracy of any appliance or equipment at any time, with or without previous notice to the Licensee, Lessee or Contractor.

Regulation 59　Accounts and Particulars

The Licensee, Lessee or Contractor shall in respect of the relevant area, in a form from time to time approved by the Authority keep full and accurate accounts of:

(a) The quantity of crude oil and casinghead spirit won and saved or recovered therefrom;

(b) The method and result of physical tests made on crude oil;

(c) The quantity of crude oil and casinghead petroleum spirit sold or exported out of the Zone and the particulars of the sale and export;

(d) The quantity of crude oil otherwise disposed of and the manner of its disposal;

(e) The quantity of natural gas sold and the price at which it has been sold;

(f) The quantity of crude oil and casinghead petroleum spirit used for drilling or pumping to storage or re – injected to a formation;

(g) The quantity of natural gas used for drilling, for production or as fuel, or reinjected into a formation; and

(h) Such further particulars and statistics relating to the operations as the Authority may from time to time require, and shall within one month after the last day of each quarter deliver to the Authority an abstract in a form from time to time approved by the Authority of the accounts for the quarter ended on that last day, together with a statement in the like form of all royalties payable in respect of the said quarter.

Regulation 60　Progress Reports

60.1　The Licensee, Lessee or Contractor shall furnish within twenty – one days after the end of each month to the Authority, in a form from time to time approved by the Authority, a report of the progress of its operations containing particulars of the contents of the record required to be kept under these Regulations, and in addition a statement of the areas in which the Licensee, Lessee or Contractor has carried out any geological or geophysical work and an account of the work in question.

60.2　The Licensee, Lessee or Contractor shall within one month after the end of each quarter furnish to the Authority a report in a form from time to time approved by the Authority of the operations conducted in the relevant area during each quarter, and a forecast of activities in the ensuing quarter, together with a plan upon a scale approved by the Authority showing the situation of all boreholes or wells.

60.3 The Licensee, Lessee or Contractor shall within two months of the end of each calendar year, or any such extended time as the Authority may allow, furnish a report containing such information regarding the progress of work in the relevant area in that year as the Authority may from time to time specify.

Regulation 61 Miscellaneous Provisions Relating to Records

61.1 The Licensee, Lessee or Contractor shall keep accurate geological and subsurface plans, maps, charts, sections and other appropriate geological records (including an estimate, revised to include information obtained up to the end of each calendar year, of the probable reserves and the recoverable amount of petroleum reasonably believed to be present as at the date of estimation or revision in the relevant area), and an extract there from or copy thereof shall form part of the annual report required to be furnished in so far as the information to which it relates has not already been furnished.

61.2 The information required to be included in the annual report by paragraph 61.1 may be submitted as a separate volume of the annual report.

61.3 The Licensee, Lessee or Contractor shall furnish to the Authority such other maps, plans and information as to the progress of operations in the relevant area as they may from time to time require, including reports on geological and geophysical surveys carried out in the relevant area.

61.4 The Licensee, Lessee or Contractor shall submit to the Authority copies of every log or borehole survey carried out in any well or borehole as soon as practicable and in any case not more than one month (or such further period as the Authority may allow), after running the log or carrying out the survey.

61.5 The Licensee, Lessee or Contractor shall submit to the Authority all seismograms and copies of all other geophysical records obtained on the relevant area.

Provided that:

(a) the Authority may direct the Licensee, Lessee or Contractor to keep the records in its custody; and

(b) any such records so kept shall be made available to the Authority on demand.

61.6 The results of all seismic surveys, including the relevant seismic map, shall be submitted to the Authority.

61.7 The Licensee, Lessee or Contractor shall submit to the Authority negatives of any aerial photographs and copies in electronic and hard copy form of any satellite imagery obtained by the Licensee, Lessee or Contractor in the course of its operations. The Authority shall be entitled to retain such negatives or copies and to make use, as it thinks fit, of them and of any information obtained from them.

61.8 The Licensee, Lessee or Contractor shall within three months of the termination of its licence or lease render a report to the Authority –

(a) giving an account of the geology of the relevant area;

(b) including an account of the stratigraphic and structural conditions, together with geological, structural and other subsurface maps, plans and sections on suitably scaled maps and charts; and

(c) including a summary of all immovable items, equipment, appliances, structures and the like in the relevant area.

61.9 No information required by these Regulations to be furnished in relation to work done or progress of operations in the relevant area shall be withheld on the grounds that the information is confidential or interpretational.

Regulation 62 Auditing of Contractors' Books and Accounts

The contractor's books and accounts shall be subject to audit by the Authority, which shall be conducted annually. The Authority may issue regulations and directions with respect to the auditing of books and accounts.

Regulation 63 Records to be Supplied at the expense of Licensee, Lessee or Contractor

All records, reports, plans, maps, charts, accounts and information which are required to be furnished under these and other Regulations shall be supplied at the expense of the Licensee, Lessee or Contractor.

Regulation 64 Confidentiality

Any information supplied by the Licensee, Lessee or Contractor shall (except as otherwise provided by these Regulations) be treated by the Authority and its officers entitled to the information as confidential PROVIDED that the Authority shall be entitled at any time to make use of any such information for the purpose of preparing or causing to be prepared aggregated returns and general reports on the extent of oil operations in the Zone and for the purposes of any arbitration or litigation between the Authority and the Licensee, Lessee or Contractor.

Regulation 65 Release of Information and Data

65.1 The Authority may make such use as it wishes of information and data contained in a report, return or other document furnished to the Authority, provided that information and data is not made publicly known by the Authority before the periods of confidentiality identified below have expired.

65.2 Basic information and data about petroleum operations in the area of a licence or lease may be released by the Authority five (5) years after it was lodged with the Authority or when the areas to which that information and data relates cease to be part of the area of the licence or lease, if earlier. However, conclusions drawn or opinions based in whole or in part on that information and data shall not be released until ten (10) years after that information and data was lodged with the Authority.

65.3 Where information and data has been released by the Licensee, Lessee or Contractor or some party acting on his behalf, the Authority shall not be obliged to maintain the confidentiality of that information and data.

65.4 Information and data relating to a seismic or other geochemical or geophysical survey shall be deemed to have been lodged no later than six (6) months after the survey has been essentially completed. Information and data on wells shall be deemed to have been lodged no later than three (3) months after the well has been essentially completed.

65.5 Access to information that is not released that relates to or is adjacent to a particular License, Lease or Contract Area shall be based on mutual agreements between the Authority and the relevant contractors.

65.6 The Authority shall be free to use any information and data relating to relinquished and surrendered blocks or relating to other blocks outside the area of the licence or lease, including releasing it to any party.

65.7 Officials of the Governments of the States Parties may have access to information and data provided to the Authority under these and other Regulations, provided such officials comply with the provisions of this Regulation applicable to the Authority itself.

Regulation 66 Special Terms

The Authority may impose on a licensee or lessee to which these Regulations apply, special terms and conditions not inconsistent with these Regulations including (without prejudice to the generality of the foregoing) the terms and conditions as to participation by the Authority in the venture to which the licence, lease or PSC relates, on terms to be negotiated between the Authority and the applicant for the licence or lease, special provisions applying to any natural gas discovered; including:

(ⅰ) the right of the Authority to take natural gas produced with crude oil by the Licensee, Lessee or Contractor free of cost at the flare or at an agreed cost and without payment of royalty;

(ⅱ) the obligation of the Licensee, Lessee or Contractor to obtain the approval of the Authority as to the price at which natural gas produced by the Licensee, Lessee or Contractor (and not taken by the Authority) is sold; and

(ⅲ) a requirement for the payment by the Licensee, Lessee or Contractor of royalty on natural gas produced and sold.

PART SIX RECRUITMENT AND TRAINING OF NATIONALS OF STATES PARTIES

Regulation 67 Training Programmes

67.1 The licensee or Operator of an oil prospecting license shall within twelve months of the grant of its licence, and the lessee of an oil mining lease shall on the grant of its lease, submit for the Authority's approval, a detailed programme for the recruitment and training of nationals of the States Parties.

67.2 The programme shall provide for the training of such nationals in all phases of petroleum operations whether the phases are handled directly by the lessee or through agents and contractors.

Regulation 68   Scholarship Schemes

All scholarship schemes prepared, and any scholarships proposed to be awarded, by the Licensee, Lessee or Contractor (whether or not related to the operations of the Licensee, Lessee or Contractor or to the oil industry generally) shall be submitted for the approval of the Authority.

Regulation 69   Variations

Once a programme under Regulation 67 of these Regulations or a scholarship scheme under Regulation 68 of these Regulations has been approved by the Authority, it shall not be varied without its written permission.

Regulation 70   Reports

A report on the execution of the programme mentioned in regulation 69 of these Regulations shall be submitted by the Licensee, Lessee or Contractor at or about the end of June and December in every calendar year.

Regulation 71 Targets

The holder of an oil mining lease shall ensure that:

(a) within ten years from the grant of its lease the number of nationals of the States Parties employed by it in connection with the lease in managerial, professional and supervisory grades (or any corresponding grades designated by it in a manner approved by the Authority) shall reach at least 75 per cent of the total number of persons employed by it in those grades;

(b) the number employed as provided for in sub-paragraph (a) of this Regulation shall be divided between nationals of Nigeria and nationals of São Tomé e Príncipe as far as reasonably practicable in line with the provision of the Treaty;

(c) within 10 years from grant of its lease, the number of nationals of the States Parties in any one such grade shall be not less than 60 percent.; and

(d) all skilled, semi-skilled and unskilled workers are citizens of the States Parties, divided between them as far as reasonably practicable in line with the provision of the Treaty.

PART SEVEN MISCELLANEOUS

Regulation 72 Datum

For the purposes of these Regulations, in determining the position of the boundaries of any Block, calculating areas, identifying any position within the Zone or any other activity relating to the identification of geodetic positions, the WGS 84 Datum shall be used.

Regulation 73 Insurance

73.1 The Authority shall require each Licensee, Lessee or Contractor to take out and maintain from the effective date of the licence or lease, to the satisfaction of the Authority, insurance on a strict liability basis and for an amount determined by the Authority in consultation with the applicant for such licence or lease. It shall also agree with the Licensee, Lessee or Contractor on a mechanism whereby compensation claims can be determined. The insurance shall cover expenses or liabilities or any other specified things arising in connection with the carrying out of petroleum operations and other activities associated with those operations in the area of the licence or lease, including expenses associated with the prevention and cleanup of the escape of petroleum.

73.2 Licensees and lessees shall ensure that transportation of petroleum in bulk as cargo from the Zone takes place only in tankers with appropriate insurance commensurate with relevant international agreements.

Regulation 74 Interference with holders of Licences, Leases or PSCs and other Offences

74.1 Any person who interferes with or obstructs the holder of a licence or lease granted under these Regulations (or his representatives or agents) in the exercise of any rights, power or liberty conferred by the licence or lease shall be guilty of an offence and on conviction shall be liable to a fine not exceeding two hundred thousand dollars or to imprisonment for a period not exceeding six months, or to both.

74.2 Any person who:

(i) Prospects for petroleum without an oil prospecting licence, or

(ii) Wins or works petroleum otherwise than in pursuance of a licence or lease granted under this Petroleum Regulation 2003,

(iii) Does, without the appropriate licence, any act for which a licence is required under any regulations, shall be guilty of an offence and shall be liable on conviction to a fine not exceeding two hundred thousand dollars.

74.3 Where a person is convicted of an offence under paragraph 74.2 in respect of any petroleum or petroleum products, then, in addition to any penalty imposed under the subsection in question, the convicting court may:

(a) Order the petroleum or petroleum products to be forfeited; or

(b) Order that person to pay to the Authority the value of the petroleum or petroleum products.

Regulation 75　Further Regulations and Power to Make Regulations

The Authority may, subject to the approval of the Council, issue guidelines:

(a) Prescribing anything requiring to be prescribed for the purposes of these Regulations;

(b) Providing generally for matters relating to licences and leases granted under these Regulations and operations carried on there under, including:

(i) safe working,

(ii) the conservation of petroleum resources,

(iii) the prevention of pollution of sea areas and the atmosphere,

(iv) the making of reports and returns (including the reporting of accidents),

(v) inquiries into accidents,

(vi) the keeping and inspection of records, books, statistics, accounts and plans,

(vii) the measurement of production, and

(c) Regulating the construction, maintenance and operation of installations used in pursuance of these and any other Regulations;

(d) Regulating the storage of petroleum and in particular (without prejudice to the generality of the foregoing);

(i) defining dangerous petroleum,

(ii) regulating the loading, unloading, and shipment of petroleum and petroleum products,

(iii) providing for the examination and testing of petroleum and prescribing the tests to be applied to ascertain its flash point and the method of applying those tests, and

(iv) regulating the transport of petroleum prescribing the quantity of petroleum and petroleum products which may be carried in any vessel, the manner in which they shall be stored when being so carried, the receptacles in which they shall be contained when being so carried and the quantities to be contained in those receptacles, and providing for the search and inspection of any such vessel;

(e) Conferring or imposing on public officers, powers and duties additional to those conferred or imposed by these Regulations;

(f) Where paragraph (a) of this subsection does not apply; prescribing;

(i) forms to be used for the purposes of these Regulations, and

(ii) fees to be charged in connection with the operation of these regulations (including, without prejudice to the generality of the foregoing, fees for the giving of any permission by the Council of Ministers and for the supplying of any document or other material, the carrying out of any examination and the doing of any other thing by him); and

(g) Providing for such other matters as in his opinion may be necessary or desirable in order to give proper effect to this Act.

Regulation 76 Publication of Regulations

These Regulations and any modification thereto adopted pursuant to paragraph 4 of Article 21 of the Treaty, shall be promptly published by the Authority, following their adoption, as provided by paragraphs 3 and 5 of Article 21 of the Treaty.

Regulation 77 Settlement of Disputes by Arbitration

77.1 Where by any provision of these Regulations or any regulations made there under a question or dispute is to be settled by arbitration, the question or dispute shall be settled in line with the provision of the Treaty

77.2 If any question or dispute arises in connection with any licence or lease to which these Regulations apply between the Authority and the Licensee, Lessee or Contractor (including a question or dispute as to the payment of any fee, rent or royalty), the question or dispute shall be settled by arbitration unless it relates to a matter expressly excluded from arbitration or expressed to be at the discretion of the Authority.

Regulation 78　Circumstances beyond Control

78.1 Failure on the part of the holder of a licence or lease to which these Regulations applies to fulfil any of the terms or conditions of the licence or lease shall not (except as may be otherwise provided for in or in relation to the licence or lease) give the Authority any claim against the Licensee, Lessee or Contractor, or be deemed a breach of the licence or lease, if the failure arises from causes beyond the control of the Licensee, Lessee or Contractor.

78.2 If from any such cause the fulfilment by any such Licensee, Lessee or Contractor of any term or condition of his licence or lease or of any provision of these Regulations is delayed, the period of delay shall be added to the period fixed for the fulfilment of the term or condition.

（十四）2001年东帝汶与澳大利亚共同开发案

1.《东帝汶政府与澳大利亚政府间帝汶海条约》

（2002年5月20日订于帝力）

董世杰译，邓妮雅校

澳大利亚政府和东帝汶政府意识到促进东帝汶经济发展的重要性；对于澳大利亚和东帝汶之间的海床区域的现有和计划石油活动的投资，有必要保证安全；认识到为澳大利亚和东帝汶之间的海床区域的石油活动按计划进行，提供一个持续的基础，将会使澳大利亚和东帝汶受益；强调以一种对自然环境损害最小且经济可持续的方式开发石油资源的重要性，推动进一步投资以及澳大利亚和东帝汶的长期发展；坚信根据本条约开发资源，将会为延续和强化澳大利亚和东帝汶之间的友好关系提供坚实基础；鉴于1982年12月10日在蒙特哥湾签署的《联合国海洋法公约》，其第83条规定海岸相向或相邻国家间的大陆架划界，应根据国际法通过协定，以公平解决；进一步考虑到，在未划界的情形下，国家有义务基于谅解和合作的精神，尽一切努力做出实际性的临时安排，不危害或阻碍最后协议的达成；注意到澳大利亚和东帝汶，愿意就澳大利亚和东帝汶之间的海床区域的石油资源的持续开发缔结条约，达成如下协议。

第一条 定义

为了本条约的目的，

(a) "条约"是指本条约，包括附件 A-G 以及此后澳大利亚和东帝汶达成的任何附件。

(b) "承包商"是指根据《石油开采规则》做承包商登记，并与指定当局订立合同的公司。

(c) "刑法"指澳大利亚和东帝汶国内有效的任何有关犯罪，或者与犯罪调查起诉有关，或者有关对罪犯的处罚（其中包括执行法院判处的刑罚）的实体或程序法。"调查"包括进入共同石油开发区设施或构筑物内，行使搜查、询问以及逮捕犯罪嫌疑人的权力。

(d) "指定当局"是指根据本条约第六条所设立的指定当局。

(e) "财政体制"是指特许权使用费，产品分成合同，或者其他决定澳大利亚和东帝汶之间的石油或石油活动收入份额的体制，但不包括根据本条约第五条 b 款规定的税收。

(f) "初步加工"是指对石油进行处理，使其准备好从生产设施中排出至某一点，可能包括除去水、挥发物和其他杂质的程序。

(g) "联合委员会"是指根据本条约第六条设立的澳大利亚—东帝汶联合委员会。

(h) "共同石油开发区"是指根据本条约第三条建立的共同石油开发区。

(i) "部长理事会"是指根据本条约第六条建立的澳大利亚—东帝汶部长理事会。

(j) "石油"是指：

ⅰ. 任何自然产生的碳氢化合物，无论是气态、液态还是固态；

ⅱ. 任何自然产生的碳氢化合物的混合物，无论是气态、液态还是固态；

ⅲ. 任何自然产生的一种或几种碳氢化合物的混合物，无论是气态、液态还是固态，也包括与这些碳氢化合物一起产生的其他物质；

以及上述 ⅰ、ⅱ、ⅲ 项中所指的被返还到自然储油层中的石油。

(k) "石油活动"是指根据合同、许可证而授权或计划从事石油生产的所有活动，包括勘探、开发、初步加工、生产、运输和销售，以及对这些活动所做的计划和准备。

（l）"石油开采规则"是指本条约第七条所指的规则。

（m）"石油规划"是指在共同石油开发区内特定区域发生的石油活动。

（n）"石油生产"是指通过石油活动，将从含油层中抽取的石油进行初步加工。

（o）"产品分成合同"是指指定当局与有限责任公司或实体间，分配共同石油开发区内特定区域的石油产品的合同。

（p）"含油层"是指由于岩石、水或其他物质的限制，无法通过气体或液体与其他石油聚集进行流通的单一地质构造内的石油聚集。

（q）"税收规则"是指本条约第十三条b款所指的规则。

第二条　不影响条款

（a）本条约是根据1982年12月10日在蒙特哥湾签署的《联合国海洋法公约》第83条的规定所缔结的，即海岸相向或相邻的国家，在未根据国际法就大陆架划界达成最终协议之前，应该达成临时性安排。本条约遵守该义务。

（b）本条约的内容以及条约生效期间所采取的行动，不应对澳大利亚和东帝汶有关大陆架划界的立场或主张，或各自海床权利造成损害或影响。

第三条　共同石油开发区

（a）建立共同石油开发区（JPDA）。该区域位于根据附件A所规定的界线的帝汶海内。

（b）澳大利亚和东帝汶基于两国人民的福祉，共同控制、管理和促进共同石油开发区石油资源的勘探、开发、利用。

（c）应当根据指定当局与专为合同目的而设立的有限责任公司之间缔结的合同，进行共同石油开发区内的石油活动。这一规定同样适用于该公司的继承者或者代理人。

（d）对于任何不根据本条约之规定，在共同石油开发区内进行石油活动的人，澳大利亚和东帝汶应将其视为犯罪。

第四条　产品分成合同

（a）澳大利亚和东帝汶对于共同石油开发区生产的所有石油享有所有

权。其中所产石油 90% 属于东帝汶，10% 属于澳大利亚。

（b）若第六条 b 款第 iii 项之规定的费用和其他收入不足以支付指定当局与条约有关的开支，缔约国应该按照本条 a 款之规定分担开支。

第五条　财政安排和税收

财政安排和税收应按照以下方式处理：

（a）除非本条约对财政制度另有规定，否则：

i．澳大利亚和东帝汶应尽一切努力，就共同石油开发区内的每一个石油项目的财政制度达成一致；

ii．如果未能对第 i 项所指之财政制度达成一致，应该共同任命一名独立专家，就适用于有关石油项目合适的共同财政计划提出建议；

iii．如果澳大利亚或者东帝汶不同意独立专家所提共同财政计划的建议，双方可根据本条约第四条中的方案所计算出的石油项目产品分配比例，分别采取各自的财政制度；

iv．如果澳大利和东帝汶根据本条之规定，就共同财政计划达成一致，除非两国都同意，否则澳大利亚或东帝汶不得在石油项目存续期间变更财政制度。

（b）根据本条约第四条中方案，以及澳大利亚和东帝汶各自国内法和税收规则，对共同石油开发区内石油活动所产生的收益以及本条约第十三条所指的活动进行征税。

第六条　管理机构

（a）建立一个由指定当局、联合委员会和部长理事会组成的三层联合管理结构。

（b）指定当局。

i．在条约生效后的 3 年内，或者澳大利亚和东帝汶另外协商的期限内，联合委员会应该任命指定当局。

ii．在第 i 项所规定的期限届满以后，指定当局应该是东帝汶负责石油活动的部门，或者是由该部门任命的一个东帝汶法定主管当局。

iii．在第 i 项所规定的期限内，指定当局具有法律人格、拥有澳大利亚和东帝汶国内法下的法律能力对其履行权力和职能是必要的。指定当局应该具有缔结合同、获得和处分动产和不动产，以及提起和参与诉讼的能力。

ⅳ. 指定当局应对联合委员会负责，并负责石油活动的日常管理事务。

ⅴ. 附件 C 对指定当局的具体权力和职能做了非排他性的列举。此外，本条约的其他附件可能还规定了指定当局其他具体的权力和职能。指定当局还拥有联合委员会授予的其他权力和职能。

ⅵ. 指定当局的经费来源于依据《石油开采规则》所征收的费用。

ⅶ. 在第 ⅰ 项所规定的期限内，指定当局免缴以下税收：

（ⅰ）在东帝汶，根据东帝汶法律征收的所得税；

（ⅱ）在澳大利亚，根据澳大利亚联邦法征收的所得税；

以及在本条约签署之后所征收的，或取代现有税种的，相同或大体类似的税收。

ⅷ. 在第 ⅰ 项所规定的期限内，指定当局的人员：

（ⅰ）为指定当局服务而获得的工资、津贴和其他报酬应当免税，不包括根据澳大利亚或东帝汶的法律，将他们视为其居民予以征税的部分；

（ⅱ）第一次任职于位于澳大利亚或东帝汶的指定当局，但不属于该国公民的公务人员，为了个人使用或居住而进口的家具，以及其所有的或订购的家庭用品和个人物品，免征关税和其他费用（服务费除外）。

这些物品应当在其第一次入境后的 6 个月内予以进口，除非澳大利亚或东帝汶政府允许延长时间。公务人员所取得或进口并且根据本项之规定免于纳税的物品，不得赠送、出卖、出借、出租或者以其他方式处置，除非其事先获得居住的澳大利亚或东帝汶政府的同意。

（c）联合委员会。

ⅰ. 联合委员会由澳大利亚和东帝汶任命的委员组成，其中东帝汶任命的委员比澳大利亚的多一名。联合委员会应该为共同石油开发区的石油活动制定政策和规则，同时监督指定当局的工作。

ⅱ. 附件 D 对联合委员会的权力和职能进行了非排他性的列举。本条约的其他附件可能还规定了指定当局其他具体的权力和职能。

ⅲ. 除了第八条 c 款规定的内容外，澳大利亚或者东帝汶任命的委员，均可在任何时候提交问题至部长理事会以求解决。

ⅳ. 联合委员会应该每年举行一次会议，或者应要求举行会议。会议由澳大利亚和东帝汶任命的委员轮流主持。

（d）部长理事会。

ⅰ. 部长理事会由澳大利亚和东帝汶相同人数的部长组成。其应研究处理澳大利亚或者东帝汶提交的有关条约运行的任何问题，应研究处理本条 c 款第ⅲ项所提及的问题。

ⅱ. 如果部长理事会无法解决问题，澳大利亚或东帝汶可将问题提交附件 B 中所规定的争端解决程序。

ⅲ. 澳大利亚或东帝汶提出要求，或者联合委员会提出要求，部长理事会应举行会议。

ⅳ. 除非澳大利亚和东帝汶另有约定，由两国至少各一名代表实际出席的部长理事会会议，应在澳大利亚和东帝汶之间轮流举行。会议由两国代表轮流主持。

ⅴ. 部长理事会可以允许其成员选择通过电话、闭路电视或者其他电子通信方式，参加一场特定的或所有的会议，这些成员视为出席会议。会议可以仅通过电子通信手段召开。

（e）联合委员会的委员以及指定当局的工作人员，必须在共同石油开发区的石油勘探和开发活动中，无个人经济利益。

第七条　《石油开采规则》

（a）澳大利亚和东帝汶应当谈判制定规范共同石油开发区石油勘探、开发和利用以及石油出口的《石油开采规则》。

（b）在条约生效时，如果澳大利亚和东帝汶两国尚未达成《石油开采规则》，那么联合委员会在其首次会议上，应采用一套临时规则，该规则直至依据 a 款制定《石油开采规则》时一直有效。

第八条　管道

（a）共同石油开发区内用于区域内出口石油的管道建设和运营，应该得到联合委员会的批准。澳大利亚和东帝汶应就从共同石油开发区到登陆点之间，出口石油的管道的条件和条款进行协商。

（b）登陆点位于东帝汶的管道受东帝汶管辖，登陆点位于澳大利亚的管道受澳大利亚管辖。

（c）若从共同石油开发区建设通往澳大利亚或东帝汶领土上的管道，管道登陆国不得反对或阻碍联合委员修建一条通往另一缔约国的管道。除非这一管道建设影响了公司的天然气的供应量。尽管有第六条 c 款第ⅲ项之规定，但部长理事会仍无权审查或改变联合委员会的决定。

（d）如果从共同石油开发区修建一条通往另一缔约国的管道，会使得有限责任公司或实体在特定期限内，根据本条约而缔结的合同从共同石油开发区的项目中获得的天然气供应量减少，那么本条 c 款之规定不适用。

（e）如果基于商业基础对共同石油开发区内的天然气进行液化并输出的建议，使得澳大利亚和东帝汶获得比通过管道运输更高的特许权使用费和税收，两国不得反对或阻碍。

（f）如果共同石油开发区内天然气液化并输出，会使得有限责任公司或实体在特定期限内，从根据本条约而缔结的合同从共同石油开发区的项目中获得的天然气供应量减少，本条 c 项不得适用。

（g）来自共同石油开发区和跨越开发区油田的石油，对于向共同石油开发区内输送石油或者从共同石油开发区向外输送石油的任何管道，拥有优先使用权。

（h）输送来自共同石油开发区的石油的管道应当是开放使用的。这种开放使用的安排应当符合良好的国际管理实践。若澳大利亚对于管道拥有管辖权，应当就管道的使用与东帝汶进行协商；如果东帝汶对于管道拥有管辖权，应当就管道的使用与澳大利亚进行协商。

第九条　统一化

（a）任何跨越共同石油开发区界线的含油层，基于管理和开发的目的，应该被视为一个实体。

（b）澳大利亚和东帝汶应该迅速和善意地，就最有效开发矿床以及公平分配开发收益的方法达成一致。

第十条　海洋环境

（a）澳大利亚和东帝汶应当合作保护共同石油开发区的海洋环境，以防止石油活动所产生的污染和其他环境损害，并将其降至最低。特别要努力保护海洋动物，包括海洋哺乳动物、海鸟、鱼类和珊瑚。澳大利亚和东帝汶应当就保护共同石油开发区海洋环境免受石油活动不利影响的最好方式进行协商。

（b）如果共同石油开发区内产生的海洋污染溢出该区，澳大利亚和东帝汶之间应当进行合作以防止、减轻和消除污染。

（c）指定当局应该发布保护共同石油开发区海洋环境的法规，并应当制订防止共同石油开发区内石油活动污染的应急计划。

（d）因共同石油开发区中的石油活动而产生的海洋环境污染所造成的损失或费用，有限责任公司或实体应依据以下规定承担责任：

ⅰ.合同、执照或者许可证，以及当局根据条约颁布的其他文件，以及

ⅱ.对赔偿请求具有管辖权的国家（澳大利亚或东帝汶）的法律。

第十一条 雇佣

（a）澳大利亚和东帝汶应当：

ⅰ.在适当考虑职位健康和安全的要求下，采取适当措施，确保共同石油开发区雇佣人员时，东帝汶的国民或永久性居民拥有优先权；

ⅱ.优先促进对东帝汶国民和永久性居民的雇佣和培训机会。

（b）对于与共同石油开发区的石油活动有关的，澳大利亚有限责任公司或实体所雇用的东帝汶国民和永久性居民，澳大利亚应当加快和便利他们在帝力的澳大利使馆申请签证的进程。

第十二条 工作人员的健康和安全

指定当局应当制定共同石油开发区雇员的职业健康安全标准和规程，并且不低于澳大利亚和东帝汶国内相似职业的人员所适用的标准和规程，有限责任公司应当适用该标准和规程。指定当局应当根据本条之规定，并考虑澳大利亚或东帝汶法律中建立的现有制度，制定该标准和规程。

第十三条 税法的适用

（a）为了税法目的，下列事项与税法直接或间接相关：

ⅰ.共同石油开发区内石油勘探或开发活动；或

ⅱ.任何勘探和开发活动有关的或产生的行动、问题和情形。

共同石油开发区应视为澳大利亚和东帝汶的一部分。

（b）附件G中的《税收规则》规定了有关石油活动免除双重征税。

（c）《税收规则》包含了自己的争端解决机制，以该机制解决的争端，条约第二十三条不予适用。

第十四条 刑事管辖权

（a）澳大利亚或东帝汶的国民或永久性居民，在共同石油开发区内与石油资源勘探开发相关的作为或不作为，适用该国的刑法；如果是一缔约国的永久性居民，同时也是另一缔约国的公民，适用后者国家的刑法。

（b）根据本条 d 款之规定，非澳大利亚或东帝汶永久性居民的第三国公民，在共同石油开发区内与石油资源勘探开发相关的作为或不作为，适用澳大利亚和东帝汶的刑法。如果一人因同一作为或不作为，已经根据其他国家的法律，受到该国有权法庭审判并且认定无罪或免除刑事责任，或者已经受到处罚，或者主管当局根据本国法律，基于公共利益，不对该人的行为提起公诉，那么该人在澳大利亚和东帝汶无须遭受刑事追诉。

（c）在上述 b 款所提情形下，澳大利亚和东帝汶在必要时，应相互协商以确定将要适用的刑事法律，并考虑受害人国籍以及受该被指控的行为影响最大的国家的利益。

（d）对于共同石油开发区内航行的船只，包括地震测量船或者钻井船上发生的作为或不作为，适用船旗国刑法；对于飞越共同石油开发区的航空器上发生的作为或不作为，适用其国籍国刑法。

（e）为了执行本条所规定的刑法，包括获得证据和信息，澳大利亚和东帝汶之间应当互助合作，其中包括通过适当的协定或安排。

（f）澳大利亚和东帝汶均承认，为该国利益，当所控罪行的受害者是一国国民时，应在法律允许范围内，将针对所控罪行所采取的措施告知该国。

（g）澳大利亚和东帝汶可做出安排，允许一国公务人员协助另一国执行刑法。若这一协助需要对依据本条 a 款另一国享有管辖权的人员进行拘留。拘留只能持续到将相关人员能移交给另一国的相关公务人员为止。

第十五条　关税、检疫和移民

（a）依据本条 c、e、f、g 款之规定，澳大利亚和东帝汶有权对从本国前往共同石油开发区，或者来自共同石油开发区进入本国领土的人、设备和货物，适用自己的关税、移民和检疫法。两国应做出必要的安排，以便利这种进出。

（b）有限责任公司或其他有限责任实体应当确保，除非有澳大利亚和东帝汶的授权，否则没有首先进入澳大利亚或者东帝汶的人员、设备和货物，不得进入共同石油开发区的构筑物内。承包商和分包商的雇员进入共同石油开发区应有指定当局的授权。

（c）为了控制这些人员、设备或货物的流动，一缔约国可以要求与另一国就特定人员、设备和货物进入共同石油开发区的构筑物事项进行协商。

（d）本条规定不得损害澳大利亚和东帝汶，对未获得其授权进入共同石油开发区的人员、设备和货物，适用其关税、移民和检疫法。澳大利亚和东帝汶之间应就行使这一权力做出协调安排。

（e）为了共同石油开发区石油活动进入该区的货物和设备，不应缴纳关税。

（f）为了石油活动的目的，而离开或途经澳大利亚或东帝汶而运输至共同石油开发区的货物和设备，无须缴纳关税。

（g）为了永久性地运往澳大利亚或东帝汶某处而离开共同石油开发区的货物和设备，应该向该国缴纳关税。

第十六条 水文和地震测量

（a）澳大利亚和东帝汶均有权在共同石油开发区进行水文调查，以促进共同石油开发区的石油活动。澳大利亚和东帝汶应就下列事项进行合作：

i. 实施水文调查，其中包括提供必要的岸上设施；

ii. 交换与共同石油开发区石油活动相关的水文信息。

（b）为了本条约之目的，澳大利亚和东帝汶应当在促进共同石油开发区内地震测量方面进行合作，其中包括提供必要的岸上设施。

第十七条 油轮的安全、运行标准和船员

除非本条约另有规定，参与石油作业的澳大利亚和东帝汶的船只应当遵守该国关于安全、运行标准和船员的法规。拥有其他国家国籍的船只，应当适用作业港口所属的澳大利亚或东帝汶关于安全、作业标准和船员的法规。进入共同石油开发区的船舶，且依据两国法律不在澳大利亚和东帝汶以外区域作业的船只，应适用相关的国际安全和作业标准。

第十八条 监督

（a）为了本条约之目的，澳大利亚和东帝汶有权对共同石油开发区的活动进行监督。

（b）澳大利亚和东帝汶应就根据本条 a 款进行的任何监督活动进行合作协调。

（c）澳大利亚和东帝汶交换以本条 a 款的监督活动中获得的信息。

第十九条 安全措施

（a）澳大利亚和东帝汶之间，应就与石油共同开发区石油资源勘探和开发有关的威胁或安全事件交换信息。

（b）澳大利亚和东帝汶之间，应就对共同石油开发区安全事件的反应做出安排。

第二十条 搜索和营救

经指定当局请求以及根据本条约之规定，澳大利亚和东帝汶应考虑普遍接受的国际法规则，以及相关国际组织制定的规范和程序，就共同石油开发区的搜索和营救安排进行合作。

第二十一条 空中运输服务

经与指定当局协调或经其请求，依据本条约，澳大利亚和东帝汶应依适用于飞往或在共同石油开发区飞行的国内法、澳大利亚和东帝汶承认的国际规则、规定和程序，对共同石油开发区内空中运输服务和航空事故调查进行合作。

第二十二条 条约期限

条约有效期至澳大利亚和东帝汶之间进行永久性的海床划界，或者条约生效后30年，以较早的日期为准。澳大利亚和东帝汶可通过协定延长条约有效期。即使条约失效，有限责任公司或实体根据条约条款所进行的石油活动，在与本条约规定的相同条件下，应当继续进行。

第二十三条 争端解决

（a）除了适用第十三条b款所指的《税收规则》解决的争端外，其余任何有关本条约解释或适用的争端，应尽可能地通过协商或谈判解决。

（b）未能以本条a款所列方式解决的争端，以及与第六条d款ⅱ项相关的未解决的问题，经澳大利亚或东帝汶请求，应该提交至附件B中规定的仲裁机构裁决。

第二十四条 修订

澳大利亚和东帝汶可在任何时候通过书面协议对条约进行修改。

第二十五条 生效

（a）在澳大利亚和东帝汶相互以书面形式通知对方，各自均已完成有关条约生效的要求之日，条约生效。

（b）条约一旦生效，本条约将会产生法律效果，本条约所有条款将被视为自签署条约之日开始适用。

本条约第三条的附件 A 石油共同开发区的确定和描述

为了本条约的目的，有必要确定地球表面的点、线和区域的位置，该位置应该根据澳大利亚大地测量基准确立，也就是参考中心在地球中心，主要（赤道）半径为 6378160 米，扁平率为 1/298.5 的球状体，以及参考位于澳大利亚北部的约翰斯顿大地测量站来确定的位置。该测量站位于南纬 25°56′54.5515″，东经 133°12′30.0771″，高于上述球体地平面 571.2 米。

区域

该区域由以下线构成：

（a）起始点为南纬 9°22′53″，东经 127°48′42″；

（b）从该点沿着球面向西南延伸至坐标点南纬 10°06′40″，东经 126°00′25″；

（c）从该点沿着球面向西南延伸至坐标点南纬 10°28′00″，东经 126°00′00″；

（d）从该点沿着球面向东南延伸至坐标点南纬 11°20′08″，东经 126°31′54″；

（e）从该点沿着球面向东南延伸至坐标点南纬 11°19′46″，东经 126°47′04″；

（f）从该点沿着球面向东北延伸至坐标点南纬 11°17′36″，东经 126°57′07″；

（g）从该点沿着球面向东北延伸至坐标点南纬 11°17′30″，东经 126°58′13″；

（h）从该点沿着球面向东北延伸至坐标点南纬 11°14′24″，东经 127°31′33″；

（i）从该点沿着球面向东北延伸至坐标点南纬 10°55′26″，东经 127°47′04″；

（j）从该点沿着球面向东北延伸至坐标点南纬 10°53′42″，东经 127°48′45″；

（k）从该点沿着球面向东北延伸至坐标点南纬 10°43′43″，东经 127°59′16″；

（l）从该点沿着球面向东北延伸至坐标点南纬 10°29′17″，东经 128°12′24″；

（m）从该点沿着球面向西北延伸至坐标点南纬 9°29′57″，东经 127°58′47″；

（n）从该点沿着球面向西北延伸至坐标点南纬 9°28′00″，东经 127°56′00″；

（o）从该点沿着球面向西北延伸至起始点。

本条约第二十三条的附件 B　争端解决程序

（a）根据第二十三条 b 款提交争端至仲裁庭，该仲裁庭由三名仲裁员按照以下方式组成：

ⅰ．澳大利亚和东帝汶各任命一名仲裁员；

ⅱ．由澳大利亚和东帝汶任命的两名裁员，在第二名任命后的 60 天内，通过协商一致选出第三名仲裁员，该仲裁员应为与澳大利亚和东帝汶均建立了外交关系的第三国的国民或永久性居民；

ⅲ．在选出第三名仲裁员后 60 天内，澳大利亚和东帝汶应该批准选择该仲裁员作为仲裁庭主席。

（b）一国通过外交途径将提起仲裁程序通知另一缔约国，仲裁程序即被启动。这种通知应当包含一项声明简要阐述主张的依据，寻求救济的性质以及任命的仲裁员的名字。在接到通知后的 60 天内，被申请方应当通知申请方，其任命的仲裁员的名字。

（c）如果在本附件 a 条 ⅱ 款和 ⅲ 款以及 b 款的期限内，无法做出所需的任命或批准，澳大利亚或东帝汶应该请求国际法院院长进行必要的任命。如果国际法院的院长是澳大利亚或东帝汶的国民或永久性居民，或者其由于其他原因无法进行任命，则请求国际法院的副院长进行任命。如果国际法院的副院长也出于这些原因无法进行任命，则请求国际法院其余法官中，既不是澳大利亚也不是东帝汶的公民或永久性居民，而且资历最老的法官，进行任命。

（d）若依本附件所任命的仲裁员辞职或无法履行职能，应按照最初仲裁员的任命方式任命继任仲裁员。继任仲裁员与最初仲裁员享有相同的权利和义务。

（e）仲裁庭在由仲裁庭主席确定的时间和地点开庭，其后由仲裁庭决定在何时何处开庭。

（f）仲裁庭根据澳大利亚和东帝汶之间的协定，审理其权限范围内的所有问题，自行决定仲裁程序。

（g）在仲裁庭做出裁决之前的任何阶段，仲裁庭可以向澳大利亚和东帝汶建议友好解决争端。仲裁庭应考虑到条约的条款和相关国际法，根据多数票做出裁决。

（h）澳大利亚和东帝汶自行承担各自任命的仲裁员、准备和提交案件产生的费用。仲裁庭主席以及仲裁活动产生的费用，由澳大利亚和东帝汶均摊。

（i）仲裁庭应该给予澳大利亚和东帝汶公平的申诉机会。在澳大利亚或东帝汶缺席的情况下，仲裁庭也会做出裁决。任何案件，自仲裁主体开庭之日起6个月内，仲裁庭应该做出裁决。任何裁决应该以书面形式做出，并且要说明法律依据。签名的裁决副本应被送达澳大利亚和东帝汶（政府）。

（j）裁决对于澳大利亚和东帝汶是终局且有约束力的。

本条约第六条 b 款 v 项下的附件 C　指定当局的权力和职能

指定当局的权力和职能应包括：

（a）依据本条约以及根据本条约而制定或生效的任何文件，包括联合委员会发布的命令，对石油活动进行日常管理和规范；

（b）准备向联合委员会提交指定当局的年度收支预算。任何开支应当符合联合委员会批准的预算，或者联合委员会批准的规范和程序；

（c）准备向联合委员会提交的年度报告；

（d）依据本条约就下列事项，向澳大利亚和东帝汶相关当局请求帮助：

ⅰ．共同石油开发区内的搜索营救活动；

ⅱ．共同石油开发区内从事石油作业的船只和构筑物受到恐怖主义威胁；

ⅲ．为共同石油开发区提供空中服务。

（e）向澳大利亚、东帝汶相关当局，或者其他机构或个人，就防止污染的措施、设备以及程序请求援助；

（f）根据国际法设立安全区和禁区，确保航行和石油作业的安全；

（g）依据国际法，管理用于石油资源勘探开发的船只、飞机、建筑物和其他设备进出共同石油开发区；根据第十五条之规定，授权承包商和分包商雇员以及其他人员进入共同石油开发区；

（h）对本条约下与石油活动监督和管理的所有事项，包括健康、安全、环保、评估以及工作实践，依据《石油开采规则》发布规范和命令；

（i）本条约其他附件列明的或者联合委员会授予的其他权力和职能。

本条约第六条 c 款 ii 项下的附件 D　联合委员会的权力和职能

1. 联合委员会的权力和职能应当包括：

（a）指导指定当局履行其权力和职能；

（b）授予指定当局其他权力和职能；

（c）必要时根据本条约第七条 b 款，制订临时石油开采规则；

（d）批准指定当局的财政收支预算；

（e）批准指定当局有效运行所需的规则、法规和程序；

（f）在第六条 b 款 i 项所规定的期限内，任命指定当局；

（g）经联合委员会成员的要求，检查和审计指定当局的账簿和账户，或对这种检查和审计做出安排；

（h）批准联合委员会对合同方账目和账户检查和审计的结果；

（i）考虑和采纳指定当局所做的年度报告；

（j）自行决定或根据指定当局的建议，为促进共同石油开发区的开采活动以不违反条约目的的方式，修订《石油开采规则》。

2. 联合委员会应当根据良好的油田、生产、运输和环境保护的实践，为了澳大利亚和东帝汶人民的利益，履行自己的权力和职能。

第九条 b 款项下的附件 E　Greater Sunrise 区域的统一开发

（a）基于 Greater Sunrise 20.1% 的储量，位于共同石油开发区内，澳大利亚和东帝汶同意统一开发 Sunrise 和 Troubadour 油田（合称 Greater Sunrise）。Greater Sunrise 产量中的 20.1% 的份额，归于共同石油开发区，而 79.9% 的份额归于澳大利亚。

（b）澳大利亚或东帝汶可以请求审查产品分享比例。根据审查结果，澳大利亚和东帝汶可以在达成一致的情况下修改产品分配比例。

（c）本附件 a 条所提的统一开发协定，不得妨碍两国间对海床进行永久性划界。

（d）一旦对海床进行永久性划界，澳大利亚和东帝汶应该重新审议本附件 a 条所提的统一开发协定。任何新的协定应该维持基于统一开发协定所缔结的产品分配合同以及发放的执照或许可证。

2. Timor Sea Treaty between the Government of East Timor and the Government of Australia

(Dili, 20 May 2002)

THE GOVERNMENT OF AUSTRALIA

and

THE GOVERNMENT OF EAST TIMOR

CONSCIOUS of the importance of promoting East Timor's economic development;

AWARE of the need to maintain security of investment for existing and planned petroleum activities in an area of seabed between Australia and East Timor;

RECOGNISING the benefits that will flow to both Australia and East Timor by providing a continuing basis for petroleum activities in an area of seabed between Australia and East Timor to proceed as planned;

EMPHASISING the importance of developing petroleum resources in a way that minimizes damage to the natural environment, that is economically sustainable, promotes further investment and contributes to the long – term development of Australia and East Timor;

CONVINCED that the development of the resources in accordance with this Treaty will provide a firm foundation for continuing and strengthening the friendly relations between Australia and East Timor;

TAKING INTO ACCOUNT the United Nations Convention on the Law of the Sea done at Montego Bay on 10 December 1982, which provides in Article 83 that the delimitation of the continental shelf between States with opposite or adjacent coasts shall be effected by agreement on the basis of international law in order to achieve an equitable solution;

TAKING FURTHER INTO ACCOUNT, in the absence of delimitation, the further obligation for States to make every effort, in a spirit of understanding and cooperation, to enter into provisional arrangements of a practical nature which do not prejudice a final determination of the seabed delimitation;

NOTING the desirability of Australia and East Timor entering into a Treaty providing for the continued development of the petroleum resources in an area of seabed between Australia and East Timor;

HAVE AGREED as follows:

Article 1　Definitions

For the purposes of this Treaty:

(a) "Treaty" means this Treaty, including Annexes A – G and any Annexes subsequently agreed between Australia and East Timor.

(b) "contractor" means a corporation or corporations which enter into a contract with the Designated Authority and which is registered as a contractor under the Petroleum Mining Code.

(c) "criminal law" means any law in force in Australia and East Timor, whether substantive or procedural, that makes provision for or in relation to offences or for or in relation to the investigation or prosecution of offences or the punishment of offenders, including the carrying out of a penalty imposed by a court. For this purpose, "investigation" includes entry to an installation or structure in the JPDA, the exercise of powers of search and questioning and the apprehension of a suspected offender.

(d) "Designated Authority" means the Designated Authority established in Article 6 of this Treaty.

(e) "fiscal scheme" means a royalty, a Production Sharing Contract, or other scheme for determining Australia's and East Timor's share of petroleum or revenue from petroleum activities and does not include taxes referred to in Article 5(b) of this Treaty.

(f) "initially processed" means processing of petroleum to a point where it is ready for off – take from the production facility and may include such processes as the removal of water, volatiles and other impurities.

(g) "Joint Commission" means the Australia – East Timor Joint Commission established in Article 6 of this Treaty.

(h) "JPDA" means the Joint Petroleum Development Area established in Article 3 of this Treaty.

(i) "Ministerial Council" means the Australia – East Timor Ministerial Council established in Article 6 of this Treaty.

(j) "petroleum" means:
i. any naturally occurring hydrocarbon, whether in a gaseous, liquid, or solid state;
ii. any naturally occurring mixture of hydrocarbons, whether in a gaseous, liquid or solid state; or
iii. any naturally occurring mixture of one or more hydrocarbons, whether in a gaseous, liquid or solid state, as well as other substances produced in association with such hydrocarbons;
and includes any petroleum as defined by sub – paragraphs (i), (ii) or (iii) that has been returned to a natural reservoir.

(k) "petroleum activities" means all activities undertaken to produce petroleum, authorised or contemplated under a contract, permit or licence, and includes exploration, development, initial processing, production, transportation and marketing, as well as the planning and preparation for such activities.

(l) "Petroleum Mining Code" means the Code referred to in Article 7 of this Treaty.

(m) "petroleum project" means petroleum activities taking place in a specified area within the JPDA.

(n) "petroleum produced" means initially processed petroleum extracted from a reservoir through petroleum activities.

(o) "Production Sharing Contract" means a contract between the Designated Authority and a limited liability corporation or entity with limited liability under which production from a specified area of the JPDA is shared between the parties to the contract.

(p) "reservoir" means an accumulation of petroleum in a geological unit limited by rock, water or other substances without pressure communication through liquid or gas to another accumulation of petroleum.

(q) "taxation code" means the code referred to in Article 13 (b) of this Treaty.

Article 2 Without prejudice

(a) This Treaty gives effect to international law as reflected in the United Nations Convention on the Law of the Sea done at Montego Bay on 10 December 1982 which under Article 83 requires States with opposite or adjacent coasts to make every effort to enter into provisional arrangements of a practical nature pending agreement on the final delimitation of the continental shelf between them in a manner consistent with international law. This Treaty is intended to adhere to such obligation.

(b) Nothing contained in this Treaty and no acts taking place while this Treaty is in force shall be interpreted as prejudicing or affecting Australia's or East Timor's position on or rights relating to a seabed delimitation or their respective seabed entitlements.

Article 3 Joint Petroleum Development Area

(a) The Joint Petroleum Development Area (JPDA) is established. It is the area in the Timor Sea contained within the lines described in Annex A.

(b) Australia and East Timor shall jointly control, manage and facilitate the exploration, development and exploitation of the petroleum resources of the JPDA for the benefit of the peoples of Australia and East Timor.

(c) Petroleum activities conducted in the JPDA shall be carried out pursuant to a contract between the Designated Authority and a limited liability corporation or entity with limited liability specifically established for the sole purpose of the contract. This provision shall also apply to the successors or assignees of such corporations.

(d) Australia and East Timor shall make it an offence for any person to conduct petroleum activities in the JPDA otherwise than in accordance with this Treaty.

Article 4　Sharing of petroleum production

(a) Australia and East Timor shall have title to all petroleum produced in the JPDA. Of the petroleum produced in the JPDA, ninety (90) percent shall belong to East Timor and ten (10) percent shall belong to Australia.

(b) To the extent that fees referred to in Article 6 (b) (vi) and other income are inadequate to cover the expenditure of the Designated Authority in relation to this Treaty, that expenditure shall be borne in the same proportion as set out in paragraph (a).

Article 5　Fiscal arrangements and taxes

Fiscal arrangements and taxes shall be dealt with in the following manner:

(a) Unless a fiscal scheme is otherwise provided for in this Treaty:

i. Australia and East Timor shall make every possible effort to agree on a joint fiscal scheme for each petroleum project in the JPDA.

ii. If Australia and East Timor fail to reach agreement on a joint fiscal scheme referred to in sub-paragraph (i), they shall jointly appoint an independent expert to recommend an appropriate joint fiscal scheme to apply to the petroleum project concerned.

iii. If either Australia or East Timor does not agree to the joint fiscal scheme recommended by the independent expert, Australia and East Timor may each separately impose their own fiscal scheme on their proportion of the production of the project as calculated in accordance with the formula contained in Article 4 of this Treaty.

iv. If Australia and East Timor agree on a joint fiscal scheme pursuant to this Article, neither Australia nor East Timor may during the life of the project vary that scheme except by mutual agreement between Australia and East Timor.

(b) Consistent with the formula contained in Article 4 of this Treaty, Australia and East Timor may, in accordance with their respective laws and the taxation code, impose taxes on their share of the revenue from petroleum activities in the JPDA and relating to activities referred to in Article 13 of this Treaty.

Article 6   Regulatory bodies

(a) A three-tiered joint administrative structure consisting of a Designated Authority, a Joint Commission and a Ministerial Council is established.

(b) Designated Authority:

i. For the first three years after this Treaty enters into force, or for a different period of time if agreed to jointly by Australia and East Timor, the Joint Commission shall designate the Designated Authority.

ii. After the period specified in sub-paragraph (i), the Designated Authority shall be the East Timor Government Ministry responsible for petroleum activities or, if so decided by the Ministry, an East Timor statutory authority.

iii. For the period specified in sub-paragraph (i), the Designated Authority has juridical personality and such legal capacities under the law of both Australia and East Timor as are necessary for the exercise of its powers and the performance of its functions. In particular, the Designated Authority shall have the capacity to contract, to acquire and dispose of movable and immovable property and to institute and be party to legal proceedings.

iv. The Designated Authority shall be responsible to the Joint Commission and shall carry out the day-to-day regulation and management of petroleum activities.

v. A non-exclusive listing of more detailed powers and functions of the Designated Authority is set out in Annex C. The Annexes to this Treaty may identify other additional detailed powers and functions of the Designated Authority. The Designated Authority also has such other powers and functions as may be conferred upon it by the Joint Commission.

vi. The Designated Authority shall be financed from fees collected under the Petroleum Mining Code.

vii. For the period specified in sub-paragraph (i), the Designated Authority shall be exempt from the following existing taxes:

(1) in East Timor, the income tax imposed under the law of East Timor;

(2) in Australia, the income tax imposed under the federal law of Australia;

as well as any identical or substantially similar taxes which are imposed after the date of signature of this Treaty in addition to, or in place of, the existing taxes.

viii. For the period specified in sub-paragraph (i), personnel of the Designated Authority:

(1) shall be exempt from taxation of salaries, allowances and other emoluments paid to them by the Designated Authority in connection with their service with the Designated Authority other than taxation under the law of Australia or East Timor in which they are deemed to be resident for taxation purposes; and

(2) shall, at the time of first taking up the post with the Designated Authority located in either Australia or East Timor in which they are not resident, be exempt from customs duties and other such charges (except payments for services) in respect of imports of furniture and other household and personal effects in their ownership or possession or already ordered by them and intended for their personal use or for their establishment; such goods shall be imported within six months of an officer's first entry but in exceptional circumstances an extension of time shall be granted by the Government of Australia or the Government of East Timor; goods which have been acquired or imported by officers and to which exemptions under this sub-paragraph apply shall not be given away, sold, lent or hired out, or otherwise disposed of except under conditions agreed in advance with the Government of Australia or the Government of East Timor depending on in which country the officer is located.

(c) Joint Commission:

i. The Joint Commission shall consist of commissioners appointed by Australia and East Timor. There shall be one more commissioner appointed by East Timor than by Australia. The Joint Commission shall establish policies and regulations relating to petroleum activities in the JPDA and shall oversee the work of the Designated Authority.

ii. A non-exclusive listing of more detailed powers and functions of the Joint Commission is set out in Annex D. The Annexes to this Treaty may identify other additional detailed powers and functions of the Joint Commission.

iii. Except as provided for in Article 8 (c), the commissioners of either Australia or East Timor may at any time refer a matter to the Ministerial Council for resolution.

iv. The Joint Commission shall meet annually or as may be required. Its meetings shall be chaired by a member nominated by Australia and East Timor on an alternate basis.

(d) Ministerial Council:

i. The Ministerial Council shall consist of an equal number of Ministers from Australia and East Timor. It shall consider any matter relating to the operation of this Treaty that is referred to it by either Australia or East Timor. It shall also consider any matter referred to in sub-paragraph (c) (iii).

ii. In the event the Ministerial Council is unable to resolve a matter, either Australia or East Timor may invoke the dispute resolution procedure set out in Annex B.

iii. The Ministerial Council shall meet at the request of either Australia or East Timor or at the request of the Joint Commission.

iv. Unless otherwise agreed between Australia and East Timor, meetings of the Ministerial Council where at least one member representing Australia and one member representing East Timor are physically present shall be held alternately in Australia and East Timor. Its meetings shall be chaired by a representative of Australia or East Timor on an alternate basis.

v. The Ministerial Council may, if it so chooses, permit members to participate in a particular meeting, or all meetings, by telephone, closed-circuit television or any other means of electronic communication, and a member who so participates is to be regarded as being present at the meeting. A meeting may be held solely by means of electronic communication.

(e) Commissioners of the Joint Commission and personnel of the Designated Authority shall have no financial interest in any activity relating to exploration for and exploitation of petroleum resources in the JPDA.

Article 7 Petroleum Mining Code

(a) Australia and East Timor shall negotiate an agreed Petroleum Mining

Code which shall govern the exploration, development and exploitation of petroleum within the JPDA, as well as the export of petroleum from the JPDA.

(b) In the event Australia and East Timor are unable to conclude a Petroleum Mining Code by the date of entry into force of this Treaty, the Joint Commission shall in its inaugural meeting adopt an interim code to remain in effect until a Petroleum Mining Code is adopted in accordance with paragraph (a).

Article 8　Pipelines

(a) The construction and operation of a pipeline within the JPDA for the purposes of exporting petroleum from the JPDA shall be subject to the approval of the Joint Commission. Australia and East Timor shall consult on the terms and conditions of pipelines exporting petroleum from the JPDA to the point of landing.

(b) A pipeline landing in East Timor shall be under the jurisdiction of East Timor. A pipeline landing in Australia shall be under the jurisdiction of Australia.

(c) In the event a pipeline is constructed from the JPDA to the territory of either Australia or East Timor, the country where the pipeline lands may not object to or impede decisions of the Joint Commission regarding a pipeline to the other country. Notwithstanding Article 6 (c) (iii), the Ministerial Council may not review or change any such decisions.

(d) Paragraph (c) shall not apply where the effect of constructing a pipeline from the JPDA to the other country would cause the supply of gas to be withheld from a limited liability corporation or limited liability entity which has obtained consent under this Treaty to obtain gas from a project in the JPDA for contracts to supply gas for a specified period of time.

(e) Neither Australia nor East Timor may object to, nor in any way impede, a proposal to use floating gas to liquids processing and off-take in the JPDA on a commercial basis where such proposal shall produce higher revenues to Australia and East Timor from royalties and taxes earned from activities conducted within the JPDA than would be earned if gas were transported by pipeline.

(f) Paragraph (e) shall not apply where the effect of floating gas to liquids processing and off-take in the JPDA would cause the supply of gas to be withheld from a limited liability corporation or limited liability entity which has obtained consent under this Treaty to obtain gas from the JPDA for contracts to supply gas for a specified period of time.

(g) Petroleum from the JPDA and from fields which straddle the boundaries of the JPDA shall at all times have priority of carriage along any pipeline carrying petroleum from and within the JPDA.

(h) There shall be open access to pipelines for petroleum from the JPDA. The open access arrangements shall be in accordance with good international regulatory practice. If Australia has jurisdiction over the pipeline, it shall consult with East Timor over access to the pipeline. If East Timor has jurisdiction over the pipeline, it shall consult with Australia over access to the pipeline.

Article 9 Unitisation

(a) Any reservoir of petroleum that extends across the boundary of the JPDA shall be treated as a single entity for management and development purposes.

(b) Australia and East Timor shall work expeditiously and in good faith to reach agreement on the manner in which the deposit will be most effectively exploited and on the equitable sharing of the benefits arising from such exploitation.

Article 10 Marine environment

(a) Australia and East Timor shall co – operate to protect the marine environment of the JPDA so as to prevent and minimise pollution and other environmental harm from petroleum activities. Special efforts shall be made to protect marine animals including marine mammals, seabirds, fish and coral. Australia and East Timor shall consult as to the best means to protect the marine environment of the JPDA from the harmful consequences of petroleum activities.

(b) Where pollution of the marine environment occurring in the JPDA spreads beyond the JPDA, Australia and East Timor shall co – operate in taking action to prevent, mitigate and eliminate such pollution.

(c) The Designated Authority shall issue regulations to protect the marine environment in the JPDA. It shall establish a contingency plan for combating pollution from petroleum activities in the JPDA.

(d) Limited liability corporations or limited liability entities shall be liable for damage or expenses incurred as a result of pollution of the marine environment arising out of petroleum activities within the JPDA in accordance with:

i. their contract, licence or permit or other form of authority issued pursuant to this Treaty; and

ii. the law of the jurisdiction (Australia or East Timor) in which the claim is brought.

Article 11   Employment

(a) Australia and East Timor shall:

i. take appropriate measures with due regard to occupational health and safety requirements to ensure that preference is given in employment in the JPDA to nationals or permanent residents of East Timor; and

ii. facilitate, as a matter of priority, training and employment opportunities for East Timorese nationals and permanent residents.

(b) Australia shall expedite and facilitate processing of applications for visas through its Diplomatic Mission in Dili by East Timorese nationals and permanent residents employed by limited liability corporations or limited liability entities in Australia associated with petroleum activities in the JPDA.

Article 12   Health and safety for workers

The Designated Authority shall develop, and limited liability corporations or limited liability entities shall apply, occupational health and safety standards and procedures for persons employed on structures in the JPDA that are no less effective than those standards and procedures that would apply to persons employed on similar structures in Australia and East Timor. The Designated Authority may adopt, consistent with this Article, standards and procedures taking into account an existing system established under the law of either Australia or East Timor.

Article 13   Application of taxation law

(a) For the purposes of taxation law related directly or indirectly to:

i. the exploration for or the exploitation of petroleum in the JPDA; or

ii. acts, matters, circumstances and things touching, concerning arising out of or connected with such exploration and exploitation the JPDA shall be deemed to be, and treated by, Australia and East Timor, as part of that country.

(b) The taxation code to provide relief from double taxation relating to petroleum activities is set out in Annex G.

(c) The taxation code contains its own dispute resolution mechanism. Article 23 of this Treaty shall not apply to disputes covered by that mechanism.

Article 14　Criminal jurisdiction

(a) A national or permanent resident of Australia or East Timor shall be subject to the criminal law of that country in respect of acts or omissions occurring in the JPDA connected with or arising out of exploration for and exploitation of petroleum resources, provided that a permanent resident of Australia or East Timor who is a national of the other country shall be subject to the criminal law of the latter country.

(b) Subject to paragraph (d), a national of a third state, not being a permanent resident of either Australia or East Timor, shall be subject to the criminal law of both Australia and East Timor in respect of acts or omissions occurring in the JPDA connected with or arising out of petroleum activities. Such a person shall not be subject to criminal proceedings under the law of either Australia or East Timor if he or she has already been tried and discharged or acquitted by a competent tribunal or already undergone punishment for the same act or omission under the law of the other country or where the competent authorities of one country, in accordance with its law, have decided in the public interest to refrain from prosecuting the person for that act or omission.

(c) In cases referred to in paragraph (b), Australia and East Timor shall, as and when necessary, consult each other to determine which criminal law is to be applied, taking into account the nationality of the victim and the interests of the country most affected by the alleged offence.

(d) The criminal law of the flag state shall apply in relation to acts or omissions on board vessels including seismic or drill vessels in, or aircraft in flight over, the JPDA.

(e) Australia and East Timor shall provide assistance to and co – operate with each other, including through agreements or arrangements as appropriate, for the purposes of enforcement of criminal law under this Article, including the obtaining of evidence and information.

(f) Both Australia and East Timor recognise the interest of the other country where a victim of an alleged offence is a national of that other country and shall keep that other country informed, to the extent permitted by its law, of action being taken with regard to the alleged offence.

(g) Australia and East Timor may make arrangements permitting officials of one country to assist in the enforcement of the criminal law of the other country. Where such assistance involves the detention of a person who under paragraph (a) is subject to the jurisdiction of the other country that detention may only continue until it is practicable to hand the person over to the relevant officials of that other country.

Article 15 Customs, quarantine and migration

(a) Australia and East Timor may, subject to paragraphs (c), (e), (f) and (g), apply customs, migration and quarantine laws to persons, equipment and goods entering its territory from, or leaving its territory for, the JPDA. Australia and East Timor may adopt arrangements to facilitate such entry and departure.

(b) Limited liability corporations or other limited liability entities shall ensure, unless otherwise authorised by Australia or East Timor, that persons, equipment and goods do not enter structures in the JPDA without first entering Australia or East Timor, and that their employees and the employees of their subcontractors are authorised by the Designated Authority to enter the JPDA.

(c) Either country may request consultations with the other country in relation to the entry of particular persons, equipment and goods to structures in the JPDA aimed at controlling the movement of such persons, equipment or goods.

(d) Nothing in this Article prejudices the right of either Australia or East Timor to apply customs, migration and quarantine controls to persons, equipment and goods entering the JPDA without the authority of either country. Australia and East Timor may adopt arrangements to co-ordinate the exercise of such rights.

(e) Goods and equipment entering the JPDA for purposes related to petroleum activities shall not be subject to customs duties.

(f) Goods and equipment leaving or in transit through either Australia or East Timor for the purpose of entering the JPDA for purposes related to petroleum activities shall not be subject to customs duties.

(g) Goods and equipment leaving the JPDA for the purpose of being permanently transferred to a part of either Australia or East Timor may be subject to customs duties of that country.

Article 16   Hydrographic and seismic surveys

(a) Australia and East Timor shall have the right to carry out hydrographic surveys to facilitate petroleum activities in the JPDA. Australia and East Timor shall co – operate on:

i. the conduct of such surveys, including the provision of necessary on – shore facilities; and

ii. exchanging hydrographic information relevant to petroleum activities in the JPDA.

(b) For the purposes of this Treaty, Australia and East Timor shall co – operate in facilitating the conduct of seismic surveys in the JPDA, including in the provision of necessary on – shore facilities.

Article 17   Petroleum industry vessel – safety, operating standards and crewing

Except as otherwise provided in this Treaty, vessels of the nationality of Australia or East Timor engaged in petroleum activities in the JPDA shall be subject to the law of their nationality in relation to safety and operating standards and crewing regulations. Vessels with the nationality of other countries shall apply the law of Australia or East Timor depending on whose ports they operate, in relation to safety and operating standards, and crewing regulations. Such vessels that enter the JPDA and do not operate out of either Australia or East Timor under the law of both Australia or East Timor shall be subject to the relevant international safety and operating standards.

Article 18   Surveillance

(a) For the purposes of this Treaty, Australia and East Timor shall have the right to carry out surveillance activities in the JPDA.

(b) Australia and East Timor shall co – operate on and co – ordinate any surveillance activities carried out in accordance with paragraph (a).

(c) Australia and East Timor shall exchange information derived from any surveillance activities carried out in accordance with paragraph (a).

Article 19   Security measures

(a) Australia and East Timor shall exchange information on likely threats to, or security incidents relating to, exploration for and exploitation of petroleum resources in the JPDA.

(b) Australia and East Timor shall make arrangements for responding to security incidents in the JPDA.

Article 20   Search and rescue

Australia and East Timor shall, at the request of the Designated Authority and consistent with this Treaty, co – operate on and assist with search and rescue operations in the JPDA taking into account generally accepted international rules, regulations and procedures established through competent international organizations.

Article 21   Air traffic services

Australia and East Timor shall, in consultation with the Designated Authority or at its request, and consistent with this Treaty, co – operate in relation to the operation of air services, the provision of air traffic services and air accident investigations, within the JPDA, in accordance with national laws applicable to flights to and within the JPDA, recognizing established international rules, regulations and procedures where these have been adopted by Australia and East Timor.

Article 22   Duration of the Treaty

This Treaty shall be in force until there is a permanent seabed delimitation between Australia and East Timor or for thirty years from the date of its entry into force, whichever is sooner. This Treaty may be renewed by agreement between Australia and East Timor. Petroleum activities of limited liability corporations or other limited liability entities entered into under the terms of the Treaty shall continue even if the Treaty is no longer in force under conditions equivalent to those in place under the Treaty.

Article 23　Settlement of Disputes

(a) With the exception of disputes falling within the scope of the taxation code referred to in Article 13 (b) of this Treaty and which shall be settled in accordance with that code, any dispute concerning the interpretation or application of this Treaty shall, as far as possible, be settled by consultation or negotiation.

(b) Any dispute which is not settled in the manner set out in paragraph (a) and any unresolved matter relating to the operation of this Treaty under Article 6 (d) (ii) shall, at the request of either Australia or East Timor, be submitted to an arbitral tribunal in accordance with the procedure set out in Annex B.

Article 24　Amendment

This Treaty may be amended at any time by written agreement between Australia and East Timor.

Article 25　Entry into force

(a) This Treaty shall enter into force upon the day on which Australia and East Timor have notified each other in writing that their respective requirements for entry into force of this Treaty have been complied with.

(b) Upon entry into force, the Treaty will be taken to have effect and all of its provisions will apply and be taken to have applied on and from the date of signature.

IN WITNESS WHEREOF the undersigned, being duly authorised thereto by their respective Governments, have signed this Treaty.

DONE at Dili, on this twentieth day of May, Two thousand and two in two originals in the English language.

Annex B　under Article 23 of this Treaty
Dispute Resolution Procedure

(a) An arbitral tribunal to which a dispute is submitted pursuant to Article 23 (b), shall consist of three persons appointed as follows:

i. Australia and East Timor shall each appoint one arbitrator;

ii. the arbitrators appointed by Australia and East Timor shall, within sixty (60) days of the appointment of the second of them, by agreement, select a third arbitrator who shall be a citizen, or permanent resident of a third country which has diplomatic relations with both Australia and East Timor;

iii. Australia and East Timor shall, within sixty (60) days of the selection of the third arbitrator, approve the selection of that arbitrator who shall act as Chairman of the Tribunal.

(b) Arbitration proceedings shall be instituted upon notice being given through the diplomatic channel by the country instituting such proceedings to the other country. Such notice shall contain a statement setting forth in summary form the grounds of the claim, the nature of the relief sought, and the name of the arbitrator appointed by the country instituting such proceedings. Within sixty (60) days after the giving of such notice the respondent country shall notify the country instituting proceedings of the name of the arbitrator appointed by the respondent country.

(c) If, within the time limits provided for in sub-paragraphs (a) (ii) and (iii) and paragraph (b) of this Annex, the required appointment has not been made or the required approval has not been given, Australia or East Timor may request the President of the International Court of Justice to make the necessary appointment.

If the Vice-President is a citizen or permanent resident of Australia or East Timor or is otherwise unable to act, the Vice-President shall be invited to make the appointment. If the Vice-President is a citizen, or permanent resident of Australia or East Timor or is otherwise unable to act, the Member of the International Court of Justice next in seniority who is not a citizen or permanent resident of Australia or East Timor shall be invited to make the appointment.

(d) In case any arbitrator appointed as provided for in this Annex shall resign or become unable to act, a successor arbitrator shall be appointed in the same manner as prescribed for the appointment of the original arbitrator and the successor shall have all the powers and duties of the original arbitrator.

(e) The Arbitral Tribunal shall convene at such time and place as shall be fixed by the Chairman of the Tribunal. Thereafter, the Arbitral Tribunal shall determine where and when it shall sit.

(f) The Arbitral Tribunal shall decide all questions relating to its competence and shall, subject to any agreement between Australia and East Timor, determine its own procedure.

(g) Before the Arbitral Tribunal makes a decision, it may at any stage of the proceedings propose to Australia and East Timor that the dispute be settled amicably. The Arbitral Tribunal shall reach its award by majority vote taking into account the provisions of this Treaty and relevant international law.

(h) Australia and East Timor shall each bear the costs of its appointed arbitrator and its own costs in preparing and presenting cases. The cost of the Chairman of the Tribunal and the expenses associated with the conduct of the arbitration shall be borne in equal parts by Australia and East Timor.

(i) The Arbitral Tribunal shall afford to Australia and East Timor a fair hearing. It may render an award on the default of either Australia or East Timor. In any case, the Arbitral Tribunal shall render its award within six (6) months from the date it is convened by the Chairman of the Tribunal. Any award shall be rendered in writing and shall state its legal basis. A signed counterpart of the award shall be transmitted to Australia and East Timor.

(j) An award shall be final and binding on Australia and East Timor.

Annex C under Article 6 (b) (v) of this Treaty Powers and Functions of the Designated Authority

The powers and functions of the Designated Authority shall include:

(a) day – to – day management and regulation of petroleum activities in accordance with this Treaty and any instruments made or entered into under this Treaty, including directions given by the Joint Commission;

(b) preparation of annual estimates of income and expenditure of the Designated Authority for submission to the Joint Commission. Any expenditure shall only be made in accordance with estimates approved by the Joint Commission or otherwise in accordance with regulations and procedures approved by the Joint Commission;

(c) preparation of annual reports for submission to the Joint Commission;

(d) requesting assistance from the appropriate Australian and East Timor authorities consistent with this Treaty

i. for search and rescue operations in the JPDA;

ii. in the event of a terrorist threat to the vessels and structures engaged in petroleum operations in the JPDA; and

iii. for air traffic services in the JPDA;

(e) requesting assistance with pollution prevention measures, equipment and procedures from the appropriate Australian and East Timor authorities or other bodies or persons;

(f) establishment of safety zones and restricted zones, consistent with international law, to ensure the safety of navigation and petroleum operations;

(g) controlling movements into, within and out of the JPDA of vessels, aircraft, structures and other equipment employed in exploration for and exploitation of petroleum resources in a manner consistent with international law; and, subject to Article 15, authorising the entry of employees of contractors and their subcontractors and other persons into the JPDA;

(h) issuing regulations and giving directions under this Treaty on all matters related to the supervision and control of petroleum activities including on health, safety, environmental protection and assessments and work practices, pursuant to the Petroleum Mining Code; and

(i) such other powers and functions as may be identified in other Annexes to this Treaty or as may be conferred on it by the Joint Commission.

Annex D under Article 6 (c) (ii) of this Treaty Powers and Functions of the Joint Commission

1. The powers and functions of the Joint Commission shall include:

(a) giving directions to the Designated Authority on the discharge of its powers and functions;

(b) conferring additional powers and functions on the Designated Authority;

(c) adopting an interim Petroleum Mining Code pursuant to Article 7 (b) of the Treaty, if necessary;

(d) approving financial estimates of income and expenditure of the Designated Authority;

(e) approving rules, regulations and procedures for the effective functioning of the Designated Authority;

(f) designating the Designated Authority for the period referred to in Article 6 (b) (i);

(g) at the request of a member of the Joint Commission inspecting and auditing the Designated Authority's books and accounts or arranging for such an audit and inspection;

(h) approving the result of inspections and audits of contractors' books and accounts conducted by the Joint Commission;

(i) considering and adopting the annual report of the Designated Authority;

(j) of its own volition or on recommendation by the Designated Authority, in a manner not inconsistent with the objectives of this Treaty amending the Petroleum Mining Code to facilitate petroleum activities in the JPDA;

2. The Joint Commission shall exercise its powers and functions for the benefit of the peoples of Australia and East Timor having regard to good oilfield, processing, transport and environmental practice.

Annex E under Article 9 (b) of this Treaty
Unitisation of Greater Sunrise

(a) Australia and East Timor agree to unitise the Sunrise and Troubadour deposits (collectively known as 'Greater Sunrise') on the basis that 20.1% of Greater Sunrise lies within the JPDA. Production from Greater Sunrise shall be distributed on the basis that 20.1% is attributed to the JPDA and 79.9% is attributed to Australia.

(b) Either Australia or East Timor may request a review of the production sharing formula. Following such a review, the production sharing formula may be altered by agreement between Australia and East Timor.

(c) The unitisation agreement referred to in paragraph (a) shall be without prejudice to a permanent delimitation of the seabed between Australia and East Timor.

(d) In the event of a permanent delimitation of the seabed, Australia and East Timor shall reconsider the terms of the unitisation agreement referred to in paragraph (a) . Any new agreement shall preserve the terms of any production sharing contract, licence or permit which is based on the agreement in paragraph (a).

3.《澳大利亚政府和东帝汶民主共和国政府关于 Sunrise 和 Troubadour 油田统一开发的协定》

(2003 年 3 月 6 日订于帝力)*

董世杰译,邓妮雅校

澳大利亚政府和东帝汶民主共和国政府,鉴于澳大利亚和东帝汶在帝汶海的勘探,证明存在跨越共同石油开发区东部边界的油田;这些油田就是 Sunrise 和 Troubadour 油田(统称 Greater Sunrise 油田);注意到在达成本协定之日,澳大利亚和东帝汶提出了海洋主张,但尚未进行海洋划界,其中就包括 Greater Sunrise 所在的帝汶海区域;希望在开始生产之前,就一体开发 Greater Sunrise 油田做出规定;承认澳大利亚和东帝汶在《帝汶海条约》附件 E 中,就统一开发 Greater Sunrise 达成一致。由于 Greater Sunrise 的 20.1% 位于共同石油开发区内,Greater Sunrise 石油产量中的 20.1% 归共同石油开发区,而 79.9% 归澳大利亚;再一次回顾 2002 年 5 月 20 日澳大利亚政府和东帝汶政府达成的谅解备忘录,两国同意迅速且善意地缔结统一开发 Greater Sunrise 的协定。双方达成协议如下。

第一条 定义

基于本协定之目的规定如下,除非条约中另有约定:

(a) "分配比例"是指本协定第七条所规定的比例,或者根据第八条重新确定的比例。

(b) "商业销售"是指与石油相关的当事方之间的所有权转移,不论是否公平。

---

* 本协定中附件 1、附件 3 涉及较多技术术语,但对协定影响不大,故未译。——译者注

(c)"开发计划"是指拟对石油储藏开发和管理的项目,其中包括详细的地下石油储量的评估和生产设施,有关计划预期年限的生产资料,涵盖该计划可行性论证、建设和设施以及计划生产前的阶段所预估的资本和非资本支出,以及对单一化储藏中开发的石油的商业性评估。

(d)"输出管道"是指任何将单一区域石油向外输送的管道。

(e)"联合委员会"是指根据《帝汶海条约》第六条设立的共同石油开发区联合委员会。

(f)"共同石油开发区"是指《帝汶海条约》第三条所指区域。

(g)"合营协议"是指与单一储藏开发相关的 Sunrise 区域合营者之间签订的协议,其中包括统一经营协议、联合作业协议以及其他与这些储藏开发相关的协议。

(h)"可销售的石油商品"是指以下从石油中生产的任何产品:

ⅰ. 稳定的原油;

ⅱ. 出售的天然气;

ⅲ. 凝析油;

ⅳ. 液化石油气;

ⅴ. 乙烷;

ⅵ. 其他管理当局宣布可以销售的石油产品。

可以销售的产品,不得为对以上 ⅰ 至 ⅵ 项所列产品进行加工后所得的产品。

(i)"可销售石油商品点"是指生产每一种可销售石油商品的点,并且可以在可销售石油商品之间变化。

(j)"石油"是指:

ⅰ. 任何自然产生的碳氢化合物,无论是气态、液态还是固态;

ⅱ. 任何自然产生的碳氢化合物的混合物,无论是气态、液态还是固态;

ⅲ. 自然产生的一种或几种碳氢化合物的混合物,无论是气态、液态还是固态,以及与这些碳氢化合物同时产生的其他物质;

包括上述 ⅰ、ⅱ、ⅲ 项中所指的已回到自然储油层中的其他石油。

(k)"管理当局"是指对单一区域中的共同石油开发区内的石油活动进行管理的主管当局,以及对共同石油开发区以外的单一区域部分内的石油活动进行管理的澳大利亚主管当局。

（l）"Sunrise 委员会"是指本协定第九条所指的委员会。

（m）"Sunrise 合营者"是指所有拥有在单一化区域内进行石油作业许可或合同的机构或个人，据该合同或许可可进行石油的勘探或开发。

（n）"单一区域"是指附件1中所指区域。

（o）"统一设施"是指基于开发计划，为了开采单一储藏的石油，而在单一化区域海床上或下所建造的设施或结构。但是不包括"估值点（Valuation Point）"之后所建造的结构或设施。

（p）"单一作业者"是指本协定第六条所指之含义。

（q）"单位石油"是指直至估值点为止，单一储藏中蕴藏的或生产的石油。

（r）"单位财产"是指单一区域的所有设施。

（s）"单一储藏"是指附件1所指含义。

（t）"估值点"是指从单一储藏生产第一批可以销售的石油的时间点，不得迟于以下较早的一个时间点：

ⅰ．石油进入输出管道的时间点，

ⅱ．可销售石油产品的时间点。

第二条　不影响条款

（1）本协定的内容，本协定生效后所实施的行为，以及根据本协定在单一化区域适用的任何法律：

（a）不得解释为损害或影响澳大利亚或东帝汶关于海洋边界的各自主张或立场；以及

（b）不得作为主张、支持否定或限制澳大利亚或东帝汶各自海洋边界主张或立场的依据。

（2）尽管有本协定的其他规定，特别是本协定第四条之规定，但是本条仍适用。

第三条　单一储藏的开发

（1）根据本协定条款之规定，单一储藏应当采取一体化方式开采。

（2）澳大利亚和东帝汶应该确保管理当局履行协定所规定的义务，即保证 Sunrise 合营者遵守本协定之规定。

第四条 适用法律

除非本协定另有规定,否则基于本协定之目的:

(a)《帝汶海条约》适用于共同石油开发区内的石油活动,以及根据本协定分配比例归于共同石油开发区的石油活动。

(b) 澳大利亚的法律,适用于根据分配比例归于澳大利亚的石油活动。

第五条 协议

(1) 澳大利亚和东帝汶应该要求 Sunrise 区域的合营者,在本协定生效之日起,根据本协定缔结合营企业协议,管理单一化储藏的开采活动。

(2) 任何合营企业协议必须含有以下条款,即如果合营企业协议与本协定冲突,以本协定为准。任何合营企业协议必须得到管理当局的批准。

(3) 除非协议有相反规定之外,任何一个合营企业协议应当包括一些条款,以确保:

(a) 任何经双方同意的,修改、变更或在其他方面改变合营协议的提议,

(b) 任何双方同意的,放弃或背离合营协议任何条款的提议,

在实施这些提议之前,必须得到管理当局的批准。管理当局应该确认收到有关这些提议的通知,并且明确接收的日期。除非自收到之日起 45 日内,单一作业者收到管理当局的相反决定,否则视为批准。

第六条 单一作业者

为了单一储藏开发目的,Sunrise 区域的合营者根据本协定通过协议任命其中一名合营者作为其代理(即"单一作业者")。单一作业者的任命和改变,应得到管理当局的批准。

第七条 单位石油的分配

从单一储藏生产的石油产品,应当根据 20.1:79.9 的比例在共同石油开发区和澳大利亚之间进行分配,其中 20.1% 归共同石油开发区,79.9% 归澳大利亚。

第八条 单位石油的重新分配

(1) 重新决定单一化储藏中石油分配的比例应遵循以下规定:

(a) 澳大利亚或东帝汶可以要求单一作业者重新决定分配比例。

（b）澳大利亚和东帝汶应考虑分配比例审查的次数降至最低的可取性。

（c）在重新决定分配比例后的 5 年内，不允许重新决定分配比例，除非重新分配比例发生于在单一化储藏开始投产后的 12 个月内。

（d）单一作业者只应运用适当的商用软件重新决定分配比例。要求进行重新分配时，只有两国政府均可以获得的数据可被单一作业者作为数据使用，根据单一作业者的拟用作重新决定分配比例的所有数据和分析，应当提供给两国政府。单一作业者应尽一切合理的努力，在 120 日内完成重新分配比例。

（e）任何根据上述 a 项之规定的要求而重新做出的分配比例，只有当管理当局同意，或若提交专家决定则在专家做出最终决定后，才生效。

（f）分配比例的任何改变具有溯及力的，过去的收支应该进行调整。

（2）根据本条第 1 款，澳大利亚或东帝汶可以请求审查分配比例。根据审查，澳大利亚和东帝汶如果达成一致，可以改变分配比例。

第九条 单一区域的管理

（1）除非本协定另有规定，根据本协定之目的，管理单一化区域或与单位石油有关的石油活动的管理当局，应该是根据第四条规定所设立的管理当局。

（2）建立 Sunrise 委员会（简称"委员会"）是为了促进本协定的实施，委员会应该就与单一化区域有关的石油勘探开发的事项进行协商。

（3）委员会应该促进管理当局之间的协作，以促进石油储藏作为单一实体的开发。

（4）委员会应当审查开发计划，并就开发计划向管理当局提出建议。

（5）委员会应该处理管理当局所提交的问题，促进对测量系统的检测，并且协调承包商向管理当局提供信息。

（6）委员会应该监督附件 2 中法律的实施，并就这些法律的实施向管理当局提出建议。

（7）管理当局应该首先将争端提交委员会，以期通过协商和谈判解决。如果委员会无法解决争端，该争端应该依据第 26 条解决。

（8）Sunrise 委员会由三名成员组成。其中两名由澳大利亚任命，一名由东帝汶任命。

第十条 收支分配

直到估值点的所有收支,应当根据分配比例进行分配。

第十一条 与单位财产有关的税收

为了征收与单位财产相关的公司税、资源税,以及成本回收和产品分成的目的:

(a) 根据分配比例,用于共同石油开发区那部分的收支,应依据《帝汶海条约》的具体安排和本协定的其他规定征收税收;

(b) 根据分配比例,用于澳大利亚的那部分收支,依据澳大利亚国内税收安排进行征税。

第十二条 开发计划

(1) 直到单一作业者提出有效的开采和开发计划(其中包括根据合资协议制订的项目和计划),并经主管当局批准,才能进行石油的生产。单一作业者应将开发计划副本提交至主管当局以获批准。

(2) 委员会可以审查开发计划,并就此向管理当局提出建议。

(3) 如果开发计划符合以下规定,管理当局应当批准:

(a) 该计划在商业上是可行的;

(b) 承包商或者许可证持有人,具备能力和财力开发储藏以实现最大的商业优势;

(c) 承包商或者许可证持有人根据良好油田实践,正在开发储藏以实现最大的商业优势;

(d) 可以合理预期承包商或者许可证持有者在特定期限内,进行储藏的开发;

(e) 承包商或者许可证持有者,已经根据公平交易原则缔结了该项目天然气的销售合同。

(4) 主管当局必须明确指出不批准开发计划的理由,包括承包商或许可证持有人没有满足的第2款之标准。

(5) 主管当局应该确保单一化区域的开采活动按照开发计划进行。

(6) 单一作业者在任何时候可以提出,若任何时候主管当局决定需要提交,有关改进或修订开发计划的建议。开发计划的所有修订或增加,需要主管当局事先批准。

(7) 如果单一作业者得到任何一个主管当局的通知,开发计划或者对于开发计划的修订没有得到批准，那么主管当局应该与另一方主管当局以及单一作业者进行协商，以达成一致。

（8）除了根据本条第 2 款之规定对开发计划进行修正外，主管当局应当要求 Sunrise 合营者不得改变单一化区域内的统一设施的地位或功能。

（9）如果 Sunrise 合营者就经批准的开发计划中的项目所产出的天然气的销售签订了合同，主管当局不得采取任何行动阻碍天然气供应。

第十三条　报废

（1）单一化区域内全部或部分单位财产进行报废，应根据本协定签订时已经生效的法律和管理当局任何时候做出的修正案来进行。

（2）报废任何单位财产，包括初步移除大型机械的任何部分或者停运任何设施或管道，单一作业者应当至少提前两年，根据本协定第十二条之规定提交一份修订的开发计划，其中包括使用单位财产进行生产的计划。

第十四条　单一化区域内的构筑物

（1）主管当局应该要求单一作业者，报告单一化区域内每一个构筑物的具体位置。

（2）为了单一化储藏开采的目的，根据本协定第二十二条和安全的需要，任何一方政府不应该阻碍单一化区域内的构筑物间人员和物资的自由流动，位于这些构筑物上的设备应可自由进入在澳大利亚和东帝汶的船只和飞行器。

第十五条　属于共同石油开发区的石油的销售时间点

（1）属于共同石油开发区的单位石油的权利，应当在估值点从两国转移至承包商。

（2）基于成本回收和产品分成的目的，依据分配比例属于石油共同开发区的单位石油，销售时间点也是对该部分石油进行征税和估值的时间点。

第十六条　为了回收成本和产品分成对单位石油的评估

（1）若澳大利亚和东帝汶同意承包商或者许可证持有人根据附件 3 规定的公平交易原则就单位石油的销售缔结合同，那么为了回收成本和产品分成的目的，对于依据分配比例归属于共同石油开发区的那部分单位石油，其交易价格就会用于石油的评估。

(2) 若澳大利亚和东帝汶不同意承包商或者许可证持有人,根据附件 3 规定的公平交易原则,就单位石油的销售缔结合同,那么对于依据分配比例归属于共同石油开发区的那部分单位石油,澳大利亚和东帝汶为了回收成本和产品分成,应根据国际接受的公平交易原则,并适当考虑附件 3 所列的履行的职能、使用的资产和承担的风险,进行石油评估。

第十七条　单位财产用于非 Sunrise 作业

(1) 澳大利亚和东帝汶承认,根据本条第 2、第 3 款之规定,除了开发单一化储藏的石油资源外,石油开发也是对单位财产的合法使用。

(2) 任何一个主管当局,在收到单一作业者使用部分单位财产的请求后,应当与另一主管当局就该请求进行协商。协商且咨询 Sunrise 区域的合营者后,若这种使用对根据本协定和开发计划,单一化区域的有效开发和石油的输送无不利影响,相关管理当局应当允许使用任何的单位财产。

(3) 根据本条第 2 款进行的协商表明,为了有效实行第 2 款之规定,有必要制定补充规定。澳大利亚和东帝汶在征询 Sunrise 区域的合营者后,应当谈判以制定补充协定。为了促进这一谈判,澳大利亚和东帝汶应当根据第二十五条之规定交换相关信息。

(4) 虽然有上述 1~3 款的规定,在澳大利亚和东帝汶就使用单位财产的征税达成一致前,两国都不得批准使用单位财产。

第十八条　雇佣和培训

适当考虑职业健康和安全要求,有效运营和良好的油田实践,澳大利亚和东帝汶应当采取适当措施保证,对单一化区域内澳大利亚和东帝汶国民或永久性居民,给予了雇佣和训练的优先权。

第十九条　安全

(1) 为了单一化区域的安全,应当适用附件 2 中所列的法律及其修正案。

(2) 主管当局应当执行单一化区域内的法律。

第二十条　职业健康和安全

(1) 为了单一化区域内的职业健康和安全,应当适用附件 2 中所列的法律及其修正案。

(2) 主管当局应当执行单一化区域内的法律。

第二十一条 环境保护

（1）为了单一化区域内的环境保护，应当适用附件2中所列的法律及其修正案。

（2）主管当局应当执行单一化区域内的法律。

第二十二条 海关

（1）为了控制人员、设备和货物的流动，在澳大利亚和东帝汶任何一方的请求下，两国应就特定货物和设备进入单一化区域进行协商。澳大利亚和东帝汶可制定安排促进人员、设备和货物的流通。

（2）根据本条第3、4、5款之规定，澳大利亚和东帝汶对从其领土进入单一化区域，或从单一化区域进入其领土的设备和货物，可适用各自的海关法。

（3）为有关石油活动的目的，进入单一化区域的货物和设备，不缴纳关税。

（4）通过澳大利亚或东帝汶，为有关石油活动的目的而进入单一化区域的货物和设备，不应缴纳关税。

（5）为永久运送至澳大利亚或东帝汶的目的，离开单一化区域的货物和设备，则应履行该国的关税义务。

第二十三条 安全安排

澳大利亚和东帝汶应就单一化区域内的安全事件做出反应，并对可能的安全威胁交换信息，做出安排。

第二十四条 测量系统

（1）在根据开发计划开始石油生产之前，主管当局应当要求单一作业者向它们提交有关测量系统的设计、安装和运行的建议以待批准。该测量系统是用于准确测量构成单位石油，或者在后续的计算过程中被视为构成单位石油的气体和液体的数量的。该测量系统被用于油田的作业、再注入、燃烧、排放或者单一矿藏的输出。

（2）主管当局应当促进：

（a）为了单位石油的测量进入任何设备；

（b）提供与单位石油测量有关的信息，包括所有系统设计和运营的详细信息；

使得检查者对澳大利亚和东帝汶在单位石油测量上的基本利益均得到

实现而感到满足。

第二十五条 信息条款

（1）应当确保有关单一化储藏中石油勘探和开发的信息，在澳大利亚和东帝汶之间自由流通。澳大利亚或东帝汶提供给对方的秘密信息，未经信息提供国的同意，不得公开。

（2）管理当局应该要求单一作业者提供以下信息：

（a）就单位财产的建设或停运的具体情况，项目花费以及做出的合同承诺，提供每月报告；

（b）用于油田的作业、再注入、燃烧、排放或从单位财产导出的单位石油，或后续计算中包括的气体和液体的数量，提供每月报告；

（c）以及以下信息的年度报告：

ⅰ．油田寿命内计划的年产量数据（提供绘制产量数据的基础）；

ⅱ．与油田有关的最新的地质、地球物理以及工程方面的信息，包括但不限于任何可能与重新决定分配比例相关的信息；以及

ⅲ．预计与单一化储藏开采有关的花费。

第二十六条 争端解决

（1）任何有关本协定解释或适用的争端，尽可能通过协商或谈判解决。

（2）根据本条第 3 款之规定，如果争端无法通过第 1 款的方式，或者任何其他协商一致的方法解决，应任何一方政府请求，应将争端提交附件 4 所规定的仲裁庭。

（3）如果根据第八条第 1 款重新决定分配比例的提案而引起的争端，或者根据第二十四条有关气体和液体产量的测量产生的争端，澳大利亚和东帝汶应该任命一名专家，解决该争端。在任何一方政府就争端发出通知后的 60 天内，两国政府应该尝试就任命专家达成一致。如果在这一期限内未能达成一致，则适用附件 5 所规定的程序。任命的专家应依据附件 5 的条款进行。专家的决定对于两国政府以及 Sunrise 区域合营公司，均为终局的和有约束力的，除非存在诈骗或明显的错误。

第二十七条 生效、修正和期限

（1）本协定在双方以书面形式通知对方均已完成各自协定生效的条件时生效。

（2）澳大利亚和东帝汶可以书面约定，于任何时候修改或终止本协定。

（3）如果就海床进行永久划界，澳大利亚和东帝汶应该重新考虑协定的条款。任何新的协定，应该确保根据本协定所进行的石油活动，得以在与本协定相同的条件下继续进行。

下列签署人，经其各自政府正式授权，在本协定上签字，以昭信守。

签订于 2003 年 3 月 16 日，帝力。原始文件为英文，一式两份。

澳大利亚代表　　　　东帝汶代表

亚历山大·唐纳　　　阿纳·佩索亚

外交部长　　　　　　国务秘书

附件 2　第 19、20 和 21 条所提及的在单一区域适用的法律

第 19 条——安全

海上石油设施安全管理法规

1989 年海上索赔责任的限制法案

1912 年航海法案

1992 年无线电通讯法案

1992 年海员康复赔偿法案

第 20 条——健康

海上石油职业健康安全法规

1993 年海洋产业职业健康安全法案

1912 年航海法案

1992 年海员康复赔偿法案

第 21 条——环境保护

1999 年海上石油环境管理法规

1981 年海洋保护法案（民事责任）

1993 年海洋保护法案（石油污染赔偿基金）

1993 年海洋保护法案（向海洋污染基金注入资金——涉及关税的规定）

1993年海洋保护法案（向海洋污染基金注入资金——涉及消费税的规定）

1993年海洋保护法案（向海洋污染基金注入资金——一般性规定）

1981年海洋保护法案（干预权）

1981年海洋保护法案（防止船舶污染）

1981年海洋保护法案（船舶运输税）

附件4 争端解决程序

（a）根据本协定第二十六条第2款将争端提交至仲裁庭，该仲裁庭的三名仲裁员应按以下方式任命：

ⅰ. 澳大利亚和东帝汶各任命一名仲裁员；

ⅱ. 由澳大利亚和东帝汶任命的两名仲裁员，在第二名任命后的60天内，通过协商一致选出第三名仲裁员，该仲裁员应为与澳大利亚和东帝汶均建立了外交关系的第三国的国民或永久性居民；

ⅲ. 在选出第三名仲裁员后60天内，澳大利亚和东帝汶应该批准选择该仲裁员作为仲裁庭主席。

（b）一国通过外交途径将提起仲裁程序通知另一缔约国，仲裁程序即被启动。这种通知应当包含一项声明简要阐述主张的依据，寻求救济的性质以及任命的仲裁员的名字。在接到通知后的60天内，被申请方应当通知申请方，其任命的仲裁员的名字。

（c）如果在本附件a条ⅱ款和ⅲ款以及b款的期限内，无法做出所需的任命或批准，澳大利亚或东帝汶应该请求国际法院院长进行必要的任命。如果国际法院的院长是澳大利亚或东帝汶的国民或永久性居民，或者由于其他原因无法进行任命，则请求国际法院的副院长进行任命。如果国际法院的副院长也是由于这些原因无法进行任命，则请求国际法院其余法官中，既不是澳大利亚也不是东帝汶的公民或永久性居民，而且资历最老的法官，进行任命。

（d）若依本附件规定所任命的仲裁员辞职或无法履行职能，应按照最初仲裁员的任命方式任命继任仲裁员。继任仲裁员与最初仲裁员享有相同的权利和义务。

（e）在仲裁庭主席确定的时间和地点召集仲裁庭，然后由仲裁庭决定其办案的时间和地点。

（f）仲裁庭根据澳大利亚和东帝汶之间的协定，审理其权限范围内的所有问题，自行决定仲裁程序。

（g）在仲裁庭做出裁决之前的任何阶段，仲裁庭可以向澳大利亚和东帝汶建议友好解决争端。仲裁庭应考虑条约的条款和相关国际法，根据多数票做出裁决。

（h）澳大利亚和东帝汶自行承担各自任命的仲裁员，准备和提交案件产生的费用。仲裁庭主席以及仲裁活动产生的费用，由澳大利亚和东帝汶均摊。

（i）仲裁庭应该给予澳大利亚和东帝汶公平的申诉机会。在澳大利亚或东帝汶缺席的情况下，仲裁庭也会做出裁决。任何案件，自仲裁主体开庭之日起6个月内，仲裁庭应该做出裁决。任何裁决应该以书面的形式做出，并且要说明法律依据。签名的裁决副本，应被送达澳大利亚和东帝汶。

（j）裁决对于澳大利亚和东帝汶是终局且有约束力的。

附件5 专家裁定程序

1. 如果在第二十六条规定的期限内，无法就专家的任命达成一致，两国政府应该立即交换一份名单，名单按照优先顺序列明不多于三名的独立专家。每份名单中第一位专家得三分，第二位得两分，第三位得一分。在两份名单中总计得分最高的被任命为专家。

2. 如果在政府交换的名单上，有两名或两名以上的专家都获得最高分数，政府应自交换名单之日起30日内，通过协商，若协商无果，则通过抽签的方式选任专家。

3. 若两国政府认为，任命的专家无法或不愿意或者没有在合理的时间内处理相关问题，那么剩下的专家中得分最高者应获任命以处理该问题。如果剩下的两名专家的分数一样，两国政府应该通过全体一致或抽签的方式，决定任命哪位专家处理问题。

4. 如果一国政府在本附件规定的时间内，对另一国任何请求或通知未进行反应，该政府视为放弃与这一请求或通知有关的权利；但仍受另一国政府选任的专家以及专家所作决定的约束。

5. 专家的任务是就任何问题做出独立的决定。如果争议的问题与本协定第八条中重新分配比例有关，专家的决定应根据相关合营协议中，重新确定的技术程序和计算公式，做出决定。

6. 专家可以雇用独立的承包商，承担专家作决定所必需的工作，只要专家为此目的指定的承包商得到两国政府的批准，承包商可从事与其自身或其工作人员没有利益冲突的工作，一旦有利益冲突则禁止其从事该项工作。

7. 以下事项所需的专家费用由政府先行垫付：

（a）要求重新计算分配比例，

（b）或者不同意本协定第二十四条所规定的气体和液体产量计量的方法，

应从单一作业者那里获得补偿。在政府支付费用后的 12 个月内，单一作业者应尽最大努力予以偿还。

8. 除非本协定另有规定，专家应该自行确定处理争端的程序。专家只能与两国政府同时会晤。政府和专家之间除会议外的所有通信应当以书面形式进行，进行通信的个人应该同时将通信的副本送往另一国。

9. 专家只应运用适当的商用软件重新决定分配比例。要求进行重新分配时，只有两国政府均可获得的数据可被专家作为数据使用，根据专家拟用作重新决定分配比例的所有数据和分析，应当提供给两国政府。

10. 专家一经任命，单一作业者应该向专家提供数据和分析。在任命后 30 日内，各政府应提交初步意见，并向另一方政府提供副本。在收到提交的副本后 20 日内，相关政府应该提出补充意见，并再次向另一方政府提供副本。

11. 专家应该在任命后 90 日内，或两国政府决定的其他日期内，做出初步决定。初步决定应该包含对其决定做出合理评价所必要的支撑性文件。在收到专家初步决定后的 90 日内，每个政府有权要求对初步决定和支撑性文件进行阐明，有权要求专家审查自己的初步决定，并且有权向专家提交自己的意见。如果一国政府提出这一要求，另一国政府自收到这些意见副本之日起 15 日内，有权提交进一步的意见。专家自做出初步决定之日起 140 日内，做出最终决定。专家的最终决定应以书面形式做出，并说明详细的理由。

12. Sunrise 区域合营者，应该在提供专家要求的信息以及便利专家做出决定的事项上，进行充分的合作。

13. 两国政府应该要求专家和专家任命的独立承包商对向专家提供的任何信息予以保密。

4. Agreement between the Government of Australia and the Government of the Democratic Republic of Timor – Leste relating to the Unitisation of the Sunrise Troubador Fields

The Government of Australia and the Government of the Democratic Republic of Timor – Leste,

Considering that the exploration in the Timor Sea between Australia and Timor – Leste has proved the existence of petroleum deposits which extend across the eastern boundary of the Joint Petroleum Development Area; those deposits being known as the Sunrise and Troubadour deposits (collectively known as Greater Sunrise);

Noting that Australia and Timor – Leste have, at the date of this agreement, made maritime claims, and not yet delimited their maritime boundaries, including in an area of the Timor Sea where Greater Sunrise lies;

Desiring, before production commences, to make provisions for the integrated exploitation of Greater Sunrise;

Acknowledging that Australia and Timor – Leste agreed under Annex E of the Timor Sea Treaty to unitise Greater Sunrise on the basis that 20.1% of Greater Sunrise lies within the JPDA and that production from Greater Sunrise shall be distributed on the basis that 20.1% is attributed to the JPDA and 79.9% is attributed to Australia;

Recalling further the Memorandum of Understanding between the Government of Australia and the Government of the Democratic Republic of Timor – Leste of 20

May 2002 in which they agreed to work expeditiously and in good faith to conclude a unitisation agreement for Greater Sunrise;

Have agreed as follows:

Article 1　Definitions

For the purposes of this Agreement, unless the context otherwise requires:

(a) "Apportionment Ratio" means the ratio as set out in Article 7 of this Agreement or such other ratio as applies from time to time as a result of any redetermination under Article 8.

(b) "Commercial Sale", in relation to Petroleum, means a transfer of title between parties, whether or not at arm's length.

(c) "Development Plan" means a description of the proposed petroleum reservoirs development and management program that includes details of the sub – surface evaluation and production facilities, the production profile for the expected life of the project, the estimated capital and non – capital expenditure covering the feasibility, fabrication, installation and pre – production stages of the project, and an evaluation of the commerciality of the development of Petroleum from the Unit Reservoirs.

(d) "Export Pipeline" means any pipeline by which petroleum is discharged from the Unit Area.

(e) "Joint Commission" means the Joint Commission of the Joint Petroleum Development Area established under Article 6 of the Timor Sea Treaty.

(f) "Joint Petroleum Development Area" ("JPDA") means the area referred to in Article 3 of the Timor Sea Treaty.

(g) "Joint Venturers' Agreement" means any agreement between all Sunrise Joint Venturers relating to the exploitation of the Unit Reservoirs including a unitisation agreement, a unit operating agreement and any other agreement relating to the exploitation of those reservoirs.

(h) "Marketable Petroleum Commodity" means any of the following products produced from petroleum:

(i) stabilised crude oil;

(ii) sales gas;

(iii) condensate;

(iv) liquefied petroleum gas;

(v) ethane;

(vi) any other product declared by the Regulatory Authorities to be a marketable petroleum commodity.

A marketable petroleum commodity cannot be a product produced from another product of a kind referred to in subparagraphs (i) to (vi) inclusive.

(i) "MPC Point" means that point where each Marketable Petroleum Commodity is produced, and may vary between Marketable Petroleum Commodities.

(j) "Petroleum" means:

(i) any naturally occurring hydrocarbon, whether in a gaseous, liquid or solid state;

(ii) any naturally occurring mixture of hydrocarbons, whether in a gaseous, liquid or solid state; or

(iii) any naturally occurring mixture of one or more hydrocarbons, whether in a gaseous, liquid or solid state, as well as other substances produced in association with such hydrocarbons;

including any Petroleum as defined in subparagraph (i), (ii) or (iii) that has been returned to a natural reservoir.

(k) "Regulatory Authorities" means the competent authority for administering petroleum activities in that part of the Joint Petroleum Development Area within the Unit Area and the competent Australian authority for administering petroleum activities in that part of the Unit Area outside of the Joint Petroleum Development Area.

(l) "Sunrise Commission" has the meaning given in Article 9 of this Agreement.

(m) "Sunrise Joint Venturers" means all those individuals or bodies corporate holding for the time being a licence or contract in respect of an area within the Unit Area under which exploration or exploitation of Petroleum may be carried out.

(n) "Unit Area" means the area described in Annex I.

(o) "Unit Installation" means any structure or device installed or to be installed above, on, or under the seabed of the Unit Area for the purpose of extracting Petroleum from the Unit Reservoirs in accordance with the Development Plan. Unit Installations exclude any structure or device after the Valuation Point.

(p) "Unit Operator" has the meaning given in Article 6 of this Agreement.

(q) "Unit Petroleum" means all Petroleum contained in or produced from the Unit Reservoirs, up to the Valuation Point.

(r) "Unit Property" means all Unit Installations in the Unit Area.

(s) "Unit Reservoirs" has the meaning given in Annex I.

(t) "Valuation Point" means the point of the first commercial sale of Petroleum produced from the Unit Reservoirs, which shall occur no later than the earlier of

(i) the point where the Petroleum enters an Export Pipeline and

(ii) the MPC point for the Petroleum.

Article 2 Without prejudice

(1) Nothing contained in this Agreement, no acts taking place while this Agreement is in force or as a consequence of this Agreement and no law operating in the Unit Area by virtue of this Agreement

(a) shall be interpreted as prejudicing or affecting the position of either Australia or Timor – Leste with regard to their respective maritime boundaries or rights or claims thereto; and

(b) may be relied on as a basis for asserting, supporting, denying or limiting the position of either Australia or Timor – Leste with regard to their respective maritime boundaries or rights or claims thereto.

(2) This article applies notwithstanding any other provision of this Agreement including, in particular, Article 4 of this Agreement.

Article 3 Exploitation of the Unit Reservoirs

(1) The exploitation of the Unit Reservoirs shall be undertaken in an integrated manner in accordance with the terms of this Agreement.

(2) Australia and Timor – Leste shall ensure that the obligations of the Regulatory Authorities contained in this Agreement, with respect to ensuring compliance by the Sunrise Joint Venturers with the terms of this Agreement, shall be fully ob-

served.

Article 4　Application of Laws

For the purposes of this Agreement but not otherwise and unless otherwise provided in this Agreement:

(a) the Timor Sea Treaty shall be deemed to apply to petroleum activities within the JPDA and petroleum activities attributed to the JPDA pursuant to the Apportionment Ratio;

(b) Australian legislation shall be deemed to apply to petroleum activities attributed to Australia pursuant to the Apportionment Ratio.

Article 5　Agreements

(1) Australia and Timor-Leste shall require Sunrise Joint Venturers, as comprised at the date on which this Agreement enters into force, to conclude Joint Venturers' Agreements to regulate the exploitation of the Unit Reservoirs in accordance with this Agreement.

(2) Any Joint Venturers' Agreement shall incorporate provisions to ensure that, in the event of a conflict between that Joint Venturers' Agreement and this Agreement, the terms of this Agreement shall prevail. Any Joint Venturers' Agreement requires the prior approval of the Regulatory Authorities.

(3) Any Joint Venturers' Agreement shall incorporate provisions to ensure that, except in so far as the contrary is expressly stated in that Agreement,

(a) any agreed proposal to amend, modify, or otherwise change the Joint Venturers' Agreement, and

(b) any agreed proposal to waive or depart from any provision of the Joint Venturers' Agreement,

shall require the approval of the Regulatory Authorities before any such proposal may be implemented. The Regulatory Authorities shall acknowledge receipt of notice of any such proposal and shall specify the date of receipt. Approval shall be deemed to have been given unless the Unit Operator has been notified to the contrary by either Regulatory Authority not later than 45 days after the later of the specified dates.

Article 6　Unit Operator

A single Sunrise Joint Venturer shall be appointed by agreement between the Sunrise Joint Venturers as their agent for the purposes of exploiting the Unit Reservoirs in accordance with this Agreement ("the Unit Operator"). The appointment of and any change of the Unit Operator shall be subject to prior approval of the Regulatory Authorities.

Article 7　Apportionment of Unit Petroleum

Production of Petroleum from the Unit Reservoirs shall be apportioned between the JPDA and Australia according to the Apportionment Ratio 20.1 : 79.9, with 20.1% apportioned to the JPDA and 79.9% apportioned to Australia.

Article 8　Reapportionment of Unit Petroleum

(1) Technical redetermination of the Apportionment Ratio from the Unit Reservoirs may take place in accordance with the following:

(a) Either Australia or Timor – Leste may request the Unit Operator to undertake a redetermination of the Apportionment Ratio.

(b) Australia and Timor – Leste shall have regard to the desirability of minimising the number of reviews of the Apportionment Ratio.

(c) Any redetermination of the Apportionment Ratio shall not occur within five (5) years of any prior redetermination, except that a redetermination may occur within twelve (12) months of the commencement of production from the Unit Reservoirs.

(d) The Unit Operator shall use only commercially available software in a redetermination of the Apportionment Ratio. Only data that is available to both Governments as at the date the redetermination is requested shall be utilised by the Unit Operator and all data and analyses pursuant to the Unit Operator's proposal for the redetermined Apportionment Ratio shall be provided to both Governments with the proposal. The Unit Operator shall use all reasonable endeavours to complete the redetermination within 120 days.

(e) Any change to the Apportionment Ratio arising from a redetermination requested under subparagraph (a) has effect when it is agreed by the Regulatory Authorities or, if referred to an expert for determination, when the expert makes a final decision.

(f) Any change to the Apportionment Ratio shall be retrospective and past receipts and expenditures shall be adjusted.

(2) Notwithstanding paragraph 1, either Australia or Timor – Leste may request a review of the Apportionment Ratio. Following such a review, the Apportionment Ratio may be altered by agreement between Australia and Timor – Leste.

Article 9　Administration of the Unit Area

(1) For the purposes of this Agreement but not otherwise and unless otherwise provided in this Agreement, the Regulatory Authorities that will regulate petroleum activities in the Unit Area or in relation to Unit Petroleum shall be those Regulatory Authorities established through application of laws as provided in Article 4.

(2) A Sunrise Commission ("the Commission") shall be established for the purpose of facilitating the implementation of this Agreement and shall consult on issues relating to exploration and exploitation of petroleum in the Unit Area.

(3) The Commission shall facilitate coordination between the Regulatory Authorities to promote the development of the petroleum reservoir as a single entity.

(4) The Commission may review, and make recommendations to the Regulatory Authorities with regard to, a Development Plan.

(5) The Commission shall consider matters referred to it by the Regulatory Authorities, facilitate inspection of measuring systems and coordinate the provision of information by contractors to the Regulatory Authorities.

(6) The Commission may monitor the application of the laws referred to in Annex II and may make recommendations to the Regulatory Authorities concerning the application of such laws.

(7) Regulatory Authorities may refer disputes to the Commission in the first instance for resolution by consultation and negotiation. In the event that the dispute cannot be resolved by the Commission, disputes shall be settled in accordance with Article 26.

(8) The Sunrise Commission shall consist of three members. Two shall be nominated by Australia and one shall be nominated by Timor – Leste.

Article 10 Apportionment of Receipts and Expenditures

All receipts and expenditures up to the Valuation Point shall be apportioned in accordance with the Apportionment Ratio.

Article 11 Taxation Applying in relation to Unit Property

For the purposes of company taxation, resource taxation, cost recovery and production sharing in relation to Unit Property,

(a) receipts and expenditures for that part of production attributed to the JPDA in accordance with the Apportionment Ratio shall be taxed in accordance with arrangements specified in the Timor Sea Treaty and elsewhere in this Agreement;

(b) receipts and expenditures for that part of production attributed to Australia in accordance with the Apportionment Ratio shall be taxed in accordance with Australia's domestic taxation arrangements.

Article 12 Development Plan

(1) Production of petroleum shall not commence until a Development Plan for the effective exploitation of the Unit Reservoirs, which has been submitted by the Unit Operator and contains a programme and plans agreed in accordance with Joint Venturers' Agreements, has been approved by the Regulatory Authorities. The Unit Operator shall submit copies of the Development Plan to the Regulatory Authorities for approval.

(2) The Commission may review, and make recommendations to the Regulatory Authorities with regard to, a Development Plan.

(3) The Regulatory Authorities shall approve the Development Plan where:

(a) the project is commercially viable;

(b) the contractor or licensee possesses the competence and resources needed to exploit the reservoir to the best commercial advantage;

(c) the contractor or licensee is seeking to exploit the reservoir to the best commercial advantage consistent with good oilfield practice;

(d) the contractor or licensee could reasonably be expected to carry out the exploitation of the reservoir during the specified period;

(e) the contractor or licensee has entered into contracts for the sale of gas from the project which are consistent with arm's length transactions.

(4) The Regulatory Authorities shall specify their reasons for not approving a Development Plan including identification of the criteria in paragraph (2) that the contractor or licensee has failed to meet.

(5) The Regulatory Authorities shall ensure that the exploitation of the Unit Area shall be in accordance with the Development Plan.

(6) The Unit Operator may at any time submit, and if at any time the Regulatory Authorities so decide may be required to submit, proposals to bring up to date or otherwise amend the Development Plan. All amendments or additions to the Development Plan require the prior approval of the Regulatory Authorities.

(7) Where the Unit Operator has been notified by either Regulatory Authority that the Development Plan or an amendment to the Development Plan has not been approved, the Regulatory Authorities shall consult with each other and with the Unit Operator with a view to reaching agreement.

(8) The Regulatory Authorities shall require the Sunrise Joint Venturers not to change the status or function of any Unit Installation in the Unit Area in any way except in accordance with an amendment to the Development Plan in accordance with paragraph (2).

(9) Where a Sunrise Joint Venturer has entered into contracts for the sale of gas from the project that are part of an approved Development Plan, no action may be taken by the Regulatory Authorities to withhold the supply of that gas.

Article 13   Abandonment

(1) The abandonment of any or all parts of Unit Property shall be undertaken in accordance with laws that have entered into force as at the date of this Agreement and as amended from time to time as applied by the Regulatory Authorities.

(2) At least two years before the abandonment of any part of Unit Property is undertaken, including the preliminary removal of any large item of machinery or the decommissioning of any installation or pipeline, the Unit Operator shall be required to submit a revised Development Plan, in accordance with the provisions of Article 12, which contains a plan for the cessation of production from Unit Property.

(3) The Sunrise Joint Venturers shall enter into an agreement to share the

costs of discharging the abandonment obligations referred to in paragraph (1) above for Unit Property.

(4) The costs of abandonment of any or all parts of Unit Property shall be apportioned in accordance with the Apportionment Ratio.

Article 14　Structures Located in the Unit Area

(1) The Regulatory Authorities shall require the Unit Operator to inform them of the exact position of every structure located in the Unit Area.

(2) For the purposes of exploiting the Unit Reservoirs and subject to Article 22 and to the requirements of safety, neither Government shall hinder the free movement of personnel and materials between structures located in the Unit Area and landing facilities on those structures shall be freely available to vessels and aircraft of Australia and Timor – Leste.

Article 15　Point of Sale for Unit Petroleum Attributed to the JPDA

(1) Title to Unit Petroleum attributed to the JPDA shall pass from Australia and Timor – Leste to the contractor acting in the JPDA at the Valuation Point.

(2) This shall be the taxing point and point of valuation of Petroleum for cost recovery and production sharing purposes, for that part of Unit Petroleum apportioned to the JPDA in accordance with the Apportionment Ratio.

Article 16　Valuation of Unit Petroleum for Cost Recovery and Production Sharing Purposes

(1) Where Australia and Timor – Leste agree that a licensee or contractor has entered into contracts for the sale of Unit Petroleum which are consistent with arm's length transactions as outlined in Annex Ⅲ, then for that part of Unit Petroleum apportioned to the JPDA in accordance with the Apportionment Ratio, the transacted price will be accepted as the Petroleum valuation for cost recovery and production sharing purposes.

(2) Where Australia and Timor – Leste do not agree that a licensee or contractor has entered into contracts for the sale of Unit Petroleum which are consistent with arm's length transactions, then for that part of Unit Petroleum apportioned to the JPDA in accordance with the Apportionment Ratio, Australia and Timor – Leste shall determine the Petroleum valuation for cost recovery and pro-

duction sharing purposes in accordance with internationally accepted arm's length principles having due regard to functions performed, assets used and risks assumed, as outlined in Annex Ⅲ.

Article 17　Use of Unit Property for non – Sunrise operations

(1) Australia and Timor – Leste recognise that, subject to paragraphs (2) and (3) below, the exploitation of Petroleum other than Petroleum from the Unit Reservoirs is a legitimate use of Unit Property.

(2) Either Regulatory Authority shall, on receipt of a request from the Unit Operator for such use of any part of Unit Property, consult with the other Regulatory Authority with regard to that request. After such consultation, and having consulted the Sunrise Joint Venturers, the relevant Regulatory Authority will allow such use of any part of Unit Property provided that such use does not adversely affect the effective exploitation of the Unit Area and the transmission of Unit Petroleum in accordance with this Agreement and the Development Plan.

(3) In the event that the consultations under paragraph (2) above indicate that any supplementary agreement to this Agreement is necessary to give effect to paragraph (2), Australia and Timor – Leste shall negotiate in order to conclude such agreement after having sought the views of the Sunrise Joint Venturers. In order to facilitate such negotiations, Australia and Timor – Leste shall, subject to Article 25, exchange any relevant information.

(4) Notwithstanding paragraphs (1) to (3) above, neither Australia nor Timor – Leste shall permit a use the subject of this Article until relevant tax authorities of Australia and Timor – Leste have reached agreement regarding the taxation of such use.

Article 18　Employment and Training

Australia and Timor – Leste shall take appropriate measures with due regard to occupational health and safety requirements, efficient operations and good oilfield practice to ensure that preference is given in employment and training in the Unit Area to nationals or permanent residents of Australia and Timor – Leste.

Article 19　Safety

(1) Legislation as set out in Annex II as amended from time to time shall

apply for the purposes of safety in the Unit Area.

(2) The Regulatory Authorities shall administer the legislation in the Unit Area.

Article 20　Occupational Health and Safety

(1) Legislation as set out in Annex II as amended from time to time shall apply for the purposes of occupational health and safety in the Unit Area.

(2) The Regulatory Authorities shall administer the legislation in the Unit Area.

Article 21　Environmental Protection

(1) Legislation as set out in Annex II as amended from time to time shall apply for the purposes of protection of the environment in the Unit Area.

(2) The Regulatory Authorities shall administer the legislation in the Unit Area.

Article 22　Customs

(1) Australia and Timor – Leste shall consult at the request of either of them in relation to the entry of particular goods and equipment to structures in the Unit Area aimed at controlling the movement of such persons, equipment and goods. Australia and Timor – Leste may adopt arrangements to facilitate such movement of persons, equipment and goods.

(2) Australia and Timor – Leste may, subject to paragraphs 3, 4, and 5, apply customs law to equipment and goods entering their respective territory from, or leaving that territory for, the Unit Area.

(3) Goods and equipment entering the Unit Area for purposes related to petroleum activities shall not be subject to customs duties.

(4) Goods and equipment leaving or in transit through either Australia or Timor – Leste for the purpose of entering the Unit Area for purposes related to petroleum activities shall not be subject to customs duties.

(5) Goods and equipment leaving the Unit Area for the purpose of being permanently transferred to either Australia or Timor – Leste may be subject to customs duties of that country.

Article 23　Security Arrangements

Australia and Timor – Leste shall make arrangements for responding to security incidents in the Unit Area and for exchanging information on likely threats to security.

Article 24　Measuring Systems

(1) Before production of Petroleum is scheduled to commence under the Development Plan, the Regulatory Authorities shall require the Unit Operator to submit to them for approval proposals for the design, installation and operation of systems for measuring accurately the quantities of gas and liquids comprising, or deemed by subsequent calculation to comprise, Unit Petroleum, which are used in the operation of the field, re – injected, flared, vented, or exported from Unit Property.

(2) The Regulatory Authorities shall facilitate:

(a) access to any equipment for Unit Petroleum measurement; and

(b) the production of information, including design and operational details of all systems, relevant to the measurement of Unit Petroleum; to enable inspectors to satisfy themselves that the fundamental interests of Australia and Timor – Leste in regard to measurement of Unit Petroleum are met.

Article 25　Provision of Information

(1) There shall be a free flow of information between Australia and Timor – Leste concerning the exploration and exploitation of petroleum in the Unit Reservoirs. Confidential information supplied by either Australia or Timor – Leste to the other shall not be further disclosed, without the consent of the supplying Government.

(2) The Regulatory Authorities shall require the Unit Operator to provide them with

(a) monthly reports recording details of the progress of the construction or decommissioning of Unit Property and project expenditure and contractual commitments entered into;

(b) monthly reports of quantities of gas and liquids comprising, or deemed by subsequent calculation to comprise, Unit Petroleum, which are used in the operation of the field, re – injected, flared, vented, or exported from Unit Property, and;

(c) annual reports setting out:

(i) projected annual production profiles for the life of the field (and referring to the basis for those production profiles)

(ii) the most recent geological, geophysical and engineering information relating to the field, including, without limitation, any information that may be relevant to a redetermination of the Apportionment Ratio; and

(iii) estimates of costs relating to the exploitation of the Unit Reservoirs.

Article 26 Settlement of Disputes

(1) Any disputes about the interpretation or application of this Agreement shall be, as far as possible, settled by consultation or negotiation.

(2) Subject to paragraph (3), if a dispute cannot be resolved in the manner specified in paragraph (1) or by any other agreed procedure, the dispute shall be submitted, at the request of either Government, to an Arbitral Tribunal set out in Annex IV.

(3) If a dispute arises concerning a proposal for a redetermined Apportionment Ratio pursuant to Article 8 (1) or concerning the measurement, pursuant to Article 24, of quantities of gas and liquids, an expert shall be appointed by Australia and Timor - Leste to determine the matter in question. The two Governments shall, within 60 days of notification by either of them of such a dispute, try to reach agreement on the appointment of such an expert. If, within this period, no agreement has been reached, the procedures specified in Annex V shall be followed. The expert appointed shall act in accordance with the terms of Annex V. The expert's decision shall be final and binding on both Governments and on the Sunrise Joint Venturers, save in the event of fraud or manifest error.

Article 27 Entry into Force, Amendment and Duration

(1) This Agreement shall enter into force upon the day on which Australia and Timor - Leste have notified each other in writing that their respective requirements for entry into force of this Agreement have been complied with.

(2) This Agreement may be amended or terminated at any time by written agreement between Australia and Timor - Leste.

(3) In the event of permanent delimitation of the seabed, Australia and Ti-

mor – Leste shall reconsider the terms of this Agreement. Any new agreement shall ensure that petroleum activities entered into under the terms of this Agreement shall continue under terms equivalent to those in place under this Agreement.

IN WITNESS WHEREOF the undersigned, being duly authorised thereunto by their respective Governments, have signed this Agreement.

DONE at Dili, on this sixth day of March, two thousand and three in two originals in the English language.

For the Government of Australia   For the Government of the Democratic Republic of Timor – Leste

Alexander Downer   Ana Pessoa

Minister for Foreign Affairs   Minister of State for the Presidency of the Council of Ministers

ANNEX II   Legislation Applicable in the Unit Area as Referred to in Articles 19, 20 and 21

Article 19   Safety

Petroleum (Submerged Lands) (Management of Safety on Offshore Facilities) Regulations

Limitation of Liability for Maritime Claims Act 1989

Navigation Act 1912

Radiocommunications Act 1992

Seafarers Rehabilitation and Compensation Act 1992

Article 20   Health

Petroleum (Submerged Lands) (Occupational Health and Safety) Regulations

Occupational Health and Safety (Maritime Industry) Act 1993

Navigation Act 1912

Seafarers Rehabilitation and Compensation Act 1992

Article 21   Environmental Protection

Petroleum (Submerged Lands) (Management of Environment) Regulations 1999

Protection of the Sea (Civil Liability) Act 1981

Protection of the Sea (Oil Pollution Compensation Fund) Act 1993

Protection of the Sea (Imposition of Contributions to Oil Pollution Compensation Fund – Customs) Act 1993

Protection of the Sea (Imposition of Contributions to Oil Pollution Compensation Fund – Excise) Act 1993

Protection of the Sea (Imposition of Contributions to Oil Pollution Compensation Fund – General) Act 1993

Protection of the Sea (Powers of Intervention) Act 1981

Protection of the Sea (Prevention of Pollution from Ships) Act 1983

Protection of the Sea (Shipping Levy) Act 1981

ANNEX IV Dispute Resolution Procedure

(a) An arbitral tribunal to which a dispute is submitted pursuant to Article 26 (2) shall consist of three persons appointed as follows:

i. Australia and Timor – Leste shall each appoint one arbitrator;

ii. the arbitrators appointed by Australia and Timor – Leste shall, within sixty (60) days of the appointment of the second of them, by agreement, select a third arbitrator who shall be a citizen, or permanent resident of a third country which has diplomatic relations with both Australia and Timor – Leste;

iii. Australia and Timor – Leste shall, within sixty (60) days of the selection of the third arbitrator, approve the selection of that arbitrator who shall act as Chairman of the Tribunal.

(b) Arbitration proceedings shall be instituted upon notice being given through the diplomatic channel by the country instituting such proceedings to the other country. Such notice shall contain a statement setting forth in summary form the grounds of the claim, the nature of the relief sought, and the name of the arbitrator appointed by the country instituting such proceedings. Within sixty (60) days after the giving of such notice the respondent country shall notify the country instituting proceedings of the name of the arbitrator appointed by the respondent country.

(c) If, within the time limits provided for in sub-paragraphs (a) (ii) and (iii) and paragraph (b) of this Annex, the required appointment has not been made or the required approval has not been given, Australia or Timor-Leste may request the President of the International Court of Justice to make the necessary appointment. If the President is a citizen or permanent resident of Australia or Timor-Leste or is otherwise unable to act, the Vice-President shall be invited to make the appointment. If the Vice-President is a citizen or permanent resident of Australia or Timor-Leste or is otherwise unable to act, the Member of the International Court of Justice next in seniority who is not a citizen or permanent resident of Australia or Timor-Leste shall be invited to make the appointment.

(d) In case any arbitrator appointed as provided for in this Annex shall resign or become unable to act, a successor arbitrator shall be appointed in the same manner as prescribed for the appointment of the original arbitrator and the successor shall have all the powers and duties of the original arbitrator.

(e) The Arbitral Tribunal shall convene at such time and place as shall be fixed by the Chairman of the Tribunal. Thereafter, the Arbitral Tribunal shall determine where and when it shall sit.

(f) The Arbitral Tribunal shall decide all questions relating to its competence and shall, subject to any agreement between Australia and Timor-Leste, determine its own procedure.

(g) Before the Arbitral Tribunal makes a decision, it may at any stage of the proceedings propose to Australia and Timor-Leste that the dispute be settled amicably. The Arbitral Tribunal shall reach its award by majority vote taking into account the provisions of this Agreement and relevant international law.

(h) Australia and Timor-Leste shall each bear the costs of its appointed arbitrator and its own costs in preparing and presenting cases. The cost of the Chairman of the Tribunal and the expenses associated with the conduct of the arbitration shall be borne in equal parts by Australia and Timor-Leste.

(i) The Arbitral Tribunal shall afford to Australia and Timor-Leste a fair hearing. It may render an award on the default of either Australia or Timor-Leste. In any case, the Arbitral Tribunal shall render its award within 6 months from the date it is convened by the Chairman of the Tribunal. Any award shall be rendered in writing and shall state its legal basis. A signed counterpart of the award shall be transmitted to Australia and Timor – Leste.

(j) An award shall be final and binding on Australia and Timor – Leste.

ANNEX V Expert Determination Procedure

1. If no agreement is reached on the appointment of an expert within the period specified in Article 26, each Government shall forthwith exchange with the other a list of not more than three independent experts, putting them in order of preference. In each list, the first shall have three points, the second two points and the third one point. The expert having the greatest number of points from the two lists shall be appointed.

2. If two or more of the experts named on the lists exchanged by the Governments share the greatest number of points, the Governments shall, within 30 days of exchange, by agreement or, failing that, by lot, select which of the experts shall be appointed to decide the matter in question.

3. If the expert to be appointed is unable or unwilling to act, or fails, in the opinion of both Governments, to act within a reasonable period of time to decide the matter in question, then the expert with the greatest number of points among the experts remaining shall be the expert to decide the matter in question. If two or more such experts share the greatest number of points, both Governments shall, by unanimous agreement or by lot, select which expert shall be appointed as the expert to decide the matter in question.

4. If a Government fails to respond to any request or notice within the time specified under this Annex, the Government shall be deemed to have waived its rights in respect of the subject of the request or notice but nevertheless shall be bound by the actions of the other Government in selecting an expert and by the decision of the expert.

5. The task of the expert is to reach an independent determination of whatever matters are in question. Where the matter in dispute is in relation to technical

redetermination of the Apportionment Ratio pursuant to Article 8, the expert's decision must be made in accordance with any technical procedures and calculation formula pertaining to redetermination as set out in the relevant Joint Venturers' Agreement.

6. The expert may engage independent contractors to undertake work which is necessary to enable the expert to reach a decision, provided that any contractor nominated by the expert for that purpose is approved by the Governments and gives an undertaking that neither it nor any of its personnel has a conflict of interest which would prevent it from undertaking the work.

7. The fees and costs of the expert shall be paid initially by the Government which first:

(a) initiated the redetermination of the Apportionment Ratio; or

(b) disagreed with the measurement, pursuant to Article 24, of quantities of gas and liquids;

and shall be recoverable from the Unit Operator. The latter shall be required to use best efforts to reimburse the initial payer within 12 months of the payment of those fees and costs.

8. Except as set out in this Agreement, the expert shall establish its own procedures. The expert shall only meet with a Government jointly with the other Government. All communications between the Governments and the expert outside those meetings shall be conducted in writing and a person making any such communication shall at the same time send a copy of it to the other Government.

9. The expert shall use only commercially available software in a redetermination of the Apportionment Ratio. Only data that was available to both Governments as at the date that the redetermination was requested shall be utilised by the expert and all data and analyses relevant to the expert's preliminary and final decisions for the redetermined Apportionment Ratio shall be provided to both Governments with those decisions.

10. Forthwith upon the appointment of the expert, the Unit Operator shall supply the expert with its data and analyses. Within 30 days of that appointment, each Government will make an initial submission and provide a copy to the other

Government. Within 20 days of receiving a copy of that submission, the Government concerned may make a supplementary submission (again providing a copy to the other Government).

11. The expert shall issue a preliminary decision within a period of 90 days, or such other period as the Governments may decide, commencing from the date the expert was appointed. The preliminary decision shall be accompanied by such supporting documentation as is necessary for the Governments to make a reasoned assessment of that decision. Each Government has the right, within 90 days of receipt of the expert's preliminary decision, to seek clarification of that decision and the supporting documentation, to request the expert to review its preliminary decision and to make submissions to the expert for its consideration. If such a request is made, the other Government shall, within a period of 15 days after receipt of a copy of those submissions, have the right to make further submissions. The expert shall issue its final decision on the matter in question no later than 140 days from the date of issue of the preliminary decision. The expert's final decision shall be in writing and the expert shall give detailed reasons for that decision.

12. The Sunrise Joint Venturers shall cooperate fully in supplying information required by the expert and otherwise in facilitating the expert to reach its decision.

13. The Governments shall require the expert and any independent contractor engaged by the expert to give an undertaking to safeguard the confidentiality of any information supplied to the expert.

5.《澳大利亚与东帝汶民主共和国关于帝汶海的特定海上安排的条约》

(2006年1月12日订于悉尼)

董世杰译，邓妮雅校

澳大利亚和政府和东帝汶民主共和国政府（下文称"一方"或"双方"）意识到它们地理邻近、双方的友谊以及经济发展的关系；注意到双方尚未进行海上划界；考虑到1982年12月10日在蒙特哥湾签署的《联合国海洋法公约》，尤其是其第74、83条规定，海岸相向或相邻的国家间划分专属经济区和大陆架，应根据国际法达成一致以求公平解决；进一步考虑到，在未进行划界的情形下，国家间有义务基于谅解和合作的精神，尽一切努力做出实际性的临时安排，不危害或阻碍最后协议的达成；认识到为澳大利亚和东帝汶之间的海床区域的石油活动提供一个长久的基础，符合澳大利亚和东帝汶的利益；强调以一种经济和环境可持续的方式开发和管理帝汶海的生物和非生物资源，以及促进在澳大利亚和东帝汶投资和长期开发的重要性；坚信根据本条约、《帝汶海条约》以及《Sunrise统一开发协定》对资源的长期开发，将会对澳大利亚和东帝汶间持续和强化友好关系提供坚实的基础；致力于维持、发展和强化澳大利亚和东帝汶间的相互尊重、友谊和合作；注意到澳大利亚和东帝汶作为邻国以及基于合作、友谊和善意的精神而分享的利益；坚信本条约将会为强化两国间的关系做出贡献；达成如下协议。

第一条　定义

基于本条约之目的：

1. "AUD"是指澳元；
2. "JPDA"是指根据《帝汶海条约》第三条设立的共同石油开发区；

3. "LIBOR"是指英国银行家协会所确定的对美元一个月期的伦敦银行同业拆息率；

4. "条约期限"是指本条约第十二条所指的条约期限；

5. "石油"是指：

（a）任何自然产生的碳氢化合物，无论是气态、液态还是固态；

（b）任何自然产生的碳氢化合物的混合物，无论是气态、液态还是固态；

（c）任何自然产生的一种或几种碳氢化合物的混合物，无论是气态、液态还是固态，以及与碳氢化合物同时产生的其他物质；

上述（a）、（b）、（c）项中已回到自然储油层中的其他石油。

6. "石油活动"是指从事石油生产的所有活动；

7. "季度"是指以3月、6月、9月、12月为结尾的三个月；

8. "Sunrise IUA"是指2003年3月6日在帝力签署的《澳大利亚政府和东帝汶民主共和国政府关于Sunrise和Troubadour油田统一开发的协定》；

9. "1982年公约"是指1982年12月10日在蒙特哥湾签署的《联合国海洋法公约》；

10. "帝汶海条约"是指2002年5月20日在帝力签署的《东帝汶—澳大利亚帝汶海条约》；

11. "单一化区域"是指Sunrise IUA附件I中所指区域；

12. "上游"是指在Sunrise IUA所规定的"估值点"之前的石油活动和设施；

13. "USD"是指美元；

14. 除非条约中另有规定，本条约中未定义的术语，但是在《帝汶海条约》和Sunrise IUA中有定义的，应该与《帝汶海条约》和Sunrise IUA中的术语具有相同含义。

第二条 不影响条款

1. 本条约的任何内容不得做如下解释：

（a）有损或影响东帝汶或澳大利亚关于海洋划界的法律立场或法律权利；

（b）放弃对帝汶海的部分或全部有关的权利或主张；

（c）承认或肯定另一方对帝汶海的部分或全部海域的权利或主张；

2. 由于本条约或者条约实施的行为或进行的活动，或者生效的法律，不得作为维护、支持、否定或者促进，另一方对帝汶海部分或全部海域有关的海洋边界主张、管辖或者权利的基础。

第三条 《帝汶海条约》的期限

对于《帝汶海条约》第二十二条规定的期限做出如下修改：

在《澳大利亚—东帝汶民主共和国关于帝汶海的特定海上安排的条约》存续期间，《帝汶海条约》有效。澳大利亚和东帝汶协商一致，可以延长本条约的期限。即使《帝汶海条约》失效，根据本条约参与的有限责任公司或实体，可在与本条约同等条件下继续进行石油活动。

第四条 冻结条款

1. 在本条约存续期间，澳大利亚和东帝汶均不得以任何方式，对另一方主张、提出海洋权利，管辖和海上边界的要求。

2. 本条第1款之规定不得妨碍一方在一些区域继续进行的，依据2002年5月19日的国内法，授权在这些区域内的海床和底土进行的与石油或其他资源相关的活动（包括管理和授权已存在的和新的活动）。

3. 尽管本条第2款做出规定，共同石油开发区继续由《帝汶海条约》及相关文件规范。

4. 虽然存在其他对双方均有约束力的双边或多边协定，或者任何一方根据这些协定所做出的宣言，但是任何一方进行司法、仲裁或其他争端解决机制之前，不得针对另一方启动或提出会直接或间接导致与帝汶海的海洋边界或划界有关的程序。

5. 任何法庭、仲裁庭或其他争端解决机制，审理包含双方的争端时，不应该考虑、评论或做出任何会直接或间接导致与帝汶海的海洋边界或划界有关的决定。任何这种评论或判决应当无效，双方不得在任何时候援引。

6. 任何一方不得在任何国际组织提出与帝汶海的海洋边界或划界直接或间接相关的问题。

7. 在本条约存续期间，双方不应承担就永久海洋划界进行谈判的义务。

第五条 单一化区域的收入分配

1. 对直接来自单一化区域内产出的石油的收入，双方在上游石油开采收入的限度内，进行公平分配。

2. 上游石油价值应在公平交易原则的基础上决定。

3. 澳大利亚的收入是指对以下事项征收的税款：

（a）石油资源租赁税，

（b）公司税（包括资本收益税），以及

（c）根据《帝汶海条约》开采的第一批石油和利润油，或后续类似性质的税收。

4. 澳大利亚收入构成应根据以下事项来决定：

（a）有关石油资源租赁税的收入，是每个季度根据以下事项调整后实际获得的收入：

ⅰ．从项目转出的与单一化区域内石油活动相关的支出，不包括转入该项目的与单一化区域内石油活动不相关的支出；

ⅱ．在项目预期的最后 5 年内，包括预估的关闭成本（一旦项目关闭，要与实际关闭成本进行对账）。

（b）有关公司税的收入是每季度的实际收入，应根据在单一化区域内上游进行石油活动相关公司的税务状况进行调整。

（c）上述 b 项所提的调整，以下列事项为基础：

ⅰ．在公司的单一区域内上游作业和其他作业之间，分配直接收入和可直接扣除的非利息性支出；

ⅱ．在公司的单一区域内上游作业和其他作业之间，以与分配直接收入和可直接扣除的非利息性支出的相同比例，分配间接收入和可间接扣除的非利益性支出；

ⅲ．在公司的单一区域内上游作业和其他作业之间，以与最终分配可扣除的非利息性支出的相同比例，分配可扣除的利息性支出。

（d）与第一批石油和利润油相关的收入是每个季度的实际收入。

5. 东帝汶的收入是由对第一批石油和利润油所征税款，以及所有以利润为基础的所得税，依据《帝汶海条约》的年度评估所征的税构成的；或者此后类似性质的税收，但是不包括每月扣缴的增值税或所得税，或者类似的税收以及类似性质的后续税收。

6. 东帝汶的收入组成应当取决于每个季度的实际收入。

7. 一方应在每个季度结束后的第 90 天或者 90 天后澳大利亚和东帝汶

的第一个工作日,将其本季度的收入总量(以本国货币为单位)通知另一方。

8. 澳大利亚的收入以美元计算应当:

(a) 在本条第 7 款的通知做出后的第 20 天或 20 天后悉尼和帝力的第一个交易日予以确定;

(b) 以澳大利亚储备银行,在澳大利亚东部标准时间当天下午 4 点以及前后两天同一时间发布的美元兑澳元的汇率的简单平均值为基础进行确定。

9. 澳大利亚应在在本条第 7 款所提通知做出后的第 30 天或 30 天后的第一个营业日,以美元向东帝汶支付一笔款项,数目为澳大利亚收入部分(以美元为单位)和东帝汶收入部分(以美元为单位)总和的一半,再减去东帝汶的收入部分(以美元为单位)。

10. 若某个季度东帝汶的收入超过澳大利亚,东帝汶不用向澳大利亚支付款项。澳大利亚再向东帝汶支付下一季度款项时,应该考虑东帝汶之前未支付的部分并加以调整。

11. 若澳大利亚和东帝汶对各自税收政策和法律的变化,可能影响到单一化区域石油生产直接获得的收入,应该立即通知对方。如果一方通知另一方,其认为另一方税法的改变对自己的收入有严重影响:

(a) 双方应将其作为紧急问题进行磋商以求解决;

(b) 如果在合理期限内,不能解决本款 a 项的问题,应将问题立即提交第九条中的海洋委员会。

12. 双方同意在条约存续期间,一方支付给另一方有关双方之间海洋区域,石油勘探开发的财政支付的总额,应该根据本条约第七条第 1 款所规定的条约和协定,以及在本条约生效时已经存在的条约和协定有关的文件,予以确定,双方不得请求额外费用。

13. 双方应当建立程序以执行本条 1~10 款的内容。

第六条 评估人员

1. 任何一方可要求任命评估人员,对第五条第 3、第 5 款中的一项或多项税收计算的调整进行审查。

2. 双方应在提出任命评估人员的请求后 30 日内,就任命评估人员寻求达成一致。如果在这一期限内不能达成一致,则应适用附件 I 中所规定的任命程序。

3. 评估人员应根据附件Ⅰ之规定进行活动。

4. 评估人员的结论，双方应当执行，除非双方间另有约定。

5. 如果根据评估员的审查结果，应当对以前的支付进行调整，应按照以下方法计算利息：

$D/360 \times LIBOR \times A$

其中：

A 是指调整的数额；

D 是指第五条第 9 款中的支付日期与支付调整数额日期之间相差的天数；

LIBOR 取决于第五条第 9 款中的支付日期。

第七条 石油资源

1. 在条约存续期间，双方关于石油勘探和开发的权利义务，存在于以下条约中：

（a）本条约；

（b）《帝汶海条约》；

（c）Sunrise IUA；

（d）澳大利亚和东帝汶未来缔结的，任何关于《帝汶海条约》第九条内容的协定。

2. 除非本条约另有规定，本条约的任何内容和依据本条约采取的任何行动，都不得被解释为对《帝汶海条约》和 Sunrise IUA 条款的修正或废除。

第八条 水域管辖权

1. 在条约存续期间：

（a）澳大利亚继续在附件Ⅱ所规定的界线以南海域，对水域行使管辖权，对水域的资源行使主权权利。

（b）东帝汶继续对附件Ⅱ所规定的界线以北海域，对水域行使管辖权，对水域的资源行使主权权利。

（c）东帝汶所行使 b 项的管辖权，不得对共同石油开发区内的石油活动造成不当妨碍。

2. 对于跨越附件Ⅱ界线的同类物种或关联物种，澳大利亚和东帝汶应直接或间接地通过该区域或次区域渔业管理组织，就协调和确保这些物种的养护和开发所需的必要措施达成一致。

3. 东帝汶和澳大利亚应尽一切努力，直接或间接地通过该区域或次区域渔业管理组织，就《海洋法公约》附件Ⅰ中的高度洄游鱼类的有效养护和管理进行合作。

第九条 东帝汶/澳大利亚海洋委员会

1. 建立东帝汶/澳大利亚海洋委员会（简称"委员会"），委员会为双方海洋利益问题进行磋商的重要中心。

2. 委员会由双方各自任命的一名部长组成，或者由双方各自任命的澳大利亚和东帝汶的其他代表组成。

3. 委员会应当：

（a）审查海上边界安排的状态；

（b）就海上安全进行磋商，其中包括石油设备和基础设施的安全；

（c）就海洋环境和保护的相关问题进行磋商；

（d）就自然资源（可再生的和非可再生的）的管理进行磋商，促进可持续的管理战略；以及

（e）就两国同意的其他海上问题进行磋商。

4. 委员会每年至少召开一次会议。

5. 委员会的活动不得损害本条约的内容，以及根据本条约的其他法律实施的行为和活动。

第十条 根据 Sunrise IUA 重新分配单位石油

尽管有 Sunrise IUA 第八条的规定，但是在本条约存续期间，双方同意不再根据第八条之规定重新确定分配比例。

第十一条 争端解决

关于本条约解释或适用的争端，应该通过协商或谈判解决。

第十二条 条约期限

1. 根据本条第 2、3、4 款之规定，本条约有效期为在其生效后 50 年，或者单一化区域开采活动终止后第 5 年，以其中较早的期限为准。

2. 若

（a）在本条约生效后的 6 年内，未能根据 Sunrise IUA 第十二条第 1 款的规定批准单一化区域的开发计划；

（b）或者在本条约生效后的10年间，单一化区域未开始石油生产；

任何一方可以书面的形式通知另一方终止本条约，自通知发出后满3个月，本条约失效。

3. 如根据上述情况条约终止后，在单一化区域又开始石油生产，自开始生产之日起，条约的所有条款恢复效力。

4. 即便条约终止，本条约以下条款仍然有效，双方在条约终止后仍受其约束：

（a）第二条；

（b）第四条第5款第2句；

（c）本条第3款；

（d）本款之规定。

5. 本条约第十二条第1款所规定的条约期限，双方可以通过书面协议延长。

第十三条　生效

条约自澳大利亚和东帝汶民主共和国以书面形式通知对方各自均已满足有关条约生效的要求之日起生效。

下列签署人，经其各自政府正式授权，在本协定上签字，以昭信守。

签订于2006年1月12日，悉尼。

澳大利亚政府	东帝汶民主共和国政府
亚历山大·唐纳阁下	乔斯·拉莫斯-霍塔
外交部长	国务资政兼外交与合作部长

附件 I　评估程序

1. 如果在第六条规定的期限内，无法就评估人员的任命达成一致，任何一方均可请求国际投资争端解决中心的秘书长任命评估人员。

2. 评估人员应该具有处理相关问题的资质。

3. 评估人员的决定应当：

（a）自任命之日起3个月内向双方提交；

（b）以书面形式并附有理由；

（c）对双方保密；

(d) 未经一方书面授权，另一方不得向第三方透露或公开。

4. 评估人员应当确立自己的程序规则，虽然：

(a) 评估人员只能与双方同时会面；

(b) 会谈以外的一方与评估人员的任何通信，应该以书面形式进行，并将副本抄送另一方。

5. 根据本国法律和政策，双方提供有助于评估人员做出评估的所有相关信息。

6. 评估人员的费用和花费由双方公平分摊。

7. 对于双方各自评估程序的花费，由双方各自承担。

8. 双方应要求评估人员和其任命的职员，提供一份书面约定，对评估保密，包括双方向评估人员及参与的职员提供的任何信息。

附件 II 条约第八条所指的界线

为了本条约的目的，有必要确定地球表面的点、线和区域的位置，该位置应该根据世界大地测量基准（WGS84）确立，也就是参考中心在地球中心，主要（赤道）半径为 6378137 米，扁平率为 100/29825.7223563 的球状体。

本条约第八条所指的界线是指以下线：

(p) 起始点为南纬 11°20′02.9″，东经 126°31′58.4″；

(q) 从该点沿着球面向东北延伸至坐标点南纬 11°19′40.9″，东经 126°47′08.4″；

(r) 从该点沿着球面向东北延伸至坐标点南纬 11°17′30.9″，东经 126°57′11.4″；

(s) 从该点沿着球面向东北延伸至坐标点南纬 11°17′24.9″，东经 126°58′17.4″；

(t) 从该点沿着球面向东北延伸至坐标点南纬 11°14′18.9″，东经 127°31′37.4″；

(u) 从该点沿着球面向东北延伸至坐标点南纬 10°55′20.8″，东经 127°47′08.4″；

(v) 从该点沿着球面向东北延伸至坐标点南纬 10°53′36.8″，东经 127°48′49.4″；

（w）从该点沿着球面向东北延伸至坐标点南纬 10°43′37.8″，东经 127°59′20.4″；

（x）从该点沿着球面向东北延伸至坐标点南纬 10°29′11.8″，东经 128°12′28.4″；

（y）从该点沿着球面向东北延伸至坐标点南纬 9°28′00″，东经 127°56′00″；此点为终点。

6. Treaty between Australia and the Democratic Republic of Timor – Leste on Certain Maritime Arrangements in the Timor Sea

(Sydney, 12 January 2006; Entry into force, 23 February 2007)

THE GOVERNMENT OF AUSTRALIA AND THE GOVERNMENT OF THE DEMOCRATIC REPUBLIC OF TIMOR – LESTE (hereinafter each referred to as "Party" or both as "Parties")

CONSCIOUS of their geographic proximity, friendship and developing economic relationship;

NOTING that the Parties have not yet delimited their maritime boundaries;

TAKING INTO ACCOUNT the United Nations Convention on the Law of the Sea done at Montego Bay on 10 December 1982 and, in particular, Articles 74 and 83 which provide that the delimitation of the exclusive economic zone and continental shelf between States with opposite or adjacent coasts shall be effected by agreement on the basis of international law in order to achieve an equitable solution;

FURTHER TAKING INTO ACCOUNT, in the absence of delimitation, the obligation for States to make every effort in a spirit of understanding and cooperation to enter into provisional arrangements of a practical nature which are without prejudice to the final determination;

RECOGNISING the benefits that will flow to both Australia and Timor – Leste by providing a long – term basis for petroleum activities in the area of seabed between Australia and Timor – Leste;

EMPHASISING the importance of developing and managing the living and nonliving resources of the Timor Sea in an economically and environmentally sustainable manner, and the importance of promoting investment and long – term development in Australia and Timor – Leste;

CONVINCED that the long – term development of the resources, in accordance with this Treaty, the Timor Sea Treaty and the Sunrise IUA will provide a firm foundation for continuing and strengthening the friendly relations between Australia and Timor – Leste;

FULLY COMMITTED to maintaining, renewing and further strengthening the mutual respect, friendship and cooperation between Australia and Timor – Leste;

MINDFUL of the interests which Australia and Timor – Leste share as immediate neighbours and in a spirit of cooperation, friendship and goodwill; and

CONVINCED that this Treaty will contribute to the strengthening of relations between the two countries;

AGREE as follows:

Article 1 Definitions

For the purposes of this Treaty:

1. "AUD" means the Australian Dollar;

2. "JPDA" means the Joint Petroleum Development Area established by Article 3 of the Timor Sea Treaty;

3. "LIBOR" means the British Bankers' Association fixing of the one (1) month London Interbank Offer Rate for USD;

4. "period of this Treaty" means the period of the duration of this Treaty referred to in Article 12;

5. "petroleum" means:

(a) any naturally occurring hydrocarbon, whether in a gaseous, liquid or solid state;

(b) any naturally occurring mixture of hydrocarbons, whether in a gaseous, liquid or solid state; or

(c) any naturally occurring mixture of one or more hydrocarbons, whether in a gaseous, liquid or solid state, as well as other substances produced in association with such hydrocarbons;

including any petroleum as defined by sub‑paragraphs (a), (b) or (c) of this paragraph that has been returned to a natural reservoir;

6. "petroleum activities" means all activities undertaken to produce petroleum;

7. "quarter" means the three months ending March, June, September and December;

8. "Sunrise IUA" means the Agreement between the Government of Australia and the Government of the Democratic Republic of Timor‑Leste relating to the Unitisation of the Sunrise and Troubadour Fields, done at Dili on 6 March 2003;

9. "the 1982 Convention" means the United Nations Convention on the Law of the Sea, done at Montego Bay on 10 December 1982;

10. "Timor Sea Treaty" means the Timor Sea Treaty between the Government of East Timor and the Government of Australia, done at Dili on 20 May 2002;

11. "Unit Area" means the area described in Annex I of the Sunrise IUA;

12. "Upstream" means the petroleum activities and facilities prior to the valuation point, as defined in the Sunrise IUA;

13. "USD" means the United States Dollar; and

14. Unless the context otherwise requires, terms which are not defined in this Treaty, but that are defined in the Timor Sea Treaty or the Sunrise IUA, shall have the same meaning in this Treaty as in the Timor Sea Treaty or the Sunrise IUA.

Article 2　Without Prejudice

1. Nothing contained in this Treaty shall be interpreted as:

(a) prejudicing or affecting Timor‑Leste, or Australia's legal position on, or legal rights relating to, the delimitation of their respective maritime boundaries;

(b) a renunciation of any right or claim relating to the whole or any part of the Timor Sea; or

(c) recognition or affirmation of any right or claim of the other Party to the whole or any part of the Timor Sea.

2. No act or activities taking place as a result of, and no law entering into force by virtue of, this Treaty or the operation thereof, may be relied upon as a basis for asserting, supporting, denying or furthering the legal position of either Party with respect to maritime boundary claims, jurisdiction or rights concerning the whole or any part of the Timor Sea.

Article 3　Duration of the Timor Sea Treaty

The text of Article 22 of the Timor Sea Treaty relating to the duration of that Treaty is replaced by the following:

"This Treaty shall be in force for the duration of the Treaty between the Government of Australia and the Government of the Democratic Republic of Timor – Leste on Certain Maritime Arrangements in the Timor Sea. This Treaty may be renewed by agreement between Australia and East Timor. Petroleum activities of limited liability corporations or other limited liability entities entered into under the terms of the Treaty shall continue even if the Treaty is no longer in force under conditions equivalent to those in place under the Treaty"。

Article 4　Moratorium

1. Neither Australia nor Timor – Leste shall assert, pursue or further by any means in relation to the other Party its claims to sovereign rights and jurisdiction and maritime boundaries for the period of this Treaty.

2. Paragraph 1 of this Article does not prevent a Party from continuing activities (including the regulation and authorisation of existing and new activities) in areas in which its domestic legislation on 19 May 2002 authorised the granting of permission for conducting activities in relation to petroleum or other resources of the seabed and subsoil.

3. Notwithstanding paragraph 2 of this Article, the JPDA will continue to be governed by the terms of the Timor Sea Treaty and associated instruments.

4. Notwithstanding any other bilateral or multilateral agreement binding on the Parties, or any declaration made by either Party pursuant to any such agreement, neither Party shall commence or pursue any proceedings against the other Party before any court, tribunal or other dispute settlement mechanism that would

raise or result in, either directly or indirectly, issues or findings of relevance to maritime boundaries or delimitation in the Timor Sea.

5. Any court, tribunal or other dispute settlement body hearing proceedings involving the Parties shall not consider, make comment on, nor make findings that would raise or result in, either directly or indirectly, issues or findings of relevance to maritime boundaries or delimitation in the Timor Sea. Any such comment or finding shall be of no effect, and shall not be relied upon, or cited, by the Parties at any time.

6. Neither Party shall raise or pursue in any international organisation matters that are, directly or indirectly, relevant to maritime boundaries or delimitation in the Timor Sea.

7. The Parties shall not be under an obligation to negotiate permanent maritime boundaries for the period of this Treaty.

Article 5　Division of Revenues from the Unit Area

1. The Parties shall share equally revenue derived directly from the production of that petroleum lying within the Unit Area in so far as the revenue relates to the upstream exploitation of that petroleum.

2. The value of petroleum upstream shall be determined on the basis of arm's length principles.

3. The Australian revenue component means taxation revenue collected from:

(a) the petroleum resource rent tax;

(b) company tax (including capital gains tax); and

(c) first tranche petroleum and profit petroleum pursuant to the Timor Sea Treaty; or subsequent taxes of a similar nature.

4. The Australian revenue component shall be determined as follows:

(a) Revenue relating to the petroleum resource rent tax is the actual revenue collected each quarter adjusted:

(i) to include expenditures related to the petroleum activities undertaken within the Unit Area transferred out of this project and to exclude expenditures not related to the petroleum activities undertaken within the Unit Area transferred into this project; and (ii) in the anticipated last 5 years of the project's life, to include estimated closing down costs (subject to reconciliation against actual closing down costs once the project has closed down).

(b) Revenue relating to company tax is the actual revenue collected each quarter adjusted to determine the company tax position of the entity's upstream operations relating to the petroleum activities undertaken within the Unit Area.

(c) The adjustment referred to in sub-paragraph (b) of this paragraph is based on:

(i) allocating direct revenues and direct deductible non-interest expenses between the upstream operations in the Unit Area and other operations of the entity;

(ii) allocating indirect revenues and indirect deductible non-interest expenses between the upstream operations in the Unit Area and the other operations of the entity in the same proportions as direct revenues and direct deductible expenses respectively; and (iii) allocating deductible interest expenses between the upstream operations in the Unit Area and the other operations of the entity in the same proportion as the final allocation of deductible non-interest expenses.

(d) Revenue relating to first tranche petroleum and profit petroleum is the actual revenue collected each quarter.

5. The Timor-Leste revenue component means taxation revenue collected from first tranche petroleum, profit petroleum and all profit-based income taxes calculated and levied by annual assessment pursuant to the Timor Sea Treaty, or subsequent taxes of a similar nature, but excludes Value Added Tax or income tax withheld monthly or similar taxes, or subsequent taxes of a similar nature.

6. The Timor-Leste revenue component shall be determined based on actual revenue collected each quarter.

7. Each Party shall notify the other Party of the revenue amount (in domestic currency terms) relating to the quarter on the first working day in both Australia and Timor-Leste on or after 90 days following the end of that quarter.

8. Australia's revenue amount in USD terms shall be:

(a) determined on the first business day in both Sydney and Dili on or after 20 days following the notification referred to in paragraph 7 of this Article; and

(b) based on the simple average of the USD/AUD exchange rate published by the Reserve Bank of Australia at 4.00 pm (Australian Eastern Standard Time) on that day, the two preceding days, and the two subsequent days.

9. Australia shall make a payment in USD to Timor – Leste equivalent to half the aggregate of the Australian revenue component (in USD terms) and the Timor – Leste revenue component, less the Timor – Leste revenue component (in USD terms), on the first business day in both Sydney and Dili on or after 30 days following notification referred to in paragraph 7 of this Article.

10. In the event that Timor – Leste, s revenue component exceeds Australia's revenue component in USD terms in a particular quarter, Timor – Leste shall not make a payment to Australia, and subsequent quarterly payments by Australia to Timor – Leste shall be adjusted to take account of the earlier payment not made by Timor – Leste.

11. Australia and Timor – Leste shall inform each other expeditiously of changes in their respective taxation policies and laws that may impact on the revenue derived directly from the production of petroleum in the Unit Area. Where one Party notifies the other that it considers that a change in the taxation laws of the other Party is likely to have a serious impact on the revenue to be received by the first Party:

(a) the Parties shall, as a matter of urgency, consult with a view to resolving the matter; and

(b) where the Parties are unable to resolve the matter pursuant to sub – paragraph (a) of this paragraph within a reasonable period, the matter shall be referred immediately to the Maritime Commission established in Article 9.

12. The Parties agree that during the period of this Treaty, the totality of financial payments from one Party to another concerning or relating to the exploration and exploitation of maritime areas between Australia and Timor – Leste are defined by the treaties and agreements referred to in paragraph 1 of Article 7 and such agreed associated documentation relating to those treaties and agreements that exists at the time of the entry into force of this Treaty, and neither Party shall seek additional payments.

13. The Parties shall establish procedures for the implementation of paragraphs 1 to 10 of this Article.

Article 6 Assessor

1. Either Party may request the appointment of an assessor to review adjustments used to calculate any one or more of the revenues referred to in paragraphs 3 and 5 of Article 5.

2. The Parties shall, within 30 days of a request being made to appoint an assessor, seek to reach agreement on the appointment of such an assessor. If, within this period, no agreement has been reached, the procedures for appointment specified in Annex I shall be followed.

3. The assessor shall act in accordance with the terms of Annex I.

4. The assessor's conclusions shall be implemented by the Parties unless the Parties agree otherwise.

5. Where adjustments are made to previous payments as the result of a review by an assessor, interest will be added, calculated as follows:

$$D/360 \times LIBOR \times A$$

where:

A is the amount of the adjustment;

D is the difference in the number of days between the payment date referred to in paragraph 9 of Article 5 and the payment of A; and

LIBOR is determined on the payment date referred to in paragraph 9 of Article 5.

Article 7 Petroleum resources

1. The applicable obligations and rights as between Australia and Timor-Leste governing the exploration and exploitation of petroleum resources during the period of this Treaty are those contained in:

(a) this Treaty;

(b) the Timor Sea Treaty;

(c) the Sunrise IUA; and

(d) any future agreement between Australia and Timor-Leste as referred to in Article 9 of the Timor Sea Treaty.

2. Except as otherwise provided for in this Treaty, nothing contained in this Treaty, and no actions taken pursuant to it, shall be interpreted as amending or revoking any terms of the Timor Sea Treaty or the Sunrise IUA.

Article 8　Water column jurisdiction

1. For the period of this Treaty:

(a) Australia will continue to exercise jurisdiction in relation to the water column, and sovereign rights over the resources of the water column, south of the line described in Annex II;

(b) Timor – Leste will continue to exercise jurisdiction in relation to the water column, and sovereign rights over the resources of the water column, north of the line described in Annex II; and

(c) the jurisdiction referred to in sub – paragraph (b) of this paragraph shall be exercised in a manner that does not unduly inhibit petroleum activities within the JPDA.

2. Where the same stock or stocks of associated species straddle the line described in Annex II, Timor – Leste and Australia shall seek, either directly or through appropriate subregional or regional fisheries management organisations, to agree upon the measures necessary to co – ordinate and ensure the conservation and development of such stocks.

3. Timor – Leste and Australia shall make every effort to pursue cooperation in relation to highly migratory fish stocks, as defined in Annex 1 to the 1982 Convention, either directly or through appropriate subregional or regional fisheries management organisations, to ensure effective conservation and management of such stocks.

Article 9　Timor – Leste/Australia Maritime Commission

1. There is hereby established a Timor – Leste/Australia Maritime Commission ("Commission"), which shall constitute a focal point for bilateral consultations with regard to maritime matters of interest to the Parties.

2. The Commission shall comprise one Minister each appointed by the Parties, or such other representative of the Governments of Australia and Timor – Leste as appointed respectively by the Parties.

3. The Commission shall:

(a) review the status of maritime boundary arrangements;

(b) consult on maritime security, including the security of petroleum facilities and infrastructures;

(c) consult on issues relating to the marine environment and its protection;

(d) consult on the management of natural resources (renewable and non-renewable), and promote sustainable management strategies; and

(e) consult on other maritime matters as appropriate as agreed by the Parties.

4. The Commission shall meet at least annually.

5. The proceedings in the Commission shall be without prejudice to the contents of this Treaty, and of any legislation, acts and activities thereunder.

Article 10　Re-apportionment of unit petroleum under the Sunrise IUA

Notwithstanding Article 8 of the Sunrise IUA, the Parties agree that there shall be no re-determination of the apportionment ratio referred to in that article during the period of this Treaty.

Article 11　Dispute Settlement

Any disputes about the interpretation or application of this Treaty shall be settled by consultation or negotiation.

Article 12　Period of this Treaty

1. Subject to paragraphs 2, 3 and 4 of this Article, this Treaty shall remain in force until the date 50 years after its entry into force, or until the date five years after the exploitation of the Unit Area ceases, whichever occurs earlier.

2. If:

(a) a development plan for the Unit Area has not been approved in accordance with paragraph 1 of Article 12 of the Sunrise IUA within six years after the date of entry into force of this Treaty; or

(b) production of petroleum from the Unit Area has not commenced within ten years after the date of entry into force of this Treaty;

either Party may notify the other Party in writing that it wishes to terminate this Treaty, in which case the Treaty shall cease to be in force three calendar months after such notice is given.

3. Should petroleum production take place in the Unit Area subsequent to the termination of this Treaty pursuant to paragraph 2 of this Article, all the terms of this Treaty shall come back into force and operate from the date of commencement of production.

4. The following provisions of this Treaty shall survive termination of this Treaty, and the Parties shall continue to be bound by them after termination:

(a) Article 2;

(b) the second sentence of paragraph 5 of Article 4;

(c) paragraph 3 of this Article; and

(d) this paragraph.

5. The period of this Treaty referred to in paragraph 1 of this Article may be extended by agreement in writing between the Parties.

Article 13 Entry into Force

This Treaty shall enter into force on the day on which the Government of Australia and the Government of the Democratic Republic of Timor – Leste have notified each other, in writing, that their respective requirements for the entry into force of this Treaty have been complied with.

IN WITNESS WHEREOF the undersigned, being duly authorised thereto by their respective Governments, have signed this Treaty.

DONE at Sydney, on this twelfth day of January, Two thousand and six.

Hon. Alexander Downer	José Ramos – Horta
Minister for Foreign Affairs	Senior Minister and Minister for Foreign Affairs and Cooperation

Annex I Assessment Procedure

1. If no agreement is reached on the appointment of an assessor within the period specified in Article 6, either Party may request the Secretary – General of the International Centre for the Settlement of Investment Disputes to appoint the assessor.

2. The assessor shall have qualifications relevant to the matter to be assessed.

3. The assessor's conclusions shall:

(a) be provided to the Parties within a period of three months from the date of appointment;

(b) be in writing and accompanied by reasons;

(c) be confidential to the Parties; and

(d) not be disclosed by a Party to any third party or publicly without the written authorisation of the other Party.

4. The assessor shall establish his or her procedures, although:

(a) the assessor shall only meet with a Party jointly with the other Party; and

(b) all communications between a Party and the assessor outside meetings shall be conducted in writing and shall be copied to the other Party.

5. Subject to national laws and policies, the Parties shall provide all relevant information to enable the assessor to carry out his or her assessment.

6. The fees and costs of the assessor shall be shared equally between the Parties.

7. Each Party shall bear its own costs of the assessment procedure.

8. The Parties shall require the assessor and any staff engaged by the assessor to provide a formal undertaking to safeguard the confidentiality of the assessment, including any information supplied to the assessor or any staff engaged by the assessor.

Annex II Line Referred to in Article 8

Where for the purposes of this Treaty it is necessary to determine the position on the surface of the Earth of a point, line or area, that position shall be determined by reference to the World Geodetic System 84 (WGS 84), a spheroid which has its centre at the centre of the Earth and a major (equatorial) radius of 6378137 metres and a flattening of 100/29825.7223563.

The line referred to in Article 8 of this Treaty is a line:

(a) commencing at the point of Latitude 11°20′02.9″South, Longitude 126°31′58.4″East;

(b) running thence north – easterly along the geodesic to the point of Latitude 11°19′40.9″South, Longitude 126°47′08.4″East;

(c) thence north – easterly along the geodesic to the point of Latitude 11°17′30.9″South, Longitude 126°57′11.4″East;

(d) thence north – easterly along the geodesic to the point of Latitude 11°17′24.9″South, Longitude 126°58′17.4″East;

(e) thence north – easterly along the geodesic to the point of Latitude 11°14′18.9″South, Longitude 127°31′37.4″East;

(f) thence north – easterly along the geodesic to the point of Latitude 10°55′20.8″South, Longitude 127°47′08.4″East;

(g) thence north – easterly along the geodesic to the point of Latitude 10°53′36.8″South, Longitude 127°48′49.4″East;

(h) thence north – easterly along the geodesic to the point of Latitude 10°43′37.8″South, Longitude 127°59′20.4″East;

(i) thence north – easterly along the geodesic to the point of Latitude 10°29′11.8″South, Longitude 128°12′28.4″East, where it terminates.

（十五）2003年圭亚那共和国和巴巴多斯国共同开发案

1.《圭亚那共和国—巴巴多斯关于在其他国家专属经济区外部界线以外两国专属经济区外部界线以内的双边重叠区中的专属经济区行使管辖权的专属经济区合作条约》

（2003年12月2日订于伦敦）

董世杰译，邓妮雅校

圭亚那共和国和巴巴多斯国（下文简称"缔约双方"）重申了两国间的友好关系；鉴于两国长期睦邻合作的精神；强调《联合国海洋法公约》（下文简称"公约"）普遍性和统一适用性的特点，以及对于维持和加强国际和平与安全以及海洋可持续发展的重要性；承认海岸相向或相邻国家的专属经济区划界，应在国际法的基础上，通过《国际法院规约》第38条中所指的条约的方式，寻求公平解决；承认公约第74条第3款的相关性和重要性，该条规定国家间在划界前，应基于谅解和合作的精神，在过渡期内尽一切努力做出实际性的临时安排，并不损害或妨碍最终协定的达成；认识到这种临时性安排不得损害最终划界；双方确信应根据广泛接受的国际法原则和公约行事；注意到其他国家的合法利益，并且有必要根据广泛接受的国际法原则和公约尊重其他国家的权利和义务；承认在其他国家专属经济区外部界线以外,在两国专属经济区外部界线以内,存在双边重叠区域;希望为了在两国专属经济区的双边重叠区域内,有序并合作地行使管辖权,同时考虑到其他国家的合法利益,建立一个明确和公平的制度;意识到有必要就该区域环境责任管理,以及生物资源和非生物资源的可持续开发达成一致;根据加勒比共同体和美洲国家组织团结友谊的精神行事;达成如下协议。

第一条 合作区

1. 依据广泛接受的国际法原则和公约,为了在其他国家专属经济区外部界线外,两国专属经济区内的重叠区域内,对生物和非生物资源行使共同管辖、控制、管理、勘探和开发,以及公约规定的其他权利和义务,本条约建立并管理一个合作区(下文称"合作区")。

2. 本条约以及其所建立的合作区,不影响双方根据广泛接受的国际法原则和公约,对双方各自海域进行最终划界。

3. 双方同意本条约的任何内容以及任何一方根据本条约内容所实施的行为,不得视为任何一方减损或放弃合作区或各自全部专属经济区内的权利。

第二条 合作区的地理范围

1. 双方同意合作区是一块位于双方专属经济区内的重叠区域。该区域位于从测量双方领海宽度的基线起算至200海里界线内,并位于从测量其他国家领海宽度的基线起算200海里界线以外。基于本条约之目的,"专属经济区"及其法律制度,应依据公约第五部分之规定。

2. 合作区的准确地理范围在本条约附件Ⅰ中做出规定。

3. 双方计划将来就它们之间的国际海洋划界达成一致。

第三条 在合作区内行使民事和行政管辖权

1. 双方应共同行使合作区内以及与合作区相关的民事、行政管辖权。双方在行使管辖权时,应依据广泛接受的国际法原则和公约行事。

2. 双方在任何特定情形下行使共同管辖权,应当以书面一致为证,其中包括外交换文的方式。

3. 进一步而言,即在任何特定情形下,如果双方未就行使共同管辖权达成书面一致,任何一方均都不得行使管辖权。

第四条 合作区内其他国家的权利和义务

1. 依据广泛接受的国际法原则和公约,尤其是公约第58条之规定,双方应适当顾及其他国家在合作区内的权利和义务。

第五条　对生物资源的管辖权

1. 双方应就合作区内的生物资源行使共同管辖权。在行使管辖权时，双方在任何时候都应依据广泛接受的国际法原则和公约，其中包括《执行 1982 年 12 月 10 日〈联合国海洋法公约〉有关养护和管理跨界鱼类种群和高度洄游鱼类种群的规定的协定》行事。

2. 为了实施环境责任管理和确保合作区内的可持续开发，在任何特殊的情形下，双方行使对生物资源的共同管辖权，应受《共同渔业许可协定》的规范，并以书面同意为证，其中包括第三条所规定的外交换文的方式。

3. 在本条约生效后的 3 个月内，双方应就合作区内的《共同渔业许可协定》进行善意的谈判。

4. 任何一方有权通过对任何人适用其相关的国内法，以执行《共同渔业学科协定》的内容。每一方如此行事时，应以书面形式通知另一方。

5. 进一步而言，在任何情形下，在双方未能就合作区内生物资源共同管辖权的行使达成书面一致时，双方均不得行使管辖权。

6. 依据双方参与的任何相关协定中的义务，双方应采取措施协调双方在合作区内生物资源的管理。

第六条　对非生物资源的管辖权

1. 双方应就合作区内的非生物资源行使共同管辖权。在行使管辖权时，双方在任何时候都应遵守广泛接受的国际法原则和公约。

2. 在任何情形下，双方对非生物资源共同管辖权的行使，应由一个非生物资源共同委员会管理，并以书面同意为证，其中包括第三条所规定的外交换文的方式。

3. 非生物资源共同委员会应依据双方协商的时间建立。

4. 进一步而言，在任何情形下，在双方未能就对合作区内非生物资源行使共同管辖权达成书面一致时，任何一方均不得行使管辖权。

5. 完全位于合作区内的非生物资源单一地质结构或矿藏，应在双方间进行公平分配。

6. 基于第六条之目的，任何全部或部分跨越合作区外部界线的非生物资源单一地质结构或矿藏，应被视为跨越了合作区。

7. 任何从一方专属经济区跨越至合作区的外部界线的，非生物资源单一地质结构或矿藏，应根据非生物资源共同委员会所作的统一安排进行分配。

8. 对于完全位于合作区内的非生物资源进行科学研究、勘探和开发，只有在第三条所规定的双方同意后方能进行。如果未能达成一致，不得进行科学研究、勘探和开发。

9. 任何一方在测量结束后，应立即将任何科学研究或者勘探结果提供给另一方。

第七条　对安全事项的管辖权

1. 诚信行事的双方应建立活动进行的程序，以维护合作区的治安。

2. 在本条约生效之日起3个月内，双方应就与合作区内活动相关的安全协定，善意开始谈判，协定可以包括以下内容：

（a）自然资源规定的执行；

（b）恐怖主义；

（c）防止非法贩卖麻醉物品；

（d）贩卖枪支、弹药、爆炸物和其他相关物品；

（e）走私；

（f）海盗；

（g）贩卖人口；以及

（h）海上治安和搜索营救。

3. 在第七条第2款所规定的安全协定生效之前，除非本条约另有规定，每一方应采取与合作区外的专属经济区内相同的方式，对合作区内以及与合作区相关的事项，单方面进行保护和行使刑事管辖权。

第八条　合作区海洋环境的保护

1. 双方依据它们的国际义务，努力协调双方的活动，以采取必要的措施保存和保护合作区的海洋环境。

2. 双方应尽早将合作区内，对海洋环境的实际或潜在威胁的相关信息，相互通知对方。

第九条　协商和沟通

1. 任何一方可就本条约或者合作区的任何问题，要求与另一方进行协商。

2. 双方应指派各自的外交部部长负责本条约所要求的所有沟通事宜，其中包括第 3、5、6、9、10 条所作之规定。任何一方经书面通知另一方，可更改指派。

第十条　争端解决

1. 任何因本条约解释或适用引起的争端，应当通过双方直接的外交谈判加以解决。

2. 如果在合理期限内双方无法达成一致，任何一方可以诉诸公约中规定的争端解决条款。

3. 依据第十条第 2 款之规定，任何法庭或仲裁庭所做出的判决或临时命令，对双方都是终局的且有约束力的。双方应善意地执行这些判决和命令。

第十一条　登记

本条约一旦生效，应当根据《联合国宪章》第 102 条之规定，在联合国秘书长和加勒比共同体秘书长处进行登记。

第十二条　生效和期限

1. 自双方以书面形式通知对方已完成本条约生效的相关要求之日起，30 天届满之日生效。

2. 双方缔结海上划界协定之日前，本条约一直有效。

3. 经任何一方请求，应对条约进行审查。

4. 对条约的任何修订，双方应通过外交换文方式达成一致。

2003 年 12 月 2 日签订于伦敦，一式两份。

圭亚那共和国代表　　　巴拉特·贾格迪奥总统阁下
巴巴多斯国代表　　　　欧文·亚瑟总理阁下

2. Exclusive Economic Zone Cooperation Treaty between the Republic of Guyana and the State of Barbados Concerning the Exercise of Jurisdiction in Their Exclusive Economic Zones in the Area of Bilateral Overlap Within Each of Their Outer Limits and Beyond the Outer Limits of the Exclusive Economic Zones of Outer States

THE REPUBLIC OF GUYANA AND THE STATE OF BARBADOS (hereinafter referred to as the Parties);

REAFFIRMING the friendly relations between them;

MINDFUL of their long – standing spirit of bilateral co – operation and good – neighbourliness;

EMPHASISING the universal and unified character of the United Nations Convention on the Law of the Sea (hereinafter referred to as the Convention) and its fundamental importance for the maintenance and strengthening of international peace and security, as well as for the sustainable development of the oceans and seas;

RECOGNISING that the delimitation of the exclusive economic zone between States with opposite or adjacent coasts shall be effected by agreement on the basis of international law, as referred to in Article 38 of the Statute of the International Court of Justice, in order to achieve an equitable solution;

RECOGNISING the relevance and applicability of paragraph 3 of Article 74 of the Convention, which establishes that, pending such delimitation, States, in a spirit of understanding and co – operation, shall make every effort to enter into provisional arrangements of a practical nature and, during this transitional period, not to jeopardize or hamper the reaching of the final agreement;

RECOGNISING that such provisional arrangements shall be without prejudice to the final delimitation;

CONFIRMING their intention to act in accordance with generally accepted principles of international law and the Convention;

MINDFUL of the legitimate interests of other States and the need to respect the rights and duties of other States in conformity with generally accepted principles of international law and the Convention;

ACKNOWLEDGING the existence of an area of bilateral overlap within the outer limits of their exclusive economic zones and beyond the outer limits of the exclusive economic zones of other States;

DESIROUS of establishing a precise and equitable regime for the orderly and co – operative exercise of jurisdiction in the area of bilateral overlap of their exclusive economic zones, whilst taking into account the legitimate interests of other States;

CONSCIOUS of the need to agree upon the environmentally responsible management and the sustainable development of living and non – living natural resources in this area; and

ACTING in accordance with the spirit of friendship and solidarity in the Caribbean Community and the Organization of American States;

HAYE AGREED as follows:

Article 1 Co – operation Zone

1. This Treaty establishes and regulates, in accordance with generally accepted principles of international law and the Convention, a co – operation zone (hereinafter referred to as the Co – operation Zone) for the exercise of joint jurisdiction, control, management, development, and exploration and exploitation of living and non – living natural resources, as well as all other rights and duties es-

tablished in the Convention, within the area over which a bilateral overlap occurs between their exclusive economic zones and beyond the outer limits of the exclusive economic zones of other States.

2. This Treaty and the Co – operation Zone established thereunder are without prejudice to the eventual delimitation of the Parties' respective maritime zones in accordance with generally accepted principles of international law and the Convention.

3. The Parties agree that nothing contained in the Treaty nor any act done by either Party under the provisions of the Treaty will represent a derogation from or diminution or renunciation of the rights of either Party within the Co – operation Zone or throughout the full breadth of their respective exclusive economic zones.

Article 2   The Geographical Extent of the Co – operation Zone

1. The Parties agree that the Co – operation Zone is the area of bilateral overlap between the exclusive economic zones encompassed within each of their outer limits measured to a distance of 200 nautical miles from the baselines from which the breadth of the territorial sea is measured, and beyond the outer limits of the exclusive economic zones of other States at a distance of 200 nautical miles measured from the baselines from which their territorial sea is measured. For the purposes of this Treaty, the term "exclusive economic zone" and its legal regime shall have the meaning ascribed to them in Part V of the Convention.

2. The precise geographical extent of the Co – operation Zone is defined in Annex 1 to this Treaty.

3. The Parties contemplate that they may, by agreement at a later date, delimit an international maritime boundary between them.

Article 3   Exercise of Civil and Administrative Jurisdiction in the Co – operation Zone

1. The Parties shall exercise joint civil and administrative jurisdiction within and in relation to the Co – operation Zone. In exercising their jurisdiction the Parties shall act at all times in accordance with generally accepted principles of international law and the Convention.

2. The exercise of joint jurisdiction by the Parties in any particular instance

shall be evidenced by their agreement in writing, including by way of an exchange of diplomatic notes.

3. For further clarity, the failure of the Parties to reach agreement in writing in relation to the exercise of their joint jurisdiction in the Co – operation Zone in any particular instance means that neither Party can exercise its jurisdiction in that instance.

Article 4   Rights and Duties of Other States in the Co – operation Zone

1. The Parties shall have due regard to the rights and duties of other States in the Co – operation Zone in accordance with generally accepted principles of international law and the Convention, and in particular the provisions of Article 58 of the Convention.

Article 5   Jurisdiction over Living Natural Resources

1. The Parties shall exercise joint jurisdiction over living natural resources within the Co – operation Zone. In exercising their joint jurisdiction, the Parties shall act at all times in accordance with generally accepted principles of international law and the Convention, including the Agreement for the implementation of the provisions of the Convention relating to the conservation and management of straddling fish stocks and highly migratory fish stocks.

2. In order to exercise environmentally responsible management and to ensure sustainable development in the Co – operation Zone, the exercise of joint jurisdiction over living resources by the Parties in any particular instance shall be governed by a Joint Fisheries Licensing Agreement and evidenced by their agreement in writing, including by way of an exchange of diplomatic notes as provided in Article 3.

3. Within three months of the date on which this Treaty enters into force, the Parties shall in good faith commence the negotiation of a Joint Fisheries Licensing Agreement within the Co – operation Zone.

4. Either Party shall be entitled to enforce the provisions of the Joint Fisheries Licensing Agreement against any persons through the application of its relevant national law. Each Party undertakes to inform the other in writing of such enforcement.

5. For further clarity, the failure of the Parties to reach agreement in writing in relation to the exercise of their joint jurisdiction over living resources in the Co-operation Zone in any particular instance means that neither Party can exercise its jurisdiction in that instance.

6. The Parties shall take steps to co-ordinate between them the management of the living natural resources within the Co-operation Zone subject to their obligations under any relevant agreement to which they are both parties.

Article 6 Jurisdiction over Non-Living Natural Resources

1. The Parties shall exercise joint jurisdiction over non-living natural resources within the Co-operation Zone. In exercising their joint jurisdiction, the Parties shall act at all times in accordance with generally accepted principles of international law and the Convention.

2. The exercise of joint jurisdiction over non-living resources by the Parties in any particular instance shall be managed by a Joint Non-Living Resources Commission and evidenced by their agreement in writing, including by way of an exchange of diplomatic notes as provided in Article 3.

3. The Joint Non-Living Resources Commission shall be established at such time as agreed by the Parties.

4. For further clarity, the failure of the Parties to reach agreement in writing in relation to the exercise of their joint jurisdiction over non-living resources in the Co-operation Zone in any particular instance means that neither Party can exercise its jurisdiction in that instance.

5. Any single geological structure or field of non-living natural resources that lies wholly within the Co-operation Zone shall be shared equally between the Parties.

6. For the purpose of this Article 6, any single geological structure or field of non-living natural resources that lies in whole or in part across the outer limit of the Co-operation Zone shall be considered to straddle the Co-operation Zone.

7. Any single geological structure or field of non-living natural resources that straddles the outer limit of the Co-operation Zone from the exclusive eco-

nomic zone of either Party shall be apportioned between them based on unitisation arrangements, as specifically provided by the Joint Non – Living Resources Commission.

8. Marine scientific research, exploration and exploitation or development of non – living natural resources that lie wholly within the Co – operation Zone shall only take place with the agreement of both Parties as provided in Article 3. If no such agreement is reached, no scientific research, exploration, exploitation or development can take place.

9. Each Party shall provide the other with the results of any scientific research or exploration as soon as possible after the conclusion of any survey.

Article 7　Jurisdiction over Security Matters

1. The Parties acting in good faith shall establish the procedures for the conduct of activities to police the Co – operation Zone.

2. Within three months of the date on which this Treaty enters into force, the Parties shall in good faith commence the negotiation of a security agreement in relation to activities to be undertaken within the Co – operation Zone, which may address among others:

a. Enforcement of regulations over natural resources;

b. Terrorism;

c. Prevention of illicit narcotics trafficking;

d. Trafficking in firearms, ammunition, explosives and other related materials;

e. Smuggling;

f. Piracy;

g. Trafficking in persons; and

h. Maritime policing and search and rescue.

3. Until a security agreement as contemplated in Article 7 (2) is in force, and unless otherwise provided for in this Treaty, each Party shall unilaterally exercise defence and criminal jurisdiction within and in relation to the Co – operation Zone to the same extent that it may do so within and in relation to that part of its exclusive economic zone that lies outside the Co – operation Zone.

Article 8   Protection of the Marine Environment of the Co-operation Zone

1. The Parties shall, consistent with their international obligations, endeavour to co-ordinate their activities so as to adopt all measures necessary for the preservation and protection of the marine environment in the Co-operation Zone.

2. The Parties shall provide each other as soon as possible with information about actual or potential threats to the marine environment in the Co-operation Zone.

Article 9   Consultation and Communications

1. Either Party may request consultations with the other Party in relation to any matter arising out of this Treaty or otherwise concerning the Co-operation Zone.

2. The Parties shall designate their respective Ministers of Foreign Affairs to be responsible for all communications required under this Treaty, including under this Article 9, and Articles 3, 5, 6 and 10. Either Party can change its designation upon written notice to the other Party.

Article 10   Dispute Resolution

1. Any dispute concerning the interpretation or application of the provisions of this Treaty shall be resolved by direct diplomatic negotiations between the two Parties.

2. If no agreement can be reached within a reasonable period of time, either Party may have recourse to the dispute resolution provisions contemplated under the Convention.

3. Any decision or interim order of any court or tribunal constituted pursuant to Article 10 (2) shall be final and binding on the Parties. The Parties shall carry out in good faith all such orders and decisions.

Article 11   Registration

Upon entry into force, this Treaty shall be registered with the Secretary-General of the United Nations in accordance with article 102 of the Charter of the United Nations and the Secretary-General of the Caribbean Community.

Article 12   Entry into Force and Duration

1. This Treaty shall enter into force 30 days after the date on which the Parties have notified each other in writing that their respective requirements for the

entry into force of this Treaty have been met.

2. This Treaty shall remain in force until an international maritime boundary delimitation agreement is concluded between the Parties.

3. This Treaty shall be subject to review at the request of either Party.

4. Any amendment to this Treaty shall be by mutual agreement through the exchange of diplomatic notes.

DONE at London on 2nd December, 2003, in two duplicate copies.

For the Republic of Guyana His Excellency Bharrat Jagdeo President

For the State of Barbados The Rt. Honourable Owen S. Arthur Prime Minister

（十六）2012 年美国和墨西哥共同开发案

1.《美利坚合众国政府与墨西哥合众国政府关于墨西哥西部海湾 200 海里以外大陆架划界条约》

（2000 年 6 月 9 日订于华盛顿）

宗吕谦译，邓妮雅校

美利坚合众国政府和墨西哥合众国政府（以下简称"双方"），鉴于 1978 年 5 月 4 日签署的美利坚合众国政府与墨西哥合众国政府海洋划界条约（以下简称"1978 年海洋划界条约"）所进行的海洋划界，双方在等距离原则的基础上，划定了从墨西哥湾和太平洋测量的领海基线外 12 海里和 200 海里的海洋边界。

回顾 1970 年 11 月 23 日签订的，美利坚合众国与墨西哥合众国解决悬而未决的边界争议和维持格兰德河及科罗拉多河作为国际边界的条约，双方的海洋边界，在等距离原则的基础上，确定了领海基线外 12 海里的海洋边界。

双方希望依据国际法，确立美利坚合众国与墨西哥合众国在西墨西哥湾距领海基线外 200 海里以外大陆架界线。

考虑到可能跨越大陆架边界的潜在油气资源，在此情形下，双方合作和定期磋商符合各方利益；考虑到睦邻友好的做法加强了双方间友好合作的关系，双方遂达成以下约定。

第一条

美利坚合众国与墨西哥合众国在西墨西哥湾距领海基线外 200 海里外的大陆架边界，为以下坐标连接而成的测地线：

1	北纬 25°42′14.1″	西经 91°05′25.0″
2	北纬 25°39′43.1″	西经 91°20′31.2″
3	北纬 25°36′46.2″	西经 91°39′29.4″
4	北纬 25°37′01.2″	西经 91°44′19.1″
5	北纬 25°37′60.7″	西经 92°00′35.5″
6	北纬 25°38′13.4″	西经 92°07′59.3″
7	北纬 25°39′22.3″	西经 92°31′40.4″
8	北纬 25°39′23.8″	西经 92°32′13.7″
9	北纬 25°40′03.2″	西经 92°46′44.8″
10	北纬 25°40′27.3″	西经 92°55′56.0″
11	北纬 25°42′37.2″	西经 92°57′16.0″
12	北纬 25°46′33.9″	西经 92°59′41.5″
13	北纬 25°48′45.2″	西经 93°03′58.9″
14	北纬 25°51′51.0″	西经 93°10′03.0″
15	北纬 25°54′27.4″	西经 93°15′09.9″
16	北纬 25°59′49.3″	西经 93°26′42.5″

第二条

（1）用于确定前述第一条规定边界的大地测量和计算的基准为 1983 年北美基准（"NAD83"）以及国际地球自转服务的地球参考框架（"ITRF92"）。

（2）为第一条之目的：

（a）NAD83 和 ITRF92 应视为有同等效力；

（b）坐标点 1 和坐标点 16 分别为 1978 年海洋划界协议中坐标点 GM.E－1（25°42′13.05″N，91°05′24.98″W）以及坐标点 GM.W－4（25°59′48.28″N，93°26′42.19″W）。上述坐标点原本基于 1927 年北美基准（NAD27），已转化为 NAD83 和 ITRF92 下的坐标。

（3）仅为说明目的，第一条规定的分界线标示于本条约附件 1 的地图上。

第三条

美利坚合众国不得以任何目的，对第一条规定的大陆架边界以南海域的海床以及底土主张或行使主权或管辖权，墨西哥合众国不得以任何目的对上述边界以北海域的海床或底土主张或行使主权或管辖权。

第四条

（1）由于潜在石油或天然气矿藏可能延伸至跨越第一条规定边界（以下简称"跨界储藏"），双方在本条约生效后10年内不得授权或者许可第一条规定边界附近1.4海里内进行大陆架油气开采或开发（上述2.8海里宽区域以下简称"区域"）。

（2）仅为说明目的，第1款规定区域在本条约附件2所附地图中标明。

（3）双方经外交照会相互协商，可修改第1款规定的期间。

（4）自该条约生效之日起，各方就第一条规定边界两侧区域，依照本国法律法规，应就对方请求授权进行地质和地球物理研究，帮助确定跨界储藏的存在和分布。

（5）自该条约生效之日起，各方就第一条规定边界两侧区域，依照本国法律法规，应对另一方授权的地质和地球物理研究的请求给予必要便利，以便确定跨界储藏的存在和分布。

（6）该条约生效之日起，若一方发现跨界油气储藏存在，或有跨界储藏的可能，应通知另一方。

第五条

（1）在第四条第1款规定的期间内，在整体区域内：

（a）若获得的地质、地球物理信息可促使双方了解可能存在跨界储藏，包括依据第四条第5款规定的双方通知，双方应定期召开会议，以识别、定位、确定上述储藏的地质特征以及地球物理特征；

（b）双方应达成协议以高效、平等地开发上述跨界储藏；

（c）在收到一方通过外交途径提交的书面请求起60日内，双方应就潜在油气储藏有关事项进行磋商。

（2）第四条第1款规定期间届满后，在整体区域内：

（a）一方应将其租赁、许可、授予特许权或以其他方式在部分区域进行石油或天然气勘探或开发的决定通知另一方，且在开始生产石油或天然气时也应通知另一方；

（b）一方应确保自己授权进行该区域开发活动的实体遵守本条约条款。

第六条

如果一方通过外交途径提出书面请求，双方应就解释和执行本条约过程中产生的问题进行磋商。

第七条

本条约确立的大陆架界线不得以任何形式损害或影响各方在内水、领海、公海的权利，以及损害或影响各方主权或管辖权。

第八条

本条约的解释和适用产生的任何争端应通过磋商或双方同意的其他和平方式解决。

第九条

本条约需经批准，并于交换批准书之日生效。

各方政府正式授权的代表在此条约上签名，以昭信守。

本条约于2000年6月9日签署于华盛顿特区，英语文本和西班牙语文本一式两份，两种文本具有同等效力。

2. Treaty between the Government of the United States of America and the Government of the United Mexican States on the Delimitation of the Continental Shelf in the Western Gulf of Mexico beyond 200 Nautical Miles, 9 June 2000

The Government of the United States of America and the Government of the United Mexican States (hereinafter "the parties").

Considering that the maritime boundaries between the parties were determined on the basis of equidistance for a distance between twelve and two hundred nautical miles seaward from the baselines from which the breadth of the territorial sea is measured in the Gulf of Mexico and the Pacific Ocean by the Treaty on Maritime Boundaries between the United States of America and the United Mexican States, signed on May 4, 1978 (the "1978 Treaty on Maritime Boundaries"),

Recalling that the maritime boundaries between the Parties were determined on the basis of equidistance for a distance of twelve nautical miles seaward from the baselines from which the breadth of the territorial sea is measured by the Treaty to Resolve pending Boundary Differences and Maintain the Rio Grande and Colorado River as the International Boundary between the United States of America and the United Mexican States, signed on November 23, 1970.

Desiring to establish, in accordance with international law, the continental shelf boundary between the United States of America and the United Mexican

States in the Western Gulf of Mexico beyond 200 nautical miles from the baselines from which breadth of the territorial sea is measure.

Taking into account the possibility that there could exist petroleum or natural gas reservoirs that extend across that continental shelf boundary, and the need for cooperation and periodic consultation between the Parties in protecting their respective interests in such circumstances; and

Considering that the practice of good neighborliness has strengthened the friendly and cooperative relations between the Parties,

Have agreed as follows:

Article 1

The continental shelf boundary between the United States of America and the United Mexican States in the Western Gulf of Mexico beyond 200 nautical miles from the baselines from which the breadth of the territorial sea is measured shall be determined by geodetic lines connecting the following coordinates:

1.	25°42′14.1″N.	91°05′25.0″W.
2.	25°39′43.1″N.	91°20′31.2″W.
3.	25°36′46.2″N.	91°39′29.4″W.
4.	25°37′01.2″N.	91°44′19.1″W.
5.	25°37′60.7″N.	92°00′35.5″W.
6.	25°38′13.4″N.	92°07′59.3″W.
7.	25°39′22.3″N.	92°31′40.4″W.
8.	25°39′23.8″N.	92°32′13.7″W.
9.	25°40′03.2″N.	92°46′44.8″W.
10.	25°40′27.3″N.	92°55′56.0″W.
11.	25°42′37.2″N.	92°57′16.0″W.
12.	25°46′33.9″N.	92°59′41.5″W.
13.	25°48′45.2″N.	93°03′58.9″W.
14.	25°51′51.0″N.	93°10′03.0″W.
15.	25°54′27.4″N.	93°15′09.9″W.
16.	25°59′49.3″N.	93°26′42.5″W.

Article 2

1. The geodetic and computational bases used to determine the boundary set forth in Article I are the 1983 North American Datum ("NAD83") and the international Earth Rotation Service's Terrestrial Reference Frame ("ITRF92").

2. For purposes of Article 1:

(a) NAD83 and ITRF92 shall be considered to be identical; and

(b) Boundary points numbers 1 and 16 are, respectively, boundary points GM. E – 1 (25°42′13.05″N., 91°05′24.89″W.) and GM. W – 4 (25°59′48.28″N., 93°26′42.19″W.) of the 1978 Treaty on Maritime Boundaries. These points, which were originally determined with reference to the 1927 North American Datum – NAD27, have been transformed to the NAD83 and ITRF92 datums.

3. For the purpose of illustration only, the boundary line in Article I is drawn on the map that appears as Annex 1 to this Treaty.

Article 3

South of the continental shelf boundary set forth in Article I, the United States of America shall not, and north of said boundary, the United Mexican States shall not, claim or exercise for any purpose sovereign rights or jurisdiction over the seabed and subsoil.

Article 4

1. Due to the possible existence of petroleum or natural gas reservoirs that may extend across the boundary set forth in Article I (hereinafter referred to as "transboundary reservoirs"), the Parties, during a period that will end ten (10) years following the entry into force of this Treaty, shall not authorize or permit petroleum or natural gas drilling or exploitation of the continental shelf within one and four – tenths (1.4) nautical miles of the boundary set forth in Article I. (This two and eight – tenths (2.8) nautical mile area hereinafter shall be referred to as "the Area".)

2. For the purpose of illustration only, the Area set forth in paragraph 1 is drawn on the map that appears as Annex 2 to this Treaty.

3. The parties, by mutual agreement through an exchange of diplomatic notes, may modify the period set forth in paragraph 1.

4. From the date of entry into force of this Treaty, with respect to the Area on its side of the boundary set forth in Article I, each Party, in accordance with its national laws and regulations, shall facilitate requests from the other Party to authorize geological and geophysical studies to help determine the possible presence and distribution of transboundary reservoirs.

5. From the date of entry into force of this Treaty, with respect to the Area in its entirety, each Party, in accordance with its national laws and regulations, shall share geological and geophysical information in its possession in order to determine the possible existence and location of transboundary reservoirs.

6. From the date of entry into force of this Treaty, if a Party has knowledge of the existence or possible existence of a transboundary reservoir, it shall notify the other Party.

Article 5

1. With respect to the Area in its entirety, during the period set forth in paragraph 1 of Article IV:

(a) as geological and geophysical information is generated that facilitates the Parties' knowledge about the possible existence of transboundary reservoirs, including notifications by Parties in accordance with paragraph 5 of Article IV, the Parties shall meet periodically for the purpose of identifying, locating and determining the geological and geophysical characteristics of such reservoirs;

(b) the Parties shall seek to reach agreement for the efficient and equitable exploitation of such transboundary reservoirs; and

(c) the Parties shall, within sixty days of receipt of a written request by a party through diplomatic channels, consult to discuss matters related to possible transboundary reservoirs.

2. With respect to the Area in its entirety, following the expiry of the period set forth in paragraph 1 of Article IV:

(a) a Party shall inform the other Party of its decisions to lease, license, grant concessions, or otherwise make available, portions of the Area for petroleum or natural gas exploration or development and shall also inform the other Party when petroleum or natural gas resources are to commence production; and

(b) a Party shall ensure that entities it authorizes to undertake activities within the Area shall observe the terms of the Treaty.

Article 6

Upon written request by a Party through diplomatic channels, the Parties shall consult to discuss any issue regarding the interpretation of implementation of this Treaty.

Article 7

The continental shelf boundary established by this Treaty shall not affect or prejudice in any manner the positions of either Party with respect to the extent of internal waters, of the territorial sea, of the high seas or of sovereign rights or jurisdiction for any other purpose.

Article 8

Any dispute concerning the interpretation or application of this Treaty shall be resolved by negotiation or other peaceful means as may be agreed upon by the Parties.

Article 9

This Treaty shall be subject to ratification and shall enter into force on the date of the exchange of instruments of ratification.

IN WITNESS WHEREOF, the undersigned having been duly authorized by their respective Governments, have signed this Treaty.

DONE at Washington, D. C. this ninth day of June 2000, in duplicate, in the English and Spanish languages, both texts being equally authentic.

3. 《美利坚合众国与墨西哥合众国之间关于墨西哥湾跨界油气储藏的协定》

(2012年2月20日订于洛斯卡沃斯)

宗吕谦译,邓妮雅校

美利坚合众国和墨西哥合众国(以下简称"双方"),鉴于1970年11月23日签订的,美利坚合众国与墨西哥合众国解决悬而未决的边界争议和维持格兰德河及科罗拉多河作为国际边界的条约(以下简称"1970年协议")以及于1978年5月4日签署的美利坚合众国政府与墨西哥合众国政府海洋划界条约(以下简称"1978年海洋划界协议")进行的海洋划界;

回顾墨西哥合众国政府与美利坚合众国政府于2000年6月9日签署的条约,划分了200海里外墨西哥西部海湾的大陆架划界(以下简称"2000年大陆架协议");

铭记2000年大陆架协议承认可能存在碳氢化合物储藏可能延伸至该条约所确定的大陆架界线;

回顾2000年大陆架协议第5条第1款b项中规定,双方应为高效、公平开发这种碳氢化合物储藏达成一致;

力求建立一个法律框架,以实现安全、高效、公平、环保地开发可能存在于美利坚合众国与墨西哥合众国在墨西哥湾海洋边界两侧的碳氢化合物储藏;

承认促进公平和合理利用跨界资源的原则,意图实现资源开发所获长期利益最大化的意愿,同时保护双方的资源;以及

承认该框架的目的是鼓励进行在联合经营这个基本原则上建立合作安排,进一步认识到在该协议框架外,双方还可能展开的其他合作安排,这些安排同样可以促进高效、公平、环保地开发跨界资源;遂达成以下

协议。

第一章 总则

第一条 范围

本协定适用于双方就位于海岸线9海里外，跨界的地质碳氢化合物结构和储层的联合勘探和开发。

若协定中任何条款规定一方在第二十二条中所规定的通知截止日期内，改变现有许可证，该条款在此情况下不适用。尽管有上述规定，双方承认该许可证符合协定所有条款有利于实现双方的共同利益，应满怀诚意地做出努力，使该许可证符合协定规定。

第二条 定义

就本协定而言：

"机密数据"指一方披露给另一方的自己非公开的且认定为机密的信息或数据，包括任何类型的、书面的或口头的地质信息；

"建设和作业"指加工、安装、铺设、使用、调整、维护、维修、关闭设备以及管道；

"边界线"指1970年协议、1978年海洋划界协议、2000年大陆架协议所划分的海洋边界，以及双方按照协议约定的新的墨西哥湾海洋边界；

"开发"指具有商业价值的油气资源被发现和界定后进行的活动，包括（但不限于）地球物理活动，钻井，平台设计，加工，运输和安装海陆、水面和水下设备以及联合区域内外用于生产已发现的碳氢化合物的设备，不包括与勘探及生产有关的活动；

"执行机构"指一方为执行该协定规定的职能而指派的机构，双方都可随时指派该机构；

"专家裁决"指有关专家依照本协定第十六条就争议做出的决议；

"开采"指与开发、生产相关的所有活动，包括（但不限于）跨界区域油井维修、油井检修、完井、油井维护、油井关闭，包括用于上述过程或该过程产生的任何物质的注入、再注入或储存，或处理从中产生的气体或液体；

"勘探"指寻找碳氢化合物资源，包括（但不限于）以下活动：（1）用于探测或发现碳氢化合物的存在，利用磁感应、重力感应、震波反射、震波折射、气体嗅探、结晶偏析等手段，进行的地质和地球物理的海洋和机载探测；（2）为寻找具有商业价值的油气，或为决定储藏是否可以继续进行开发和生产而进行的钻探；

"设施"指任何用于勘探或开发的设备、基础设施及装置，包括（但不限于）钻井船、固定式平台或浮动平台、钻井平台、浮式生产设备、储存器、海上或海底井口、油田集输管线、油田内电缆，以及其他钻井、测井、修井、试井所需的附属设施和用于从海上设施转移产品且物理上属于该设备的船只；

"边界线附近设施"指在任何一方管辖范围内，且距离边界15法定哩以内的任何设施，以及任何一方管辖范围内的跨界管道，但不包括供给船；

"地质资料"指勘探或开发过程中产生的关于地质、地球物理、地球化学的信息和数据，包括（但不限于）已完钻井资料及根据该数据做出的解释，上述资料可以由一国依照本国法律进行披露；

"碳氢化合物"指任何形态的石油、天然气，包括天然地层中存在的或提取的混合物；

"边界附近碳氢化合物"指在钻井作业过程中探测出的边界两侧3法定哩以内的碳氢化合物；

"检查员"指经任何一方主管当局授权，对下列有关事项进行检查的人：

(a) 跨界区域设施的建设和作业；

(b) 跨界区域有关生产的计量系统；

(c) 健康与安全；或

(d) 环境保护；

"许可证"指由执行机构签发的在指定区域勘探或开发、设施建设和作业的授权证明，包括美国执行机构签发的租契；

"许可证持有者"指任何持有许可证的个人和实体；

"许可"指任何一方依照法律签发的有关碳氢化合物的勘探或开发以及/或设施和/或管道建设与作业有关的许可证、授权、同意书或批准；

"管道"指配备流量阀门、传输平台、压缩机站、通信系统等设备的连续管道，用于将碳氢化合物、采出水或其他液体和气体从一点输送至另一点，通常从油田或石油加工厂输送至其他管道或输送至使用和储存的地点。

"生产"是指包括（但不限于）处理油气和其他物质，注入、再注入或储存用于此类活动或从该活动中产生的物质的活动，提高碳氢化合物回收的活动，碳氢化合物运输或出口至陆地的活动，以及其他与油井维修、油井维护、油井养护、油井检修、再完井、检查有关的所有操作，不包括将油气从跨界油气储藏中分离的勘探和开发活动；

"储藏"指碳氢化合物在聚集于地质或地层结构中，具有多孔和可渗透的介质的单一连续的矿床；

"跨界储藏"指任何跨越边界线，全部位于海岸线9海里外，在边界两侧整体或部分可开发的储藏；

"跨界联合区"指跨越边界线且全部位于海岸线9海里外的单一地质碳氢结构或储藏，且依据联合开发协议的条款经执行机构批准用于共同勘探和/或开发。

"联合区域"指在联合开发协议中所述的跨界联合区的地理区域；

"联合作业协议"指许可证持有者与联合经营人间签署的，明确双方权利义务的，包括（但不限于）分担和分享联合区域作业产生支出和债务以及所获收益的协议。

第三条 管辖权

协定中任何内容不应解释为，影响任何一方在国际法下享有的对邻接的大陆架的主权和管辖权。

第四条 边界线附近活动

1. 在协定生效后90日内及此后每年，双方应就边界线3法定哩以内的勘探与开发活动进行磋商。磋商内容包括交换与上述活动有关，以及从上述活动中获取的可用的和所有相关的地质信息。

2. 虽然本条第1款有磋商的规定，但需符合本国法律：

（a）若一方发现可能存在跨界储藏，该方应在发现之日起60日内以书面形式告知另一方；

（b）若一方批准在边界线3法定哩内收集地震数据的方案，或一方许可证持有人提交上述方案，该方需在方案提交或者批准之日起30日内，以书面形式告知另一方；

（c）若一方已经批准在边界线3法定哩内的勘探方案，或一方许可证持有者提交上述方案，该方应在方案提交或者批准之日起 30 日内，以书面形式告知另一方。

（d）若一方在边界线附近发现油气分布，需在发现之日起 60 日内以书面形式告知另一方；

（e）若一方许可证持有者所提交的钻井方案中，井口或井眼的任何部分位于边界附近 3 法定哩内，该方需在获知该情况之日起 30 日内以书面形式告知另一方；

（f）若任何许可证持有者提交方案，开发和生产位于边界线 3 法定哩内的区域，收到该方案的一方需在收到方案之日起 30 日内，将该方案提交给另一方。

第五条 跨界储藏的确定

1. 双方在收到第四条第 2 款 a 项和 d 项中规定的通知后 30 日内，双方应通过其执行机构启动磋商，以确定是否存在跨界储藏。执行机构应要求许可证持有者提供一切与上述决定有关的地质信息，并提交自己掌握的所有可用地质信息。

2. 若双方在本条第 1 款规定的提起磋商的最后期限后 60 日内，仍未做出是否存在跨界油气储藏的决定，任何一方的执行机构可以将该问题提交给联合委员会。

3. 在本条第 1 款规定的磋商期间，以及本协定第十四～十七条所规定的程序过程中，相关执行机构应依照本国法律，向对方执行机构提交关于其管辖范围内，许可证持有者进行的有关潜在跨界储藏的勘探和开发活动或作业的季度报告。

第二章 跨界油气储藏或跨界联合区的勘探与开发

第六条 联合经营协议

1. 跨界油气储藏与跨界油气联合区的共同勘探和/或开发，需遵守由双方共同批准的联合经营协议中的规定。这种联合勘探和/或开发应依据，由许可证持有者提出和商定的，经执行机构批准的联合经营协议的规定进行。执行机构应依据本协定提供一个或多个联合经营协议的范本。

2. 联合经营协议应包括，特别是：

（a）确定联合区域与跨界储藏的范围；

（b）许可证持有者身份以及其各自参与的利益；

（c）计算产量分配的方法；

（d）联合区域的勘探或开发方案，包括预估油井数量和时间，以及针对该计划后续变更如何交付和批准的有关机制；

（e）联合经营协议条款和协议生效日期；

（f）联合经营者的身份和任命，辞职和免职的程序，以及继任联合经营者的任命程序；

（g）有关权益转移的规定；

（h）有关产量精确测量的规定；

（i）确保准确支付特许权收益及其他的有关程序；

（j）依照各方法律采取的安全措施与环保措施；

（k）联合经营者与各方共享相关信息的规定；

（l）生产分配重新确定的程序，包括引起这种重新分配的时间表和事件。

3. 各方应要求许可证持有者，或与联合经营人共同作业的许可证持有人提交联合经营协议草案时，同时提交一方要求的所有可用数据，以用于审核协议草案，各方需确保上述数据和资料向另一方公开。

4. 各执行机构应在收到联合经营协议草案后 120 日内，做出批准、修改或否决的决定。各执行机构可延长上述期间，但总附加审查期间不得超过 120 日。若一个执行机构最后的审查期间已过，各执行机构仍未做出批准、修改或否决的决定，则该联合经营协议草案被视为被否决。在该款规定的审议期内，各执行机构可以在余下的时间内将审议草案提交至联合委员会审查。

5. 已获批准的联合经营协议的任何修正都需经执行机构批准。各执行机构应在收到修正草案后 30 日内，做出批准、修改或否决的决定。各执行机构可延长上述期限，但总附加审查期不得超过 30 日。若一个执行机构最后的审查期间已过，各执行机构仍未做出批准、修改或否决的决定，则该提案被视为被否决。在该款规定的审议期内，各执行机构可以在余下的时间内将审议草案提交至联合委员会审查。

第七条 跨界联合区形成前跨界油气储藏的管理

1. 若经第五条第 1 款规定的磋商或第十四～十七条的程序后，确定了跨界油气储藏的存在，在双方未就联合经营协议达成一致的情况下，各方应采取措施，促进跨界储藏作为一个跨界联合区进行开发。其促进措施包括，在确定跨界油气储藏之日起至适用本条第 2 款至第 5 款规定的最后期限，禁止对跨界油气储藏开始生产。若上述生产已开始，相关方应采取其认为依据该国法律适当的措施，提供相关法律，证明其正在进行的生产没有不适当地妨碍本协定的执行。

2. 若跨界储藏确定之日起 6 个月期间届满，或在期间届满之前，相关许可证持有者告知执行机构其不参与联合经营协议，或执行机构为许可证持有者参与联合协议另行确定期限的，联合协议视为未通过：

（a）各方应要求其许可证持有者在 60 日内，向各执行机构提交联合经营协议草案以及联合作业协议草案；

（b）执行机构应在 30 日内共同确定跨界储藏在原始条件下，在边界两侧可采碳氢化合物的预计量，以及共同确定相关的产量分配。

3. 若执行机构无法达成本条第 2 款 b 项所规定的决议，该决议应提交专家决定。

4. 在收到本条第 2 款 a 项规定的联合经营协议草案以及联合作业协议草案后，或者在期限届满之前双方都没有收到联合经营协议以及本条第 2 款 b 项以及该条第 3 款规定产量分配的决议，执行机构应在 90 日内批准提交的联合经营协议草案或联合作业协议草案，或是批准双方制定的替代性联合经营协议或联合作业协议。若 90 日届满仍未批准联合经营协议或联合作业协议，应将该问题提交至联合委员会。该问题提交至联合委员会 90 日内，若联合委员会仍没有批准联合经营协议或联合作业协议，跨界储藏的开发依照本条第 5 款的规定进行。

5. 若任何一方或其许可证持有者未签订，由执行机构批准或联合委员会在 60 日内批准的联合经营协议或联合作业协议，或若执行机构或联合委员会未批准联合经营协议或联合作业协议，各方可授权许可证持有者根据本条第 2 款 b 项及第 3 款规定，或在双方同意的情况下，依据跨界储藏联合管理方案，包括达成一致的管理再分配和测量的条款，就相关跨界储藏进行开发。上述方案可包括第十六条所规定的争端解决条款。进行上述开发时，双方需按月交换生产数据。

6. 联合委员会应尽力解决本条未载明的有关跨界储藏产量分配的问题。

第八条 产量分配

1. 执行机构应要求联合经营人在跨界储藏进行生产前 60 日，代表许可证持有者提交生产分配方案，就边界两侧的生产分配进行磋商，以获得执行机构批准，其后适用该区域第一次生产。执行机构在做出批准协议的决定之前，应与联合经营人进行协商。

2. 各执行机构应确保联合区域中与草案有关的所有相关的和获得的信息应及时提供给其他执行机构。

3. 从本条第 1 款规定的磋商开始之日起 30 日内，如果执行机构不能就产量的初始分配问题达成一致，则该事项应提交联合委员会。

第九条 产量分配的重新确定

1. 跨界储藏产量的再分配应依照联合经营合同或本协定第七条第 5 款的规定进行。双方应努力确保重新确定的条款可为跨界储藏产量提供公正、平等分配方案。此类条款应在联合协议中载明，且在有效期内可适用。

2. 各执行机构应确保，依照本国法律，与跨界储藏分配的重新确定有关的所有相关和获得的信息，及时披露给其他执行机构。执行机构在做出不同意联合经营者重新确定的提议之前，应与联合经营者进行协商。

3. 从本条第 1 款规定的重新确定的程序开始之日起 60 日内，执行机构不能就重新确定的问题达成一致的，应将该问题提交联合委员会解决。

第三章 作业协议

第十条 联合经营人

1. 执行机构应确保跨界联合区域内联合经营人，可由许可证持有者之间协议指定。指定和更换联合经营人需经执行机构批准。

2. 联合经营人将代表许可证持有者行事。

第十一条 联合作业协议

1. 各执行机构应要求其许可证持有者依据本协议，签订一份关于跨界联合区勘探开发的联合区作业协议。

2. 执行机构要求许可证持有者，在联合经营协议被批准之前，先提交一份已生效的联合区作业协议。

3. 若联合区作业协议与联合经营协议相冲突，以联合经营协议为准；

若联合经营协议与本协定相冲突，以本协定为准。

第十二条 边界线附近的设施

1. 双方应尽最大努力促进许可证持有者，在跨界联合区有关勘探和开发活动中的合作，包括提供使用边界线附近设施的便利，禁止在不必要时对此类活动做出不合理的阻止和妨碍。

2. 使用边界线附近的设施，特别是使用管道、通过管道，并在适当情况下，为其使用提供技术服务上的便利。

3. 双方应依照本国法律，为参与跨界联合区有关活动的工人提供操作设备上的便利。

第十三条 财税条款

跨界油气储藏开采所获收益，分别按照墨西哥合众国和美利坚合众国的法律征税，1992年9月18日墨西哥合众国政府与美利坚合众国政府就收入和资本税避免双重征税防止逃税公约、公约修正案（以后可能再修订），以及将来双方签订的任何取代该公约的协定。

第四章 制度安排

第十四条 联合委员会

1. 应在本协定生效后90日内成立一个联合委员会，以协助执行机构管理本协定。

2. 各方通过其执行机构，指派联合委员会代表、副代表各一名。在必要时，各方可通过包括提供专家在内的方式，对联合委员会代表提供必要的支持。

3. 为行使其职能，联合委员会可以设立工作小组或专家小组，听取非政府组织和个人的建议，在双方同意下，也可以采取其他类似措施。

4. 联合委员会应在其成立后90日内通过其议事规则。

5. 联合委员有权审查执行机构提交的，有关本协定解释和适用的争端或其他事项，或本协定下其他不可预见的问题。

6. 若联合委员会在60日内未解决第8条规定的产量分配有关争议，以及与第9条规定的产量分配重新确定有关的争议，各方可将该争议提交专家裁决。若联合委员会在60日内未解决第5条第2款规定的确定跨界储藏有关争议，以及与未解决边界线两侧潜在的跨界储藏的油井相关的数据有关的争议，各方可将该争议提交专家裁决。

7. 若联合委员会在 60 日内未解决执行机构提交的本条约解释和适用中产生的，非本条第 6 款的争端，或依据第六条第 4 款、第六条第 5 款、第七条第 4 款提交的争端，任何一方可诉诸第十五条和第十七条的争端解决条款。联合委员会应在 30 内依照第十七条做出最终仲裁。若联合委员会在该期限届满后仍未解决争议，该争议将被退回双方。

8. 双方对提交给联合委员会或专家裁决的或依据本协定争端解决的任何争端，不得采取任何行动——若可以合理预见到这些行动，在争端解决程序完成之前会妨碍与争端有关的决定的实施。

第五章　争端解决

第十五条　协商和调解

1. 双方需尽最大可能尽早通过协商解决本条约解释和适用中产生的争议。各方可提出书面请求，要求进行磋商。除非双方另做约定，磋商应在请求提出后 20 日内进行。

2. 若提出协商请求后 120 日内，双方仍未解决不属于专家裁决的争议，任意一方可在 30 日内依据第十七条规定将该争议提交仲裁。

3. 双方也可将本条约解释和适用中产生的任何争端提交中立的第三方进行不具有约束力的调解，以作为本条及第十七条规定程序的补充或替代。

第十六条　专家裁决

1. 联合委员会应通过有关议事规则在 180 日内建立专家任命和雇佣条款的安排，包括特别是赔偿规则和机密保护条款。

2. 若争议提交专家裁决时，联合委员会还未制定本条第 1 款规定的安排：

（a）各方应在争议提交后 30 日内，选择一名指派专家，费用由各方共同承担；

（b）指派专家应在 30 日内任命专家、制定聘任专家有关条款，包括依照现行标准确定的薪水以及机密数据的严格保护条款；

（c）此情形下做出专家裁决的有关费用，由双方分担。

3. 各方应及时提供自己享有的所有信息，或其有法律权限从许可证持有人获得的信息，或专家要求提供用于做出决议的信息。

4. 双方应确保专家保持严格的公正度和透明度。一方与专家之间任何形式的沟通，除机密信息以外，应披露给另一方。

5. 双方应规定，在指定专家后90日内，专家应向联合委员会提交做出的初步裁决以及做出该初步裁决的详细说明。之后，从初步裁决通知联合委员会之日起60日内，或者联合委员会约定的其他期限内，任意一方可以要求专家做出说明，或提出深入意见供专家参考。在上述期限届满前30日内，专家做出的最终裁决以及做出该裁决的详细说明将以书面形式告知联合委员会。

6. 尽管有本条第5款的规定，双方应规定依据第七条第3款提交至专家解决的争端，专家应在收到之日起30日内做出裁决，专家裁决应直接提交给执行机构。

7. 专家裁决过程将严格保密。除非任何一方法律要求双方将确保并保证专家对为裁决提供的信息，与裁决、初步决定、最终决定有关的书面和口头信息均保密。

8. 尽管有本条第4款和第7款的规定，专家做出跨界储藏存在的初步决议后，专家做出该决议使用的所有信息以及在确定上述跨界油气储藏日期之后提供给专家的信息，应提供给双方。双方应依照本协定条款及本国法律对上述信息保密。

9. 专家裁决是终局的，对双方都具有约束力。

第十七条　仲裁

1. 本协定的解释和适用中产生的且不能由专家裁决的争端，若不能通过联合委员会或者协商解决，任何一方可将争议提交仲裁。

2. 联合委员会应在确定其议事程序后180日内，建立仲裁机制以履行本条之规定的。

第六章　检查、安全和环境保护

第十八条　设备检查

1. 根据可适用的本国法律，各方依据本协定制定和达成一致的程序，有权检查本协定规定的联合区域的有关设施。

2. 为使各方检查员更好地维护各方在安全、环境以及财政方面的利益，执行机构应依照本国法律，制定有关以下事项的详细程序：

（a）各方检查员之间的协商；

（b）及时获知相关检查活动信息；以及

（c）在联合检查制度下有权进入联合区域进行检查活动，包括进入所有位置的计量系统。

3. 双方检查员应相互合作、共同协商，以达到相应安全标准和环保标准。

4. 联合区域有关设施，一方检查员可在情况需要时要求另一方检查员行使职权，确保设施达到相应安全标准和环保标准。若双方检查员产生分歧，或一方检查员在收到另一方检查员的请求时，拒绝采取行动，则应将该事项提交执行机构解决。

5. 若为避免发生危害生命、严重的人身损害或环境破坏之必要，且当时条件不允许检查员与执行机构进行协商，有管辖权的检查员可应其他检查员要求，依照本国法律，立即停止任何或全部引发上述风险活动的操作。在责令停止活动后4小时内，检查员应立即通知执行机构所采取的措施并说明理由，执行机构应立即商议消除上述风险的必要措施。本款的任何规定不妨碍各方恢复使用相关设施的权力。

第十九条　安全和环境保护

1. 双方应适时为在本协定下进行的活动采取共同的安全和环境标准以及规定。在任何情况下，双方应努力确保各自标准相协调，保障本协定安全、高效、环保地施行。

2. 执行机构应制订施行本条的有关程序。

3. 双方承认在油污防备、油污应急响应以及油污处理合作方面的国际义务的重要性，双方将审议进行本协定活动时相关义务的履行情况，确保合作在适当的框架下进行。

第七章　最终条款

第二十条　保密

依照本国法律，双方应对从另一方或其许可证持有者处依照本协定获取的保密数据及其他信息予以保密，并责成其许可证持有者履行保密义务。

第二十一条　修正案

1. 经双方共同书面同意，本协定可随时进行修正。

2. 修正案通过本协定第二十二条规定的程序方能生效。

第二十二条　生效

双方应在完成使本协定生效的国内程序后相互通知对方。本协定在最后一份通知发出后 60 日开始生效。

第二十三条　终止

1. 本协定可经双方书面协议终止，也可由协议任何一方发出书面通知 180 天后，随时予以终止。

2. 即使本协定终止，除非双方有相反约定：

（a）联合经营协议、联合作业协议，或其他根据本协定制定且在协定终止时仍然有效的协议，或者是在本协定终止时依据本协定提交至双方或由双方审核的协议，在这些协议的有效期间仍然适用本协定的规定；

（b）有关联合经营协议、联合作业协议以及其他根据本协定制定的其他协议上双方的关系，在这些协议有效期间，仍然适用本协定的规定；

（c）一方在本协定生效后有效期届满前签发的许可证，仍然适用本协定规定；

（d）依据第七条第 5 款进行的跨界储藏开发活动应继续适用本协定规定；

（e）第二十条规定的双方保密义务需继续适用。

3. 经本条第一款规定的通知，双方可就制定跨界油气储藏共同勘探开发的新协议展开初步磋商。

第二十四条　墨西哥湾西部缺口边界区域碳氢化合物活动暂停的终止

随着本协定生效，在依据 2000 年大陆架协议第 4 条第 1 款建立的"区域"内的大陆架上石油或天然气开采或开发的授权或许可的暂停期，以及后续换文延长的期，应当终止。

第二十五条　与其他协议的关系

除第二十四条外，本协定任何条款都不影响双方签署的其他国际协议中双方的权利和义务。

(十六) 2012 年美国和墨西哥共同开发案

本协定于 2012 年 2 月 20 日签署于洛斯卡沃斯，英语和西班牙语文本一式两份，两文本具有同等效力。

美利坚合众国　　　　　墨西哥合众国
希拉里·罗德姆·克林顿　帕特里夏·埃斯皮诺萨·坎特利亚诺
国务卿　　　　　　　　外交部长

4. Agreement between the United States of America and the United Mexican States Concerning Transboundary Hydrocarbon Reservoirs in the Gulf of Mexico

The United States of America and the United Mexican States (hereinafter, "the Parties");

Considering that the maritime boundaries between the Parties were delimited by the Treaty to Resolve Pending Boundary Differences and Maintain the Rio Grande and Colorado River as the International Boundary signed on November 23rd, 1970 (hereinafter, "the 1970 Treaty") and the Treaty on Maritime Boundaries between the United Mexican States and the United States of America signed on May 4th, 1978 (hereinafter, "the 1978 Treaty on Maritime Boundaries");

Recalling that the continental shelf in the Western Gulf of Mexico beyond 200 nautical miles was delimited by the Treaty between the Government of the United Mexican States and the Government of the United States of America signed on June 9th, 2000 (hereinafter, "the 2000 Treaty on the Continental Shelf");

Bearing in mind that the 2000 Treaty on the Continental Shelf recognizes the possible existence of hydrocarbon reservoirs that may extend across the continental shelf boundary established in that Treaty;

Recalling also that Article 5, paragraph 1, subparagraph (b) of the 2000 Treaty on the Continental Shelf provides that the Parties shall seek to reach agreement for the efficient and equitable exploitation of such transboundary reservoirs;

Desiring to establish a legal framework to achieve safe, efficient, equitable and environmentally responsible exploitation of transboundary hydrocarbon reservoirs that may exist along the maritime boundaries established between the United Mexican States and the United States of America in the Gulf of Mexico;

Recognizing principles that promote equitable and reasonable utilization of transboundary resources, and desiring to maximize the long term benefits from their exploitation, as well as to protect the resources of both Parties; and

Recognizing that this framework is intended to encourage the establishment of cooperative arrangements based primarily on principles of unitization, and further recognizing that additional cooperative arrangements may be developed outside of the framework of this Agreement and that such arrangements may also promote efficient, equitable, and environmentally responsible exploitation of transboundary reservoirs,

Have agreed as follows:

CHAPTER 1 GENERAL PRINCIPLES

Article 1 Scope

This Agreement shall apply to cooperation between the Parties with regard to the joint Exploration and Exploitation of geological Hydrocarbon structures and Reservoirs that extend across the Delimitation Line, the entirety of which are located beyond 9 nautical miles from the coastline.

If any provision in this Agreement would require a Party to alter the terms of any License existing as of the date of the last notification provided under Article 22, such provision shall not apply in such case. Notwithstanding the foregoing, the Parties recognize that it is in their interest that such Licenses be subject to all terms of this Agreement, and shall undertake good faith efforts to bring those Licenses under this Agreement.

Article 2 Definitions

For the purposes of this Agreement:

"Confidential Data" means any information or data, including Geological Information, of any type, kind or character, whether written or oral, disclosed by one Party to the other that is not publicly available and which information or data has been identified by the disclosing Party as confidential;

"Construction and Operation" means the fabrication, installation, laying, use, modification, maintenance, repair and decommissioning of Facilities and/or Pipelines;

"Delimitation Line" means the maritime boundaries in the Gulf of Mexico delimited in the 1970 Treaty, the 1978 Treaty on Maritime Boundaries and the 2000 Treaty on the Continental Shelf, and any future maritime boundary in the Gulf of Mexico delimited between the Parties, as agreed;

"Development" means those activities that take place following discovery and delineation of commercial quantities of Hydrocarbons, including, but not limited to, geophysical activities, drilling, platform design, fabrication and transportation, and installation of all Facilities, whether onshore or offshore, surface or subsea, and which are for the purpose of producing the discovered Hydrocarbons, whether on or off the Unit Area, excluding any activity related to Exploration or Production;

"Executive Agency" means the Agency of the Party designated to carry out the functions specified in this Agreement, as each Party may designate from time to time;

"Expert Determination" means the resolution of a dispute by an expert in accordance with Article 16 of this Agreement;

"Exploitation" means Development, Production, and all associated activities, including, but not limited to, workover, servicing, completion, maintenance, and decommissioning of wells in a Transboundary Unit, including treatment and processing of gas or liquids from and/or the injection, reinjection or storage of any substance used for or derived from the aforementioned processes;

"Exploration" means the search for Hydrocarbons including, but not limited to, activities such as: (1) geological and geophysical marine and airborne surveys where magnetic, gravity, seismic reflection, seismic refraction, gas sniffers, coring, or other systems are used to detect or imply the presence of Hydrocarbons; and (2) any drilling conducted for the purpose of searching for commercial quantities of Hydrocarbons or needed to delineate any Reservoir to decide whether to proceed with Development and Production;

"Facility" means any equipment, infrastructure or installation used for Exploration or Exploitation including, but not limited to, drilling vessels, fixed or floating platforms, platform installed drilling rigs, floating production systems, storage units, Hotels, surface or seafloor well heads, intra-field gathering Pipelines, intra-field cables, and all the accessories necessary for well drilling, well logging, well intervention, well repair and well testing and includes any vessel used to transfer production from an offshore facility while it is physically attached to the Facility;

"Facilities near the Delimitation Line" means any Facility under the jurisdiction of either Party within a distance of 15 statute miles from the Delimitation Line or further for transboundary Pipelines, but excluding supply and support vessels;

"Geological Information" means geological, geophysical or geochemical information and data resulting from Exploration or Exploitation, including, but not limited to, information from drilled wells and interpretations derived from such data, and which, subject to its national law, may be disclosed by a Party.

"Hydrocarbon" means all oil and natural gas, regardless of form, including any mixture thereof, existing in or derived from natural strata;

"Hydrocarbon Occurrence near the Delimitation Line" means a detection of Hydrocarbons during drilling operations within 3 statute miles on either side of the Delimitation Line;

"Inspector" means any person authorized by the competent authority of either Party to carry out inspection activities relating to:

(a) the Construction and Operation of Facilities related to a Transboundary Unit;

(b) any metering system relating to production associated with a Transboundary Unit;

(c) health and safety; or

(d) protection of the environment.

"License" means the authorization issued by an Executive Agency to carry out Exploitation or Exploration in a given area, and for the Construction and Operation of a Facility. The term License includes a "lease" issued by the U. S. Executive Agency;

"Licensee" means any person or entity holding a License;

"Permit" means any permit, authorization, consent or approval issued under the law of either Party, relating to the Exploration or Exploitation of Hydrocarbons and/or the Construction and Operation of Facilities and/or Pipelines;

"Pipeline" means a continuous conduit, complete with such equipment as valves for flow control, transmission platforms, compressor stations, and communications systems, for transporting Hydrocarbons, produced waters or other fluids and gases from one point to another, usually from a point in the producing field or processing plant to another Pipeline or to points of utilization or storage;

"Production" means those activities, excluding Exploration and Development activities, for the removal of Hydrocarbons from a Transboundary Reservoir, including, but not limited to, treatment and processing of Hydrocarbons or other substances, the injection, reinjection or storage of any substance used for or derived from such activities, enhanced Hydrocarbon recovery activities, transfer and export of Hydrocarbons to shore, and all operations associated with well intervention, repair, maintenance, servicing, re-completion, and workovers;

"Reservoir" means a single continuous deposit of Hydrocarbons in a porous and permeable medium, trapped by a structural or stratigraphic feature;

"Transboundary Reservoir" means any Reservoir which extends across the Delimitation Line and the entirety of which is located beyond 9 nautical miles from the coastline, exploitable in whole or in part from both sides of the Delimitation Line;

"Transboundary Unit" means a single geological Hydrocarbon structure or Reservoir which extends across the Delimitation Line the entirety of which is located beyond 9 nautical miles from the coastline, approved by the Executive Agencies for joint Exploration and/or Exploitation pursuant to the terms of a unitization agreement;

"Unit Area" means the geographical area described in a Transboundary Unit, as set out in the unitization agreement; and

"Unit Operating Agreement" means an agreement made between the Licensees and the unit operator that, among other things, establishes the rights and obligations of the Licensees and the unit operator including, but not limited to, the allocation of costs and liabilities incurred in and benefits derived from operations in the Unit Area.

Article 3　Jurisdiction

Nothing in this Agreement shall be interpreted as affecting the sovereign rights and the jurisdiction which each Party has under international law over the continental shelf which appertains to it.

Article 4　Activity Near the Delimitation Line

1. Within 90 days following the entry into force of this Agreement and annually thereafter, the Parties shall consult on Exploration and Exploitation activities carried out within 3 statute miles of the Delimitation Line. Such consultation shall include the exchange of all relevant and available Geological Information associated with and derived from such activities.

2. Notwithstanding the consultation set forth in paragraph 1 of this Article, and subject to its national law:

a. if either Party is aware of the likely existence of a Transboundary Reservoir, that Party shall provide written notice to the other Party within 60 days of the date on which such Party became aware of such likely existence;

b. if either Party has approved or its Licensee has submitted for approval a plan for the collection of seismic data in an area within 3 statute miles of the Delimitation Line, that Party shall provide written notice of such plan to the other Party within 30 days of the submission and, as applicable, approval of such plan;

c. if either Party has approved or its Licensee has submitted an exploration plan applicable to an area within 3 statute miles of the Delimitation Line, that

Party shall provide written notice to the other Party within 60 days of the submission and, as applicable, approval of such plan;

d. if either Party is aware of a Hydrocarbon Occurrence near the Delimitation Line, that Party shall provide written notice to the other Party within 60 days of the date such Party becomes aware of such Hydrocarbon Occurrence;

e. if either Party's Licensee has submitted a plan to drill a well, the wellhead or borehole any portion of which will be within 3 statute miles of the Delimitation Line, that Party shall provide written notice of such fact to the other Party within 30 days of the date such Party becomes aware of such plan; and

f. if any Licensee has submitted a plan for the Development or Production of an area within 3 statute miles of the Delimitation Line, the receiving Party shall provide such plan to the other Party within 30 days of the acceptance of the submission by the receiving Party of such plan.

Article 5 Determination of Transboundary Reservoirs

1. Within 30 days following receipt of a communication under paragraph 2 subparagraphs a or d of Article 4, the Parties, through their Executive Agencies, shall initiate consultations with a view to determine whether a Transboundary Reservoir exists. The Executive Agencies shall request their Licensees to provide all Geological Information relevant to such determination and shall submit to each other all available Geological Information in their possession.

2. If the Parties have not reached a determination on the existence of a Transboundary Reservoir within 60 days of the deadline for initiating consultations in paragraph 1 of this Article, either Executive Agency may submit the issue to the Joint Commission.

3. During the consultations referred to in paragraph 1 of this Article and the pendency of further proceedings under Articles 14 through 17 of this Agreement, the relevant Executive Agency shall, subject to its national law, deliver quarterly reports to the other Executive Agency on Exploration and Exploitation activities or operations carried out by Licensees within its jurisdiction in relation to the potential Transboundary Reservoir.

CHAPTER 2　EXPLORATION AND EXPLOITATION OF ATRANSBOUNDARY RESERVOIR OR UNIT

Article 6　Unitization Agreement

1. Any joint Exploration and/or Exploitation of a Transboundary Reservoir or Unit Area pursuant to the terms of a unitization agreement must be approved by the Parties. Such joint Exploration and/or Exploitation shall be conducted pursuant to the terms of a unitization agreement negotiated and proposed by the Licensees and approved by the Executive Agencies. The Executive Agencies should develop one or more model unitization agreements for use under this Agreement.

2. The unitization agreement shall include, Inter alia:

a. The identification of the limits of the Unit Area and that of any Transboundary Reservoir;

b. The identity of the Licensees and their respective participating interests;

c. The methodology used to calculate the allocation of production;

d. A development plan for the Exploration or Exploitation of the Unit Area, including the estimated number and timing of wells, and a mechanism for delivery and approval of subsequent changes to such plan;

e. The effective date and term of the unitization agreement;

f. The identity and appointment of the unit operator, the process for resignation and removal of the unit operator, and the process for appointment of a successor unit operator;

g. Provisions regarding the transfer of interests;

h. Provisions for an accurate measurement of production;

i. Procedures for ensuring accurate payments of royalties and other proceeds;

j. Safety and environmental measures to be taken under the national laws of each Party;

k. Provisions for appropriate information sharing between the unit operator and each Party;

l. Procedures for the redetermination of the allocation of production, including a timetable or the events that trigger such redetermination.

3. Each Party shall require that, together with the submission of a proposed unitization agreement, its Licensee or the Licensees acting together through the unit operator, shall provide all available data required by a Party in order for it to review the proposed unitization agreement, and each Party shall ensure that such files and data are available to the other Party.

4. Each Executive Agency shall approve, approve with modifications or reject the proposed unitization agreement within 120 days of its receipt. Either Executive Agency may extend this period, provided that the total additional period for consideration shall not exceed 120 days. If after the end of the latest period applicable for consideration by an Executive Agency either Executive Agency has not approved, approved with modifications, or rejected the proposal, the unitization agreement shall be deemed to be rejected. At any point during the period contemplated under this paragraph either Executive Agency may refer the issue to the Joint Commission for its consideration within the remaining portion of the period.

5. Any amendment to an approved unitization agreement shall be subject to approval by the Executive Agencies. Each Executive Agency shall approve, approve with modifications or reject any proposed amendment within 30 days of its receipt. Either Executive Agency may extend this period provided that the total additional period for consideration shall not exceed 30 days. If after the end of the latest period applicable for consideration by an Executive Agency either Executive Agency has not approved, approved with modifications, or rejected the proposal, the unitization agreement shall be deemed to be rejected. At any point during the period contemplated under this paragraph either Executive Agency may refer the issue to the Joint Commission for its consideration within the remaining portion of the period.

Article 7 Management of a Transboundary Reservoir Prior to the Formation of a Transboundary Unit

1. If it is determined as a result of consultations pursuant to paragraph 1 of Article 5 or following further proceedings under Articles 14 to 17 of this Agreement that a Transboundary Reservoir exists, and a unitization agreement has not

been approved by the Parties, each Party shall take steps to facilitate Exploitation of the Transboundary Reservoir as a Transboundary Unit. Such facilitation shall include a prohibition by each Party on the commencement of production of such Transboundary Reservoir for a period from the date of determination of the Transboundary Reservoir to the end of the final period for consideration contemplated in paragraphs 2 through 5 of this Article, as applicable. If production of a Transboundary Reservoir has already commenced, the relevant Party shall take steps it deems appropriate under national law to provide that ongoing production does not unduly prejudice implementation of this Agreement.

2. If, six months following the date of determination of a Transboundary Reservoir or, alternatively, an earlier date on which the relevant Licensees have each notified the Executive Agencies that they have decided not to enter into a unitization agreement or a subsequent date agreed by the Executive Agencies in order to provide additional time for the Licensees to pursue a unitization agreement, a unitization agreement has not been approved:

a. each Party shall require its Licensee, within 60 days, to submit a proposed unitization agreement and associated Unit Operating Agreement to each Executive Agency; and

b. the Executive Agencies shall, within 30 days, jointly determine an estimate of the recoverable Hydrocarbons in the Transboundary Reservoir, under the original conditions of such Reservoir, on each side of the Delimitation Line, and jointly determine the associated allocation of production.

3. If the Executive Agencies are unable to reach the determination set out in paragraph 2 subparagraph b of this Article, such determination shall be referred to Expert Determination.

4. Following the receipt of both unitization agreements and associated Unit Operating Agreements under paragraph 2 subparagraph a of this Article, or the expiration of such period without the receipt by the Parties of both unitization agreements, and determination of the allocation of production under paragraph 2 subparagraph b or paragraph 3 of this Article, the Executive Agencies shall have 90 days to approve one of the submitted unitization agreements and associated U-

nit Operating Agreement, or an alternative unitization agreement and Unit Operating Agreement developed by the Parties. If no unitization agreement and associated Unit Operating Agreement has been approved at the end of this 90 – day period, the issue shall be referred to the Joint Commission for consideration. If no unitization agreement and associated Unit Operating Agreement has been approved within 90 days of submission of the issue to the Joint Commission, Exploitation of the Transboundary Reservoir may proceed pursuant to paragraph 5 of this Article.

5. Should any Party or Licensee fail to sign a unitization agreement or Unit Operating Agreement, as applicable, approved by the Executive Agencies or the Joint Commission within 60 days of its approval, or should the Executive Agencies or the Joint Commission fail to approve a unitization agreement and an associated Unit Operating Agreement, each Party may authorize its Licensee to proceed with Exploitation of the relevant Transboundary Reservoir subject to the determination of the recoverable Hydrocarbons pursuant to paragraph 2 subparagraph b or paragraph 3 of this Article and any plan for joint management of the Transboundary Reservoir, including any provisions agreed governing redetermination and metering, as may be agreed between the Parties. Such plan may contain provisions for the resolution of disputes pursuant to Article 16. In the event of such Exploitation, Parties will exchange production data on a monthly basis.

6. The Joint Commission shall endeavor to resolve issues related to the allocation of production of a Transboundary Reservoir not otherwise addressed in this Article.

Article 8　Allocation of Production

1. The Executive Agencies shall require the unit operator, on behalf of the Licensees and 60 days prior to the commencement of production from a Transboundary Reservoir, to initiate consultations on the allocation of production to each side of the Delimitation Line by submitting a proposal for the allocation of production for approval by the Executive Agencies to be applied from first production. The Executive Agencies shall, prior to any decision not in agreement with the proposal, jointly consult with the unit operator.

2. Each Executive Agency shall ensure that all relevant and available infor-

mation from the Unit Area related to the proposal is made available in a timely manner to the other Executive Agency.

3. If the Executive Agencies are unable to reach agreement on this initial allocation of production within 30 days from the date of the initiation of consultations in accordance with paragraph 1 of this Article, the matter shall be addressed by the Joint Commission.

Article 9　Redetermination of the Allocation of Production

1. Any redetermination of the allocation of production of a Transboundary Reservoir shall be conducted pursuant to the unitization agreement or as agreed pursuant to Article 7 paragraph 5. The Parties shall endeavor to ensure that provisions for redetermination shall provide for fair and equitable allocation of production of each Transboundary Reservoir. Such terms shall be contained in the unitization agreement and shall be applicable over its full term.

2. Each Executive Agency shall ensure that, subject to national law, all relevant and available information related to a redetermination of allocation of a Transboundary Reservoir is made available in a timely manner to the other Executive Agency. The Executive Agencies shall, prior to any decision not in agreement with a redetermination proposal from a unit operator, jointly consult with the unit operator.

3. If the Executive Agencies are unable to reach agreement on any redetermination of the allocation of production within 60 days following the initiation of a process for redetermination as contemplated under paragraph 1 of this Article, the matter shall be addressed by the Joint Commission.

CHAPTER 3　OPERATING AGREEMENT

Article 10　Unit Operator

1. The Executive Agencies shall ensure that a unit operator for a Transboundary Unit is designated by agreement between the Licensees. The designation or change of the unit operator shall be subject to the approval of the Executive Agencies.

2. The unit operator will act on behalf of the Licensees.

Article 11 Unit Operating Agreement

1. Each Executive Agency shall require its Licensees to enter into a Unit Operating Agreement for the Exploration or Exploitation of a Transboundary Unit in accordance with this Agreement.

2. The Executive Agencies shall require that the Licensees submit an executed Unit Operating Agreement prior to the approval of the unitization agreement.

3. In case of a conflict between the Unit Operating Agreement and the unitization agreement, the unitization agreement shall prevail, or between the unitization agreement and this Agreement, the provisions of this Agreement shall prevail.

Article 12 Faculties near the Delimitation Line

1. The Parties shall use their best efforts to facilitate cooperation between Licensees in activities related to the Exploration and Exploitation of a Transboundary Unit, including the facilitation of access to and use of Facilities near the Delimitation Line, and shall not prevent or impede such cooperation by unreasonably withholding necessary Permits.

2. The use of Facilities near the Delimitation Line may include, inter alia, access to and interconnection with a Pipeline and physical access to Pipeline capacity and, where appropriate, to Facilities supplying technical services incidental to such access.

3. The Parties shall facilitate, subject to their respective national law, access to Facilities for workers engaged in any activities related to a Transboundary Unit.

Article 13 Fiscal Terms

Income arising from the Exploitation of Transboundary Reservoirs shall be taxed in accordance with the legislation of the United Mexican States and the United States of America respectively, as well as the Convention between the Government of the United States of America and the Government of the United Mexican States for the Avoidance of Double Taxation and the Prevention of Fiscal Evasion with respect to Taxes on Income and Capital, signed on September 18th, 1992, as amended (and as may be amended in the future), or any Convention superseding that Convention as the Parties may enter into in the future.

CHAPTER 4　INSTITUTIONAL ARRANGEMENTS

Article 14　Joint Commission

1. A Joint Commission shall be established no later than 90 days after entry into force of this Agreement to assist the Executive Agencies in administering this Agreement.

2. Each Party, through its Executive Agency, shall appoint one representative and one alternate representative to the Joint Commission. Each Party may provide assistance, including experts, to its representative as it deems necessary.

3. In exercising its functions, the Joint Commission may establish working groups or expert groups, seek the advice of non-governmental groups or individuals, and take such other actions as the Parties may agree.

4. The Joint Commission should endeavour to adopt its rules of procedure no later than 90 days after it is established.

5. The Joint Commission shall be the competent body to examine any dispute or other matter referred to it by either Executive Agency relating to the interpretation and implementation of this Agreement, or any unforeseen issues arising under this Agreement.

6. If the Joint Commission is unable within 60 days to resolve all differences concerning the allocation of production pursuant to Article 8, or the reallocation of production pursuant to Article 9, either Party may submit the dispute for Expert Determination. If the Joint Commission is unable within 60 days to resolve all differences related to the determination of a Transboundary Reservoir pursuant to paragraph 2 of Article 5, and relevant data is available from a well in the prospective Transboundary Reservoir on each side of the Delimitation Line, either Party may submit the dispute for Expert Determination.

7. If the Joint Commission is unable within 60 days to resolve all differences concerning any dispute referred to it by the Executive Agencies relating to the interpretation and implementation of this Agreement that is not addressed in paragraph 6 of this Article or referred to it under paragraphs 4 or 5 of Article 6 paragraph 4 of Article 7, either Party may resort to the dispute settlement provisions

in Articles 15 or 17. The Joint Commission will have 30 days in which to consider the final recommendation in any arbitration instituted pursuant to Article 17. If the Joint Commission is unable to resolve any remaining differences within that time, the dispute will be returned to the Parties.

8. The Parties will refrain from action with regard to any dispute referred to the Joint Commission or to Expert Determination or dispute resolution under this Agreement where it is reasonably foreseeable that such action would prejudice the implementation of any decision related to the dispute until the dispute resolution procedures are complete.

CHAPTER 5 SETTLEMENT OF DISPUTES

Article 15 Consultations and Mediation

1. The Parties shall make every effort to resolve any disagreement relating to the interpretation and implementation of this Agreement through consultations as rapidly as possible. Either Party may initiate consultations through a written request to the other Party. Unless the Parties otherwise agree, the Parties shall consult within 20 days of delivery of the request.

2. If the Parties do not resolve a disagreement that is not subject to Expert Determination within 120 days of the delivery of the request for consultations, either Party may refer the disagreement to arbitration pursuant to Article 17 within 30 days.

3. The Parties may also agree to submit any disagreement relating to the interpretation and implementation of this Agreement to non – binding mediation by a neutral third party in addition to, or in lieu of, the procedures set out in this Article and in Article 17.

Article 16 Expert Determination

1. The Joint Commission shall, within 180 days of the adoption of its rules of procedure, establish arrangements for the appointment of the expert and terms of engagement, including, in particular, provisions governing compensation and the protection of confidentiality.

2. In the event a dispute is submitted to Expert Determination and the Joint

Commission has not established the arrangements set out in paragraph 1 of this Article:

a. each Party shall, within 30 days of the date of submission of the dispute and at its own expense, choose an appointing expert.

b. the appointing experts shall, within 30 days, appoint the expert and determine the terms of engagement of the expert, including compensation, according to prevailing standards and strict protections of Confidential Data.

c. in such circumstances the costs of Expert Determination shall be shared equally by the Parties.

3. Each Party shall promptly provide all information in its possession, or that it has the legal authority to obtain from its Licensees, that exists and is required by the expert in order to reach a decision.

4. The Parties shall ensure that the expert will maintain the strictest impartiality and transparency. All communications between a Party and the expert, in any form, other than Confidential Data, shall be provided to the other Party.

5. The Parties shall provide that, within 90 days of the expert's appointment, the expert will provide a preliminary decision to the Joint Commission together with a detailed explanation of how the decision was reached. Thereafter, there will be a period of 60 days, or such other period as the Joint Commission may agree, from the date that the preliminary decision is communicated to the Joint Commission during which either Party may seek clarification and/or make further submissions to the expert for his consideration. The final determination of the expert along with a detailed explanation shall be communicated in writing to the Joint Commission within 30 days of the end of this period.

6. Notwithstanding paragraph 5 of this Article, the Parties shall provide that referrals to the expert under Article 7 paragraph 3 shall be resolved within 30 days of their receipt by the expert and that the expert's determination shall be provided directly to the Executive Agencies.

7. Expert Determination proceedings will be confidential. Except as required by either Party's domestic law, the Parties shall treat, and shall ensure that the expert treats, any information provided for the determination, any written and oral

communications related to the determination, and both the preliminary decision and final decision as confidential.

8. Notwithstanding paragraphs 4 and 7 of this Article, upon any preliminary determination by the expert that a Transboundary Reservoir exists, all information used by the expert in reaching such determination and all information provided to the expert after such date with respect to such Transboundary Reservoir shall be provided to both Parties. Such information shall be maintained as confidential by the Parties pursuant to the terms of this Agreement, subject to national law.

9. Determinations of the expert shall be final and binding on the Parties.

Article 17　Arbitration

If any dispute regarding the interpretation and implementation of this Agreement that is not subject to Expert Determination cannot be resolved by the Joint Commission or through consultations, either Party may submit the dispute to arbitration.

The Joint Commission shall, within 180 days of the adoption of its rules of procedure, establish an arbitration mechanism for the implementation of this Article.

CHAPTER 6　Inspections, Safety, and Environmental Protection

Article 18　Inspections

1. Subject to applicable national law, each Party shall, under procedures to be developed and agreed under this Agreement, have the right to inspect Facilities in a Unit Area approved pursuant to this Agreement.

2. To enable Inspectors of each Party to safeguard their respective interests with respect to safety, environmental and fiscal matters, the Executive Agencies shall develop specific procedures, subject to national law, for:

(a) consultation among Inspectors of each Party;

(b) timely access to information relevant to inspection activities; and

(c) physical access to Unit Areas for the purpose of inspecting activities therein under a joint inspection regime, including access to metering systems, wherever located.

3. The Inspectors of each Party shall act in cooperation and consult with In-

spectors of the. other Party to achieve compliance with applicable safety and environmental standards.

4. An Inspector of one Party may, with regard to Facilities located in the Unit Area, request an Inspector of the other Party to exercise his or her powers to ensure compliance with the applicable safety and environmental standards and requirements whenever it appears that circumstances so warrant. In the event of any disagreement between the Inspectors of the Parties, or the refusal of the Inspector of one Party to take action at the request of the Inspector of the other Party, the matter shall be referred to the Executive Agencies.

5. If it appears that it is necessary for the purpose of averting risk to life or serious personal injury or significant damage to the environment, and that circumstances do not permit the Inspectors to consult with the Executive Agencies, the Inspector with jurisdiction over the activities giving rise to such risk shall, as authorized under national law, order the immediate cessation of any or all operations upon the request of the other Inspector. Immediately thereafter, but not more than 4 hours following the ordered cessation of activity, the Inspectors shall notify the Executive Agencies of such action and the reasons therefore, and the Executive Agencies shall immediately consult regarding actions necessary to address the risk. Nothing in this paragraph shall prevent the right of each Party to authorize the resumption of operations of the relevant Facilities.

Article 19 Safety and Environmental Protection

1. The Parties shall adopt, where appropriate, common safety and environmental standards and requirements applicable to activity contemplated under this Agreement. In any event, the Parties shall strive to ensure that their respective standards and requirements are compatible where necessary for the safe, effective, and environmentally responsible implementation of this Agreement.

2. The Executive Agencies shall develop procedures for the implementation of this Article.

3. The Parties recognize the importance of their existing international obligations with respect to oil pollution preparedness, response, and cooperation, and are to review their implementation of such obligations in light of the activity con-

templated under this Agreement in order to ensure an appropriate framework for ongoing cooperation.

CHAPTER 7 FINAL CLAUSES

Article 20 Confidentially

To the extent consistent with their national laws, the Parties shall maintain confidential, and obligate their Licensees to maintain confidential, all Confidential Data and other information obtained from the other Party or its Licensees in accordance with this Agreement.

Article 21 Amendments

1. This Agreement may be amended at any time by mutual written agreement of the Parties.

2. Amendments shall enter into force in accordance with the procedure established under Article 22 of this Agreement.

Article 22 Entry into force

The Parties shall so notify each other in writing when the necessary internal procedures have been completed to bring this Agreement into force. This Agreement shall enter into force 60 days after the date of the later notification.

Article 23 Termination

1. This Agreement may be terminated by mutual written agreement or by either Party at any time upon 180 days written notice to the other Party.

2. Notwithstanding termination of this Agreement, unless otherwise agreed by the Parties:

a. the provisions of this Agreement shall continue to apply to any unitization agreement, Unit Operating Agreement, or other agreement entered into under this Agreement and in effect at the time of termination, for the duration of such agreement, and to any such agreement submitted to or otherwise under review by the Parties pursuant to this Agreement at the time of termination, for the duration of such agreement;

b. the provisions of this Agreement shall continue to govern the relationship between the Parties with respect to any unitization agreement, Unit Operating Agreement, or other agreement entered into under this Agreement and in effect at the time of termination for the duration of such agreements;

c. the provisions of this Agreement shall continue to apply to any License issued by a Party after entry into force and prior to termination of this Agreement;

d. the provisions of this Agreement shall continue to apply to the Exploitation of any Transboundary Reservoir undertaken pursuant to paragraph 5 of Article 7; and

e. the obligations of the Parties set forth in Article 20 concerning confidentiality shall continue to apply.

3. Upon any notice provided under paragraph 1 of this Article, the Parties shall initiate consultations for the development of a new agreement to address the joint exploration and exploitation of transboundary reservoirs.

Article 24　Termination of the Moratorium on Hydrocarbon Activity in the Boundary Area in the Western Gap of the Gulf of Mexico

Upon entry into force of this Agreement, the period of any moratorium on the authorization or permitting of petroleum or natural gas drilling or exploration of the continental shelf within the boundary "Area" as established by Article 4, paragraph 1, of the 2000 Treaty on the Continental Shelf and extended by any subsequent exchanges of notes shall be terminated.

Article 25　Relationship with other Agreements

With the exception of Article 24, nothing in this Agreement shall affect the rights and obligations of the Parties with respect to other international agreements to which they are both party.

Done at Los Cabos on the twentieth day of February of two thousand and twelve, in the English and Spanish languages, both texts being equally authentic.

For the United States of America:
Hillary Rodham Clinton
Secretary of State

For the United Mexican States:
Patricia Espinosa Cantellano
Minister of Foreign Affairs

（十七）2012年塞舌尔和毛里求斯共同开发案

1.《塞舌尔共和国政府与毛里求斯共和国政府关于共同管理马斯克林高原地区大陆架的条约》

（2012年3月13日订于瓦克阿克拉里斯官）

申钟秀译，黄文博校

为了促进两个岛国各自经济与社会的长期可持续发展，以保护当代人与后代的利益；

为了维护、重申与深化两国之间的相互尊重、善意、友谊与合作；

鉴于大陆架重叠区域延伸到两国依据2008年7月29日《毛里求斯共和国政府与塞舌尔共和国政府关于两国间专属经济区划界条约》建立的专属经济区之外；

考虑到两国基于《塞舌尔共和国政府与毛里求斯共和国政府关于向联合国大陆架界限委员会联合注册的框架条约》进行的合作，该条约签订于2008年9月18日，随后进行了修订，依据1982年12月10日在蒙特哥湾签署的《联合国海洋法公约》（《公约》）第76条第8段，两国于2008年12月1日向联合国大陆架界限委员会（委员会）提出关于马斯克林地区的联合注册（联合注册）；

还考虑到2011年3月30日委员会采纳了这两个国家的建议，确认了其对大陆架地区拥有的权利，正如《大陆架界限委员会对2008年12月1

日毛里求斯与塞舌尔关于马斯克林高原地区的联合注册的建议》中所包含的权利；

根据《公约》第 83 条规定，海岸相向国家间大陆架的界线应在国际法的基础上以协定划定，以便得到公平的解决，并且在没有划界的情况下有关各国应基于谅解与合作的精神，尽一切努力做出实质性的临时安排，并且这种安排并不影响对大陆架延伸区域进行划界的最后决定；

认识到为两国在马斯克林高原地区大陆架依照国际法共同行使主权权利和管辖权提供一项公平与合作的法律依据的重要性；

重申 2012 年 3 月 13 日《关于共同行使马斯克林高原地区大陆架主权权利的条约》，依据该条约缔约各方划定马斯克林高原地区大陆架的外部界线，并就旨在共同探索大陆架与开发自然资源的共同行使主权权利达成协议；

认识到以符合可持续与预防原则保护大陆架海洋环境与生物多样性的方式来共同管理大陆架自然资源的重要性；

致力于达成一项国际协定，以便为共同管理马斯克林高原地区大陆架提供一个公平有效的框架；

双方达成协定如下。

第一部分 初步措施

第一条 定义

依本条约：

（a）"当局"指条约第四条中的指定当局；

（b）"生物勘探"指对生物资源的查明，这些资源包括但不限于化合物，基因及产品，以及对商业发展有价值的物理性能；

（c）"委员会"指依据条约第四条设立的联合委员会；

（d）"大陆架"的含义见《公约》第 76 条中所包含的内容；

（e）"承包人"指某个法人、公司或者其他实体，这些实体能够承担同被充分授权的指定当局进行缔约的有限责任；

（f）"《公约》"指 1982 年 12 月 10 日缔结于蒙特哥湾的《联合国海洋法公约》；

（g）"刑法"指在任一缔约方领土范围内生效的刑事法律，包括对涉及犯罪，调查、起诉犯罪，或处罚罪犯（包括执行法院判决）的事项做出安排的实体法与程序法，以及为了这一目的，调查包括进入共同管理区的设施与结构，对犯罪嫌疑人实施搜查、审问与逮捕；

（h）"理事会"指根据条约第四条设立的部长理事会；

（i）"初步加工"指已经进行到可以将石油从生产设备移走的加工过程，还可能包括诸如排除水、挥发物及其他杂质的过程；

（j）"JMA"指根据条约第三条设立的共同管理区；

（k）"矿物"包括任何自然形成的元素、化合物与混合物，经过地理或生物化学过程形成的非结晶体与结晶体（包括液态结晶化合物），以及任何自然形成的混合物，包括煤炭、黏土、蒸发岩、砂砾、石灰岩、油页岩、岩石以及多金属结核；

（l）"自然资源"指大陆架海床及其底土中的矿物、石油和其他非生物资源，以及正处于捕捞阶段的定栖于海床，或处于海床之下，或除非与海床或底土有持续物理作用而不可移动的生物组织；

（m）"自然资源活动"指经授权的或者依据合同、许可或特许实施的在共同管理区勘探和开发自然资源的各种活动，包括但不限于开发、初步加工、捕捞、生产、运输和交易，也包括为此所做的计划和准备活动；

（n）"自然资源法规"指条约第八条提及的法规；

（o）"自然资源项目"指任何经共同管理区指定当局批准而进行的自然资源活动；

（p）"石油"指任何自然形成的气态的、液态的或者固态的碳氢化合物，及任何自然形成的气态的、液态的或者固态的碳氢化合物的混合物，以及与这些碳氢化合物相关的其他物质，包括已经进入（油气）储藏的石油；

（q）"石油生产"指通过石油活动对从（油气）储藏中提取的石油进行初步加工；

（r）"油气储藏"意指存在于由岩石、水及其他物质构成的地理单元中的石油堆积物，这一堆积物与另一石油堆积物之间没有液体或者气体的压力连通；

（s）"税收法规"指条约第六条提及的法规；

（t）"条约"指本条约，包括附件A－D及缔约方接下来将缔结的成为条约组成部分的任何附件。

第二条　条约不得损害任何一方的权益

（a）该条约使《公约》中所包含的国际法得以实施，《公约》第83条要求海岸相向或相邻国家间在国际法的基础上尽一切努力以实质性的临时协议对大陆架的最后划界做出临时性的安排，该条约旨在履行这一义务。

（b）条约中所包含的任何事项，及条约生效期间发生的任何行为，都不应做出损害或者影响缔约方关于其大陆架权利与大陆架划界的法律地位或权利的解释。

第二部分　共同管理区

第三条　共同管理区

（a）共同管理区（JMA）根据2012年3月13日缔结的《关于共同行使马斯克林高原地区大陆架主权权利的条约》第2条中描述的共同区块而建立，附件A中的地图有描述。

（b）缔约方应共同控制、管理与促进共同管理区大陆架的勘探及对其自然资源的保护、开发与开采。

（c）在共同管理区开展自然资源活动应遵照指定当局的指令，通过符合条约规定的方式，包括许可或遵照当局与承包人之间的合同。本条同样适用于继承者或此类合同的受托人。

（d）缔约方应认定任何人在共同管理区里依据其本国法律从事资源活动为犯罪，除非依据本条约。

第三部分　机构与管理安排

第四条　管理部门

（a）设立由部长理事会、共同委员会和指定当局组成的三级联合管理结构。

（b）部长理事会：

ⅰ. 设立部长理事会。部长理事会应由缔约国任命的相同数目的部长组成。

ⅱ. 部长理事会应处理任一缔约方提起的与条约的执行有关的任何问题。其也应处理本条（c）项下的任何问题。

ⅲ．任一缔约方或委员会有要求，部长理事会都应召开会议。

ⅳ．部长理事会的所有决议须经协商一致通过。如果理事会不能解决某一问题，任一缔约方可援引第二十一条规定的争端解决程序。

ⅴ．部长理事会的决议唯有以书面记录的方式且由每一缔约方至少一名成员签字方有效。

ⅵ．部长理事会应设定其运行的程序，包括休会时的决议程序及组织电视电话会议的程序。

（c）联合委员会

ⅰ．联合委员会由缔约双方任命的数目相同的委员组成。联合委员会应为共同管理区内的石油与其他自然资源活动制定政策法规并监督指定当局的工作。

ⅱ．附件 C 中不完全列举了联合委员会的权力和职能，且在必要时可随时做出修改。

ⅲ．联合委员会可将问题提交给部长理事会解决。

ⅳ．联合委员会应轮流或按约定的其他方式在缔约方至少一年开会一次，并且每次会议由双方共同主持。

ⅴ．联合委员会的决议须经一致同意方得通过。

（d）指定当局

ⅰ．联合委员会应设立指定当局（简称"当局"）。

ⅱ．指定当局应为独立法人，因为该法定资格是其依据缔约国法律行使权力和职能所必需的。其有权缔结、获得和处置动产和不动产，并有权制定并参与诉讼程序。

ⅲ．指定当局应对联合委员会负责，并执行共同管理区的日常监督与管理工作。

ⅳ．附件 D 不完全列举了更多的指定当局的具体权力和职能，并确认了指定当局其他额外的一些权力和职能。指定当局也具有委员会可能授予的其他权力和职能。

ⅴ．指定当局的费用由缔约方平等承担，包括最终通过自然资源法所募集到的款项。

ⅵ．指定当局在下列事项上享有豁免：

（1）收入所得税或营业税，根据情况而定，及

（2）依据缔约国领土范围内现行有效的法律征收的关税、消费税、增值税（VAT）、捐税和其他类似为官方用途而进口的税，以及条约签字之日以后征收的新增的或取代现有收税的任何相同或相似的税收。

ⅶ. 指定当局的人员

（1）如果其为一方当事国国民，其收入、津贴及指定当局给付的与其受雇佣相关的其他报酬便受该国税收法律的支配。为此，"国民"一词包括任一缔约国在本国税收法规中定义的居民。

（2）首次赴任一缔约方境内的指定当局就职时，如果不是访缔约方的居民，依据联合委员会制定的条款，对进口家具及其他家庭和个人用品（包括他们自己的或他们订购的归个人或单位使用的一台机动车辆）应免除关税、消费税、增值税、捐税及其他类似税种（服务付费除外）。这些物品应于该官员首次入境后6个月内进口，但在特殊情况下缔约国应分别准予延期。对于那些应官员们要求而已获取的或已进口的免税物品不应以抛弃、出售、出借和出租及其他方法处理，除非经其所在国的事前同意。

（e）部长理事会、联合委员会及指定当局的任何成员对共同管理区的自然资源都不享有财政及个人利益。

第五条　收益的分配

（a）缔约方应平等分享从共同管理区开展的自然资源活动中获取的利益，因此，收益的50%应交予毛里求斯，另50%交予塞舌尔。

（b）第十条第（d）款、第（v）款中的费用与其他收益不足以弥补指定当局依据条约支出的费用时，该差额由双方依照（a）项中的相同比例承担。

（c）第十条中的联合经营产生的收益不适用（a）项，除非经缔约方同意。

第六条　税收法规

（a）缔约方应就适用于共同管理区自然资源活动收入的税收法规达成协议。

（b）自然资源项目进行期间，任一缔约方都不得违反适用于该项目的税收法规，缔约方相互同意的除外。

第七条　国内法的适用

与以下内容直接或间接相关的事项适用任一缔约国的国内法：

ⅰ. 共同管理区大陆架的勘探与共同管理区自然资源的开发与开采，及

ⅱ. 关于、涉及或产生于共同管理区自然资源活动的行为、问题、情况与事项。

任一缔约国都应把共同管理区视为和作为自身领土的组成部分。

第八条 自然资源法规

（a）缔约方应就包括开发、开采、收获、保存及出口共同管理区的自然资源在内的勘探共同管理区大陆架的法规达成协议。

（b）必要时联合委员会应采取临时性的安排以待符合（a）项的自然资源法规的适用。

第四部分 管道与联合经营

第九条 管道

（a）从共同管理区输出石油的输油管道的建设和运营应经联合委员会的批准。

（b）缔约国应对从共同管理区输出石油的管道的安置点到其着陆点的条款和条件互相协商。

（c）一国对位于其领土内的管道行使管辖权。

（d）如果建设一条从共同管理区到任一缔约国的输油管道，管道经过的国家不应反对或阻碍联合委员会关于管道的决定，除非管道建设对共同管理区现存自然资源项目有不利的经济或物理影响。

（e）产自共同管理区的石油与产自跨越共同管理区边界线油田的石油在任何时间都有权经共同管理区内的管道运输及从共同管理区运输。

（f）管道对产自共同管理区的石油必须是开放使用的。这种开放使用的安排应符合良好的国际实践。如果某一缔约方拥有对管道的管辖权，其应就管道的使用同另一缔约方协商。

第十条 联合经营

（a）任何延伸出或跨越了共同管理区边界线进入缔约双方或一方专属经济区内的油气储藏或单一矿床，在勘探、开发和管理的目的下都应被视为单一实体。

（b）缔约方应秉承善意，果断行动，就最有效管理和开发（a）项中

提及的油气储藏和矿床及公平分享开发收益的方式达成协议。

第十一条 调查

任一缔约方都拥有调查权,包括对促进共同管理区自然资源活动的水道学的、地理学的、地球物理学的和地震学的调查。在行使这些权力的过程中,缔约方应:

ⅰ. 将任何拟进行的调查通知给指定当局;

ⅱ. 在调查的过程中进行合作,包括提供必要的陆上设施;及

ⅲ. 交换与共同管理区自然资源活动相关的信息。

第五部分 环境保护、生物多样性与生物勘探

第十二条 海床海洋环境保护

(a) 缔约国应在保护共同管理区自然资源活动上加强合作,以确保海床生物多样性,防止污染及其他由共同管理区自然资源活动产生的或与之相关的对环境的不良风险。

(b) 缔约国应在合作保护共同管理区海底环境与海洋生物多样性中坚持预防原则。这应包括对在共同管理区海床的上覆水域捕鱼活动采取的预防措施,如果区域内类似捕鱼的活动对共同管理区海床与底土的自然资源产生了直接影响,或带来重要风险的话。

(c) 缔约国应加强合作以保护共同管理区海底的海洋栖息地与相关的生态群落。这应包括识别环境标准与识别海底海洋保护区,参考下列要素:

ⅰ. 海床海洋物种与生物群落的地理分布;

ⅱ. 这些生物群落的结构;

ⅲ. 与物理环境及化学环境的关系;

ⅳ. 自然生态与基因变异性,及

ⅴ. 包括捕鱼与自然资源活动在内的对生态系统构成的自然和人为影响。

(d) 当发生于共同管理区的海洋环境污染扩散超出共同管理区之时,缔约国应依据最佳国际实践、标准和程序加强合作,采取果断有效的行动阻止、减轻和消除这种污染;

(e) 指定当局应颁布规定以保护共同管理区的生物资源与海底环境,

并应制订意外事故应对方案以应对共同管理区自然资源活动中可能产生的污染；

（f）缔约方应对共同管理区内自然资源活动造成的海洋污染所带来的损失和费用承担责任，依据

ⅰ．它们的合同、特许、许可或其他类型的依据条约授予的权利；及

ⅱ．提出要求的缔约一方的法律。

第十三条 生物调查与生物勘探

（a）任一缔约方都有权为了条约第十二条的目的进行生物调查和生物勘探，以识别和检查对共同管理区商业发展有价值的或有保护意义的生物资源。

（b）缔约方应：

ⅰ．将拟进行的调查通知指定当局；

ⅱ．在这种生物调查与生物勘探中进行合作，包括提供必要的陆上设施；及

ⅲ．交换与共同管理区生物调查与生物勘探有关的信息。

第六部分 雇佣、健康与安全及国内法的适用

第十四条 雇佣

缔约方应采取合适的措施确保缔约国国民在共同管理区工作的优先权，促进国民在培训与雇佣机会上享有优先权。

第十五条 工人的健康与安全

（a）指定当局应为在共同管理区设施与构筑物上工作的工人制定符合国际公认的标准与最佳实践的职业健康与安全标准和程序，缔约国在需要时应适用。

（b）相似的职业健康、安全标准和程序应适用于共同管理区内从事自然资源活动的所有工人。

第十六条 刑事管辖权

（a）缔约国应为处理发生于共同管理区的犯罪查明不同的选项，在此项工作完成之前，本条规定应适用于发生于共同管理区的犯罪行为。

（b）缔约国的公民或居民关于或发生于共同管理区自然资源活动的作为与不作为犯罪，应受其国籍国或居住国刑事法律的管辖。

（c）尽管有（e）项的规定，非任一缔约国居民的第三国国民，应受任一缔约国关于或发生于共同管理区自然资源活动的作为与不作为犯罪的刑事法律的管辖。如果因同一作为与不作为依据其他国家的法律或主管当局所在国的法律，此人已被判决免于处罚，或被主管法庭无罪释放，或已经接受了处罚，则不应受任一缔约国刑事程序法律的管辖。

（d）（c）项提到的案件中，如有必要缔约方应共同协商适用何国刑事法律，应考虑受害人的国籍与所涉犯罪影响最大国的利益。

（e）行驶于共同管理区上覆水域的船舶上的作为与不作为犯罪，应受船旗国刑事法律的管辖。

（f）缔约国应彼此给予帮助与合作，包括通过协商一致或酌情安排执行本条规定的刑事法律，包括获取证据与信息。

（g）任一缔约国都应识别所涉犯罪的受害人所属国的利益，应在法律允许的范围内将对所涉犯罪采取的行动通知该国。

（h）缔约国应对允许一方公务员帮助另一国执行刑事法律做出安排。这些帮助包括拘留依据（b）项属另一缔约国管辖的人，这种拘留持续到将此人实际上移交给该另一缔约国为止。

第十七条　海关法、移民与检疫

（a）依据（c）、（e）、（f）与（g）项，缔约国应对进入其领土或离开其领土进入共同管理区的人员、设备与货物，适用符合国际通用标准与最佳实践的海关、移民与检疫法律；缔约国应做出安排以方便这种进出。

（b）除非有缔约国的特殊授权，缔约国应确保没有首先进入缔约国的人员、设备与货物，不得进入共同管理区内，并确保其雇员与其转包商的雇员得到指定当局的授权方可进入共同管理区。

（c）任一缔约国可要求另一缔约国就特定人员、设备与货物进入共同管理区的问题进行协商，以管理这些人员、设备与货物的转移。

（d）该条的任何规定都不影响任一缔约国对未经其授权而进入共同管理区的人员、设备与货物适用海关、移民与检疫管理。缔约国可制定安排以协调此项权力的行使。

（e）为了与自然资源活动相关的目的而进入共同管理区的货物与设备免征关税、消费税、增值税及其他类似税收。

（f）为了与自然资源活动相关的目的进入共同管理区的货物与设备离

开或经过任一缔约国领土时免征关税、消费税、增值税及其他类似税收。

（g）为了永久进入缔约国而离开共同管理区的货物与设备可被征收关税、消费税、增值税、捐税及该缔约国的其他类似税收。

第十八条　资源产业船舶的安全、操作标准及其船员

（a）除非有条约的相反规定，具有从事共同管理区自然资源活动的缔约国国籍的船舶应受其国籍国关于安全和操作标准及船员法规的约束。

（b）悬挂非缔约国国旗从事共同管理区自然资源活动的船舶，应受相关的国际安全和操作标准及船员法规的约束。

第七部分　监督、安全与救援

第十九条　监督与安全措施

（a）为了本条约的目的，缔约国应具有对共同管理区自然资源活动进行监督的权力。

（b）缔约国应合作与协调任何依据（a）项进行的监督活动，并交换共同管理区自然资源活动可能受到的威胁或安全事故的信息。

（c）缔约方应为迅速有效应对共同管理区的安全事故做出安排。

第二十条　搜索与营救

经指定当局的要求及依照本条约规定，缔约方应在共同管理区的搜索与营救行动中开展合作与援助，考虑适用由有资质的国际组织确立的通行的国际法、规定与程序。

第八部分　争端的解决，条约的有效期及生效

第二十一条　争端的解决

（a）除属于条约第六条涉及的税收法规范围内的争端及应依照缔约方协商一致的法规解决的争端外，与条约的解释和适用有关的任何争端都应尽可能地通过互相协商友好地解决。

（b）任何未通过（a）项所列的方式解决的争端，及任何未能依据第四条第（b）款第（ⅱ）项解决的与条约的执行有关的问题，经任一缔约方的要求，均应提交给依据附件B所列程序设立的仲裁法庭。

第二十二条　条约的修订

本条约可于任何时间通过缔约国间的协议进行修订。

第二十三条 条约的有效期

（a）本条约在缔约国对大陆架的永久划界达成协议之前或自条约生效之日起 30 年内持续有效，以时间早者为准。

（b）本条约可通过缔约国间的协定更新。

（c）本条约失效后根据本条约开启的自然资源项目应依据条约规定的条件继续进行。

第二十四 条约的生效

（a）任一缔约方都应通过互换外交照会的方式，将法律规定的条约生效所需程序的完成告知对方。条约自后收到通知的日期生效。

（b）条约生效后，即发生效力，自签字之日起所有条文都应适用。

由各国政府完全授权的签署人签署条约，可兹证明。

2012 年 3 月 13 日，签署于毛里求斯瓦克阿克拉里斯宫，约文采用英语，一式二份。

毛里求斯共和国	塞舌尔共和国政府
H. E. 詹姆斯·阿里克斯·米歇尔	翁·纳温卡德拉·兰古利博士，GCSK，FRCP
总统	首相

附件 A （条约第三条）

共同管理区的划设与描述

第三条中提及的共同管理区，包含 2012 年 3 月 13 日缔结的《关于共同行使马斯克林高原地区大陆架主权权利的条约》第二条中的列出的大陆架地区。插图如下：

附件 B （条约第二十一条）

争端解决程序

（a）依据第二十一条第（b）款，争端应提交给的仲裁法庭（仲裁庭）应由三人组成，该三人的任命如下：

（i）任一缔约方均应任命一名仲裁员；

（ii）在第二个仲裁员被任命 60 日以内，由缔约国任命的该两名仲裁

员应挑选一名第三国的国民或永久居民为第三个仲裁员；以及

（ⅲ）在第三名仲裁员被选定 60 日以内，缔约国应批准关于由哪个仲裁员担任仲裁庭主席的选定。

（b）仲裁程序的建立在通过外交渠道给予通知的基础上，应由提起程序的缔约国通知另一缔约国。通知应包括：

ⅰ．主张根据的总结性陈述；

ⅱ．救济的性质；及

ⅲ．由提起程序的缔约方任命的仲裁员的名字。

在被通知后的 60 天内，被诉缔约方应将其任命的仲裁员的名字通知给提起程序的缔约方。

（c）如果在（a）款（ⅱ）与（ⅲ）项及（b）款规定的期限内，必需的任命还没有任命或必需的批准还没有批准，缔约方可要求国际海洋法法庭（ITLOS）庭长做出必要的任命；如果庭长为缔约国的国民或永久居民或因其他原因不能做出任命，应由副庭长做出任命。如果副庭长为缔约方的国民或永久居民，则由非为缔约方国民或永久居民的国际海洋法法庭成员做出任命。

（d）当依据该附件规定任命的仲裁员辞职或不能行使职权时，应以与规定的任命原仲裁员相同的方式任命新的仲裁员，新仲裁员享有原仲裁员享有的全部权利与义务。

（e）此时，仲裁庭主席应拟定召集会议的时间和地点，由仲裁庭最终决定。

（f）依据缔约方达成的协议，仲裁庭裁决与其权限相关的各种问题并决定其程序。

（g）在裁决做出前的任何诉讼阶段都应建议缔约方善意解决争端。仲裁庭应依据条约和相关国际法的规定，通过多数票做出裁决。

（h）缔约方均应承担与任命仲裁员相关的费用，及其自身准备和提起仲裁的费用。与仲裁庭主席及与仲裁有关的费用应由缔约方平等负担。

（i）仲裁庭应对缔约方公平聆讯。仲裁庭可在任一缔约方违约的情况下做出裁决。任何情况下仲裁庭都应在仲裁庭主席召集会议的 6 个月内做出裁决。裁决应以书面形式做出并陈述其法律依据。应发给缔约方签章的裁决副本。

（j）仲裁裁决是终局性的并对缔约方具有法律效力。

附件 C 【条约第四条第（c）款第（ⅱ）项】

联合委员会的权力与职能

1. 联合委员会的权力与职能包括：

（a）设立指定当局；

（b）对指定当局行使权力与履行职务做出指令；

（c）授予指定当局其他权力与职能；

（d）颁布应用于共同管理区的税收法规与自然资源法规，包括必要时的修正案与临时性安排；

（e）批准指定当局财政收支评估报告；

（f）批准指定当局现行有效的规则、规定与程序；

（g）要求对指定当局进行账册审计；

（h）审议与采纳指定当局的年度报告。

附件 D 【条约第四条第（d）款第（ⅳ）项】

指定当局的权力与职能

指定当局的权力与职能包括：

（a）依据条约及任何依据条约做出的文书（包括联合委员会做出的指令）对自然资源活动进行日常管理与调控；

（b）编制年度收支评估报告并提交给联合委员会；任何支出均须与经联合委员会通过的评估报告一致，并遵守联合委员会通过的法规和程序；

（c）编制提交给联合委员会的年度报告；

（d）要求主管部门在下列情况下依据条约提供帮助：

ⅰ．当共同管理区开展搜索和营救行动时；

ⅱ．当共同管理区内从事自然资源石油作业的船舶与构筑物遭遇海盗或恐怖主义威胁时；

（e）要求主管部门、其他主体或个人在防止污染的措施、设备和程序上提供援助；

（f）依据国际法设立安全区和限制区，以确保与自然资源活动相关的航行安全；

（g）按照符合国际法的方式管理进出共同管理区及位于共同管理区的船舶、飞行器、设施及其他从事自然资源活动的设备，及依据条约第十五条授权雇员与承包人及其分包人和其他人进入共同管理区；

（h）对与监督和管控自然资源活动相关的一切问题，适用联合委员会批准的法规与指令，包括健康、安全、环境保护与评估及工作实践均应以自然资源法规为依据；

（i）充当共同管理区的数据信息库；

（j）进行与共同管理区自然资源活动相关的检查和审计；

（k）缔约方确认的或联合委员会授予的其他权力与职能。

2. Treaty Concerning the Joint Management of the Continental Shelf in the Mascarene Plateau Region

THE GOVERNMENT OF THE REPUBLIC OF SEYCHELLS

and

THE GOVERNMENT OF THE REPUBLIC MAURITIUS

(the Contracting Parties)

SEEKING to promote the sustainable and long – term economic and social development of their respective small island countries for the benefit of present and future generations;

COMMITTED to maintaining, renewing and further strengthening the mutual respect, goodwill, friendship and co – operation between their two countries;

ACKNOWLEDGING the existence of an overlapping area of continental shelf extending beyond the Exclusive Economic Zone boundaries established by their two countries under the Treaty between the Government of the Republic of Mauritius and the Government of the Republic of Seychelles on the Delimitation of the Exclusive Economic Zone between the two States dated 29 July 2008;

RECALLING that both countries co – operated on the basis of the Treaty between the Government of the Republic of Seychelles and the Government of the Republic of Mauritius on the Framework for a Joint Submission to the United Nations Commission on the Limits of the Continental Shelf dated 18 September 2008, as subsequently amended, to lodge on 1 December 2008 the Joint Submission to the United Nations Commission on the Limits of the Continental Shelf ("the Commission") concerning the Mascarene Plateau region "Joint Submission") under Article 76, paragraph 8 of the United Nations Convention on the law of the Sea done at Montego Bay on 10 December 1982 ("the Convention");

RECALLING ALSO on 30 March 2011, the Commission adopted recommendations confirming the entitlement of their two countries to the area of continental shelf as contained in the Commission document entitled Recommendations of the Commission on the Limits of the Continental Shelf in regard to the Joint Submission made by Mauritius and Seychelles in respect of the Mascarene Plateau Region on 1 December 2008;

CONSCIOUS that the Convention provides in Article 83 that the delimitation of the continental shelf between States with opposite coasts shall be effected by agreement on the basis of international law in order to achieve an equitable solution and, in the absence of delimitation, that States shall make every effort in a spirit of understanding and co-operation to enter into provisional arrangements of a practical nature which do not prejudice a final determination of the extended continental shelf delimitation;

RECOGNISING the importance of providing an equitable and co-operative legal basis for the exercise by their two countries of their sovereign rights and jurisdiction over the continental shelf in the Mascarene Plateau Region in accordance with international law;

REAFFIRMING the Treaty Concerning the Joint Exercise of Sovereign Rights over the Continental Shelf in the Mascarene Plateau Region of 13 March 2012, under which the Contracting Parties established the outer limits of the continental shelf in the Mascarene Plateau Region and agreed to exercise sovereign rights jointly for the purpose of exploring the continental shelf and exploiting its natural resources;

MINDFUL of the importance of jointly managing the natural resources of the continental shelf in the Mascarene Plateau Region in a manner that is sustainable and consistent with the precautionary principle and the protection of the marine environment and the biological diversity of the continental shelf;

DESIRING to enter into an international agreement to provide an effective and equitable framework to govern the joint management of the continental shelf in the Mascarene Plateau Region;

HAVE AGREED as follows:

PART 1   PRELIMINARY

Article 1   Definitions

For the purposes of this Treaty:

(a) "Authority" means the Designated Authority established in Article 4 of this Treaty;

(b) "bioprospecting" means the examination of biological resources for features including but not limited to chemical compounds, genes and their products and physical properties that may be of value for commercial development;

(c) "Commission" means the Joint Commission established under Article 4 of this Treaty;

(d) "continental shelf" has the meaning contained in Article 76 of the Convention;

(e) "contractor" means a corporation, company or other legal entity or entities with limited liability that enter into a contract with the Designated Authority and which are duly regulated;

(f) "Convention" means the United Nations Convention on the Law of the Sea done at Montego Bay on 10 December 1982;

(g) "criminal law" means any law in force in the territory of either of the Contracting Parties, whether substantive or procedural, that makes provision for, or in relation to offences, or for or In relation to the investigation or prosecution of offences or the punishment of offenders, including the carrying out of a penalty imposed by a court. For this purpose, "investigation" includes entry to an installation or structure in the JMA, the exercise of powers of search and questioning and the apprehension of a suspected offender;

(h) "Council" means the Ministerial Council established in Article 4 of this Treaty;

(i) "initially processed" means processing of petroleum to a point where it is ready for off-take from the production facility and may include such processes as the removal of water, vola6les and other impurities;

(j) "JMA" means the Joint Management Area established in Article 3 of this Treaty;

(k) "minerals" means any naturally occurring element, compound or substance, amorphous or crystalline (including liquid crystalline compounds), formed through geological or biogeochemical processes and any naturally occurring mixture of substances, including in the form of coal, clay, evaporates, gravel, limestone, oil – shale, sand, shale, rock, and polymetallic nodules;

(l) "natural resources" means the mineral, petroleum and other non – living resources of the seabed and subsoil of the continental shelf together with living organisms belonging to sedentary species that are at the harvestable stage either immobile on or under the seabed or are unable to move except in constant physical contact with the seabed or subsoil;

(m) "natural resource activities" means all activities authorised or contemplated under a contract, permit or licence that are undertaken to explore and exploit natural resources in the JMA including but not limited to development, initial processing, harvesting, production, transportation and marketing, as well as the planning and preparation for preparation for such activities;

(n) "natural resource codes" means codes referred to in Article 8 of this Treaty;

(o) "natural resources project" means any natural resource activity taking place with the approval of the Designated Authority in a specified area of the JMA;

(p) "petroleum" means any naturally occurring hydrocarbon, whether in a gaseous, liquid, or solid state and any naturally occurring mixture of hydrocarbons, whether in a gaseous, liquid or solid stale, together with other substances produced in association with such hydrocarbons, and includes any petroleum that has been returned to a reservoir;

(q) "petroleum produced" means initially processed petroleum extracted from a reservoir through petroleum activities;

(r) "reservoir" means an accumulation of petroleum in a geological unit limited by rock, water or other substances without pressure communication through liquid or gas to another accumulation of petroleum;

(s) "Taxation Code" means the Code referred to in Article 6 of this Treaty;

(t) "Treaty" means this Treaty, including Annexes A – D and any Annex that may subsequently be agreed by the Contracting Parties to form a part of this Treaty.

Article 2   Treaty without Prejudice

(a) This Treaty gives effect to international law as reflected in the Convention which under Article 83 requires States with opposite or adjacent coasts to make every effort to enter into provisional arrangements of a practical nature pending agreement on the final delimitation of the continental shelf between them in a manner consistent with international law. This Treaty is intended to adhere to such obligation.

(b) Nothing contained in this Treaty, and no act taking place while this Treaty is in force, shall be interpreted as prejudicing or affecting the legal position or rights of the Contracting Parties concerning their respective continental shelf entitlements or the delimitation of the continental shelf.

PART 2   THE JOINT MANAGEMENT AREA

Article 3   Joint Management Area

(a) The Joint Management Area (JMA) is established in respect of the Joint Zone described in Article 2 of the Treaty Concerning the Joint Exercise of Sovereign Rights over the Continental Shelf in the Mascarene Plateau Region, done on 13 March 2012 and as depicted in the map at Annex A.

(b) The Contracting Parties shall jointly control, manage and facilitate the exploration of the continental shelf within the JMA and the conservation, development and exploitation of its natural resources.

(c) Natural resource activities in the JMA shall be carried out under the direction of the Designated Authority, by such means as it may determine in accordance with this Treaty, including where appropriate through the issue of licences or pursuant to contracts between the Authority and a contractor. This provision shall also apply to the successors or assignees of such contractors;

(d) The Contracting Parties shall each make it an offence under their respective national laws for any person to conduct resource activities in the JMA otherwise than in accordance with this Treaty.

PART 3　INSTITUTIONAL AND REGULATORY ARRANGEMENTS

Article 4　Regulatory Bodies

(a) A three – Tiered joint administrative structure consisting of a Ministerial Council, a Joint Commission and a Designated Authority, is established.

(b) Ministerial Council:

i. A Ministerial Council for the JMA is hereby established. The Ministerial Council shall consist of an equal number of Ministers designated by the Contracting Forties.

ii. The Ministerial Council shall consider any matter relating to the operation of this Treaty that is referred to it by either of the Contracting Parties. It shall also consider any matter referred to under sub – paragraph (c) (iii).

iii. The Ministerial Council shall meet at the request of either Contracting Party or at the request of the Commission.

iv. All decisions of the Ministerial Council shall be adopted by consensus. In the event the Council is unable to resolve a matter, either of the Contracting Parties may invoke the dispute resolution procedure provided under Article 21.

v. No decision of the Ministerial Council shall be valid unless it is recorded in writing and signed by at least one member from each Contracting Party.

vi. The Ministerial Council shall establish its own procedures, including those in relation to taking decisions out of session and for conducting meetings by means of telephonic and electronic communication.

(c) Joint Commission:

i. The Joint Commission shall consist of an equal number of commissioners appointed by the Contracting Parties. The Joint Commission shall establish policies and regulations relating to petroleum and other natural resource activities in the JMA and shall oversee the work of the Authority.

ii. A non-exhaustive list of more detailed powers and functions of the Joint Commission is set out in Annex C. This list may be amended from time to time as necessary.

iii. The Joint Commission may at any time refer a matter to the Ministerial Council for resolution.

iv. The Joint Commission shall meet at least once a year in the Contracting Parties on an alternate basis, or otherwise as agreed, and each meeting shall be co-chaired.

v. Decisions of the Joint Commission shall be made by consensus.

(d) Designated Authority:

i. The Joint Commission shall establish the Designated Authority ("Authority").

ii. The Authority shall have juridical personality and such legal capacities under the law of the Contracting Parties as are necessary for the exercise of its powers and the performance of its functions. It shall have the capacity to contract, to acquire and dispose of movable and immovable property and to institute and be party to legal proceedings.

iii. The Authority shall be responsible to the Joint Commission and shall carry on the day-to-day regulation and management of natural resource activities in the JMA.

iv. A non-exhaustive list of more detailed powers and functions of the Authority is contained in Annex D. The Annexes to this Treaty may identify other additional powers and functions of the Authority. The Authority also has such other powers and functions as may be conferred upon it by the Commission.

v. The Authority shall be financed on an equal basis by the Contracting Parties, including eventually through the remittance of fees collected under natural resource codes.

vi. The Authority shall be exempt from:

(1) income tax or business tax, as the case may be; and

(2) customs duties, excise tax, Value Added Tax (VAT), levy and other similar taxes on imports for official use, imposed under the law in force in the territory of each of the Contracting Parties, as well as any identical or substantially similar taxes that are imposed after the date of signature of this Treaty in addition to, or in place of, the existing saxes.

vii. Personnel of the Authority:

(1) shall be subject to taxation in the Contracting Party of which they are a national and in accordance with the tax law of that Contracting Party in respect of salaries, allowances and other payments made to them by the Authority in connection with their employment with the Authority. For the purposes of this paragraph the term "national" includes a resident of either Contracting Party as defined in the income tax law of that Contracting Party; and

(2) shall, at the time of the first taking up the post with the Authority located in either of the Contracting Parties in which they are not resident, be exempt from customs duties, excise tax, VAT, levy and other similar taxes and other such charges (except payments for services) in respect of imports of furniture and other household and personal effects including one motor vehicle in their ownership or possession or already ordered by them and intended for their personal use or for their establishment, subject to terms and conditions established by the Joint Commission. Such goods shall be imported within six months of an officers first entry but in exceptional circumstances an extension of time shall be granted by the Contracting Parties respectively. Goods that have been acquired or imported by officers and to which exemptions under this sub‑paragraph apply shall not be given away, sold, lent or hired out, or otherwise disposed of except under conditions agreed in advance depending on in which country the officer is located.

(e) No member of the Ministerial Council, Joint Commission and personnel of the Authority shall have any financial or personal interest in any natural resource project in the JMA.

Article 5 Sharing of Revenue

(a) The Contracting Parties shall share revenue received in respect of natural resource activities carried out in the JMA equally, whereby fifty (50) per cent of revenue received shall be remitted to Mauritius and fifty (50) percent of revenue received shall be remitted to Seychelles.

(b) To the extent that fees referred to in Article 4 (d) (v) and other income are inadequate to cover the expenditure of the Authority in relation to this Treaty, that expenditure shall be borne by each of the Contracting Parties in the same proportion as set out in paragraph (a).

(c) Paragraph (a) shall not apply to the equitable sharing of the benefits arising from unitisation under Article 10 unless mutually agreed by the Contracting Parties.

Article 6　Taxation Code

(a) The Contracting Parties shall agree upon a Taxation Code applicable to income derived from natural resource activities in the JMA.

(b) Neither Contracting Party may during the life of a natural resource project vary any of the provisions of the Taxation Code applicable to it except by mutual agreement.

Article 7　Application of Domestic Law

For the purposes of the application of the domestic laws of each contracting Party related directly or indirectly to:

i. the exploration of the continental shelf within the JMA and the development and exploitation of natural resources in the JMA; and

ii. acts, matters, circumstances and things touching, concerning, arising out of or connected with. natural resource activities in the JMA.

the JMA shall be deemed to be and treated by each Contracting Party as forming part of its respective territory.

Article 8　Natural Resource Codes

(a) The Contracting Parties may agree upon natural resource codes concerning the exploration of the continental shelf within the JMA and the development, exploitation, harvesting, conservation and export of natural resources from the JMA.

(b) The Commission shall, where necessary, adopt interim arrangements to be applied pending the adoption of natural resource codes in accordance with paragraph (a).

PART 4   PIPELINES AND UNITISATION

Article 9   Pipelines

(a) The construction and operation of a pipeline within the JMA for the purposes of exporting petroleum from the JMA shall be subject to the approval of the Commission.

(b) The Contracting Parties shall consult each other on the terms and conditions for laying of pipelines exporting petroleum from the JMA to the point of landing.

(c) A pipeline landing in the territory of a Contracting Party shall be under the jurisdiction of the country of landing.

(d) In the event a pipeline is constructed from the JMA to the territory of either of the Contracting Parties, the country where the pipeline lands may not object to or impede decisions of the Commission regarding that pipeline except where the construction of a pipeline would have an adverse economic or physical impact upon an existing natural resource project in the JMA.

(e) Petroleum from the JMA and from fields which straddle the boundaries of the JMA shall times have priority of carriage along any pipeline carrying petroleum from and within the JMA.

(f) There shall be open access to pipelines for petroleum from the JMA. The open access arrangements shall be in accordance with good international regulatory practice. If one Contracting Party has jurisdiction over the pipeline, it shall consult with the other Contracting Party over access to the pipeline.

Article 10   Unitisation

(a) Any reservoir of petroleum or unitary mineral deposit that extends across or straddles the boundary of the JMA into the Exclusive Economic Zone of either or both Contracting Parties shall be treated as a single entity for exploration, development and management purposes.

(b) The Contracting Parties shall work expeditiously and in good faith to reach agreement on the manner in which the petroleum field or mineral deposit referred to in paragraph (a) will be most effectively managed and developed and on the equitable sharing of revenue arising from such development.

Article 11　Surveys

Each of the Contracting Parties has the right to conduct surveys including hydrographic, geological, geophysical and seismic surveys to facilitate natural resource activities in the JMA.

In the exercise of such right, the Contracting Parties shall:

i. notify the Authority of any proposed survey;

ii. cooperate on the conduct of such surveys, including the provision of necessary on - shore facilities; and

iii. exchange information relevant to natural resource activities in the JMA.

PART 5　PROTECTION OF THE ENVIRONMENT. BIODIVERSITY AND BIOPROSPECTING

Article 12　Protection of the Seabed Marine Environment

(a) The Contracting Parties shall co - operate to protect natural resources in the JMA so as to secure seabed biodiversity and prevent pollution and other risks of harm to the environment arising from, or connected with, natural resource activities in the JMA.

(b) The Contracting Parties shall apply the precautionary principle in co - operating to conserve and protect the environment and biodiversity of the seabed in the JMA. This shall include measures concerning fishing activity in the waters superjacent to the seabed in the JMA where such activity is having a direct impact upon, or poses a significant risk to, the natural resources of the seabed and subsoil in the JMA.

(c) The Contracting Parties shall co - Operate to protect seabed marine habitats and associated ecological communities of the seabed in the JMA. This shall include the identification of environmental benchmarks and the identification of seabed marine protected areas, having regard to the following:

I. geographical distribution of seabed marine species and biological communities;

ii. the structure of these communities

iii. their relationship with the physical and the chemical environment;

iv. the natural ecological and genetic variability; and

v. the nature and the effect of the anthropogenic influences including fishing and natural resource activities on these ecosystem components.

(d) Where pollution of the marine environment occurring in the JMA spreads beyond the JMA, the Contracting Parties shall co‐operate in taking prompt and effective action 1o prevent, mitigate and eliminate such pollution in accordance with international best practices, standards and procedures.

(e) The Authority shall issue regulations to protect the living natural resources and seabed environment in the JMA. It shall establish a contingency plan for combating pollution from natural resource activities in the JMA.

(f) Contractors shall be liable for damage or expenses incurred as a result of pollution of marine environment arising out of natural resource activities within the JMA in accordance with:

i. their contract, licence or permit or other form of authority issued pursuant to this Treaty; and,

ii. the law of the jurisdiction of the Contracting Party in which the claim is brought.

Article 13 Biological Surveys and Bioprospecting

(a) Each of the Contracting Parties has the right to carry out biological surveys for the purposes of Article 12 of this Treaty and to engage in bioprospecting to identify and examine living natural resources that may be of value for commercial development in the JMA or of conservation significance.

(b) The Contracting Parties shall:

i. notify the Authority of any proposed survey;

ii. co‐operate in the conduct of such biological surveys and bioprospecting, including the provision of necessary on‐shore facilities; and

iii. exchange information relevant to biological surveys and bioprospecting in the JMA.

PART 6 EMPLOYMENT, HEALTH AND SAFETY AND APPLICATION OF DOMESTIC LAWS

Article 14 Employment

The Contracting Parties shall take appropriate measures to ensure that preference is given in employment in the JMA to nationals of both Contracting Parties and to facilitate, as a matter of priority, training and employment opportunities for those nationals.

Article 15 Health and Safety for Workers

(a) The Authority shall develop, and contractors shall apply where required, occupational health and safety standards and procedures for persons employed on installations and structures in the JMA in accordance with internationally accepted standards and best practices.

(b) Similar occupational health, safety standards and procedures shall apply to all workers engaged in natural resource activities in the JMA.

Article 16 Criminal Jurisdiction

(a) The Contracting Parties shall examine different options for addressing offences committed in the JMA. Pending the completion of such exercise, the provisions of this Article shall apply with respect to offences committed in the JMA.

(b) A national or resident of a Contracting Party shall be subject to the criminal law of the country of nationality or residence in respect of acts or omissions occurring in the JMA connected with or arising out of natural resource activities.

(c) Notwithstanding paragraph (e), a national of a third state, not being a resident of either Contracting Party, shall be subject to the criminal law of either Contracting Party in respect of acts or omissions occurring in the JMA connected with or arising out of natural resource activities. Such person shall not be subject to criminal proceedings under the law of either Contracting Party if he or she has already been tried and discharged or acquitted by a competent tribunal or already undergone punishment for the same act or omission under the law of the other country or where the competent authorities of one country, in accordance with its law, have decided in the public interest to refrain from prosecuting the person for that act or omission.

(d) In cases referred to in paragraph (c), the Contracting Parties shall, as and when necessary, consult each other to determine which criminal law is to be applied, taking into account the nationality of the victim and the interests of the country most affected by the alleged offence.

(e) The criminal law of the flag state shall apply in relation to acts or omissions on board vessels operating in the waters superjacent to the JMA.

(f) The Contracting Parties shall provide assistance to and co-operate with each other, including through agreements or arrangements as appropriate, for the purposes of enforcement of criminal law under this Article including the obtaining of evidence and information.

(g) The Contracting Parties each recognise the interest of the other country where a victim of an alleged offence is a national of that other country and shall keep that other country informed, to the extent permitted by its law, of action being taken with regard to the alleged offence.

(h) The Contracting Parties may make arrangements permitting officials of one country toassist in the enforcement of the criminal law of the other country. Where such assistance involves the detention of a person who under paragraph (b) is subject to the jurisdiction of the other country, that detention may only continue until it is practicable to hand the person over to the relevant officials of that other country.

Article 17 Customs, Migration and Quarantine

(a) The Contracting Parties may, subject to paragraphs (c), (e), (f) and (g), apply customs, migration and quarantine laws in accordance with internationally accepted standards and best practices to persons, equipment and goods entering its territory from, or leaving its territory for, the JMA. The Contracting Parties may adopt arrangements to facilitate such entry and departure.

(b) Contractors shall ensure, unless otherwise authorised by the Contracting Parties, that persons, equipment and goods do not enter structures in the JMA without first entering the Contracting Parties, and that their employees and the employees of their subcontractors are authorised by the Authority to enter the JMA.

(c) Either Contracting Party may request consultations with the other Contracting Party in relation to the entry of particular persons, equipment and goods to structures in the JMA aimed at controlling the movement of such persons, equipment and goods

(d) Nothing in this Article prejudices the right of either Contracting Party to apply customs, migration and quarantine controls to persons, equipment and goods entering the JMA without the authority of either Contracting Party. The Contracting Parties may adopt arrangements to co – ordinate the exercise of such rights.

(e) Goods and equipment entering the JMA for purposes related to natural resource activities shall not be subject to customs duties, excise tax, VAT, levy and other similar taxes.

(f) Goods and equipment leaving or in transit through the territory of the Contracting Parties for the purpose of entering the JMA for purposes related to natural resource activities shall not be subject to customs duties, excise tax, VAT, levy and other similar taxes.

(g) Goods and equipment leaving the JMA for the purpose of being permanently transferred to a part of the territory of the Contracting Parties may be subject to customs duties, excise tax, VAT, levy and other similar taxes of that Contracting Party.

Article 18 Safety, Operating Standards and Crewing of Resource Industry Vessels

(a) Except as otherwise provided in this Treaty, vessels of the nationality of a Contracting Party engaged in natural resource activities in the JMA shall be subject to the law of their nationality in relation to safety and operating standards and crewing regulations.

(b) Vessels flying the flag of States other than the Contracting Parties and which are engaged in natural resource activities in the JMA shall be subject to the relevant international safety and operating standards and crewing regulations.

PART 7 SURVEILLANCE, SECURITY AND RESCUE

Article 19 Surveillance and Security Measures

(a) For the purposes of this Treaty, the Contracting Parties shall have the right to carry out surveillance activities in the JMA in relation to natural resource activities.

(b) The Contracting Parties shall co-operate on and co-ordinate any surveillance activities carried out in accordance with paragraph (a) and shall exchange information on likely threats to, or security incidents relating to, natural resource activities in the JMA.

(c) The Contracting Parties shall make arrangements for responding promptly and effectively to security incidents in the JMA.

Article 20 Search and Rescue

The Contracting Parties shall, at the request of the Authority and consistent with this Treaty, co-operate and assist in the conduct of search and rescue operations in the JMA, taking into account generally accepted international rules, regulations and procedures established through competent international organisations.

PART 8 SETTLEMENT OF DISPUTES, DURATION AND ENTRY INTO FORCE

Article 21 Settlement of Disputes

(a) With the exception of disputes falling within the scope of the Taxation Code referred to in Article 6 of this Treaty and which shall be settled in accordance with that Code as agreed by the Contracting Parties, any dispute concerning the interpretation or application of this Treaty shall, as far as possible, be settled amicably through mutual consultation.

(b) Any dispute which is not settled in the manner set out in paragraph (a) and any unresolved matter relating to the operation of this Treaty under Article 4 (b) (ii) shall, at the request of either of the Contracting Parties, be submitted to an Arbitral Tribunal established in accordance with the procedure set out in Annex B.

Article 22 Amendment

This Treaty may be amended at any time by written agreement between the Contracting Parties.

Article 23 Duration of the Treaty

(a) This Treaty shall remain in force until a permanent delimitation of the continental shelf is agreed between the Contracting Parties or for thirty (30) years from the date of its entry into force, whichever is sooner.

(b) This Treaty may be renewed by agreement between the Contracting Parties.

(c) Natural resource projects commenced under this Treaty shall continue, notwithstanding that this Treaty is no longer in force, under conditions that are consistent with those that are provided for under this Treaty.

Article 24 Entry into Force

(a) Each of the Contracting Parties shall notify the other, by means of exchange of diplomatic notes, the completion of the procedures required by its law for the bringing into force of this Treaty. The Treaty shall enter into forte on the date of receipt of the later notification.

(b) Upon entry into force, the Treaty shall be taken to have effect, and all of its provisions shall be taken to have applied, from the date of signature.

IN WITNESS WHEREOF the undersigned, being duly authorised thereto by their respective Governments, have signed this Treaty.

DONE at Clarisse House, Vacoas, Mauritius in duplicate on this 13th day of March Two Thousand and Twelve in the English language.

For the Government of the Republic of Mauritius	For the Government of the Republic of Seychelles
H. E. Mr. James Alix Michel	Dr the Hon Navinchandra Ramgoolam, GCSK, FRCP
President	Prime Minister

Annex A   under Article 3 of this Treaty

Designation and Description of the JMA

The JMA referred to in Article 3 comprises the area of continental shelf set out in Article 2 of the Trealy Concerning the Joint Exercise of Sovereign Rights over the Continental Shelf in the Mascarene Plateau Region, done on 13 March 2012, as depicted in the map below.

Annex B   under Article 21 of this Treaty

Dispute Resolution Procedure

(a) An Arbitral Tribunal ("Tribunal") to which a dispute is submitted pursuant to Article 21 (b) shall consist of three persons appointed as follows:

i. the Contracting Parties shall each appoint one arbitrator;

ii. the arbitrators appointed by the Contracting Parties shall, within sixty (60) days of the appointment of the second of them, by agreement, select a third arbitrator who shall be a citizen, or permanent resident of a third country which has diplomatic relations with both the Contracting Parties; and

iii. the Contracting Parties shall, within sixty (60) days of the selection of the third arbitrator, approve the selection of that arbitrator who shall act as Chairman of the Tribunal.

(b) Arbitration proceedings shall – be instituted upon notice being given through the diplomatic channel by the Contracting Party instituting such proceedings to the other Contracting Party. Such notice shall contain:

i. a statement setting forth in summary form the grounds of the claim;

ii. the nature of the relief sought; and,

iii. the name of the arbitrator appointed by the Contracting Party instituting such proceedings.

Within sixty (60) days after the giving of such notice, the respondent Contracting Party shall notify the Contracting Party instituting proceedings of the name of the arbitrator appointed by the respondent Contracting Party.

(c) If, within the time limits provided for in sub-paragraphs (a) (ii) and (iii) and paragraph (b) of this Annex, the required appointment has not been made or the required approval has not been given, the Contracting Parties may request the President of the International Tribunal of the Law of the Sea ("ITLOS") to make the necessary appointment. If the President is a citizen or permanent resident of the Contracting Parties or is otherwise unable to act, the Vice – President shall be invited to make the appointment. If the Vice – President is a citizen or permanent resident of the Contracting Parties or is otherwise unable to act, the Member of the ITLOS next in seniority who is not a citizen or permanent resident of the Contracting Parties shall be invited to make the appointment.

(d) In case any arbitrator appointed as provided for in this Annex resigns or becomes unable to act, another arbitrator shall be appointed in the same manner as prescribed for the appointment of the original arbitrator and the new arbitrator shall have all the powers and duties of the original arbitrator.

(e) The Tribunal shall convene at such time and place as shall be fixed by the Chairman of the Tribunal. Thereafter, the Tribunal shall determine where and when it shall sit.

(f) The Tribunal shall decide all questions relating to its competence and shall, subject to any agreement between the Contracting Parties, determine its own procedures.

(g) Before the Tribunal makes a decision, it may at any stage of the proceedings propose to the Contracting Parties that the dispute be settled amicably. The Arbitral Tribunal shall reach it award by majority vote, taking into account the provisions of this Treaty and relevant international law.

(h) Each Contracting Party shall bear the costs incurred in relation to its appointed arbitrator and its own costs in preparing and presenting cases. The cost incurred in relation to the Chairman of the Tribunal and the expenses associated with the conduct of the arbitration shall be borne in equal parts by the Contracting Parties.

(i) The Tribunal shall afford to the Contracting Parties a fair hearing. It may render at award on the default of either of the Contracting Parties. In any case, the Arbitral Tribunal shall render its award within six (ti) months from the date it is convened by the Chairman of the Tribunal. Any award shall be rendered in writing and shall state its legal basis. A signer counterpart of the award shall be transmitted to the Contracting Parties.

(j) An award of the Tribunal shall be final and binding on the Contracting Parties.

Annex C under Article 4 (c) (ii) of this Treaty

Powers and Functions of the Joint Commission

1. The powers and functions of the Joint Commission shall include:

(a) establishing the Authority;

(b) giving directions to the Authority on the exercise of its powers and performance of its functions;

(c) conferring additional powers and functions to the Authority;

(d) adopting taxation and natural resource codes applicable to the JMA including amendments and interim arrangements as necessary;

(e) approving financial estimates of income and expenditure of the Authority;

(f) approving rules, regulations and procedures for the effective functioning of the Authority;

(g) calling for the auditing of the Authority's books and accounts;

(h) considering and adopting the annual report of the Authority.

Annex D under Article 4 (d) (iv) of this Treaty

Powers and Functions of the Authority

The powers and functions of the Authority shall include:

(a) day-to-day management and regulation of natural resource activities in accordance with this Treaty and any instruments made or entered into under this Treaty. including directions given by the Joint Commission;

(b) preparation of annual estimates of income and expenditure of the Authority for submission to the Joint Commission. Any expenditure shall only be made in accordance with estimates approved by the Joint Commission or otherwise in accordance with regulations and procedures approved by the Joint Commission;

(c) preparation of annual reports for submission to the Joint Commission;

(d) requesting assistance from the appropriate authorities consistent with this Treaty:

i. for search and rescue operations in the JMA;

ii. in the event of piracy or terrorist threats to vessels and structures engaged in natural resource petroleum operations in the JMA;

(e) requesting assistance with pollution prevention measures, equipment and procedures from the appropriate authorities or other bodies or persons;

(f) establishment of safety zones and restricted zones, consistent with international law, to ensure the safety of navigation connected with natural resource activities;

(g) controlling movements into, within and out of the JMA of vessels, aircraft, structures and other equipment engaged in natural resource activities in a manner consistent with international law; and, subject to Article 15, authorising the entry of employees and contractors and their subcontractors and other persons into the JMA;

(h) applying regulations and giving directions as approved by the Commission under this Treaty, on all matters related to the supervision and control of natural resource activities including on health, safety, environmental protection and assessments and work practices, pursuant to natural resource codes;

(i) acting as a repository of all data and information pertaining to the JMA;

(j) conducting inspections and audits concerning natural resource activities in the and

(k) such other powers and functions as may be identified by the Contracting Parties or as may be conferred on it by the Joint Commission.

3. 《塞舌尔共和国政府与毛里求斯共和国政府关于共同行使马斯克林高原地区大陆架主权权利的条约》

(2012年3月13日订于瓦克阿克拉里斯官)

申钟秀译,黄文博、杨泽伟校

考虑到两个国家均为沿海国,基于2008年9月18日签订的《塞舌尔共和国政府与毛里求斯共和国政府关于向联合国大陆架界限委员会联合共同提交(大陆架划界案)的框架条约》进行合作,随后进行了修订,并依据1982年12月10日于蒙特哥湾签署的《联合国海洋法公约》(简称《公约》)第76条第8款,于2008年12月1日向联合国大陆架界限委员会(简称"委员会")共同提交(大陆架划界案);

亦考虑到2011年3月30日委员会通过了"建议",肯定了缔约方在共同提交(大陆架划界案)中他们所提出的本大陆架区域的权利,它包含在名为《大陆架界限委员会对2008年12月1日毛里求斯与塞舌尔关于马斯克林高原地区的共同提交案的"建议"》的委员会文件中;

注意到《公约》第76条规定沿海国在委员会的"建议"的基础上划定的大陆架界线应是终局性的和有约束力的;

亦注意到《公约》第83条规定海岸相向国家间大陆架的界线应在国际法的基础上以协定划定,以便得到公平的解决,并且在没有划界的情况下有关各国应基于谅解与合作的精神,尽一切努力做出实质性的临时安排,这种安排并不影响最后界线的划定;双方协定如下。

第一条 共同行使大陆架主权权利

缔约方应本着勘探和开发大陆架自然资源的目的,在第2条描述的区块(共同区块)里共同行使主权权利。

第二条　共同区块的划定

共同区块由以下各点确定，这些点的纬度与经度坐标［参照世界大地测量系统（WGS84）］详见该条约附件1的表格，插图详见该条约的附件2的地图。

区块的边界线始于塞舌尔专属经济区边界线上的点 ECS1，经 ECS2～ECS44 各点延伸，再至点 ECS45，再至点 ESC46，然后经 ECS47～ECS105 各点，然后至点 ECS106，再经 ECS107～ECS123 各点，然后经 ECS124～ECS186 各点，然后至点 ECS187，再至点 ECS188，然后经 ECS189～ECS220 各点，然后至点 ECS221，然后经 ECS222～ECS269 各点，然后经 ECS270～ECS275 各点，然后至点 ECS276，再经 ECS277～ECS296 各点，然后经 ECS297～ECS321 各点，然后经 ECS322～ECS362 各点，然后至点 ECS363，然后经 ECS364～ECS395 各点，然后至点 ECS396，然后至毛里求斯专属经济区边界线上的 ECS397～ECS453 各点，然后沿着毛里求斯专属经济区边界线至点 34，然后经 35～41 各点，然后经 42～47 各点，然后经点 48 至塞舌尔与毛里求斯两国经济专属区交界上的点 MS1，然后沿着塞舌尔专属经济区边界线经 EZ1～EZ5 各点，然后沿着塞舌尔专属经济区边界线回到位于塞舌尔专属经济区边界线上的点 ECS1 处的起始线。

上文所列各点之间的边界线为测地线。

第三条　条约不得损害任何一方的权益

条约中所包含的任何事项与条约生效期间发生的任何行为，都不得做出损害或者影响缔约方关于未来两国间在马斯克林高原地区大陆架划界的法律地位或权利的解释。

第四条　条约的生效

（a）缔约方任何一方都应通过互换外交照会的方式，将法律规定条约生效所需程序的完成告知对方。条约自后收到通知的日期开始生效。

（b）条约生效后，即应发生效力，自签字之日起所有条文都应适用。

经各国政府完全授权的签署人签署条约，以昭信守。

2012年3月13日签署于毛里求斯瓦克阿克拉里斯宫，约文采用英语，一式二份。

毛里求斯共和国政府	塞舌尔共和国政府
H.E. 詹姆斯·	翁·纳温卡德拉·
阿里克斯·米歇尔	兰古利博士，GCSK，FRCP
总统	首相

4. Treaty Concerning the Joint Exercise of Sovereign Rights over the Continental Shelf in the Mascarene Plateau Region

THE GOVERNMENT OF THE REPUBLIC OF SEYCHELLS

and

THE GOVERNMENT OF THE REPUBLIC MAURITIUS

(the Contracting Parties)

RECALLING that both countries being coastal States co – operated on the basis of the Treaty between the Government of the Republic of Seychelles and the Government of the Republic of Mauritius on the Framework for a Joint Submission to the United Nations Commission on the Limits of the Continental Shelf dated 18 September 2008, as subsequently amended, to lodge on 1 December 2008 the Joint Submission to the United Nations Commission on the Limits of the Continental Shelf ("the Commission") under article 76, paragraph 8 of the United Nations Convention on the Law of the sea done at Montego Bay on 10 December 1982 ("the Convention");

RECALLING ALSO that on 30 March 2011, the Commission adopted the recommendations confirming the entitlement of the Contracting Parties to the area of continental shelf submitted by them in the joint submission, as contained in the Commission document entitled Recommendations of the the Commission on the Limits of the Continental Shelf in regard of the Joint Submission made by Mauritius and Seychelles in respective of the Mascarene Plateau Region on 1 December 2008;

NOTING that Article 76 of the Convention provides that the limits of the continental shelf established by coastal States on the basis of the recommendations of the Commission shall be final and binding;

NOTING ALSO that Article 83 of the Convention provides that the delimitation of the continental shelf between States with opposite coasts shall be effected by agreement on the basis of international law in order to achieve an equitable solution and, in the absence of delimitation, that States shall make every effort in a spirit of understanding and co-operation to enter into provisional arrangements a practical nature which do not prejudice a final delimitation of the continental shelf;

HAVE AGREED as follows:

Article 1 Joint Exercise of Sovereign Rights over the Continental Shelf

The Contracting Parties shall exercise sovereign rights jointly for the purpose of exploring the continental shelf and exploiting its natural resources in the area described in Article 2 (the Joint Zone).

Article 2 Delineation of the Joint Zone

The Joint Zone is defined by the following points, the coordinates of latitude and longitude [referred to the World Geodetic System (WGS84)] of which are set out at Annex 1 to this Treaty, and as illustrated in the map at Annex 2 of this Treaty:

Commencing at point ECS1 on Seychelles Exclusive Economic Zone Boundary, the boundary line runs through points ECS2 to ECS44, thence to point ECS45, thence to point ECS46, thence through points ECS47 to ECS105, thence to point ECS106, thence through points ECS107 to ECS123, thence through points ECS124 to ECS186, thence to point ECS187, thence to point ECS188, thence through points ECS189 to ECS220, thence to point ECS221, thence through points ECS222 to ECS269, thence through points ECS270 to ECS275, thence to point ECS276, thence through points ECS277 to ECS296, thence through points ECS297 to ECS321, thence through points ECS322 to ECS362, thence to point ECS363, thence through points ECS364 to ECS395, thence to point ECS396, thence through points ECS397 to ECS453 on Mauritius Exclusive Economic Zone boundary, thence along Mauritius Exclusive Economic Zone boundary to point 34, thence through points 35 to 41, thence through points 42 to 47, thence through point 48 to MS1 on the intersection of the Seychelles and Mauritius Exclusive Economic Zone boundaries, thence along the Seychelles Exclusive Economic Zone boundary through points EZ1 to EZ5, thence along the Seychelles Exclusive Economic Zone boundary to the starting point at ECS1 on Seychelles Exclusive Economic Zone boundary.

The boundary line between the above listed points is a geodesic.

Article 3　Treaty without Prejudice

Nothing contained in this Treaty, and no act taking place whilst this Treaty is in force, shall be interpreted as prejudicing or affecting the legal position or rights of the Contracting Parties concerning any future delimitation of the continental shelf between them in the Mascarene Plateau Region.

Article 4　Enter into Force

(a) Each Contracting Party shall notify the other, by means of exchange of diplomatic notes, the completion of the procedures required by its law for the bringing into force of this Treaty. The Treaty shall enter into force on the date of receipt of the later notification.

(b) Upon entry into force, the Treaty shall be taken to have effect and all of its provisions shall be taken to have applied, from the date of signature.

IN WITNESS WHEREOF the undersigned, being duly authorised thereto by their respective Governments, have signed this Treaty.

DONE at Clarisse House, Vacoas, Mauritius in duplicate on this 13th day of March Two Thousand and Twelve in the English language.

For the Government of the Republic of Mauritius	For the Government of the Republic of Seychelles
H. E. Mr. James Alix MICHEL	Dr the Hon Navinchandra RAMGOOLAM, GCSK, FRCP
President	Prime Minister

四

海上共同开发协定示范文本

1990年英国国际法与比较法研究所的修订示范文本

1.《X国和Y国共同开发两国大陆架和/或专属经济区区域内石油的修订示范协定》

邓妮雅译，黄文博校

X国和Y国为了促进两国的友好关系，承认两国邻接的大陆架和/或专属经济区尚未划定界线，且存在主张重叠区。两国注意到，在主张重叠区内，可能存在石油资源。考虑到两国以适当方式勘探和开发石油资源符合两国的最大利益，且相信这种活动最好由两国共同进行，考虑到1958年《日内瓦大陆架公约》和1982年《联合国海洋法公约》，双方申明本协定没有规定的问题继续受国际法规则规范，遂达成如下约定。

第一条 术语的使用

根据本协定：

（1）"可适用的法律"是指本协定的条款、开发合同的条款以及专门的石油法案；

（2）"承包人"是指与开发当局签订开发合同的任何国民；

（3）"开发合同"是指根据第十一条规定，由开发当局与承包人签订的协议；

（4）"合同区域"是指根据当前的开发合同确定的一块开发区域，排除了承包人已经放弃的区域；

(5)"开发区域"是指开发当局间为了分配石油活动的监督、管理和规制，划分的区域（如果有的话）；

(6)"开发当局"是指依据本协定就区域内或相关开发区域内的石油活动，签订开发协议的一方当事国、多方当事国，或者联合委员会：

（ⅰ）"并行的开发当局"是指有权依据本协定与其选定的申请者，就任何开发区域签订开发合同的一方当事国。该当事国反过来也需要在同样的开发区域内，与享有相同权利的另一当事国的承包人，达成共同开发协议；

（ⅱ）"共同开发当局"是指有权依据本协定，与其选定的申请者及另一当事国任命的联合经营者，就任何开发的区域签订开发合同的一方当事国。联合经营人双方都需要与另一国签订同样的开发合同；

（ⅲ）"单一开发当局"是指根据本协定的唯一授权，就任何开发区域签订开发合同的联合委员会或一方当事国；

(7)"设备"是指在海床上方、内部或下方安装的，供在石油活动中使用的任何设施、装置或人工岛屿，包括在当地的钻井船；

(8)"联合委员会"是指根据第五条设立的行使第六条职权的委员会；

(9)"国民"是指按照相关当事国的法律和法规，享有一方或双方国籍的自然人或法人；

(10)"经营协议"是指开发合同持有人之间，为了开展区域内的石油开发活动签订的合同；

(11)"经营人"是指持有与开发当局签订的开发合同，并依据适格开发当局批准的经营协议条款，被指定和充当经营者的主体；

(12)"石油"是指与其他衍生的地下矿物质结合产生的、沉积于地下的原油和天然气；

(13)"石油活动"是指与区域内石油勘探和开发相关的所有活动；

(14)"区域计划"是指当事国政府根据第六条和第七条达成的，关于区域内石油活动的开发计划；

(15)"污染"是指区域内石油活动引起的物质或能源进入海洋环境，包括河口，对生物资源、海洋环境造成或可能造成有害影响，危害人类健康、海水使用的质量和环境舒适程度；

(16)"专门的石油法"是指在区域、开发区，或者依据第七条和第八条区域计划建立的合同区内，适用于石油活动或与之相关活动的法律体系；

（17）"区域"是指海床、海底和底土区域；

（a）以……为基准，由按顺序连接以下点的测地线构成：

（ⅰ）纬度……　经度……

（ⅱ）纬度……　经度……

（ⅲ）纬度……　经度……

（b）海底的界线由海平面界线的垂直线构成；以及

（c）区域可以做必要的延伸，以包括为了石油活动目的，在区域内的安全设备周围设立合理的安全区域。

第二条　共同开发区

（1）建立开发区的目的是在其界线内进行石油开发活动。区域内所有的石油活动应遵守本协定规定。

（2）当事国可以通过后续协定对区域内其他矿物资源和非生物资源做出安排。

（3）联合委员会应当，仅为说明的目的，用适当的比例尺在一幅或多幅海图上绘制区域的界线。

第三条　共同开发原则

（1）当事国应按照本协定建立的制度，分享和分担（平等，或按双方同意的比例）石油活动中的权利和义务，促进区域内石油的共同开发。

（2）区域内的所有石油活动应按照本协定的规定和采纳的相应措施进行。

（3）当事国应当：

（a）在石油活动监管和实施上采取全面合作，促进区域内石油的共同开发；

（b）产生影响任一当事国利益的事项时，通过联合委员会进行协商；

（c）尽可能协调好区域内共同开发的利益。

（4）应当有效开采区域内的石油资源，并与普遍接受的、良好的石油工业实践保持一致，并适当考虑海洋环境保护。

（5）依据本协定对当事国石油活动的规定，区域内的共同开发应适当尊重区域内其他国家的利益。

第四条 不损害条款

(1) 本协定的任何条款不应当解释为,任何国家放弃区域内的权利或主张,也不能解释为承认或支持其他相关国家在区域内的任何权利或主张。

(2) 根据本协定或者协定执行引起的任何行为或活动,不构成对任何国家在区域内权利或主张的确定、支持或否认的根据。

(3) 除非当事国间达成一致,最终的划界谈判应推迟到本协定期满之后。

第五条 联合委员会

(1) 联合委员会的职责是全面监管区域内的石油活动,编制区域计划,承担根据本协定第六条和区域计划可能赋予的管理区域内石油活动的职能。

(2) 联合委员会由每个当事国同等数量的代表组成。联合委员会的所有决定,无论是实质性事项还是程序性事项,都必须获得双方当事国代表的同意。

(3) 联合委员会应当任命一个技术委员会,由各方当事国任命同等数量的、具有石油活动相关资质的技术顾问组成。本协定生效后,该技术委员会应一直处于会话状态。

(4) 技术委员会的任务是对共同开发进行日常监督,包括审查开发合同,就技术问题和联合委员会交付的其他问题向联合委员会提供建议和咨询。

(5) 联合委员会应当于本协定生效后[6]个月内召开会议,此后每年或双方一致同意或在任意一方要求下或者有必要行使本协定规定的职责时召开会议。

(6) 联合委员会可以设定一个常设秘书处,执行联合委员会的行政工作。若联合委员会不是开发当局,应首先考虑其他方法满足行政工作需要,否则不能设立常设秘书处。联合委员会必须在秘书处所在地召开会议,如果没有秘书处,则应轮流在当事国决定的领土内召开会议。

(7) 联合委员会应该具有法律人格,且应在任意一方领土范围内享有,执行本协定赋予或可能赋予的,或达到本协定的目标所必需的法律能力。

（8）除非当事国另有约定，联合委员会产生的合理行政支出，应从联合委员会建立之日开始支付。这些费用应由当事国平等分担，当事国应按照协商一致达成的预算程序定时缴纳以建立基金。联合委员会应当遵守预算程序，并有效利用可使用的资源。联合委员会可以通过收取开发合同申请费或租金补偿自己的开支，但不能超过合理的手续费数额。

（9）委员会的官方语言是 X 和 Y，或者是委员会决定的其他语言。

（10）为了履行本协定下联合委员会的职责，当事国的代表、联合委员会的职员以及所有的技术顾问，不应对区域内的石油活动享有经济利益。依据他们对当事国的责任，即使在职责终止后，也不应当公开提交给联合委员会的任何工业秘密或专利数据，以及他们作为联合委员会的成员或雇员而获得的其他保密信息。

（11）依据公布和使用的合法限制，当事国应当交换承包人提交的与区域有关的信息。当事国应当保证将这种信息视为保密信息，除了联合委员会或技术委员会使用，不得违背限制性规定进一步公开或使用。

第六条 联合委员会的职能

（1）联合委员会的职责是：负责为当事国计划、协调以及监督区域内石油的共同开发，以促进本协定目标的实现和第二条原则的实施。

（2）除了上述第（1）款的一般功能，联合委员会应当具有以下职能：

（a）准备向当事国提交按照第一条确定的区域范围，以及开展任何附带的调查工作；

（b）收集和交换区域内与石油开发相关的科学、技术和其他数据；

（c）编制和提交区域计划，以获得当事国的共同批准；

（d）执行根据区域计划，为区域或其他开发区域的联合委员会分配的任务；

（e）为了促进区域内石油开发之必要，向当事国推荐应当适用和修改的专门的石油法；

（f）监督和实施本协定；

（g）审议任意一方当事国提交的事项；

（h）对区域内渔业、海洋科学调查、海底电缆和管道的铺设和维护，以及海洋环境的保护的管理事项提出建议，要考虑到促进石油开发的需要，以及当事国间已生效的条约中包含的相关国际法的标准和规则；

(i) 除石油资源，对区域内可能发现的任何矿物资源，做出安排建议；

(j) 本协定可能规定的其他职责，或当事国认为履行其目标和原则所必需的职责。

第七条 区域计划的编制

(1) 本协定实际生效之后，联合委员会应召开会议编制区域计划，计划中应规定区域内石油开发的方式和石油活动的管理方式。联合委员会应依据第六条向当事国提交完整的区域计划以获得批准。

(2) 编制区域计划应要求解决第（3）、（4）、（5）款框架内提出的问题。联合委员会可以按照任何顺序审议这些问题，但是除非当事国另有约定，联合委员会需仅就这几个条款中确定的选择方案，做出决定。联合委员会在编制区域计划时，需以本协定第三条作为指导原则。

(3) 当事国应当互相通知对方，在本协定签订时，按照现行的国内法，在区域内石油活动连续性权利的所有主张，并提出处理这些主张的方法。当事国应就与此主张相关的区域计划的运营，尽力达成一项协定，该协定不损害第三条第（2）项规定的原则。

(4) 联合委员会可以将区域视为单一区域，也可以为了分配其与当事国依据第（5）款对区域内石油活动的管理责任，划分为若干开发区。联合委员会在做出决定时，应当考虑以下相关因素，包括区域的面积和位置、已知悉的特性（包括地质结构和环境敏感度）、石油活动商业利益的大小，以及潜在许可区的数量。区域内划分的任何开发区，应当由一个或多个合同区组成，合同区的大小由有关当局决定。

(5) 区域或其划分的任何开发区内的区域计划应当指定：

(a) 联合委员会作为单一开发当局（这种情形下，它可以授予任意当事国一部分或全部行政或管理职能）；或者

(b) 任意一方当事国作为单一开发当局；或

(c) 双方当事国作为并存的或联合开发当局。

开发当局的权力和责任源于本协定的规定，并且其代表双方政府行使。

(6) 联合委员会应按照以下方式，在区域计划中建立适用于区域、开发区或合同区的专门的石油法案（本协定条款和开发合同条款均为规制开发区内的石油活动所适用的法律）：

（a）联合委员会作为整个区域或任何开发区的单一开发当局时，应尽力商定选择任意一方当事国石油活动的法律，作为区域或相关区域的专门石油法。在没有达成协议的情况下，联合委员会应当推定其国民是承包人，或者（存在多个承包人时）其国民是经营者的国家的法律，作为相关开发区或合同区的专门石油法。

（b）任意一个当事国作为任何开发区域的单一开发当局时，应当推定该国有关石油活动的法律作为该区域的专门石油法。

（c）如果在任何开发区域存在并存的或联合开发当局，则同一合同区内开发合同持有人应当达成一个经营协议，应当推定被指定为经营者的国民，其本国有关石油活动的法律作为相关合同区的专门石油法。

（7）实施按照第（6）款确定的专门石油法，不应当影响任何当事国在受区域影响的海洋划界上的主张，其除了临时管理便利外不具有任何含义。开发当局按照本协定，在石油活动上行使管辖权应当被视为代表双方当事国行使。

第八条 遵守与实施

（1）区域内所有石油活动应当遵守可适用的法律。

（2）当事国应当在国内法律体系中采取一切适当措施，以实施可适用的法律。

（3）当事国应当向联合委员会和其他开发当局提供一切必要和合理的帮助和支持，以保证承包人遵守可适用的法律。其支持的方式应由联合委员会不时决定。

（4）适用依据第九条采用的税收制度，若与专门石油法有抵触之处，以该税收制度为准。当事国，特别是每个当事国的国内的税收当局，应当适用依据第九条采用的税收制度。

（5）第二十二条第（1）款规定的检查权，当事国根据第二十条为设备安全和人员安全健康，以及根据二十一条为防止污染和保护环境一致同意的程序规则，如果与专门石油法抵触，以前者为准。

第九条 开发合同的财政条款

（1）财政义务，包括区域内承包人向当事国承担的、与区域内的石油活动相关的财政义务，应当依本协定签订的开发合同财务条款做出排他性规定。开发当局（经联合委员会同意适用第3款和第4款），可以同意列入可替代性财政条款,以鼓励对区域或相关区域的投资。"财政条款"应当包括所有具有税收性质的义务(无论是基于产量还是收入),以及其他义务,包括但不限于特许权费、实物支付、产品分成安排、收入和企业税及资源租赁费。

(2) 并存的开发当局与承包人的开发合同中的财政条款,应当遵守并存的开发当局的税收制度安排。作为区域或者部分区域并存管理当局的当事国,不应当向没有与之签订开发合同的承包人征税。任何当事国都不能依据本条向任何承包人,就用于区域内石油活动的设施和设备等资产征税,除非符合资产中承包人的利益。

(3) 当事国可以同意,将一方当事国在离岸勘探和开采活动上的税收制度,适用于区域内的石油活动。

在这种情形下:

(a) 开发当局应当代表本国将税收制度列入共同开发合同条款中;

(b) 采用其税收制度国家的税收当局应当负责为当事国(联合委员会代表当事国)管理和征收区域内石油活动相关的所有税收,且应当与另一当事国的税收当局进行合作;

(c) 除非另有约定,任何税收当局依据本条所得的财政收入应归当事国所有,并平等分配给当事国。

一方当事国根据本条采用的税收制度,除了便利和简化行政管理之外,不应当带来任何其他的后果。

(4) 替代性方法是,当事国可以授予联合委员会起草和谈判开发合同中财务条款的权利。在这种情形下:

(a) 联合委员会应适当顾及和平衡以下需要:

(ⅰ) 为当事国从石油商业开采中获得最佳收入;

(ⅱ) 鼓励商业开发和刺激投资;

(ⅲ) 确保经营活动的透明度和确定性;

(ⅳ) 保证依据财务条款,承包人支出的税款是合理和实际的,可以避免相关第三方国家双重征税。

(b) 在联合委员会的要求下,一方或双方当事国的税收当局应当执行开发合同的财务条款,向联合委员会筹集并核算从承包人收取的费用。获得的所有收入应当由当事国平等分享,除非双方另有约定。

（5）除非适用第（2）、（3）、（4）款的情形，承包人应当履行每个当事国有关国内勘探和开发的税收制度下的财税义务，但是降低的税率也应保证，在每个财务体系的规定下，承包人的纳税都不应当超过，其按照任一特殊的财务体系应缴税额的 50%（或者其他商定的份额）。每个当事国本国的税务局应当：

（a）依据双重财务条款中本国的那部分，向承包人征税，并向联合委员会做账目陈述报告；

（b）在财务条款的行政事务上，与联合委员会进行合作并进行协助。

（6）除非主体另有约定，开发合同的财务条款只能依据合同条款进行修改。任何变化应当获得联合委员会的同意。

（7）当事国应当在国内法律体系中，采取一切合适的措施以执行财务条款。除此之外，当事国应当采取一切适当的步骤（包括为避免双重征税进行协商或修改协议），以保证（在合理和现实范围内）承包人按照财务条款缴纳的税收可以免除第三方国家的双重征税。

（8）依据本条制订的开发合同的财务条款，旨在成为适用于区域的单一税收制度。除非本条另有规定，当事国不应当向区域内的石油活动或者与之相关的活动征税。本条的任何内容都不应当影响，当事国对石油的加工和再处理（超出了石油作为原材料销售所必需的处理）所得收益征税。

（9）按照本条的税收分享的规定，不应当从一个当事国交付给另一国的款项中扣除任何管理费，除非联合委员会另有合意。

第十条 区域计划的批准

（1）区域计划的执行需要当事国的共同批准。当事国应当以适当方式公布此项批准。

（2）如果一方当事国没有在……月内批准联合委员会提交的区域计划，联合委员会应当重新考虑区域计划，并做出适当修改。

（3）如果在本协定生效后两年内，区域计划仍然没有获得共同批准，当事国应当会面以促成批准的达成。

（4）区域计划内没有包含的事项应按照本协定规定处理，本协定没有规定的，当事国应当达成补充协议。

第十一条 开发合同

（1）任何石油活动都应当依据开发合同进行，开发合同可以采取许可证制、租让制、产品分成合同或者其他合同安排。

（2）任何一个当事国的国民，可以向适格的开发当局申请签订一个包含部分或全部石油活动的开发合同。申请应当包括一个详细的工作计划、环境影响评估，以及开发当局要求的其他信息。

（3）联合委员会之外的开发当局，应当根据本协定条款可能要求的任何修改，或者联合委员会可能公布的指导原则，处理本国国民的申请、筛选和签约程序。

（4）联合委员会或作为区域或开发区域开发当局的任何当事国，应当处理申请、筛选和签约程序，这些规定可以源于，也可以不源于专门石油法，但是应当公布。

（5）开发当局在执行过程中，联合委员会可以将任何事项提交技术委员会审议或建议（关于承包人或开发合同）。

（6）所有的开发当局，包括联合委员会，在决定是否订立开发合同时，除了要注意可适用的石油法的要求，也要考虑以下事项：

（a）区域内的前期开发和花费；

（b）实施申请人的工作计划可能给当事国增加的经济利益；

（c）保护海洋环境的令人满意的保护措施条款；

（d）对区域的合法使用或其他国家的利益造成的不合理干扰；

（e）申请人的经济和技术资质，包括拟荐经营者的相关的经验；

（f）工作计划给当事国当地的雇佣和培训政策带来的贡献。

所有的开发合同应当包含遵守本协定条款和专门石油法的条款。

（7）在竞争申请的情形下，作为开发当局的联合委员会可以：

（i）自由裁量授予一个申请人一项开发合同；

（ii）邀请申请人在指定的时间内按照自己的选择解决竞争性的问题，如果没有解决，联合委员会可以根据第（6）款（e）项的考量，授予一个申请人一项开发合同；或者

（iii）不能根据（i）和（ii）进行授权，邀请申请人对合同区进行竞争性投标，联合委员会授予满足合同区其他要求并出价最高的投标人以开发合同。

（8）当事国或者联合委员会处理申请和授予开发合同时，应当按照第十条下的区域计划的共同批准公布后迅速进行。如果在申请提交［2年］

后，对任何申请都没有答复，应当视为申请被拒绝。

（9）开发当局应当允许潜在的承包人查阅注册内容，注册内容应包括申请人或承包人的最新的身份信息，开发合同或申请包含的区域和位置，合同转让与合同条款。工作计划和商业条款应当保密。

第十二条 行使

为了保证实施本协定第二条的共同开发原则的适用，每个当事国除了具有第二十二条授予的权利，还应当具有下列权利：

（a）对国民共同开发合同的申请进行非歧视性的考虑；

（b）监督经营者，经营者应定期通报区域或相关开发区的石油活动的进程；

（c）可以获取本协定的保密条款中的地质数据；

（d）独立监测各种石油活动，包括必要时进入设备。

本条款的任何内容都不能赋予非相关区域开发当局的当事国干涉日常经营活动的权利，第二十二条规定除外。当事国应当采取产量监测措施，以保证对提高石油产量达成协议。

第十三条 承包人的权利和义务

（1）承包人在合同期限内，依据合同条款和专门石油法，享有开展石油活动的排他性权利。

（2）承包人应当有权处置其依据开发合同享有的石油，只要遵守开发当局对卸货、购买者身份、增加产量的核实等方面的非歧视性限制。

第十四条 开发合同的取消或中止

（1）开发合同不应当被取消、终止或修改，除非承包人被告知且有机会补救时，仍然不能履行开发合同的条款。

（2）本条的任何内容都不应当影响，承包人的作业对海洋环境造成严重威胁或者危害健康和安全时，开发当局或当事国有权中止承包人的权利。

（3）任何违反本条第1款的行为，应当进行补偿。

（4）开发当局取消了由多个承包人共同持有的开发合同时，开发当局应依据与原合同相似的条款，与未违约的承包人签订新的开发合同，且接受与违约承包人相同国籍的替代承包人。

（5）若并存开发当局取消一个开发合同，它应当确保有替代性的承包人与其他并存开发当局的承包人，在与现存联合经营协议相似的条件下，达成新的开发协议。达成新协议之前，除非联合委员会另有指令，余下的承包人可以在现存联合经营协议的单一风险经营条款下，继续进行石油活动。

第十五条 分配

开发合同下承包人的权利和义务，未经相关开发当局允许，不能转让。如果拟受让者具备经济和技术上的资质，并能满足开发当局或本协定的要求（在非歧视性基础上实行的），开发当局不应当无理保留其同意。

第十六条 关税与税收豁免

（1）除非联合委员会另有合意，不应当对区域内使用的石油设备，或者与使用引起的在任意当事国管辖权区域内的进出口活动，征收任何关税或其他税款。本条的任何内容不应当影响当事国，对区域已使用完的本国生产的石油设备出口有关的权利。

（2）将区域内石油运输至一方当事国管辖权范围内，应当免除所有的费用和税收，除非相关的开发合同的财务条款有其他规定。根据本条规定，"石油设备"应当包括区域内石油活动所必需的设施、设备和装备（包括钻探装置），以及材料和其他物品。

第十七条 承包人在当事国领土内的作业活动

承包人可以在任意当事国领土内，依据正在开展辅助性石油活动的当事国的法律法规，获得、建设、维护、使用以及处分建筑、平台、油槽、管道、终端站和其他区域内石油活动的必要设施。

第十八条 统一性

（1）如果任何单一石油地质结构或油田跨越了非以下第 2 款的边界线，当事国应当按照第二十三和二十四条进行适当的协商。

（2）如果任何单一石油地质结构或油田跨越了区域内开发区或合同区的界线，或者跨越了区域内与当事国任何无争议的专属海洋区域的界线，位于上述边界线一侧的这部分地质构造或油田，从边界线的另一侧整体或部分可开采的，当事国应当在承包人未达成一致（如果有的话）的情况下，就地质结构或油田最有效开采的方式以及由此获得收益分配的方式达成一致。

第十九条 人员的雇佣和培训

联合委员会可以对区域内承包人应当遵守的雇佣和培训政策颁布指导准则，以达成如下目的：

（a）高效安全地开展石油活动，增加国民的就业机会；

（b）帮助在当事国间平等地分配雇佣和培训利益。

开发合同的条款应当与指导准则保持一致。当事国将应当在移民法和就业法的实施上进行合作，以促进签证和工作许可证问题的协调。

第二十条 健康与安全

（1）当事国应采取一切合理的措施确保参与石油活动的人员的健康和安全，以及区域内设备和管道的安全。

（2）遵照第 1 款的规定，当事方根据联合委员会的推荐，应就区域内人员健康和安全，所有石油活动设备和管道的设计、建设和维护相关的标准和程序达成一致。特别是这些措施应当：

（a）考虑到相关国际机构建立的被普遍接受的国际标准；

（b）依据第七条同意的专门石油法规定，以及联合委员会认为达成这些标准和程序所必需的修改规定来执行，包括弃权声明。

（3）为了确保上述第 2 款的措施得到实施，当事国应当按照联合委员会的建议，采用行政程序以交换与健康、安全和建设标准有关的信息。

第二十一条 防止污染和保护海洋环境

（1）当事国应当尽一切合理努力确保区域内的石油活动，或者与此相关的任何设备和管道的运行，不会也不可能污染海洋环境。

（2）遵照第 1 款的规定，当事国应当按照联合委员会的建议，就防止和消除区域内石油活动引起的海洋污染而采取的必要措施和程序达成一致。

特别是，这些措施应当：

（a）依据第七条同意的专门石油法规定，以及联合委员会认为达成这些标准和程序所必需的修改规定来执行，包括弃权声明；

（b）以良好的石油领域的实践为基础，并考虑特别是联合国环境规划署、国际海事组织和其他相关的国际机构制定的国际规则、标准以及推荐的实践和程序；

（c）纳入防止井喷、防止和控制石油从设备或管道中泄漏，或倾倒垃圾，或废弃设备和管道的条款；

（cc）制订一个应急计划以应对石油作业的污染；

（d）确保当事国管辖下的自然人和法人因海洋污染造成的损害，应依据当事国的法律制度，获得迅速和充分的补偿或其他救济。

（3）为了促进有效监督区域作业对环境的影响，双方当事国应当定期向联合委员会提供，其从承包人或检查员获得的与石油泄漏和污染相关的信息。特别是，如发生下列事件，必须立即通知联合委员会：

（a）石油泄漏或类似的可能会引起污染的事件；

（b）设备和管道上泄漏大量的石油；

（c）与设备和管道相关的碰撞事件；

（d）由于不可抗力、危难或其他紧急情况，设备上人员撤离的事件。

通知应包括处理该事件应采取的措施。

（4）本协定的任何内容不应当影响，任何当事国或双方当事国在本区域内共同采取或实施，与实际损害或可能的损害相应的措施，以保护其海岸线或相关利益，包括渔业，免受上述3款（a）至（d）项事件合理预期可能造成的重大损害性后果，造成污染或污染的威胁。

第二十二条　检查权

（1）法律为专门石油法的当事国（"责任国"），应当对设备和管道的检查，以及依据该法在区域内、开发区或合同区的设备上作业的检查，负有单一责任。当事国间应当就本款所指的检查和监管事项，与另一国商定检查员的资格认证程序并交换信息。

（2）责任国应当授予另一当事国的检查员进入的权利，并配备设备以使检查员对第二十条和二十一条的要求得到遵守。若另一方的检查员认为，第二十条或二十一条的要求没有得到遵守，该当事国可以书面通知责任国进行补救。

（3）双方当事国的检查员存在分歧，或者一个当事国的检查员拒绝另一方检查员的要求，不采取行动，则相关的事项应当提交联合委员会。

（4）任意当事国的检查员在以下情形下，可以命令立即停止全部或部分作业：

（a）检查员认为为了下述目的，这样做是必需的或是权宜之计：

（i）避免造成丧生或有生命危险的事件（无论危险是否紧急）；

（ⅱ）避免对当事国造成实际损害或损害威胁，以保护其海岸线或者相关利益，包括渔业，免受不可抗力、危难或紧急情况合理预期可能造成的重大损害性后果，造成的污染或污染的威胁；

（ⅲ）将事故或事件的后果降至最低；并且

（b）时间和情形不允许双方当事国的检查员进行协商；且

（c）立即向联合委员会报告该命令的内容和原因，联合委员会随后立即召开会议，商量采取必要的行动以安全快速地恢复作业。

第二十三条　争端解决

（1）下述所有争端：

（a）当事国间关于本条约解释和适用的争端；或

（b）开发当局与承包人间关于开发合同解释和适用的争端；或

（c）并存或联合开发当局的承包人关于联合经营协议解释和适用的争端；

除了上述（b）款联合委员会作为开发当局的争端以外，争端应当首先提交联合委员会调解，再按照本条后续条款解决。

（2）除非当事国间达成其他合意，第（1）款（a）项的争端应由任一当事国提交仲裁庭裁决。任一当事国通知另一当事国其依据第（2）款（a）项任命的仲裁员，并依第（1）款（a）项提交联合委员会后60天内任何时间，提交仲裁庭。仲裁庭应当按照下列方式构成和裁决：

（a）任一当事国应当任命一个仲裁员，两名仲裁员应当在第二名仲裁员任命后60天内，指定第三国国民作为第三名仲裁员，且作为仲裁庭主席；

（b）在收到另一国任命仲裁员的通知后60天内，一方当事国没有指定仲裁员，或者两名仲裁员在第二名仲裁员任命后60天内没有指定第三名仲裁员，国际法院院长应在任一当事国的请求下，指定第三国的国民填补空缺；

（c）若国际法院院长是任一当事国的国民或者领土上的常住居民，或因其他原因不能任命仲裁员，应当由不是任一当事国的国民或者不能承担此任的高级法官来任命；

（d）除非当事国通过本协定议定书的方式，制定了仲裁庭程序的相关规则，由仲裁庭自行决定仲裁庭程序，仲裁庭的所有决定须遵循多数表决制；

（e）仲裁庭应当依据本协定可适用的条款，以及国际法相关规则和原则，对争端进行裁决；

（f）为了保护当事国的相关权利或者防止争端扩大化，仲裁庭在最后裁决之前可以采取临时措施。

争端方应当依据善意执行仲裁庭所有的裁决，包括临时措施的命令。仲裁庭的裁决对当事国具有终局性和约束力。

（3）第（1）款（b）项下开发当局和承包人的争端，或者第（1）款（c）项下承包人间的争端，除非达成其他合意，应当按照相关开发合同或联合经营协议的相关条款，提交有约束力的商业仲裁。但是，任何仲裁委员会对下列提交的争端没有管辖权：

（a）关于本条约解释和适用的问题，如果与仲裁委员会的裁决有关，应当将此问题提交当事国按照上述第2款解决，并将上款仲裁庭的裁决写入本裁决书中；

（b）争议属于第（1）款（b）项的争端，开发当局根据开发合同的条款或专门石油法具有专属裁量权的事项。

依据本条行使管辖权的仲裁委员会，应当依据第一条规定的可适用的法律，对争端进行裁决。

（4）任何情况都不应当阻止，在第（3）款（a）项的情形下，当事国共同授予仲裁委员会对本条约的解释和适用问题的管辖权，以代替根据第（2）款组成的仲裁庭。在这种情形下，双方当事国有权参与仲裁委员会的诉讼，提交本条所指的解释和使用问题的口头和书面证据。

（5）第3款下的任何商业仲裁，应当在1958年《承认与执行外国仲裁公约》（也称《纽约公约》）签订国的领土内或仲裁员同意的地方进行。当事国应当承认和执行商业仲裁做出的裁决，本国的法律制度与《纽约公约》第五条的规定不一致的情形除外。

第二十四条 第三方权利

（1）当事国按照本协定行使权力，不得不公平地干涉其他国家在区域内依据普遍接受的国际法原则享有的权利和自由。

（2）任何第三方国家主张的权利，与本协定规定的当事国的权利相冲突时，当事国应当通过合适的渠道进行协商，以协调一致地做出回应。

第二十五条　生效和期限

（1）双方当事国交换批准文书时条约生效，互换批准文书应于条约签署之后两年内进行。

（2）本协定无期限限制。但是，条约生效［45］年后，任意当事国可以提出［5］年后终止本协定。依据本规定终止协定不应当影响尚未到期的开发合同。本协定只为既存合同的目的而继续有效。最后一个继续有效的合同到期或提前终止，本协定随即终止。

（3）虽然有第2款的规定，当事国可以在任何时候以书面协议的方式修改或终止协定。

（4）一旦发出终止的通知，当事国间应当不予延迟地协商本区域的未来安排问题。

（5）本协定的终止不应当影响终止前当事方应承担的财政义务，也不影响终止前依据本协定开发合同所规定的权利和义务。除非当事国达成其他合意，联合委员会应继续履行实施既存合同可能必需的剩余职责。

2. The Revised Model Agreement between State X and State Y on the Joint Development of Petroleum in Areas of the Continent Shelf and /or the Exclusive Economic Zone of the Two Countries

STATE X AND STATE Y

Desiring to promote the friendly relations between them,

Recognizing that the continent shelf and/or the exclusive economic zone adjacent to the two States have not been delimited and or may be subject of overlapping claims,

Noting the possibility that petroleum resources may exist in the area subject to such overlapping claims,

Considering that it is in the best interests of the two States to explore for and exploit any petroleum resources in an orderly fashion,

Convinced that such activities could be best carried out jointly,

Taking into consideration that Geneva Convention on the Continent Shelf of 1958 and the United Nations Convention on the Law of the Sea of 1982,

Affirming that the rules of international law will continue to govern questions not regulated by the provisions of this Agreement.

HAVE AGREED AS FOLLOWS:

Article 1 USE OF TERMS

For the purpose of the Agreement:

(1) "applicable law" means the provisions of this Agreement, the terms of the development contract and the specified petroleum law;

(2) "contractor" means any national which is a party to a development contract with a development authority;

(3) "development contract" means the agreement entered into between the development authority and a contractor pursuant to Article 11;

(4) "contract area" means that part of a development area which is currently the subject of a development contract and excludes areas which have been relinquished by the contractor;

(5) "development area" means the areas (if any) into which the Zone is divided for the purpose of apportioning the supervision, administration and regulation of petroleum activities between the development authorities;

(6) "development authority" means the State Party, States Parties, or the Joint Commission which is empowered pursuant to this Agreement to enter into development contracts in respect of petroleum activities in the Zone or the relevant development area;

(i) "concurrent development authority" means a State Party which is in respect of any development area is empowered under this Agreement to enter into a development contract with an applicant selected by it which in turn is required to enter into a joint operating agreement with the contractor of the other State Party exercising identical authority in the same development area;

(ii) "joint development authority" means a State Party which in respect of any development area is empowered under this Agreement to enter into a development contract with the applicant of its choice and with the nominee of the other State Party as joint contractor each of which is required to obtain a similar development contract from that other State Party;

(iii) "sole development authority" means the Joint Commission or a State Party which in respect of any development area is alone empowered under this Agreement to enter into development contracts;

(7) "installation" means any structure, device or artificial island utilized in petroleum activities, installed above, in, on or under the seabed including drilling vessels in situ;

(8) "joint commission" means the Commission established by Article 5

with functions set out in Article 6;

(9) "national" means a natural or juridical person having the nationality of one or both of the States Parties in accordance with the laws and regulations of the relevant State Party;

(10) "operating agreement" means a contract concluded between the holders of development contracts, for the purpose of carrying out petroleum activities in the Zone;

(11) "operator" means the holder of a development contract with a development authority appointed and acting as operator under the terms of the operating agreement which has been approved by the appropriate development authority or authorities;

(12) "petroleum" means crude oil and natural gas deposited beneath the subsurface together with other underground minerals which are produced in association with them;

(13) "petroleum activities" means all activities of exploration for and exploitation of the petroleum of the Zone;

(14) "Zone Plan" means the development plan agreed by the State Parties pursuant to Article 6 and 7 for the petroleum activities in the Zone;

(15) "pollution" means the introduction by reason of petroleum activities in the Zone of substances or energy into marine environment, including estuaries which results or is likely to result in such deleterious effects as harm to living resources and marine life, hazards to human health, impairment of quality for use of sea water and reduction of amenities;

(16) "specified petroleum law" means the system of law applicable to petroleum activities or activities in connection therewith in the Zone, development area or contract area as established in the Zone Plan by virtue of the provisions of Articles of 7 and 8;

(17) "Zone" means that area of seabed, ocean floor and subsoil;

(a) bounded by geodesic lines joining the following points using the ······ Datum in the order listed:

(i) Lat ······ Long ······

(ⅱ) Lat …… Long ……

(ⅲ) Lat …… Long ……

(b) the sea floor limits of which are set by perpendicular lines dropped from the sea level boundary; and

(c) extended where necessary to include a reasonable safety zone around any installation constructed within the Zone for purpose of petroleum activities.

Article 2 JOINT DEVELOPMENT ZONE

(1) The Zone is hereby established for the purpose of developing petroleum within its boundaries and all petroleum activities in the Zone shall be governed by this Agreement.

(2) The State Parties by subsequent agreement may make arrangements for the development for the development of other mineral and non-living resources of the Zone.

(3) The Joint Commission shall, for illustrative purposes only, depict the boundaries of the Zone on a chart or charts of appropriate scale.

Article 3 PRINCIPLES OF JOINT DEVELOPMENT

(1) The State Parties shall promote the joint development of petroleum of the Zone and share [equally or in such other agreed proportion] the rights and obligations arising from petroleum activities through the mechanism established by this Agreement.

(2) No petroleum activities shall be conducted in the Zone excepted in accordance with this Agreement and measures adopted pursuant to it.

(3) The State Partied shall:

(a) further joint development of the Zone's petroleum by cooperating fully in the supervision and conduct of petroleum activities;

(b) consult through the medium of the Joint Commission when matters arise which may affect the interests of either State Party;

(c) wherever possible co-ordinate their interests in the joint development of the Zone.

(4) the petroleum of the Zone shall be exploited efficiently and in a manner consistent with generally accepted good oilfield practice and with due regard to

the protection of the marine environment.

(5) Subject to the petroleum activities of the States' Parties under this Agreement the joint development of the Zone shall be carried on with due respect to the rights of other states in the Zone.

Article 4 WITHOUT PREJUDICE CLAUSE

(1) Nothing contained in this Agreement shall be interpreted as a renunciation of any right or claim relating to the Zone by either State Party or a recognition of or support for the other State Party's position with regard to any right or claim to the Zone.

(2) No act or activities taking place as a consequence of this Agreement or its operation shall constitute a basis for asserting, supporting or denying the position of either State Party with regard to rights or claims over the Zone.

(3) Unless otherwise agreed between the State Parties negotiations on the issue of final delimitation shall be postponed for the duration of this Agreement.

Article 5 THE JOINT COMMISSION

(1) The Joint Commission is hereby established as the body responsible for the overall supervision of petroleum activities in the Zone, for the preparation of the Zone Plan and such functions in respect of the administration of petroleum activities in the Zone as may be devolved upon it pursuant to the Zone Plan and Article 6 of this Agreement.

(2) The Joint Commission shall consist of an equal number of representatives of each State Party and all decisions of the Joint Commission whether on matters of procedure or of substance shall require the consent of the representatives of both State Parties.

(3) The Joint Commission shall appoint a Technical Committee composed of equal numbers of technical advisers nominated by each State Party and possessing appropriate qualifications relevant to petroleum activities. On entry into fore of this Agreement the Technical Committee shall be in continuous session.

(4) The tasks of the Technical Committee shall be the day to day supervision of joint development including the examination of development contracts, the provision of advice and recommendations to the joint commission on technical

matters and other issues referred to it by the Joint Commission.

(5) The Joint Commission shall meet within [six] months of the entry into force of this Agreement and thereafter once annually or as it may agree, or on the request of either State Party or as necessary to perform its functions under this Agreement.

(6) The Joint Commission may establish a permanent secretariat to carry out the administrative work of the Joint Commission. Where the Joint Commission is not a development authority it shall not establish a permanent secretariat without first investigating other methods of servicing its administrative needs. The Joint Commission shall meet at the site of Secretariat or if none is established at such places alternating between the territories of State Parties as they may determine.

(7) The Joint Commission shall have such legal personality and shall enjoy in the territory of each of the State Parties such legal capacity as may be necessary to perform those functions which are, or may be, devolved to it under the Agreement and to enable it to achieve the objectives of this Agreement.

(8) Unless otherwise agreed reasonable administrative expenses incurred by the Joint Commission shall be paid from the date of establishment of the Joint Commission. These expenses shall be shared equally between the State Parties which shall make timely contributions to its funds in accordance with budgetary procedures to be agreed between them. The Joint Commission shall comply with the budgetary procedures and make efficient use of its available resources. The Joint Commission may defray its costs by charging fees or rentals in respect of applications for development contracts which shall not exceed the reasonable costs of their processing.

(9) The official languages of the Commission shall be X, Y or such other language as the Commission may decide.

(10) In fulfilling the functions of the Joint Commission under this Article, the representative members of the State Parties, staff of the Joint Commission and any technical advisers shall have no financial interest in petroleum activities in the Zone. Subject to their responsibilities to the State Parties, they shall not dis-

close, even after the termination of their functions, any industrial secret or proprietary data which are transferred to the Joint Commission, or any other confidential information coming to their knowledge by reason of their membership of or employment with the Commission.

(11) Subject to lawful restrictions as to disclosure and use the State Parties shall exchange information received by contractors in respect if the Zone. Each State Party undertakes to receive such information as confidential and, except for the use of the Joint Commission or the Technical Committee, not further to disclose or use it inconsistently with such restrictions.

Article 6 FUNCTION OF THE JOINT COMMISSION

(1) The Joint Commission shall be the body responsible to the State Parties for planning, co-ordinating and supervising the joint development of the petroleum of the Zone in furtherance of the objectives of this Agreement and in application of the principles set out in Article 2 above.

(2) In addition to its general role under paragraph 1 above the Joint Commission shall have the following functions:

(a) the preparation of submissions to the State Parties in respect of the determination of the Zone under Article 1 together with the carrying out of any incidental survey work;

(b) the collection and exchange of scientific, technical and other data concerning petroleum in the Zone;

(c) the preparation and submission of the Zone Plan for the State Parties' joint approval;

(d) the carrying out of such tasks as development authority for the Zone or any development area as may be allocated to it under the Zone Plan;

(e) the recommending to the State Parties the proper application of and such changes to the specified petroleum law as may be necessary to promote the development of the petroleum of the Zone;

(f) the supervision and implementation of this Agreement;

(g) the consideration of matters referred to it by either State Party;

(h) the submission of proposals for the regulation of fishing, marine scientific research, the laying and maintenance of submarine cables and pipelines and the preservation of the marine environment in the Zone, having regard both to the need to facilitate the development of petroleum and to the relevant standards and rules of international law including any treaty provisions in force between the State Parties;

(i) the recommendation of arrangements for the joint exploitation of any mineral resource, apart from petroleum, which may be discovered within the Zone;

(j) such other functions as may be specified elsewhere in this Agreement or which the State Parties may regard as necessary to fulfill its objects and principles.

Article 7 PREPARATION OF THE ZONE PLAN

(1) As soon as practicable following the entry into force of this Agreement the Joint Commission shall meet in order to prepare the Zone Plan which shall establish the manner in which the petroleum of the Zone shall be developed and petroleum activities regulated. The Joint Commission shall submit the completed Zone Plan to the States Parties for their approval under Article 6 above.

(2) Preparation of the Zone Plan shall require determination of the matters set out n paragraph 3, 4 and 5 within the framework of those provisions. The Joint Commission may consider them in any order but unless otherwise agreed by the States Parties the Joint Commission shall in making its determination be limited to the various alternative specified in those paragraph. The Joint Commission in preparing the Zone Plan shall be guided by the principles established in Article 3.

(3) The States Parties shall inform each other if all claims to continuing rights in respect of petroleum activities in the Zone arising under their national laws existing at the date of this claims. The States Parties shall endeavor to reach agreement on the operation of the Zone Plan in relation to those claims without prejudice to the principle contained in Article 3 (2) above.

(4) The Joint Commission may treat the Zone as a single area or divide it into development areas for the purpose of allocating responsibility for the administration of petroleum activities in the Zone between itself and the States Parties un-

der paragraph 5 below. In reaching its decision the Joint Commission shall take into account such factors as appear relevant to it including the size and location of the Zone, its known characteristics (including geological structure and environmental sensitivity), the degree of commercial interest in petroleum activities, and the number if potential licensing areas. Any development area into which the Zone is divided may consist of one or more contract areas whose size shall be determined by the competent development authority.

(5) The Zone Plan shall in respect of the Zone or any development area into which it is divided designate:

(a) the Joint Commission are sole development authority (in which case it may delegate some or all of its administrative or regulatory functions to either States Party); or

(b) either States Party as sole development authority; or

(c) both States Parties, as concurrent or joint development authorities.

A development authority's power and responsibilities shall derive from this Agreement and be exercised on behalf of both States Parties.

(6) The Joint Commission shall in the Zone Plan establish the specified petroleum law for the zone, development areas or contract areas as appropriate (which together with the provisions of this Agreement and the terms of the development contract shall be the applicable law governing petroleum activities in the Zone) in the following manner:

(a) where the Joint Commission is to be the sole development authority for the whole Zone or any development area it shall endeavor to agree on the selection of the law of either State Party in respect of petroleum activities as the specified petroleum law for the Zone or area in question. Falling agreement the Joint Commission shall be deemed to have selected the law of the State Party whose national is the contractor or (if more than one contractor) whose national is the operator as the specified petroleum law for the relevant development or contract area where appropriate;

(b) where a State Party is sole development authority for any development area its laws in respect of petroleum activities shall be deemed to have been selected as the specified petroleum law for the area;

(c) where there are concurrent or joint development authorities in respect of any development area the holders of development contracts over the same contract area shall enter into an operating agreement, and the law in respect of petroleum activities of the State Party whose national is appointed operator shall be deem to have been selected as the specified petroleum law for the relevant contract area.

(7) The operation of the specified petroleum law as established pursuant to paragraph 6 shall be without prejudice to either State Party's claim in respect of the delimitation of its maritime boundaries affected by the Zone and shall carry no implication other than of temporary administrative convenience. Furthermore the exercise under this Agreement of any jurisdiction in respect of petroleum activities by a development authority shall be deemed to be on behalf of both States Parties.

Article 8 COMPLIANCE AND ENFORCEMENT

(1) All petroleum activities in the Zone shall be carried on in accordance with the applicable law.

(2) States Parties shall take all appropriate measures within their national legal systems to enforce the applicable law.

(3) States Parties shall render all necessary and reasonable assistant and support to the Joint Commission or any other development authority in ensuring that contractors comply with the applicable law. The manner of such support shall be decided by the Joint Commission from time to time.

(4) The taxation regime adopted pursuant to the provisions of Article 9 shall apply and prevail to the extent of any inconsistency with the specified petroleum law. States Parties, and in particular each States Party's national taxation authority, shall apply the taxation regime adopted pursuant to the provisions of Article 9.

(5) Inspection rights pursuant to Article 22 paragraph 1 and the procedures agreed by the States Parties pursuant to Article 20 for the safety of installations and the health and safety of personnel and Article 21 for the prevention of pollution and the protection of the marine environment shall apply and prevail to the extent of any inconsistency with the specified petroleum law.

Article 9 FINANCIAL TERMS OF DEVELOPMENT CONTRACTS

(1) The financial including fiscal obligations of contractors to the States Parties in respect of petroleum activities in the Zone shall be exclusively determined by the financial terms of development contracts established under this Article. Development authorities (subject to the consent of the Joint Commission where paragraph 3 or 4 apply) may agree to incorporate alternative financial terms in order to encourage investment in the Zone or relevant development area. "Financial terms" shall include all obligations in the nature of taxation (whether production or income based) and other financial obligation including but not limited to royalties, payments in kind, production sharing arrangements, income and corporation taxes and resources rentals.

(2) The financial terms of a development contract between a concurrent development authority and a contractor shall be those imposed by the taxation regime of that concurrent development authority. A State Party which is a concurrent development authority for the Zone or any part thereof shall not tax a contractor with whom it does not have a development contract. Neither State Party shall tax any contractor pursuant to this paragraph in respect of installations plant and equipment used in petroleum activities in the Zone other than on proportion to the interest held by the contractor in those assets.

(3) The States Parties may agree to adopt the taxation regime of one State Party in respect of offshore exploration or exploitation activities for application to petroleum activities in the Zone.

In this event:

(a) the development authority or authorities shall on behalf of the State Parties incorporate the taxation regime so chosen into the terms of all development contracts;

(b) the taxation authorities of the State Party whose taxation regime is so chosen shall be responsible to the State Parties (represented for this purpose by the Joint Commission) for the administration and collection of all taxation in respect of petroleum activities in the Zone, and shall enjoy the cooperation of the taxation authorities of the other State Party;

(c) all revenues received by any taxation authorities pursuant to this provision shall be accounted for and divided equally between the State Parties unless otherwise agreed.

The adoption of a State Party's taxation regime pursuant to this provision shall carry no implication other than convenience and ease of administration.

(4) Alternatively the State Parties may delegate to the Joint Commission powers to formulate and negotiate the financial terms of development contract. In this event:

(a) the Joint Commission shall take due account of and balance the needs to:

(i) obtain optimum revenues for the State Parties from commercial exploitation of the petroleum;

(ii) encourage commercial exploitation and provide incentives for investment;

(iii) ensure clarity and certainty of operation;

(iv) ensure to the extent reasonable and practicable that the contractors' tax payments under the financial terms qualify for double taxation relief in relevant third State Parties;

(b) at the request of the Joint Commission the taxation authorities of either or both State Parties shall administer the financial terms of the development contracts and collect and account to the Joint Commission for all payments received from the contractors. All monies so received shall be divided equally between the State Parties unless otherwise agreed.

(5) Unless paragraph 2, 3 or 4 apply, the financial obligations under each of State Parties' taxation regimes in respect of national exploration and exploitation shall apply to contractors but at reduced rates calculated to ensure that liability of the contractor under each of dual sets of financial conditions does not exceed fifty per cent (or other agreed share) of that which would obtain if the contractor were subject to the particular set of financial conditions alone. Each State Party's own taxation authorities shall:

(a) collect the payments due from the contractor under its part of the dual financial terms and provide statements of account to the Joint Commission;

(b) cooperate with and assist the Joint Commission in the administration of the financial terms.

(6) Unless the parties otherwise agree the financial terms of a development contract may be varied only in accordance with its provisions. Any such variation shall also require the consent of the Joint Commission.

(7) The State Parties shall take all appropriate measures within their national legal systems to enforce the financial terms. In addition to the State Parties shall take such steps as seem to them appropriate (including the negotiation or amendment of agreements for avoidance of double taxation) to ensure (to the extent reasonable and practical) that contractors' tax payments under the financial terms qualify for double taxation relief in relevant third party State.

(8) The financial terms of development contracts established under this Article are intended to be the sole taxation system applicable to the Zone. Neither State Party shall tax petroleum activities in the Zone or the proceeds deriving therefrom except in accordance with this Article. Nothing in this provision shall affect the State Parties' rights to tax any profits arising from the processing or further treatment of petroleum beyond the initial treatment necessary to effect its sale as a raw material.

(9) Any sums due from one State Party to the other under the revenues sharing provisions of this Article shall not be subject to any deduction for administrative expenses except as agreed by the Joint Commission.

Article 10　APPROVAL OF THE ZONE PLAN

(1) The Zone Plan shall require the joint approval of the State Parties for its implementation. Any such approval shall be published in an appropriate manner by the State Parties.

(2) In the event that either State Party has not approved the Zone Plan within …… months of its submission the Joint Commission shall reconsider the Zone Plan and where appropriate revise it.

(3) If joint approval has not been obtained within two years of this Agreement's entry into force the State Parties shall meet with a view to facilitating

such approval.

(4) Matters which are not included in the Zone Plan shall be governed by this Agreement, or in the absence of any provision in this Agreement by supplemental agreement between the State Parties.

Article 11　DEVELOPMENT CONTRACTS

(1) No petroleum activities may be undertaken other than pursuant to a development contract, which may take the form of a license, concession, production sharing contract or other contractual arrangement.

(2) Nationals of either State Party may apply to the appropriate development authority for a development contract covering any or all petroleum activities. Applications shall include a detailed work programme, environmental impact statement and such other information as the development authority may determine.

(3) Development authorities other than the Joint Commission shall apply their own national application, selection and contracting procedures with such modifications as may be required by the terms of this Agreement or such guidelines as the Joint Commission may publish.

(4) The Joint Commission or State Party acting as development authority for the Zone or a development area shall apply application, selection and contracting procedures which may or may not derive from the specified petroleum law and which it shall publish.

(5) In exercising its development authority, the Joint Commission may refer any matter to the Technical Committee for consideration and recommendation (as to contractor or development contract).

(6) All development authorities, including the Joint Commission, shall in addition to the requirements of the applicable petroleum law have regard to the following matters when deciding whether or not to enter into a development contract:

(a) prior exploration and expenditure in the Zone;

(b) economic benefits to the State Parties likely to accrue from the implementation of the applicants' work programme;

(c) provision of satisfactory safeguard for the protection of the marine environment;

(d) any unreasonable interference with the interests of other States or other lawful uses of the Zone;

(e) financial and technical qualifications of the applicants including the relevant experience of the proposed operator;

(f) contribution of the work programme to the local employment and training policies of the State Parties.

All development contracts shall contain undertakings to comply with the provisions of this Agreement and the specified petroleum law.

(7) In the event of competing applications the Joint Commission as development authority may:

(i) in its discretion grant to one applicant a development contract;

(ii) invite the applicants to resolve the competition within a prescribed time amongst themselves by means of their own choice falling which the Joint Commission may, having regard to the considerations referred to in paragraph 6 (e) above, award a development contract to an applicant; or

(iii) where no grant can be achieved by (i) and (ii) above, invite the applicants to make competitive bids for contracts in which case the Joint Commission shall award a development contract to the highest bidder who satisfies the other requirements of the contract.

(8) The processing of applicants and the granting of development contracts whether by the State Parties or the Joint Commission shall proceed expeditiously following publication of the joint approval of the Zone Plan under Article 10. Where no decision has been reached on any application within [two years] of the date of its submission, such application shall be deemed to have been rejected.

(9) Development authorities shall maintain a register open to inspection by potential contractors which shall contain up-to-date details of the identity of applicants or contractors, location and area covered by development contracts or applications, transfers and terms of contracts. The work programme and commer-

cial terms shall remain confidential.

Article 12　ACCESS TO OPERATIONS

In order to ensure the application of the principles of joint development under Article 2 above each State Party shall in addition to its rights under Article 22 be entitled to:

(a) non-discriminatory consideration of its nationals' applications for the development contracts;

(b) monitor operations and be kept regularly informed on the progress of petroleum activities in the Zone or relevant development areas;

(c) obtain access to geological data subject to the confidentiality provisions of this Agreement;

(d) independently meter any petroleum activities including necessary access to installations.

Nothing in this provision shall entitle a State Party which is not a development authority for the relevant area to interfere in day to day operations except as provided in Article 22. The State Parties shall adopt procedure in respect of metering production designed to ensure agreement on the quantities of petroleum uplifted.

Article 13　RIGHTS AND DUTIES OF CONTRACTORS

(1) Contractors shall have exclusive rights to carry out the petroleum activities authorized under the development contract for its duration subject to compliance with its terms and the specified petroleum law.

(2) The contractor shall be titled to dispose of any petroleum to which it is entitled under the development contract subject only to any non-discriminatory restrictions the development authority may impose on landing, identity of the purchaser and verification of the volumes uplifted.

Article 14　CANCELLATION OF SUSPENSION OF DEVELOPMENT CONTRACTS

(1) Development contracts shall not be cancelled, suspended or revised other than for the contactor's failure to comply with the terms of the development contract of which it has notice and opportunity to remedy.

(2) Nothing in this Article shall affect a development authority's or State Parties' rights to suspend a contractor's rights under a development contract in the event of a serious threat to the marine environment or danger to health and safety arising out of the contractor's operations.

(3) Any breach of paragraph 1 of this Article shall entitle compensation.

(4) In the event that a development authority cancels a development contract held jointly by more than one contractor the development authority shall offer a new development contract to the contract (s) not in default on similar terms to those of the previous development contract subject to their acceptance of a replacement contractor of the same nationality as the defaulting contract (s).

(5) Should a concurrent development authority cancel a development contract it shall be responsible for ensuring that a replacement contractor enters into a new joint operating agreement with the contractor of the other concurrent development authority on similar terms to that of the existing joint operating agreement. Until this is done and unless the Joint Commission directs otherwise the remaining contractor may continue petroleum activities under the sole risk operating provisions of the existing joint operating agreement.

Article 15 ASSIGNMENT

A contractor's rights and obligations under a development contract shall not be transferred without the consent of the relevant development authority. The development authority shall not unreasonable withhold its consent where the proposed transferee is financially and technically qualified and otherwise meets the requirements of the development authority (administered on a non-discriminatory basis) and this Agreement.

Article 16 CUSTOMES AND DUTY EXEMPTIONS

(1) Petroleum equipment shall not be subject to any customs duties or other taxes and duties in respect of its use in the Zone or import or export incidental to that use from or to areas within the jurisdiction of either State Party unless and to the extent the Joint Commission otherwise agrees. Noting in this Article shall affect a State Party's rights in respect of the export following the completion of its use in the Zone of petroleum equipment having the territory of that State Party as

its country of origin.

(2) The shipment of petroleum extracted from the Zone to areas within the jurisdiction of the State Parties shall be free of all taxes and duties other than those provided for in the financial terms of the relevant development contract. For the purposes of this Article "petroleum equipment" shall include installations, plant and equipment (including drilling rigs) together with materials and other goods necessary for the conduct of petroleum activities in the Zone.

Article 17 OPERATIONS BY CONTTACTORS IN THE TERRITORY OF THE STATES PARTIES

Contractor may acquire, construct, maintain, use and dispose of in the territory of either State Party, buildings, platform, tanks, pipelines, terminals and other facilities necessary for petroleum activities in the Zone in accordance with the laws and regulations of the State Party in whose territory such ancillary petroleum activities are being undertaken.

Article 18 UNITISATION

(1) If any single geological petroleum structure or petroleum field extends across any dividing line not being one covered by paragraph 2 below, the State Parties shall consult together in accordance with Article 23 and 24 as appropriate.

(2) If any single geological petroleum structure or petroleum field extends across any dividing line between any development or contract areas within the Zone or across the dividing line between the Zone and any undisputed exclusive maritime area of one of the State Parties, and the part of such structure or field which is situated on one side of the said dividing line is exploitable, wholly or in part, from the other side of the said dividing line, the State Parties shall, on failure of the contractors (if any) to agree among themselves, seek to reach agreement as to the manner in which the structure or field shall be most effectively exploited and the manner in which the proceeds deriving therefrom shall be appointed.

Article 19 EMPLOYMENT AND TRAINING OF PERSONNEL

The Joint Commission may issue guideline in respect of the employment and training policies to be followed by contractors in the Zone for the purposes of :

(a) enhancing the employment opportunities of nationals consistent with the efficient and safe conduct of petroleum activities;

(b) assisting to the extent practicable the equitable division of employment and training benefits between the State Parties.

The terms of development contracts shall comply with such guidelines. The State Parties shall cooperate in the administration of their immigration and employment laws so as to facilitate the issue of visas and work permits.

Article 20 HEALTH AND SAFETY

(1) The State Parties undertake to make every reasonable endeavor to secure the health and safety of personnel engaged in petroleum activities and safety of the installations and pipelines in the Zone.

(2) In accordance with paragraph 1, the State Parties on the recommendation of the Joint Commission shall agree standards and procedures in respect of health and safety of personnel, design, construction, and maintenance of installations and pipelines for all petroleum activities in the Zone. In particular these measures shall:

(a) take into account generally accepted international standards established through a competent international body;

(b) be implemented under the specified petroleum law agreed under Article 7 supplemented by such modifications including waivers as the Joint Commission may recommend as necessary to achieve those standards and procedures.

(3) In order to ensure the implementation of the measures under paragraph 2 above the State Parties on recommendation of the Joint Commission undertake to adopt administrative procedures for the exchange of information concerning health, safety and construction standards.

Article 21 PREVENTION OF POLLUTION AND PROTECTION OF THE MARINE ENVIRONMENT

(1) The State Parties shall use all reasonable endeavors to ensure that petroleum activities in the Zone or the operation of any installation or pipeline involved in those activities shall not cause nor be likely to cause pollution of the marine environment.

(2) In accordance with paragraph 1 the State Parties on the recommendation of the Joint Commission shall agree necessary measures and procedures to prevent and remove pollution of the marine environment resulting from petroleum activities in the Zone.

In particular those measures shall:

(a) be implemented under the specified petroleum law agreed under Article 7 supplemented by such modifications, including waivers, as the Joint Commission may recommend as necessary for such agreed measures and procedures;

(b) be based on good oilfield practice taking account of any international rules, standards, recommended practices and procedures, in particular those promulgated by the United Nations Environmental Programme, the International Maritime Organisation and other relevant international bodies;

(c) include provision for the prevention of blow-outs, prevention or control of discharge of petroleum from an installation or pipeline, discharge or dumping of waste, or abandonment of an installation or pipeline;

(cc) establish a contingency plan for combatting pollution from petroleum operations;

(d) ensure recourse in accordance with State Parties' legal systems for prompt and adequate compensation or other relief in respect of damage caused by pollution of the marine environment by natural or juridical persons under their jurisdiction.

(3) In order to facilitate the effective monitoring of the environmental impact of operations in the Zone both State Parties shall regularly provide the Joint Commission with relevant information obtained from their contractors or inspectorate concerning levels of petroleum discharge and contamination. In particular the Joint Commission shall be immediately informed of the occurrence of the following events:

(a) petroleum spillage or event likely to cause pollution;

(b) discharge of large quantities of petroleum from an installation or pipeline;

(c) collision involving an installation or pipeline;

(d) evacuation of personnel from an installation due to force majeure, distress or other emergency.

The notification shall include any measures taken with respect to such events.

(4) Nothing in this Agreement shall prejudice the taking or enforcement by each State Party or by the State Parties jointly of measures in the Zone proportionate to the actual or threatened damage to protect their coastline or related interests, including fisheries, from pollution or threat of pollution from events of the type referred to in paragraph 3 (a) to (d) above which may reasonable be expected to result in major harmful consequences.

Article 22 INSPECTION RIGHTS

(1) The State Party whose laws constitute the specified petroleum law ("the responsible State Party") shall have sole responsibility for the inspection of installations and pipelines and for the supervision of operations carried out on such installations situated in the Zone, development area or contract area subject to that law. The State Parties undertake to argue certification procedures for inspectors and exchange information with each other regarding inspection and supervision pursuant to this paragraph.

(2) The responsible State Party shall grant access to the inspectors of the other State Party and for their equipment to enable its inspectors to satisfy themselves that the requirements of Article 20 and 21 of this Agreement are being observed. Where, in the opinion of the inspectors of the other State Party, the requirements of Article 20 and 21 are not being observed, that State Party may by written notice request the responsible State Party to remedy the situation.

(3) In the event of disagreement between the inspectors of the two State Parties, or if the inspector of the one State Party refuses to take action at the request of the inspector of the other, the matter shall be referred to the Joint Commission.

(4) An inspector of either State Party may order the immediate cessation of any or all operations in the Zone provided:

(a) such a course appears to him necessary or expedient for the purpose of:

(ⅰ) avoiding an accident involving loss of life or danger to life (whether the danger is immediate or not);

(ⅱ) avoiding actual or threatened damage to protect the coastline or related interests of the State Party, including fishing, pollution or threat of pollution due to force majeure distress or an emergency which may reasonably be expected to result in major harmful consequences;

(ⅲ) minimizing the consequences of such a casualty or other accident; and

(b) time and circumstances do not permit consultation between the inspectors of the two State Parties; and

(c) the issue and reasons for such an order are reported immediately to the Joint Commission which shall thereafter meet promptly to consider the actions necessary for the sale and speedy resumption of operations.

Article 23 SETTLEMENT OF DISPUTES

(1) All disputes between:

(a) the State Parties concerning the interpretation or application of this Agreement; or

(b) a development authority and a contractor concerning interpretation or application of a development contract; or

(c) contractors of concurrent or joint development authorities concerning the interpretation or application of a joint operating agreement,

other than those within (b) in which the Joint Commission is the development authority, shall be referred first to the Joint Commission for its mediation before resolution under the ensuring paragraphs of this Article.

(2) Unless the State Parties otherwise agree, disputes between them under paragraph 1 (a) shall at the instance of either be referred to an arbitral tribunal ("the Tribunal") for resolution. Referral shall be made at any time following 60 days from referral to the Joint Commission under paragraph 1 (a) by either State Party's notice to the other of its appointment under paragraph 2 (a). The Tribunal shall be constituted and determine the dispute in the following manner:

(a) each State Party shall appoint one arbitrator and the two arbitrators so appointed shall within 60 days of the appointment of the second arbitrator appoint a national of a third State as third arbitrator who shall act as Chairman of the Tribunal;

(b) in the event that a State Party fail to appoint an arbitrator within 60 days of receiving notice of other State Party's appointment or the two arbitrators fail to appoint a third arbitrator within 60 days of the appointment of the second, then the President of the International Court of Justice at the request of either State Party shall fill the vacancy by appointing a national of a third State;

(c) should the President of the International Court of Justice be a national of either State Party or habitually resident in the territory of a State Party or otherwise unable to act then the appointment shall be made by the next most senior judge who is not a national of either State Party or otherwise unable to act;

(d) the Tribunal shall determine its own procedures unless the State Parties by protocol to this Agreement establish rules of arbitration in which case its procedures shall be governed by those rules. All decisions of the Tribunal shall be by majority vote;

(e) the Tribunal shall determine the dispute by application of the provisions of this Agreement and relevant rules and principles of the international law;

(f) the Tribunal pending its final award may issue an order indicating the interim measures which must be taken to preserve the respective rights of either State Party or prevent the aggravation or extension of the dispute.

The State Parties shall carry out in good faith all decisions of the Tribunal including any orders for interim measures. Decisions of the Tribunal shall be final and binding on the State Parties.

(3) Disputes between a development authority and a contractor under paragraph 1 (b) or between contractors under paragraph 1 (c) shall unless otherwise agreed between the parties thereto be subject to binding commercial arbitration pursuant to the terms of the relevant development contract or joint operating agreement. However, any arbitral panel to which the dispute is submitted shall have no jurisdiction to the determine:

(a) questions concerning the interpretation or application of this Agreement but insofar as they arise in connection with its decision the arbitral panel shall refer them to the State Parties to resolve pursuant to paragraph 2 above and incorporate the ruling of Tribunal in its award;

(b) in the case of disputes falling within paragraph 1 (b), matters which are properly within the sole discretion of the development authority under the terms of the development contract or the specified petroleum law.

Any arbitral panel exercising jurisdiction pursuant to this provision shall determine the dispute in accordance with the applicable law as defined in Article 1.

(4) Nothing shall prevent the States Parties in situations where the proviso referred to in paragraph 3 (a) applies from jointly consenting to the jurisdiction of the panel over questions involving the interpretation or application of this Agreement in place of that of the Tribunal which would otherwise be constituted under paragraph 2. In this event the States Parties may participate in proceedings before the panel by the submission of oral and written evidence on the question of interpretation referred to in this paragraph.

(5) Any commercial arbitration under paragraph 3 shall be located at such place in a country being a party to the 1958 New York Convention on Recognition and Enforcement of Foreign Arbitral Awards as the parties or failing them the arbitrators may agree. The States Parties shall recognize and enforce any award made pursuant to the commercial arbitration referred to subject only to such rights of refusal under their respective legal systems as are not inconsistent with those contained in Article V of that New York Convention.

Article 24 THIRD PARTY RIGHTS

(1) States Parties shall exercise their rights under this Agreement in such a manner as not to interfere unjustifiably with the rights and freedoms of other States in respect of the Zone as provided under generally accepted principles of international law.

(2) In the event that any third party claims rights inconsistent with those of the States Parties under this Agreement then the States Parties shall consult through appropriate channels with a view to co – ordinating a response.

Article 25 ENTRY INTO FORCE AND DURATION

(1) This Agreement shall enter into force on the exchange of instruments of

ratification by both States Parties which shall take place within two years from the date of signature hereof.

(2) This Agreement shall be of unlimited duration. However, after [45] years have elapsed from the date of its entry into force, either States Party may give [5] years' notice of termination of this Agreement. Termination pursuant to this provision to this provision shall not affect development contracts with an expiry date after that termination and this Agreement shall remain in force for the sole purpose of administering the existing contracts. On the expiry or earlier termination of the last remaining existing contract this Agreement shall terminate forthwith.

(3) Notwithstanding the provision of paragraph 2 hereof this Agreement may be amended or terminated at any time by written agreement between the States Parties.

(4) If notice of termination is given, the States Parties shall consult without delay about the question of further arrangements for the area of the Zone.

(5) Termination of this Agreement shall not affect the financial obligations of the States Parties incurred prior to termination nor the rights and obligation under development contracts granted pursuant to this Agreement prior to that date. Unless otherwise agreed between the States Parties the Joint Commission shall continue to exercise such residual functions as may be necessary in respect of the continuing administrative of existing contracts.

图书在版编目（CIP）数据

海上共同开发协定汇编：全2册：汉英对照 / 杨泽伟主编．
—北京：社会科学文献出版社，2016.1
（武汉大学边界与海洋问题研究丛书）
ISBN 978－7－5097－8313－9

Ⅰ.①海… Ⅱ.①杨… Ⅲ.①海洋开发-国际法-海洋法-汇编-汉、英 Ⅳ.①D993.5

中国版本图书馆CIP数据核字（2015）第261599号

·武汉大学边界与海洋问题研究丛书·
海上共同开发协定汇编（汉英对照）（全2册）

主　　编 / 杨泽伟
副 主 编 / 邓妮雅　黄文博

出 版 人 / 谢寿光
项目统筹 / 高明秀
责任编辑 / 许玉燕　赵子安　卢敏华

出　　版 / 社会科学文献出版社·当代世界出版分社（010）59367004
　　　　　　地址：北京市北三环中路甲29号院华龙大厦　邮编：100029
　　　　　　网址：www.ssap.com.cn
发　　行 / 市场营销中心（010）59367081　59367090
　　　　　　读者服务中心（010）59367028
印　　装 / 三河市尚艺印装有限公司
规　　格 / 开　本：787mm×1092mm　1/16
　　　　　　印　张：47.25　字　数：817千字
版　　次 / 2016年1月第1版　2016年1月第1次印刷
书　　号 / ISBN 978－7－5097－8313－9
定　　价 / 128.00元（全2册）

本书如有破损、缺页、装订错误，请与本社读者服务中心联系更换

▲ 版权所有 翻印必究